RESEARCH HANDBOOK ON INTELLECTUAL PROPERTY EXHAUSTION AND PARALLEL IMPORTS

RESEARCH HANDBOOKS IN INTELLECTUAL PROPERTY

Series Editor: Jeremy Phillips, *Intellectual Property Consultant, Olswang, Research Director, Intellectual Property Institute and co-founder, IPKat weblog*

Under the general editorship and direction of Jeremy Phillips comes this important new *Handbook* series of high quality, original reference works that cover the broad pillars of intellectual property law: trademark law, patent law and copyright law – as well as less developed areas, such as geographical indications, and the increasing intersection of intellectual property with other fields. Taking an international and comparative approach, these *Handbooks*, each edited by leading scholars in the respective field, will comprise specially commissioned contributions from a select cast of authors, bringing together renowned figures with up-and-coming younger authors. Each will offer a wide-ranging examination of current issues in intellectual property that is unrivalled in its blend of critical, innovative thinking and substantive analysis, and in its synthesis of contemporary research.

Each *Handbook* will stand alone as an invaluable source of reference for all scholars of intellectual property, as well as for practising lawyers who wish to engage with the discussion of ideas within the field. Whether used as an information resource on key topics, or as a platform for advanced study, these *Handbooks* will become definitive scholarly reference works in intellectual property law.

Titles in the series include:

Research Handbook on Cross-border Enforcement of Intellectual Property
Edited by Paul Torremans

Research Handbook on Human Rights and Intellectual Property
Edited by Christophe Geiger

International Intellectual Property
A Handbook of Contemporary Research
Edited by Daniel J. Gervais

Indigenous Intellectual Property
A Handbook of Contemporary Research
Edited by Matthew Rimmer

Research Handbook on Intellectual Property and Geographical Indications
Edited by Dev S. Gangjee

The History of Copyright Law
A Handbook of Contemporary Research
Edited by Isabella Alexander and H. Tomás Gómez-Arostegui

Research Handbook on Intellectual Property and Climate Change
Edited by Joshua D. Sarnoff

Research Handbook on Intellectual Property Exhaustion and Parallel Imports
Edited by Irene Calboli and Edward Lee

Research Handbook on Intellectual Property Exhaustion and Parallel Imports

Edited by

Irene Calboli

Professor of Law, Texas A&M University School of Law, USA; Visiting Professor and Deputy Director, Applied Research Centre for Intellectual Assets and the Law in Asia, Singapore Management University School of Law

Edward Lee

Professor of Law and Director, Program in Intellectual Property Law, Illinois Institute of Technology, Chicago-Kent College of Law, USA

RESEARCH HANDBOOKS IN INTELLECTUAL PROPERTY

Edward Elgar
PUBLISHING

Cheltenham, UK • Northampton, MA, USA

© The Editors and Contributors Severally 2016

All rights reserved. No part of this publication may be reproduced, stored in a retrieval system or transmitted in any form or by any means, electronic, mechanical or photocopying, recording, or otherwise without the prior permission of the publisher.

Published by
Edward Elgar Publishing Limited
The Lypiatts
15 Lansdown Road
Cheltenham
Glos GL50 2JA
UK

Edward Elgar Publishing, Inc.
William Pratt House
9 Dewey Court
Northampton
Massachusetts 01060
USA

A catalogue record for this book
is available from the British Library

Library of Congress Control Number: 2016931741

This book is available electronically in the Elgaronline
Law subject collection
DOI 10.4337/9781783478712

MIX
Paper from
responsible sources
FSC
www.fsc.org FSC® C013056

ISBN 978 1 78347 870 5 (cased)
ISBN 978 1 78347 871 2 (eBook)

Typeset by Servis Filmsetting Ltd, Stockport, Cheshire
Printed and bound in Great Britain by TJ International Ltd, Padstow

Contents

List of editors and contributors	viii
Foreword by Jerome H. Reichman	xv
Preface by Irene Calboli and Edward Lee	xvii

PART I THE THEORETICAL FRAMEWORK OF INTELLECTUAL PROPERTY EXHAUSTION

1 Incentives, contracts, and intellectual property exhaustion   3
  Shubha Ghosh

2 The economic rationale for exhaustion: distribution and post-sale restraints   23
  Ariel Katz

3 Exhaustion and personal property servitudes   44
  Molly Shaffer Van Houweling

4 "Exhaustion" in the digital age   64
  Reto M. Hilty

PART II INTELLECTUAL PROPERTY EXHAUSTION AND PARALLEL IMPORTS: THE INTERNATIONAL CONTEXT

5 International intellectual property rules and parallel imports   85
  Susy Frankel and Daniel J. Gervais

6 Economic perspectives on exhaustion and parallel imports   106
  Keith E. Maskus

7 Working toward international harmony on intellectual property exhaustion (and substantive law)   125
  Vincent Chiappetta

8 Parallel trade in pharmaceuticals: trade therapy for market distortions   145
  Frederick M. Abbott

PART III INTELLECTUAL PROPERTY EXHAUSTION AND PARALLEL IMPORTS: REGIONAL AND NATIONAL APPROACHES

9 The European internal market: exhaustion plus   169
  Christopher M. Stothers

10 The exhaustion doctrine in Singapore: different strokes for different IP folks   185
   Ng-Loy Wee Loon

11	Parallel imports and the principle of exhaustion of rights in Latin America *Carlos M. Correa and Juan I. Correa*	198
12	Exhaustion of intellectual property rights and the principle of territoriality in the United States *John A. Rothchild*	226

PART IV SELECTED ISSUES (AND CHALLENGES) ON PATENT EXHAUSTION

13	Patent exhaustion and free transit at the interface of public health and innovation policies: lessons to be learned from EU competition law practice *Josef Drexl*	249
14	Regulatory responses to international patent exhaustion *Sarah R. Wasserman Rajec*	271
15	Patent exhaustion rules and self-replicating technologies *Christopher Heath*	289
16	Development of patent exhaustion in Mainland China *Xiang Yu and Conghui Yin*	308
17	The hermeneutics of the patent exhaustion doctrine in India *Yogesh Pai*	324

PART V SELECTED ISSUES (AND CHALLENGES) ON TRADEMARK EXHAUSTION

18	Trademark exhaustion and its interface with EU competition law *Apostolos G. Chronopoulos and Spyros M. Maniatis*	343
19	Trademark exhaustion and free movement of goods: a comparative analysis of the EU/EEA, NAFTA and ASEAN *Irene Calboli*	367
20	Using trademark law to override copyright's first sale rule for imported copies in the United States *Mary LaFrance*	390
21	New developments in trademark exhaustion in Korea *Byungil Kim*	408
22	Trademark exhaustion and the Internet of resold things *Yvette Joy Liebesman and Benjamin Wilson*	422

PART VI SELECTED ISSUES (AND CHALLENGES) ON COPYRIGHT EXHAUSTION

23 How could the Taiwan Copyright Act follow the patent and trademark regime and adopt international copyright exhaustion? 443
Kung-Chung Liu

24 The Marrakesh Treaty and the targeted uses of copyright exhaustion 461
Marketa Trimble

25 From importation to digital exhaustion: a Canadian copyright perspective 478
Pierre-Emmanuel Moyse

26 Exhaustion and the Internet as a distribution channel: the relationship between intellectual property and European law in search of clarification 498
Guido Westkamp

27 Digital copyright exhaustion and personal property 518
Aaron Perzanowski and Jason Schultz

Index 537

Editors and contributors

Frederick M. Abbott is Edward Ball Eminent Scholar Professor of International Law at Florida State University College of Law, U.S. He has served as expert consultant for numerous international and regional organizations, governments and nongovernmental organizations, mainly in the fields of intellectual property, public health, trade and sustainable development. Recent books include *International Intellectual Property in an Integrated World Economy* (3d ed. 2015, with T. Cottier and F. Gurry), *Emerging Markets and the World Patent Order* (2013, edited with C. Correa and P. Drahos), and *Global Pharmaceutical Policy* (2009, with G. Dukes).

Irene Calboli is Deputy Director of the Applied Research Centre for Intellectual Assets and the Law in Asia, School of Law, Singapore Management University, where she is Visiting Professor and Lee Kong Chian Fellow. She is also Professor of Law at Texas A&M University School of Law, and Transatlantic Technology Law Forum Fellow at Stanford Law School. She teaches and writes in the areas of intellectual property and international trade law. Her recent publications include *Diversity in Intellectual Property* (2015, edited with S. Ragavan), and *The Law and Practice of Trademark Transactions* (2016, edited with J. de Werra). She is an elected member of the American Law Institute.

Vincent Chiappetta is Professor of Law at Willamette University College of Law in Oregon, U.S. He teaches and writes in the areas of U.S. and international intellectual property and business law. He has also served as in-house counsel for multinational corporations and spent a number of years in private practice.

Apostolos G. Chronopoulos is Lecturer in Trade Mark Law at the Centre for Commercial Law Studies, Queen Mary University of London. He has studied law at the National and Kapodistrian University of Athens (LL.B), the University of London (LL.M. Lond.), and the Ludwig-Maximilians University of Munich (LL.M. Eur. and Dr. jur.). He is also a member of the Athens Bar. His research interests focus on intellectual property and competition law. His recent publications address issues related to trademark law and include *Goodwill Appropriation as a Distinct Theory of Trademark Liability: A Study on the Misappropriation Rationale in Trademark and Unfair Competition Law*, 22 TEX. INTELL. PROP. L.J. 253–310 (2013–14).

Carlos M. Correa is Special Advisor on Intellectual Property and Trade to the South Centre and Director of the Center for Interdisciplinary Studies on Industrial Property and Economics at the Faculty of Law, University of Buenos Aires. He held visiting positions at several universities and has been a consultant to governments as well as to regional and international organizations on matters related to intellectual property, innovation policy, and public health. He was a member of the U.K. Commission on Intellectual Property, the Commission on Intellectual Property, Innovation and Public Health established by the World Health Assembly, and the FAO Panel of Eminent Experts on Ethics in Food and Agriculture.

Juan I. Correa graduated from the Faculty of Law of the University of Buenos Aires and is currently pursuing a Master Program in intellectual property at the Facultad Latinoamericana de Ciencias Sociales (FLACSO). He has undertaken research at the University of Buenos Aires and is the editor of the Revista Temas de Derecho Industrial y de la Competencia. He is also an advisor on intellectual property at the Office of Policy Coordination of the Ministry of Agriculture and Fisheries of Argentina.

Josef Drexl is Director of the Max Planck Institute for Innovation and Competition in Munich, Honorary Professor at the Law Faculty of the University of Munich, and a member of the Bavarian Academy of Sciences. He also chairs the Managing Board of the Munich Intellectual Property Law Center (MIPLC) in Munich, which offers an international Master's program in intellectual property. He regularly teaches in a Master's course in European law at Université de Paris II, Panthéon Assas. His major research interests are in European and international competition law and European and international intellectual property law.

Susy Frankel is Professor of Law and Director of the New Zealand Centre of International Economic Law, at Victoria University of Wellington. Since 2008 she has been Chair of the NZ Copyright Tribunal. She is President of the International Association for the Advancement of Teaching and Research in Intellectual Property (ATRIP) 2015–2017. She was Assistant Commissioner of Trade Marks, Patents and Designs, Hearings Officer for the Intellectual Property Office of NZ, from 1998–2006. Research appointments have included Project Leader of the NZ Law Foundation Regulatory Reform Project and Consultant Expert to Waitangi Tribunal on the WAI 262 flora fauna and indigenous intellectual property claim (Waitangi Tribunal Report, 2011 Ko Aotearoa Tēnei).

Daniel J. Gervais is Professor of Law at Vanderbilt University Law School and Director of the Vanderbilt Intellectual Property Program. He is Editor-in-Chief of the *Journal of World Intellectual Property* and editor of www.tripsagreement.net. Before joining academia, he was Legal Officer at the GATT (now WTO); Head of Section at WIPO; and Vice-President of Copyright Clearance Center, Inc.. In 2012, he was elected to the Academy of Europe. He is a member of the American Law Institute and, as of 2015, President Elect of the International Association for the Advancement of Teaching and Research in Intellectual Property (ATRIP).

Shubha Ghosh is Crandall Melvin Professor of Law and Director, Technology Commercialization Law Program, at the Syracuse University College of Law. His scholarship focuses on competition policy and intellectual property, innovation, freedom of expression and data access, and legal and economic analysis of the exhaustion doctrine. He has published articles in the many leading journals and authored several casebooks. His book *Identity, Invention, and the Culture of Personalized Medicine Patenting* was published in 2012. In 2014–15, he was the inaugural AAAS Law and Science Fellow at the Federal Judicial Center in Washington, D.C. In 2016, he was the Fulbright-Nehru Scholar at the National Law University, Delhi, where he studied developments in the interface between competition law and patent law and the growth of intellectual property professionalization in India.

Christopher Heath is currently a Member of the Boards of Appeal at the European Patent Office in Munich and co-editor of *International Review of Intellectual Property and Competition Law* (I.I.C.). He studied at the Universities of Konstanz, Edinburgh, and the London School of Economics. He lived and worked in Japan for three years, and between 1992 and 2005 headed the Asian Department of the Max Planck Institute for Patent, Copyright and Competition Law in Munich (now Max Planck Institute for Innovation and Competition). Dr. Heath wrote his Ph.D. thesis on Japanese unfair competition prevention law.

Reto M. Hilty is Director of the Max Planck Institute for Innovation and Competition. He is also Professor at the Universities of Zurich and Munich. He studied mechanical engineering at the Swiss Federal Institute of Technology, Zurich, and law at the University of Zurich, school of law. He was head of department and member of board of Directors at the Swiss Federal Institute of Intellectual Property, Berne (1994–97) and received his postdoctoral lecture qualification at the University of Zurich in 2000. Subsequently, he became Full Professor at the Swiss Federal Institute of Technology, Zurich, before joining the Max Planck Institute in 2002.

Ariel Katz is Associate Professor at the Faculty of Law, University of Toronto, where he holds the Innovation Chair in Electronic Commerce. From 2009 to 2012 he was the Director of the Centre for Innovation Law and Policy. He received his LL.B and LL.M from the Faculty of Law at the Hebrew University of Jerusalem and his SJD from the Faculty of Law, University of Toronto. He studies, writes, speaks, teaches, and advises on competition law and intellectual property law, with allied interests in electronic commerce, the regulation of international trade, and particularly the intersection of all these fields.

Byungil Kim is Professor of Intellectual Property Law, Hanyang University Law School, Korea. He is also the Co-Director of Hanyang IP and Information Law Centre, Hanyang University. Prior to taking a position at Hanyang, he held visiting research positions at the Universities of Munich, Houston, and Oxford. He holds a Dr. jur (Munich), LL.M (Yonsei University), and a DBA (Yonsei University). His research focuses on patent law, competition law, information technology law, and licensing law.

Mary LaFrance is the IGT Professor of Intellectual Property Law at the William S. Boyd School of Law, University of Nevada, Las Vegas. A *summa cum laude* graduate of Bryn Mawr College, she received her J.D. with High Honors from Duke University, where she served as Executive Editor of the *Duke Law Journal*. Prior to teaching, she clerked for the U.S. Court of Appeals for the D.C. Circuit, and practiced law for three years in Washington, D.C. Professor LaFrance has authored or co-authored six books as well as numerous articles and book chapters on intellectual property and entertainment law.

Edward Lee is Professor of Law and the Director of the Program in Intellectual Property Law at IIT Chicago-Kent College of Law. He is the co-author of the leading casebook *International Intellectual Property: Problems, Cases, and Materials* (2012, with Daniel C.K. Chow). He founded The Free Internet Project, a nonprofit organization whose mission is to provide the public with information about the latest legal and technological efforts to protect Internet freedoms around the world. He is a *cum laude* graduate of

Harvard Law School, where he was an editor of the *Harvard Law Review*. He graduated Phi Beta Kappa and *summa cum laude* from Williams College.

Yvette Joy Liebesman is Professor of Law at Saint Louis University School of Law, where she focuses her scholarship on the interaction of technology with trademark and copyright. Her recent publication, *When Does Copyright Law Require Technology Blindness? Aiken Meets Aereo*, BERKELEY TECH. L.J. 30:2 (2015), was awarded the University of Houston's Institute for Intellectual Property and Information Law's 2015 Sponsored Scholarship Grant for the Legal Academy. *The Mark of a Resold Good*, 20 GEO. MASON L. REV. 157 (2012), upon which her and co-author Benjamin Wilson's chapter is based, won the 2013 INTA Ladas Award for Trademark Scholarship.

Kung-Chung Liu received an LL.B and LL.M from National Taiwan University, and a Doctor of Law degree from the Ludwig Maximilian Universität in Munich. He has been affiliated with Academia Sinica in Taiwan since 1992 and has been a Research Fellow at Institutum Iurisprudentiae since 2002. He is currently the External Director of the Applied Research Center for Intellectual Assets and the Law in Asia, Singapore Management University. His teaching and research focus on intellectual property, antitrust, and unfair competition law, and communications law. He has authored fourteen books in Chinese, over 110 peer-reviewed articles in Chinese and English, and edited eight books in English.

Spyros M. Maniatis is Professor of Intellectual Property Law and Head of the Centre for Commercial Law Studies, Queen Mary University of London. His expertise and research interests cover trademark and unfair competition law as well as the interaction between intellectual property and competition law. His work on *Trade Marks in Europe: A Practical Jurisprudence* (now co-authored with Dimitris Botis, Alexander von Mühlendahl, and Imogen Wiseman) reached its third edition with Oxford University Press in January 2016.

Keith E. Maskus is Arts and Sciences Professor of Distinction at the University of Colorado, Boulder. He has been a Lead Economist in the Development Research Group at the World Bank. He is also a Research Fellow at the Peterson Institute for International Economics and a consultant for the World Trade Organization and the World Intellectual Property Organization. Maskus received his Ph.D. from the University of Michigan and has written extensively about various aspects of international trade and technology. His most recent book is *Private Rights and Public Problems: The Global Economics of Intellectual Property in the 21st Century* (2012).

Pierre-Emmanuel Moyse is Associate Professor at the McGill Faculty of Law and the Director of the Center for Intellectual Property Policy. He is the founder and editor of the Thémis Competition and Innovation Series and Director of publications of the *Jurisclasseur Propriété Intellectuelle* published in Québec by LexisNexis. In 2014–15, he taught a course on the Laws of Innovation at the Buchmann Faculty of Law of the University of Tel Aviv and was visiting scholar at the University of Paris II Panthéon-Assas and Paris XI. He is currently researching the social and legal costs of innovation.

Ng-Loy Wee Loon is Professor at the Faculty of Law, National University of Singapore. Amongst her academic publications is her text on *Law of Intellectual Property of Singapore*. Outside of the university, her involvement in the legal landscape of Singapore includes the following: member of the Board of Directors of the Intellectual Property

Office of Singapore (2000–01); member of the Board of Governors of the IP Academy (2007–11); member of Singapore's Copyright Tribunal (since 2009); member of the Singapore Domain Name Dispute Resolution Policy Panel (since 2014); IP Adjudicator with the Intellectual Property Office of Singapore (since 2014).

Yogesh Pai is Assistant Professor of Law at National Law University, Delhi. He teaches and writes in the area of intellectual property law and policy. He has previously worked with the South Centre in Geneva, Centad, New Delhi, and was Assistant Professor of Law at National Law University, Jodhpur. Yogesh serves as legal member in an ad hoc committee constituted by the Government of India to assess the granting of compulsory licenses for affordable healthcare in India. Previously, he was part of an ad hoc expert committee formed in order to examine the need for utility models in India.

Aaron Perzanowski is Professor of Law at the Case Western Reserve University School of Law, where he teaches courses on intellectual property and technology law. His recent publications include *Creativity Without Law* (2016, edited with Kate Darling) and *The End of Ownership* (2016, with Jason Schultz).

Sarah R. Wasserman Rajec is Assistant Professor of Law at William and Mary Law School. Her research focuses on patent law and international trade law. Her recent publications include *Free Trade in Patented Goods: International Exhaustion for Patents*, 28 BERKELEY TECH. L.J. 317 (2014) and *Evaluating Flexibility in International Patent Law*, 65 HASTINGS L.J. 153 (2013). Previously, Professor Rajec practiced patent litigation and served as a law clerk to Judge Donald C. Pogue of the U.S. Court of International Trade and to Judge Alan D. Lourie of the U.S. Court of Appeals for the Federal Circuit.

Jerome H. Reichman is Bunyan S. Womble Professor of Law at Duke University School of Law. He has written and lectured widely on diverse aspects of intellectual property law, including comparative and international intellectual property and the connection between intellectual property and international trade. His recent publications include *Governing Digitally Integrated Genetic Resources, Data, and Literature: Global Intellectual Property Strategies for a Redesigned Microbial Research Commons* (2016, with P.F. Uhlir and T. Dederwaerdere). He is consultant to numerous intergovernmental and nongovernmental organizations, a member of the Board of Editors for the *Journal of International Economic Law*, and the Scientific Advisory Board of *Il Diritto di Autore*. He is a graduate of the University of Chicago, where he was a Hutchins Scholar and an early entrant, and Yale Law School.

John A. Rothchild is Associate Professor at Wayne State University Law School, where he teaches in the areas of intellectual property law and Internet law. He is a co-author of the law school casebook *Internet Commerce* (2d ed. 2006, edited with Margaret J. Radin, R. Anthony Reese, and Gregory M. Silverman), and the editor of the forthcoming *Research Handbook on Electronic Commerce Law* (2016). Previously he was an attorney in the Federal Trade Commission's Bureau of Consumer Protection.

Jason Schultz is Professor of Clinical Law and Director of NYU's Technology Law and Policy Clinic. Previously, he was an Assistant Clinical Professor at Berkeley Law, where he directed the Samuelson Law, Technology and Public Policy Clinic. Before joining academia, he was a senior staff attorney at the Electronic Frontier Foundation, an associate at Fish & Richardson, and a clerk for Judge D. Lowell Jensen of the Northern District of California. He holds a JD from the University of California, Berkeley, and a BA with honors in public policy and women's studies from Duke University.

Christopher M. Stothers is an Intellectual Property Litigation Partner at Arnold & Porter (UK) LLP in London and a Visiting Lecturer in Intellectual Property and Competition Law at University College London. Christopher is an experienced litigator on strategic, cross-border patent disputes, including oppositions before the European Patent Office. He also litigates and arbitrates other types of intellectual property (trademark, copyright, and designs), antitrust (including follow-on damages claims), pharmaceutical regulation, European Union law and commercial disputes. His 2007 practitioner textbook, *Parallel Trade in Europe: Intellectual Property, Competition and Regulatory Law*, has been cited by the U.K. Supreme Court.

Marketa Trimble is the Samuel S. Lionel Professor of Intellectual Property Law at the William S. Boyd School of Law of the University of Nevada, Las Vegas. She teaches and writes in the area of intellectual property law. Her major areas of expertise are public and private international law of intellectual property, including conflict of laws, transnational litigation, and enforcement of intellectual property rights on the Internet. She has authored numerous articles and book chapters. Her publications include the book *Global Patents: Limits of Transnational Enforcement* (2012) and the casebook *International Intellectual Property Law: Cases and Materials* (4th ed. 2016, with P. Goldstein).

Molly Shaffer Van Houweling is Professor of Law and Associate Dean at the University of California, Berkeley. She teaches and writes about property law and intellectual property and is a Faculty Co-Director of the Berkeley Center for Law and Technology. She also serves as Associate Reporter for the American Law Institute's *Restatement of the Law, Copyright*, and as advisor to the *Restatement of the Law Fourth, Property*. She is a founding director of the non-profit Authors Alliance and past executive director of Creative Commons. She graduated from Harvard Law School and clerked for Judge Michael Boudin and Justice David Souter.

Guido Westkamp holds a Chair in Intellectual Property and Comparative Law and is Co-Director of the Queen Mary Intellectual Property Research Institute at Queen Mary University of London. His research and teaching interests are in the areas of comparative copyright, trademark, competition, personality, and media law. He holds degrees from both Germany and the U.K. and is also a Co-Director of the European Intellectual Property Institutes Network (EIPIN).

Benjamin Wilson is an associate at HeplerBroom L.L.C. Before joining HeplerBroom, he clerked for the Hon. William D. Stiehl and Hon. David R. Herndon in the U.S. District Court for the Southern District of Illinois. His publications include *The Mark of a Resold Good*, 20 GEO. MASON L.REV. 157 (2012), with Prof. Yvette Liebesman; *Notice, Takedown, and the Good-Faith Standard: How to Protect Internet Users from Bad-Faith Removal of Web Content*, 29 ST. LOUIS UNIV. PUB. L. REV. 613 (2010); and *Lu Junhong: The Seventh Circuit Stirs the Waters of Maritime Removals*, IDC QUARTERLY (2015).

Conghui Yin is a doctoral candidate at the Chinese-German Institute for Intellectual Property at Huazhong University of Science and Technology (HUST) in Wuhan, China.

Her research fields are intellectual property and technological innovation. She is one of the core members of the Chinese IP Group for the US-China CERC Project and the Chinese IP Group for the China-EU/EEA NZEC-CCS Project.

Xiang Yu is Director and Professor at the Chinese-German Institute for Intellectual Property at Huazhong University of Science and Technology (HUST) in Wuhan, China. He is also a German Humboldt Scholar and a member of the European Academy of Sciences and Arts. He teaches patent related courses in many universities in different countries and has published about 120 research articles in the fields of intellectual property in English, German, Japanese, and Chinese. He is now acting as Director of the Chinese IP Group for the US-China CERC Project, as well as Director of the Chinese IP Group for the China-EU/EEA NZEC-CCS Project.

Foreword

The principle of exhaustion is a well-established concept in the intellectual property laws of the member states of the World Trade Organization (WTO). By means of explicit legislative provisions or judicial precedents, most countries use the principle of exhaustion to limit the rights of intellectual property owners and to advance diverse public policy objectives. For example, some countries rely on this principle to regulate competition in the domestic marketplace and to enhance consumer welfare; other countries invoke the concept of exhaustion as a mechanism to promote trade and the free movement of goods. Typically, governments will adapt national laws on exhaustion to pursue some combination of these goals.

Today, however, there is still no international consensus concerning a uniform policy justification for the principle of exhaustion, nor is there any consensus about uniform rules to be adopted either for exhaustion in general or even for specific applications of this doctrine to patents, trademarks, copyrights, and related intellectual property regimes.

In particular, two diverging paradigms continue to influence opposing views about the exhaustion of intellectual property rights. One is the free trade paradigm—implemented under the General Agreement on Tariffs and Trade (GATT 1994) and the General Agreement on Trade in Services—which supports a system of international exhaustion. Another is the independence of intellectual property rights paradigm—embodied in the Paris Convention for the Protection of Industrial Property and the Berne Convention for the Protection of Literary and Artistic Works—which has been invoked to defend a system of national or regional exhaustion.

Contrasting views about these diverging paradigms made it impossible to reach a consensus on the issue of exhaustion during the multilateral trade negotiations that produced the Agreement on Trade Related Aspects of Intellectual Property Rights ("TRIPS Agreement") in 1994. Hence, even though the language in Article 6 of the TRIPS Agreement expressly leaves members of the WTO free to determine their national policies on intellectual property exhaustion, existing national practices remain open to challenges and questions under GATT 1994. In the recent past, many of these challenges and questions have been addressed by national and international policy-makers, regulatory authorities, and the courts.

The contributors to this book address these issues in depth. Chapter by chapter, the authors explore and analyse the theoretical and normative framework supporting the principle of exhaustion. They discuss existing controversies in detail, with particular regard to the impact of different systems of exhaustion on international trade. To their credit, the authors also reach beyond the traditional—but still unresolved—areas of disputes, in order to consider applications of the principle of exhaustion to new fields of technology, such as self-replicating technologies, digital goods, and their distribution via the Internet. The end result is a provocative and informative work that instructs and challenges readers, whether experts or novices in this field. I congratulate the editors for having compiled this comprehensive and valuable set of materials on such an important topic, the product of a team of stellar contributors.

Jerome H. Reichman
March 2016

Preface

I. INTELLECTUAL PROPERTY EXHAUSTION AND PARALLEL IMPORTS: *QUO VADIS*?

Supap Kirtsaeng, an enterprising graduate student from Thailand, needed money to pay his university tuition in the United States (U.S.). He asked family and friends to purchase English-language textbooks in Thailand that were sold at cheaper prices compared to the U.S., and send him the books. He then re-sold the books for a profit in the U.S. The book publisher, however, sued him for copyright infringement under U.S. law. Mr. Kirtsaeng denied the infringement claim and argued that the publisher's rights to control the distribution of the books in the U.S. was exhausted after the first sale of the books in Thailand. After several years of litigation, the case reached the U.S. Supreme Court.[1] To the surprise of many copyright experts, the Supreme Court agreed with now Dr. Kirtsaeng. The Court rejected the views of the lower courts that the sales in Thailand did not exhaust the publisher's rights in the U.S. The Court held that authorized foreign sales of U.S. copyrighted works constituted a lawful first sale under U.S. copyright law, thereby exhausting the copyright owner's distribution right with respect to those copies also in the U.S.[2]

The effects of this decision, *Kirtsaeng v. John Wiley & Sons*, were felt far beyond the shores of North America. At the time the Supreme Court ruled on the case in March 2013, U.S. trade negotiators were lobbying for national exhaustion as part of the intellectual property obligations to be adopted by countries negotiating the Trans-Pacific Partnership Agreement (TPP). The adoption of these provisions would have imposed changes in national laws in many TPP members that followed a system of international exhaustion.[3] Yet, U.S. negotiators could no longer plausibly support a principle of national exhaustion for other countries' copyright laws after the Supreme Court held that the U.S. Copyright Act adopted a principle of international exhaustion. Ultimately, when the TPP negotiations were finalized in October 2015, the exhaustion provision in the Intellectual Property Chapter left TPP members free to adopt their preferred approaches.[4]

The story of Dr. Kirtsaeng and the unsettled legal treatment of parallel imports—unauthorized imports of genuine products first sold in a foreign country—is not unique to the U.S. Indeed, the legal treatment of parallel imports, and the principle of intellectual property exhaustion—in copyright, trademark, patent law, and other intellectual property

---

[1] Kirtsaeng v. John Wiley & Sons, Inc., 133 S. Ct. 1351 (2013).
[2] *Ibid.* at 1371.
[3] Wikileaks, *Trans-Pacific Partnership Agreement: Intellectual Property [Rights] Chapter Consolidated Text*, available at https://wikileaks.org/tpp/static/pdf/Wikileaks-secret-TPP-treaty-IP-chapter.pdf (August 30, 2013, released November 13, 2013).
[4] Wikileaks, *Trans-Pacific Partnership Agreement (TPP): Intellectual Property [Rights] Chapter, Consolidated Text*, available at https://wikileaks.org/tpp-ip3/WikiLeaks-TPP-IP-Chapter/WikiLeaks-TPP-IP-Chapter-051015.pdf (October 5, 2015, released October 9, 2015).

rights—continues to be unsettled in many countries today. The divide between levels of development in different regions of the world also magnifies the differences in national views. The uncertainty and the controversy that surround the application of the principle of exhaustion are captured in Article 6 of the Agreement on Trade Related Aspects of Intellectual Property Rights (TRIPS)—which expressly leaves the issue undecided: "nothing in this Agreement shall be used to address the issue of the exhaustion of intellectual property rights."[5] Over two decades after the adoption of TRIPS, the language, and the spirit, of Article 6 of TRIPS continues to apply not only at the multilateral level, but also, as noted above, has been transplanted in the TPP and other international trade agreements.

Hence, from the Americas to Europe, Asia-Pacific, and Africa, countries around the world are facing increased pressure to clarify the application of the principle of exhaustion in their national laws. Courts and policy-makers in many jurisdictions are asking similar basic questions, notably: Should the principle of intellectual property exhaustion apply at the national, regional, or international level? Should countries attempt to harmonize their approaches to exhaustion internationally? Should copyright, patent, and trademark laws follow the same principle of exhaustion? For example, in February 2016, the U.S. Court of Appeals for the Federal Circuit Federal ruled that foreign sales of patented products do *not* exhaust the right of patentees in the U.S., thus rendering U.S. patent law's treatment of unauthorized imports (national exhaustion) different from copyright law's treatment (international exhaustion).[6] But why?

The expansion of intellectual property protections in new fields, such as biotechnology, has added to the complexities of the debate. This field presents new challenges for a traditional interpretation of exhaustion, particularly with respect to self-replicating "technologies" like seeds, plants, and animals, and post-sale distribution of these "products." Judges in several jurisdictions have already decided several cases related to the exhaustion of genetically modified patented seeds. Similar cases will certainly continue to be litigated in the future.[7] Besides biotechnology-related new technologies, the rise of other types of technologies, including the growing number of digital goods and online distribution platforms, often referred to as the "Internet of things," has further complicated the debate by challenging the traditional concepts of materiality of products and territoriality of laws. Here again, the treatment of exhaustion in the digital environment has led to court decisions. And it will continue to be a topic of discussion and litigation for years to come.[8]

The objective of this Handbook is to explore these and other vexing questions that

---

[5] Agreement on Trade-Related Aspects of Intellectual Property Rights, April 15, 1994; Marrakesh Agreement Establishing the World Trade Organization, Annex 1C, 1869 U.N.T.S. 299, 33 I.L.M. 1197, art. 6 (1994).

[6] Lexmark International, Inc., v. Impression Products, Inc., Case Nos. 14-1617, 1619 (Fed Cir, Feb. 12, 2016) (en banc) (holding that a foreign sale of a U.S. patented article, when made by or with the consent of the U.S. patentee, does not exhaust the rights of the patentee in the U.S. and excluding the application of the decision of the Supreme Court in Kirtsaeng with respect to patent exhaustion).

[7] See e.g. Bowman v. Monsanto Co., 133 S. Ct. 1761 (2013); Case C-428/09, Monsanto v. Cefetra, [2010] E.C.R. I-09961; Monsanto v. Schmeisser, [2004] 1 S.C.R. 902, 2004 SCC 34.

[8] See e.g. Capitol Records, L.L.C. v. ReDigi Inc., 934 F. Supp. 2d 640 (S.D.N.Y. 2013); Case C-128/11, UsedSoft GmbH v. Oracle Int'l Corp., 2012 E.C.R. I-0000 (July 3, 2012).

surround the application of the principle of intellectual property exhaustion at the national and international level, with the caveat, however, that no single book can address all aspects of this complex topic, and that a one-size answer cannot likely be found to many questions. Notably, the objective of this Handbook is to offer insights to several of the traditional and more recent challenges that characterize intellectual property exhaustion by considering many different elements including the specific circumstances, market size, and economic development of individual jurisdictions, as well as the different types of intellectual property rights and technology examined.

II. METHODOLOGY AND STRUCTURE OF THE BOOK

Academic discussions on the principle of exhaustion date back several decades. However, no academic collection or book has systematically addressed the various issues related to this topic to date, including the various theories at the basis of the principle of exhaustion and parallel imports. This Handbook fills this void by offering a systematic analysis of the application of this principle in the context of national economies and international trade. The Handbook combines a comprehensive analysis of the doctrinal and critical interpretations of intellectual property exhaustion with a comparative analysis of the treatment of exhaustion under the national law of several countries in North and South America, Europe, and Asia.

To address the various issues related to the topic, we structured the Handbook in six specific Parts. In particular, Parts I, II, and III focus on the theoretical framework of the principle of exhaustion and its application in the context of international trade. Parts IV, V, and VI address specific themes relating to the principle of exhaustion as it is applied to patents, trademarks, and copyrights, respectively. Despite this formal division, all Parts and contributions are closely linked together, as many concepts (incentive theories, price discrimination, integration of regional markets, and so on) apply across the various topics and the general themes addressed in the Handbook.

Part I provides background on the policy justifications and concerns over the exhaustion doctrine. This Part focuses on utilitarian and property theories, as well as on economic analysis. This Part also addresses the growing discussion over the application of exhaustion to digital goods, or "digital exhaustion." Building on these concepts, Part II discusses the application of intellectual property exhaustion and its challenges in the context of international trade. Contributions to this Part elaborate on the reasons for the absence of harmonized international rules on parallel imports, the role of national and regional exhaustion rules as a calibration tool for different size economies, and the economic analysis of parallel imports. In this respect, this Part questions the seemingly pervasive benefits of parallel trade, giving particular attention to the issue of parallel imports of pharmaceuticals. Part III continues the analysis at the regional level and elaborates on the systems of exhaustion adopted in the European Economic Area (EEA), the Common Market of the South (MERCOSUR), and the Andean Community of Nations. This Part also discusses the national systems adopted in Singapore and the U.S. Chapters in this Part also reflect on the potential benefits of harmonization and the equally relevant benefits of maintaining a diversity of national or regional exhaustion policies, including with respect to separate types of intellectual property rights.

Part IV begins the specialized part of the Handbook and focuses on selected issues on patent exhaustion. Among these issues is the treatment of parallel imports of pharmaceutical products, not only under intellectual property law, but also under the perspective of EU competition law and the regulatory regime for pharmaceuticals in the United States. This part also addresses the challenges of applying the traditional concepts of patent exhaustion to self-replicating technologies. Last, but not least, this part focuses on the application of the principle of patent exhaustion and its ambiguities in two of the largest emerging economies, India and China.

Part V then focuses on trademark exhaustion, starting with a discussion of the relationship between trademark exhaustion and the free movement of goods in free trade areas and custom unions, namely the EU/EEA, the North American Free Trade Area (NAFTA), and the Association of Southeast Asian Nations (ASEAN). The principle of trademark exhaustion in the EU/EEA is specifically addressed under the lens of EU competition law. This part also reviews the application of the principle of trademark exhaustion in South Korea; explores how, post *Kirtsaeng*, U.S. trademark owners can use trademark law to control parallel imports of copyrighted goods; and analyzes the challenges surrounding the application of trademark exhaustion in cyberspace. Part VI concludes the Handbook with a series of selected issues on copyright exhaustion. Several of the contributions in this Part focus specifically on digital copyright exhaustion, with emphasis on the current situations in Canada, the EU, and the U.S. This Part also discusses copyright exhaustion in Taiwan and explores the targeted use of copyright exhaustion as means to implement the recently adopted Marrakesh Treaty to Facilitate Access to Published Works for Persons Who Are Blind, Visually Impaired, or Otherwise Print Disabled adopted under the aegis of the World Intellectual Property Organization (WIPO) in 2013.[9]

III. ACKNOWLEDGMENTS

This Handbook benefited from, and would not have been possible without, the contributions of many. We would like to express our gratitude to all those who have assisted us in the various phases of the production of the Handbook and made its publication possible.

First and foremost, we would like to thank the impressive array of scholars from many countries who contributed to the Handbook, and whose insightful ideas stream the pages of this collection from beginning to end. We are thrilled—and humbled—by the opportunity to have worked with them. The readers will greatly benefit from the wealth of information and variety of perspectives offered in every chapter. This Handbook is also a significant example of international cooperation among scholars from different countries and legal systems. In addition to our contributors, we are indebted to Jeremy Phillips, the Editor of Edward Elgar's Research Handbook Series, for his suggestions and comments on the structure of the Handbook. We also thank our research assistants, all

---

[9] Marrakesh Treaty to Facilitate Access to Published Works for Persons Who are Blind, Visually Impaired, or Otherwise Print Disabled, June 27, 2013, available at www.wipo.int/treaties/en/text.jsp?file_id=301016.

graduate students, who have supported us during the editing process of the manuscript before its submission to the publisher. We particularly want to thank Yanbing Li, Molly Madonia, Lori Shaw, and Jia Wang. Furthermore, we would like to acknowledge the work of Edward Elgar's editorial team, and in particular Rebecca Stowell, in preparing this Handbook for publication.

We are additionally grateful for the opportunity to collaborate in designing and editing on this Handbook. This is the second book that we have edited together and we look forward to more collaboration in the future. The idea of editing a collection on the topic of "Intellectual Property Exhaustion and Parallel Imports" began with a conversation with Edward Elgar's editor Luke Adams in July 2013 in Oxford, during the 32nd ATRIP Congress hosted by the Faculty of Law of the University of Oxford. In early 2014, the idea translated into a Handbook project and, during the following months, we refined the structure and topics, following the suggestions and comments of our contributors. Today, several months, many edits, and proof corrections later, we celebrate the publication of this Handbook. We are also delighted to see that questions related to intellectual property exhaustion are, more than ever, at the forefront of debates of intellectual property and international trade. We conclude by thanking our readers. We are indebted to you for your interest and welcome all comments you may have.

Irene Calboli and Edward Lee
March 2016

PART I

THE THEORETICAL FRAMEWORK OF INTELLECTUAL PROPERTY EXHAUSTION

1. Incentives, contracts, and intellectual property exhaustion
*Shubha Ghosh**

I. INTRODUCTION

This chapter examines the claim that the exhaustion doctrine reduces incentives for the creation of new works and inventions. In order to make the strongest argument in favor of intellectual property exhaustion, I will be working solely within the incentives-based justification for intellectual property. Since the claims for evisceration of incentives are most often made for copyright and patent, I will focus on copyright and patent exhaustion in the last section of this chapter. The positive conclusion is that intellectual property exhaustion is consistent with incentives-based justifications for intellectual property rights.

For the purposes of this chapter, I define incentives-based rationale for intellectual property rights[1] as the view that rights of exclusivity are needed in order to promote creativity and invention and their dissemination. This exclusivity allows the creator to sell rights of access or use to the work. With this ability to commercialize rights in a creative work, the creator can develop a market, and possibly an industry, within which the works can propagate under the control and management of the rights holder. Through these mechanisms, exclusivity creates incentives for the creative person (who harnesses the legally provided exclusivity to exploit the work) and the public (who can benefit from the work through market exchange).

However, the incentives theory can become groundless and unprincipled if taken too far. Law-makers, whether in the legislature or the courts, might fall victim to the claim that if some exclusivity is needed for creativity, then more exclusivity can produce more creative and innovative works. Since exclusive rights are relatively costless to provide and the potential upside for consumers and culture is great, the temptation readily arises for establishing expansive rights. Although it is easy to challenge the incentives argument from outside its terms, what is most compelling is that the terms of the incentives

---

* Crandall Melvin Professor of Law & Director Technology Commercialization Law Program, Syracuse University College of Law.

[1] See e.g. Benjamin N. Roin, *Intellectual Property Versus Prizes: Reframing the Debate*, 81 U. CHI. L. REV. 999, 1018 (2014) (discussing incentives); Eric E. Johnson, *Intellectual Property and the Incentive Fallacy*, 39 FLA. ST. U. L. REV. 623, 624 (2012) (discussing the fallacy of incentive theory); Jeanne C. Fromer, *Expressive Incentives in Intellectual Property*, 98 VA. L. REV. 1745, 1760 (2012) (showing the complementarities of utilitarian and moral theories with respect to copyright incentives). For an economic discussion of incentives generally, see DONALD CAMPBELL, INCENTIVES: MOTIVATIONS AND THE ECONOMICS OF INFORMATION 514 (2006). For an economic analysis of incentives in intellectual property, see SUZANNE SCOTCHMER, INNOVATION AND INCENTIVES 98–103 (2004) (asking how profitable should intellectual property rights be).

justification compels at some point limitations on exclusivity. Incentives are diverse and multifarious. Therefore, one needs to carefully consider the subsidiary incentive questions of "for whom?" and "for what?" This chapter unpacks the meaning of incentives and the implication for intellectual property exhaustion.

An exchange from the oral argument in the 2013 dispute over patent exhaustion and self-replicating seeds, *Bowman v. Monsanto*,[2] illustrates the claim that exhaustion undermines intellectual property incentives. During the oral argument, Justice Kagan raised the question of incentives.[3] The petitioner, urging a finding of exhaustion, pointed out that contract remedies can serve to compensate the patent owner once the rights are exhausted upon an initial sale. Justice Kagan questioned whether contract remedies would provide enough of an incentive to create and distribute a seed that can be readily replicated after public distribution.[4] The final opinion, authored by Justice Kagan, rested on the premise that contract remedies would not provide enough incentive for creation. While the Court's ruling has its strength, the reasoning ignored the larger question of incentives "for whom?" and "for what?"

The roadmap for this chapter is as follows. The next section addresses several cases in which the U.S. Supreme Court has confronted questions of incentives and intellectual property broadly. The third section places the problem of exhaustion in the context of these broader cases. The fourth section concludes and analyzes the implications for policy.

II. ON INCENTIVES AND INTELLECTUAL PROPERTY

The word "incentive" is used synonymously with motivation, but has many nuances that are relevant to intellectual property law and policy.[5] Intellectual property incentives are most often external and monetary.[6] Packaged as legal rights to exclude, intellectual property incentives tap into the quest for money and wealth by encouraging individuals to focus their energies on creation. The size of the monetary reward depends on the scope of exclusivity, determined by the subject matter of the right, the range of potential markets to which the rights attach, and the types of uses that must be licensed by third parties. Intellectual property incentives fashion these dimensions of exclusive rights into a monetary reward as a beacon for a creatively-inclined person to pursue. To use the

---

[2] Bowman v. Monsanto Co., 133 S. Ct. 1761 (2013).
[3] Transcript of Oral Argument, Bowman v. Monsanto Co., 133 S. Ct. 1761 (2013) (No. 11-796), available at www.supremecourt.gov/oral_arguments/argument_transcripts/11-796-1j43.pdf.
[4] *Ibid.* at 19: "Mr. Walters, could you go back to the Chief Justice's opening question because the Chief Justice asked you what incentive Monsanto would have to produce this kind of product if you were right. And you said, well, they can protect themselves by contract. Actually, it seems to me that that answer is peculiarly insufficient in this kind of a case because all that has to happen is that one seed escapes the web of these contracts, and that seed because it can self-replicate in the way that it can, essentially makes all the contracts worthless. So again, we are back to the Chief Justice's problem, that Monsanto would have no incentive to create a product like this one."
[5] See e.g. Fromer, *supra* note 1.
[6] See Johnson, *supra* note 1 (discussing internal and external motivations).

language of economics, intellectual property incentives are signals to which opportunities to pursue, alongside market wages, for early stage careerists on their desired paths, whether law, medicine, business, or artistic.

One criticism of intellectual property incentives is that direct rewards might be more effective and efficient.[7] If society seeks a cure for a disease, then the state should offer a set of monetary rewards financed by tax revenues rather than grant exclusionary rights. If one views creativity and invention as serendipitous rather than planned, exclusionary rights may offer more freedom and openness to pursue creative pathways than targeted rewards. But acknowledging serendipity in the creative process may further undermine arguments for the incentive theory of intellectual property. Incentives do not work in a deterministic fashion. Instead, they set parameters within which individuals act in pursuit of creativity and its rewards.

A pure pecuniary conception of incentives must confront elements of randomness and serendipity in creation. One accommodation is to posit incentives in aggregate terms: a society with intellectual property will tend to create more creative works and inventions because of the play of incentives on all members of society. This accommodation suggests that intellectual property incentives may not work as direct motivations, but as defining the rules of society, like the use of social norms to guide good behavior. We can contrast these soft incentives with the tactile and compelling lure of monetary rewards. But once we move to this broader conception of incentives one has to ask, first, what is the purpose of the incentives and, second, how do they function? The cases to be discussed in the rest of this section address these questions. But one critical question illustrates these two subsidiary questions: how big should incentives be?

The simple answer to the last question is: as big as society wants. However, stating the question in the converse might be more instructive: when are incentives insufficient? One response is that anything short of full appropriation of the value of a creative work or invention is insufficient. But full appropriation cannot be the right measure of incentives. The value of a work, such as a vaccine or a movie, depends on factors that may be out of the control of the creator. In a market system, rewards are set by prices that reflect transactions of demanders and suppliers aggregating into a marketplace. But by definition, a unique creation may not support a thick market. There may be only a few demanders and only one seller. Negotiated prices will not be the result of a competitive dynamic. Consequently, we are left with this question: how much of a reward is enough? This question first depends upon what we are trying to incentivize through reward, and secondly, the manner in which incentives function.

With this conceptual background, we can turn to concrete cases, including the Supreme Court's review of copyright term extension, the escalator clauses conditional on patent grant in licensing arrangements, and the relationship between licenses and contracts. These concrete cases both illustrate the concept of incentive in action and set a background against which to examine exhaustion.

---

[7] See Roin, *supra* note 1.

A. Eldred v. Ashcroft

In 2002, the Supreme Court ruled that Congress has wide latitude in expanding the term of copyright (and arguably other forms of intellectual property) in *Eldred v. Ashcroft*.[8] This latitude includes extending the copyright for existing works. Constitutional language like "promoting progress" and "limited terms" were given a liberal interpretation.[9] Congress was given deference on how best to promote progress through limited terms of exclusivity, as long as there was some rationale for the legislative choices. In the case of a twenty-year retroactive extension, the relevant rationales included conformity with international law, accommodation of increased life expectancy of authors, and the need of copyright owners to develop new digital markets on the Internet.[10] The added years served as an incentive for the last set of goals.

Consider the Court's lack of attention to the motives of the plaintiff in the case. Eldred was waiting for certain works to fall into the public domain precisely so they could be distributed digitally, as would be permissible once the copyright expired.[11] His business model involved transforming public domain works for consumption by the digiterati.[12] With the extension of copyright, works about to be in the public domain fall within the exclusive rights of copyright owners. Eldred did not need the incentive of copyright to digitize already created works. The question is, why did the ex-copyright owners need additional exclusive rights to digitize existing works? The Court's answer seems to be that it is up to Congress to determine how incentives are set.[13] That determination cannot be second-guessed by the Court.

A prominent criticism of the *Eldred* decision stems from the minimal incentives that are provided by adding twenty years to an already long term of life of the author plus fifty years. Drawing on the *amicus* brief of Nobel Laureate economists, critics of *Eldred* emphasize that it is irrational to conclude that twenty years of exclusivity added more than fifty years away would provide adequate incentives for additional creativity.[14] Congress, therefore, did not have sufficient rationale to justify its decision. This argument is compelling in terms of the mathematics of incentives. But for three equally compelling reasons, it does not slay the beast of deference that the Court released through its opinion.

First is the problem of the metric used to gauge incentives. Within the logic of the incentive rationale for copyright, even an iota of extra reward might compel some new works to be produced. Unless one has a measure of how much progress is desirable, it is hard to judge the amount of incentives Congress should pursue. It may not seem cost-effective

---

[8] Eldred v. Ashcroft, 537 U.S. 186 (2003).
[9] *Ibid.* at 223, 245, and 247.
[10] Eldred v. Reno, 74 F. Supp. 2d 1 (D.D.C. 1999), *rev'd sub nom.* Eldred v. Ashcroft, 537 U.S. 186 (2003).
[11] *Ibid.*
[12] *Eldred, supra* note 8, 537 U.S. at 222.
[13] *Ibid.*
[14] Brief of George A. Akerlof, Kenneth J. Arrow, Timothy F. Bresnahan, James M. Buchanan, Ronald H. Coase, Linda R. Cohen, Milton Friedman, Jerry R. Green, Robert W. Hahn, Thomas W. Hazlett, C. Scott Hemphill, Robert E. Litan, Roger G. Noll, Richard Schmalensee, Steven Shavell, Hal R. Varian, and Richard J. Zeckhauser as Amici Curiae in Support of Petitioners at 13–16, Eldred v. Ashcroft, *supra* note 8.

to impose an additional twenty years if only one new work is produced. Ultimately, this calculus assumes that years of exclusivity should translate into a quantity of new works. What if that new work is on the scale of "Remembrance of Things Past" (or pick your own example of a mega opus)? Would the minimal incentives somehow be justified? My point is not to defend the reasoning of *Eldred* or to detract from the rhetoric of the *amicus* brief. Instead, I would like to illustrate the poverty of the incentives justification for copyright both to defend the enactment of copyright term extension and to attack it. To say that, on its face, the incentive of twenty additional years is too small or meaningless is to make assumptions about the scale and scope of desirable incentives. The adequacy of incentives perhaps can only be ascertained by looking outside the incentive justification for copyright.

Secondly, and more realistically, the force of the twenty-year extension benefited already existing copyright owners. Needless to say, such owners may not be incentivized to create extant works. But, the Court's argument is that the twenty years may create incentives for more intensive use of the work. Rather than having the works go into desuetude, the Court believes copyright owners will revive the works and given them new life and new uses. As stated above, this argument ignores incentives outside of copyright that also permit such intensive uses. *Eldred* seemingly was driven by such incentives. Furthermore, scholars Mark Lemley and Paul Heald have independently shown how this justification for intensive usage of created works is flawed as theoretical and empirical matters.[15] Professor Lemley argues against *ex post* rationales for copyright, suggesting that copyright is limited for the purposes of promoting originality.[16] Professor Heald shows that extensive copyright has created gaps in the usage and marketing of copyrighted works in favor of public domain works.[17] These two arguments taken together highlight the error of talking about incentives as "freely floating mechanisms" for Congress to deploy as it sees fit. Incentives are used to achieve certain ends, and those ends need to be kept in mind while assessing the adequacy of the means.

Finally, critics of *Eldred* who point to the irrationality of an additional twenty years as a meaningful incentive ignore half of the argument in the economists' *amicus* brief. The brief begins with an analysis of the presently discounted value of an additional term of protection twenty years in the future.[18] But the brief then compares these minimal benefits with the costs of exclusivity in terms of limiting use by individuals like Eldred.[19] At the heart of the economists' argument is the conclusion that the benefits are outweighed by the costs. To separate the parts of the argument by focusing solely on the minimal incentives ignores the central question of the goals for which incentives are set.

As I stated earlier in this chapter, the challenging and critical questions are determining incentives for whom and for what ends. The academic economists' brief fairly and

---

[15] See *infra* notes 16 and 17.
[16] See Mark A. Lemley, *Ex Ante Versus Ex Post Justifications for Intellectual Property*, 71 U. CHI. L. REV. 129 (2004).
[17] See Paul J. Heald, *Does the Song Remain the Same?: An Empirical Study of Bestselling Musical Compositions (1913–1932) and Their Use in Cinema (1968–2007)*, 60 CASE WES. RES. L. REV. 1 (2009).
[18] Amicus Brief in Support of Petitioners, *supra* note 14, at 9–13.
[19] *Ibid.* at 23–24.

rigorously states the problem of copyright incentives and contextualizes that problem within the larger set of actors who engage with copyrighted works. This set not only includes the creators, but also subsequent innovators, re-users, retrofitters, and consumers. The Court, to its fault, adopts a narrower domain for the role of incentives, one that includes only authors and their publishers. Consequently, the incentives rationale and copyright policy are less powerful than they could be for creating a marketplace and community of creative talent.

B. *Aronson v. Quick Point* and the Pre-emption Issue

As further illustration of the range of incentives that inform intellectual property systems consider the Supreme Court's decision in *Aronson v. Quick Point*.[20] At issue in this 1979 ruling is the interplay between contract and patent law for the incentives to create and propagate new technologies. Just as *Eldred* does not directly confront the question of exhaustion, so *Aronson* deals with the separate issue of conflict between federal and State law under the United States (U.S.) system of federalism. Both *Eldred* and *Aronson*, however, teach about incentives and have implications, as I address in the next section, about limitations on intellectual property rights and the perceived loss of incentives.

When Aronson invented a new key chain, consisting of a sliding ring locking onto a curved metal holder, she did not realize that her acts and the ensuing litigation would produce a critical case relating to intellectual property and commercialization. Aronson negotiated a manufacturing license with Quick Point while her patent application was pending.[21] Under the terms of this license, Quick Point would produce the key chains and distribute them in exchange for a payment of royalties from its sales.[22] The royalties were subject to an escalator clause which set a specific rate if the patent were issued and a lower rate if the patent was denied.[23] The United States Patent and Trademark Office (USPTO) rejected Aronson's application, but Quick Point manufactured and sold the key chains for several years. After about fourteen years, at the point when the patent would have expired if it had been granted, Quick Point questioned why it should have to pay under the license.[24] The license was of unspecified duration, and Quick Point was finding that there were numerous competitors who simply copied Aronson's unprotected design.[25] The Supreme Court ruled against Quick Point, holding that contractual obligations can complement patent law without conflict.[26]

Both the *Eldred* and *Aronson* decisions center on the temporal limitations of intellectual property rights. *Eldred* questioned when Congress has the power to extend the term. In *Aronson*'s predecessor, *Brulotte v. Thys*, the Supreme Court ruled that an obligation to pay royalties post-patent expiration was invalid because of conflict with the limited

---

[20] Aronson v. Quick Point Pencil Co., 440 U.S. 257, 99 S. Ct. 1096, 59 L. Ed. 2d 296 (1979).
[21] *Ibid*. at 259.
[22] *Ibid*.
[23] *Ibid*.
[24] *Ibid*. at 260.
[25] *Ibid*.
[26] *Ibid*. at 266.

Incentives, contracts, and intellectual property exhaustion 9

patent term.[27] The core issue was the ability of private parties to extend the effective term through contract. When the Court created a *per se* rule against post-expiration royalty payments in *Brulotte*, the concern then became the patent owner leveraging its exclusive rights to expand the scope of the patent beyond the statutory grant.

Quick Point's argument in *Aronson* extended the reasoning of *Brulotte* to the scenario when a patent was not granted. If a patent on an invention is denied, and the invention is not otherwise protected, there is no consideration for the royalty payments. Aronson was effectively leveraging the promise of a patent to obtain exclusive rights she did not have. Furthermore, if any inventor was allowed to do what Aronson had done, namely obtain protection for an unpatentable invention through contract, then Quick Point questioned what incentive would exist to enter the patent system at all.[28] Quick Point argued that enforcing contracts like the one between it and Aronson conflicts with the incentives of the patent system to obtain exclusive rights for inventions.[29]

The Court rejected the conflict argument, concluding that contract incentives complemented those provided by patent law.[30] In broad terms, contracts facilitate the commercialization of patented inventions by allowing patentees to monetize rewards that flow from exclusivity. Even in the case of nonpatentable inventions, contracts can create incentives for an inventor to pursue a patent grant through escalating licensing terms. Although parties may not always be able to predict whether a patent will be granted, the possibility of obtaining a higher royalty rate or other contractual payment is an incentive for an inventor to file an application. Furthermore, even if an invention is nonpatentable, contracting for the use of the invention can help defray any expenses associated with producing the work. Since an inventor may invest in a range of inventions, some patentable, some not, entering into a contract allows the recoupment of fixed costs associated with research and development. Since the exclusivity established by contract is much narrower than that created by property, which creates rights against the world, the contract provides benefits without attendant costs from exclusivity. If there is a concern with abusive leveraging, the licensee can always propose terms for time-limiting the contract or lessening its burden through other means. In short, contract creates its own set of incentives that work in tandem with patent incentives for the creation and dissemination of new works.

As many scholars have pointed out, even before the Supreme Court's decision in *Aronson*, the complementarity of contract and patent counters the reasoning of the *Brulotte* ruling. Post-expiration royalties may serve many valid purposes that reinforce the goals of patent law. By potentially lowering payments over time, licensees may be more willing to enter into agreements with patentees for use of a technology. Royalty payments, although enforceable by patent law remedies, arise from contracting terms that bind only the parties and not the rest of the world. Should post-expiration payments be burdensome or the product of abusive leveraging, contract law doctrines can serve to limit their enforcement and antitrust law can sanction the patentee.

With the decision in *Aronson* as the applicable guide for how we should understand

---

[27] Brulotte v. Thys Co., 379 U.S. 29, 85 S. Ct. 176, 13 L. Ed. 2d 99 (1964).
[28] *Aronson, supra* note 20, 440 U.S. at 263.
[29] *Ibid.*
[30] *Ibid.* at 266.

intellectual property incentives, the Court emphasizes the importance of contract law to provide incentives for inventors and patent owners. As pointed out above, these incentives complement the exclusivity of patents. But these incentives also exist absent the grant of a patent. Even for unpatentable inventions, contract law provides incentives for undertaking the quest for a novel and nonobvious invention. Should that quest succeed, then contract law offers tools for commercializing patent rights. But even if the quest fails, contracts can provide alternatives that aid in obtaining a return on the research and development investment. For Eldred, returns through contract may have spurred his decision to pursue a business model based on public domain works. More generally, the ability to contract is available for all unprotected creations, including those that have fallen out of protection and those not eligible for protection because of failure to meet legal standards.

One may wonder whether contracts provide as much incentive as exclusive property rights. But this query again raises the issue, discussed in section II.A above, of how to gauge the magnitude and effectiveness of incentives. Exclusive property rights may create incentives for creation and invention. But they may also serve as disincentives for those who are seeking new business models or forms of creativity and invention. In the case of Eldred, a digital publisher was willing to undertake a venture absent any ostensible intellectual property protection. Instead, working with contract and other business tools, Eldred was drawing on public domain works to cultivate and distribute them. Similarly, Quick Point was manufacturing and marketing an unpatented invention for the commercial life of the ungranted patent. It was only the expiration of the shadow patent term which spurred Quick Point to rely on the highly criticized precedent in *Brulotte* to escape from its contractual obligations. While Quick Point argued that Aronson's contract undermined incentives for patenting the keychain, it could equally be argued that nonenforcement of the contract undermined incentives for Aronson to seek commercialization of her creation.

A skeptical reader may cast my argument as suggesting that contract law is a substitute for patent law. No such argument is being made. Justice Kagan characterized the exhaustion argument in *Bowman* as promoting substitution of contract protection for patent protection. But that is a mischaracterization of how contract and patent work together, whether in the context of pre-emption, as in *Aronson*, or in the context of exhaustion (as I will explain in more detail in section III). As the Court in *Aronson* emphasized, contract law does not displace patent law. Instead, the bodies of law complement each other, even in cases where no patent is granted.

To understand that point more fully, note that the process of invention and product development is a risky one. The question is who should bear the risk. If a patent is granted, the patentee can, in theory and often in practice, recoup the costs of development. The risk undertaken by the inventor is effectively spread through the commercialization of a patent to the rest of society. Rights against the world can be characterized as a form of risk spreading. Users of the patented product bear the risk through higher prices. However, they gain reward through presumably useful, novel, and nonobvious products (if these gains are not present, the patent is invalid). Contract allows risk sharing for specific ventures within the commercialization process between the inventor, manufacturers, and distributors. What *Aronson* allows is for the inventor to share the risk of the failure of patent issuance with a licensee. An inventor, like Aronson, bears the risk of non-issuance in the form of lower royalties. A licensee bears the risk of paying for an invention that others may be able to copy for free. But one advantage the licensee might gain is that of being first to market and being able to claim authorization from the inventor. Contract and patent work in tandem to allocate these and other identifiable risks in the development and commercialization process.

To summarize, contract and patent are complements. This conclusion should not be surprising. The counter-intuitive point is that contract law can complement patent law even if a patent is not granted. Contrary to Justice Kagan's doubt about contract in the *Bowman* oral argument, the complementary role of contract as incentive exists even when patent rights are exhausted. This last point is critical to the argument in section III.

III. EXHAUSTION AND INCENTIVES

We now turn to the question of incentives and intellectual property exhaustion. Two broad lessons follow from the previous discussion about intellectual property incentives. First, a critical part of the intellectual property incentive is that intellectual property rights are limited, certainly with respect to duration, but also respect to other dimensions of the right. Second, these limitations reflect a complex set of incentives targeted not only to owners of intellectual property but also to other creators and inventors. The doctrines of copyright and patent exhaustion reflect these two lessons.

The incentive argument needs to be acknowledged but also placed in the broader context of the impact of intellectual property rights on markets and other institutions. Debates over the exhaustion doctrine highlight the need to place the incentive arguments in the proper context so as to assess claims that intellectual property rights are being eviscerated. In the next subsection, we consider specifically the cases of copyright and patent exhaustion as canonical examples.

A. U.S. Approach to Copyright and Patent Exhaustion

Under U.S. law, exhaustion exists separately within copyright and patent, reflecting different policy goals for each type of intellectual property. Although courts and legislatures do refer to general exhaustion principles, the exhaustion doctrine is tailored to different intellectual property regimes.

(1) Copyright exhaustion

Exhaustion of copyright first arose in the U.S. in the 1908 decision by the U.S. Supreme Court in *Bobbs-Merrill v. Strauss*.[31] Prior to this decision, there is evidence of an aftermarket for copyrighted materials, particularly books, suggesting that copyrighted works could be resold. But there are no reported cases on the issue, perhaps because the practice of resale itself was not seen as controversial. This hypothesis is consistent with the specific controversy in *Bobbs-Merrill*. The publisher had distributed its books on the condition that the books not be sold for less than a specific price.[32] The question before the Court

---

[31] Bobbs-Merrill Co. v. Strauss, 210 U.S. 339, 28 S. Ct. 722 (1908).
[32] *Ibid*. at 341–42.

was whether this contractual term was enforceable, not whether resale in general would be permitted.[33] The two issues were related to each other, but the specific legal issue was the legality of the practice of maintaining the price at which books could be sold and resold.

The Court held that the contract term was unenforceable on the grounds of exhaustion.[34] Although the Court did analogize to price maintenance practices and other contractual restrictions under patent law (citing many of the cases discussed in the next subsection on U.S. patent exhaustion), the Court ultimately concluded that these patent law cases were inapposite to the copyright context.[35] The patent context was different because copyright was statutory, the Court deemed, although it is not completely clear from the opinion why that distinction is relevant.[36]

Nonetheless, the Court based its decision on the reading of the copyright statute in light of the language in the U.S. Constitution that copyright and patent are enacted in order to "promote progress in science and the useful arts."[37] The Copyright statute in force in 1908 did not mention exhaustion. Nonetheless, the Court read broadly the effective statute's language about the owner's right to vend the copyrighted work as promoting wide dissemination of the work without private contractual restrictions. Such wide, unfettered dissemination, the Court concluded, fulfills the goals of copyright law to benefit the public.[38]

Revisions to the Copyright Act in 1909 included an express provision regarding exhaustion. Section 41 of the 1909 Copyright Act stated: "[N]othing in this Act shall be deemed to forbid, prevent, or restrict the transfer of any copy of a copyrighted work the possession of which has been lawfully obtained."[39] This provision allows the transfer of a copy of a copyrighted work by someone who has lawfully obtained that copy. This provision is the first statutory codification of exhaustion under U.S. copyright law.

This version of exhaustion, referred to as the first sale doctrine, was recodified in the Copyright Act of 1976 under section 109(a), which has been in effect from 1978 to the present. This section provides that:

> the owner of a particular copy or phonorecord lawfully made under this title, or any person authorized by such owner, is entitled, without the authority of the copyright owner, to sell or otherwise dispose of the possession of that copy or phonorecord.[40]

The statute expressly states that this term is a limitation on the exclusive right of the copyright owner "to distribute copies or phonorecords of the copyrighted work to the public by sale or other transfer of ownership, or by rental, lease, or lending" under section 106(3) of the Copyright Act.[41]

While the understanding of section 109(a) limits the legal reselling of a copy of a

---

[33] *Ibid.* at 350.
[34] *Ibid.* at 346.
[35] *Ibid.*
[36] *Ibid.*
[37] *Ibid.* (citing U.S. Const. art. I, § 8).
[38] *Ibid.* at 351.
[39] Copyright Act of 1909, § 41 (repealed and superseded by the Copyright Act of 1976, in effect January 1, 1978).
[40] Copyright Act of 1976, 17 U.S.C. § 109(a).
[41] See *ibid.*

copyrighted work that has been lawfully purchased (e.g., reselling a purchased book or DVD), the statutory language is fairly complex. Although section 109(a) is presented as a limitation on section 106(3), the limitation does not apply to the portion of section 106(3) that provides an exclusive right "for rental, lease, or lending." This limitation on a limitation, so to speak, is an inference from the use of the word "owner" in section 109(a). Someone who obtains possession through rental, lease or lending would not be an owner of the copy. Section 109(d) clarifies this reading by expressly stating that section 109(a) does not apply to rental, lease or lending.[42]

Exhaustion principles arise in other provisions of section 109. These further limitations illustrate the work- and industry-specific nature of copyright exhaustion. Section 109(b) provides that the copyright owner retains the rental right in copyrighted software and phonorecords even after a first sale.[43] This retention of rights effectively prohibits a rental market for software and phonorecords even if a purchaser buys a copy of software or a phonorecord, unless authorized by the copyright owner. Section 117, however, does allow the owner of a copy of software to make copies for archival purposes or for booting up or running requisite hardware. Under section 117, the owner is also allowed to make copies for the purpose of maintaining or repairing a machine that contains authorized copies of the software.[44] Section 109(c) allows a purchaser of a pictorial, graphic or sculptural work to publicly display the work without needing to obtain a license from the copyright owner.[45] Furthermore, section 109(e) allows the purchaser of an "electronic audiovisual game," which was "lawfully made under this title," to publicly perform and display the copyrighted content in the game, although this right does not extend to any content that might be infringing within the game, i.e., content that the creator of the game infringed.[46]

Lower courts in the U.S. have addressed issues of copyright exhaustion in response to particular industry practices.[47] Courts have found that copyright exhaustion applies when there is a sale based on the economic and business realities of a transaction.[48] Therefore, exhaustion has applied to a transaction in which resale rights were purportedly limited by contractual provisions. Such contractual limitations on resale do not apply if the court finds under the circumstances that the copyright has transferred its rights in a particular copy to the acquiring party. However, right to resell digital content (works subject to technology protection measures) is an ongoing issue in the U.S. One district court ruling against exhaustion of digital works based its decision on the recopying of the work by the purchaser in reselling the technologically protected work.[49] According to the court, copyright exhaustion does not permit recopying the work since unlimited copying would lower the demand for the original work.[50] However, the purchaser could

---

[42] 17 U.S.C. § 109(d).
[43] 17 U.S.C. § 109(b).
[44] 17 U.S.C. § 117.
[45] 17 U.S.C. § 109(c).
[46] 17 U.S.C. § 109(e).
[47] UMG Recordings, Inc. v. Augusto, 628 F.3d 1175 (9th Cir. 2011); MDY Indus., LLC v. Blizzard Entm't, Inc., 629 F.3d 928 (9th Cir. 2010).
[48] See discussion in Vernor v. Autodesk, 621 F.3d 1102 (9th Cir. 2010).
[49] Capitol Records, LLC v. Redigi Inc., 934 F. Supp. 2d 640 (S.D.N.Y. 2013).
[50] *Capitol Records*, 934 F. Supp. 2d at 654.

resell the protected work embodied in a physical medium (such as a digital player or a personal computer) as long as no new copies were made. The application of copyright exhaustion to digital works will be of continued importance as more content migrates to electronic formats.

The contemporary version of copyright exhaustion in the U.S. dates back at least a century and illustrates the tailoring of the doctrine to specific works and uses. One overarching question that was resolved by the U.S. Supreme Court in 2013 is the application of copyright exhaustion to cross-border transactions. Although this question has been controversial for over a decade, the Court decided in favor of the principle of international exhaustion through its decision in *Kirtsaeng v. Wiley Publishing*.[51]

The debate over international copyright exhaustion began in the 1997 case *Quality King v. L'Anza*, a controversy over the gray market sales of cosmetics bearing labels copyrighted in the U.S.[52] In *Quality King*, a parallel importer who had bought U.S. cosmetics overseas, resold the cosmetics bearing copyrighted labels, and was arbitraging the global price differential for the products.[53] The products themselves were initially exported from the U.S., but made their way back into the U.S. market through the round trip of global sales. While the owner of the copyright in the labels (also the manufacturer of the cosmetics) claimed that the act of importing the products into the U.S. was a violation of the distribution right, the importer asserted the exhaustion doctrine through the first sale defense.[54] However, it was not clear as a matter of statutory interpretation whether the first sale doctrine under section 109(a) applied to the importation right under section 601. For the courts, the issue was purely one of statutory interpretation. Since section 109(a) was stated as a limitation on section 106(3), it was not clear that the limitation would apply to the separate statutory provision establishing the importation right. The Supreme Court ultimately ruled that section 109(a) was a limitation on the rights under section 601, since section 601 was written to be a part of the distribution rights under section 106(3).[55]

Although a relatively straightforward matter of statutory interpretation, several controversies were buried within the *Quality King* case. First, the U.S. government's position was that the first sale defense did not apply to the importation right because importation entailed the movement of goods across borders, which is to be considered as different than the sale of goods.[56] The Court in *Quality King* rejected this view since the first sale doctrine would apply to the sale of a work.[57] Application of the first sale doctrine would rest on whether there had been a sale triggering exhaustion. A separate importation right involving the movement of goods would not negate any application of exhaustion to the sale of the imported goods. Although the Court in *Quality King* seemingly gave a definitive negative response to the U.S. government's view, Justices Kagan and Alito in the 2013 *Kirstaeng* decision authored a concurrence suggesting that perhaps the U.S. government

---

[51] Kirstaeng v. John Wiley & Sons, Inc., 133 S. Ct. 1351 (2013).
[52] Quality King Distribs. v. L'Anza Research Int'l, 523 U.S. 135, 118 S. Ct. 1125 (1998).
[53] *Ibid.* at 139.
[54] *Ibid.* at 152.
[55] *Ibid.* at 152–53.
[56] *Ibid.* at 146.
[57] *Ibid.* at 151–52.

was correct.[58] Therefore, the issue of treatment of importation as physical movement of goods still potentially remains open.

The second controversy arises from the nature of the transaction triggering exhaustion. At issue in *Quality King* was a round trip, meaning that the goods were originally exported from the U.S. before, after several transactions overseas, being imported back into the country. Justice Ginsburg in a separate opinion stated that the first sale doctrine applied only to this scenario.[59] Subsequently, lower courts followed Justice Ginsburg's analysis to conclude that the first sale doctrine applied only to goods that originated from the U.S. Some courts adopted an even stronger limitation that requires the copyrighted works be manufactured in the U.S. in order for exhaustion to apply to the importation of the goods into the country. A few courts, however, held that the first sale doctrine applied to all copyrighted goods regardless of place of manufacture or sale. This last position is referred to as international exhaustion, which is the principle adopted by the Court in the 2013 *Kirstaeng* decision.

At issue in *Kirstaeng* was the purchase overseas of textbooks manufactured and marketed by the copyright owner Wiley Publishers for the Thailand market.[60] Kirstaeng, a Thai student in the U.S., had bought large quantities of textbooks for a low price in Thailand and imported them into the U.S. for resale at the higher price in the U.S. market.[61] Wiley, as copyright owner, asserted violation of the importation and distribution rights.[62] Kirstaeng asserted exhaustion through the first sale doctrine.[63] The majority of the Supreme Court found for Kirstaeng on the grounds that there was no geographic limitation on the first sale doctrine in the statute, in case law, and in policy.[64]

With respect to the statute, the Court addressed the language "lawfully made under this title," which some courts had interpreted to mean "made in the United States." The Court rejected this reading because "under this title" does not have a geographic meaning.[65] Instead, the phrase referred to the source of legal authority for making a work. Such legal authority would not extend to pirated or counterfeited works. In this case, Wiley had authorized the manufacture and sale of the books in Thailand. Furthermore, the roots of the first sale doctrine in case law did not support a geographic limitation. To this point, the Court majority refers to precedent in *Bobbs-Merrill* and the broad policy goals of dissemination to the public.[66] Finally, as a policy matter, the Court majority expressed concern regarding the uncertainty created in domestic markets as to the applicability of the first sale doctrine to copyrighted works that have multiple countries of origin, either with respect to manufacture or to sale.[67] For example, if there were a geographic limitation, a purchaser of an automobile containing copyrighted software may not be able to

---

[58] *Kirstaeng*, *supra* note 51, 133 S. Ct. at 1372.
[59] *Quality King*, *supra* note 52, 523 U.S. at 153–54.
[60] *Kirstaeng*, *supra* note 51, 133 S. Ct. at 1356.
[61] *Ibid.*
[62] *Ibid.* at 1357.
[63] *Ibid.*
[64] *Ibid.* at 1371.
[65] *Ibid.* at 1361.
[66] *Ibid.* at 1363.
[67] *Ibid.* at 1362.

resell the car domestically if the software originated overseas. International exhaustion was held to be consistent with the statute, judicial precedent, and copyright policy.

The three dissenting judges (Justices Ginsburg, Scalia, and Kennedy) read the statute as limiting first sale to works that originated in the U.S.[68] They emphasized the policy concern expressed by copyright owners and by the U.S. government: permitting imported works would lead to the introduction of pirated or counterfeit works within the U.S. Limiting the U.S. copyright owners' rights to prevent imports would allow unscrupulous importers to bring in unauthorized works. Therefore, the three justices advocated for a much narrower exhaustion principle, one limited to national boundaries. Even though Justices Kagan and Alito agreed with the majority on adopting international exhaustion, their concurring opinion expresses sympathy for the dissenting argument.[69] But ultimately, Justices Kagan and Alito concluded that adopting international exhaustion was consistent with precedent. However, their concurrence and the opinion of the three dissenters suggest that the issue of international exhaustion may be settled only temporarily.

There are, however, two lessons to be gleaned from the discussion of U.S. copyright exhaustion. The first is the basis of the doctrine in policies and principles of public dissemination. The second is the tailoring of the exhaustion doctrine to different works, industries, and uses. These potentially competing principles will be important in drawing broader policy implications for the exhaustion doctrine.

(2) Patent exhaustion

Like copyright exhaustion, patent exhaustion originates in judicial decisions. But unlike copyright exhaustion, patent exhaustion has not been codified in the statute. Instead, the case law is based on a mixture of patent law, antitrust law, and common law principles of property, and continues to be the basis for applying the patent exhaustion doctrine. Recent U.S. Supreme Court decisions have addressed novel issues of patent exhaustion, demonstrating both the doctrine's continued viability and evolution. Given the complexities of patent exhaustion, I break the analysis into parts.

(a) What is patent exhaustion? The grant of a patent to a useful, novel, and nonobvious invention is one step in the development of a free and competitive marketplace. The exclusive rights to make, use, sell, and offer to sell provided by 35 U.S.C. § 154(a)(1)[70] and enforced through 35 U.S.C. § 271(a)[71] allow the patent owner to distribute the patented invention. The exclusive rights also allow the patent owner to enter into transactions permitting the dissemination of the protected product through a chain of manufacture and into the hands of many users. In this way, the existence of a patent is no different from any other legal rule that facilitates the working of a vibrant market. Just as the rules of property, contract, tort, and the sundry federal and State statutory schemes strive to protect consumers, investors, and manufacturers, the laws of patents (and its cousin of copyright law) set ground rules for competition.

---

[68] *Ibid.* at 1375.
[69] *Ibid.* at 1372.
[70] Patent Act, 35 U.S.C § 154(a)(1).
[71] 35 U.S.C. § 271(a).

The patent exhaustion doctrine is one of the key elements of these ground rules. Under the patent exhaustion doctrine, once the invention is distributed through a lawful transaction, the invention passes into the hands of the purchaser, no longer subject to the exclusive rights of the patent owner. Like any other commodity, a patented invention enters into commerce and can be further distributed without the original seller encumbering and raising the costs of subsequent transactions. Put simply, the principle underlying the exhaustion doctrine is that the patent owner obtains "one bite at the apple" by first permitting the owner to extract the commercial returns in the first sale of a patented invention and then by preventing him from erecting a "tollgate" at each subsequent transaction.

While copyright exhaustion extinguishes the distribution right after the first sale, patent exhaustion applies to both the patent owner's exclusive right to sale and the right to use. To the last point, the purchaser of a patented invention has an implied license to use the patented invention for the purposes intended. In addition, the purchaser has the right to repair the invention in order to "preserve the fitness for use."[72] However, a reconstruction entails the making of another copy of the patented invention, while repair entails reconstituting an existing invention.[73] The Supreme Court has distinguished a reconstruction from repair as an impermissible making of the invention.

(b) Origins of patent exhaustion The Supreme Court has recognized that the patent exhaustion doctrine is important for a functioning market shaped by patent law. The Court first articulated the broad contours of the doctrine in *Bloomer v. McQuewan*:

> The inventor might lawfully sell it to him, whether he had a patent or not, if no other patentee stood in his way. And when the machine passes to the hands of the purchaser, it is no longer within the limits of the monopoly. It passes outside of it, and is no longer under the protection of the act of Congress.[74]

In *Adams v. Burke*, the Court recognized the patent exhaustion doctrine as essential to the nature of transactions transferring patented inventions.[75] In *Burke*, the Court was faced with a territorial use restriction on the manufacturer-assignee, who was not permitted to distribute patented coffin lids outside a ten-mile radius of the City of Boston.[76] When a subsequent assignee of the patent owner sued an undertaker who had purchased the lids and removed them from the territory, the Court found that patent exhaustion barred the claim.[77] This out-of-territory purchaser, the Court reasoned, had "acquired the right to use that coffin for the purpose for which all coffins are used."[78] "[I]n the essential nature of things," the Court wrote, "when the patentee, or the person having his rights, sells a machine or instrument whose sole value is in its use, he receives the consideration

---

[72] See discussion in Aro Manufacturing Co. v. Convertible Top Replacement Co., 365 U.S. 336, 374 (1961).
[73] Ibid.
[74] Bloomer v. McQuewan, 55 U.S. 539, 549 (1852).
[75] Adams v. Burke, 84 U.S. 453, 456 (1873).
[76] Ibid.
[77] Ibid.
[78] Ibid.

for its use and he parts with the right to restrict that use."[79] The protected work passes "without the limit of the monopoly."[80]

The exhaustion doctrine, in patent as well as copyright law, rests on a carefully constructed balance between property and contract rights. The doctrine recognizes that transactions between patent/copyright owners and their purchasers will be subject to a myriad of negotiated terms. In *Bobbs-Merrill*, for example, the Court applied the first sale doctrine to sales "without restriction."[81] This qualifying language recognizes that the copyright or patent owner can impose contractual restrictions on the initial purchaser, including, presumably, clear limitations on the right to resell the intellectual property. In this way, for example, the owner can create a rental market for intellectual property analogous to rental markets for real or personal property. But as the Court of Appeals for the Federal Circuit has acknowledged, "patented articles when sold 'become the private individual property of the purchasers, and are no longer specifically protected by the patent laws.' The fact that an article is patented gives the purchaser neither more nor less rights of use and disposition."[82] In other words, limitations imposed in the sale of a patented invention are a matter of contract law, not patent law. The exhaustion doctrine tells the purchaser of a patent-protected work and all subsequent distribution parties that the work has been transferred free of any patent claims of the original owner on the use or disposition of the work, although not necessarily of contract claims.

Both the *Bloomer* and *Adams* decisions were rendered before the enactment of the Sherman Act in 1890. The Supreme Court's decision in *United States v. Univis Lens Co.*[83] illustrates how the exhaustion doctrine complements the antitrust treatment of use restrictions. At issue in *Univis Lens* was an alleged antitrust violation arising from resale restrictions imposed by a manufacturer patentee. The manufacturer argued under the rule of *General Electric* that it was engaged in a licensing transaction that allowed it to impose the resale restrictions.[84] The Court found that the transaction was a sale, and not a license, and therefore was outside the scope of the patent monopoly, reasoning:

> [W]here one has sold an uncompleted article which, because it embodies essential features of his patented invention, is within the protection of his patent . . . The reward he has demanded and received is for the article and the invention which it embodies and which his vendee is to practice upon it. He has thus parted with his right to assert the patent monopoly with respect to it.[85]

In short, the exhaustion doctrine made the legal issue a pure question of how the contractual restriction would be treated under antitrust law. The Supreme Court affirmed this approach to the patent exhaustion doctrine through the lens of antitrust law in its 2008

---

[79] Ibid.
[80] Ibid.
[81] *Bobbs-Merrill*, supra note 31, 210 U.S. at 350.
[82] Jazz Photo Corp. v. Int'l Trade Comm'n, 264 F.3d 1094, 1102 (Fed. Cir. 2001) (quoting Mitchell v. Hawley, 83 U.S. 544, 548 (1873)).
[83] United States v. Univis Lens Co., 316 U.S. 241, 62 S. Ct. 1088 (1942).
[84] *Ibid.* at 247.
[85] *Ibid.* at 250–51.

decision in *Quanta v. LG Electronics*,[86] and it is the subject of the recent 2013 decision in *Bowman v. Monsanto*.

(c) Recent Supreme Court developments: Quanta and Bowman In *Quanta*, LG Electronic's licensee, to quote the language from *Univis Lens*, sold an article that "embodies essential features" of the patented invention and "has destined the article to be finished by the purchaser in conformity to the patent."[87] LG Electronics had acquired a large patent portfolio of technologies used in the manufacturing of computer chips. After a dispute with Intel, the company manufacturing the chips, the respondent entered into a complex licensing agreement with Intel that allowed Intel to use the technology in the construction and sale of chips. These chips in turn were sold to petitioners and incorporated as components in computer hardware systems. LG Electronics subsequently sought to enforce its patent rights against the petitioners based on their alleged violation of "conditions" placed on the original agreement with Intel.[88]

The patent exhaustion doctrine was designed to prohibit precisely this type of "reach-through" by the patent owner to enforce its patent rights. Accordingly, in *Quanta*, the Supreme Court affirmed the long recognized patent exhaustion doctrine. Citing its precedents at the intersection of antitrust and patent laws, the Court stated the first sale doctrine broadly, holding that "[t]he authorized sale of an article that substantially embodies a patent exhausts the patent holder's rights and prevents the patent holder from invoking patent law to control post sale use of the article."[89]

In *Bowman v. Monsanto*, the Supreme Court considered the applicability of patent exhaustion to genetically modified seeds.[90] At issue in the case were two patents owned by Monsanto that read on a type of gene and a type of synthase, respectively. Monsanto's patent claim was limited to its "chimera gene" sequence that allows the resulting plant to be pesticide resistant. Monsanto sold the genetically modified seeds directly to purchasers and licensed its patent to seed producers to manufacture and sell the genetically modified seeds.[91]

Monsanto did contractually restrict the right of the seed purchaser to replant the second generation seeds from the germinated plant. The patented gene sequence is sold and licensed subject to an agreement which states: (1) that the purchaser will plant the seed for only one growing season; (2) that the purchaser will not supply the seed to any other grower for planting; (3) that the purchaser will not save any crop from the planting for replanting or transfer the crop to a third party for replanting; and (4) that the purchaser will not use the seed or allow the seed to be used for research, crop breeding, or crop production.[92] Bowman, a soybean farmer, planted seeds he had obtained from grain elevators to which other farmers had sold the second-generation seeds. Monsanto sued Bowman for patent infringement.

---

[86] Quanta Computer, Inc. v. LG Elecs., Inc., 553 U.S. 617, 128 S. Ct. 2109 (2008).
[87] *Ibid.* at 627–28.
[88] *Ibid.* at 624.
[89] *Ibid.* at 631.
[90] Monsanto Co. v. Bowman, 657 F.3d 1341 (Fed. Cir. 2011).
[91] *Ibid.* at 1345–46.
[92] *Ibid.*

Bowman raised the exhaustion defense in accordance with the Supreme Court's ruling in *Quanta*. The U.S. Court of Appeals for the Federal Circuit rejected the defense on two grounds. First, the court reasoned that the exhaustion doctrine would not apply to self-replicating technologies, like genetically modified seeds.[93] Applying exhaustion, the court reasoned, would permit reuse and thereby limit the patent owner's ability to profit from the patented technology. Second, the Federal Circuit reasoned that exhaustion would not apply to Bowman because exhaustion permits reselling the seed and not making another copy of the patented technology.[94] By growing a third generation of plants containing the seeds, the Federal Circuit concluded, Bowman went beyond his rights under the exhaustion doctrine to make an unauthorized copy of the patented technology.[95]

In its decision for Monsanto, the Federal Circuit created an exception to the patent exhaustion doctrine for the *sui generis* category of self-replicating technologies, meaning inventions that recreate themselves through reproduction. The court repeated its reasoning in *Monsanto v. Scruggs* that "[a]pplying the first sale doctrine to subsequent generations of self-replicating technology would eviscerate the rights of the patent holder."[96]

The Federal Circuit rejected Bowman's argument that the seed sold by Monsanto contained all future generation seeds and thereby embodied Monsanto's patent fully. First, the court characterized the reproduction from the seed of a new plant as constructing an essentially new article, infringing the patent owner's right to exclude others from making the patented invention.[97] Second, the court rejected Bowman's argument that the only reasonable and intended use of the seed was for replanting them to create new seeds.[98] The Court suggested other use of the seeds, such as for feed. Consequently, the Court rejected the exhaustion argument because the patented technology at issue is one that recreates itself.[99] The application of the patent exhaustion doctrine to such a technology, the Federal Circuit concluded, would eviscerate patent rights over such technology.[100]

The Supreme Court affirmed the Federal Circuit's ruling in favor of Monsanto, although through different reasoning. Writing for an unanimous court, Justice Kagan concluded:

> Under the patent exhaustion doctrine, Bowman could resell the patented soybeans he purchased from the grain elevator; so too he could consume the beans himself or feed them to his animals. Monsanto, although the patent holder, would have no business interfering in these uses of Roundup Ready beans. But the exhaustion doctrine does not enable Bowman to make additional patented soybeans without Monsanto's permission (either express or implied).[101]

Citing precedent from 1882, the Court reasoned that the exhaustion doctrine did not permit the making of another copy of the patented invention without the patent owner's permission. As the Court explained:

---

[93] *Ibid.* at 1347 (citing Monsanto v. Scruggs, 459 F.3d 1328, 1336 (Fed. Cir. 2006)).
[94] *Ibid.* at 1349.
[95] *Ibid.* at 1348.
[96] *Ibid.* at 1347 (citing Monsanto v. Scruggs, 459 F.3d 1328, 1336 (Fed. Cir. 2006)).
[97] *Ibid.* at 1348.
[98] *Ibid.*
[99] *Ibid.*
[100] *Ibid.*
[101] Bowman v. Monsanto Co., 133 S. Ct. 1761, 1766 (2013).

> [I]f simple copying were a protected use, a patent would plummet in value after the first sale of the first item containing the invention. The undiluted patent monopoly, it might be said, would extend not for 20 years (as the Patent Act promises), but for only one transaction. And that would result in less incentive for innovation than Congress wanted. Hence our repeated insistence that exhaustion applies to the particular item sold, and not to reproductions.[102]

While the Court's reasoning echoes the concerns of the Federal Circuit in its decision, with the possibility of boundless copying after the first sale, the Court fell short of adopting an exception to patent exhaustion for self-replicating technologies. The Court concluded its opinion by stating that the holding "is limited" to the particular facts of the *Bowman* case.[103] As for other types of self-replicating technologies, such as software or digital content, "the article's self-replication might occur outside the purchaser's control. Or it might be a necessary but incidental step in using the item for another purpose."[104] Therefore, the Supreme Court's decision leaves open the question of how the patent exhaustion doctrine would apply to cases other than genetically modified soybeans.

One controversy left open by the Court's decision is the source of a farmer's right to plant the genetically modified seed. In an elaborate footnote, the Court states that its conclusion about exhaustion is applicable regardless of how a farmer acquires the patented seed.[105] Whether the farmer bought the seed directly from the patent owner or indirectly from a granary, the farmer cannot plant the seed to grow another generation of the patented germplasm. The Court does point out that a purchase directly from the patent owner would be subject to an express license that the patent owner uses to distribute the seeds.[106] But even absent such an express license, the Court suggests, "the farmer might reasonably claim that the sale came with an implied license to plant and harvest one soybean crop."[107] The language regarding implied license is confusing. It is not clear whether the Court is saying that exhaustion is a matter of implied/express license or a matter of the purchaser's rights to be free from restraints on alienation. The possibility of an implied license suggests that the patent owner could further restrict the farmer through contractual use of the patented seeds. How far a patent owner can limit the exhaustion doctrine through contract is an unclear question under the decision in *Bowman*.

IV. CONCLUSION: TOWARDS THE DIGITAL FUTURE

This chapter presents the arguments why placing limits on intellectual property rights does not undermine the incentives for creation and invention. These arguments have salient application to the doctrines of copyright and patent exhaustion. The points defended in this chapter will have ongoing implications for the continuing debate over the scope of intellectual property exhaustion as applied to the distribution of digital works. As courts and legislatures struggle over the scope of digital rights, their attention

---

[102] *Ibid.* at 1768.
[103] *Ibid.* at 1769.
[104] *Ibid.*
[105] *Ibid.* at n. 3.
[106] *Ibid.*
[107] *Ibid.*

will undoubtedly turn to exhaustion. Lower courts have been hesitant to recognize digital exhaustion because the transfer of digital works often entails making a new copy of the work.[108] Their reasoning, steadfast but incorrect, is that permitting exhaustion would undermine incentives.

What this chapter advocates is a richer understanding of incentives, one that looks beyond incentives for creation and invention to include incentives for consumers, resellers, and other actors necessary for the active, competitive exchange of the fruits of intellectual property. An expansion of how we recognize incentives is not a rhetorical move. Instead, understanding incentives broadly is consistent with the incentives rationale for copyright and patent in promoting progress in the development of new works and inventions. While courts may have narrowed the meaning of incentives, a broader conception of incentives is present in Supreme Court precedent. What this chapter has done is identify and support a more complete formulation of intellectual property incentives. Such a formulation, grounded in legal traditions, can guide our approach to the digital future.

---

[108] See Capitol Records v. ReDigi, 934 F. Supp. 2d 640 (S.D.N.Y. 2013). But see also Case C-128/11 UsedSoft v. Oracle International, European Court of Justice, 2012 ECLI:EU:C:2012:407 (finding exhaustion in resale of digital licenses).

2. The economic rationale for exhaustion: distribution and post-sale restraints
*Ariel Katz**

I. INTRODUCTION

The first sale doctrine, also known as the exhaustion rule of intellectual property (IP) rights, limits an IP owner's power to control the downstream distribution and use of its intellectual goods. Despite its common law origins, "an impeccable historic pedigree,"[1] and over a hundred years of adjudication, courts have never been able to draw the exact contours of the first sale doctrine or fully articulate its rationale.

Proponents of narrow (or no) exhaustion rules began harnessing insights from modern antitrust law and economics to suggest that, just as antitrust law has recognized the efficiency of some post-sale restraints and relaxed its hostility toward them, so should IP law permit their imposition and provide remedies for their breach. This chapter challenges this position. It shows that post-sale restraints can be beneficial, mostly in situations of imperfect vertical integration between coproducing or collaborating firms, when used to solve organizational problems that occur during the production and distribution phases or shortly thereafter. In such situations, the law should allow IP owners and those with whom they collaborate to contract around the first sale doctrine. Beyond such limited circumstances, however, the first sale doctrine promotes important social and economic goals: it promotes efficient use of goods embodying IP, guarantees their preservation, and facilitates user innovation, while minimizing transaction costs that otherwise might impede those goals. Therefore, rather than undermining it, the economics of post-sale restraints confirm the validity of the first sale doctrine and support its continued vitality.

This chapter focuses on the first sale doctrine in copyright law, but most of the analysis is applicable to other IP rights.[2] It also focuses mainly on U.S. law, yet most of its lessons can be applied elsewhere as well. The chapter proceeds as follows: section II briefly describes different existing and possible formulations of the first sale doctrine to set the stage for the discussion that follows. Sections III and IV present arguments in favor of the first sale doctrine and against it, while section V shows how those conflicting views can be reconciled and emphasizes how the first sale doctrine, properly understood, enables

---

   * Associate Professor, Innovation Chair Electronic Commerce, Faculty of Law, University of Toronto. This chapter is based on an earlier article, Ariel Katz, *The First Sale Doctrine and the Economics of Post-Sale Restraints*, 2014 BYU L. REV. 55 (2014). I thank Michael Stenbring for his research assistance.
   [1] Kirtsaeng v. John Wiley & Sons, Inc., 133 S. Ct. 1351, 1353 (2013).
   [2] Moreover, since the first sale doctrine is merely a manifestation of "a common-law doctrine with an impeccable historic pedigree," *Kirtsaeng, supra* note 1, 133 S. Ct. at 1363, the analysis can apply even more broadly to all restraints on alienation of property, whether or not IP rights are involved.

23

short-term post-sale restraints (where they are most likely to be beneficial) while guaranteeing the long-term benefits that exhaustion supports.

II. FIRST SALE DOCTRINE: DIFFERENT FORMULATIONS

Part of the difficulty in the debate about the first sale doctrine stems from ambiguity surrounding its meaning and scope: how strong it is, whether it is a mandatory or merely a default rule, and if it is a default rule, how sticky that default rule is. In order to begin answering these questions, it may be useful to recognize that there might be at least five possible formulations of the doctrine based on perceived strength.

Level 0: At one end of the spectrum lies the option of no first sale doctrine, meaning that it is up to the IP owner to decide whether the first-authorized sale or any subsequent sale would exhaust the IP right. This option is included not merely for the elegance of the model, but also because in some instances this is (or might be) the law.[3]

Level 1: A weak formulation views the first sale doctrine as a simple default rule: the IP owner's exclusive right is exhausted after the first *unconditional* sale. However, it may not be exhausted if the transaction is conditional and conditions were imposed by license, contract, or, possibly, even mere notice. Breach of any such conditions (by a contracting party, a licensee, or a purchaser who had notice of the restriction) would trigger liability for infringement.[4]

Level 2: Under a moderate first sale doctrine the first authorized sale still exhausts the IP right but the buyer may still be bound by contractual post-sale restraints.[5]

Level 3: A strong formulation of the rule treats the first sale doctrine as a sticky default rule.[6] This means that the first authorized sale exhausting the IP rights and attempting to work around exhaustion rules would be invalidated in the absence of a compelling case-specific explanation as to why the work-around should be upheld.[7]

Level 4: Under the strongest formulation of the first sale doctrine, not only does the sale exhaust the IP right, but also all attempts to work around the doctrine would be held invalid, and might even constitute IP misuse[8] or a *per se* antitrust violation.

---

[3] See e.g. Vernor v. Autodesk, Inc., 621 F.3d 1102 (9th Cir. 2010) (holding that the owner of the copyright in a computer program can escape its limitations by "licensing" copies instead of selling them); *Capitol Records, L.L.C. v. ReDigi Inc.*, 934 F. Supp. 2d 640 (S.D.N.Y. 2013) (finding that the doctrine does not apply to digital copies resold apart from the medium in which they are embedded); *Kirtsaeng, supra* note 1, 133 S. Ct. at 1376 (Ginsburg J., dissenting) (regarding copies made outside of the U.S.).

[4] See e.g. Herbert Hovenkamp, *Post-Sale Restraints and Competitive Harm: The First Sale Doctrine in Perspective*, 66 N.Y.U. ANN. SURV. AM. L. 487, 541 (2010).

[5] See Brief of Amicus Curiae United States in Support of Petitioners, Quanta Computer, Inc. v. LG Elecs., 553 U.S. 617 (2008) (No. 06-937), 2007 WL 3353102, at *29.

[6] On sticky default rules, see generally Cass R. Sunstein, *Switching the Default Rule*, 77 N.Y.U. L. REV. 106 (2002).

[7] This can be analogous to how the scope of fair use in copyright law develops, see Peter DiCola & Matthew Sag, *An Information-Gathering Approach to Copyright Policy*, 34 CARDOZO L. REV. 173 (2012).

[8] See Omega S.A. v. Costco Wholesale Corp., 776 F.3d 692 (9th Cir. 2015) (Wardlaw J., concur-

III. THE CASE FOR EXHAUSTION

The first sale doctrine has been justified on several grounds, economic and otherwise. Some arguments outline the ways in which the first sale doctrine benefits not only consumers, but also the public at large and even, in certain ways, creators and innovators. Exhaustion mitigates some of the deadweight loss that results from the grant of exclusive IP rights and the associated power to price intellectual goods above the competitive level, increasing access to and availability of intellectual goods mainly through secondary markets or parallel trade.[9] These markets make works sold through these channels more affordable, and therefore more accessible, and they also put competitive pressure on the prices that IP owners can set through their primary distribution channels.[10] Exhaustion also allows consumers who are unwilling or unable to pay the IP owner's market price to access the work through alternative channels such as rental, or borrowing from public institutions like libraries.[11] Perzanowski and Schultz offer another justification. According to them, exhaustion plays an important part in reducing consumer lock-in and thereby encourages platform competition; that is, competition between systems that can be used for different and changing applications.[12]

However, the effects of exhaustion on static efficiency are not unambiguously salutary. If IP owners respond to those competitive pressures by abandoning some markets or focusing only on "premium" high-margin markets, consumers who otherwise might be served will be worse off,[13] and because supply in the primary markets will be more limited, the quantities available through the secondary markets will be limited as well. That said, exhaustion may also benefit IP owners because it may assist them to implement *unofficial* price discrimination schemes, where official action may be more costly or even backfire on them. For example, students in a given geographical market may vary in their willingness and ability to pay for textbooks. Some can and would purchase a highly priced new textbook, while others cannot or would not. Ideally, the publisher would like to set different prices for each type, but it may be difficult to identify which student belongs to which type. Preventing the low-price types from reselling their books to the high-price types might prove difficult to enforce, even if such resale constituted

---

ring) (describing copyright misuse as an attempt to gain control over acts that fall outside the scope of the statutory grant).

[9] See e.g. Joseph P. Liu, *Owning Digital Copies: Copyright Law and the Incidents of Copy Ownership*, 42 WM. & MARY L. REV. 1245 (2001); R. Anthony Reese, *The First Sale Doctrine in the Era of Digital Networks*, 44 B.C. L. REV. 577 (2003); Aaron Perzanowski & Jason Schultz, *Digital Exhaustion*, 58 UCLA L. REV. 889 (2010) [hereinafter Perzanowski & Schultz, *Digital Exhaustion*]; Aaron Perzanowski & Jason Schultz, *Legislating Digital Exhaustion*, 29 BERKELEY TECH. L.J. 1535 (2015).

[10] Ariel Katz, *The First Sale Doctrine and the Economics of Post-Sale Restraints*, 2014 B.Y.U. L. REV. 55, 76 (2014).

[11] Reese, *supra* note 9, at 587–89.

[12] Perzanowski & Schultz, *Digital Exhaustion*, *supra* note 9, at 900 (exhaustion encourages platform competition by preventing lock-in, which occurs when "the costs of switching to a new vendor or technology platform are sufficient to discourage consumers from adopting an otherwise preferable competitive offering," by allowing consumers to recoup some of the costs they sunk into a platform through the resale of the platform itself, or the resale of applications which function on that platform, thereby making the switch to a new platform more affordable).

[13] Guy A. Rub, *Rebalancing Copyright Exhaustion*, 64 EMORY L.J. 741, 763 (2015).

infringement. Moreover, high-price types might resent being charged a higher price for the same product, decreasing their own willingness to pay, or even increasing their willingness to consider obtaining pirated copies by reducing the moral cost of piracy.[14] Exhaustion offers the publisher a solution to this dilemma. First, it lets consumers sort themselves out. High-price types might be happy to pay for the ease, convenience, and value of a brand new book, which they might keep in their library after the course ends. Medium-priced types might value a brand new book, even one they do not intend to keep, knowing they can offset the high cost of buying by reselling it later. The low-price types might tolerate some inconvenience of obtaining a used book. While the publisher earns nothing from the sale of a used book, it earns it indirectly when it sells to the medium-price type at a price that otherwise they would not be willing or able to pay. When implementing official price discrimination schemes is costly, exhaustion can provide an effective second-best alternative, and because the secondary transactions occur irrespective of the IP owner's wishes, they are able to avoid some of the possible negative repercussions from officially condoning it.[15]

The effects of the first sale doctrine on dynamic efficiency are also ambiguous. To the extent that exhaustion constrains IP owners' market power and the profit that they may generate, it might reduce their incentive to invest in creating the intellectual good in the first place, making them, consumers, and society at large, worse off. However, the first sale doctrine can and does promote dynamic efficiency in certain ways. As discussed above, rather than impeding price discrimination, in some cases it might achieve similar, or even superior results, thus allowing the IP owner to earn higher profits and encouraging more investment in innovation rather than less.

Even if exhaustion increases competition from secondary markets, and even if this results in lower profit, it might actually accelerate the rate of innovation. Instead of investing in costly price discrimination schemes, some producers entice high-price types to continue paying premium prices by innovating and releasing new or upgraded products, which render last month's glitzy top-of-the-line product obsolete in comparison. The ability to resell the existing models makes even the medium-price types more inclined to pay a premium price and upgrade to the newest model.[16]

The first sale doctrine also contributes to dynamic efficiency by permitting secondary market channels to enable access to and use of intellectual goods and the ideas or technologies embedded therein, even if the IP holder ceases production or distribution of the good.[17] In a related vein, exhaustion serves an important purpose in preserving culture and knowledge in the long term by preventing the complete disappearance of works.

---

[14] Ariel Katz, *A Network Effects Perspective on Software Piracy*, 55 U. TORONTO L.J. 155, 181 (2005).

[15] *Compare ibid.* at 179–86 (discussing how tolerating piracy allows software companies to implicitly price discriminate while avoiding some of the downsides of overt price discrimination).

[16] Margeurite Reardon, *Can Samsung Phone Trade-In Values Ever Match Apple's?*, CNET (February 7, 2014, 12:00 am PST), available at www.cnet.com/news/can-samsung-phone-trade-in-values-ever-match-apples/ (noting that "Savvy smartphone owners know that trading in their existing smartphone can help finance the purchase of their next device").

[17] Eric Matthew Hinkes, *Access Controls in the Digital Era and the Fair Use/First Sale Doctrines*, 23 SANTA CLARA COMPUTER & HIGH TECH. L.J. 685, 689 (2006).

While the first sale doctrine cannot be relied on for reprinting works that go out of print, it plays an important role in mitigating the potential cultural loss associated with such works. Exhaustion rules open up the possibility of a secondary market and assure that the artefacts embedding protected works remain available to the public over time.[18] Instead of discarding an item when it is no longer useful and becomes costly to keep or preserve, the first sale doctrine makes it legal to sell or donate a used copy of an intellectual good.[19] This way, the first sale doctrine enshrines preference for the garage sale over the garbage bin and for the library over the landfill.[20]

As Mulligan argues, the first sale doctrine reflects the *numerus clausus* principle, limiting the types of property rights exercised by producers and lowering the transaction costs of obtaining and using them.[21] Without the principle, significant costs would exist for consumers purchasing even simple low-cost products, such as books or CDs, because each item could be burdened with entirely different and fragmented terms and conditions.[22]

Exhaustion also safeguards consumer privacy.[23] Because they are able to use and transfer works without the permission of the producer, consumers are not subject to potentially intrusive monitoring mechanisms that can seem decidedly *1984*-esque.[24] Even without such aggressive monitoring, the simple fact is that "any system trying to answer the question of who can use what, when, where and under what circumstances will have to know where the object in question is, who is using it or whom it is being transferred to, and other details."[25] The first sale doctrine means that this kind of data collection is simply unnecessary.

Lower transaction costs and privacy also contribute to dynamic efficiency. Recent research on user innovation shows that important innovation often occurs outside the producer-firm. These studies challenge the producer-centric view of innovation, and the traditional belief that strong IP rights are necessary to spur innovation.[26] Strong IP

---

[18] Reese, *supra* note 9 at 592; see generally Diane L. Zimmerman, *Cultural Preservation: Fear of Drowning in a Licensing Swamp*, in WORKING WITHIN THE BOUNDARIES OF INTELLECTUAL PROPERTY (Rochelle C. Dreyfuss, Diane L. Zimmerman, & Harry First eds., 2010) [hereinafter Zimmerman, *Cultural Preservation*]; Hinkes, *supra* note 17, at 685; Margaret Jane Radin, *Regulation by Contract, Regulation by Machine*, 160 J. INST. & THEORETICAL ECON. 1 (2004); Diane Leenheer Zimmerman, *Can Our Culture be Saved? The Future of Digital Archiving*, 91 MINN. L. REV. 989 (2006) [hereinafter Zimmerman, *Digital Archiving*].

[19] Reese, *supra* note 9, at 607–8.

[20] Katz, *First Sale*, *supra* note 10.

[21] Christina M. Mulligan, *A Numerus Clausus Principle for Intellectual Property*, 80 TENN. L. REV. 235, 252 (2012–2013).

[22] Christina M. Mulligan, *Personal Property Servitudes on the Internet of Things*, GA. L. REV. (forthcoming 2016), BROOKLYN LAW SCHOOL, LEGAL STUDIES PAPER NO. 400, at 32–36, available at http://ssrn.com/abstract=2465651; see also Molly Shaffer Van Houweling, *The New Servitudes*, 96 GEO. L.J. 885, 897 (2008); Perzanowski & Schultz, *Digital Exhaustion, supra* note 9.

[23] Julie E. Cohen, *A Right to Read Anonymously: A Closer Look at "Copyright Management" in Cyberspace*, 28 CONN. L. REV. 981 (1996); Julie E. Cohen, *Some Reflections on Copyright Management Systems and Laws Designed to Protect Them*, 12 BERKELEY TECH. L.J. 161, 183–87 (1997).

[24] See Mulligan, *Personal Property, supra* note 22, at 46–47.

[25] *Ibid.* at 52.

[26] Carliss Baldwin & Eric von Hippel, *Modeling a Paradigm Shift: From Producer Innovation to User and Open Collaborative Innovation*, 22 ORG. SCI. 1399 (2011).

rights may encourage innovation by producer-firms, but increase the cost of innovation that occurs outside those firms. Therefore, sensible innovation policies would also seek to maintain conditions that facilitate user-innovation, and should refrain from adopting rules that favor one model of innovation over others. The first sale doctrine supports user-innovation because it frees innovators who use existing intellectual goods from the need to obtain others' permission. Thus, exhaustion contributes to preserving the "Innovation Wetlands," a term coined by Andrew Torrance and Eric Von Hippel, to draw attention to the importance of various rules that foster "conditions that enable innovation by individuals to flourish."[27]

Finally, the first-sale doctrine also reflects constitutional norms of the rule of law and due process. Allowing IP owners to impose on others restraints beyond those that the statute specifically provides, to control what people can do with their own goods and then call upon the courts to enforce those restraints, delegates state power to private parties without any constraint and accountability. Such concerns influenced the U.S. Supreme Court's decision in some of the seminal exhaustion cases.[28]

IV. THE CASE AGAINST EXHAUSTION

The argument in favor of exhaustion set out in the previous section can be contrasted with the perspective of IP owners seeking greater control over their works, and, more recently, of some scholars, mainly from law and economics, seeking to highlight the efficiencies that can result from post-sale restraints. These theories draw in large part from developments in antitrust law and the economic theories that drove them. They contend that just as antitrust law has abandoned its earlier hostility to post-sale restraints, IP law should embrace them as well and allow IP owners greater, or even full, freedom to impose such restraints using the full arsenal of remedies available against infringers of IP rights, including third parties. In other words, the first sale doctrine should be narrowed, if not abolished altogether.

Post-sale restraints are a subset of a broader type of restraints, known as vertical restraints. They may restrict what a buyer can do with the goods she purchased—where she can resell them, to whom, at what prices, and whether she will have to provide pre- or post-sale services, repairs, warranties, etc. Antitrust law's attitude towards agreements imposing such restraints (e.g., between manufacturers and distributors) has seen remarkable changes throughout its history. Early antitrust law was as averse to vertical restraints as it was hostile to horizontal restraints,[29] and treated many agreements imposing verti-

---

[27] Andrew W. Torrance & Eric von Hippel, *The Right to Innovate*, 2015 MICH. ST. L. REV. 793, 798 (2015). See also Katz, *First Sale*, *supra* note 10; Pamela Samuelson, *Freedom to Tinker*, 17(2) THEOR. INQ. L. (forthcoming 2016), UC BERKELEY PUBLIC LAW RESEARCH PAPER NO. 2605195, available at http://papers.ssrn.com/sol3/papers.cfm?abstract_id=2605195.
[28] Ariel Katz, *IP and the Rule of Law*, 17(2) THEOR. INQ. L. (forthcoming 2016).
[29] Horizontal agreements are those entered between actual or potential competitors (i.e., firms at the same level of the distribution chain), whereas vertical agreements are those entered between firms at different levels of the distribution chain (e.g., manufacturer-wholesaler; wholesaler-retailer; retailer-customer).

cal restraints, such as exclusive dealing, tying, and resale price maintenance (RPM), as *per se* illegal.[30] Over time, however, antitrust scholarship began to recommend that horizontal and vertical restraints be treated differently because vertical restraints more likely enhance efficiency, prevent opportunism, and otherwise advance procompetitive outcomes than they are implemented for anticompetitive ends.[31] Jurisprudence followed scholarship, and since the late 1970s,[32] the Supreme Court has gradually abolished virtually all *per se* rules applying to vertical restraints.[33] The last bastion fell in 2007 in *Leegin*, which overruled an almost century-old *per se* prohibition on RPM.[34] This reflects the prevailing wisdom that frequently such restraints might be beneficial rather than harmful.

The argument relies in part on the important insight that unlike competitors who share a common interest in reducing competition among themselves at the expense of consumers, vertically situated parties do not share a common interest in reduced competition. Quite the contrary, a manufacturer benefits both when competition among its suppliers is intense and when market power among its distributors is limited.[35] Similarly, distributors would rather be free to deal with competing manufacturers upstream and competing retailers downstream than with monopolistic firms. In other words, the divergence of interests inherent in vertical relationships serves as a check on anticompetitive practices.[36]

A growing body of literature has identified a myriad of reasons supporting the proposition that they often serve procompetitive goals.[37] For example, vertical restraints may encourage dealers to invest in developing a local market (by advertising or other means) or to supply pre- or post-sale services (such as training or repairs). They may also be required to implement beneficial price discrimination schemes. As modern antitrust law has opened up to vertical restraints and their positive impact on competition, it has grown to tolerate agreements that govern and monitor them. In the case of goods in which no IP rights subsist, contracts and the mere threat of termination serve as the main tools for enforcing such restraints. But if IP rights can be relied on to enforce the restraints, the additional set of remedies could make those restraints more effective.[38]

---

[30] Leegin Creative Leather Prods., Inc. v. PSKS, Inc., 551 U.S. 877, 888 (2007).
[31] *Ibid.* at 889.
[32] Continental T.V., Inc. v. GTE Sylvania Inc., 433 U.S. 36 (1977).
[33] *Leegin, supra* note 30, 551 U.S. at 900–904.
[34] A nominally *per se* rule against tying still exists, but it has been watered down so significantly that it is questionable whether it is different from a rule of reason. See Ariel Katz, *Making Sense of Nonsense: Intellectual Property, Antitrust, and Market Power*, 49 ARIZ. L. REV. 837, 896 (2007).
[35] KEITH N. HYLTON, ANTITRUST LAW: ECONOMIC THEORY AND COMMON LAW EVOLUTION 253 (2003).
[36] *Leegin, supra* note 30, 551 U.S. at 896 ("[I]n general, the interests of manufacturers and consumers are aligned with respect to retailer profit margins. The difference between the price a manufacturer charges retailers and the price retailers charge consumers represents part of the manufacturer's cost of distribution, which, like any other cost, the manufacturer usually desires to minimize.").
[37] See e.g. MICHAEL J. TREBILCOCK et al., THE LAW AND ECONOMICS OF CANADIAN COMPETITION POLICY 373–99 (2003).
[38] Hovenkamp, *supra* note 4, at 492.

From this perspective, courts' stubborn adherence to the first sale doctrine undermines the efficacy of post-sale restraints, entrenches an inefficient IP rule, and preserves a relic from an era in which the economics of vertical restraints were not well understood.[39] Such courts fail to see that if IP rights subsist in the goods and can be relied on to enforce post-sale restraints, producers would have a more powerful and arguably more effective tool to enforce them. If post-sale restraints could be a good thing, the argument goes, then endowing IP owners with more powerful tools to impose and enforce them is a good thing too. Section IV.B below explains the basic flaw of this logical equation, but before doing that, let me present the argument in favor of enforceable post-sale restraints in greater detail in the context of parallel trade. This is a contentious phenomenon that attracts many of those arguments, though many of them are not limited to this context.

A. Parallel Trade

The term "parallel trade" (or "gray market") describes situations where goods sold abroad at a lower price are imported (or reimported) by an unauthorized dealer and compete domestically with the local authorized distribution system.[40] When such goods embed some protected IP, owners sometimes invoke IP law to ban the unauthorized importation. Whether IP law should be used for this purpose is subject to a heated debate and the actual rules are often inconsistent among nations, as well as between different IP laws within a nation (i.e., different rules for patents, copyrights, and trademarks) and even within a specific national IP law.[41] One question that plagues this debate is whether the IP right is exhausted only upon the first *domestic* sale authorized by the IP owner (national exhaustion) or whether the IP right is exhausted upon the first sale authorized by the IP owner regardless of the country in which it occurs (international exhaustion). Indeed, the difference between national exhaustion and international exhaustion was the dividing line between the majority and the dissenting opinions in *Kirtsaeng*.[42]

(1) Price discrimination
Proponents of national exhaustion often cite the benefits of international price discrimination when they argue that IP owners should be able to prohibit parallel trade. They maintain that because demand for an intellectual good (or the ability to pay) varies across countries, allowing producers to set different prices promotes both efficiency and social justice. Price discrimination may be more efficient because it may lead to higher output and greater incentive to innovate.[43] It may also be socially progressive because it might

---

[39] See e.g. Rub, *supra* note 13, at 754–59.
[40] See *Kirtsaeng, supra* note 1, 133 S. Ct at 1379.
[41] See e.g. Euro-Excellence Inc. v. Kraft Canada Inc., [2007] 3 S.C.R. 20 (Can.).
[42] *Kirtsaeng, supra* note 1, 133 S. Ct. at 1384 ("[I]n my view, [section 602(a)(1)] ties the United States to a national-exhaustion framework. The Court's decision, in contrast, places the United States solidly in the international-exhaustion camp.") (Ginsburg, J., dissenting).
[43] *Kirtsaeng, supra* note 1, 133 S. Ct. at 1390 (Ginsburg, J. dissenting); Katz, *supra* note 10, at 77; Rub, *supra* note 13.

help consumers with low willingness or ability to purchase goods, from which they would otherwise be excluded.[44] On this view, the first sale doctrine—a form of arbitrage that jeopardizes the producers' ability to price discriminate—leads to economically inferior and socially regressive results.[45]

Post-sale restraints may facilitate price discrimination in additional ways, for example, through the practice of tying, where a manufacturer sells Good A only on condition that the buyer use it with Component B, which can only be purchased from the manufacturer or from its designated suppliers. Tying can facilitate price discrimination when different buyers use different quantities of Component B with one unit of Good A. If Good A is worth more to the intensive users than to the less intensive users, tying Component B to Good A can effectively achieve the goal of discriminatory pricing for Good A. Component B, the tied product, serves as a counting device to measure how intensively Good A is being used.[46] For example, the demand for a patented machine may vary among different users. Instead of attempting to sell the machine to different users at different prices (and encountering the problems of determining in advance how much each buyer would be willing to pay and how to prevent those who paid a low price from reselling to those who paid a high price), the patentee may resort to tying: it can sell the machine at cost, or even for free "on condition that the unpatented staples used in the machine be bought from the patentee . . . Hence by charging a higher than competitive price for the staples, the patentee could receive the equivalent of a royalty from his patented machines."[47]

(2) Impact on local dealer investment

Antitrust scholarship has identified a variety of other benefits arising from post-sale restraints. Most of the benefits relate to guaranteeing local dealers a level of profitability in order to encourage them to make various investments in the distribution or the servicing of the product. Presumably, local dealers (distributers or retailers) would be reluctant to invest in promoting the product or in providing pre- and post-sale services if, after incurring these costs, consumers could buy the goods at a lower price from other dealers who free ride on their investments. To mitigate such concerns, a manufacturer may then impose various vertical restraints, such as territorial restraints (limiting the dealers to sell only within a designated territory) or price restraints (RPM). If the purpose of such restraints is indeed to guarantee investment and those investments are indeed necessary to increase output, then these restraints are efficient because they will result in more units sold and better services delivered.[48]

From this perspective, parallel trade is a cause for concern because it allows the parallel importer and the foreign dealer to free ride on the investments of the local dealer. Parallel trade, thus, could undermine the incentive to invest in building the local market and to

---

[44] See e.g. *Kirtsaeng*, *supra* note 1, 133 S. Ct. at 1390 (Ginsburg, J., dissenting).
[45] Rub, *supra* note 13.
[46] Ward S. Bowman Jr., *Tying Arrangements and the Leverage Problem*, 67 YALE L.J. 19, 23 (1957).
[47] *Ibid.* at 23–24.
[48] Edward Iacobucci, *The Case for Prohibiting Resale Price Maintenance*, 19 WORLD COMP. L. & ECON. REV. 71 (1995).

provide pre-sale and post-sale services, ultimately to the detriment of the local dealer, local consumers, and the manufacturer. To the extent that the first sale doctrine makes it more difficult to curb such parallel trade, it should be limited.

(3) Other benefits

Post-sale restraints may be used in distributing "positional goods," such as luxury brands, whose appeal lies in the exclusive status that their high prices confer.[49] Preserving the appeal of such goods requires an ability to maintain their high prices; parallel trade could undermine an effort by a producer of such a status good to maintain *different* high prices in different countries.[50]

Post-sale restraints may be used to achieve goals other than preventing arbitrage. For example, manufacturers sometimes argue that they need to exercise downstream control over the use and disposition of their products to ensure a guaranteed level of quality or safety.[51]

B. Limited Relevance of the Antitrust Insights to the Question of Exhaustion

From price discrimination to brand image, modern antitrust scholarship has identified a variety of benefits that post-sale restraints promote. These insights, which have contributed to the gradual erosion of antitrust law's hostility towards vertical restraints, have been carried over to the debates around exhaustion generally, and more specifically to debates around parallel imports. This section explains why, notwithstanding the importance of these insights, they have very limited bearing on the question of what model of exhaustion, national or international, IP law should adopt, and for deciding the scope of exhaustion more generally. In brief, those who rely on those economic insights to justify a legal position generally overshoot the mark.

Consider the following price discrimination argument. Price discrimination is good. Arbitrage frustrates price discrimination, therefore arbitrage is bad. An international exhaustion rule facilitates parallel trade, hence it supports arbitrage, which is bad. It follows that international exhaustion should be rejected and nations adopt only a national exhaustion rule. The flaw in the argument is threefold: first, it assumes that price discrimination is more efficient than uniform pricing, but no such general rule exists. Price discrimination may increase efficiency or it may not.[52] Second, it assumes that the benefits of legal rules facilitating price discrimination outweigh their costs; and third, it mismatches the symptom it identifies (arbitrage) and the remedy it prescribes (national exhaustion).

---

[49] Barak Y. Orbach, *The Image Theory: RPM and the Allure of High Prices*, 55 ANTITRUST BULL. 277, 279 (2010).

[50] See e.g. NAT'L ECON. RESEARCH ASSOCS. et al., THE ECONOMIC CONSEQUENCES OF THE CHOICE OF A REGIME OF EXHAUSTION IN THE AREA OF TRADEMARKS 104 (1998), available at http://ec.europa.eu/internal_market/indprop/docs/tm/report_en.pdf.

[51] Edward Iacobucci, *Tying as Quality Control: A Legal and Economic Analysis*, 32 J. LEGAL STUD. 435 (2003) (arguing that tying is not necessarily the optimal way for providing such assurances).

[52] TREBILCOCK et al., *supra* note 37, at 371.

If price discrimination is desirable, arbitrage is a problem, and IP law should be harnessed to prevent it, then the logical conclusion is to reject all exhaustion, not only international exhaustion. If the goal is preventing arbitrage, it seems odd to design rules that target only one type of arbitrage (cross-border), but remain agnostic towards all other forms. Efficient price discrimination requires an ability to sort consumers according to their willingness or ability to pay. Sometimes national borders would provide a close proxy to different consumer attributes, but in many cases the preferences and attributes of consumers within a nation will be just as varied as the preferences of consumers across nations. There is no general *a priori* reason to assume that international arbitrage is a problem that requires legal intervention, while domestic arbitrage is not.[53] If anything, transportation costs, regulatory differences, language, and various border measures limit international arbitrage irrespective of the IP regime, rendering IP law intervention less necessary. At the same time, the ubiquity of price discrimination schemes that occur domestically, notwithstanding the first sale doctrine, indicate that the supposed benefits of IP intervention are overblown. Thus, the price discrimination argument only explains why sometimes post-sale restraints may be justified, but it provides no coherent basis for choosing between national or international exhaustion.

Similar flaws plague most of the other legal arguments that rely on the benefits of vertical restraints to support limiting the first sale doctrine. Establishing and maintaining efficient distribution systems clearly benefits producers and consumers alike, and as I note in the previous sections, this goal often requires the imposition of enforceable post-sale restraints. If IP law should be asked to play a role in achieving better efficiency, national exhaustion provides only a very partial tool. For example, a manufacturer might assign exclusive territories or allocate types of customers to different dealers. Each of these dealers might need to make specific investments and might be reluctant to do so without being offered credible protection against free riding by other dealers or the manufacturer. Arguably, the first sale doctrine undermines the credibility of such guarantees because third parties might be able to obtain the goods and undercut the local dealer. If exhaustion rules should be curtailed to prevent that scenario, national exhaustion seems like an arbitrary and unprincipled choice because it targets only one type of arbitrage, not necessarily the most significant one. As a general matter, and in the absence of rules seeking to regulate particular industries under specific market circumstances to solve concrete problems,[54] the only principled choices are either no exhaustion at all or international (or indeed universal) exhaustion. Indeed, the logic of the economic arguments should result in empowering IP owners to impose all types of restraints.

As tempting as this position might be, the economic insights provide only limited normative guidance. They explain why there are circumstances under which post-sale restraints might be a good thing and, therefore, a sensible legal system might not seek

---

[53] Katz, *supra* note 10, at 86–88.
[54] It is always possible to conceive of specific situations where parallel trade exists to such an extent that the absence of legal tools to prevent it results in unambiguously undesirable results. See Katz, *supra* note 10, at 79–81.

to outlaw them altogether and adopt the strongest of the five formulations of the first sale doctrine mentioned above.[55] But other than that, the economic insights fall short of supporting the weakest formulations. More precisely they fail to: (a) establish that IP owners, as a general matter, should be entitled to rely on their IP rights to impose and enforce such restraints; and (b) identify the optimal legal tool for enforcing such restraints. Without more, the economic arguments do not tell us whether the power to control downstream use or dispossession of intellectual goods should be part of the IP bundle of rights or whether a more limited power should suffice.

Many of the economic arguments against exhaustion rely on a similar logic applied with respect to the "red wine" fallacy. Many people believe that drinking red wine confers protection against heart disease and hence is good for your health. This might not be true,[56] but even if drinking some red wine is good, it is false to conclude that drinking more red wine is better. Indeed, consuming a lot of red wine can be quite bad. Just as it does not follow from the general economic justification for IP rights that their scope and duration should be as broad and long as possible, it does not follow that granting greater powers to impose and enforce post-sale restraints might be a good thing. Like many questions of policy, economic analysis can be useful in assessing the implications of various alternatives and whether, relative to a certain baseline, the benefits that a proposed change might bring about will outweigh its costs, or vice versa. As the next section explains, the first sale doctrine (even in its strong formulations) does not prohibit all post-sale restraints, nor does it make it impossible to implement them effectively. Instead, it provides a general rule that balances the costs and the benefits that the power to control downstream uses of intellectual goods entails. Thus, the first sale doctrine assists IP owners in implementing post-sale restraints where their social benefits may likely be greater than their social costs. However, post-sale restraints limit their power where downstream control will likely yield smaller social benefits relative to the social harms that they might entail. Therefore, to choose among the formulations along the spectrum, from level 0 to level 4, it is not enough to point out that moving towards the weaker formulations (i.e., allowing IP owners to exercise greater control downstream) may yield some benefits, but it also requires accounting for the social costs that such a move would entail and whether the benefits outweigh the costs. In the following sections, I explain why this is unlikely.

V. RECONCILING CONFLICTING VIEWS

A. Exhaustion Does Not Mean the End of Efficient Distribution

Before we can choose the optimal strength level of the first sale doctrine, it may be useful to recall that the doctrine neither prohibits IP owners from achieving the benefits that post-sale restraints might bring about, nor does it totally impair their ability to do so. The first sale doctrine only ordains that as a matter of IP law, the owner's exclusive rights

---

[55] See II *supra*.
[56] Malcolm Law & Nicholas Wald, *Why Heart Disease Mortality is Low in France: The Time Lag Explanation*, 318 BMJ—BRIT. MED. J. 1471 (1999).

do not include the power to impose the restraint, and therefore those rights cannot be relied on to enforce them. Even the strongest formulation does not prohibit all means of achieving the benefits of post-sale restraints.

Consider, for example, the case of a firm that owns a copyright in every country and is vertically integrated into production and distribution. Such a firm can achieve the same benefits from post-sale restraints by relying on its internal governance. It can implement internal rules and procedures to ensure that all its salespersons adhere to different retail prices that it chooses for different territories, conform to its quality standards, etc. The firm's ability to structure its preferred production and distribution system depends on how effectively its management can implement it. As a legal matter, corporate law, contract law, or labour law will be much more determinative of the firm's success, than copyright law's choice of any particular exhaustion rule.

While vertical integration may provide the firm considerable ability to structure its production and distribution system as it sees fit, it may have some shortcomings. First, the firm's internal controls do not bind anyone else, and therefore, once it sells the goods, they may circulate freely in a way that could undermine the goals that it sought to achieve. Therefore, the firm might wish to have some ability to control its goods even after it has sold them. Second, vertical integration may not always be possible or desirable. A firm might have an advantage in developing new intellectual goods, but not in producing, distributing, or providing post-sale service. Or it might be more efficient to collaborate with other players to provide some or all of these services than to do it alone. In such cases, the firm will not be able to rely on its internal command and control procedures but will need to resort to other legal tools, such as licensing agreements, to structure an efficient production or distribution system with restraints on some or all of its collaborators. If the law categorically prohibited any type of restraint, it would drive firms into greater vertical integration, even when it is inefficient to do so, or to forgo the benefits altogether. This may not be a good idea.[57]

Therefore, the firm might attempt to impose contractual restraints on its downstream collaborators or customers. But contractual obligations can only bind those who voluntarily assumed them, and therefore cannot bind third parties, such as the purchaser's own customers, users, or service personnel.[58] In theory, the manufacturer could require its contracting party to insert the same restrictions in the latter's contract with downstream buyers, but such obligations will be increasingly difficult to enforce. Moreover, remedies for breach of contract, which tend to be limited to expectation damages,[59] are usually weaker than remedies available for infringement of an IP right. Proponents of weak or no exhaustion rules usually invoke the shortcomings of contracts when they argue that IP owners should be able to use the more potent rules of IP law to impose and enforce the restraints.

But relying on contracts or any other legal tool also entails willingness to incur the costs of enforcing them and manufacturers can resort to various unilateral non-legal techniques

---

[57] Stephen M. Maurer & Suzanne Scotchmer, *Profit Neutrality in Licensing: The Boundary Between Antitrust Law and Patent Law*, 8 AM. L. & ECON. REV. 476, 481 (2006).
[58] Hovenkamp, *supra* note 4, at 541.
[59] *Ibid.* at 539.

that make arbitrage more costly and less attractive. For example, they may refuse to sell to arbitrageurs or the buyers whom they suspect might immediately resell the goods. They might also limit the quantities sold to untrustworthy buyers or they might use different versions of the product to make the cheaper version less attractive or incompatible with the more expensive ones. Finally, they might delay the sale of the cheaper products and keep innovating and releasing newer products that render the older ones less attractive.

Moreover, resellers and arbitrageurs can only deal with goods that were made and put on the market by the IP owner or with its authorization, meaning that the supply of goods to the secondary market depends on supply to the primary one. Therefore, because the IP owner is the exclusive source of goods to the primary market, its decisions also influence the supply to the secondary market. Even though, at the margin, resold goods may compete with those sold by the IP owner, resellers operate (all things equal) at a cost disadvantage. Their supply of goods depends, albeit indirectly, on the IP owner whose decisions are made upstream. They may lack access to technical expertise, and they may not have access to the most lucrative distribution channels. Consequently, the IP owner has some control over its downstream competitors and some ability to prevent the growth of their market share at its expense. Granted, this power is indirect and imperfect, but in many cases, and especially when the lifecycle of goods is short, an ability to delay the growth of the secondary market, however temporary and imperfect, may be all that the IP owner needs to prevent exhaustion from having devastating consequences. In sum, exhaustion does not mean the end of efficient distribution systems, and in many cases IP owners can set them up even if they cannot rely on the remedial tentacles of IP law to enforce them.

B. Focusing the Debate on the Margin

Nevertheless, what may be good enough in many cases may not be good enough at the margin, and consequently, in theory, some efficient restraints will not be implemented unless IP owners can resort to the more potent tool of IP law to enforce them. Efficient business arrangements that depend on the enforceability of such restraints might be forgone. If so, then the inability to enforce the restraints would prevent efficient business schemes from being implemented.

Rational debate about the scope of exhaustion should focus on this margin. Proponents of weak exhaustion rules should be able to show that the marginal social benefits stemming from greater powers to control downstream uses outweigh the marginal losses, while supporters of strong exhaustion rules should be able to demonstrate that the additional marginal benefits are minor compared to the social losses that they might inflict. Unfortunately, we do not have the empirical data that would allow us to quantify and compare these effects. But fortunately, we can soundly predict their respective magnitudes by focusing more closely on the type of situations where the ability to impose restraints might be beneficial, the types of costs they inflict, and the likelihood that IP owners and others who might bear the costs of the downstream restraints will be able to agree on socially efficient outcomes. Such a closer look reveals that granting IP owners greater powers to impose and enforce post-sale restraints is likely to cause more harm than good.

All the economic justifications for enforceable post-sale restraints share two common features: (1) they primarily involve settings of joint-production and incomplete vertical integration; and (2) they seek to address short-term concerns. In other words, the economic justifications for post-sale restraints describe them as solutions to concerns arising during production, initial distribution, or shortly thereafter, and as solutions to organizational problems between non-integrated or imperfectly integrated firms along the production and distribution chain. Whether post-sale restraints are imposed in the provision of pre-sale or post-sale services or to facilitate price discrimination, to maintain the status of a luxury good, or to encourage investment in building a distribution system, a closer look at the antitrust scholarship reveals that it has focused on the relationships between collaborating firms attempting to organize an efficient production and distribution system.

For obvious reasons, IP owners would prefer the ability to enforce post-sale restrictions through property mechanisms,[60] but while the availability of remedies for IP infringement reduces the costs of enforcing post-sale restrictions, such remedies may increase the associated social costs.

Modern antitrust teaches us that post-sale restraints are not necessarily harmful. They may actually be quite beneficial and necessary to organize sophisticated distribution systems when a manufacturer is not fully integrated into distribution and retail.[61] The following line of reasoning may thus be adopted: if post-sale restrictions are efficient, they should be enforceable. If enforcing them on the grounds of IP infringement is easier than on the grounds of breach of contract, an IP remedy should be available. Unfortunately, this line of reasoning is flawed. Remedies for infringement of an IP right may be more effective than those available for breach of contract. However, whether greater efficacy is desirable depends not only on the benefits of more compliance, but also on the costs that may be externalized to third parties.[62] Therefore, before concluding that greater enforceability is better, it is important to carefully understand why and against whom post-sale restrictions may need to be enforced.

C. Short-term and Long-term Costs and Benefits

The organizational problems that post-sale restraints might solve occur mainly at the early stages of the product lifecycle:[63] production problems disappear immediately after the good is produced[64] and distribution problems largely disappear upon the distribution of the good, or shortly thereafter. Notably, these problems cease to exist long before the IP rights expire (particularly in the case of copyright). Moreover, as co-producers, the firms are in privity, which enables them to rely on contracts for addressing many of the organizational problems associated with efficient distribution.[65] Further, because the standard remedy for breach of contract is only damages, and the plaintiff needs to prove actual

---

[60] See Part VI of Katz, *supra* note 10, at 89–94.
[61] See e.g. Hovenkamp, *supra* note 4, at 489.
[62] Henry E. Smith, *Toward an Economic Theory of Property in Information*, in RESEARCH HANDBOOK ON THE ECONOMICS OF PROPERTY LAW 104 (Kenneth Ayotte & Henry E. Smith eds., 2011), available at http://ssrn.com/abstract=1712089.
[63] Ariel Katz, *Substitution and Schumpeterian Effects Over the Life Cycle of Copyrighted Works*, 49 JURIMETRICS J. 113 (2009).
[64] *Ibid.*
[65] As opposed to organizational problems during the development and production stages, which contract law alone may not solve and which IP rights may help to ameliorate. *Ibid.* at 141–42.

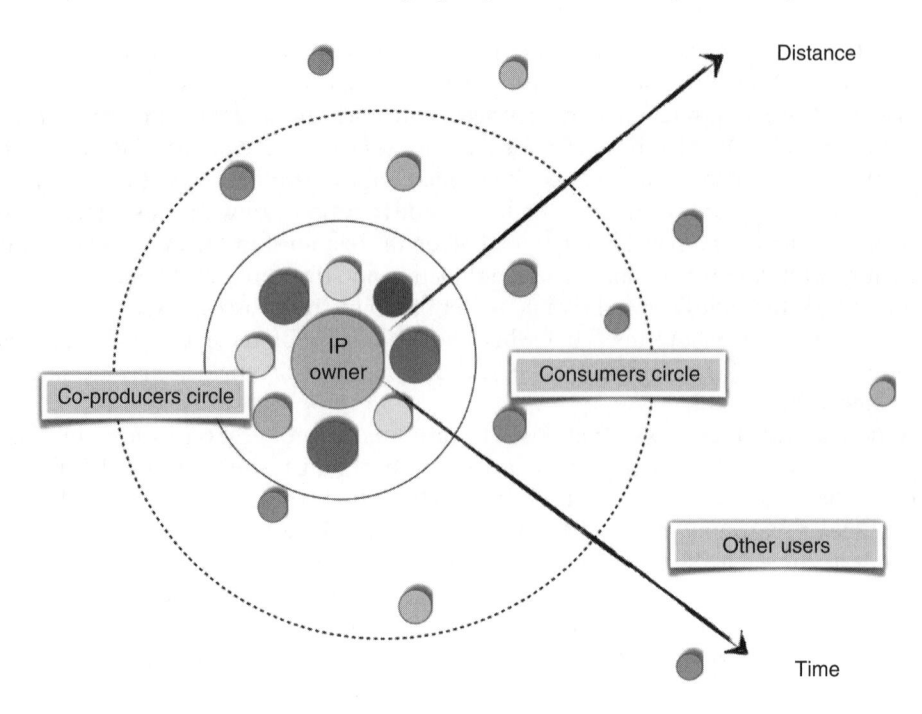

Figure 2.1   An IP owner, co-producers, and users

damage, a party bound by a contractually valid post-sale restraint may be able to put the good to better use when no damage can be shown or otherwise when the breach is efficient. Thus, while IP remedies may increase the enforceability of post-sale restraints, granting those additional powers yields marginally decreasing benefits.

Figure 2.1 represents the circles of relationship between an IP owner and interested parties through the lifecycle of an innovative good. The inner circle comprises the IP owner and the several firms that participate in the production or initial distribution of an innovative good. The second circle depicts the consumers who buy the goods produced in the inner circle. The third circle shows users who may at one point be interested in obtaining and using the innovative good but do not obtain it directly from the inner circle. Two vectors—distance and time—are also presented. Distance reflects the transactional proximity between the IP owner and the user. As the distance between the user and the IP owner increases, concerns about opportunism diminish. The time vector reflects temporal proximity between production, distribution, and use.

As noted above, the benefits of post-sale restraints are concentrated primarily within the inner circle. Hence, the marginal benefit from having enforceable restraints diminishes as we move along the vectors of distance and time.

In contrast, many of the benefits of exhaustion are long-term and distributed. Exhaustion frees users from the need to determine whether a product can be used without restriction and from the need to locate the IP owner and negotiate a license for reserved uses. The associated costs likely increase as we move along the distance and time vectors. When users contemplate combining various intellectual goods, those costs compound.

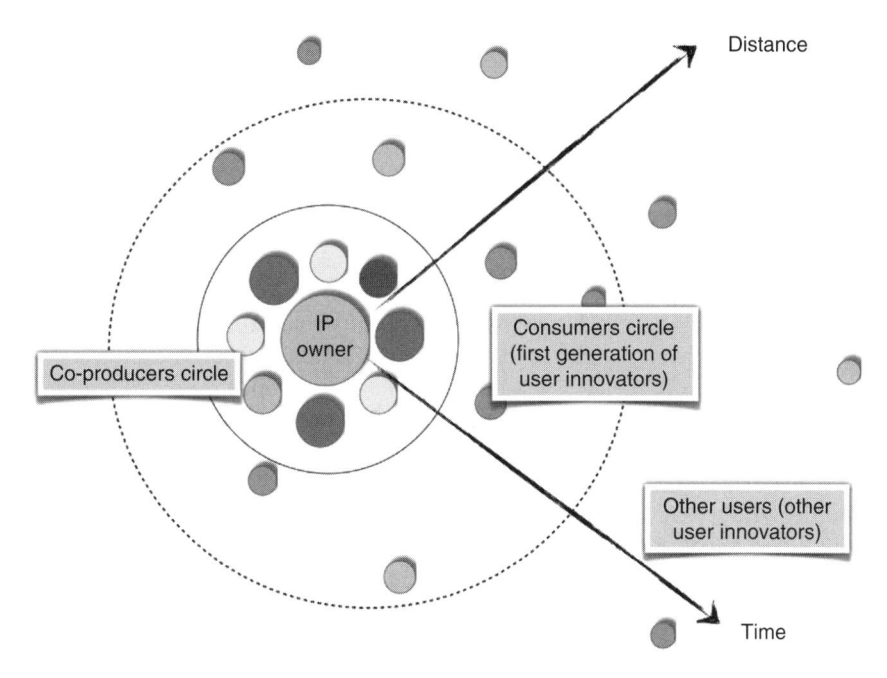

Figure 2.2   An IP owner, co-producers, and user innovators

Since users are not only consumers but also actual or potential innovators, granting IP owners an extended power (over time and distance) to restrain the use of goods embodying their innovation will impede users' ability to innovate or transfer the goods to others who might innovate. Figure 2.2 graphically depicts this assertion.

Moreover, the proximity between the IP owner and the players in the inner circles and the fact that they have already established business relationships for fairly well-defined goals imply that the transaction costs needed in order to structure efficient deals among themselves are relatively low. In contrast, the temporal and spatial distance between the IP owner and generations of consumers and future innovators, and the fact that the uses in which they might wish to engage are varied and sometimes unpredictable, imply that the costs of obtaining permission, if necessary, are likely to be fairly high.

It follows that it would make sense to allow IP owners to impose restraints where such restraints may result in significant marginal benefits, and limit such powers when the restraints will likely result in decreasing social benefits and increasing social costs. The first sale doctrine does exactly that. The law grants strong property rights that enable IP owners to enter into license agreements that can promote efficient production and distribution at the early and critical stages of production and distribution and to rely on the full range of the more potent remedies that IP law provides to enforce them. But the law, through the first sale doctrine, also limits IP owners' ability to exercise downstream control when the marginal utility of such control is diminishing. This way, the first sale provides room for efficient organization, but it also guarantees that trade will not be encumbered through durable, but often unnecessary, restraints later on.

VI. WHY EXHAUSTION SHOULD BE A STICKY DEFAULT RULE

The preceding discussion supports the existence of a first sale doctrine, but it does not yet fully answer how strong it should be. It explains why the grant of property rights that empower IP owners to impose restraints on third parties beyond the inner circle of co-producers (and after production or initial distribution) might cause more harm than good. It therefore suggests that the power to enforce post-sale restraints should not normally be part of the property bundle. Even under an assumption that post-sale restraints are efficient, they should generally be imposed and enforced as a matter of contract law, not property.[66] Assuming therefore that exhaustion is the default rule, the next question is how strong or sticky this default rule should be. Under what conditions should courts enforce deviations from the default and what are the grounds for invalidating such deviations? The issue is less about a categorical choice between IP remedies and contract remedies (and whether clever drafting can guarantee that a restriction is found to be a license condition rather than contractual covenant),[67] than about the design of default exhaustion rules.

I need first to reject the view that exhaustion provides no more than a simple default rule that can be easily modified by contract. Current case law tends to reflect this paradigm[68] and as a result, many cases are decided on the basis of relatively marginal legal questions, such as what constitutes a valid contract,[69] whether a first conditional sale pre-empts exhaustion,[70] whether there was a sale or just a license,[71] and whether restraints imposed by notice are sufficient.[72] Such decisions do not get to the heart of the problem.

The economic arguments in favor of easily contracting around exhaustion rely on the logic of the Coase Theorem that asserts that in the absence of transaction costs, bargaining will lead to an efficient outcome regardless of the initial allocation of property rights.[73] In a Coasian world, it does not matter whether the first sale doctrine exists or not because transacting parties will always be able to efficiently bargain about the rights to resale or otherwise use an item. If resale is efficient, the owner and the user will enter into a contract permitting it, and if it is not, the contract will restrict it, regardless of which party has the initial right to resale. If some consumers value the ability to resale the good more than others, then sellers would be happy to sell the goods with or without such rights at different prices.

While attractive, this policy prescription is flawed—the real world is not Coasian and

---

[66] Katz, *supra* note 10, at 100. There might be some exceptions that could justify resort to IP remedies. *Ibid.* at 100–101.
[67] MDY Indus. v. Blizzard Entm't., Inc., 629 F.3d 928 (9th Cir. 2010).
[68] For more detailed examination of how the courts have dealt with these issues, including an in depth discussion of *ProCD*, see Part VII of Katz, *supra* note 10, at 100–109.
[69] See e.g. ProCD v. Zeidenberg, 86 F.3d 1447 (7th Cir. 1996) (discussing the validity of shrink-wrap licenses and holding that they are valid, as long as the buyer can return the product after having an opportunity to read the terms).
[70] Quanta Computer, Inc. v. LG Elecs., Inc., 553 U.S. 617 (2008) (leaving the question open).
[71] Vernor v. Autodesk, Inc., 621 F.3d 1102 (2010).
[72] UMG Recordings, Inc. v. Augusto, 628 F.3d 1175, 1180 (9th Cir. 2011) (distinguishing *Vernor* on, among other things, lack of acceptance of the restrictions).
[73] Ronald Coase, *The Problem of Social Cost*, 3 J.L. & Econ. 1 (1960).

the world of IP is even less so.[74] The need for IP rights, and the need to define their limits, arises precisely because transacting around information, the subject matter of IP, is replete with all sorts of market failures.[75]

Therefore, we cannot assume that IP law provides only the baseline from which bargaining will necessarily, or even presumptively, increase social welfare.[76] This does not mean that contracting out of limitations on IP rights cannot increase social welfare; we have no reason to assume that the initial allocation is always optimal and we have grounds to believe that sometimes it may not be. However, it does not follow that whenever IP owners and the parties with whom they transact agree to work around the initial allocation of right, social welfare presumptively increases. The reason is simple: IP owners and their immediate transacting parties may rationally impose and agree to restraints that maximize their short-term private benefits, while ignoring the short- and long-term externalities that such restraints may generate. Since the terms of the transaction between the IP owner and her transacting party are unlikely to reflect what is socially optimal, contracting around the first sale doctrine should be met with a healthy dose of legal skepticism. Contrary to some views, the problem extends beyond mere notice.[77] Full notice of the restraint does not remedy the problem; it may only improve the bargaining between the parties. Notice does not address the externalities.

It follows that exhaustion should be treated as a sticky default rule. The law should not categorically invalidate any attempt to contract around the first sale doctrine, but it should also require those who seek to enforce the restraints to justify their efficiency and reasonableness before a court will uphold them. When the restraints purport to bind third parties or have long-term effects, the dose of suspicion should increase.

This view would be consistent with the common law historical treatment of agreements in restraint of trade. As Judge Taft explained in *Addyston Steel*,[78] the early common law treated all contracts in restraint of trade as wholly illegal but gradually, the common law began recognizing several categories of contracts in partial restraint of trade which, when reasonable, were generally upheld as valid.[79] A partial restraint of trade would be reasonable not only if it protects the interests of the parties, but also if it does not interfere with the interests of the public.[80] A reasonable restraint would be one that is merely ancillary to an otherwise legitimate contract and where it is:

---

[74] The term "Coasian" is misleading because it actually ignored Coase's main contribution, namely, that transaction costs are pervasive and important and that the law does matter. As Coase himself wrote, "[t]he world of zero transaction costs has often been described as a Coasian world. Nothing could be further from the truth. It is the world of modern economic theory, one which I was hoping to persuade economists to leave." See RONALD H. COASE, THE FIRM, THE MARKET, AND THE LAW 174 (1988).
[75] Katz, *supra* note 10, at 104–8.
[76] Except, perhaps, in the case of questions of who is the first owner, as opposed to the question of what this ownership entails. IP law clearly contemplates assignments of ownership, or the grant of licenses, which, by definition, presuppose the possibility that the owner is not necessarily the best exploiter.
[77] Hovenkamp, *supra* note 4, at 516–21; Rub, *supra* note 13, at 793–94.
[78] United States v. Addyston Pipe & Steel Co., 85 F. 271 (6th Cir. Court of Appeals 1898).
[79] *Ibid*. at 281.
[80] *Ibid*. at 282 (citing Horner v. Graves, 131 E.R. 284, 287 (1831)).

inserted only to protect one of the parties from the injury which, in the execution of the contract or enjoyment of its fruits, he may suffer from the unrestrained competition of the other. The main purpose of the contract suggests the measure of protection needed, and furnishes a sufficiently uniform standard by which the validity of such restraints may be judicially determined. In such a case, if the restraint exceeds the necessity presented by the main purpose of the contract, it is void."[81]

Taft's judgment and the notion of "ancillary restraints" became the cornerstone for antitrust law's relaxed stance towards vertical restraints,[82] but its common law basis and logic are equally applicable to the issue at hand. Contracts limiting exhaustion will be reasonable if they are (a) ancillary to an otherwise legitimate business enterprise, and (b) do not impose restraints exceeding what is necessary to protect the interests of the one or both contracting parties and do not impose externalities that interfere with the interests of the public. The first sale doctrine, when coupled with rule that allows parties to contract around it if they can demonstrate that the restraint thereby imposed meets the same reasonableness standard, therefore rests on sound economic and legal grounds.

This brief discussion of the history of the common law doctrine of restraint of trade highlights a final crucial point for the formulation of optimal exhaustion rules: the question of burdens of proof. Under modern antitrust law, vertical restraints are subject to rule of reason analysis, meaning that the burden is on the plaintiff to show that an agreement in restraint of trade produces the requisite anticompetitive effect. Proponents of weak exhaustion rules, who uncritically apply the lessons from the development of antitrust law, maintain that IP owners too should be able to impose post-sale restraints unless it can be shown that those restraints result in a concrete harm to competition or to innovation.[83]

However, the logic of antitrust with respect to burdens of proof does not carry over to the context of IP. First, the goals and focus of IP laws are not the same as those of antitrust. As noted above, IP laws' own logic requires some stickiness to its allocation of rights between owners, users, and the general public. Second, in addition to invalidating the agreement, a finding of an antitrust violation may result in civil and potentially criminal liability. Generally, the rule of law mandates that a person cannot be held liable unless that person's liability has been established under the appropriate standard of proof. In contrast, strong exhaustion rules, as this chapter suggests, do not result in liability, but only in incapacity. An IP owner who attempts to impose an unreasonable restraint is not, as a matter of IP law, guilty of any offense or liable to pay damages, but is merely incapable of harnessing the court to impose its wishes on others. Because exhaustion, under this formulation, merely sets a limit on the scope of the IP owner's statutory grant in order to preserve larger public interests, rule of law considerations do not require any particular burden of proof.

---

[81] *Ibid.* at 282.
[82] Robert H. Bork, *Ancillary Restraints and the Sherman Act*, 15 SEC. ANTITRUST L. 211 (1959).
[83] CHRISTINA BOHANNAN & HERBERT HOVENKAMP, CREATION WITHOUT RESTRAINT: PROMOTING LIBERTY AND RIVALRY IN INNOVATION 393 (2011).

VII. CONCLUSION

Despite over a hundred years of adjudication, courts have never been able to draw the exact contours of the first sale doctrine or fully articulate its rationale. Recently, insights borrowed from modern antitrust law and economics have been invoked to provide a seemingly robust theoretical foundation for undermining exhaustion rules or narrowing their scope, thereby strengthening IP owners' control over downstream distribution and use of the goods they produce. It has been suggested that just as antitrust law has recognized the efficiency of post-sale restraints and relaxed its hostility toward them, so should IP law permit their imposition and provide remedies for their breach. This chapter shows that, with the exception of certain instances, this trend is misguided and should be resisted, not because the insights from modern antitrust are irrelevant, but because insights from modern antitrust do not support the case against the first sale doctrine. The main benefits of post-sale restrictions involve situations of imperfect vertical integration between co-producing or collaborating firms, which occur during the production and distribution phases or shortly thereafter. In such situations, contracting around the first sale doctrine should be permitted, and agreements containing such restraints should not be automatically condemned. Beyond such limited circumstances, however, the first sale doctrine promotes important social and economic goals: it promotes efficient use of goods embodying IP, guarantees their preservation, and facilitates user innovation, while minimizing transaction costs that otherwise might impede those goals. A closer look at what the insights from modern law and economics can teach reveals that rather than undermining the first sale doctrine they confirm its validity and support its continued vitality.

3. Exhaustion and personal property servitudes
Molly Shaffer Van Houweling*

I. INTRODUCTION

The intellectual property (IP) exhaustion doctrine helps to determine the extent to which IP owners can control how other people use objects in their lawful possession—control that would otherwise be enforced (if at all) through generally applicable bodies of contract, property, and commercial law. Exhaustion can thus properly be understood, at least in part, as helping to define the boundary between IP and these other areas of law.

This boundary notion might suggest a sharp distinction between IP and the laws on the other side of the exhaustion line.[1] But courts and commentators have long suggested that the exhaustion doctrine in fact owes its origins to these bodies of law. Specifically, the argument goes that exhaustion is a version of a generally applicable common law prohibition on restrictions that run with objects other than land, that is, "personal property servitudes." This chapter revisits that claim in light of recent jurisprudence and scholarship.

The chapter starts with an abridged history of the law and policy of servitudes, explaining how these running restrictions on resource use have been somewhat reluctantly enforced when applied to land and largely resisted when applied to chattels. It explains how concerns about notice and information costs, dead hand control and the "problem of the future," and negative externalities have shaped this evolving body of law. It then explains the historical, doctrinal, and theoretical links between resistance to chattel servitudes and intellectual property exhaustion. Next it reviews several recent strands of scholarship. One strand claims that resistance to chattel servitudes was ill-considered in its heyday and is anachronistic today, and that exhaustion should be revisited in light of this critique. The second strand of scholarship claims that resistance to chattel servitudes reflected legitimate policy concerns that should continue to shape exhaustion doctrine today—and even that exhaustion itself is an evolving common law doctrine. The third, most recent strand argues that exhaustion does not reflect a common law tradition at all, but is rather an independent doctrine defined and influenced only by the IP statutes themselves. I conclude with my own arguments about the continued relevance of the policy lessons of personal property servitudes to the future of exhaustion.

---

* Professor of Law, University of California, Berkeley.
[1] John F. Duffy & Richard Hynes, *Statutory Domain and the Commercial Law of Intellectual Property*, 102 VA. L. REV. 1 (2016).

II. A BRIEF HISTORY OF SERVITUDES[2]

Before launching into a brief history of servitudes, it is worth explaining why I find servitudes so relevant not just to the doctrine of IP exhaustion, but also to intellectual property more generally. Start by considering a classic passage from Justice Holmes' 1908 concurrence in *White-Smith Music Publishing Co. v. Apollo*, in which he considers that nature of copyright as a property right:

> The notion of property starts, I suppose, from confirmed possession of a tangible object and consists in the right to exclude others from interference with the more or less free doing with it as one wills. But in copyright property has reached a more abstract expression. The right to exclude is not directed to an object in possession or owned, but is in vacuo, so to speak. It restrains the spontaneity of men where but for it there would be nothing of any kind to hinder their doing as they saw fit. It is a prohibition of conduct remote from the persons or tangibles of the party having the right. It may be infringed a thousand miles from the owner and without his ever becoming aware of the wrong. It is a right which could not be recognized or endured for more than a limited time, and therefore, I may remark in passing, it is one which hardly can be conceived except as a product of statute, as the authorities now agree.[3]

In drawing the contrast between copyright and paradigmatic possessory property rights in tangible objects, Justice Holmes here emphasizes the non-possessory, "in vacuo" nature of copyright and the way in which copyright owners can control strangers from afar, unconnected to any object possessed by the copyright owner. Copyright owners are thus unlike owners of possessory fee simple interests in land, whose rights to exclude generally impact the limited universe of people who come into contact with the physical boundaries of the owner's parcel.

Justice Holmes alludes to another apparent copyright anomaly: although copyright owners are not necessarily possessors, the people whose spontaneity is restrained by copyright *are* typically in possession of tangible objects—books, sheet music, or other manifestations of the copyrighted work. As to these tangible objects, copyright operates not as an instrument of freedom from interference for the possessor but rather the opposite: an instrument of restraint wielded by strangers (copyright owners) via remote-control. Copyright thus strikes Justice Holmes as an odd sort of property right in that instead of liberating people to use their possessions it "restrains [their] spontaneity . . . where but for it there would be nothing of any kind to hinder their doing as they saw fit."

Copyright owners' power to control how remote strangers use objects in their possession is not as extraordinary as this passage suggests, however. Of course, copyright shares this characteristic with patent and trademark. Beyond IP, copyrights are similar in this regard to a whole set of "remote-control" property interests that give their owners the

---

[2] Parts of this section are adapted from my previous work on servitudes. See Molly Shaffer Van Houweling, *The New Servitudes*, 96 Geo. L. Rev. 885 (2008); Molly Shaffer Van Houweling, *Cultural Environmentalism and the Constructed Commons*, 70 Law & Contemp. Prob. 23 (2007); Molly Shaffer Van Houweling, *Touching and Concerning Copyright, Real Property Reasoning in MDY Industries, Inc. v. Blizzard Entertainment, Inc.*, 51 Santa Clara L. Rev. 1063 (2011); Molly Shaffer Van Houweling, *Technology and Tracing Costs: Lessons from Real Property*, in Intellectual Property and the Common Law 385 (Shyamkrishna Balganesh ed., 2013).

[3] White-Smith Music Pub. Co. v. Apollo Co., 209 U.S. 1, 19 (1908) (Holmes, J., concurring).

right to control use of assets possessed by other people.[4] Servitudes are the most prominent example.

A servitude (which can take the form of an easement, real covenant, or equitable servitude[5]) is a non-possessory property interest that gives its holder the right to use an asset (typically land) in specified ways, or to object to specified uses of it, or to insist on specified behavior connected to it. The asset is encumbered by the servitude, such that the servitude's burdens "run with" the asset, "pass[ing] automatically to successive owners or occupiers."[6] Unlike a mere contractual agreement to, say, refrain from operating a gas station in a residential neighborhood, a servitude is enforceable against successors in interest. Therefore, if you grant your neighbor an effective servitude she will be able to enforce the restriction against you and subsequent owners of your land. The benefit of a servitude typically runs to successors as well—from your neighbor to the next owner of her house. As Carol Rose puts it, "[t]he greatest overall advantage of servitudes is that they give stability to property arrangements over both time and space."[7]

The stability that servitudes produce can be especially valuable for land use planning. Land is, of course, immobile and enduring. It is therefore often important for people who invest in land to be able to predict how surrounding land will be used far into the future, in order to make investments that will coordinate rather than conflict with adjacent activities.[8]

In recognition of these benefits, land servitudes and some other varieties of remote-control property rights have long been enforced by courts. Nonetheless, Justice Holmes' contention that property rights with such features could only be the product of statute rings somewhat true. Judges have greeted most non-possessory property rights with suspicion and hemmed them in with doctrinal limitations. Understanding some of this history and doctrine can help us to understand the challenges posed by intellectual property law's remote-control property rights—and the origins of the exhaustion doctrine as a limitation on that remote-control.

---

[4] See generally Gerald Korngold, *For Unifying Servitudes and Defeasible Fees: Property Law's Functional Equivalents*, 66 TEX. L. REV. 533 (1988).

[5] The *Restatement* simplifies this traditional three-part classification into two: affirmative easements and covenants running with the land (the latter category including servitudes that had traditionally been classified as negative easements, real covenants, and equitable servitudes). RESTATEMENT (THIRD) OF PROP.: SERVITUDES §§ 1.1–1.4 (2000).

[6] RESTATEMENT (THIRD) OF PROP.: SERVITUDES § 1.1 (2000).

[7] Carol Rose, *Servitudes*, in RESEARCH HANDBOOK ON THE ECONOMICS OF PROPERTY LAW 296, 297 (Kenneth Ayotte & Henry E. Smith, eds., 2011).

[8] See, e.g., Henry Hansmann & Reinier Kraakman, *Property, Contract, and Verification: The Numerus Clausus Problem and the Divisibility of Rights*, 31 J. LEGAL STUD. 373, 407 (2002) (observing that "the spatial fixity of individual parcels of real property causes the value of those parcels to be necessarily dependent on the uses made of neighboring parcels"); Henry Hansmann & Marina Santilli, *Authors' and Artists' Moral Rights: A Comparative Legal and Economic Analysis*, 26 J. LEGAL STUD. 95, 101 (1997) (noting "the potentially large advantages in coordinating the uses of parcels of property that are, by their nature, bound in a spatial relationship to each other regardless of their separate ownership").

A. Evolution of Land Servitudes

The land-use planning needs of the Industrial Revolution triggered the development of modern Anglo-American servitude law.[9] Increased urban density and the potential for conflicts between neighboring property owners prompted a variety of attempts to coordinate land uses through durable private arrangements.[10] Nineteenth-century English courts reacted with ambivalence, however, establishing a complicated scheme of servitude classifications and accompanying doctrinal limitations.

Servitudes came to be classified into the three major categories of easements, real covenants, and equitable servitudes, with each category subject to convoluted rules limiting formation, subject matter, and enforceability.[11] As I describe in prior work,[12] tracing the evolution of modern servitude law reveals several rationales for this type of hostility and the limiting doctrines that it produced. I have organized these rationales into three broad categories: those related to notice and information costs; those related to dead-hand control and other aspects of the "problem of the future";[13] and those related to harmful externalities.[14]

B. Notice and Information Costs

Servitudes, like other remote-control property rights, raise special concerns about notice and information costs. Consider the counter-factual: if the person in possession of land necessarily had all rights to control its use, then it would be easy for someone else acquiring possession from that person to understand exactly what they were getting.[15] Where, by contrast, the law recognizes servitudes that allow one person to own and possess the land while someone else has the right to control its use, the newcomer who acquires possession does not automatically know what use rights he has acquired. If servitudes could be imposed to benefit strangers without any doctrines promoting or requiring notice to

---

[9] Easements existed in Roman law and running covenants were recognized as early as Spencer's Case in 1583, but "[u]ntil the Industrial Revolution greatly increased the use of servitudes, the common law did not develop a general theory of easements or servitudes." Susan F. French, *Design Proposal for the New Restatement of Property—Servitudes*, 21 U.C. DAVIS L. REV. 1213, 1214 (1998); see also Uriel Reichman, *Toward a Unified Concept of Servitudes*, 55 S. CAL. L. REV. 1177, 1183 (1982).

[10] See, e.g., A.W.B. SIMPSON, A HISTORY OF THE LAND LAW 262 (2d. ed. 1986); French, *supra* note 9, at 1262; James L. Winokur, *The Mixed Blessings of Promissory Servitudes: Toward Optimizing Economic Utility, Individual Liberty, and Personal Identity*, 1989 WIS. L. REV. 1, 13 (1989).

[11] See generally Susan F. French, *Toward a Modern Law of Servitudes: Reweaving the Ancient Strands*, 55 S. CAL. L. REV. 1261 (1982) (reviewing the rules governing the three types of servitudes).

[12] See Van Houweling, *The New Servitudes*, *supra* note 2.

[13] I borrow this useful terminology from Julia Mahoney. Julia D. Mahoney, *Perpetual Restrictions on Land and the Problem of the Future*, 88 VA. L. REV. 739 (2002).

[14] Carol Rose offers a similar but not identical categorization, identifying the concerns as involving information or notice, renegotiability, and value (including third-party effects). Rose, *supra* note 7.

[15] See generally Hansmann and Kraakman, *supra* note 8, at 384–85 (describing "the rule of possession" and observing that "[t]he advantages of this system are obvious. It is easy to understand, cheap to administer, and generally unambiguous").

people acquiring the burdened land, then transfers of possession would be plagued by confusion and/or costly investigation to discover hidden encumbrances. In *Keppell v. Bailey*,[16] one of the seminal nineteenth-century English servitude cases,[17] Lord Brougham famously expressed his concern about this possibility.

> Great detriment would arise and much confusion of rights if parties were allowed to invent new modes of holding and enjoying real property, and to impress upon their lands and tenements a peculiar character, which should follow them into all hands, however remote. Every close, every messuage, might thus be held in a several fashion; and it would hardly be possible to know what rights the acquisition of any parcel conferred, or what obligations it imposed.[18]

This kind of hostility toward the rude surprise of remote-control property runs throughout the law and scholarship on servitudes, with courts and commentators agreeing that servitudes should not generally bind purchasers who acquire land with no notice of the encumbrance and no reasonable opportunity to acquire notice.

The importance of notice is, accordingly, often identified as a rationale for the common law's limitations on servitudes.[19] For example, by requiring that servitudes have some connection to the land that they burden, and (typically) to a neighboring benefited parcel, the "touch and concern" doctrine helps to ensure that servitudes will be relatively easy to discover upon physical inspection and that the owner of the beneficial interest will be relatively easy to identify and locate.[20] By limiting the subject matter of servitudes, the doctrine also shapes and reinforces expectations in a way that limits surprise.[21] In their influential work explaining the role of property standardization in limiting information costs, Thomas Merrill and Henry Smith point to the touch and concern requirement as an example of a doctrinal technique that standardizes servitudes and thus limits the information costs they impose.[22]

Other doctrines that emerged from the seminal nineteenth-century English servitudes case law, including the requirements of appurtenance and horizontal privity, similarly limited servitudes to those that were relatively easy to discover.[23] When the landmark decision of *Tulk v. Moxhay* eliminated the horizontal privity requirement for equitable servitudes, it did so only in cases in which there was actual notice.[24]

---

[16] 39 Eng. Rep. 1042 (Ch. 1834).

[17] See generally Rose, *supra* note 7, at 298, n. 7 (citing *Keppell* as an example of "nineteenth century judges sharply criticiz[ing] [servitudes] for stirring confusion about and tying up real estate").

[18] *Keppell*, *supra* note 16, 39 Eng. Rep. at 1049. Keppell was superseded to some extent by the landmark case of Tulk v. Moxhay, 41 Eng. Rep. 1143 (1848), discussed below.

[19] See, e.g., French, *supra* note 11, at 1283–86; see also Rose, *supra* note 7, at 299.

[20] See generally Hansmann and Kraakman, *supra* note 8, at 402 ("Servitudes that meet this [touch and concern] requirement are much easier to verify by physical inspection of the property and its surroundings").

[21] See generally French, *supra* note 11, at 1290.

[22] Thomas W. Merrill & Henry E. Smith, *Optimal Standardization in the Law of Property: The Numerus Clausus Principle*, 110 YALE L.J. 1, 17 (2000).

[23] See generally Van Houweling, *The New Servitudes*, *supra* note 2, at 893–95; Rose, *supra* note 7, at 299–300.

[24] Tulk v. Moxhay, 41 Eng. Rep. 1143, 1144 (1848) ("[T]he question is . . . whether a party shall be permitted to use the land in a manner inconsistent with the contract entered into by his vendor,

Recording acts—which provide for public recording of interests in land and protect bona fide purchasers from some unrecorded encumbrances—represent another notice-facilitating mechanism. There was no recording system in England when the seminal nineteenth-century servitude cases were decided. There were, however, recording systems in every U.S. State. One might therefore have expected the U.S. courts to take a more accommodating and less convoluted approach to servitudes. To the contrary, they initially adopted the English categories and many of the corresponding doctrinal limitations, most of which made their way into the first *Restatement of Property* in 1944 and subsequent case law, despite fierce opposition by those who saw the restrictions as anachronistic solutions to a notice problem that no longer existed in the U.S., if it ever did.[25]

Criticism of the law's complexity and needless hostility toward certain types of servitudes persisted, and over the course of the twentieth century courts in the U.S. gradually relaxed some of the most controversial limitations.[26] This evolution is reflected (and perhaps outpaced) by the 2000 *Restatement (Third) of Property: Servitudes*, which abandons the horizontal privity requirement, "touch and concern," and all limitations on benefits held in gross.[27] Restatement Reporter Susan French explained in advance of the project that alternative mechanisms for providing notice justified eliminating unnecessary rules:

> Servitudes law may be simplified substantially because particular rules designed to give notice are no longer needed. The modern technology of record systems and title search procedures, together with the protection recording acts afford, have made these rules superfluous.[28]

This evolution of servitude doctrine demonstrates, first, that remote-control property comes with special notice and information costs; and, second, that those costs can be addressed with a number of different mechanisms. Subject matter limitations like touch and concern are one mechanism; actual notice requirements as in *Tulk v. Moxhay* are another; and recording systems are a third. As we will see when we turn to personal property, the comparative availability of these mechanisms differs across the types of resources

---

and with notice of which he purchased.").

[25] Regarding horizontal privity, *see* CHARLES E. CLARK, REAL COVENANTS AND OTHER INTERESTS WHICH "RUN WITH LAND" 117 (1929); Lawrence Berger, *A Policy Analysis of Promises Respecting the Use of Land*, 55 MINN. L. REV. 167, 193–95 (1970). On the persistence of limitations in U.S. servitude law "notwithstanding persistent criticism from the academic community," see Merrill and Smith, *supra* note 22, at 16–17.

[26] See generally Van Houweling, *The New Servitudes*, *supra* note 2; Rose, *supra* note 7.

[27] RESTATEMENT (THIRD) OF PROP.: SERVITUDES §§ 2.4, 2.6, 3.2 and introductory notes to chs. 2 and 3 (2000).

[28] French, *supra* note 9, at 1225; see also Richard Epstein, *Notice and Freedom of Contract in the Law of Servitudes*, 55 S. CAL. L. REV. 1353, 1358 (1983) (arguing that "with notice secured by recordation, freedom of contract should control"); Hansmann and Kraakman, *supra* note 8, at 407 (explaining that "registries developed for verifying ownership of land" avoid "many of the additional system and nonuser costs that effective verification of these rights would otherwise require"); Merrill and Smith, *supra* note 22, at 40 (noting that "recording acts ... lower the costs of notice [and are] an alternative method of lowering information costs"). On recording acts generally, see RICHARD R. POWELL, POWELL ON REAL PROPERTY § 82.01 (2005). On marketable title acts, see *ibid.* § 82.04.

that might be burdened by remote-control property rights, and so does the intensity of concern about notice and information cost problems.

C. Problem of the Future

Assuring adequate and meaningful notice and minimizing information costs are not the only justifications for standardizing property rights and restricting servitudes. There is another constellation of concerns for which I have borrowed Julia Mahoney's useful term: "the problem of the future."[29] Within this constellation I include a number of related issues regarding the extent to which enforcement of servitudes undesirably limits the freedom of future generations to manage resources wisely and autonomously.[30] The theme is excessive control by one generation over the freedom and flexibility of the next. The specific concerns are that excessive control will limit autonomy and recreate feudal incidents, impose inefficient land-use choices, and threaten freedom of alienation. These problems arise not only from manipulation of property rights by an earlier generation but also from the transaction costs that make that manipulation difficult to undo. In her classification of concerns about servitudes, Carol Rose thus groups many of the same problems under the heading "renegotiability."[31]

One feature of servitudes that contributes to these concerns about the future is the aforementioned remoteness between burdened and benefited parties who may be complete strangers—a remoteness that can contribute to the difficulty of renegotiating an obsolete servitude. Another important servitude feature that underlies the problem of the future is durability. Unlike a living party to a contract, a parcel of land that carries its terms with it can interact with generations of people over time, increasing the likelihood that unforeseen circumstances will render those terms obsolete.[32] The problem of the future is further compounded when a servitude arises in a context of rapid and unpredictable change, making unforeseen obsolescence especially likely.[33]

Concerns about the problem of the future resonate with the larger jurisprudence and literature on "dead-hand control" in the law of property. A classic statement on dead-hand control comes from Lewis Simes, who argued in his lectures on "Public Policy and

---

[29] Mahoney, *supra* note 13; see also Susan F. French, *Perpetual Trusts, Conservation Servitudes, and the Problem of the Future*, 27 CARDOZO L. REV. 2523 (2006); cf. Merrill and Smith, *supra* note 22, at 4–7 (surveying the literature and observing that "[t]he primary candidate for an economic expression [of the numerus clausus principle] has been the suggestion that the numerus clausus is a device for minimizing the effects of durable property interests on those dealing with assets in the future").

[30] See generally MARGARET JANE RADIN, REINTERPRETING PROPERTY 112–19 (1993) (discussing ways in which restraints on alienation and servitudes may "enhance or inhibit freedom or personhood systematically over time").

[31] Rose, *supra* note 7.

[32] See Stewart E. Sterk, *Foresight and the Law of Servitudes*, 73 CORNELL L. REV. 956 (1988); see also Glen O. Robinson, *Personal Property Servitudes*, 71 U. CHI. L. REV. 1449, 1489 (2004) (observing that "[a] restriction on the use (or sale) of Blackacre can limit the use of a valuable resource for a very long time").

[33] Cf. Julia D. Mahoney, *The Illusion of Perpetuity and the Preservation of Privately Owned Lands*, 44 NAT. RESOURCES J. 573, 584.

the Dead Hand," that "[i]t is socially desirable that the wealth of the world be controlled by its living members and not by the dead."[34] Simes went on to quote Thomas Jefferson, who insisted in a letter to James Madison that "[t]he earth belongs always to the living generation. They may manage it then, and what proceeds from it, as they please during their usufruct."[35]

This preference for the living over the dead is often justified in terms of autonomy and contrasted with feudal serfdom.[36] According to this view, controlling people who are distant in time and space—not family members or contractual privies—is a power associated with government (or with undesirable feudal hierarchy). Such control should not be unilaterally imposed by private parties merely on the basis of their property ownership and informed only by their "whim and caprice."[37]

The concern with dead-hand control is also often discussed in utilitarian terms: the land-use choices of previous generations may turn out to be inefficient ones in light of changed circumstances.[38] Where voluntary termination of servitudes is allowed by law (as it typically but not always is[39]) the mechanism by which dead-hand control limits autonomy or efficiency requires further explanation. The potential problem is that transaction costs may block a negotiated solution—even when all affected parties would, in theory, agree to extinguish the unwanted servitude. The current holders of the servitude's beneficial interest may be difficult to identify and locate, and they may be so numerous as to make contact and negotiation infeasible. Defenders of limitations on servitudes often point to this specter of transaction-cost-insulated servitudes as a justification for policies that either constrain the subject matter of servitudes or enable judges to terminate the detrimental ones.[40]

Inefficient but transaction-cost-insulated servitudes represent a species of the anticommons problem described by Michael Heller with regard to fragmentation of property interests more generally. Servitudes divide rights in a single parcel of land among multiple

---

[34] LEWIS M. SIMES, PUBLIC POLICY AND THE DEAD HAND 59 (1955).

[35] *Ibid.* (quoting *Letter from Thomas Jefferson to James Madison (Sept. 6, 1789)*, in 5 WRITINGS OF THOMAS JEFFERSON 121 (Paul Leicester Ford ed., 1895)).

[36] As Uriel Reichman puts it in his discussion of servitudes, "Private property is sanctioned by society not only to promote efficiency, but also to safeguard individual freedom. Servitudes are a kind of private legislation affecting a line of future owners. Limiting such 'legislative powers'... eliminates the possibility of creating modern variations of feudal serfdom." Reichman, *supra* note 9, at 1233. For a skeptical view, see Gregory S. Alexander, *The Dead Hand and the Law of Trusts in the Nineteenth Century*, 37 STAN. L. REV. 1189, 1258 (1985); Gregory S. Alexander, *Freedom, Coercion, and the Law of Servitudes*, 73 CORNELL L. REV. 883, 891 (1988).

[37] Copelan v. Acree Oil Co., 290 S.E.2d 94, 96 (Ga. 1982).

[38] Mahoney, *supra* note 13, at 744; see also Gerald Korngold, *Privately Held Conservation Servitudes: A Policy Analysis in the Context of in Gross Real Covenants and Easements*, 63 TEX. L. REV. 433, 457 (1984) (arguing that "[t]he market response of a future property owner to the future needs of society is likely to be more effective than a past owner's fixed blueprint").

[39] In some states, statutes make it difficult to terminate a conservation easement even if the easement holder agrees. But usually conservation easements, like other types of servitudes, can be voluntarily extinguished by negotiation with the holder of the non-possessory interest. See generally ELIZABETH BYERS & KARIN MARCHETTI PONTE, THE CONSERVATION EASEMENT HANDBOOK 195–96 (2005).

[40] See e.g. Reichman, *supra* note 9, at 1233.

owners. If it is later desirable to consolidate those rights in order to put the resource to its best use, fragmentation of the property bundle (and the transaction costs involved in re-bundling) can make consolidation difficult. Heller cites restrictions on servitudes among "numerous restraints [that] limit an individual's capacity to break up property bundles too much."[41]

Heller's concern with fragmentation offers an interesting way to think about the classic but under-theorized concern with restraints on alienation, which is also often cited as a rationale for limiting servitudes. Many legal mechanisms that are criticized for restraining alienation do not in fact directly restrain transfer. They merely limit the rights that can be acquired from any single owner. So a subsequent user who wants to reassemble property rights into a useful bundle must tackle the transaction costs involved in multiple negotiations. Often the problem is not so much restraint on alienation as restraint on acquisition: every individual stick in the property can be sold; the difficulty is in buying a bundle that is useful to own.

These various concerns associated with "the problem of the future" have long motivated common-law restrictions on servitudes.[42] And contemporary property theorists point to them to justify a variety of doctrines that serve to standardize and consolidate property rights.[43]

As with the problem of notice, however, multiple mechanisms could be employed to address the problem of the future. The view adopted by the current *Restatement* is that concerns with the future are best addressed in the future—by marketable title acts and by doctrines that allow judicial modification or termination of obsolete servitudes—instead of through doctrines that limit servitude subject matter *ex ante*. The *Restatement* uses the availability of these alternative approaches to justify discarding the common law rules (like touch and concern) that addressed the problem of the future indirectly.[44]

Although the mechanisms used to address the issue have shifted over time, it is clear that the problem of the future is a recurring justification for servitude skepticism. As with the problems of notice and information costs, it is a problem that is endemic to durable remote-control property rights, but one that can be alleviated using a variety of doctrinal techniques.

D. Externalities

A final set of problems often associated with servitudes involves their impact on third parties. Restrictions that run with land can impose significant and harmful externali-

---

[41] Michael Heller, *The Tragedy of the Anticommons: Property in the Transition from Marx to Markets*, 111 Harv. L. Rev. 621, 666 (1998). See generally Ben W.F. Depoorter & Francesco Parisi, *Fragmentation of Property Rights: A Functional Interpretation of the Law of Servitudes*, 3 Global Jurist Frontiers 1 (2003) (available at www.bepress.com/gj/frontiers/vol3/iss1/art2); Francesco Parisi, *Entropy in Property*, 50 Am. J. Comp. L. 595 (2002).
[42] See generally Van Houweling, *The New Servitudes*, supra note 2, at 904.
[43] See e.g. Reichman, *supra* note 9, at 1232–33.
[44] See Restatement (Third) of Prop.: Servitudes ch. 3, introductory note (2000).

ties.[45] Both the problem of the future and the problem of notice can be understood (at least in part) as externality problems. Inadequate or costly information about the nature of property rights in a specific parcel of land can produce confusion about property rights more generally. When one landowner's parcel is burdened by a strange and confusing covenant, the rest of the neighborhood's residents may become concerned and confused about the nature of their own rights. They bear an information-cost externality, to use Merrill and Smith's terminology.[46] Similarly, the costs imposed by servitudes that will burden future generations in unpredictable ways may not be accounted for in today's land transactions.

There are additional categories of externalities that have generated servitude skepticism. A servitude that prohibits land from being used in a way that subjects a neighboring business to competition, for example, may harm third-party competitors and consumers.[47] A racially-restrictive covenant may harm third parties who suffer its discriminatory impact.[48] The third-party effects of servitudes are likely to be especially pronounced (compared, for example, to the third-party effects of bilateral contracts imposing similar restrictions) because of the features of remoteness and durability. Servitudes can reach out over time and space in a way that tends in general to expand their impact and thus to intensify the externality problem.[49]

In addition to its other functions, the touch and concern requirement has sometimes seemed like a catch-all doctrinal hook used by courts to weed out servitudes that impose harmful externalities. The new *Restatement* opts to address such harms more directly, by invalidating those servitudes that "violate public policy" because, for example, they are "arbitrary, spiteful, or capricious," or "unreasonably burden a fundamental constitutional right," or "impose an unreasonable restraint on trade or competition."[50]

As we will see, the externality problem is one that features prominently in the analysis of whether and how the law of servitudes (and its limiting doctrines) should be applied outside of the land context.

---

[45] See e.g. Stewart E. Sterk, *Freedom from Freedom of Contract: The Enduring Value of Servitude Restrictions*, 70 IOWA L. REV. 615, 617 (1985).

[46] Cf. Merrill and Smith, *supra* note 22, at 8 ("The existence of unusual property rights increases the cost of processing information about all property rights. Those creating or transferring idiosyncratic property rights cannot always be expected to take these increases in measurement costs fully into account, making them a true externality.").

[47] See e.g. Sterk, *supra* note 45, at 622; cf. Norcross v. James, 2 N.E. 946, 949 (Mass. 1885) (using the touch and concern doctrine to invalidate running covenant against competition), *overruled in part by* Whitinsville Plaza, Inc. v. Kotseas, 390 N.E.2d 243, 246–49 (Mass. 1979). See generally Susan F. French, *Can Covenants Not to Sue, Covenants Against Competition and Spite Covenants Run with Land? Comparing Results Under the Touch or Concern Doctrine and the Restatement Third, Property (Servitudes)*, 38 REAL PROP. PROB. & TR. J. 267, 280–90 (2003) (reviewing two cases concerning whether covenants against competition run with the land).

[48] See e.g. Shelley v. Kraemer, 334 U.S. 1, 20 (1948).

[49] Contracts that happen to affect many third parties might trigger the same level of concern. Cf. Merrill and Smith, *supra* note 22, at 57; Richard A. Epstein, *Covenants and Constitutions*, 73 CORNELL L. REV. 906, 917 (1988).

[50] RESTATEMENT (THIRD) OF PROP.: SERVITUDES § 3.1 (2000).

E. Personal Property Servitudes

The gradual erosion of traditional limitations on land servitudes can be explained in part by the development of alternative methods for ensuring notice, by the adoption of *ex post* solutions to the problem of the future, and by the replacement of vague requirements like touch and concern with more focused doctrines addressing specific types of harmful externalities caused by certain types of servitudes. During the course of this evolution, property owners, commentators, and occasionally courts raised the question whether property doctrine that increasingly accommodated land servitudes could also be applied to enforce running restrictions attached to items of personal property.

English equity courts initially extended the equitable servitude reasoning of *Tulk v. Moxhay* to personal property, holding in *De Mattos v. Gibson*[51] in 1858 that the principle applied "alike . . . to movable and immovable property."[52] But in the early twentieth century, English courts stepped back from this position, holding instead that a manufacturer's resale conditions attached to product packages "do not run with goods, and cannot be imposed upon them. Subsequent purchasers, therefore, do not take subject to any conditions which the Court can enforce."[53]

In several early twentieth-century cases, U.S. courts similarly refused to enforce running restrictions that imposed resale conditions on chattels. *John D. Park & Sons v. Hartman*[54] involved a manufacturer of unpatented medicine who attempted to fix retail prices by only selling to wholesalers who agreed to sell only to approved retailers who had agreed to the manufacturer's minimum prices. The defendant, a retailer who was not on the manufacturer's approved list, nonetheless managed to acquire a supply of the medicine, which it sold for less than the minimum price despite knowledge of the minimum price regime. The manufacturer apparently cited *De Mattos* "to support the notion that a covenant may attach to chattels which pass by delivery from hand to hand and bring any one who buys with notice under the restrictions against a resale at less than a dictated price."[55] Judge (later Justice) Lurton rejected that proposition, instead citing contrary cases (including *Taddy & Co.*) and declaring sweepingly that:

> It is . . . a general rule of the common law that a contract restricting the use or controlling sub-sales cannot be annexed to a chattel so as to follow the article and obligate the subpurchaser

---

[51] 45 Eng. Rep. 108 (Ch. App. 1858).

[52] *Ibid.* at 110; see also SIMPSON, *supra* note 10, at 259; Zechariah Chafee, Jr., *Equitable Servitudes on Chattels*, 41 HARV. L. REV. 945, 953–54 (1928); Andrew Tettenborn, *Covenants, Privity of Contract, and the Purchaser of Personal Property*, 41 CAMBRIDGE L.J. 58 (1982).

[53] Taddy & Co. v. Sterious & Co., [1904] 1 Ch. 354, at 358 (U.K.). See also McGruther v. Pitcher, [1904] 2 Ch. 306 (A.C.) (U.K.). In this case, Lord Justice Vaughan Williams declared Taddy "perfectly right." *Ibid.* at 309. Lord Justice Romer also elaborated that: "[a] vendor cannot . . . by printing the so-called condition upon some part of the goods or on the case containing them, say that every subsequent purchaser of the goods is bound to comply with the condition, so that if he does not comply with the condition he can be sued by the original vendor. That is clearly wrong. You cannot in that way make conditions run with goods." *Ibid.* at 311.

[54] 153 F. 24 (6th Cir. 1907).

[55] *Ibid.* at 40.

by operation of notice. A covenant which may be valid and run with land will not run with or attach to a mere chattel.[56]

In *Dr. Miles Medical Co. v. John D. Park & Sons*,[57] the Supreme Court considered the enforceability of a similar price-fixing scheme, explaining that "[t]he basis of the argument appears to be that, as the manufacturer may make and sell, or not, as he chooses, he may affix conditions as to the use of the article or as to the prices at which purchasers may dispose of it."[58] Like its predecessors, the Court rejected this chattel servitude logic: "[w]hatever right the manufacturer may have to project his control beyond his own sales must depend not upon an inherent power incident to production and original ownership, but upon agreement."[59]

These and similar cases are the bases for the conventional wisdom among academic commentators that chattel servitudes, while not unheard of, are much less likely to be enforced than land servitudes.[60] Commentators are less uniform in their assessment of whether, and if so why, this should be the case.

Contemporary scholarship about personal property servitudes owes a debt to two foundational articles by Zechariah Chafee. In 1928, Chafee provided a comprehensive analysis of the topic in *Equitable Servitudes on Chattels*. The article surveyed the case law, based on which Chafee observed that "[i]n view of these decisions it might well be maintained that the doctrine of equitable servitudes on chattels has been effectively killed by the courts."[61] But Chafee found the courts' reasoning conclusory and unpersuasive.[62] Further, he observed that most of the cases involved restrictions that restrained trade in one way or another (by, e.g., fixing prices, tying goods, or dividing territories), possibly leaving open the question of the validity of restrictions not subject to that objection.[63] In the meantime, manufacturers continued to attempt to impose restrictions, suggesting a

---

[56] *Ibid.* at 39.
[57] 220 U.S. 373 (1911), *overruled in part by* Leegin Creative Leather Prods., Inc. v. PSKS, Inc., 127 S. Ct. 2705 (2007).
[58] *Ibid.* at 404.
[59] *Ibid.* at 405.
[60] Merrill and Smith, *supra* note 22, at 18 ("[A]lthough the case law is rather thin, it . . . appears that one cannot create servitudes in personal property"); Hansmann and Kraakman, *supra* note 8, at 407 (noting that the law "makes it much simpler to establish partial rights in real property than in personal property").
[61] Chafee, *supra* note 52, at 955.
[62] For example, as to the oft-recited policy in favor of free alienation, Chafee observed that restraints on the alienation of land "were also regarded as objectionable at common law" and yet cases like Tulk v. Moxhay enforced use restrictions that made land less alienable as a practical matter. So "[j]ust as modern needs have brought equitable restrictions on land, of which the old common law knew nothing, into existence, they may also call for a limited departure from the free transfer of chattels for the sake of promoting desirable business practices wholly strange to Coke's day." Chafee, *supra* note 52, at 983.
[63] *Ibid.* at 1007 ("In many situations where manufacturers have endeavored to employ this device, the courts have refused to allow them to do so because it would unreasonably restrain trade. However, it seems possible that restrictions on the area and the form of resale may not always be open to such an objection.").

live question.[64] So Chafee went on to consider and evaluate normative arguments in favor and against enforcing chattel servitudes.

I will describe some of Chafee's specific arguments below. For now suffice it to say that he found servitudes attached to personal property more likely to be costly, and less likely to be necessary, than land servitudes. Although he was unwilling to condemn chattel servitudes across the board, he put the burden on anyone seeking to enforce a running restriction on a chattel to show that theirs was a special case in which the benefits outweighed the costs, or that something in the business and/or legal environment had changed so dramatically as to make chattel servitudes desirable in general. Chafee did not think that the time for enforceable chattel servitudes had come, as a general matter, in 1928, nor when he revisited the question in 1956.[65]

Some contemporary commentators argue that the time for chattel servitudes has now come. Referring to Chafee's 1928 article and his 1956 second thoughts, Glen Robinson argues in his 2004 article "Personal Property Servitudes" that: "Nearly a half century later, there is reason to entertain third thoughts on the matter despite the general disposition of courts and commentators to be content with Chafee's judgment."[66] Robinson suggests that personal property servitudes should be enforceable as a general matter, with any concerns about restrictions with anti-competitive terms left to be addressed by antitrust law—now more mature than it was when the early twentieth-century chattel servitude cases were decided.[67]

In 2007, I took up the question myself, arguing—contra Robinson—that judicial skepticism is justified by a somewhat different mix of the concerns with notice and information costs, dead-hand control over the future, and externalities that motivated skepticism of land servitudes.

This renewed interest in chattel servitudes is due in part to the historical, doctrinal, and theoretical connections with current controversies about the scope of IP exhaustion, as the next section explains.

III. SERVITUDES AND THE COMMON LAW ORIGINS OF INTELLECTUAL PROPERTY EXHAUSTION

In the midst of early twentieth-century cases questioning the enforceability of chattel servitudes as a general matter, several cases arose that posed an added complication: the chattels in question embodied copyrighted works or patented inventions. Against the backdrop of courts refusing to enforce servitudes on ordinary chattels, IP owners argued that their exclusive rights should give them extra power to control downstream resale and use of the embodiments of their intangible property.

---

[64] *Ibid.* at 956 ("[T]he wide prevalence of these restrictions in business practice indicates that they embody a strong and definite commercial policy which, despite its previous checkered career, may eventually succeed in obtaining judicial recognition, perhaps with legislative aid.").
[65] Zechariah Chafee, Jr., *The Music Goes Round and Round: Equitable Servitudes and Chattels*, 69 HARV. L. REV. 1250 (1956).
[66] See e.g. Robinson, *supra* note 32, at 1451.
[67] *Ibid.* at 1494–515.

The seminal case taking up this question in the copyright context was *Bobbs-Merrill Co. v. Straus*,[68] in which a book publisher attempted to enforce a restriction printed inside books, to wit: "The price of this book at retail is one dollar net. No dealer is licensed to sell it at a less price, and a sale at a less price will be treated as an infringement of the copyright."[69]

The Second Circuit understood this as an "attempt of an owner of an ordinary chattel to impose by contract restrictions upon its use or sale binding upon third parties, and which, it is claimed, may operate as a sort of ambulatory covenant annexed to the chattel."[70] The court rejected that attempt, albeit rather timidly in light of the conflicting case law it cited on the topic (including both *De Mattos* and *Taddy & Co*).[71]

But the plaintiff in *Bobbs-Merrill* did not rely exclusively on the equitable servitude notion from *De Mattos*. It also argued that as the copyright holder it had an exclusive right to "vend" the copyrighted work embodied in its books. By distributing books subject to restrictive terms, it was granting purchasers only a conditional license to exercise that vending right; vending outside the terms of that license (that is, selling books for less than one dollar) therefore amounted to copyright infringement.[72] The Copyright Act, according to this logic, provides a mechanism for imposing running restrictions on chattels that the common law lacks. The Second Circuit rejected that argument, and the Supreme Court affirmed.[73]

On this point, both *Bobbs-Merrill* opinions purport merely to interpret the language of the Copyright Act, concluding that the right to "vend" granted in the Act is exhausted as to a given copy of a copyrighted work once that copy is sold.[74] But the reasonableness of that interpretation gains strength from the notion that to interpret the right to vend beyond the first sale would do violence to the common law.[75] For example, the Supreme Court's opinion notes with apparent alarm:

What the complainant contends for embraces not only the right to sell the copies, but to *qualify the title of a future purchaser* by the reservation of the right to have the remedies of the statute

---

[68] Bobbs-Merrill Co. v. Straus ("*Bobbs-Merrill I*"), 147 F. 15 (2d Cir. 1906), *aff'd*, 210 U.S. 339 (1908).
[69] *Ibid.* at 17.
[70] *Ibid.* at 24.
[71] *Ibid.* at 25–28.
[72] *Ibid.* at 17.
[73] Bobbs-Merrill Co. v. Straus ("*Bobbs-Merrill II*"), 210 U.S. 339, 351 (1908).
[74] See *ibid..* at 350 ("It is not denied that one who has sold a copyrighted article, without restriction, has parted with all right to control the sale of it"); *Bobbs-Merrill I*, *supra* note 68, 147 F. at 22 ("If the statutory owner desires after publication to control the lawfully published copies, such control can only be secured by means of positive contract or conditions.").
[75] Cf. *Bobbs-Merrill I*, *supra* note 68, 147 F. at 20 ("The law of copyright also gives privileges to authors and publishers that do not pertain to property which anybody may make and sell if he can; but even under the law of copyright, when the owner of a copyright and of a particular copy of a book to which it pertains, has parted with all his title to the book, and has conferred an absolute title to it upon a purchaser, he cannot restrict the right of alienation, which is one of the incidents of ownership in personal property") (quoting Garst v. Hall & Lyon Co., 61 N.E. 219, 220 (Mass. 1901)); see also Joseph P. Liu, *Owning Digital Copies: Copyright Law and the Incidents of Copy Ownership*, 42 WM. & MARY L. REV. 1245, 1248–49 (2001).

against an infringer because of the printed notice of its purpose so to do unless the purchaser sells at a price fixed in the notice.[76]

The Court refused to interpret the Copyright Act to include such a right.[77] Although (unlike the Second Circuit) it did not cite *Taddy & Co* or any other cases addressing chattel servitudes, the Court's narrow interpretation of the vending right suggests an undercurrent of hostility toward running restrictions on chattels that made it difficult to persuade the Court that Congress intended to part ways with the common law.[78]

Of course, the statutory rights granted to copyright holders supersede the hostility to running restrictions to some extent: there are some things that the owner of a copyright-embodying chattel is not permitted to do with it (for example, reproduce each of its pages) on account of the non-possessory intellectual property rights created by copyright. But *Bobbs-Merrill* (and, later, the statutory codification of the "first sale" doctrine[79]) articulates one limit on even a copyright holder's power to impose running restrictions on personal property.

In the patent context, the Supreme Court initially accepted the idea that a patent owner's right to control "use" of a chattel embodying his invention could be leveraged into the type of running restriction that would not be enforced on a non-patented article. In *Henry v. A.B. Dick Co.*,[80] the Court held that a patent owner could use an express conditional license to impose a running restriction on a chattel embodying a patented invention against a purchaser with notice;[81] specifically, the Court enforced a restriction stamped on a mimeograph machine which said: "This machine is sold by the A.B. Dick Company, with the license restriction that it may be used only with the stencil, paper, ink, and other supplies made by A.B. Dick Company."[82]

Justice Lurton, who had rejected the notion of a use restriction "annexed to a chattel" in *John D. Park & Sons v. Hartman*, explained that the patent law (unlike the common law of personal property[83] and unlike copyright) separates ownership of a chattel from the right *to use* that chattel, and that the right to use can be granted conditionally so as to allow use subject to running restrictions.[84] The opinion suggested that other restrictions—even resale price-fixing restrictions of the type rejected in *Dr. Miles* and *Bobbs-Merrill*—could be enforced via an express restriction imposed by a patent holder against a chattel owner with notice.[85] Indeed, Justice Lurton cited an English case,

---

[76] *Bobbs-Merrill II*, *supra* note 73, 210 U.S. at 351 (emphasis added).
[77] See *ibid*.
[78] See *ibid*. See generally Robinson, *supra* note 32 (describing links between the first sale doctrine and common law principles).
[79] 17 U.S.C. § 109 (2000).
[80] See 224 U.S. 1 (1912), *overruled by* Motion Picture Patents Co. v. Universal Film Mfg. Co., 243 U.S. 502, 517 (1917).
[81] Henry v. A.B. Dick Co., *supra* note 80, 224 U.S. at 12.
[82] *Ibid*. at 26.
[83] *Ibid*. at 39.
[84] *Ibid*. at 24–25.
[85] See *ibid*. at 26.

Incandescent Gaslight Co. v. Cantelo, which held that a patentee's restrictive terms were enforceable with notice and that "[i]t does not matter how unreasonable or how absurd the conditions are."[86]

But the distinction that Justice Lurton drew between common law chattel servitudes and running restrictions imposed via patent law on the use of chattels embodying patented inventions was short-lived. Just one year later, the Court refused to enforce express retail price limitations printed on packaging for patented medicine in *Bauer v. O'Donnell*.[87] The Court confirmed the *Bauer* result in *Straus v. Victor Talking Machine Co*[88] (refusing to enforce price restrictions attached to patented record players). And in *Motion Picture Patents Co. v. Universal Film Manufacturing Co*,[89] the Court expressly overruled *A.B. Dick*, refusing to enforce a trying restriction imposed via a label on a movie projector.[90]

My claim here is not that these seminal cases establishing the doctrines of copyright and patent exhaustion were mere applications of a common law prohibition on chattel servitudes. They were primarily exercises in statutory interpretation—determining the meaning of the exclusive rights to vend copies of copyrighted works and to use and sell articles embodying patented inventions. But these exercises in statutory interpretation were conducted in the shadow of the common law hostility to chattel servitudes, which made the question of statutory interpretation partly whether Congress had spoken clearly enough to invade what would otherwise be the province of the common law, and to validate a legal mechanism that the common law had rejected.[91]

IV. CONTEMPORARY CRITIQUES

The contemporary commentary on personal property servitudes has been motivated in part by controversies about the scope of IP exhaustion, with its historical and doctrinal connection to the servitude case law. Among the most pressing questions is whether exhaustion is a default rule that IP owners can avoid merely by attaching restrictive labels to objects embodying their IP or by characterizing distribution of those objects as "licenses" rather than sales. The commentators who address this and related questions

---

[86] *Ibid.* at 40 (quoting Incandescent Gas Light Co. v. Cantelo, (1895) 12 R.P.D.T.M.C. 262, 264 (Q.B.) (U.K.)).
[87] 229 U.S. 1, 17 (1913).
[88] 243 U.S. 490, 501 (1917) (concluding that the case fell "within the principles of" Adams and Bauer).
[89] 243 U.S. 502 (1917).
[90] *Ibid.* at 518–19; see also Mallinckrodt I, No. 89 C 4524, 1990 WL 19535, at *5 (N.D. Ill. Feb. 16, 1990), *rev'd*, 976 F.2d 700 (Fed. Cir. 1990).
[91] Cf. Kirtsaeng v. John Wiley & Sons, Inc., 113 S.Ct. 1351, 1363 ("'[W]hen a statute covers an issue previously governed by the common law,' we must presume that 'Congress intended to retain the substance of the common law.' Samantar v. Yousuf, 560 U.S. 305, 320, n. 13, 130 S.Ct. 2278, 2289–90, n. 13, 176 L.Ed.2d 1047 (2010). See also Isbrandtsen Co. v. Johnson, 343 U.S. 779, 783, 72 S.Ct. 1011, 96 L.Ed. 1294 (1952) ('Statutes which invade the common law . . . are to be read with a presumption favoring the retention of long-established and familiar principles, except when a statutory purpose to the contrary is evident').").

come to dramatically different conclusions about the implications of the chattel servitude connection.

As noted above, Glen Robinson finds arguments against enforcement of chattel servitudes unpersuasive. He therefore contends that the doctrinal prohibition should be abandoned and that chattel servitudes should be enforced much as land servitudes are. And because Robinson sees IP exhaustion as sharing the same origins and logic as the ban on chattel servitudes, he suggests that exhaustion should not operate to invalidate IP-owner-imposed restrictions on use and resale, which should generally be enforceable with IP and state law remedies.[92]

In their work on copyright exhaustion, Aaron Perzanowski and Jason Schultz also emphasize the common law origins of the IP exhaustion concept, but their origin story is somewhat different. They point not only to the common law's general hostility to chattel servitudes,[93] but also to common law reasoning within copyright itself—cases preceding the seminal chattel servitude decisions in which judges permitted downstream owners of copyrighted works to do a variety of things without the authority of copyright owners. They argue that the justifications motivating this common law reasoning should continue to shape the law of copyright exhaustion in the courts, even beyond the codification of copyright first sale as a specific limitation on the rights of distribution and display.[94] In addition, Perzanowski and Schultz harness the common law rationales for exhaustion to resist attempts by copyright owners to avoid exhaustion by recharacterizing sales as licenses. Beyond that, they argue that the user privileges associated with exhaustion should sometimes extend beyond copy owners in a digital age in which physical copies are increasingly irrelevant.[95]

In a recent contribution to this debate, John Duffy and Richard Hynes make a break with those who trace the origins of exhaustion to the common law of either chattel servitudes or IP.[96] They argue instead that the doctrine is exclusively a matter of statutory interpretation. Its only connection to the law of chattel servitudes is as a "boundary doctrine" that prevents IP law from interfering more than Congress intended with generally applicable commercial law.[97] As to the substance of that commercial law, Duffy and Hynes point out that distributors of chattels (including IP embodying chattels) can in fact impose running restrictions by complying with the Uniform Commercial Code's rules governing secured transactions.[98] They argue that IP owners should also be able to seek contractual (but not IP) remedies against users who violate terms attached to IP embodiments.[99] This is not to say, however, that exhaustion lacks teeth. Duffy and Hynes

---

[92] See e.g. Robinson, *supra* note 32, at 1505 (approving of the result in Adobe Systems Inc. v. One Stop Micro, Inc., 84 F. Supp. 2d 1086 (N.D. Cal. 2000)).
[93] Aaron Perzanowski & Jason Schultz, *Digital Exhaustion*, 58 UCLA L. REV. 889, 910–11 (2011).
[94] Ibid. at 912–18.
[95] Aaron Perzanowski & Jason Schultz, *Reconciling Intellectual and Personal Property*, 90 NOTRE DAME L. REV. 1211 (2015).
[96] Duffy and Hynes, *supra* note 1.
[97] Ibid. at 7.
[98] Ibid. at 35, 60–64.
[99] Ibid. at 8, 37, 58.

point out that the notice and other formal requirements of these bodies of state law are more onerous and the remedies less generous than those of IP.[100]

My own view is that the information costs, problems of the future, and externalities that long motivated doctrinal restrictions on land servitudes are all the more relevant to both chattel servitudes and IP. I am concerned, in particular, with notice and information costs, including the costs involved in identifying and locating servitude beneficiaries for the purposes of renegotiating.[101] Notice and information costs are minimized for land servitudes by recording systems, but no comprehensive recording system exists for chattels outside of the secured transactions context. And recording of IP is notoriously imperfect. When IP owners are permitted to impose running restrictions notwithstanding exhaustion, the ultimate recipient of the burdened object may be remote in time and place, with little hope of identifying and communicating with the current owner of the IP right for purposes of renegotiating the restriction once it becomes obsolete. This is of course a problem that plagues remote-control IP rights generally, including the core rights of reproducing copies of copyrighted works and making patented inventions. But at least with regard to the generally inexhaustible rights of reproduction and making, there is a strong case that the costs imposed by the remote-control property rights are outweighed by the benefits (as where land servitudes are enforced to serve important land-use planning goals). That is the basic logic of IP protection: the incentive effect relies on IP owners controlling the proliferation of embodiments that might compete in the marketplace with their authorized embodiments.[102] That type of control limits the ruinous competition that could make it impossible for at least some creators and inventors to garner returns on their investments. It is much less clear that adequate incentives depend on IP owners' ability to control downstream use and transfer of authorized embodiments (including use and transfer that requires some *de minimis* reproduction).[103] And so, to me, the argument for exhaustion stems in part from the costs that are imposed by chattel servitudes, and in part from the lack of justification for enduring those costs except in the limited circumstances in which creators' and inventors' incentives would be undermined in a way that inhibits progress in science and the useful arts.[104] The proper reach of the exhaustion doctrine is thus a question for copyright policy, in Congress and the courts, not for IP

---

[100] *Ibid.* at 61–62 (regarding notice requirements for security interests); *ibid.* at 58–59 (regarding contract remedies).

[101] Van Houweling, *Technology and Tracing Costs*, *supra* note 2. Guy Rub also emphasizes these costs in his recent work on copyright exhaustion. Guy A. Rub, *Rebalancing Copyright Exhaustion*, 64 EMORY L.J. 741, 788–89 (2015).

[102] Cf. Perzanowski and Schultz, *supra* note 95, at 915 ("Of course, title to a copy cannot confer on its owner an unbounded privilege to reproduce the work. Complete exhaustion of the reproduction right would undermine the incentive structure at the heart of copyright law.").

[103] See *Kirtsaeng*, *supra* note 91, at 1371 ("[T]he Constitution's language nowhere suggests that its limited exclusive right should include a right to divide markets or a concomitant right to charge different purchasers different prices for the same book, say to increase or to maximize gain."); Ariel Katz, *The First Sale Doctrine and the Economics of Post-Sale Restraints*, 2014 B.Y.U. L. REV. 55.

[104] Cf. Katz, *supra* note 103, at 99–100 ("[T]he marginal benefit from having enforceable restraints diminishes as we move along the vectors of distance and time. At the same time, the marginal social costs associated with goods encumbered by restraints could easily increase over distance and time because any use inconsistent with the restraint would require the IP owners' permission, yet the cost of obtaining such permission could easily increase over time and distance.").

owners unilaterally deciding that exhaustion should not apply to them—either by unilaterally re-characterizing sales as licenses or by imposing nominally contractual restrictions that are so adhesive and ubiquitous that they function like property rights.[105] Exhaustion should be subject to relaxation only if information costs problems are addressed.[106] Even then, there should be a screen, akin to the touch and concern requirement,[107] that would help ensure that running restrictions backed by the force of IP rights promote progress rather than imposing negative externalities. These negative externalities could include waste of physical resources, destruction of cultural heritage, and diminution of opportunities for innovation and expression.[108] If running restrictions promote progress but only in the short term (or only when enforced against intermediaries but not end-users) then they should be subject to durational limits and/or a "changed circumstances" doctrine designed to address the problem of the future.[109]

V. CONCLUSION

The law of IP exhaustion is rightly informed by a long history of skepticism toward what I call remote-control property rights. Property rights that give owners the ability to control how other people use assets in their rightful possession are potentially confusing, subject to obsolescence, and sometimes burdensome to third parties. In some cases, these costs can be mitigated in ways that make remote-control property rights beneficial on balance. The evolution of the law of land servitudes, which can be very useful tools for long-term land-use planning, demonstrates this possibility. By contrast, longstanding judicial hostility toward personal property servitudes suggests that the game of remote control property may not always be worth the candle.

So what about remote-control IP? The entire logic of this field of law is based on the notion that remote-control property rights can be worthwhile. Every copyright, patent, and trademark gives its owner some ability to control how other people use things they rightly possess. But where IP owners try to exercise remote control over uses and transfers that do not cut to the core of their need to limit ruinous competition, exhaustion can step in to maintain IP's balance between remote-control property's benefits and costs. These costs and benefits are not just a matter of concern to IP owners and users: like the costs associated with personal property servitudes, they have implications for a property system that is beset by high information costs, for future generations burdened by obsolete restrictions, and for third parties harmed by other externalities.

Although looking to the law of tangible property helps us to recognize these costs, we should also keep in mind their unique character in the IP context. Restrictions on the use of works of creativity and invention have implications for the promotion of progress of

---

[105] See generally Van Houweling, *The New Servitudes*, *supra* note 2, at 934–35.
[106] Van Houweling, *Technology and Tracing Costs*, *supra* note 2.
[107] Van Houweling, *Touching and Concerning Copyright*, *supra* note 2.
[108] Katz, *supra* note 103, at 109–17.
[109] I explore this idea in ongoing work. Molly Shaffer Van Houweling, *Disciplining the Dead Hand of Copyright: Durational Limits on Remote Control Property* (unpublished manuscript on file with author).

science and the useful arts. They therefore should not be ratcheted up solely at the whim of IP owners attaching labels to embodiments of their works. Nor should they be left solely to generally applicable commercial law without regard to IP's special policy concerns. Instead, courts and Congress should continue to absorb the wisdom of the common law of tangible property while crafting an IP-specific exhaustion policy that is attentive to the specific costs and benefits of remote-control IP.

4. "Exhaustion" in the digital age
Reto M. Hilty*

I. INTRODUCTION

In its judgment of July 3, 2012 in *UsedSoft v. Oracle*, the Court of Justice of the European Union (CJEU) ruled:

> that the right of distribution of a copy of a computer program is exhausted if the copyright holder who has authorised, even free of charge, the downloading of that copy from the internet onto a data carrier has also conferred, in return for payment of a fee intended to enable him to obtain a remuneration corresponding to the economic value of the copy of the work of which he is the proprietor, a right to use that copy for an unlimited period.[1]

This decision opened up an intense debate about the applicability of this "exhaustion rule" to copyright-protected digital products other than software, particularly since the CJEU based its judgment on Directive 2009/24,[2] which is *lex specialis* in relation to the InfoSoc Directive 2001/29.[3]

This chapter provides an analysis of the comparability and distinction of the different types of digital products from a legal point of view, including reflections on the factual circumstances, as well as the economic impacts of a broader application of the aforementioned CJEU ruling.

II. TECHNICAL DEVELOPMENTS IN THE DIGITAL AGE

In order to spot the questions involved, it is essential first to trace the development of digital products over the past few years and the exact ways of their commercialization. The digital age can broadly be divided into three (partially still on-going) periods.

In the initial period, digital copies of works took the place of analogue copies. Their distribution was—and to some extent still is—carried out via tangible carriers (e.g., DVDs and CDs). In this process, the tangible carriers remain in the main focus of trade. This

---

* Director, Max Planck Institute for Innovation and Competition, Munich; Professor at the Universities of Zurich and Munich. The author wishes to thank Oliver Schmid, LL.M., Research Assistant at the University of Zurich, for his valuable support, especially in document enquiry and analysis.

[1] Case C-128/11, UsedSoft GmbH v. Oracle Int'l Corp., 2012 E.C.R. I-0000 (July 3, 2012), available at http://curia.europa.eu/juris/document/document.jsf?docid=124564&doclang=en.

[2] Directive 2009/24 of the European Parliament and of the Council of April 23, 2009 on the legal protection of computer programs, [2009] O.J. L111/16 (EC) [hereinafter Software Directive].

[3] Directive 2001/29 of the European Parliament and of the Council of May 22, 2001 on the harmonization of certain aspects of copyright and related rights in the information society, [2001] O.J. L167/10 (EC) [hereinafter InfoSoc Directive].

traditional way of distributing works via physical data carriers is mainly classified as a sales contract; consequently sales contract legislation applies in practice—at least analogically.[4]

In the second period, the downloading of works (and therewith creation of a copy of the work) by the user himself on his own physical device (any data carrier) via the Internet began to replace the distribution of works via tangible carriers. Also in this period, the prevailing opinion assumes analogue application of sales contract legislation due to the permanent copy ultimately ending up on a physical device.[5]

The third period is characterized by a replacement of downloading works by streaming. Having access to digital works increasingly becomes more important to users than ownership of tangible copies of the protected work.[6] Mere access requires neither a distribution of works via tangible carriers nor a download by the user. At this point the legal doctrine has begun to assess the applicability of sales contract legislation more critically. In fact, without a physical copy even an analogical applicability fails.

It should be noted, however, that certain types of digital products cannot perfectly be

---

[4] See Reto M. Hilty, Kaya Köklü, & Fabian Hafenbrädl, *Software Agreements: Stocktaking and Outlook—Lessons from the UsedSoft v. Oracle Case from a Comparative Law Perspective*, 44 INT'L REV. INTELL. PROP. & COMPETITION L. 263, 266 (2013); see also Reto M. Hilty, *Die Rechtsnatur des Softwarevertrags*, COMPUTER & RECHT 625 (2012).

[5] Jochen Schneider & Gerald Spindler, *Der Erschöpfungsgrundsatz bei "gebrauchter" Software im Praxistest*, COMPUTER & RECHT 214 (2014); Helmut Redeker, *Das Konzept der digitalen Erschöpfung—Urheberrecht für die digitale Welt*, COMPUTER & RECHT 74 (2014); see also implicit Damien Riehl & Jumi Kassim, *Is "Buying" Digital Content Just "Renting" for Life? Contemplating a Digital First Sale Doctrine*, 40 WILLIAM MITCHELL L. REV. 807 (2014). However, Yin Harn Lee, *UsedSoft GmbH v. Oracle International Corp. (Case C-128/11): Sale of "Used" Software and the Principle of Exhaustion*, INT'L REV. INTELL. PROP. & COMPETITION L. 846 (2012), points out the importance of the involved copyright. In U.S. courts, Vernor v. Autodesk, Inc., 621 F.3d 1102 (9th Cir. 2010), 42 INT'L REV. INTELL. PROP. & COMPETITION L. 231–32 (2011); UMG Recordings Inc. v. Augusto, 628 F.3d 1175, 1180 (9th Cir. 2011); and DSC Communs. Corp. v. Pulse Communs., Inc., 170 F.3d 1354 (Fed. Cir. 1999) distinguish between transfers where the copyright owner dictates how media can be used (license) and transfers free from restrictions regarding use (sale). Even over a century ago in *Bobbs-Merrill*, the U.S. Supreme Court noted that, "[t]here is no claim in this case of contract limitation, nor license agreement controlling the subsequent sales of the book," implying that customers' rights would differ in case of a contractual relationship in terms of a license agreement as opposed to transferring ownership of a tangible object. Bobbs-Merrill Co. v. Straus, 210 U.S. 339, 350 (1908); see also Monica L. Dobson, *ReDigi and the Resale of Digital Media: The Courts Reject a First Sale Doctrine and Sustain the Imbalance Between Copyright Owners and Consumers*, 7 AKRON INTELL. PROP. J. 179, 190 (2015); John Villasenor, *Rethinking a Digital First Sale Doctrine in a Post-Kirtsaeng World: The Case for Caution*, 2 COMP. POLICY INT'L ANTITRUST CHRONICLE 8 (2013); Alandis Kyle Brassel, *Confused, Frustrated, and Exhausted: Solving the U.S. Digital First Sale Doctrine Problem Through International Lens*, 48 VAND. J. TRANSNAT'L L. 245, 261 (2015). Lukas Feiler, *Birth of the First-Download Doctrine: The Application of the First Sale Doctrine to Internet Downloads Under EU and US Copyright Law*, J. INTERNET L. 1 (2012), however, classifies contracts regarding downloads of digital content not as sales contracts but as licenses.

[6] Samuel Perkins, *"Fixing" the First Sale Doctrine: Adapting Copyright Law to the New Media Distribution Paradigm*, 6 N. ILL. U. L. REV. 7, 14 (2014), available at http://papers.ssrn.com/sol3/papers.cfm?abstract_id=2616008; Riehl & Kassim, *supra* note 5, at 809; Kristin Cobb, *The Implications of Licensing Agreements and the First Sale Doctrine on U.S. and EU Secondary Markets for Digital Goods*, 24 DUKE J. COMPARATIVE & INT'L L. 529, 530 (2014).

assigned to a specific period. This for example applies to "hybrid" business models—such as Spotify—where access is not (necessarily) granted through real-time use (i.e., streaming). Instead, users are enabled to download files temporarily on their own device. Such downloads, however, cannot be copied and do not remain permanently stored. The files are rather deleted on a specific date (e.g., in the case of timestamps) or at the end of a subscription as soon as the user is online again. Despite possible temporary downloads, such business models at their core need to be allocated to the third period rather than the second.

On the other hand, even if a permanent copy remains available to the user, the prevailing habit of qualifying either the distribution of digital products in the first period or downloads by the user in the second period as sales contract results from an underlying misconception from the outset. Although a sales contract exists for the physical carrier in the first period, the relationship between right holder and user with respect to the copyright-protected work is not a sales contract.[7] If a book is sold, the work as such (in terms of the copyright to the work) is not sold. All rights remain with the right holder.[8] However, the sale of the physical carrier, containing the copy of the work, implies a right to use it. Such a right to use granted to someone who is not the holder of the right is commonly known as a license. We will return to this issue.

III. "EXHAUSTION" IN THE FIRST AND SECOND PERIOD OF THE DIGITAL AGE

A. Terminology

According to the first sale doctrine originating from the Anglo-American legal area, once an intellectual property (IP)-protected product is lawfully sold, the acquirer of this product is allowed to distribute this product further—even if this transaction in principle constitutes a relevant act under the respective IP law—and is not subject to restrictions by the copyright owner.[9] The doctrine only applies, however, to the distribution right. It does not enable users to reproduce the copyright-protected work, for instance.

---

[7] Unclear in this sense, for instance, Sarah Reis, *Toward A "Digital Transfer Doctrine"? The First Sale Doctrine in the Digital Era*, 103 Nw. U. L. Rev. 175 (2015).

[8] In line with this, the copyright holders in Bobbs-Merrill Co. v. Straus, 210 U.S. 339, 350–51 (1908) asked "Who can own a copyright protected work but the copyright holder?"; but see Capitol Records, LLC v. ReDigi Inc., 934 F.Supp.2d 640 (S.D.N.Y. 2013), which held that "a ReDigi user owns the phonorecord that was created when she purchased and downloaded a song from iTunes to her hard disk"; however, according to Reis, *supra* note 7, at 174, the user receives ownership rights over the digital files.

[9] The "first sale doctrine" was first recognized by the U.S. Supreme Court in Bobbs-Merrill Co. v. Straus, 210 U.S. 339, 350–51 (1908); one year following the *Bobbs-Merrill* decision, the U.S. Congress codified the first sale doctrine in the Copyright Act of 1909. 17 U.S.C. § 109(a) states in relevant part: "Notwithstanding the provisions of section 106(3), the owner of a particular copy or phonorecord lawfully made under this title, or any person authorized by such owner, is entitled, without the authority of the copyright owner, to sell or otherwise dispose of the possession of that copy or phonorecord." *Ibid*. The purpose behind this provision was to allow a resale after the right

In Europe, "first sale doctrine" is not a common term. Instead the ability to resell an IP-protected product is captured by the term "exhaustion." This term, however, also covers what in the Anglo-American legal area is known as "implied license," which is the power to use a protected subject matter (although being a legally relevant activity) if the right holder has taken measures to factually enable such use. The implied license is a legal fiction and a recognized explanation in patent law in particular, as it would be pointless to sell a patent-protected machine without the permission to use that machine.[10] As we will see later, it may also be useful to explain the right to use in copyright law based on the implied license (e.g., if the right holder enables the download of certain content).[11]

In this respect, the imprecise legal term "exhaustion" mixes up the resale right and the right to use. In copyright law, however, this is not readily apparent because use as such is only a legal issue in the case of software, whereas reading a book, watching a movie or listening to music—the mere enjoyment of a work—is not a legal issue, according to the common view. Of course, the right holder is free to take measures to make the use of a work—in terms of an enjoyment of the work—dependent on an advance payment (e.g., entrance fee at the cinema). The circumvention of such payment mechanisms may conflict with house rules or contractual obligations, but it does not infringe copyright.

The use of software, in contrast, constitutes a copyright-relevant activity. Accordingly, the user needs a right to use the work, which may be based on legislation (any explicit provision of law[12]), on a legal principle (e.g., the implied license) or on an explicit agreement with the right holder. This particular setting related to software makes visible the mentioned lack of distinction inherent in the term "exhaustion." Both the right to use software and the right to resell an acquired copy of it can be explained equally as long as a physical carrier is involved: it is the fact that this carrier is sold by the right holder or with his consent. In the third period at the latest, however—if the respective data are only temporarily on the device of the user but a permanent download does not necessarily take place—the term "exhaustion" becomes misleading since it presupposes a sale which does not happen. Therefore, the first sale doctrine obviously may not apply in the third period, whereas the implied license is a helpful concept since this doctrine does not necessarily require the sale of a physical copy. Any other measure taken by the right holder to factually enable such use activities gives rise to the right to do so.

At first glance this distinction seems not to be an issue for any categories of works other than software. The term "exhaustion" explains at least that a carrier containing a copy of a work (e.g., CDs and DVDs of films or music) may be resold (in the sense of the first sale doctrine) whereas use—in terms of an enjoyment of the work—according to the common

---

holder has received an appropriate remuneration for a copy of the work. The Registrar of the U.S. Copyright Office stated in 1996 that "the first sale doctrine was developed to avoid restraints on the alienation of physical property, and to prevent publishers from controlling not only initial sales of books, but the after-market for resales." See Marybeth Peters, *The Spring 1996 Horace S. Manges Lecture—The National Information Infrastructure: A Copyright Office Perspective*, 20 COLUM.-V.L.A. J.L. & ARTS 341, 356 (1996).

[10] Hilty, Köklü, & Hafenbrädl, *supra* note 4, at 276; Orit Afori, *Implied License: An Emerging New Standard in Copyright Law*, 25 SANTA CLARA HIGH TECH. L.J. 279 (2008).
[11] See *infra* IV.A.
[12] In the EU, for instance, certain use activities are allowed by legislation. See Software Directive, art. 5(1).

view does not need to be explained from the outset. A closer look at the reality of the third period, however, reveals the shortcomings of the ambiguous term "exhaustion." In this period, the factual possibility to use the work no longer coincides with the ownership of a copy of the work. Therefore, if no physical carrier can be transferred to another party, it also cannot be explained without further reflections as to why (or why not) the possibility to use the work may be conveyed to another party. We will return to that issue.[13]

B. Second versus Third Period

As to the second period—characterized by the production of copies by the user by way of downloading—the main question at issue is whether the first sale doctrine should apply as well. If it does apply, the resale right of the buyer of a copy in the first period would be extended to such downloads, meaning that the related carrier would be subject to free distribution by the initial user.

Two situations regarding the means of transferring downloaded data need to be distinguished. Data may indeed be transferred from the first to the second user on a physical data carrier on which the copy was downloaded by the first user. This situation actually characterizes the second period. The other situation, however, concerns business models such as the one used in *UsedSoft*, *Capitol Records v. ReDigi*,[14] etc. where no physical data carrier is transferred. Rather, a further download is undertaken (and thus a further copy produced) by the second user, while at the same time the first user deletes his own copy. Since no ownership of any physical good is transferred in such business models, the first sale doctrine *a priori* cannot apply.[15]

Consequently, such cases are better assigned to the third period. The same classification applies to "hybrid" business models related to other categories of copyright-protected works like texts or music—such as Spotify—by which users are enabled to temporarily download files on their own devices in order to avoid the necessity of permanent online access. Such files cannot be copied and do not remain permanently stored, but rather are deleted at a specific date or at the end of a subscription, as already described. Since no transferable download on a device of the user exists, but access to data constitutes the core of such business models, they likewise must be allocated to the third period. In other words, the question about the applicability of the first sale doctrine to the second period only arises regarding transfers of physical data carriers including the downloaded copy of the work.

C. Opinions and Evaluation

In the United States (U.S.), the DMCA Section 104 Report states that:

> [p]hysical copies of works in a digital format, such as CDs or DVDs, are subject to section 109 in the same way as physical copies of works in analog form. Likewise, a lawfully made tangible

---

[13] See *infra* IV.C.
[14] See *infra* IV.B.
[15] In this sense, see *ReDigi*, *supra* note 8, 934 F.Supp.2d 655 (S.D.N.Y. 2013) (holding that "the first sale defense is limited to material items, like records, that the copyright owner put into stream of commerce"); see also Dobson, *supra* note 5, at 190.

copy of a digitally downloaded work, such as an image file downloaded directly to a floppy disk, is subject to section 109.[16]

This clearly affirms the applicability of the first sale doctrine to products of the second period. Right in line with this, the Court of the Southern District of New York held in *ReDigi* that owners could sell or trade the device to which those digital copies were downloaded.[17]

In Europe, a part of the legal doctrine denies the applicability of the first sale doctrine to digital products with reference to Recitals 28[18] and 29[19] to Directive 2001/29.[20] Recital 29 to the Directive explicitly excludes exhaustion for online services. The CJEU however ruled:

> that the existence of a transfer of ownership changes an "act of communication to the public" provided for in Article 3 of that Directive [2001/29] into an act of distribution referred to in Article 4 of the Directive which, if the conditions in Article 4(2) of the Directive are satisfied, can, like a "first sale . . . of a copy of a program" referred to in Article 4(2) of Directive 2009/24, give rise to exhaustion of the distribution right.[21]

On the other hand, Recital 28 to Directive 2001/29 limits the first sale doctrine to the transfer of tangible objects. It is, however, disputed to what extent recitals of a Directive have binding effect, particularly if they no longer sufficiently cover the current state of the art related to forwarding data and Internet technologies.[22] Some authors in the field deny

---

[16] U.S. COPYRIGHT OFFICE, DCMA SECTION 104 REPORT 78 (2001), available at http://copyright.gov/reports/studies/dmca/sec-104-report-vol-1.pdf; see also Reis, *supra* note 7, at 194.

[17] *ReDigi, supra* note 8, 934 F.Supp.2d 656 (S.D.N.Y. 2013) (reasoning that "Section 109(a) still protects a lawful owner's sale of her 'particular' phonorecord, be it a computer hard disk, iPod, or other memory device onto which the file was originally downloaded").

[18] InfoSoc Directive, recital 28 reads as follows: "Copyright protection under this Directive includes the exclusive right to control distribution of the work incorporated in a tangible article. The first sale in the Community of the original of a work or copies thereof by the right holder or with his consent exhausts the right to control resale of that object in the Community. This right should not be exhausted in respect of the original or of copies thereof sold by the right holder or with his consent outside the Community. Rental and lending rights for authors have been established in Directive 92/100/EEC. The distribution right provided for in this Directive is without prejudice to the provisions relating to the rental and lending rights contained in Chapter I of that Directive."

[19] InfoSoc Directive, recital 29 reads as follows: "The question of exhaustion does not arise in the case of services and online services in particular. This also applies with regard to a material copy of a work or other subject-matter made by a user of such a service with the consent of the right holder. Therefore, the same applies to rental and lending of the original and copies of works or other subject-matter which are services by nature. Unlike CD-ROM or CD-I, where the intellectual property is incorporated in a material medium, namely an item of goods, every online service is in fact an act which should be subject to authorisation where the copyright or related right so provides."

[20] See e.g. Oberlandesgericht (OLG, Court of Appeals) Stuttgart (Ger.), decision of November 3, 2011, Aktenzeichen 2 U 49/11, COMPUTER & RECHT 299 (2012); Oberlandesgericht (OLG, Court of Appeals) Hamm (Ger.), decision of May 15, 2014, 22 U 60/13, COMPUTER & RECHT 498 (2014).

[21] *UsedSoft, supra* note 1, 2012 E.C.R., para. 52; see also Feiler, *supra* note 5, at 8; Laura Kubach *Musik aus zweiter Hand – Ein neuer digitaler Trödelmarkt?*, COMPUTER & RECHT 283 (2013).

[22] Nikita Malevanny, *Die Usedsoft-Kontroverse: Auslegung und Auswirkungen des EuGH-Urteils*, COMPUTER & RECHT 426 (2013); Thomas Hartmann, *Weiterverkauf und "Verleih" online*

the applicability of the first sale doctrine to digital products with reference to Article 6 of the WIPO Copyright Treaty[23] (WCT), as well as the joint declarations concerning Articles 6 and 7 of the WCT.[24] The German Federal Court of Justice, in the meantime, rejected this argumentation in its judgment of July 17, 2013.[25] According to the Court, the WCT lays down only minimum obligations. The parties to this agreement are free to extend the first sale doctrine to non-physical copies.

In its judgment of May 15, 2014, the Higher Regional Court Hamm nevertheless denied the transferability of the CJEU jurisprudence in *UsedSoft* to audio books. The argument was that in the case of distribution via the Internet, no distribution under Article 4(2) of Directive 2009/24 takes place, but "making content publicly available" under Article 3(1) of Directive 2001/29.[26] The Court, however, mixed up two different actions. The upload of a file on the right holder's webpage is indeed "making the work publicly available." The download process by a single user, on the other hand, is not an act of making content publicly available. This process is a reproduction and the whole act in the result resembles a distribution since the download to a device provides the user with a digital copy with usability comparable to that of a purchased data carrier.[27] This view is also in line with the jurisprudence in *UsedSoft*, where the CJEU rejected the argument that the download of publicly available files is "making the work publicly available" (which would exclude the exhaustion of the right of distribution).[28] Although the business model in that case was different (no carrier was transferred to the second user, but he downloaded once again), the legal classification of the download as such is the same.

A further part of the legal doctrine rejects the applicability of the first sale doctrine to digital products of the second period with the argument that this would affect the marketplace.[29] After several transactions a digital product of the second period might be transferred for a fractional amount of the initial price, while qualitatively still being identical to the copies offered by the right owner for the full price.[30] It should not be

---

vertriebener Inhalte. Zugleich Anmerkung zu EuGH, Urteil vom 3. Juli 2012, Rs. C-128/11 – UsedSoft./.Oracle, GRUR INT. 982 (2012); Kubach, *supra* note 21, at 282; Marco Ganzhorn, *Ist ein E-Book ein Buch? Das Verhältnis von Büchern und E-Books unter besonderer Berücksichtigung der UsedSoft-Rechtsprechung*, COMPUTER & RECHT 495 (2014); Schneider & Spindler, *supra* note 5, at 223.

[23] WIPO Copyright Treaty, December 20, 1996, 36 I.L.M. 65 (1997) [hereinafter WCT].

[24] Thomas Vinje, Vanessa Marsland, & Anette Gärtner, *Software Licensing after Oracle v. Usedsoft: Implications of Oracle v. Usedsoft (C-128/11) for European Copyright Law*, 4 COMPUTER L. REV. INT'L 97, 100 (2012); Truiken Heydn, *EuGH: Handel mit gebrauchter Software – UsedSoft*, MULTIMEDIA & RECHT 591 (2012); Truiken Heydn, *BGH: Handel mit "gebrauchten" Softwarelizenzen – UsedSoft*, MULTIMEDIA & RECHT 310 (2011).

[25] Bundesgerichtshof (BGH, Federal Court of Justice), decision of July 17, 2013, I ZR 129/08, *UsedSoft II* (Ger.).

[26] Oberlandesgericht (OLG, Court of Appeals) Hamm (Ger.), decision of May 15, 2014, 22 U 60/13, COMPUTER & RECHT 498 (2014); see also Landgericht (LG, District Court) Bielefeld (Ger.), decision of March 5, 2013, 4 O 191/11.

[27] See also Kubach, *supra* note 21, at 283.

[28] *UsedSoft*, *supra* note 1, 2012 E.C.R., para. 50 et seq.

[29] Dobson, *supra* note 5, at 193.

[30] Reis, *supra* note 7, at 195; Riehl & Kassim, *supra* note 5, at 793. It has been suggested to introduce a resale royalty scheme allowing right holders to get resale royalties for their products

ignored, however, that this is also the case for (digital) products in the first period. Furthermore, the copyright holder typically earns most through new releases. Thus, the "lion's share" of his income is paid by customers eager to get the product around its release date.[31] Through time, the worth of a copyrighted work will, as a general rule, decrease. Consequently, the copyright industries adjust their prices after a certain period of time in order to keep attracting customers even where the release happened a long time ago.

Another argument related to the marketplace should be considered instead. If the first sale doctrine applies, a secondary market of data carriers develops and the crucial question is to what extent this secondary market impacts the primary market. Right holders allowing (or at least not restricting) the copying of original carriers in the first period (or unlimited downloads in the second period) will hardly have this secondary market in mind. Rather, they may allow such copying or downloads for the purpose of enabling users to consume the corresponding content on several devices or to recover an accidentally destroyed copy. What the right holders have in mind, however, is not that such copies on physical carriers should be distributed to third parties. Nevertheless, if this is done and if the first sale doctrine applies based on the consent of the right holder to produce such copies or downloads (although for other purposes[32]), it will be difficult to limit this consent to the production of one single physical carrier only. Rather, a large number of carriers with copies or downloads might be repeatedly produced and distributed to third parties and consequently a sizeable secondary market could evolve. With this, the right holder risks losing adequate compensation on the primary market and ultimately might have strong incentives to avoid the emergence of a secondary market from the outset. He would no longer consent to copies or downloads—thus excluding the application of the first sale doctrine—but he might be tempted to apply technological protection measures (e.g., allowing for one download only),[33] thus confronting users with undesirable factual restrictions.[34] In other words, the application of the first sale doctrine at least in the second period (and possibly even in the first period, concerning copies lawfully produced by the buyer of an original physical carrier[35]) might lead to dysfunctional effects ultimately to the detriment of consumers.

---

sold on the secondary market; Theodore Serra, *Rebalancing At Resale: ReDigi, Royalties and the Digital Secondary Market*, 93 B.U.L. REV. 1798 (2013); Cobb, *supra* note 6, at 553; Reis, *supra* note 7, at 205.

[31] Serra, *supra* note 30, at 1777; see also Reis, *supra* note 7, at 195.

[32] In this sense, *ReDigi*, *supra* note 8, 934 F.Supp.2d 640, 656 (S.D.N.Y. 2013).

[33] "Digital rights management" (DRM) enables right holders to control access to digital products as well as tracking and limiting uses of digital products. See AMERICAN LIBRARY ASSOCIATION, DIGITAL RIGHTS MANAGEMENT (DRM) & LIBRARIES, available at www.ala.org/advocacy/copyright/digitalrights.

[34] Reto M. Hilty & Kaya Köklü, *Limitations and Exceptions to Copyright in the Digital Age: Four Cornerstones for a Future-Proof Legal Framework in the EU*, in THE FUTURE OF COPYRIGHT: A EUROPEAN UNION AND INTERNATIONAL PERSPECTIVE (Irini Stamatoudi ed., forthcoming 2016). A detailed analysis on the (non-) applicability of the first sale doctrine on software agreements is provided by Hilty, Köklü, & Hafenbrädl, *supra* note 4, at 275.

[35] It should be noted, however, that such "private copying," if ever allowed based on a statutory exception or limitation in certain legislations, does not take place with the consent of the right holder anyway.

After all, the question concerning the (non-)applicability of the first sale doctrine to downloaded works on a user's own physical device is a political rather than a legal question. Accordingly, all the involved interests need to be taken into consideration. The above-mentioned argument of an uncontrollable increase of the number of copies on a secondary market speaks against the application of the first sale doctrine to digital products in the second period. At the same time, it is obvious that a secondary market creates more competition and pressure on the—possibly excessive—prices on the primary market. It is questionable, however, whether copyright law (and in particular the first sale doctrine) is an appropriate tool to counter anticompetitive behavior of right holders and copyright industries, respectively.[36]

IV. TRANSFER OF CAPACITY TO BE A LICENSEE IN THE THIRD PERIOD OF THE DIGITAL AGE

A. Software

If it is already doubtful whether the first sale doctrine should apply to the second period (characterized by physical data carriers including downloads that are transferred to a new user) it is even less justifiable to base transactions on this legal principle in the third period of the digital age.[37] If no—transferable—carrier exists from the outset, the legal question needs to be another one: is a change of party on the user's side allowed without consent by the right holder? In fact, although not explicitly asked that way, this was also the relevant issue in the *UsedSoft* case in respect of which the CJEU ruled affirmatively. Of course, the underlying Directive 2009/24 interpreted by the CJEU, which, in truth, reflects the technical status of the early 1990s (the current Directive did not amend the relevant provisions compared to the replaced Directive 91/250), when software could indeed be purchased on data carriers only, did not leave much leeway.[38] Nevertheless, the CJEU explicitly (and throughout the whole decision) used the term "license" without touching upon the issue of physical carriers, but rather by answering the question whether or not the capacity to be a licensee can be transferred to a third party. The effect of such transfer of capacity is that the third party—as new licensee—is allowed to use the work instead of the first user (and right holder's initial contractual partner).[39]

---

[36] With a different approach, see Reis, *supra* note 7, at 189; Perkins, *supra* note 6, at 23. The U.S. Court of Appeals for the Ninth Circuit stated that secondary markets, "contribute . . . to the public good by (1) giving consumers additional opportunities to purchase and sell copyrighted works, often at below-retail prices; (2) allowing consumers to obtain copies of works after a copyright owner has ceased distribution; and (3) allowing the proliferation of businesses." Vernor v. Autodesk, Inc., 621 F.3d 1102, 1115 (9th Cir. 2010).

[37] LUCIE GUIBAULT, COPYRIGHT LIMITATIONS AND CONTRACTS 197 (2002).

[38] The provision the CJEU had to interpret reads as follows: "The first sale in the Community of a copy of a program by the rightholder or with his consent shall exhaust the distribution right within the Community of that copy, with the exception of the right to control further rental of the program or a copy thereof." Software Directive, art. 4(2).

[39] According to *UsedSoft*, *supra* note 1, 2012 E.C.R., paras. 85 and 88, the "new acquirer" obtains a "user license" in the meaning of a "right to use."

It is obvious that the question about the change of party on the user's side cannot be answered based on the first sale doctrine. The first user's right to use as such needs to be explained differently. This is even true in the first period; although a carrier including the software may have been sold to the user, the question is not whether this carrier may be resold but rather whether the software on the carrier can be used. In this case, the answer would be affirmative because the carrier was sold by the right holder or with his consent. This, however, is only part of the explanation, which in truth is that the right holder has taken measures to factually enable such use. Such a measure may be the sale of the carrier, but it may also be the fact that the right holder enables the download of the software as is the case in the second period.

As mentioned earlier, the particularity of software is that its use constitutes a copyright-relevant activity. Therefore, it matters whether the first user—and right holder's initial contractual partner—uses the work or whether any subsequent user does. At the same time, we need to keep in mind that the right to use does not necessarily derive from the implied license; it may also be established (or concretized) by law or by contract.[40] However, we shall ignore these two alternatives for the moment and concentrate on the principle of the implied license, including in particular its relationship to other categories of copyright-protected works than software. In other words, the question at stake is whether or not the first user's right to use can—even without the consent of the right holder—be transferred to a third party.

In fact, only if we answer in the affirmative can we achieve a comparable situation to those we know from the first and the second period, in which a physical data carrier is transferred. In case of transfers of products of the first and second period, the right holder also does not consent to the use by the third party—the later acquirer of the carrier. The right to use of the acquirer therefore needs to be construed based on a line of arguments:

- The right to use of the first user derives from the implied license based on measures taken by the right holder to factually enable such use.
- The factual enabling of use of a third party arises from the first sale doctrine, meaning that the data carrier may be transferred to that third party (even without the consent of the right holder) because the carrier has been sold by the right holder or with his consent.
- The first sale doctrine, however, would simply be "pointless"[41] if the third party from a legal point of view was not allowed to use the acquired data carrier. For this reason, the right to use of the first user (based on the implied license) must be transferable to the third party.

The consequence is that measures taken by the right holder to factually enable the use affect not only the legal situation of the first user, but any subsequent user; in other words, the implied license continues to exist even if the beneficiary of the measures taken by the right holder changes. If we assume that copyright law is—or should be—technologically

---

[40] See *supra* III.A.
[41] *UsedSoft*, *supra* note 1, 2012 E.C.R., para. 44.

neutral, there is no reason why this principle should not apply in the third period, although a physical carrier no longer exists, for which reason the first sale doctrine may not apply.

We will see whether this line of arguments applies as well if other categories of works than software are involved. First, however, we will review the different opinions in the legal doctrine.

B. Opinions Regarding Works Other than Software

It should be noted first that neither the legal doctrine nor the jurisprudence distinguishes clearly between the different periods. Rather, the question is discussed whether or not the first sale doctrine should apply if solely digital data are forwarded (but no physical carrier transferred), eventually leading to a change of party on the user's side.

In the *UsedSoft* decision, the CJEU left open whether its jurisprudence applies to works other than software. The CJEU, however, emphasizes that from an economic point of view it does not make any difference whether software is transferred in a physical or non-physical way.[42] This may indicate that the CJEU might not distinguish between physical and non-physical transfers even in the case of works other than software. At the same time the CJEU emphasizes the *lex-specialis* character of Directive 2009/24 in relation to Directive 2001/29.[43] With reference to this paragraph, some voices of the legal doctrine deny the transferability of the *UsedSoft* decision of the CJEU to works other than software.[44] Also, the Bielefeld Regional Court held that the *UsedSoft* decision was based on Directive 2009/24 and thus applies solely to software. The court stated that the provisions concerning exhaustion in Directive 2001/29 did not contain wordings comparable to the relevant provisions in Directive 2009/24 and therefore rejected the permissibility of forwarding e-books to a third party.[45]

In the *ReDigi* case,[46] the New York District Court decided that the transfer of digital media infringed the right holder's reproduction right because a new copy is unavoidably created[47] despite the fact that ReDigi applied a technology not only enabling users to transfer their copies of digital music, but at the same time ensuring that only one copy continued to exist[48] and the software ensured that files copied from a CD or downloaded were ineligible for transfer. The New York District Court thus (implicitly) rejected a right to transfer the capacity to be a licensee.[49] Several scholars have affirmed this point

---

[42] *Ibid.* para. 61.
[43] *Ibid.* para. 56.
[44] See e.g. Schneider & Spindler, *supra* note 5, at 222; Redeker, *supra* note 5, at 76.
[45] Landgericht (LG, District Court) Bielefeld (Ger.), decision of March 5, 2013, 4 O 191/11.
[46] *ReDigi, supra* note 8, 934 F.Supp.2d 640 (S.D.N.Y. 2013). ReDigi enabled users to forward music files they had acquired from iTunes or from another ReDigi user to third parties.
[47] See *ibid.* at 649–50 ("Because the reproduction right is necessarily implicated when a copyrighted work is embodied in a new material object, and because digital music files must be embodied in a new material object following their transfer over the Internet, the Court determines that the embodiment of a digital music file on a new hard disk is a reproduction within the meaning of the Copyright Act."); see also U.S. COPYRIGHT OFFICE, *supra* note 16, at 79.
[48] *ReDigi, supra* note 8, 934 F.Supp.2d 640 (S.D.N.Y. 2013); see also Cobb, *supra* note 6, at 532.
[49] *ReDigi* seems to have been a rather political decision, however. The court believed it lacked authority to expand the exhaustion rule by concluding that it "cannot of its own accord condone

of view.[50] This is also in line with the Digital Millennium Copyright Act (DCMA) Section 104 Report. This Report explicitly advised against expanding 17 U.S.C. § 109 to transfers of digital content, indicating that sufficient forward-and-delete technology, ensuring only one copy exists at a time, did not exist at the time the report was written.[51] ReDigi has meanwhile changed its business model by going one step further: users may now download their music files directly to a "cloud". The file on the "cloud" does not need to be copied, but remains on the server in case of a change of licensee.[52] It remains unclear, however, whether the courts would allow this business model.

In contrast, the District Court of Amsterdam declined a request to shut down an e-book "reselling" website.[53] Before transferring an e-book on the website, the user has to declare that he obtained his copy legally and agree to delete that copy once he enables another user to make a copy. The website marks the e-book with a digital watermark and stores this watermark information in a database to prevent illegal distribution of e-books. However, the service was unable to verify whether a copy was legally obtained or whether the transferring party actually deleted his copy after the transfer. The court therefore noted that it was not clear whether the rights of the right holder were infringed.[54]

Parts of the legal doctrine deny the permissibility of transfers of capacity to be a licensee, because forwarding digital data is much easier and faster than transferring physical copies, like books or CDs.[55] The burden of transporting physical carriers is thus seen as a natural break restricting the number of sales on the secondary market.[56] Right holders

---

the wholesale application of the first sale defence [meaning however the permissibility of change of party] to the digital sphere, particularly when Congress itself has declined to take that step." *ReDigi, supra* note 8, 934 F.Supp.2d 660 (S.D.N.Y. 2013).

[50] Serra, *supra* note 30, at 1763; MELVILLE B. NIMMER & DAVID NIMMER, NIMMER ON COPYRIGHT § 8.12[E]; Reis, *supra* note 7, at 200; Jonathan C. Tobin, *Licensing as a Means of Providing Affordability and Accessibility in Digital Markets: Alternatives to a Digital First Sale Doctrine*, 93 J. PAT. & TRADEMARK OFF. SOC'Y 172 (2011); Riehl & Kassim, *supra* note 5, at 793.

[51] U.S. COPYRIGHT OFFICE, *supra* note 16, at 98. In contrast, a "Benefit Authors without Limiting Advancement or Net Consumer Expectations (BALANCE) Act" of 2003 sought to add a provision to 17 U.S.C § 109 allowing digital forwarding of copyright-protected content. This Act would have enabled a user of a digital data to: "sell . . . or otherwise dispose . . . of the work by means of a transmission to a single recipient, if the owner does not retain the copy or phonorecord in a retrievable form and the work is so sold or otherwise disposed of in its original format." H. R. 1066, 108th Cong. § 4 (2003–04). This Act, however, never came into force, at least partially because it benefited consumers one-sidedly and did not sufficiently take into consideration copyright holders' interests. See Serra, *supra* note 30, at 1783; Reis, *supra* note 7, at 203.

[52] See John T. Soma & Michael K. Kugler, *Why Rent When You Can Own? How ReDigi, Apple, and Amazon Will Use the Cloud and the Digital First Sale Doctrine to Resell Music, E-Books, Games, and Movies*, 15 N.C.J. L. & TECH. 445 (2014).

[53] *Uitgeversverbond and Groep Algemene Uitgevers v. Tom Kabinet*, Case C/13/567567/KG ZA 14-795 SP/MV, District Court of Amsterdam, July 21, 2014.

[54] Loek Essers, *Dutch Courts Lets Ebook Reseller Stay Online*, TECH WORLD (July 22, 2014), available at www.techworld.com.au/article/print/550527/dutch_courts_lets_ebook_reseller_stay_online/; Andreas Udo de Haes, *Ebook Reselling Dispute Erupts in the Netherlands*, PC ADVISOR (July 3, 2014), available at www.pcadvisor.co.uk/news/tech-industry/3528449/ebook-reselling-dispute-erupts-in-the-netherlands/.

[55] U.S. COPYRIGHT OFFICE, *supra* note 16, at 99; see also Reis, *supra* note 7, at 194.

[56] U.S. COPYRIGHT OFFICE, *supra* note 16, at 82; see also Perkins, *supra* note 6, at 7; Riehl & Kassim, *supra* note 5, at 792.

are, however, free to limit the possibility of forwarding digital data by way of technical protection measures.

Furthermore, it is argued that digital products do not degrade through time, unlike analogue physical copies (e.g., scratched vinyl records, highlighted textbooks, etc.).[57] According to that view, degradation of analogue copies tempers a secondary market and consumers are more likely to obtain a new copy of a physical product, even if the price is higher.[58] However, these concerns would not only speak against the transferability of the capacity to be a licensee; arguing that way would ultimately exclude the first sale doctrine even in the first and the second period, since digital physical data carriers (such as CDs and DVDs) also hardly degrade through time if handled carefully. Nevertheless, the applicability of the first sale doctrine to products of the first period is undisputed.

Another argument against the permissibility of transfers of capacity to be a licensee arises from the increased risk of unauthorized copying and forwarding of digital data.[59] An increased risk of piracy, however, can hardly be decisive. The ability to pirate works exists in all three periods as soon as digital products are involved.[60] Although the transfer of capacity to be a licensee may involve a higher vulnerability, it should also be noted that DRM nowadays may largely protect right holders from piracy in the third period.[61]

In contrast to these views, parts of the legal doctrine affirm the applicability of the *UsedSoft* decision of the CJEU to works other than software with reference to the underlying economic perspective of the CJEU. These authors would have the statement of the CJEU that "a restriction of the resale of copies [meaning the possibility to forward data] would go beyond what is necessary to safeguard the specific subject-matter of the intellectual property concerned"[62] apply *mutatis mutandis* to copyright-protected works other than software.[63]

C. Evaluation

As far as can be seen, neither the legal doctrine nor those juridical decisions available at present seem to resort to the argument of the implied license. Related to works other than software, this may indeed not be obvious, at least if one follows the common view that the mere enjoyment of a work—such as reading a book, watching a movie or listening to music—is not an issue of copyright law. It is, however, questionable whether this view is persuasive, for three reasons.

First, there are rather obscure borderline cases that suggest that things might be more complicated.[64] It is, for example, comprehensible that a private person does not need

---

[57] U.S. COPYRIGHT OFFICE, *supra* note 16, at 82; Andrew Harmeyer, *Can Digital Music Files Really be Considered "Used"? Online Market Place ReDigi Sued by Capitol Records*, COLUM. BUS. L. REV. (February 2, 2012), http://cblr.columbia.edu/archives/11955; Riehl and Kassim, *supra* note 5, at 793; Reis, *supra* note 7, at 194; Dobson, *supra* note 5, at 189.
[58] Riehl & Kassim, *supra* note 5, at 791; Dobson, *supra* note 5, at 189.
[59] U.S. COPYRIGHT OFFICE, *supra* note 16, at 88; Riehl & Kassim, *supra* note 5, at 792.
[60] Dobson, *supra* note 5, at 192.
[61] See Perkins, *supra* note 6, at 25.
[62] *UsedSoft*, *supra* note 1, 2012 E.C.R., para. 63.
[63] See e.g. Feiler, *supra* note 5, at 7; Malevanny, *supra* note 22, at 426.
[64] See also RETO M. HILTY, URHEBERRECHT, para. 151 (2011).

any permission to read a book and tell his friends about the story he has read. But is it similarly obvious that an attorney may read a legal book and use the information in it (commercially) to advise his clients or to draft his own statement of claim (beyond strict quoting)? May a needlewoman sew a dress using a dressmaking pattern (assuming that this pattern is copyright protected)—and does it make a difference whether she does it for herself, for friends or as a professional dressmaker? How about cooking according to a (creative) cooking recipe? On the other hand, it might be agreed that a construction plan may be "read"—be it by a private person or an architect—but that no one may use it for the purpose of building the corresponding house.

Such examples indicate that the criterion of pure enjoyment ("*Werkgenuss*"), which is deemed to lie outside of the applicability of copyright law, implies normative differentiations. In this respect, one may ask whether it would not be more plausible to apply the principle of the implied license instead; if the right holder takes measures to factually enable certain use activities related to a protected subject matter, and if he reasonably must foresee that the buyer of that subject matter would make the respective use, it is assumed that the right holder (implicitly) licensed that use. This logic applies in patent law[65]—irrespective of the person using a patent-protected machine—and it is hard to see why it could not apply in copyright law as well. Indeed, the author of a legal book reasonably must foresee that not only law students, but also attorneys, would make use of his work, whereas the architect handing over a construction plan may not assume that another person would apply it for construction purposes.

Secondly, particularly in the third period in which users no longer dispose of physical copies, right holders increasingly try to prevent users from taking advantage of the whole range of factual possibilities to use a work. Indeed, such possibilities—technically—may go beyond the mere reading of a book or listening to music played from a CD. For this reason, right holders tend to do both, imposing contractual restrictions as well as applying technical protection measures.

This is also the case regarding software, but the use of software is deemed to be an issue of copyright law. Accordingly, the legislature is free to implement certain—mandatory—exceptions or limitations. The effect of such a statutory use authorization is that users can be protected against overly restrictive terms and conditions. Right in line with this, U.S. copyright law, as well as EU law, both allow making copies necessary for the use of the program.[66] This approach obviously is not available if a use activity is deemed to take place outside of the applicability of copyright law.

In fact, various court decisions have already dealt with the question of the validity of terms and conditions imposed by the right holders.[67] Specifically, the question was whether or not the contractual partner of the right holder may be prohibited from

---

[65] See *supra* III.A.
[66] 17 U.S.C § 117; Software Directive, art. 5(1).
[67] For such terms, see e.g. Amazon MP3 Store, Terms of Use: "Upon payment for Music Content, we grant you a non-exclusive, non-transferable right to use the Music Content only for your personal, non-commercial purposes, subject to the Agreement," available at www.amazon.com/gp/help/customer/display.html?nodeId=200154280; Google Play, Terms of Service: "You may not sell, rent, lease, redistribute, broadcast, transmit, communicate, modify, sublicense or transfer or assign your rights to products to any third party without authorization, including with regard

78 *Research handbook on intellectual property exhaustion and parallel imports*

enabling a third party to copy the work in question by simultaneously deleting his own copy. Not surprisingly, courts only consider such cases under contractual perspectives and tend to validate such terms and conditions.[68]

Thirdly, if technical protection measures hinder undesired use activities, this should not *a priori* be rejected, since right holders may legitimately try to sustain their business models to ensure appropriate returns on their investments. However, a legal protection against the circumvention of such technical protection measures presupposes the legal protection of the content, which at the same time requires that:

> technological measures . . . are used by authors in connection with the exercise of their rights under this Treaty or the Berne Convention and that [these measures] restrict acts, in respect of their works, which are not authorised by the authors concerned or permitted by law.[69]

If, however, "use" activities are deemed to lie outside of the applicability of copyright law, users legally may circumvent such technical protection measures. On the other hand, if a legislature is of the opinion that certain protection measures should not apply,[70] it may only prohibit this by stating that certain exceptions or limitations (in terms of usage permissions) may not be overridden. This, however, presupposes—in principle—the applicability of copyright law.

All these reflections show that users would not lose but, rather, be supported by a similar approach to the one we know in the field of patent law or related to software. This is that uses of protected subject matters are not simply "free"—they do not lie outside the applicability of copyright law. Certain uses, however, need to be classified as a consequence of measures taken by the right holder. Under certain circumstances, he implicitly licenses such uses. Reading an e-book, for instance, will hardly explicitly be allowed in the terms and conditions. Rather, the right holder reasonably foresees that after he takes appropriate measures (e.g., providing access to a database) the e-book will be read.

Admittedly, it sounds contrived to argue based on the implied license as long as it concerns the reading of a printed book. When it comes to e-books, however, the implied license has the great advantage that it provides an answer to our question—namely,

---

to any downloads of products that you may obtain through Google Play," available at http://play.google.com/intl/en_us/about/play-terms.html.

[68] See e.g. ProCD, Inc. v. Zeidenberg, 86 F.3d 1447, 1449 (7th Cir. 1996); Specht v. Netscape Communications Corp., 306 F.3d 17, 32 (2d Cir. 2002); Davidson & Assocs. v. Jung, 422 F.3d 630, 638 (8th Cir. 2005); Vernor v. Autodesk, Inc., 621 F.3d 1102, 1115 (9th Cir. 2010), 42 INT'L REV. OF INTELL. & COMPETITION 231–32 (2011); UMG Recordings, Inc., v. MP3.com, Inc., 92 F.Supp.2d 349, 352 (S.D.N.Y. 2000) (citing Castle Rock Entm't, Inc. v. Carol Publ'g Grp., Inc., 150 F.3d 132, 145–46 (2d Cir. 1998)); Salinger v. Random House, Inc., 811 F.2d 90, 99 (2d Cir. 1987) ("[A] copyrighterholder's [sic] 'exclusive' rights, derived from the Constitution and the Copyright Act, include the right, within broad limits, to curb the development of such a derivative market by refusing to license a copyrighted work or by doing so only on terms the copyright owner finds acceptable."); Landgericht (LG, District Court) Bielefeld (Ger.), decision of March 5, 2013, 4 O 191/11; Landgericht (LG, District Court) Berlin (Ger.) decision of July 14, 2009, 16 O 67/08.

[69] WCT, art. 11; see also WIPO Performances and Phonograms Treaty, December 20, 1996, art. 18, 36 I.L.M. 76 (1997) (WPPT).

[70] See e.g. Council Directive 2001/29, [2001] O.J. L167, art. 6(4) (EC).

whether or not a third party may read the same e-book if the corresponding data have been forwarded instead of the right holder's contractual partner. The answer is the same as that relating to software, for which we said that, irrespective of the period and whether or not a physical carrier is involved, the implied license continues to exist even if the beneficiary of the measures taken by the right holder changes. In other words, the transfer of the capacity to be licensee is permitted if the third party takes over the legal position of the (first) licensee. Consequently, all acts by the third party necessary for the designated use (e.g., temporary reproduction of the work in case of hybrid business models) would be allowed based on the implied license.[71]

It goes without saying that this is a purely theoretical reasoning: it ignores the possibilities of right holders to technically prevent any third party from actually using a given work. At the same time, we need to recall that all these questions, ultimately, are of a political nature. It is up to the legislature to balance the interests of right holders and their contractual partners. With respect to the implied license, however, the perspective might change. If above we concluded that an application of the first sale doctrine might lead to dysfunctional effects because right holders increasingly might be tempted to apply technical protection measures to save their business models, we are one step further at this point: technical protection measures are indeed applied in order to undermine the principle of the implied license. Thus, the question is rather whether or not such technical protection measures may apply without restriction. The answer to this question is not obvious. Three reflections, however, suggest caution.

First, the transfer of the capacity to be a licensee does not lead to an augmentation of the number of copies of the work available on the (secondary) market if a third party actually replaces the right holder's contractual partner.[72] As long as the legitimate interests of the right holder are not harmed by a change of party, the right holder has no justified or equitable interest to prevent the transfer of this capacity. In fact, in copyright law, it is usually not important to the right holder which person is licensee and thus (end-) user of the work. Exceptions may apply if a licensee exploits the work commercially, or in the field of patent law, where the suitability ("*Eignung*") of the licensee can be essential to the right holder. In that case, the licensor may have a justified and equitable interest in retaining a particular licensee.[73]

Secondly, an argument brought forward by the CJEU in the *UsedSoft* judgment is worth considering. The CJEU ruled that forwarding software is lawful if (among other points):

> the first sale of the copy had already enabled the right holder to obtain an appropriate remuneration. Such a restriction of the resale of copies of computer programs downloaded from

---

[71] Hilty, Köklü, & Hafenbrädl, *supra* note 4, at 288; see also Perkins, *supra* note 6, at 19. For instance, digital movie files and digital music files need to be modified and converted to different formats and resolutions depending on the device used to play them; in this sense, see also Riehl & Kassim, *supra* note 5, at 804; Cobb, *supra* note 6, at 533 (basing the permissibility of the reproduction on the "fair use doctrine"). But see Bob Hyde, *The First Sale Doctrine and Digital Phonorecords*, 2001 DUKE L. & TECH. REV. 0018, para. 25, available at http://scholarship.law.duke.edu/cgi/viewcontent.cgi?article=1017&context=dltr.
[72] In this sense see also Perkins, *supra* note 6, at 22.
[73] RETO M. HILTY, LIZENZVERTRAGSRECHT 754 (2001).

the internet would go beyond what is necessary to safeguard the specific subject-matter of the intellectual property concerned.[74]

This argument goes beyond the wording of the relevant provisions of Directive 2009/24, taking into consideration the interests of the involved parties from an economic point of view. Not surprisingly, the statement opened up an intense discussion about the applicability of this jurisprudence to copyright-protected works other than software, like music, movies or e-books.[75] However, it is precisely the fact that the CJEU balances the involved interests "freehand" which makes it seem not *a priori* out of the question to extend it to other copyright industries.[76]

Thirdly, not all technical protection measures have the same purpose. Whereas some may be directed at saving specific business models, possibly unduly affecting competitors or consumer interests, other measures may have the purpose of preventing abusive behavior of users. It is, however, questionable whether such a distinction is feasible from a practical perspective—and if so, to what extent a right holder should in fact be in the position to undermine a transfer of the capacity to be a licensee.[77] In any case, methods ensuring that users can no longer access a file after enabling a third party to use it are meanwhile available.[78] For instance, in 2013, Amazon registered a patent describing "an electronic marketplace facilitating a secondary market for digital objects,"[79] including a system using deletion to avoid duplications of digital objects. An Apple patent application published in March 2013 describes techniques allowing "access to a digital content item (such as an e-book, music, movie, software application) to be transferred from one user to another. The transferor is prevented from accessing the digital content item after the transfer occurs."[80]

---

[74] *UsedSoft*, *supra* note 1, 2012 E.C.R., para. 61. The opposite perspective, namely, that the inability to forward digital data lowers the value of this data to the detriment of customers (in that sense, see Riehl & Kassim, *supra* note 5, at 812), may be true as well, but it seems questionable whether this argument is conclusive.

[75] Feiler, *supra* note 5, at 6; Cobb, *supra* note 6, at 544 and 549; Malevanny, *supra* note 22, at 426; Ganzhorn, *supra* note 22, at 493.

[76] Hilty, Köklü, & Hafenbrädl, *supra* note 4, at 284.

[77] See also Brian Mencher, *Digital Transmissions: To Boldly Go Where No First Sale Doctrine has Gone Before*, 10 UCLA ENT. L. REV. 47, 61 (2002); Davis Nakimuli, *Reselling Digital Music: Is There a Digital First Sale Doctrine*, LOY. L.A. ENT. L. REV. 372 (2009). The Library Associations proposed that section 109(a) of Title 17 of the United States Code should be amended as follows: "[n]otwithstanding the provisions of section 106(3), the owner of a particular copy or phonorecord lawfully made under this title, or the owner of any right of access to the copyrighted work, or any person authorized by such owner, is entitled, without the authority of the copyright owner, to sell or otherwise dispose of the possession of that copy, phonorecord, or right of access." United States Copyright Office and Department of Commerce, National Telecommunications and Information Administration, Washington, D.C., *Reply Comments of the Library Associations Before the Library of Congress*, available at www.arl.org/storage/documents/publications/dmca-section109-comments-05jun00.pdf; Cobb, *supra* note 6, at 554.

[78] Dobson, *supra* note 5, at 197.

[79] Eric Ringewald, Secondary Market for Digital Objects, U.S. Patent No. 8,364,595 col. 2 ll 9–10 (issued January 29, 2013), available at www.google.com/patents/US8364595; see also Riehl & Kassim, *supra* note 5, at 805; Soma and Kugler, *supra* note 52, at 452.

[80] Eliza C. Block & Macel van Os, Managing Access to Digital Content Items, U.S. Patent Application No. 13/531,280, Publication No. 20130060616, Abstract (published March 7, 2013),

The consequence of not allowing such technical protection measures, however, would be far-reaching if this ultimately would mean that an application of such measures preventing uses by other parties than the right holder's contractual partner could be interdicted. In the *UsedSoft* decision, the CJEU did not go that far. The question was limited to contractual restrictions regarding the transfer of software (or rather the capacity to be a licensee) to a third party insofar as the CJEU treated the new user as a "lawful acquirer" in the sense of Article 5(1) of Directive 2009/24.[81] This decision had an impact, since at that time the plaintiff did not apply technical protection measures to undercut third-party downloading—but the company naturally signalled that it would do so in the future.

V. OUTLOOK

One certainly may hesitate to decide whether it would be an advisable strategy for the future to (legally) restrict the right holder's possibilities of factually controlling "use" activities related to digital data under his control. On the one hand, such an approach seems to be the other side of the coin if we accept that contractual restrictions may be rejected. In fact, mandatory exceptions or limitations allowing certain use activities would become meaningless if right holders could nevertheless enforce the same restrictions technically.

At the same time it is not less doubtful to overburden copyright law with the objective of establishing workable competition on copyright-related markets; we have mentioned it above with respect to the applicability of the first sale doctrine to downloads in the second period. If we are of the opinion that things go wrong in such markets, it might be more appropriate to find more efficient legal tools to counter misguided behavior of right holders. Admittedly, antitrust law may not help much since in most cases the requirements for intervention are not met. But at the same time we should critically scrutinize whether interventions are needed at all.

In the near future, the question of transferability to third parties—be it of physical carriers with downloads produced by a user or be it the capacity to be a licensee—might lose its relevance. Such transfers are only attractive when the subject matter of the transfer has some remaining value. If copyright-protected works will increasingly be used by way of streaming, comparatively low prices could be charged. Spotify may serve as the prime example, even though it is not yet granted that this concrete business model will survive. It has, however, demonstrated that alternative approaches—and, in contrast to former times, extremely cheap approaches—to provide access to content are possible. If that is the case, a "resale" value would hardly continue to exist—and the transfer of capacity to be a licensee would become meaningless. The necessary expenses would not lead to any advantage compared to a user's own—direct—contracting with the right holder.

We are certainly not there yet. It is also true that right holders will find new ways of optimizing their business models. This however could—and should—hardly be stopped.

---

available at www.google.com/patents/US20130060616; see also Soma & Kugler, *supra* note 52, at 449; Riehl & Kassim, *supra* note 5, at 806.

[81] *UsedSoft*, *supra* note 1, 2012 E.C.R., para. 81.

In particular, if streaming technologies increasingly apply, it will be easy—and doubtless lawful—for right holders to conclude short-term contracts only, which periodically need to be renewed. This would make the value of a remaining period of such a term very low from the outset and no third party would be willing to step in. And this might be the crucial point: it is ultimately up to consumers to decide which kinds of business models are worth accepting. At the end of the day, consumer preferences should point the way for copyright holders. Consumers "succeeded," for instance, by refusing to buy CDs with copy protection—after a short time, the music industry gave up that kind of technical protection measure.

At the same time, it is manifest that consumers are not always in the position of freely choosing what they want, particularly if there is real demand for certain products but no acceptable offers are available on the market. Such scarcities may also happen in the case of copyright-protected content, in particular if certain business models impede workable competition. At this point, however, we should be aware that consumer protection laws might be a more appropriate way of balancing disparate interests. Copyright regulation certainly may also produce some side-effects on related markets, but being subject to permanently new technological challenges and innovative business models, copyright law could hardly ever be designed in a way to sufficiently balance all interests involved.

PART II

INTELLECTUAL PROPERTY EXHAUSTION AND PARALLEL IMPORTS: THE INTERNATIONAL CONTEXT

5. International intellectual property rules and parallel imports
Susy Frankel* and Daniel J. Gervais**

I. INTRODUCTION

There is much international disagreement about the merits or otherwise of parallel importing. As the phrase "parallel importing" suggests, an import (of a good that is protected as a patent or copyright or bearing a protected trademark) is "parallel" to a domestic intellectual property (IP) right in the country of importation. Put differently, there is a parallel IP right in the country from which the good is exported. The owner or exclusive licensee of the right in both territories may or may not be the same. The price at which the good is sold is often different (reflecting market conditions), thus creating an "arbitrage" incentive for export to a higher priced market.

There is a relationship between the legal concept of parallel importing and exhaustion of rights in domestic law. When IP is embodied in a physical product, the sale of that product transfers ownership rights in the product, but not the underlying IP. For example, the person who purchases a copy of a copyright book cannot make and sell new copies of the book. However, the distribution-related IP rights are said to be "exhausted," by which we mean that *that copy* of the book can be resold or otherwise treated as the property of the purchaser. If a country or trade territory allows the importation of a copy sold in another country or trade territory, then it is said to allow parallel importing. In this way the IP rights in both countries, or trade territories, are put in "parallel."

There are few internationally agreed rules about parallel importing. There are different rationales and related narratives used to justify parallel importing, or to justify a ban on parallel imports. Broadly speaking, one could see a primary rationale for allowing parallel importing as being a way for developing countries to obtain cheaper goods and goods not otherwise put on the market in their territory. Not surprisingly, many developing countries allow some kind of parallel importing. This may increase access to global knowledge, ideas, and innovation and spur local development.[1] This rationale and its supporting developmental narrative are not discussed in further detail in this chapter. Instead, this chapter focuses on why more economically advanced countries allow parallel importing.

There is no harmonization or even coordination among developed countries on the issue of parallel importing. Indeed, there is no enforceable multilateral agreement on the parameters of parallel importation. This may seem surprising because trading in IP across borders is one of the key features of the purpose of the Agreement on Trade Related

---

* Professor of Law, Victoria University of Wellington.
** Professor of Law, Vanderbilt Law School.
[1] See generally, THE DEVELOPMENT AGENDA: GLOBAL INTELLECTUAL PROPERTY AND DEVELOPING COUNTRIES (Neil W. Netanel ed., 2009).

Aspects to Intellectual Property Rights (TRIPS),[2] which is part of the World Trade Organization's (WTO) package of agreements.[3] While TRIPS provides that a patent owner has the exclusive right to control imports of a patented product or processes,[4] it does not refer to import rights in relation to other types of IP. Moreover, TRIPS also provides that no disputes may be brought in relation to exhaustion of rights.[5] The territorial barriers erected in IP in order to maintain parallel import bans (where they exist) act effectively as trade barriers that the WTO has not interfered with, but rather recognizes as some kind of exception to the free movement of goods principle enshrined in the General Agreement on Tariffs and Trade (GATT).[6]

The notion of parallel importing is not limited to physical products. Electronic transmissions of copyright works and even services that can involve IP, for example, can be parallel imported. While there is disagreement over parallel importing regimes in relation to physical products, the disagreement is likely to intensify with regard to electronic products and transmissions. By way of example, on April 3, 2014, the United States (U.S.) International Trade Commission (ITC) issued a Summary Notice of Determination affirming an administrative law judge's conclusion that electronically transmitted information could constitute an "article,"[7] thereby asserting ITC jurisdiction over electronic transmissions across borders.[8] The ruling extends not to copyright content *per se*, but it does seem potentially applicable to digital files that contain information that might infringe a patent, especially patents including computer programs and, perhaps, also files containing instructions to 3D print patented objects. In the particular case, the transmission contained digital models of teeth that might infringe a patent claiming steps and methods involving use of a computer to create digital models for sequential dental appliances.[9] What is imported is a file, as the stream of packets containing that information is progressively sent across the border. The ITC's jurisdiction was challenged in court.[10]

The broader issue requires deeper analysis. A simple effects-based test might support

---

[2] Agreement on Trade-Related Aspects of Intellectual Property Rights, April 15, 1994; Marrakesh Agreement Establishing the World Trade Organization, Annex 1C, Legal Instrument—Result of the Uruguay Rounds Vol. 31, 33 I.L.M. 83, 1869 U.N.T.S. 299 (1994) [hereinafter TRIPS Agreement].

[3] The TRIPS Agreement is not a standalone agreement. It is part of the World Trade Organization (WTO) Agreements, which are a single package of agreements to which all members must belong and there can be no reservations.

[4] TRIPS Agreement, art. 28.

[5] TRIPS Agreement, art. 6.

[6] General Agreement on Tariffs and Trade, October 30, 1947, 61 Stat. A-11, 55 U.N.T.S. 154 [hereinafter GATT].

[7] As defined by 19 U.S.C. § 1337(a)(1)(B) (2004).

[8] In the Matter of Certain Digital Models, Digital Data, and Treatment Plans for Use in Making Incremental Dental Positioning Adjustment Appliances, the Appliances Made Therefrom, and Methods of Making the Same, Inv. No. 337-TA-833 (April 10, 2014). Under s. 337 (19 U.S.C. § 1337, as amended) "[t]he *importation* into the United States, the sale for importation, or the sale within the United States after importation by the owner, importer, or consignee, of *articles that . . . infringe a valid and enforceable United States patent*" is prohibited (emphasis added).

[9] See generally In the Matter of Certain Digital Models, *supra* note 8.

[10] ClearCorrect v. International Trade Commission, Inv. No. 337-TA-833 (USITC), *appeal docketed*, No. 14-1527 (Fed. Cir. October 9, 2014).

the ITC determination. After all, IP is, at its core, information. Hence, when that information crosses a border in one form or another, one could argue that "importation" has taken place. Yet, that analysis displaces the traditional linkage between a physical product and the intellectual property it contains. Products are typically owned while files containing data are rarely sold, though they may be licensed. Products cannot be copied (at least until 3D printing, that is), but digital files can be. While the ITC measure was ostensibly taken to protect right holders, it may backfire. If digital files crossing borders are a form of importation, then measures will be used to defeat that form of IP right infringement as they have been for more than fifteen years for file-sharing.[11] This, in turn, is liable to call into question the importation right in its entirety.

The effect of not having a multilaterally agreed rule is that parallel importing is largely permitted. In various jurisdictions parallel imports are permitted in all fields of IP. Other jurisdictions allow parallel imports in one area of IP but not in another. Some countries, for example, allow parallel imports of copyright goods and related trademarks, but not patented goods. Some jurisdictions prevent imports of new goods, but allow imports of second-hand goods. In short, there is a patchwork of arrangements around the globe.

There are many rationales for *preventing* parallel importing in developed countries. First, one argument is that local markets will thrive in preference to imports if parallel importing is prohibited, thus allowing the right holder to charge higher prices. This produces a "subsidy effect," which, in turn, one may argue will allow the right holder to develop new or improved products and be (even) more competitive globally. This phenomenon is visible, for example, in the U.S., where prices for pharmaceutical products are high compared to world standards and may contribute to increasing the research budget of pharmaceutical companies. The U.S. consumer and/or taxpayer (where the buyer is a government-run healthcare system) may be said to "subsidize" this research.[12] A prohibition on parallel importing enables IP owners to maximize profits in as many export markets as possible, either through price-discrimination or through controlled release. Sometimes a ban on parallel importing has been used for a different purpose, namely, to maintain varying qualities of products in different markets depending on consumer demand.[13]

There are also three compelling rationales to *allow* parallel importing: first, to obtain cheaper goods by importing them from a market where they are sold at a lower price; second, to introduce competition into an otherwise non-competitive market, which should also exert a downward pressure on price; third, a country might want to compare and expand the range of available products and their varying qualities if only a limited

---

[11] See Daniel Gervais, *The Price of Social Norms*, 12 J. INTELL. PROP. L. 40, 49–51 (2005).

[12] The WTO prohibits some subsidies and allows others. These are primarily governed by the Agreement on Subsidies and Countervailing Measures, April 15, 1994, 1869 U.N.T.S. 183, 33 I.L.M. 1167 [hereinafter SCM]. The WTO has effectively chosen rules of intellectual property in preference to allowing subsidies to promote innovation, even when the intellectual property rights have a subsidizing effect in an economic sense, which is wider than the subsidies which are prohibited or actionable under the SCM. See SUSY FRANKEL, TEST TUBES FOR GLOBAL INTELLECTUAL PROPERTY ISSUES: SMALL MARKET ECONOMIES 159 (2015).

[13] Arguably this rationale does not work when goods are available online and can be wholly electronic.

range is locally available.[14] These rationales are easily and directly linked to consumer welfare narratives.

While TRIPS has been in force, parallel importing issues have arguably intensified. Dividing markets is often attempted, for example, through technological protection mechanisms rather than parallel import rules.[15] As noted above technology brings its own tensions and new possibilities for those who seek to divide markets territorially.

In section II of this chapter we discuss the international rules relating to parallel importing. We then analyze developed country and trade territory approaches to parallel importing. This includes an overview of the areas of IP where parallel importing is allowed and the areas where it is prohibited, and related justifications for the policies. In particular, in section III, we consider the laws of the U.S., the European Union (EU), New Zealand, Singapore, Israel, and Australia and how those different countries and trade territories use variants on exhaustion to calibrate their IP laws according to their interests. From this comparative approach we conclude with an overview of how developed countries use parallel importation as a calibration tool.

II. INTERNATIONAL RULES

A. Exhaustion and First Sale

In any jurisdiction there is a question about how an IP right survives a transfer of ownership of an object that embodies the IP. A basic principle of IP law is that IP is an *intangible* property right which frequently finds a host in tangible goods. The literary work is separate in legal analysis from the book, a sound recording has copyright interests that are separate from the record or CD, and the patent is separate from the pill purchased at the local pharmacy. It is odd to talk of IP goods, such as a download of a song, as tangible but from a property law point of view that is exactly what they are the equivalent of. This underscores the principle of *first sale*, which, while articulated in slightly different ways around the world, is broadly the principle that a purchaser of an IP product can make use of that product and on sell it and so forth. The purchaser of the product does not purchase the copyright or the patent right or indeed any trademark, but the first sale exhausts the distribution-related rights, such as right of distribution in copyright.[16] As a result, the right of distribution gives the copyright owner (or assignees) control over first distribution, but not subsequent distribution. That is a simple principle, but its nuances are less than simple, particularly when cross-border trade is added, including cross-border trade in second-hand goods.

The first sale principle is distinct from the exhaustion principle. First sale is relevant to

---

[14] Countries can use trade barriers to limit that range. Cheese and meat are typical examples.
[15] Region coding is an obvious example.
[16] In some jurisdictions this is called the right to issue to the public. See, e.g., Copyright, Designs and Patents Act 1988 § 18(2) (UK) and Copyright Act 1994 (NZ), § 16(1)(b) and § 9(1)(a) which provides "References in this Act to the issue of copies of a work to the public mean the act of putting into circulation copies not previously put into circulation; and do not include the acts of subsequent distribution or sale of those copies."

parallel importing, although terminological fog shrouds the real issue. A country that recognizes that first sale exhausts distribution-related rights does not have to allow imports of products from other markets, even where those products have been put on the market in that other country by the same right holder or with her consent. First sale can thus be combined with national exhaustion or international exhaustion, and the notions are, therefore, distinct. For example, a country might decide that only a first sale *in the country or territory* exhausts distribution-related rights. In such a case that country would be said to be applying national exhaustion. Alternatively, a country might decide that a first sale anywhere in the world exhausts the distribution-related rights in that country. In such a case that country would be said to be applying international exhaustion.[17]

The legal principle, which is central to how parallel importing works, is the rule of exhaustion that a country chooses to apply to IP rights. Broadly, countries apply either rules of national, regional, or international exhaustion to prevent or allow parallel importation.[18] National exhaustion means that parallel importing is not permitted because the rights of the IP owners are treated as having a wholly independent existence in each national market. This means that the placing on the market of products in one national territory does not exhaust the distribution right in another national territory. National exhaustion can be extended to a group of countries (typically a customs territory or free trade area), in which case it becomes regional.

B. GATT Pre-TRIPS

The key purpose of GATT and its successor, the WTO, was and is to remove trade barriers.[19] The main GATT text from 1947 recognized that IP could form a trade barrier. GATT also provides that IP laws could be a *legitimate* trade barrier. It uses the mechanism of providing that IP rules can be exceptions to the other requirements of GATT. GATT provides:

> Subject to the requirement that such measures are not applied in a manner which would constitute a means of arbitrary or unjustifiable discrimination between countries where the same conditions prevail, or a disguised restriction on international trade, nothing in this Agreement shall be construed to prevent the adoption or enforcement by any contracting party of measures . . . (d) *necessary* to secure compliance with laws or regulations *which are not inconsistent with the provisions of this Agreement*, including those relating to customs enforcement . . . the protection of patents, trade marks and copyrights, and the prevention of deceptive practices.[20]

There is a considerable body of GATT/WTO jurisprudence about the meaning of "necessary," particularly as used in other parts of the GATT exceptions.[21] The key feature

---

[17] Typically, a condition would be that the copy has been legally put on the market. We come back to this issue later.
[18] The European Union (EU) regime, which is generally referred to as regional exhaustion, is complex. In relation to trademarks, see e.g. Thomas Hays, *The Free Movement (or Not) of Trademark Protected Goods in Europe, in* TRADEMARK LAW AND THEORY: A HANDBOOK OF CONTEMPORARY RESEARCH (Graeme Dinwoodie & Mark Janis eds., 2008).
[19] See GATT.
[20] *Ibid*. art. XX(d) (emphasis added).
[21] For discussion in the IP context, see Susy Frankel & Daniel Gervais, *Plain Packaging and the Interpretation of the TRIPS Agreement*, 46(5) VAND. J TRANSNAT'L L. 1149 (2013).

is that "necessary" is connected to the requirement to comply with IP laws, provided that those laws are "not inconsistent with other provisions of the Agreement." Were it not for TRIPS, one could argue that the prevention of parallel importation is "necessary" for the protection of IP rights. Some people disagree.[22]

The most relevant other GATT provisions, as far as parallel imports are concerned, are the parts of GATT that embody the principle of free movement of goods.[23]

GATT Article XX (which overall is the general exception provision to the GATT principles) was raised in two GATT panel disputes before the WTO was formed. In *United States—Imports of Certain Automotive Spring Assemblies*, the panel concluded that contracting parties could take measures to protect patents that otherwise would not be in conformity with their GATT obligations.[24]

In *United States—section 337 of the Tariff Act of 1930*, the panel concluded that GATT could not be used to challenge the substantive patent law of a contracting party because of the Article XX(d) exception.[25] Importantly, however, members of GATT had an obligation to try to enforce their patents law in a way that was not inconsistent with GATT provisions.[26]

In addition, Article IX of GATT is arguably the only GATT provision dealing directly with the protection of an IP right.[27] Article IX:6 states that:

> The contracting parties shall co-operate with each other with a view to preventing the use of trade names in such manner as to misrepresent the true origin of a product, to the detriment of such distinctive regional or geographical names of products of the territory of a contracting party as are protected by its legislation. Each contracting party shall accord full and sympathetic consideration to such requests or representations as may be made by any other contracting party regarding the application of the undertaking set forth in the preceding sentence to names of products which have been communicated to it by the other contracting party.[28]

---

[22] Daniel J. Gervais, The TRIPS Agreement: Drafting History and Analysis 100 (4th ed., 2012).

[23] See Susy Frankel, *The Applicability of GATT Jurisprudence to the Interpretation of the TRIPS Agreement*, in Research Handbook on Intellectual Property Law and the WTO (Carlos M. Correa ed., 2010); see also Paul J. Heald, *Trademarks and Geographical Indications: Exploring the Contours of the TRIPS Agreement*, 29 Vand. J. Transnat'l L. 638, 658 (1996), where he suggests that "protecting the profit margin of certain producers by stopping goods at the border is precisely the sort of activity that the GATT was meant to discourage."

[24] *United States—Imports of Certain Automotive Spring Assemblies*, Panel Report, L/5333-30S/107 (May 26, 1983).

[25] *United States—Section 337 of the Tariff Act of 1930*, Panel Report, L/6439-36S/345 (November 7, 1989).

[26] In the particular dispute, the provisions allowing the International Trade Commission (ITC) to suspend the importation of goods allegedly infringing a U.S. patent were said to violate GATT. One of the reasons given was that the alleged infringer could not benefit from the same procedural rights as the plaintiff (e.g., the right to file a cross-complaint). Both ITC officials and attorneys who practice in this area debated for a number of years over the best way to amend § 337 patent-related procedures.

[27] GATT, art. IX.

[28] *Ibid.* art. IX:6.

This provision was given a restrictive interpretation in a panel report on *Japan—Customs Duties, Taxes and Labelling Practices on Imported Wines and Alcoholic Beverages*, where the panel found that the use of marks such as "Riesling" or "chateau" by Japanese manufacturers was not established to be to the detriment of distinctive regional or geographical names of products.[29] Japan's participation in the Madrid Agreement for the Repression of False or Deceptive Indications of Source was accepted as evidence that it had met its obligation to cooperate pursuant to Article IX:6.[30]

There are two further points that should be noted. First, GATT does not make all IP laws immune to GATT principles under the Article XX(d) exception mechanism. That is, some IP law arguably would not fall under the GATT exception, which may include aspects of parallel importing. Second, the TRIPS Agreement became the primary code (or *lex specialis*) regarding IP at the WTO. It is, therefore, the first place for interpretation of IP rights and the WTO, in as far as is possible, requires that its agreements are interpreted so they do not conflict.[31]

Before turning to the TRIPS Agreement it is important to recognize that the very existence of the TRIPS Agreement is a recognition that IP rights, although they form barriers to trade, are to a certain degree an acceptable barrier to trade.[32] What that degree is and the discretion countries have form the central issues relating to parallel importing.

C. Paris Convention and Berne Convention

There are rules concerning importation that can be found in, or at least derived from, the Paris Convention for the Protection of Industrial Property (Paris Convention) and the Berne Convention for the Protection of Literary and Artistic Works (Berne Convention).[33] Both instruments support the territoriality of rights. Territoriality works in two complementary ways. It restricts the effects of national laws of a given country to the territory of that country (thus preventing or limiting extra-territorial effects) and it allows countries to make decisions about, for example, the validity of rights in their territory. This is true even within the EU.[34] In the field of copyright, each country party to

---

[29] *Japan—Customs Duties, Taxes, and Labelling Practives on Imported Wines and Alcoholic Beverages* (November 10, 1987), GATT BISD 34S/83 (1983).

[30] It was agreed at the First Session of the ITO Preparatory Committee (London) that the words "deceptive practices" in art. XX covered the false marking of geographical origin. A contracting party could therefore protect indications of geographical origin under GATT. Under the TRIPS Agreement, WTO members have an obligation to provide that protection. See TRIPS Agreement, arts. 22–24.

[31] JOOST PAUWELYN, CONFLICT OF NORMS IN PUBLIC INTERNATIONAL LAW: HOW WTO LAW RELATES TO OTHER RULES OF INTERNATIONAL LAW (2009).

[32] Susy Frankel, *The WTO's Application of "the Customary Rules of Interpretation of Public International Law" to Intellectual Property*, 46 VA. J. INT'L L. 365 (2005).

[33] Paris Convention for the Protection of Industrial Property, 20 March 1883, 21 U.S.T. 1583, 828 U.N.T.S. 305 (revised 1967) [hereinafter Paris Convention]; Berne Convention for the Protection of Literary and Artistic Works, July 24, 1971, 1161 U.N.T.S. 3 [hereinafter Berne Convention].

[34] See PAUL GOLDSTEIN & BERNT HUGENHOLTZ, INTERNATIONAL COPYRIGHT 97 (2d ed., 2010).

the Berne Convention (that is, member of the Berne Union) is free to impose a fixation requirement as a threshold condition to obtain protection, or to exclude official texts (such as legislative instruments) from the realm of protected works.[35]

The Paris Convention also contains a number of relevant provisions such as Article 4*bis*, which provides in part that patents "applied for in the various countries of the [Paris] Union by nationals of countries of the Union shall be independent of patents obtained for the same invention in other countries."[36] This independence applies, *inter alia*, "as regards the grounds for nullity and forfeiture."[37] Article 5*quater* is even more directly relevant. It applies to the importation of products made from a patented process, but in a different country, and makes clear that the matter is left to the country of importation.[38] We see an example of this rule in 35 U.S.C. § 271(g). As Bodenhausen explains:

> Before the [1958] Lisbon Conference the Convention left complete freedom to the member States to define in their national legislation the acts of third parties by which a patent would be infringed. At the Conference of Lisbon it was proposed to change this situation rather drastically ... the proposal was not accepted and the adopted Article has a considerably narrower scope.[39]

In truth, however, the increasing degree of harmonization of public international IP and of standard term agreements used by worldwide Internet giants (a form of private international IP law) have significantly reduced disparities between, and flexibilities available, for national legislation, and, thus, the impact of territoriality.

D. TRIPS Agreement

For reasons that we have outlined in the Introduction, at both the national and international level there is disagreement over whether parallel importing should be permitted or not.

Internationally, no agreement has been reached on what is the appropriate rule globally for parallel importation.[40] This lack of international agreement is reflected in Article 6 of TRIPS,[41] which provides that nothing in the Agreement "shall be used to address the issue of the exhaustion of intellectual property rights."[42] Although, as one of us has noted, the inclusion of Article 6 indicates that parallel importing falls under TRIPS.[43]

However, as there is no agreement on any minimum standard relating to exhaustion of rights, the members of TRIPS have agreed that recourse to the WTO dispute settlement

---

[35] Berne Convention, arts. 2(2), 2(4).
[36] Paris Convention, art. 4*bis*(1); see also Philippe Baechtold, Tomoko Miyamoto, & Thomas Henninger, *International Patent Law: Principles, Major Instruments and Institutional Aspects*, in RESEARCH HANDBOOK ON INTERNATIONAL INTELLECTUAL PROPERTY 43 (D. Gervais ed., 2015).
[37] Paris Convention, art. 4*bis*(2).
[38] *Ibid.* art. 5*quater*.
[39] G.H.C. BODENHAUSEN, GUIDE TO THE APPLICATION OF THE PARIS CONVENTION FOR THE PROTECTION OF INTELLECTUAL PROPERTY 85 (1969).
[40] See Vincent Chiappetta, *The Desirability of Agreeing to Disagree: The WTO, TRIPS, International IPR Exhaustion and a Few Other Things*, 21 MICH. J. INT'L L. 333 (2000).
[41] TRIPS Agreement, art. 6.
[42] *Ibid.*
[43] GERVAIS, *supra* note 22, para. 2.99.

mechanism is not appropriate. Therefore, although TRIPS does not include general determinative and enforceable rules about parallel importing, the subject is relevant to TRIPS.

Other than Article 6, TRIPS contains no general rule concerning *parallel* importing or exhaustion of rights. That said, certain obligations of the Agreement may raise issues about parallel imports, for example, the rental right and whether that applies to parallel imported products.[44]

As far as patents are concerned there are two relevant obligations. The first is found in Article 28.1(a), which gives patent owners an import right.[45] The scope of the import right is critical. Article 28.1(a) must be read in conjunction with Article 6, as the footnote to the Article makes clear. To understand Article 28 it is useful to consider that copyrights and patents are different. Because there are no formalities to acquire copyright,[46] a copyright work will typically be protected more or less worldwide automatically upon creation.[47] Patents, however, are granted territory by territory. A parallel importing situation occurs where a patent owner owns patents in different territories, relating to a similar or the same product, and that owner sells or authorizes someone else to sell that product in those territories. In that case, if the price of the product is lower in one territory, a WTO member may apply international exhaustion and allow the importation of the lower priced product. This is the situation where the footnote to Article 28.1(a) applies. If, however, the product is made in a territory where the product is not patented (because no patent was applied for or a patent was refused), then there is no "parallel" right in that country and importing the unpatented version into a territory where a patent has issued would violate Article 28.1(a). That leaves a third situation, namely, where the product is manufactured under a compulsory license in a territory and imported into another. This issue will be discussed below. A right to prevent importation is also contained in respect of articles bearing or embodying a protected industrial design[48] and protected layout-designs of integrated circuits.[49]

As was discussed in the WTO dispute settlement report concerning the Canadian pharmaceutical related patent exceptions,[50] making and stockpiling prior to the expiry of the patent to have copies ready to sell is not allowed under Article 30.[51] Providing protection against making for export would similarly infringe (as is made clear by interpretation of

---

[44] See discussion below.
[45] TRIPS Agreement, art. 28. Article 28 provides that: "1. A patent shall confer on its owner the following exclusive rights: (a) where the subject matter of a patent is a product, to prevent third parties not having the owner's consent from the acts of: making, using, offering for sale, selling, or importing for these purposes that product; (b) where the subject matter of a patent is a process, to prevent third parties not having the owner's consent from the act of using the process, and from the acts of: using, offering for sale, selling, or importing for these purposes at least the product obtained directly by that process." *Ibid*.
[46] Berne Convention, art. 5(2), as incorporated into TRIPS Agreement, art. 9.1. See Berne Convention, art. 5(2); see also TRIPS Agreement, art. 9.1.
[47] Fixation is required in some jurisdictions, including the United States, the UK, and New Zealand.
[48] TRIPS Agreement, art. 26.1.
[49] *Ibid.* art. 36.
[50] *Canada—Patent Protection of Pharmaceutical Products, Complaint by the European Communities and Their Member States*, Panel Report, WT/DS114/R (March 17, 2000).
[51] TRIPS Agreement, art. 30.

Article 31(f)).[52] Article 31(f) is significant when compared to the Paris Convention, which basically left the matter up to national legislators while providing for certain very specific exceptions.[53] The Paris Convention did, however, accord rights in respect to products obtained by a patented process,[54] but those rights were still limited to what the national legislation provided.

Articles 31 and 31*bis* of TRIPS provides for situations where compulsory licenses for pharmaceuticals can be granted. Article 31(f) requires that such licenses are made predominantly for the domestic market.[55] As lifesaving drugs are often needed in countries that have no manufacturing capacity for pharmaceuticals, the WTO members agreed to amend TRIPS[56] to allow pharmaceuticals made under compulsory license in one country and to be parallel imported into another country, provided that both countries met certain criteria as an eligible importer[57] and eligible exporter.[58]

There are at least three different situations that arise from compulsory licenses. First, a product made for export under Article 31*bis* is subject to detailed rules that it must not be diverted into other markets (that is, the only import is to the eligible importing member named in the license). This is a *lex specialis* on importation that WTO members agreed to, and which specifically provides "members shall ensure the availability of effective legal

---

[52] *Ibid*. art. 31(f).
[53] Paris Convention, art. 5*ter*.
[54] *Ibid*. art. 5*quater*.
[55] TRIPS Agreement, art. 31(f), which states "any such use shall be authorized predominantly for the supply of the domestic market of the Member authorizing such use."
[56] The amendment was the introduction of art. 31*bis*, which allows members of the TRIPS Agreement to manufacture and import, under compulsory license, certain pharmaceuticals in specified circumstances. This amendment followed the Doha Declaration on Public Health, see WTO, Ministerial Declaration of November 14, 2001, WTO Doc. WT/MIN(01)/Dec/1, 41 I.L.M. 746 (2002); General Council, *Implementation of Paragraph 6 of the Doha Declaration on the TRIPS Agreement and Public Health*, WTO Doc. WT/L/540 (August 30, 2003); General Council, *Amendment to the TRIPS Agreement*, WTO Doc. WT/L/641 (December 8, 2005). Implementation requires that two-thirds of the WTO members ratified the Article by December 1, 2007, which did not happen. The deadline was extended to December 31, 2009; December 31, 2011; December 31, 2013; and the latest General Council decision of November 26, 2013, WT/L/899, extended the deadline to December 31, 2015 (General Council, *Amendment to the TRIPS Agreement—Fourth Extension of the Period for the Acceptance by Members of the Protocol Amending the TRIPS Agreement*, WTO Doc. WT/L/899 (November 27, 2013)). Until then, a "waiver" has been in place since 2003; General Council, *Implementation of Paragraph 6 of the Doha Declaration on the TRIPS Agreement and Public Health*, WTO Doc. WT/L/540 (August 30, 2003).
[57] An eligible importing member is defined as "any least-developed country Member, and any other Member that has made a notification to the Council for TRIPS of its intention to use the system set out in Article 31*bis* and this Annex ('system') as an importer, it being understood that a Member may notify at any time that it will use the system in whole or in a limited way, for example only in the case of a national emergency or other circumstances of extreme urgency or in cases of public non-commercial use. It is noted that some Members will not use the system as importing Members and that some other Members have stated that, if they use the system, it would be in no more than situations of national emergency or other circumstances of extreme urgency." See General Council, *Amendment of the TRIPS Agreement*, WT/L/641, art. 1(b) (December 8, 2005).
[58] "Exporting Member" means "a Member using the system to produce pharmaceutical products for, and export them to, an eligible importing Member." *General Council, Amendment of the TRIPS Agreement*, WT/L/641, art. 1(c) (December 8, 2005).

means to prevent the importation into, and sale in, their territories of products produced under the system and diverted to their markets inconsistently with its provisions."[59] When WTO members put in place the so-called "paragraph 6 system" (reflected in Article 31*bis*), the WTO General Council Chair read a statement noting that "all reasonable measures" should be taken to prevent diversion and directed WTO members to a set of guidelines developed by the pharmaceutical industry and attached to the Chair's statement.[60] It seems unlikely that a panel would apply Article 6 in a way that contradicts that agreement. This system applies to importation in least developed countries that are not the focus of this chapter and, in any event, are not subject to substantive TRIPS obligations.[61] Developed countries have a choice whether to agree to use the Article 31*bis* as exporters. Because Article 31*bis* does not allow developed countries to import products made under it we do not focus on this point further.

Second, a patented product may be made under an Article 31 compulsory license not caught by Article 31*bis*, for example, to remedy an anticompetitive practice.[62] If the products made thereunder then supply a different market this might be a breach of the license, for a product made under Article 31 is typically subject to rules in the license that it must not be diverted into other markets. This is confirmed by Article 31(f).[63] In both of these situations, Article 6 is not applicable and the matter can be brought to dispute settlement.

Finally, a compulsory license, which is not otherwise prohibited by TRIPS, may be issued for rights other than patents, for example, under the Appendix to the Berne Convention in the field of copyright. What happens then? This again seems to have a *lex specialis*, namely, Article 4(4)(a), which specifically prohibits compulsory license for export and then provides specific exceptions to cases where sending copies to another country may be allowed.

There are two competing principles at play here. First, if a compulsory license is issued, it is presumably because a parallel right exists in the country of manufacture and first sale. Hence, one could argue that parallel importation of such copies should be allowed. The second principle, which in this case clashes with the first, is of a normative nature. If parallel imports are allowed when a product is put on the market in one country and imported into another, it is arguably because the right holder has consented to the first sale. In the case of a compulsory license, that is not the case. There is, therefore, no "right" answer

---

[59] *Ibid.*

[60] WTO General Council Chairman, Press Release, The General Council Chairperson's Statement (August 30, 2003), available at www.wto.org/english/news_e/news03_e/trips_stat_28aug03_e.htm.

[61] TRIPS Agreement, art. 66. Article 66 provides a transition period for least developed countries to comply with TRIPS. "This transition period has been extended twice for all LDC members in response to a specific request by the LDC Group. In its decision of 29 November 2005, the TRIPS Council extended the period until 1 July 2013, and on 11 June 2013, it extended this further until 1 July 2021—or when a particular country ceases to be in the least developed category if that happens before 2021." See WTO, *Responding to Least Developed Countries' Special Needs in Intellectual Property* (October 16, 2013), available at www.wto.org/english/tratop_e/trips_e/ldc_e.htm.

[62] TRIPS Agreement, art. 31.

[63] The same could be said of the protection for semiconductor chips. See TRIPS Agreement, art. 37.2.

as a matter of principle. However, if the situation that justified the issuance of the license in country A exists in country B, then, as a matter of principle, one could support the parallel importing as a matter of efficiency without contravening the normative principle outlined above. This is supported by the text of Article IV(4)(b) of the Berne Convention's Appendix, which allows certain exports of copies produced under a compulsory license if the importing country is eligible to import as provided in the Appendix.

E. Conclusions about TRIPS and GATT

Although some countries oppose international exhaustion, the wording and the object and purpose of TRIPS do not support that conclusion.[64] The Preamble to TRIPS includes that IP should not become a barrier to trade.[65] This reflects the broad role of the WTO to reduce tariffs and non-tariff barriers. IP is, to a degree, an acceptable trade barrier.[66] TRIPS not only requires countries to provide IP rights, but its objectives and principles include that IP should be for "the mutual advantage of producers and users of technological knowledge in a manner conducive to social and economic welfare, and to a balance of rights and obligations."[67] This objective arguably supports parallel importing.[68] One could not say that permitting parallel importing is required. The position is that a country will be TRIPS compliant if it applies either national or international exhaustion. As noted, however, under TRIPS the rules are not the same for patents as for other areas of IP.

Parallel importing is part of a country's toolkit to allow for calibration. Domestically, the calibration process is one by which countries and regions tailor policy to their potential strengths in innovation while alleviating negative welfare costs. Finding a proper admixture of international IP disciplines and endogenous contextual realities *requires* calibration. Each country is different and, therefore, should tailor its IP policy to its own needs. This must be done within the constraints of TRIPS rules to avoid WTO disputes, and often in the face of political pressure from multinational stakeholders who prefer globally harmonized norms and practices. Moreover, IP policy forms part of a broader set of policies designed to maximize domestic innovation while taking due account of welfare costs in key areas such as access to pharmaceutical products and the development of vibrant marketplaces for products services and ideas. Calibration is not simple, but it is essential. Policies designed to optimize innovation while minimizing welfare costs should enhance economic growth, facilitate cultural prosperity, and foster human development.

---

[64] These are the rules of the Vienna Convention on the Law of Treaties, May 23, 1969, 1115 U.N.T.S. 331, art. 31. See Frankel, *supra* note 32; see also Frankel and Gervais, *supra* note 21.
[65] There are several important statements in the Preamble.
[66] See discussion *supra* II.B. GATT Pre-TRIPS.
[67] TRIPS Agreement, art. 7.
[68] For a discussion of the object and purpose of the TRIPS Agreement see Frankel, *supra* note 32.

III. JURISDICTIONAL APPROACHES TO PARALLEL IMPORTING

In this section, we compare the different parallel importing approaches of several developed countries. We do not underestimate the importance of parallel importing to developing countries. Our focus is, however, on developed countries because of the distinct differences in approaches indicating that parallel importing is not primarily a "North-South divide," as is often the case with other IP issues. Additionally, this comparative analysis demonstrates the purpose of calibration that we state above as allowing for policies designed to optimize innovation while minimizing welfare costs in order to enhance economic growth, facilitate cultural prosperity, and foster human development. We do this first by outlining how different countries and trade territories approach each of the three main areas of IP (trademarks, copyright, and patent).

A. United States

U.S. import rules concerning goods embodying one or more IP rights are fairly complex. As noted already, in 2014, the ITC issued a Summary Notice of Determination affirming an administrative law judge's conclusion that electronically transmitted information could constitute an "article," thereby asserting ITC jurisdiction over electronic transmissions across borders.[69] However, the parallel importation of copyrighted goods manufactured legally in a foreign country is legal under U.S. law. In *Kirtsaeng*, the U.S. Supreme Court aligned 17 U.S.C. § 602(a)(1), which prohibits importing a copy without permission and 17 U.S.C. § 106(3) (distribution right), which is "[s]ubject to the various doctrines and principles contained in §§ 107 through 122, including § 109(a)'s 'first sale' limitation."[70] The Court then decided that a copy made in a foreign country, but with permission of the local right holder, was "lawfully made under" the U.S. Copyright Act and, consequently, that the first sale doctrine contained in 17 U.S.C. § 109(a) was not geographically constrained.[71] Interestingly, the Court noted that "reliance upon the 'first sale' doctrine is deeply embedded in the practices of those, such as booksellers, libraries, museums, and retailers, who have long relied upon its protection."[72] The Court also stated that:

> a copyright law that can work in practice only if unenforced is not a sound copyright law. It is a law that would create uncertainty, would bring about selective enforcement, and, if widely unenforced, would breed disrespect for copyright law itself.[73]

The last quote suggests the difficulty of enforcing copyright against imports. While this does not seem entirely convincing for physical books (though it may be for *de minimis* imports, e.g., in travelers' luggage), the statement does ring true for digital imports.

---

[69] See In the Matter of Certain Digital Models, *supra* note 8.
[70] Kirtsaeng v. John Wiley & Sons, Inc., 133 S. Ct. 1351, 1355 (2013).
[71] *Ibid.*
[72] *Ibid.* at 1366.
[73] *Ibid.*

In the area of trademark, the Supreme Court distinguished among three types of "gray market" goods in the *K Mart* case.[74] The first, "prototypical gray market" case is the:

> domestic firm that purchases from an independent foreign firm the rights to register and use the latter's trademark as a United States trademark and to sell its foreign-manufactured products here ... If the foreign manufacturer could import the trademarked goods and distribute them here, despite having sold the trademark to a domestic firm, the domestic firm would be forced into sharp intrabrand competition.[75]

The second case is a "situation in which a domestic firm registers the United States trademark for goods that are manufactured abroad by an affiliated manufacturer," generally a subsidiary, although it could be an American-based firm with a manufacturing subsidiary corporation or unincorporated manufacturing division overseas to produce its U.S. trademarked goods.[76]

The third case is that of a:

> domestic holder of a United States trademark who authorizes an independent foreign manufacturer to use it ... If the foreign manufacturer or a third party imports into the United States, the foreign-manufactured goods will compete on the gray market with the holder's domestic goods.[77]

The Court then determined which of these cases were compatible with U.S. law, in particular section 526 of the 1930 Tariff Act, which prohibits importing into the U.S. any merchandise of foreign manufacture bearing a trademark owned by a U.S. citizen or corporation and registered at the U.S. Patent and Trademark Office (USPTO) without the consent of such person.[78] Applicable regulations provide a "common control exception" to section 526's prohibition. The regulation furnishes a "common control" exception from the ban, permitting the entry of gray market goods manufactured abroad by the trademark owner or its affiliate.[79] The Court found the "common control" exception consistent with section 526, but the authorized-use exception inconsistent with said provision. In other words, the first and second cases are legal, but not the third.

Another series of cases dealt with a fourth scenario, namely, where a "domestic firm manufactures a product in the United States for sale abroad and that good is re-imported to the United States for later sale without the trademark owner's permission."[80] This is considered under section 337 of the Tariff Act of 1930, which requires the goods to be materially different for the import prohibition to apply.[81] The Court of Appeals for the Federal Circuit found that:

---

[74] K Mart Corp. v. Cartier, Inc., 108 S. Ct. 1811 (1988).
[75] *Ibid.* at 1815.
[76] *Ibid.*
[77] *Ibid.*
[78] 19 U.S.C. § 1526 (1996).
[79] 19 C.F.R. § 133.21(c)(3) (1995).
[80] Bourdeau Bros. v. Int'l Trade Comm'n, 444 F.3d 1317, 1322 (Fed. Cir. 2006).
[81] 19 U.S.C.A. § 1337 (2004).

gray market law is concerned with whether the trademark owner has authorized use of the trademark on that particular product in the United States and thus whether the trademark owner has control over the specific characteristics associated with the trademark in the United States.[82]

The court in *Lever Bros. Co. v. United States*[83] interpreted section 42 of the Lanham Act, which provides that:

> [N]o article of imported merchandise which shall copy or simulate the name of . . . any domestic manufacture, or manufacturer . . . or which shall copy or simulate a trademark registered in accordance with the provisions of this chapter . . . shall be admitted to entry at any customhouse of the United States.[84]

In the wake of those cases, the U.S. Customs Service published regulations on the so-called "affiliate exception" to gray market imports.[85] The Customs rule restricts importation of certain gray market articles that bear genuine trademarks identical to or substantially indistinguishable from those appearing on articles authorized by the U.S. trademark owner that thereby create a likelihood of consumer confusion, in circumstances where the gray market articles and those bearing the authorized U.S. trademark "are physically and materially different."[86] The "restrictions are not applicable if the otherwise restricted articles are labeled in accordance with a prescribed standard under the rule that eliminates consumer confusion."[87]

This leaves the area of patent law. The U.S. Patent Act was amended in 1996 (coinciding with TRIPS entering into force in the U.S.) to include an exclusive right of importation.[88] The statute does not, however, deal explicitly with parallel imports.

To answer whether a foreign sale exhausts U.S. patent rights, one must consider two well recognized principles of patent law. First, the initial, authorized sale of a patented item terminates the patent owner's right to control the distribution of that item.[89] The sale need not be of the complete patented article, but includes the sale of an item that "sufficiently embodies the patent—even if it does not completely practice the patent—such that its only and intended use is to be finished under the terms of the patent."[90]

Second, patents are necessarily territorial. They may differ in scope and ownership from one territory to another. The question that connects the two principles, therefore, is whether exhaustion happens in country A only when it is related to the patent issued in that territory or whether a good that is legally produced in another territory may be imported. A variation on this theme is whether the sale of a product made by a patented process exhausts the rights in the same way as a patent on the product itself. As the Supreme Court

---

[82] *Bourdeau Bros.*, *supra* note 80, 44 F.3d at 1323.
[83] 981 F.2d 1330 (D.C. Cir. 1993).
[84] 15 U.S.C. § 1124 (1999).
[85] For more information on Gray Market Imports and Other Trademarked Goods, see Tres. Reg. § 64 FR 9058-01 (1999).
[86] Tres. Reg. § 64 FR 9058-01 (1999).
[87] *Ibid*.
[88] 35 U.S.C. § 154(a)(1) (2015); 35 U.S.C. § 271(a) (2010).
[89] Bowman v. Monsanto Co., 133 S. Ct. 1761, *reh'g denied*, 134 S. Ct. 24 (2013). See also United States v. Univis Lens Co., 316 U.S. 241, 249–51 (1942).
[90] Quanta Computer, Inc. v. LG Electronics, Inc., 553 U.S. 617, 627–28 (2008).

noted in that respect, patent exhaustion applies to method patents, meaning that a method patent is exhausted by sale of the item that embodies the method.[91]

Under U.S. law, exhaustion of patent rights occurs when a sale authorized by the U.S. patent holder takes place in the U.S.[92] A foreign first sale does not affect exhaustion of that patentee's rights in the U.S.[93] The exhaustion following a U.S. sale "survives," however, if the item is exported and reimported in the U.S. to be resold, for example, if refurbished overseas,[94] in some cases this is an application of the so-called "repair defense."

B. European Union

In examining the treatment of parallel imports of goods protected in the EU, it is important to bear in mind that goods normally can circulate freely within the EU.[95]

The principal EU legislative instrument concerning border measures was Regulation (EC) 1383/2003.[96] This Regulation excludes goods produced outside the EU with the consent of the right holder, but not intended for the EU market, from the scope of its application.[97] This leaves it up to individual Member States to decide whether to empower their customs authorities to enforce IP rights in such cases. Germany and the United Kingdom (U.K.), for example, do allow for customs seizure of parallel imported goods.[98]

Regulation 1383/2003 was repealed and replaced by Regulation (EU) 608/2013 of June 12, 2013, which went into effect on January 1, 2014.[99] Among the extensions is an application to rights and goods previously excluded from border measures, including goods that are designed to circumvent technological measures and trade names, semiconductor topographies, and utility models.[100] The new Regulation did not change the status of parallel imports despite significant lobbying by major multinational IP right holders.[101] The key recital on this point excludes illegal parallel trade (goods that have been manufactured with the consent of the right holder but placed on the market for the first time in the European Economic Area without consent), and overruns (goods that are manufactured

---

[91] *Ibid.*

[92] Fujifilm Corp. v. Benun, 605 F.3d 1366, 1372–73 (Fed. Cir. 2010), *cert. denied*, 79 U.S.L.W. 3254 (U.S. December 13, 2010).

[93] But see LG Electronics, Inc. v. Hitachi, Ltd., 655 F.Supp.2d 1036, 1046 (N.D. Cal. 2009).

[94] Jazz Photo Corp. v. Int'l Trade Comm'n, 264 F.3d 1094 (Fed. Cir. 2001).

[95] Case C-115/02, Administration des douanes et droits indirects v. Rioglas S.A. & Transremar S.L., [2003] E.C.R. I-2705, para. 28. See also Gabriël Moens & John Trone, *Free Movement of Goods*, in COMMERCIAL LAW OF THE EUROPEAN UNION 39, 54 (Gabriël Moens & John Trone eds., 2010).

[96] [2003] O.J. L196/7.

[97] *Ibid.* art. 3(1).

[98] Robert G. Krupka, Christian W. Liedtke, & Peter J. Corcoran, *Patent Parallel Imports in the United States and Germany: Shedding Light on the Grey*, 33 EUR. INTELL. PROP. REV. 613, 618 (2011).

[99] [2013] O.J. L181/15.

[100] See *ibid.* recital 5.

[101] Séamus David Long, *Regulation 5129/2013: The Protection It Offers Intellectual Property Right Holders*, 36 EUR. INTELL. PROP. REV. 785, 786 (2012).

by a person duly authorized to manufacture a certain quantity of goods in excess of the agreed quantities) from the scope of the Regulation.[102]

The law governing parallel imports reveals differences among EU Member States.

The first issue is whether transit is sufficient to trigger an infringement of the importation right. In a case involving trademarks, the Court of Justice of the European Union (CJEU) held that transit without more (that is, the more physical introduction of goods into the EU) was not importation.[103] The issue became controversial in a case involving pharmaceuticals in transit through a Dutch port.[104] If those goods were put in the market in the EU, then the exclusive rights of the trademark owner would apply.[105] Similarly, a British court held that the simple use of the postal service of a Member State for reshipment outside the EU did not amount to importation.[106] What courts look for is actual interference with the "specific subject matter (or the essential function) of the right."[107]

Beyond this issue of goods in transit, EU Member States are also bound by the Trade Marks Directive 2008/95/EC, which provides for regional (EU-wide) exhaustion and, specifically, precludes Member States from adopting international exhaustion in the trademark area.[108] Goods put into circulation in the EU with the trademark owner's consent can typically, therefore, no longer be prevented from crossing borders within the Union. Article 7(2) of the Trade Marks Directive does allow in certain cases the retention on further commercialization ("*commercialisation ultérieure*" in French) for a legitimate reason,[109] for example, allowing the seller of pharmaceutical products to oppose the selling of repackaged goods, in part because pharmaceuticals are particularly "sensitive goods."[110] The existence of price controls in a Member State is not a legitimate reason.[111]

Goods manufactured with the authorization of the trademark owner outside the EU

---

[102] Regulation (EU) 608/2013 concerning customs enforcement of intellectual property rights and repealing Council Regulation (EC) 1383, recital 6, [2013] O.J. L181/15 (EU).

[103] Case C-405/03, Class Int'l B.V. v. Colgate-Palmolive Co., [2005] E.C.R. I-8735, para. 44.

[104] Manoranjan Ayilyath, *EU Border Measure Regulation: A Threat to Access to Public Health in Developing Countries and Least Developed Countries*, 35 EUR. INTELL. PROP. REV. 212, 217 (2013).

[105] Directive 2008/95/EC of the European Parliament and of the Council of October 22, 2008 to approximate the laws of the Member States relating to Trade Marks, art. 5(1), [2008] O.J. L299/25 [hereinafter Trade Marks Directive]; and Council Regulation (EC) 207/2009 of February 26, 2009 on the Community Trade Mark, art. 9(1), [2009] O.J. L78/1 [hereinafter CTMR].

[106] Eli Lilly Co. et. al. v. 8PM Chemist Ltd., [2008] EWCA Civ 24, paras. 17, 35–45.

[107] Marius Schneider & Olivier Vrins, *Regulation (EC) 1383/2003*, in ENFORCEMENT OF INTELLECTUAL PROPERTY RIGHTS THROUGH BORDER MEASURES 109, 151 (2d ed., Oliver Vrins & Marius Schneider eds., 2012); see also Guido Westkamp, *Intellectual Property, Competition Rules, and the Emerging Internal Market: Some Thoughts on the European Exhaustion Doctrine*, 11 MARQ. INTELL. PROP. L. REV. 291, 296 (2007).

[108] Trade Marks Directive, art. 7(1), (2). See also CTMR, art. 13(1). See Case C-355/96, Silhouette Int'l Schmied GmbH & Co. K.G. v. Hartlauer Handelsgesell-schaft mbH, [1998] 2 C.M.L.R. 953. The *Silhouette* case dealt with reimportation, not first importation, however. See Thomas Hays, *Silhouette is Not the Proper Case upon which to Decide the Parallel Importation Question*, 20 EUR. INTELL. PROP. REV. 277, 279 (1998).

[109] See Thomas Hays, *Paranova v. Merck and Co-Branding of Pharmaceuticals in the European Economic Area*, 94 TRADEMARK REP. 821, 853 (2004).

[110] Case C-427/93, Bristol-Myers Squibb v. Paranova, [1997] E.C.R. I-03457.

[111] Case 15-74, Centrafarm B.V. v. Winthrop B.V., [1974] E.C.R. I-01147.

can be imported into the EU (or, more broadly, the European Economic Area) if consent to such importation has been given. The burden to show consent is on the importer, and this rule is uniform across the EU.[112] This does not, however, allow "artificial partitioning" of the internal market.[113] Repackaging of trademarked goods is allowed under certain conditions. A repackager must, among other conditions, take care not to damage the reputation of the trademark and its owner and give notice to the trademark owner.[114]

EU-wide exhaustion also applies to goods protected by copyright.[115]

This is also largely true in the field of patents. A product put into circulation in a Member State, either with the consent of the patent holder or in a Member State where no patent protection existed, can be exported to and sold in other Member States.[116] An exception to this principle would be goods that the manufacturer was under a legal obligation to supply.[117]

C. Israel, New Zealand, and Singapore

Israel, New Zealand, and Singapore all apply international exhaustion to some intellectual property rights. As one of us has discussed, the policy in all three of these small market economies is international exhaustion, but, in order to secure trade agreements, parallel importing is limited, particularly in relation to patents and patented pharmaceuticals.[118] The main reason these countries apply an international exhaustion rule to allow parallel imports is connected to their trade-related focus. Parallel importation is a calibration device to create competition in small markets where otherwise size often dictates a small number of players. Allowing parallel imports treats the world as the marketplace in which there are many competitors and ultimately lower prices for consumers. A concern often expressed about parallel importing is the effect on local businesses. In New Zealand, studies that have assessed the effect of parallel importing on local businesses, such as bookshops and music producers, concluded that the difficulties faced by booksellers are primarily due to technology and not just parallel importing.[119] In addition, New Zealand's film industry is not thought to be adversely affected by parallel importing.

---

[112] Case C-414/99, Zino Davidoff v. A&G Imports, [2001] E.C.R. I-08691.
[113] See *ibid*.
[114] Case C-348/04, Boehringer Ingelheim K.G. v. Swingward Ltd., [2007] E.C.R. I-03391. On the matter of damage to the reputation more specifically, see Boehringer Ingelheim K.G. v. Swingward Ltd., [2008] E.T.M.R. 38. See also Irene Calboli, *Reviewing the (Shrinking) Principle of Trademark Exhaustion in the European Union (Ten Years Later)*, 16 MARQ. INTELL. PROP. L. REV. 257, 273 (2012).
[115] Case C-337, Parfums Christian Dior v. Evora, [1998] E.C.R. I-06013.
[116] Case C-267-268/95, Merck & Co. Inc. et al. v. Primecrown Ltd. et al., [1996] E.C.R. I-06285.
[117] See Andreas Reindl, *Intellectual Property and Intra-Community Trade*, 20 FORDHAM INT'L L.J. 819, 826 (1997); see also Daniel J. Gifford, *Government Policy Towards Innovation in the United States, Canada, and the European Union as Manifested in Patent, Copyright, and Competition Laws*, 57 S.M.U.L. REV. 1339, 1357 (2004).
[118] See FRANKEL, *supra* note 12, at 159. Also, a number of other jurisdictions, including Japan and Switzerland, apply international exhaustion in the patent area. Krupka, Liedtke, and Corcoran, *supra* note 98, at 618.
[119] See Susy Frankel *et al.*, *The Challenges of Trans-Tasman Intellectual Property Coordination*, in RECALIBRATING BEHAVIOUR: SMARTER REGULATION IN A GLOBAL WORLD 17–62 (Susy Frankel & D. Ryder eds., 2013), where the studies are summarized and discussed.

In New Zealand, the copyright legislation defines "infringing copy" so that parallel imports are not infringing.[120] Thus:

> an object that a person imports or proposes to import into New Zealand is not an infringing copy if it was made by or with the consent of the owner of the copyright, or other equivalent intellectual property right, in the work in question in the country in which the object was made.[121]

Additionally, if any dispute arises, the burden of proof falls on the importer to show the imports are legitimate rather than requiring the copyright owner to prove infringement (as would be the norm in other sorts of infringement cases).[122] After the law was reformed to allow parallel importation of copyright works, trademark law was also reformed to allow parallel imports.[123] Patented products are not parallel imported into New Zealand.

In Singapore, copyright works and trademarked products can be parallel imported.[124] Singapore law permits parallel importation of patented products even when the owner outside of Singapore is different from the owner in Singapore.[125] These are general rules. After the conclusion of a free trade agreement with the U.S., different rules apply to pharmaceuticals.[126] If "the product has not previously been sold or distributed in Singapore" it cannot be parallel imported.[127] This amounts to a first sale right for pharmaceuticals in Singapore, but that first sale right does not prevent subsequent parallel importation. In addition, a patent owner also has a right against a parallel importer who has actual or constructive knowledge that the pharmaceutical product has been distributed in breach of a distribution agreement.[128]

In Israel, as long as the copy of a copyright work imported is made legitimately in the country of origin then the copyright work can be parallel imported into Israel. *Dyson Ltd. v. Y Shalom Ltd.*, a case that involved industrial design and copyright, is illustrative.[129] In that case, the overseas manufacturer and local exclusive distributor of Dyson products tried to prevent parallel imports of Dyson vacuum cleaners and an

---

[120] For a full discussion of the old regimes see Susy Frankel, Intellectual Property in New Zealand 94–96 (2d ed., 2013). Copyright Act 1994, s. 12(3)(b) (N.Z.) now limits "infringing copying" to situations in which, "The importer would have infringed the copyright in the work in question in New Zealand had the importer made the object in New Zealand, unless the object is one to which subsection (5A) or subsection (6) applies."

[121] Copyright Act 1994, s. 5(A) (N.Z.).

[122] Copyright (Parallel Importation of Films and Onus of Proof) Amendment Act 2003 (N.Z.). The Amendment was incorporated into the 1994 Copyright Act. For further discussion see Frankel, *supra* note 120.

[123] Trade Marks Act 2002, s. 97(A) (N.Z.).

[124] Television Broadcasts Ltd. v. Golden Line Video & Marketing Pte. Ltd., [1988] S.L.R. 930, 937.

[125] Ng-Loy Wee Loon, Intellectual Property Law of Singapore 34.3.13–34.3.23 (2009).

[126] EU-Singapore Free Trade Agreement, art. 16.7.2 (September 20, 2013), available at http://ec.europa.eu/trade/policy/countries-and-regions/countries/singapore/.

[127] Patents Act, s. 63(3) (Sing.).

[128] *Ibid.* s. 63(b)–(c). See also discussion in Ng-Loy Wee Loon, *supra* note 125, at 34.3.1–34.3.6.

[129] Case 1089/05, Dyson Ltd. v. Y Shalom Ltd., November 14, 2007.

unauthorized translation of the manufacturer's user manual into Hebrew.[130] The Court allowed the parallel imports and concluded that other IP rights should not be used to inhibit the parallel importation of trademarked products that could be imported.[131] The Supreme Court of Israel has held that patented goods, and pharmaceuticals in particular, could be parallel imported into Israel.[132]

D. Australia

In contrast to the above described approaches in New Zealand and other small market economies, Australia generally applies a rule of national exhaustion. After much debate, restrictions on parallel imports of computer programs and sound recordings were removed to allow parallel imports, but print music and books cannot be parallel imported. Books privately purchased over the Internet and eBooks[133] fall outside of the prohibition. A Productivity Commission report published in 2009 recommended reform of parallel importing relating to books on economic grounds and cited New Zealand as a successful model.[134] The different approaches of New Zealand and Australia have been analyzed and the suggestion made that this was an area where better coordination between the two countries would likely have produced better results for both.[135]

In recent years, a number of studies have been conducted to investigate the impact of removing parallel import restrictions on books, music, sound recordings, DVDs, and computer software.[136] Protecting the local book business was a position that the Australian government followed when it did not lift restrictions on parallel imports of books.[137]

---

[130] Ibid.
[131] Ibid. citing Case 471/70, Geigy v. Pazchim and Case 371/89, Leibovitch v. Eliyahu.
[132] Bristol Myers Squib Co. v. Minister of Health, 5379/00.
[133] See Copyright Act 1968 (Cth), ss. 37–38 (44A and following) and 102–103 (102C and following). There are other qualifications on parallel imports of books in the current provisions, including a "30-day rule" and the "90-day resupply rule," which effectively mean that if a book is not released in Australia within 30 days of its being published elsewhere or there is no capacity to resupply it within 90 days, the parallel import restrictions do not apply.
[134] See AUSTRALIAN PRODUCTIVITY COMMISSION, RESTRICTIONS ON THE PARALLEL IMPORTATION OF BOOKS (June 2009), available at www.pc.gov.au/projects/study/books/report.
[135] See Frankel et al., supra note 119, at 101–38.
[136] See e.g. NETWORK ECONOMICS CONSULTING GROUP, THE IMPACT OF PARALLEL IMPORTS ON NEW ZEALAND'S CREATIVE INDUSTRIES (Ministry of Economic Development, Wellington, 2004); NEW ZEALAND INSTITUTE OF ECONOMIC RESEARCH, PARALLEL IMPORTING: A THEORETICAL AND EMPIRICAL INVESTIGATION (February 1998); NEW ZEALAND INSTITUTE OF ECONOMIC RESEARCH, PARALLEL IMPORTING REVIEW: THE ECONOMIC EFFECTS OF LIFTING THE BAN IN NZ (February 2000); AUSTRALIAN PRODUCTIVITY COMMISSION, COPYRIGHT RESTRICTIONS ON THE PARALLEL IMPORTATION OF BOOKS (June 2009), available at www.pc.gov.au/inquiries/completed/books.
[137] AUSTRALIAN PRODUCTIVITY COMMISSION, supra note 134. The Productivity Commission recommended that all remaining parallel importing restrictions be repealed. As an illustration, the report's findings showed that Australian book prices were, on average, 35 percent higher than in the United Kingdom and United States.

IV. PARALLEL IMPORTATION AS A CALIBRATION TOOL

As noted above, allowing calibration of local laws,[138] within the international rules, where those calibrations are designed to meet domestic or regional policy goals is an integral part of the IP framework. Pinpointing how parallel imports in developed countries achieve calibration is perhaps challenging. However, as the above survey shows, that is exactly why most developed countries allow some parallel importation. Other drivers, such as trade deals in the case of small developed countries and the push of technology making barriers to online imports inefficient, may be a motivating force. Where physical barriers to importation remain effective (at least for the time being) parallel importing restrictions remain strong in developed countries. The most obvious example is in the case of patented pharmaceuticals. Most of the developed countries do not allow for parallel importation of many patented products. Where they do allow for it, the parallel importation of pharmaceuticals has been pared back, as is illustrated in Singapore in particular. And for the time being that remains likely, but as we are at the dawn of 3D printing of pharmaceuticals (and other patented products) technology may continue to make parallel import restrictions progressively redundant. For better or for worse, the end, however, is a long way off.

---

[138] For a detailed discussion about calibration on international intellectual property rules in domestic law see Daniel Gervais, *Intellectual Property Calibration, in* INTELLECTUAL PROPERTY, TRADE AND DEVELOPMENT 86–116 (2d ed., Daniel Gervais ed., 2014).

6. Economic perspectives on exhaustion and parallel imports
*Keith E. Maskus**

I. INTRODUCTION

Parallel imports (PI) are legitimately sourced goods brought into a country, without the authorization of the entity owning some form of intellectual property rights (IPRs) to those goods, after they have been placed into circulation in another nation. Whether such trade is legally permitted depends on the geographic scope within which the IPR, whether patent, copyright, trademark or other exclusive right, is exhausted upon first sale. Typically when a commodity is first sold within a country the IPR holder cannot prevent its owner from reselling it within that market. The exhaustion doctrine governs the ability of such goods to be imported legally into another market. Some countries give the IPR owner in the target market the right to exclude such goods sold abroad from importation, a situation referred to as *national exhaustion*. The United States (U.S.) adopts this policy in most areas.[1] Others permit parallel imports, which are called that because by definition they occur within a parallel distribution channel outside the control of the originator. This is the case of *international exhaustion*, which may be found for certain types of IPR in Brazil, New Zealand, and elsewhere.[2] The European Union (EU) and other members of the European Economic Area (EEA) pursue an intermediate policy of *regional exhaustion*, under which IPR owners may exclude PI from outside the EU geographical area but such trade is fully legal inside the region.

Under the terms of Article 6 of the Agreement on Trade-Related Aspects of Intellectual Property Rights (TRIPS) at the World Trade Organization (WTO), member nations are given full latitude to select their own exhaustion regimes. It is not surprising that a global rule could not be reached, given the complexity of the subject. There are marked differences across markets in the permissibility of this trade.[3] Moreover, for any country the law may vary across types of IPRs. For example, Japan traditionally followed national exhaustion in patents until recent court decisions opened the market in certain circumstances.[4]

---

* Professor of Economics, Department of Economics, University of Colorado Boulder.
[1] Keith E. Maskus, *Parallel Imports*, 23 THE WORLD ECONOMY 1269, 1272–74 (2000).
[2] STANDING COMMITTEE ON THE LAW OF PATENTS, WORLD INTELLECTUAL PROPERTY ORGANIZATION (WIPO), EXCEPTIONS AND LIMITATIONS TO PATENT RIGHTS: EXHAUSTION OF PATENT RIGHTS (2000), available at www.wipo.int/edocs/mdocs/scp/en/scp_21/scp_21_7.pdf.
[3] Carsten Fink, *Entering the Jungle of Intellectual Property Rights Exhaustion and Parallel Imports*, in INTELLECTUAL PROPERTY RIGHTS AND DEVELOPMENT: LESSONS FROM RECENT ECONOMIC RESEARCH, 174 (Carsten Fink & Keith E. Maskus eds., 2004).
[4] SECRETARIAT, WORLD INTELLECTUAL PROPERTY ORGANIZATION, INTERFACE BETWEEN EXHAUSTION OF INTELLECTUAL PROPERTY RIGHTS AND COMPETITION LAW (2011), available at www.wipo.int/edocs/mdocs/mdocs/en/cdip_4/cdip_4_4rev_study_inf_2.pdf.

However, it is open to parallel imports in copyrighted goods except motion pictures. Australia has a mixed regime, being open to PI in trademarks but closed in patented goods (with limitations) and in copyrighted products, except for compact disks and books.

As might be surmised from this variation, decisions regarding legalized PI are complex and often arise from judicial actions, making it impossible to characterize them in a simple yet accurate way across countries.[5] To a first approximation, however, the primary economic determinant of the regime choice is the extent to which a country has a comparative advantage in producing intellectual property of various types. For example, the U.S. is a major producer and net exporter of patented technologies and copyrighted goods. Its policy permits exclusion of patented and copyrighted items on the principle that the rights to exploit such products should be fully exclusive throughout the term of protection.[6] Similarly, the bulk of the high-income economies in the Organization for Economic Cooperation and Development (OECD) favor limits on international exhaustion in patents and copyrights, though there are many exceptions. In contrast, India is generally open to PI because its domestic firms register relatively few patents, meaning that parallel trade competes largely with foreign-owned IPR.[7] However, India bans PI in copyrights, reflecting the importance of its software and cinematic industries. More generally, poorer countries are more open to PI in order to promote import competition with IPR-protected goods, though again there are many detailed exceptions.

In economic terms, parallel imports are a form of cross-border arbitrage.[8] As will be discussed below, owners of a product patented or copyrighted in multiple locations profit from setting market-specific launch dates and prices, which vary according to country characteristics. It follows immediately that banning PI is a means of sustaining this market segmentation, while permitting such trade should reduce or eliminate it. Indeed, to the great majority of economists specializing in international trade it seems intuitively obvious that PI, by generating another source of competition in high-priced markets, must be procompetitive. That intuition carries over to official policies in the EU, where parallel trade within the region is seen as a key means of integrating the single market and generating consumer benefits.[9]

While this idea is appealing and correct in its simplest form, it is misleading in important ways. Such is the basic conclusion of serious economic analysis of the sources and impacts of PI. This analysis is surprisingly recent, given that exhaustion has been an element of IPR policy for a long time. Growing interest in the subject may be attributed largely to three closely interrelated factors. First, the entire subject of intellectual property rights as a matter of trade policy was ignored by international economists until after

---

[5] For a review of practices in a range of countries, see Mattias Ganslandt & Keith E. Maskus, *Intellectual Property Rights, Parallel Imports, and Strategic Behavior*, in INTELLECTUAL PROPERTY, GROWTH, AND TRADE 267–68 (Keith E. Maskus ed., 2008).

[6] The fact that this exclusive right is limited in trademarks stems from their different legal foundations: so long as consumers are not confused regarding the true origin of goods, PI should be permitted if the mark owner placed them into circulation abroad with a related party.

[7] Ganslandt & Maskus, *supra* note 5, at 267.

[8] Maskus, *supra* note 1, at 1274.

[9] Ganslandt & Maskus, *supra* note 5, at 269–72.

TRIPS.[10] Now it is a mainstream area of trade analysis as economists have come to see its importance for innovation, technology transfer, and market power. In this context, PI form perhaps the most interesting element of international marketing strategies affected by regulatory policy.[11]

Second, the intense globalization associated with the spread of multinational enterprises and international production chains, largely driven by technological advantages combined with factor-cost differences, have roused the interest of trade analysts in all forms of international technology and cultural markets.[12] Whether PI are permitted matters for many strategic decisions, ranging from first-stage investments in research and development (R&D) to the timing of market entry.

Finally, the subject of price differences across markets has taken on direct urgency as a matter of development policy. Consider, for example, the issue of "tiered pricing" in essential medicines, or the idea that segmented markets should support lower prices of patented drugs in poor countries, thereby raising market access.[13] While a powerful prescription in theory, the idea does not seem to hold much water in practice, raising basic questions about the efficacy of bans on parallel trade as a means of beneficial market segmentation.

Because space is limited in a single chapter, it will not be possible to do justice to what is now a deep and important economics literature. Rather, I will focus on three key questions that have been the subject of close study and highlight the central lessons emerging from that work. After a brief review of basic facts the subsequent sections cover these questions, which may be introduced as follows. First, what do our core economic models predict about the impacts of parallel trade on competition and prices under different circumstances? What little empirical evidence there is in this regard is also discussed. Second, how does the permission of PI affect dynamic decisions regarding R&D investment and product entry, and what is the role of national price regulation in this context? Third, are there important linkages between trade policy and the choice of exhaustion regime, at least in theory?

As we will see, there is a great deal of ambiguity about the potential competitive and welfare impacts of parallel trade. For example, economic theory shows that it is quite possible for IPR owning firms to profit from the existence of PI when they are subject to rigorous price controls. Moreover, there are realistic circumstances in which openness to PI may actually cause prices to diverge across markets when distributors act strategically to maximize profits. Thus, exhaustion and parallel trade are far more complex than simple arbitrage theory might suggest and subtleties of this kind should be kept in mind by policy-makers and legal scholars.

---

[10] Keith E. Maskus, Intellectual Property Rights in the Global Economy 6–7 (2000).
[11] See generally Keith E. Maskus, Private Rights and Public Problems: The Global Economics of Intellectual Property in the 21st Century 140–231 (2012).
[12] Ibid. at 35–81, 294–312.
[13] Ibid. at 258–70.

II. BASIC FACTS AND EVIDENCE ABOUT PARALLEL IMPORTS

The most frustrating feature of parallel imports for researchers is that data about them are extremely scarce and hard to locate. The reason is pragmatic: because PI are legal and entail trade in legitimate (that is, not counterfeited) goods they attract no particular attention from customs authorities despite the fact that they are traded in parallel distribution channels. Distributors of PI pay any required tariffs but there is no customs-related purpose to collect figures on parallel trade flows. The primary exception, which supports some analysis discussed below, is that public health authorities must track the origins of medicines and other goods that may affect public health. Thus, customs may be asked to identify certain import transactions as parallel imports. However, such data are almost always confidential and unavailable to researchers. Thus, there are no systematic databases on PI by commodity, source, or destination.

A. Stylized Facts

Despite this lacuna, occasional surveys have been undertaken that help characterize parallel imports. The most comprehensive one, now quite dated, was performed by National Economic Research Associates (NERA) at the request of the European Commission. The survey found that intra-EU PI accounted for different shares of sales in ten industries in 1993, though there is reason to suspect the figures were under-reported by respondents.[14] PI were greatest in compact disks (10–20 percent of EU sales), cosmetics and perfumes (up to 13 percent), and soft drinks (up to 15 percent). Each of these types of commodities reflect characteristics giving rise to the potential for PI. Compact disks are copyrighted goods subject to substantial increasing returns, fashion goods are subject to heavy marketing (and potential free riding), and soft drinks intensively use trademarks. Other sectors with significant intra-EU parallel trade included automobiles, consumer electronics, clothing, and confectionery. Thus, one stylized fact is that PI can account for significant shares of trade in IPR-intensive goods within regions where they are permitted.

The NERA survey pointed out another important stylized fact, which is that the great bulk of PI are undertaken by organized parallel trading firms, who operate at the distributor level.[15] A good example is soft drinks, which are far likelier to be traded in bulk form as syrup than as final packaged goods. These PI firms seek stable sources of supply among authorized wholesalers in lower-priced countries for resale to retailers in higher-priced locations. Stability and volume are important, for parallel-trading firms need to be viewed as reliable sources of legitimate products for retailers to be willing to enter into delivery contracts with them. In contrast, despite the usual depiction of parallel trade as the practice of individuals buying a car or a watch in a cheaper location for use at home,

---

[14] NATIONAL ECONOMIC RESEARCH ASSOCIATES (NERA), THE ECONOMIC CONSEQUENCES OF THE CHOICE OF REGIME IN THE AREA OF TRADEMARKS: FINAL REPORT FOR DG XV OF THE EUROPEAN COMMISSION 76–100 (1999), available at http://ec.europa.eu/internal_market/indprop/docs/tm/report_en.pdf.

[15] *Ibid.* at 32.

individual-level and even retail-level PI is rare.[16] The basic reason is simple: engaging in international trade requires payment of significant fixed costs for firms, in terms of finding suppliers, meeting regulatory requirements in import markets, and dealing with customs and taxes.[17] These costs need to be spread over large volumes, implying that PI is largely done in bulk at the wholesale level.

A third important fact is that PI volumes are sensitive to international price changes. For example, an early survey found that substantial increases in such imports into the U.S. emerged after large increases in the international exchange value of the dollar.[18] Parallel trade also seems sensitive to variations in exchange rates within East Asia.[19] On the other hand, available evidence in the European Union, where this trade is legal among Member States, suggests that parallel imports are not sufficient to push price levels together as a result of arbitrage.[20] This is a loose claim, for it relies on the observation that price convergence of commodities across European cities is considerably less than one might expect within a single market connected by zero tariffs and the threat of PI.[21] This claim has not yet been subjected to serious statistical analysis, however.

B. Empirical Evidence

Given the data scarcity in this area, there are no rigorous statistical studies of the extent and effects of PI across industries, a real shortcoming in the literature. However, some progress has been made specifically in pharmaceuticals where, as noted above, health authorities must keep track of the sources of traded medicines. Ganslandt and Maskus offered the first statistical analysis of actual data on parallel imports and prices of original manufacturers' patented pharmaceuticals.[22] They gained access to detailed and high-frequency data on prescription-drug sales in Sweden from 1994 to 1998, broken down at the product level into brand-name, original manufacturers' sales, and chemically identical products brought in through parallel channels from other markets in the EU. Sweden was an ideal natural experiment for this study because it had to switch from national exhaustion to regional exhaustion when it joined the EU in 1995. By mid-1966, after a period of eighteen months during which PI firms gained certification as suppliers of legitimate versions of patented drugs, PI began entering Sweden. By 1998 such sales comprised up to two-thirds of the market for large-volume drugs. In this regard their analysis unearthed a fifth stylized fact, which is that distributor-level parallel trade

---

[16] Mattias Ganslandt & Keith E. Maskus, *Vertical Distribution, Parallel Trade, and Price Divergence in Integrated Markets*, 51 EUR. ECON. REV. 943 (2007).

[17] NERA, *supra* note 14, at 68.

[18] John C. Hilke, *Free Trading or Free Riding: Examination of the Theories and Available Empirical Evidence on Gray Market Imports* 75 (U.S. Free Trade Commission, Working Paper No. 150, 1987).

[19] Aspy P. Palia & Charles F. Keown, *Combating Parallel Importing: Views of U.S. Exporters to the Asia-Pacific Region*, 8 INT'L MARKETING REV. 4 (1991).

[20] John H. Rogers, *Monetary Union, Price Level Convergence and Inflation: How Close is Europe to the USA?*, 54 J. MONETARY ECONOMICS 784 (2007).

[21] Ganslandt & Maskus, *supra* note 16.

[22] Mattias Ganslandt & Keith E. Maskus, *The Price Impact of Parallel Imports in Pharmaceuticals: Evidence from the European Union*, 23 J. HEALTH ECON. 1035 (2004).

is far more common in products with large markets and significant international price disparities.

In their analysis the authors specified a model in which changes over time in the wholesale prices of patented drugs were affected by entry of PI firms, controlling for various determinants of pricing.[23] The authors controlled for the obvious potential reverse causality, in which PI entry itself would vary with market conditions. In their preferred estimates they found that original manufacturers' prices are pushed downward by competition from parallel imports, with the reduction getting stronger as more PI firms entered. Overall, the pricing power of brand-name firms was reduced by 12 to 18 percent on average due to PI competition, suggesting that this form of competition exerts a strong price-moderating impact.

Did these price effects translate into significant savings for patients and public-health budgets? In an extended paper, Ganslandt and Maskus argued that the actual cost savings were small in Sweden because the wholesale price reductions were not passed on to hospitals and patients at the retail level, rather retailers and PI firms made larger margins.[24] This finding of a limited beneficial impact of PI on final patient costs has been found in other studies as well. For example, Kanavos and Costa-i-Font, again using detailed data, found that the gains from PI accrue largely to trading firms, which price their versions marginally below the often controlled prices in destination countries.[25] In a related survey of six high-priced pharmaceutical markets in the EU these and other authors found that direct savings from PI totaled around 45 million Euros in 2002, ranging from 0.3 percent of the market in Norway to 2.2 percent in Denmark, though various clawback regulations raised these benefits somewhat.[26] In contrast, the profit margins enjoyed by PI firms ranged from 46 to 60 percent, suggesting that parallel trade is lucrative, if not that effective in reducing actual patient costs, while it poses little competitive threat to incumbents. Indeed, this pessimistic finding might be considered yet a sixth stylized fact about PI, at least in medicines.[27]

While this insight is suggestive, there are simply too few serious studies to support any confident conclusions about the impacts of PI on prices and competition in drugs, much less in other goods. Much more research should be done to develop a full picture of what

---

[23] *Ibid.* at 1049–54.

[24] Mattias Ganslandt & Keith E. Maskus, The Price Impact of Parallel Imports in Pharmaceuticals: Evidence from the European Union 28 (manuscript on file with University of Colorado, 2002).

[25] Panos Kanavos & Joan Costa-i-Font, *Pharmaceutical Parallel Trade in Europe: Stakeholder and Competition Effects*, ECON. POL'Y 758, 772–75 (October 2005).

[26] PANOS KANAVOS, JOAN COSTA-I-FONT, SHERRY MERKUR, & MARIN GEMMILL, THE ECONOMIC IMPACT OF PHARMACEUTICAL PARALLEL TRADE IN EUROPEAN MEMBER STATES: A STAKEHOLDER ANALYSIS 15 (2004), available at www.researchgate.net/profile/Panos_Kanavos/publication/48909718_The_economic_impact_of_pharmaceutical_parallel_trade_in_European_union_member_states_a_stakeholder_analysis/links/02bfe51076f921d6d7000000.pdf.

[27] However, another survey claimed that direct cost savings in five of these countries in 2002 amounted to 635 million Euros, a significantly higher figure. This finding is questionable because the authors appear to have ascribed the entire price gap between retail prices in destination countries and distribution prices in source countries to savings from PI, a highly unlikely assumption. See PETER WEST & JAMES MAHON, BENEFITS TO PAYERS AND PATIENTS FROM PARALLEL TRADE 67–69 (2003).

drives parallel imports and the impacts they have on important variables. For example, there is no econometric study available that considers the potential effects of PI on decisions of IPR-owning firms to invest in R&D. This is a fundamental question, reflected in the fact that U.S. research-based pharmaceutical firms oppose opening the U.S. border to re-importation of patented and brand-name drugs from Canada, partly on the grounds that resulting lost profits would reduce their ability to develop new medicines.[28] This ignorance represents a considerable gap in the literature on parallel trade. Policy-makers concerned with PI and competition in IPR-protected markets might therefore consider directing their statistical authorities to collect more data in order to lift this veil of uncertainty.

III. INTERNATIONAL PRICE DISCRIMINATION, ARBITRAGE, AND EXHAUSTION POLICY

In this section I return to the basic economic theory of parallel trade as international commodity arbitrage and discuss its implications for how countries might choose their exhaustion policies. Again, PI arise in principle as a form of competitive pressure against firms having market power as a result of owning a territorial intellectual property right, or a basket of rights. Firms with market power maximize profits by choosing prices that reflect the economic valuation of specific consumers, thereby extracting higher amounts of surplus. Put differently, firms set higher prices where demand for a good is inelastic and lower prices where demand is elastic.

Price discrimination is ubiquitous in today's markets, ranging from different airline ticket prices to varying discounts for purchasing electronic goods and medicines. To sustain it requires that the scope for arbitrage among consumers or markets is limited. If there were fully frictionless arbitrage among consumers facing different prices firms would be forced to set uniform prices. At the international level, frictionless arbitrage would refer to parallel trade that faces no trade taxes, transport costs, supply restrictions, or regulatory costs that would support higher prices in some markets than others. Of course, one such regulation would be national exhaustion, which effectively segments markets by barring PI.

It is useful to start this discussion by defining specific forms of price discrimination used in the economics and marketing literatures. First-degree (or "perfect") price discrimination refers to the ability to set different prices for individual consumers arrayed along a common demand curve.[29] Second-degree price discrimination occurs where consumers along a demand curve may be arranged into single-price blocks. Neither concept relies on a specific geographical dimension. These forms are best illustrated by the varying ticket prices paid by passengers for the same service on an airplane flight or by age-related discounts. In contrast, third-degree price discrimination refers to a situation in which groups of consumers have different demand characteristics, typically across locations,

---

[28] MASKUS, PRIVATE RIGHTS, *supra* note 11, at 185–88.
[29] These concepts are more precisely defined in FREDERIC M. SCHERER, INDUSTRIAL MARKET STRUCTURE AND ECONOMIC PERFORMANCE 315–17 (2d ed. 1980).

and a single price is charged in each market. The markets are separated by some kind of trade barrier or transport costs permitting oligopolistic firms to engage in "pricing to market."[30] This is the primary concept analyzed in the exhaustion context, with national exhaustion supporting such price segmentation across countries.[31]

Basic theory shows that profits of IPR owners are generally higher the greater the scope for third-degree price discrimination in international markets.[32] Thus, we would expect original manufacturers owning the relevant IPR to prefer bans on parallel trade, as they generally do. In turn, if profitability is an important factor in setting policy we should expect IPR-generating nations to erect restrictions against PI, as noted earlier. This observation surely animates the U.S. position that permitting firms to block parallel trade constitutes a natural extension of their rights to control distribution. However, profits are not synonymous with economic welfare, which depends also on competition and price, with more competition generating greater consumer gains. In fact, the welfare results of price discrimination, and therefore of PI, are complex and the net effects on any particular country are theoretically ambiguous.[33]

To appreciate this ambiguity at its simplest level, consider the effects of price discrimination across markets on global well-being. Differential prices distort global consumption decisions in the sense that they frustrate consumers in higher-priced locations who would buy the good if it were available through trade at a lower charge. At the same time, total global consumption could be higher with differentiated prices as additional consumers in more price-sensitive markets can afford to buy the good. In pragmatic terms, market segmentation offers incentives to originator firms to sell their goods at lower prices in poorer markets, where demand is likely to be more elastic. If parallel trade shifted products from these markets to higher-priced ones, consumers in the source countries would be harmed. Indeed, even the threat of PI could deter firms from engaging in otherwise beneficial price segmentation.

In this context, it is important to note that where parallel trade is legal we may not see any actual trade arise. The reason is that the competitive threat of PI would induce originator firms to set uniform prices, or more accurately prices that differ across borders only by the costs of organizing and shipping goods, leading to no net trade. It is ironic that legalized PI would actually generate little or no actual trade, an important observation for scholars seeking to understand the phenomenon.

The basic condition under which third-degree price discrimination reduces total global welfare is that total consumption would be at least as large without segmentation, that is, under a globally uniform price.[34] Put differently, price discrimination can increase total welfare if it raises total world consumption by serving higher-elasticity consumer groups

---

[30] Price segmentation can result from many factors and can persist for considerable time periods. See Paul R. Krugman, *Pricing to Market when the Exchange Rate Changes* 15–20 (Cambridge, MA, National Bureau of Economic Research, Working Paper No. 1926, 1986).
[31] Ganslandt & Maskus, *supra* note 5, at 274.
[32] Krugman, *supra* note 30, at 16.
[33] SCHERER, *supra* note 29, at 317 regarding a simple welfare analysis and Ganslandt & Maskus, *supra* note 5, at 274–75 concerning parallel imports.
[34] Richard Schmalensee, *Output and Welfare Implications of Monopolistic Third-Degree Price Discrimination*, 71 AM. ECON. REV. 242 (1981).

and markets.[35] It should be noted that this primary result is static and does not consider any potentially negative effects of uniform pricing (under PI) on R&D and growth. Moreover, it depends on the ability of PI to equalize prices at low costs. If arbitrage wastes resources, as noted in the next section, PI can be harmful.

More broadly, price discrimination may encourage firms to open new markets in lower-income countries, which they would be willing to do if the price they command exceeds the marginal costs of supplying those locations. If they were forced to charge an equal international price it may not be worthwhile to serve such markets. Thus, in this context market segmentation may be strictly preferred to market integration through PI, because the new markets raise both consumer benefits and profits, without damaging consumers in existing markets. Note further that where there are multiple markets, and therefore multiple potential prices and entry decisions, the possibility that uniform pricing could restrain welfare is yet higher.

This complex nature of the exhaustion doctrine was captured well in a canonical model by Malueg and Schwartz.[36] They present a theory with many countries and compare three potential regimes regarding exhaustion: price discrimination (segmented markets), a uniform price (integrated markets), and a mixed situation with identical prices in subsets of markets but potential price discrimination between different groups of markets. In their model total output does not depend on the degree of price discrimination as long as all countries are served, meaning that price discrimination is only beneficial if it opens new markets. This implies that demand conditions must be quite different across countries for price discrimination to increase world welfare. They show that a mixed regime, with uniform prices within groups of markets with similar demand patterns and price differences across country groupings with dramatically different patterns, raises global economic well-being compared to either a uniform price or price discrimination across all countries. This result suggests that it could be globally optimal to have regional IPR exhaustion within groups of countries with similar demand characteristics but to permit price segmentation across groups. This insight offers support for the EU's policy of regional exhaustion, while pointing out the potential importance for similar developing countries to consider permitting PI among them, perhaps in a preferential trading arrangement.

Such observations motivated Richardson[37] to ask a fundamental question about global exhaustion policies. He set out a multiple-country model in which each country engages in Nash bargaining to maximize its own welfare, assuming the policies of other nations to remain fixed. His basic question was whether countries of the world, characterized by different demand conditions and comparative advantage in IP-sensitive goods, could jointly agree either on total market segmentation (national exhaustion in all) or globally uniform prices (international exhaustion in all). His finding was striking: neither extreme

---

[35] Hal R. Varian, *Price Discrimination and Social Welfare*, 75 AM. ECON. REV. 870 (1985); see also Marius Schwartz, *Third-Degree Price Discrimination and Output: Generalizing a Welfare Result*, 80 AM. ECON. REV. 1259 (1990).

[36] David A. Malueg & Marius Schwartz, *Parallel Imports, Demand Dispersion, and International Price Discrimination*, 37 J. INT'L ECON. 187 (1994).

[37] Martin Richardson, *An Elementary Proposition Concerning Parallel Imports*, 56 J. INT'L ECON. 233 (2002).

could be sustained as an equilibrium outcome in bargaining among disparate nations. This finding is significant for it explains why TRIPS negotiators could not agree on an international exhaustion rule. Rather, Article 6 of TRIPS leaves the choice up to each individual country or region, which is eminently sensible in economic terms.[38]

IV. CURIOUS ECONOMICS OF PARALLEL IMPORTS

The analysis to this point views PI as simple and low-cost arbitrage against international price differences. While generating important insights this approach is misleading for it assumes that originator firms simply place their goods into circulation and do not react when there is a change in the exhaustion regime, other than to set prices that differ by the trade-cost margin when PI are permitted. Surely, however, IPR-owning firms, which by definition embody market power, would adopt different distribution and pricing strategies in a situation where PI are banned compared to where they are legal. This basic observation generates considerably wider insights, sometimes counter-intuitive, about the impacts of parallel trade.

A. Profit-Increasing Parallel Imports

It seems evident that firms would gain maximal profits if they can separate markets and price according to local demand. However, this simple observation rests on the notion of third-degree price discrimination, in which there is a single price in each market because all consumers are homogeneous. In markets where consumers have heterogeneous demands, meaning different valuations for a particular good, and those consumer types can be segregated the situation changes. In these cases firms can set a menu of prices in different markets to separate consumers into types, such as those who value higher quality or want the good quickly and those who prefer lower quality or prefer to wait. Consumers sorting through this form of second-degree discrimination makes it possible for originator firms to see higher profits if international arbitrage through PI is permitted. Moreover, parallel imports actually may exist in equilibrium as they flow to where consumers have higher valuations.

Consider a simple example supporting PI that are profitable for the originator firms.[39] Suppose that in one market a firm can set a high price to a price-inelastic group, the members of which find it too costly to engage in arbitrage. It can also set a low price to a price-elastic group, which for some reason faces low arbitrage costs. The firm now has the option of opening a second market abroad at an even lower price and permitting PI between the countries. Under these circumstances it is possible for PI to increase the firm's global profits by raising price in the second (source) market while not diminishing profits derived from the high-price segment of the first market. This scenario seems consistent

---

[38] This analysis was extended to more general circumstances by Kamal Saggi, *Regional Exhaustion of Intellectual Property*, 10 INT'L J. ECON. THEORY 125 (2014).

[39] This description is adapted from the logic in Simon P. Anderson & Victor A. Ginsburg, *International Pricing with Costly Consumer Arbitrage*, 7 REV. INT'L ECON. 126 (1999).

with the common observation that pharmaceutical prices in high-income (and inelastic) private market segments are sustainable in poor countries despite the potential threat of parallel trade.[40] Many variations on this story, in which consumers in different markets may be segmented by type, are possible in theory.[41]

A completely different example of how PI can profit the originator firm was set out by Raff and Schmidt.[42] Consider a case where demand levels for a good are both unknown and different across countries, while unused inventories have little direct value to the manufacturer. In this situation, parallel trade potentially increases competition among retailers that sell the good but it also raises the expected value of inventories because they can be sold to other markets. Banning PI causes prices to fall when retailers have large stocks on hand and demand is low. This effect diminishes the retailers' willingness to purchase large volumes and can reduce the manufacturing firm's profits. However, allowing parallel trade may keep retail prices from falling sharply when demand falls, which sustains order volumes and increases the originator's profits. Logic of this kind may explain why some industries, such as automobiles, take a relatively benign attitude toward parallel trade.

B. Vertical Pricing and Distributor-Level Parallel Trade

It is natural to conceive of PI as arbitrage against retail price differences across countries. However, as noted earlier, surveys suggest that the bulk of such trade happens at the wholesale level. This is true of both consumer goods, such as fashions, cosmetics, pharmaceuticals, and automobiles, and intermediate goods, including machinery and chemicals. There are three practical reasons why parallel trade by direct consumers is small.[43] First, there are significant costs associated with finding reliable supplies and getting goods across borders, deterring small volumes. Second, there may be complementary services sold with the physical goods, such as calling plans for mobile phones, which are sacrificed through trades outside authorized channels. Third, consumer-level parallel trade may be illegal in order to protect public health. This is the case for pharmaceuticals in the EU, for example, and for alcoholic beverages in the U.S. Thus, the simple idea that manufacturers discriminate in prices among international retailers and individuals easily trade against these differences is wrong. Instead, firms sell to (often independent) wholesale distributors, which then deal with retailers. The bulk of PI entails specialized trading firms buying at the distributor level in cheap markets.

In this context, IPR owners generally wish to maintain a large degree of vertical control over its licensed distributors. In the U.S., for example, firms are permitted to establish

---

[40] KEITH E. MASKUS, PARALLEL IMPORTS IN PHARMACEUTICALS: IMPLICATIONS FOR COMPETITION AND PRICES IN DEVELOPING COUNTRIES: FINAL REPORT 28–34 (April 2001), available at www.wipo.int/export/sites/www/about-ip/en/studies/pdf/ssa_maskus_pi.pdf.

[41] The most recent example is Keith E. Maskus & Frank Staehler, *Retailers as Agents and the Limits of Parallel Trade*, 70 EUR. ECON. REV. 186 (2014). These authors analyze a case in which there is uncertainty about which consumers have high valuations and which have low valuations for a good. Firms can hire independent local retailers, which can help resolve this problem, but it is still possible for no PI to actually emerge.

[42] Horst Raff & Nicolas Schmitt, *Why Parallel Trade May Raise Producers' Profits*, 71 J. INT'L ECON. 434 (2007).

[43] Ganslandt & Maskus, *supra* note 16, at 946–47.

exclusive territories for their distributors, which can be efficient in terms of serving consumers across disparate locations.[44] European firms also often set up national or regional distributors, attempting to control trading among them through contractual terms. However, this sets up the possibility that differential wholesale prices set across markets could generate incentives for PI between them, sourced at the distributor level. One means that original firms can use to manage this problem is through vertical price control (VPC), or setting wholesale prices that can endogenously limit or deter PI.

The primary economic theory of PI and VPC was developed by Chen and Maskus.[45] In this framework, a manufacturer protected by IPR in both a home and foreign market has one independent distributor in each location. The firm needs to set its wholesale prices to induce profit-maximizing retail prices, which vary between markets according to demand conditions. If PI are legal, however, these distributors compete with each other in the higher-priced location.

This basic setup reveals several interesting tradeoffs. First, parallel trade generates more competition, reducing profits of the original firm. Second, this firm, in maximizing its profits, will choose to limit or even eliminate PI by setting a menu of wholesale prices. While these prices deal with the PI problem, they reduce overall profitability compared to the case where no PI are threatened. Thus, in VPC models parallel trade follows the usual intuition in that it reduces profitability of IPR owners. Finally, and this is an important point, parallel trade itself incurs real resource costs, which is costly in welfare terms. This latter observation might be considered yet another stylized fact: PI can be competitive but the simple act of hauling goods across borders uses up labor, capital, and other inputs, solely to arbitrage against prices.

This analysis was extended by later authors,[46] who took fuller account of the strategic effects of market power at the distributor level. They closely studied the effects of diminished PI trade costs, which could arise from greater market integration or more efficient transportation systems. Working through the various cases, they demonstrate the curious possibility that, as the costs of shipping goods fall toward zero and the volume of PI increases, the manufacturer would react by raising its wholesale price in the import market even as it reduces the wholesale price in the export market. This happens because it becomes profitable at some point to push one of the distributors out of the market by raising the price it is charged, leaving the joint region open for the remaining distributor.

This is an important finding in policy terms. It suggests that an open regime of PI, coupled with declining trade costs, could cause greater concentration of the wholesaler market while inducing retail price divergence rather than convergence. Indeed, this may be one reason for the observed failure of retail prices within the EU to move together as much as anticipated. A deeper implication is that legalized PI, in an environment where trading partners actively seek to reduce the costs of trade, can be anticompetitive in its impacts at the distributor level. In fact, this problem can be exacerbated by a well-meaning competition rule requiring that manufacturers set uniform wholesale prices across

---

[44] Ganslandt & Maskus, *supra* note 5, at 269–70.
[45] Yongmin Chen & Keith E. Maskus, *Vertical Pricing and Parallel Imports*, 14 J. INT'L TRADE & ECON. DEV. 1 (2005).
[46] Ganslandt & Maskus, *supra* note 16, at 946.

international markets, which is found in EU policy. Predictions of this kind, along with others that will emerge as this literature deepens, are ripe for empirical testing.

V. PARALLEL TRADE, R&D, AND POLICY SPILLOVERS

Static economic analysis shows that PI ordinarily reduce the profits made by an original manufacturer owning some form of protected IPR. How does this insight carry over to dynamic markets? To an important degree, expected profitability determines how much firms are willing to invest in new technologies and products. Accordingly, innovative firms would take the legal treatment of PI into account in determining their R&D programs.

One of the primary arguments against legalizing parallel trade is that it would diminish investments in new technologies. This claim is prominent in the U.S. debate over whether to legalize PI (called "re-imports") of pharmaceuticals from Canada and Western Europe.[47] Research-based pharmaceutical firms have lobbied successfully to defeat such legislation or its implementation. More generally, originator firms in any IPR-based industry tend to oppose the opening of markets to PI.[48] For example, major music publishers strongly opposed the liberalization of import barriers in Australia in 1998, though they lost that battle.[49]

Despite its importance, the theoretical economics literature on this point is limited and empirical analysis is absent. A few insights are worth highlighting, however, including the strong linkages among price controls, R&D, and parallel trade, especially in pharmaceutical products.

A. Models of R&D and Parallel Trade

Li and Maskus[50] published the first theoretical model linking PI to investments in R&D in the vertical control model described above, adding an R&D stage prior to the competition between distributors. Thus, in a first stage the manufacturer decides how much to invest in a technology that, if successful, will reduce its marginal production costs. Depending on the amount of R&D, the firm chooses its vertical price structure either on the basis of a high marginal cost or a low marginal cost. The differences in these costs and prices determine the volume and impacts of PI. Their basic conclusion is that PI would reduce final-stage profits of the manufacturer, leading it to invest less initially. However, the extent of this impact on R&D depends on numerous factors, including the transportation cost in parallel trade. Thus, legalizing PI does not necessarily reduce economic welfare even though it diminishes the equilibrium expenditures on innovation. Indeed, it can raise

---

[47] MASKUS, PRIVATE RIGHTS, *supra* note 11, at 183–85.
[48] Claude E. Barfield & Mark A. Groombridge, *The Economic Case for Copyright Owner Control over Parallel Imports*, J. WORLD INTELLECTUAL PROPERTY 1, 903 (1998).
[49] MASKUS, GLOBAL ECONOMY, *supra* note 10, at 211.
[50] Changying Li & Keith E. Maskus, *The Impact of Parallel Imports on Investments in Cost-Reducing Research and Development*, 68 J. INT'L ECON. 443 (2006).

well-being if trade costs are small. At larger transport costs, however, the combination of resources used up in parallel trade and diminished R&D reduces welfare.[51]

In a different theoretical framework, Valletti[52] showed in a basic arbitrage model with a single monopolist and segmented markets that a policy mandating a uniform international price, such as a rule for global exhaustion of intellectual property rights, increases welfare *ex post* but may reduce *ex ante* investment in quality-enhancing R&D. More specifically, suppose differential pricing is based on variations in demand characteristics, meaning that some consumers in high-price markets go unserved. In this model the uniform price from unimpeded PI ultimately raises static welfare but reduces prior innovative investments due to diminished profitability. Whether overall welfare, in the *ex ante* expected sense, rises or falls when costless PI are permitted, depends on market parameters. In a related paper a similar model is used to illustrate a welfare tradeoff in which international exhaustion and uniform pricing can raise static welfare but reduce investments in product quality.[53] Overall, then, while parallel trade tends to diminish incentives for R&D, the full impacts cannot be readily characterized. On these grounds I hesitate to predict that exhaustion policies have an identifiable causal impact on economic growth.

B. Price Controls and Parallel Trade

I noted earlier the obvious point that government price controls in different countries can generate parallel imports. Things could go both ways, of course, for PI in turn could impact the ability to sustain these regulated pricing regimes. Consider, for example, the fact that in the EU each country has full authority over its public health policy, including choosing price regulations in pharmaceuticals that vary markedly across Member States.[54] Some countries, generally in lower-income southern Europe, set price ceilings that are substantially lower than prices in higher-income northern Europe. Despite this sovereignty in health policy, EU law is committed to permitting free circulation of goods as part of the Single Market. In consequence, parallel trading firms respond to these price differences and medicines move from countries with lower regulated prices, such as Spain, Portugal, Italy, and Greece, to markets with laxer regulations, such as the United Kingdom (U.K.), Netherlands, Germany, Sweden, and Denmark. It is reasonable to claim that the great bulk of PI in pharmaceuticals within the EU stem from such differences in policy.

On its face this remarkable juxtaposition of national sovereignty in health policy and the inability of governments to regulate PI seems inconsistent. If parallel imports withdraw supplies of medicines from highly regulated economies toward less regulated markets they should reduce the price gaps between markets. This would frustrate the

---

[51] Similar results were found for product-improving innovation in Changying Li & John Robles, *Product Innovation and Parallel Trade*, 25 INT'L J. INDUS. ORG. 417 (2007).
[52] Tommaso M. Valletti, *Differential Pricing, Parallel Trade, and the Incentive to Invest*, 70 J. INT'L ECON. 314 (2006).
[53] Tommaso M. Valletti & Stefan Szymanski, *Parallel Trade, International Exhaustion and Intellectual Property Rights: A Welfare Analysis*, 54 J. INDUS. ECON. 499 (2006).
[54] Ganslandt & Maskus, *supra* note 22, at 1036; see also KANAVOS ET AL., *supra* note 26, at 26–27.

intentions of the regulations in source countries and push economies toward policy harmonization.[55] Further, shifting from a regime of no PI to legalized trade would change incentives for innovative firms to undertake R&D in pharmaceuticals. Indeed, the presence of rigorous price regulations is sometimes blamed for declining investments in medical R&D in Europe relative to the U.S. in recent decades, a factor that should be exacerbated by unrestricted PI.[56] Thus, PI in markets subject to price regulations could have markedly different effects than arbitrage in cases where the IPR-owning firm can adjust prices without worrying about price limits.

Once again, however, general conclusions are elusive, even in theory. Regarding the pricing issue, there is little evidence in the EU that PI has the effect of reducing international price differences, which remain large in pharmaceuticals. As noted above, studies suggest that, despite the elastic responses of PI to price differentials, the primary effects are to afford significant price-cost markups for parallel traders within the EU. In turn, there is little effective pressure on governments to change their regulatory systems, which are markedly stable. The reasons for this insensitivity are straightforward.[57] First, price regulations in higher-price countries tend to stabilize retail and pharmacy prices, meaning they do not necessarily fall in the presence of PI. Second, PI volumes are rarely sufficient to place real pressure on price controls. Third, firms are permitted under EU law to set contractual limits on supplies sent to their distributors in various markets, so long as they do not explicitly aim to restrict PI. Combined with differential packaging and a natural tendency for patients and pharmacists to consider PI goods to be of lower quality, this permits sustainable brand-name pricing.

The issue of PI and R&D investments in the context of pharmaceutical price regulation has attracted attention among economists. The simplest analyses accord with intuition: international exhaustion should reduce incentives for R&D in the face of rigorous price controls. For example, in a horizontal arbitrage model Rey[58] takes government policy as given and shows that parallel trade should cause retail prices in unregulated markets to fall and thereby reduce the global incentives to invest in R&D. Similarly, Danzon[59] argues forcefully that permitting PI, at least among advanced economies, is unwise in a dynamic sense. In her view, international price discrimination is beneficial in that it reflects differences in elasticity of demand, making it an efficient means of allocating the costs of R&D among markets.[60] Such discrimination, supported by market segmentation, is

---

[55] This possibility explains the considerable concern on behalf of Canadian public health authorities whenever the U.S. contemplates removing its restrictions on re-imports; see MASKUS, PRIVATE RIGHTS, *supra* note 11, at 183–85.

[56] Joseph H. Golec & John A. Vernon, *European Pharmaceutical Price Regulation, Firm Profitability and R&D Spending* 3, NATIONAL BUREAU OF ECONOMIC RESEARCH, WORKING PAPER No. 12676 (2006).

[57] MASKUS, PRIVATE RIGHTS, *supra* note 11, at 179–82.

[58] Patrick Rey, The Impact of Parallel Imports on Prescription Medicines 10 (manuscript on file with the University of Toulouse, 2003), available at http://citeseerx.ist.psu.edu/viewdoc/download?doi=10.1.1.493.1937&rep=rep1&type=pdf.

[59] Patricia M. Danzon, *The Economics of Parallel Trade*, 13 PHARMACOECONOMICS 293 (1998).

[60] Here she refers to market segmentation as supporting "Ramsey pricing," which means permitting differential pricing across users of the services of a public good as the most efficient means of financing its development. This interpretation is problematic for many reasons.

therefore globally optimal from a social point of view. Such thinking militates against international exhaustion, at least where R&D costs are high and the innovative products of research bear global welfare spillovers. However, Danzon's analysis is limited in that it fails to consider that price differences in medicines are generally associated with price regulations, not profit-maximizing price setting by pharmaceutical companies. In this decidedly second-best world of multiple distortions and policies, defining optimality is rarely that straightforward.

The most rigorous theoretical analysis of these tradeoffs is found in Grossman and Lai.[61] These authors develop a two-country (or region) North-South model in which the South government chooses its optimal price-control policy, given the prior choice by the North government of an exhaustion regime.[62] This is the first paper in economics to recognize explicitly that price controls and world exhaustion regimes are jointly determined, given fundamental welfare tradeoffs. They show that the North's choice of PI regime can change the South's government policy equilibrium through its induced impacts on innovation. Suppose that innovation of new medicines occurs solely in the North but these products are consumed in both locations. The South faces a basic tradeoff: by relaxing its price controls this country gains from access to new products but suffers higher consumer welfare costs from higher prices on patented goods already in the market. This tradeoff is altered by a shift in the North's exhaustion policy. When the North chooses to permit PI, it becomes the potential destination of parallel exports of local supplies from the South. Because this reduces profits of the Northern pharmaceutical firms they may choose not to serve the South at all if prices in that market are capped below certain threshold levels. This lack of access is detrimental to the South, so its government reacts by relaxing its price controls, which in turn raises profits of the Northern firms. Under some market parameters it is possible for this profit gain to be larger than the costs of competition from PI.

In this way parallel trade weakens the incentives of lower-income economies to impose the aggressive price regulations that would maximize static consumer welfare in the absence of such trade. In turn, a low price cap in one country reduces incentives for R&D investment worldwide, which is harmful for future consumers even in the low-price countries. Arbitrage through PI thus makes government policies interdependent and forces every government to consider the consequences of its price regulation on global incentives to invest in new products. In their model this effect can be so important that permission of PI reduces free riding (that is, the ability of low-priced nations to benefit from research abroad) and ultimately strengthens the incentives for innovation. In equilibrium, global investment in research increases. The authors conclude that legalized parallel trade is actually pro-innovation, rather than a factor that restrains R&D in controlled goods.

There are other mechanisms under which exhaustion policies interact with other IPR

---

[61] Gene M. Grossman & Edwin L.-C. Lai, *Parallel Imports and Price Controls*, 39 RAND J. ECON. 378 (2008).

[62] This paper is an extension of the seminal theory in Gene M. Grossman & Edwin L.-C. Lai, *International Protection of Intellectual Property*, 94 AM. ECON. REV. 1635 (2004). In that model the North and South non-cooperatively choose optimal patent lengths, which depend on their innovative capacities, market sizes, and demand patterns.

standards and generate international policy spillovers.[63] One important question is the degree to which exhaustion policies affect the strength of IPRs themselves. Consider a situation in which the South must decide whether or not to provide patents, depending on the exhaustion regime of the North.[64] If it does not protect patents the South permits local imitation of the North's good, but this is likely to be a low-quality version. If the South has stronger preferences for the original, higher-quality version, it may have to offer patent protection in order to get the firm to provide it in their market. But its willingness to do so depends on the North's exhaustion regime. If there is free PI into the North the degree of patent protection in the South would have to be correspondingly larger to induce entry of new goods. Again, we see that the WTO-provided flexibility of Northern governments to choose an exhaustion regime, while sensible on many grounds, is not innocent when it comes to inducing patent law changes around the world.

As in the case of vertical price control models of PI, the literature on arbitrage, dynamic innovation incentives, and policy interdependence is in its infancy. Considerably more research could be devoted to fleshing out relevant market characteristics that would affect the returns to R&D under parallel trade and how responsive IPR policies are to shifts in exhaustion regimes (and trade policy more generally). This analysis is important to sort out the likely relationships among IPR, competition and price regulation, parallel trade, and innovation policies. This research agenda remains important despite the absence to date of sound empirical evidence that PI in fact has such impacts. Indeed, one of the most pressing unanswered questions in the literature on parallel trade is its role in encouraging or discouraging innovation. While this project would pose formidable issues to resolve in terms of identifying the relevant effects, it is well worth pursuing.

VI. CONCLUSION

The exhaustion doctrine is a legal construct with complex implications, as noted in the other contributions to this volume. As a matter of economics, it may be construed simply in its essence as a regulatory decision regarding whether to keep a market open or closed to parallel imports. Countries with a strong comparative advantage in innovation and creation, such as the U.S. and the European Union as a whole, tend to see national exhaustion as an important component of an IPR owner's right to control distribution across borders for the duration of her protection. Other countries tend to view openness to PI as an important means of sustaining competition and access to goods.

This chapter has reviewed the primary outcomes of economic theory analyzing PI as a form of international commodity arbitrage. At its simplest level PI imposes, in principle, considerable discipline on the ability of firms to separate markets and establish differential prices. Whether this outcome is globally and nationally beneficial or harmful depends on various features of market size, demand, and production capacity. Even in its most

---

[63] A fuller description and analysis may be found in Kamal Saggi, *Trade, Intellectual Property Rights and the WTO*, in HANDBOOK OF COMMERCIAL POLICY (K. Bagwell & R. Staiger eds., 2016).
[64] This model is due to Kamal Saggi, *Market Power in the Global Economy: The Exhaustion and Protection of Intellectual Property*, 123 ECONOMIC J. 131 (2013).

elemental form, the welfare effects of parallel trade are ambiguous. When additional complications arising from market power and the ability to set strategic prices to limit or deter PI are added to this mix the story becomes yet more involved. In theory, moving from national to international exhaustion could be procompetitive in its price effects or anticompetitive in its impacts on distributor margins and concentration. This policy change could reduce profits and R&D incentives, thereby diminishing prospects for innovation and growth. Perhaps surprisingly, it could actually raise R&D incentives under important circumstances, by placing pressure on countries to relax their price controls in key commodities in order to sustain access to goods. These complexities and ambiguities arise everywhere in the analysis of parallel trade, itself a new scholarly endeavor with much more to learn. This is why one keen observer refers to the economics of exhaustion as a "jungle," with little in the way of clear lessons though much to think about for scholars and policy-makers.[65]

In making this review I have left aside some important questions that embody broader policy elements than IPR exhaustion but are clearly related to this issue. Two questions in particular should be mentioned, which have received only the briefest of treatments here. First, some analysts argue that, at least in the area of ensuring access to essential medicines, a global policy of national exhaustion (or perhaps regional exhaustion with a limited geographical scope) would be beneficial.[66] The notion is that strict market segmentation would induce pharmaceutical originators to engage naturally in tiered pricing, with extensive discounts for poor countries. This might be of particular utility in so-called "Type 2" diseases, such as heart ailments and cancer, which are prevalent in both rich and poor nations. A companion suggestion would be for wealthier governments to abandon their linkage of price controls to "reference pricing" in which domestic price ceilings depend partially on the lowest prices found elsewhere, including in developing countries. This policy is thought to discourage firms from charging low prices in the latter markets for fear of cannibalizing their price negotiations in larger and more lucrative locations. Our evidentiary basis to assess such claims is limited.

A second related area is the extent to which exhaustion policies, perhaps in conjunction with pricing regulations, affect decisions of firms to delay the launches of new products in various markets or alter their R&D incentives in particular goods. Available evidence indicates that such impacts could be significant, raising consequent concerns about the ultimate impacts of parallel trade on public health status.[67] Again, however, far more research is called for.

There are two central lessons to be drawn from this review. First, there are numerous complex and diverse potential impacts of exhaustion policies and PI, which could in principle be of considerable importance for the global economy. This situation argues for far more close empirical work, tied to economic theory, in order to sort out just which

---

[65] Fink, *supra* note 3, at 174.
[66] Various arguments are reviewed in detail in MASKUS, PRIVATE RIGHTS, *supra* note 11, at 263–65, including a critical discussion of the empirical basis for this claim.
[67] Regarding price controls see Margaret K. Kyle, *Pharmaceutical Price Controls and Entry Strategies*, 89 REV. ECON. & STAT. 88 (2007). The same issue is considered in the context of PI in Margaret K. Kyle, *Strategic Responses to Parallel Trade*, 11 B.E.J. ECON. ANALYSIS & POL'Y, 20–25 (2011).

factors are important and how responsive market forces and government policies are to parallel trade. The unfortunate implication arises from the second lesson. The extreme scarcity of solid data on parallel trade places considerable limits on our abilities to answer such basic questions. Thus, it seems important to conclude the chapter by appealing to authorities and international organizations to devote more effort to collecting such databases, at least in sectors of considerable importance for public policy, and making them available for research.

7. Working toward international harmony on intellectual property exhaustion (and substantive law)
*Vincent Chiappetta**

I. INTRODUCTION

The Agreement on Trade-Related Aspects of Intellectual Property Rights (TRIPS)[1] was an important watershed in the international law of intellectual property rights (IPRs). It moved the effort to harmonize transnational intellectual property (IP) beyond regime specific agendas to setting standards governing all IPRs. It also created a unique dispute resolution process for addressing complaints regarding member nations' non-compliance and, by connecting it to the World Trade Organization (WTO), explicitly tied IP law to international trade. Although the parties reached agreement regarding a wide array of significant substantive points, one issue proved intractable. They could not reach consensus regarding IPR exhaustion—how an IPR owner putting goods into one WTO member's domestic market would affect its parallel IPRs in other WTO nations. That point might seem a mere matter of detail in the context of such an overwhelmingly successful negotiation. However, examining the reasons behind the failure to agree on exhaustion explains not only why the issue remains so divisive, but also why the domestic implementation of TRIPS has proven so problematic. More importantly, that understanding provides a way forward regarding both exhaustion and harmonization.

II. CONTEXT

A. Definitions

In a topic fraught with complexity, starting with a few definitions helps avoid the further distraction of semantic confusion. An IPR owner generally has the right to make and distribute or authorize others to make or distribute physical goods that incorporate the IPR in question and to prevent others from doing the same. The "exhaustion doctrine" applies when goods incorporating the IPR are put into the marketplace by or with the authorization of the IPR owner (the alternative label, the "first sale doctrine," specifically refers to that triggering event). Despite its comprehensive connotation, exhaustion does

---

[*] Professor of Law, Willamette University College of Law.
[1] Agreement on Trade-Related Aspects of Intellectual Property Rights, April 15, 1994; Marrakesh Agreement Establishing the World Trade Organization, Annex 1C, 1869 U.N.T.S. 299 [hereinafter TRIPS].

not entirely eliminate the IPR owner's legal rights. It only prohibits the owner from using the IPR to prevent the initial acquirer and any subsequent owners of authorized goods from transferring them to others or repairing them during their useful life. The IPR owner retains the right to prevent anyone, including owners of authorized goods, from making or distributing additional goods incorporating the IPR or from reconstructing authorized goods to extend their useful life.

"National exhaustion" means a country's IP regime contains a statutory or judicial rule that only applies the exhaustion doctrine to authorized goods initially distributed in its domestic market, not those first distributed outside its borders. A "regional exhaustion" rule applies exhaustion to goods initially placed on the market in any one of a specific group of countries, usually those belonging to a geographic, treaty-based trading group such as the European Union (EU). A country whose IP law incorporates that rule allows the resale of authorized goods initially put into any regional group member's market free of domestic IPR interference, but not those first distributed elsewhere. Finally, a rule of "international exhaustion" allows all authorized goods to be freely resold in the nation's domestic market regardless of where they were first put on the market.

B. Transnational IPRs and Exhaustion Under and After TRIPS

A brief look at the structure and operation of TRIPS provides similarly helpful common ground. The bulk of the TRIPS provisions establish agreed minimum standards regarding IPR protection under the four core IPR regimes: patents, copyrights (and related rights), trademarks, and undisclosed information (trade secrets). One group of standards sets out the requirements governing substantive issues, such as qualifying subject matter, legal rights and permissible exceptions, and the minimum duration of protection. Others address the remedies and procedures that must be made available to IPR owners seeking to enforce their legal rights.

Two points about TRIPS have particular relevance to this discussion. First, the TRIPS mandated rights, remedies, and procedures are designed to foster the economically efficient operation of the overall global marketplace, thus maximizing its aggregate output in those terms. They are indifferent to, much less promote, other normative values (specific distributional outcomes, individual natural rights) or social policy priorities (domestic economic development, other cultural or political norms). Recognizing that many developing countries did not yet have market-based economies or a related efficiency-driven IPR system, the "least developed countries" (LDCs) were given until 2005 to fully comply.

Second, TRIPS did not create supra-national rights enforced by new international institutions. Instead, it requires each WTO member to enact legislation incorporating the mandated standards into its domestic IP laws and enforce the resulting rights within its jurisdiction.[2] The transnational legal ramifications of this approach were recently given a thorough airing by the United States (U.S.) Supreme Court in *Kirtsaeng v. John Wiley &*

---

[2] To be effective, a mechanism to ensure national implementation must exist. As noted in the introduction, TRIPS specifically includes such a procedure, with art. 64 making non-compliance subject to the WTO dispute settlement procedures.

Sons,[3] which addressed whether the exhaustion doctrine applied to goods made and first sold elsewhere and then imported into and resold in the U.S. The majority found that the language of the U.S. Copyright Act, which applies exhaustion to copies "lawfully made under [the Act],"[4] covered goods manufactured and first distributed outside the U.S. (a rule of international exhaustion). It reasoned that as IP rights are determined under national law, U.S. copyright law determines the domestic rights of copyright owners regarding any goods that ultimately come within its jurisdiction, regardless of where they were manufactured. As such, U.S. copyright law applies to every good from the moment of its creation, and in that sense every good is "made under" U.S. copyright law.[5]

The dissent interpreted the national nature of IP law very differently. It pointed out that jurisdictional limitation means U.S. copyright law does not and cannot prevent any non-domestic manufacture of goods, even if they would otherwise be infringing. The legality of that activity is determined exclusively by reference to the copyright law of the jurisdiction of manufacture. That means foreign manufactured goods are most logically legally (and semantically) viewed as "made under" the copyright law of the nation in which they are created.

Taken together, the *Kirtsaeng* majority and dissent identify an important practical consequence of the TRIPS reliance on national implementation. In order to obtain transnational IPR protection, those engaged in international commerce must own a portfolio of individual national IPRs on the same subject matter—one for each jurisdiction in which it wishes to enforce the right. For example, a pharmaceutical company doing business in the U.S., Germany, and China must obtain separate domestic patents on its drug innovations in each of those jurisdictions. To challenge a particular activity it must assert the patent held in the jurisdiction where it is occurring. If the troublesome activity involves the sale of a product in China, only the company's rights under the Chinese patent apply. Similarly, if the activity is the sale of a product in the U.S. or Germany, the only recourse is through its U.S. or German patent, respectively.

The national implementation-portfolio situation explains why the TRIPS negotiators needed to address IPR exhaustion. Absent a treaty obligation, each nation unilaterally decides whether and if so how it chooses to apply exhaustion to the goods that come within its jurisdiction. For example, assume a copyright owner has obtained domestic copyrights in Brazil, the U.S., and Japan. It makes and sells a product in Brazil, which the purchaser then seeks to resell in the U.S. If the copyright owner wishes to challenge that resale it must look to its rights under its U.S. copyright. The *Kirtsaeng* decision held that the U.S. Copyright Act applies international exhaustion. That rule prevents the copyright owner from asserting its U.S. copyright against the resale of authorized goods in the U.S. despite their having been made and first sold elsewhere, in this case under the owner's Brazilian copyright. But as the *Kirtsaeng* dissent points out, that domestic rule has no effect regarding activities occurring in other countries. So Japan could limit its copyright law to national exhaustion, thus allowing the owner to use its Japanese copyright to

---

[3] Kirtsaeng v. John Wiley & Sons, Inc., 133 S. Ct. 1351 (2013).
[4] 17 U.S.C. § 109(a).
[5] As John Wiley & Sons had authorized the making of the goods in question, the "lawfulness" of their manufacture was not in issue.

prevent the resale of the same, authorized Brazilian made goods in Japan. To create a uniform transnational rule regarding exhaustion, every country must agree to adopt the same approach in their domestic IP law.

In response to that reality, the developed nations, including notably the U.S., proposed a TRIPS provision that would have prevented any WTO member from adopting a rule of international exhaustion (referred to below as "international non-exhaustion"). Under that rule, the authorized first sale of a good embodying a domestic IPR owned in one WTO member would not affect the owner's rights under its corresponding national IPRs in any other member. As a result anyone holding a portfolio of parallel national IPRs who puts products onto one WTO member's market could prevent their resale in any other member's market in which it owned a corresponding national IPR.

The proposal was vigorously resisted, most particularly by the developing nations. The final outcome is found in Article 6 of TRIPS, which reads in relevant part: "nothing in this Agreement shall be used to address the issue of the exhaustion of intellectual property rights." That agreement to disagree left each WTO member free not to apply the doctrine at all or, if it wished to do so, to apply it nationally, regionally, or internationally.

The TRIPS negotiators' failure to agree on IPR exhaustion had the outward appearance of a minor detail that could be followed-up at a later time. The next step should have been to move on to the members' domestic implementation of the otherwise highly successful accord. That is not what happened. A number of developing countries, most particularly the LDCs, have failed to comply and, to date, the original 2005 grace-period deadline has been extended three times. The first was under the 2001 Doha Ministerial Declaration on TRIPS and the Public Health, formally adopted by the TRIPS Council in 2002, which extended the deadline in regard to pharmaceuticals until 2016.[6] The second, adopted by the Council in 2005, extended the general deadline until July 2013.[7] In June 2013, that date was pushed back to July 2021 or such earlier date as the member ceases to be an LDC.

The latest extension is unlikely to resolve the matter. The final Article of the June 2013 Council Decision expressly notes it is without prejudice to the LDCs' right to seek further extensions. Even more revealing is why the extension was granted. The WTO expressly acknowledges the root cause of the delay is not the demands of technical implementation, but the TRIPS standards themselves. More specifically, for real progress to occur, "cooperation should aim for more than simply translating TRIPS provisions into national law—an overarching theme concerns how best to tailor and apply IP mechanisms judiciously to serve the development objectives, policy priorities and domestic situation of individual LDCs."[8]

The post-TRIPS experience makes it apparent that far from being a "done deal" on international IPR harmonization, the agreement was only an initial step in a much more complicated undertaking. For those who considered the matter when the accord was finalized in 1996, the failure to reach consensus on exhaustion was an obvious harbinger of

---

[6] World Trade Organization, Ministerial Declaration of November 14, 2001, WTO Doc. WT/MIN(01)/DEC/2 [hereinafter Doha Ministerial 2001].

[7] See World Trade Organization, Responding to least developed countries' special needs in intellectual property, available at www.wto.org/english/tratop_e/trips_e/ldc_e.htm.

[8] See *ibid.*

future difficulties. Rather than an isolated detail, it represented the developing countries' "last stand" resistance to IPR standards they were unprepared to adopt for the very reasons the WTO has now officially recognized some twenty years later—they do not serve their domestic "development objectives, policy priorities [or] domestic situations."

The following discussion identifies why agreement on exhaustion proved so elusive, explains how those same issues provide important insights regarding the reasons driving the current delays in implementing the TRIPS IPR standards, and, finally, what can be done to address and progress these two interrelated issues.

III. THE DISTRIBUTIONAL PROBLEM

A. Exhaustion

The exhaustion issue arose in the domestic IP context well before its appearance on the international stage. IPRs are commonly justified based on their ability to improve efficient market operation. For example, patent law grants an individual the legal right to prevent others' use of the claimed invention thus ensuring capture of all related market returns. That capture, in turn, provides an incentive to invest in innovation, mitigating the underinvestment otherwise caused by free riding. For such a regime to produce a net efficiency gain, however, the costs of the exclusionary right's interference with competition must not overwhelm the benefits of increased innovation. In patent law that is avoided (in part) by requiring novelty/non-obviousness to ensure the regime produces a social benefit and limiting the right to a fixed term, after which the invention becomes available for general use, to mitigate costs.

The exhaustion doctrine reflects a refinement of that benefit–cost optimization.[9] Patent law again provides a good illustration. When a patent owner sells a good incorporating the invention, his willingness to complete the transaction indicates he accepts the price paid as the appropriate patent return with regard to the particular good. As the regime has thus fulfilled its incentive "capture" function, permitting use of the patent to constrain post-sale (re)distribution of that good would create unjustified social costs. Exhaustion eliminates those costs by preventing the owner's assertion of the patent to block the good's transfer to others. The "one payment" rationale also explains why the doctrine does not fully exhaust the patent owner's rights. As the original sale price only covers the value of the patent in connection with the particular authorized good, the regime's incentive objective requires that the patent owner retains the right to prevent even owners of authorized goods from making additional goods incorporating the patent.

The exhaustion rationale has been refined over time to more specifically reflect the patent regime's objective of maximally improving the net (benefit–cost) efficient market outcome. Most relevant to the present discussion, the purchaser's right to transfer authorized goods allows a secondary market to develop which competitively constrains the IPR owner's pricing of new goods. In particular, because that secondary market is

---

[9] See generally, Vincent Chiappetta, *Patent Exhaustion: What's It Good For?*, 51 SANTA CLARA L. REV. 1087 (2011).

available to all users, it limits an IPR owner's ability to segment markets and charge different prices to capture varying demand among users. The inability to price discriminate reduces the market price to the marginal cost of production, helps output to rise to meet actual demand, and increases overall consumer surplus. In addition, the secondary market increases allocative efficiency, allowing existing goods to flow to higher uses in response to changed circumstances and avoids the disposal waste that would otherwise occur when an initial purchaser has no further use for a good still having remaining useful life. Finally, by eliminating the need for subsequent purchasers to determine whether IPR restrictions "run with the good," the doctrine reduces confirmation transaction costs, facilitating the efficient operation of the secondary market.

For nations adopting the efficient market as their domestic economic model, these arguments provide a powerful case for adopting a rule of national IPR exhaustion. As the decision to adopt an IP regime is justified by the related improvements in the efficient operation of that market, the exhaustion doctrine's further optimization of the related benefits and costs makes it a logical limitation on an IPR owner's rights.

Another consideration, however, must be taken into account when a nation decides to adopt efficiency-based IPRs and the related exhaustion doctrine. Although an efficient market maximizes aggregate domestic economic output, its operation is indifferent to distributive outcomes beyond those produced by the competitive ability to pay. That market dynamic creates widely varying access to resources among the society's members. IP law exacerbates this effect, with IPR owners' legal rights enabling them to demand significant transfers from would-be consumers, putting the related goods out of many individuals' economic reach. That can produce social dissatisfaction and even unrest. Within a single country the issue can be addressed through redistribution. As domestic economic activity occurs within the nation's jurisdictional reach, virtually all the resulting outputs remain available to make mitigating adjustments. Most commonly those take the form of taxes generating the public resources necessary to provide for citizens who fall below acceptable access thresholds. This intra-community ability to adjust makes it politically possible to enact market efficiency-based IP laws despite the system's distribution consequences. For example, health-related IPRs can be justified by the combination of the incentive to their creation and the mitigation of distributional concerns through tax-subsidized access to essential pharmaceuticals, devices, or diagnostic testing.

The logic of this combination has not been lost on countries using the market model and has led to their adoption of efficiency-based IP regimes including a rule of national exhaustion. The paradigmatic example is the U.S., but almost every nation with a developed market economy has such a system. However, when those nations sought to transplant the market-efficiency IP law paradigm into the global market context during the TRIPS negotiation the developing nations balked, with resistance coming to a head regarding IPR exhaustion.

Examination of the developed nations' position in the exhaustion debate provides the explanation for the developing nations' reaction.[10] The developed countries forcefully

---

[10] See generally Vincent Chiappetta, *The Desirability of Agreeing to Disagree: The WTO, TRIPS, International IPR Exhaustion and a Few Other Things*, 21 MICH. J. INT'L L. 333, 370–74 (2000).

argued the aggregate economic performance virtues of efficiency-based international IPR harmonization. For the reasons outlined above, those arguments also logically supported a rule of international exhaustion. Treating the first sale of an authorized good in any WTO member as exhausting the IPR owner's entire portfolio of parallel national rights with regard to that good allows cross-border market competition to develop, reduces prices, increases output, and maximizes access throughout the global economy. But, oddly, the developed nations instead vigorously advocated for a rule of international non-exhaustion.

The explanation is found by examining how transplanting the efficient-market IPR paradigm into the global context affects a particular country. In both the national and global markets the approach maximizes aggregate economic output. But as explained above, within a single nation the vast majority of its economic outputs are then available to mitigate any undesirable distributional consequences. That is not true in the international context. In the global market, each nation acts as an autonomous competitor and its success and distributional share, is determined by its relative ability to capture economic returns. However, the absence of effective international redistributional mechanisms makes any adjustment to account for shortfalls highly unlikely. Consequently, the argument that exhaustion maximizes aggregate global economic output is not convincing. A nation is far more interested in determining which rule allows it to capture the largest absolute amount of that aggregate output. In more colloquial terms, nations acting as self-interested competitors in the global marketplace are not focused on which rule will produce the largest overall pie, they want the rule that gives them the biggest individual serving.

The above analysis explains the developed nations' insistence on a TRIPS provision calling for a standard of international non-exhaustion despite its obvious inconsistency with their advocacy of the efficient market IPR paradigm. Under that rule the sale of IPR-based goods in one WTO member has no effect on the IPR owner's ability to exercise its parallel IPRs held in other members. The owner would thus be able to use those IPRs to prevent the resale of such goods in any other country in which it holds such rights. As a result IPR owners can isolate individual national markets by preventing the development of a secondary import market. That, in turn, permits profit maximizing price discrimination because leakage from lower priced national markets cannot undermine its returns from higher priced markets. The IPR owners' augmented returns, of course, come at the expense of those in the higher priced markets, who pay more to purchase IPR-based goods.

A nation's position on exhaustion, therefore, depends on how it fares on net. When the increased returns from a country's IPR owners' market segmentation-price discrimination exceeds the increased domestic cost of acquiring goods based on IPRs that are owned by citizens of other nations (for ease of reference, a "net IPR-producer"), its economy will receive a greater absolute share of the global market IPR returns under a rule of international non-exhaustion. Conversely, a country whose citizens own relatively small IPR portfolios and are heavy domestic consumers of foreign IPR-based goods will be a "net IPR-consumer." Such nations will strongly prefer the secondary import market competition created by a rule of international exhaustion.

This distinction explains the developed nations' change of heart regarding exhaustion. As they have the mature market economies and established innovation-base that create high levels of domestic price competition and IPR ownership, they are generally net IPR-producers. Because they benefit distributionally from international non-exhaustion, they will prefer that rule despite its negative effect on overall global output. It also explains the developing nations' resistance. Their nascent economies and innovation bases make them net IPR-consumers. As such, they not only fail to garner the domestic IPR-based inflows under a rule of international non-exhaustion but also to bear its transfer costs.

The distribution-based, developed country versus developing country alignment was clearly visible in the exhaustion debate in TRIPS, but it can also be seen in the post-TRIPS domestic decisions on the issue. Developing nations overwhelmingly favor international exhaustion and developed nations generally continue to hold out for international non-exhaustion.[11] However, the most convincing empirical evidence of the net IPR-producer versus net IPR-consumer explanation is found by looking at the exceptions: developing nations that have adopted a rule of international non-exhaustion and countries with highly developed market economies and robust innovation infrastructure that have nonetheless favored international exhaustion.

Developing nations have generally adopted a rule of international non-exhaustion in two instances, both of which produce a net positive domestic "share" outcome despite their net IPR-consuming status. Most frequently, a developing country adopts the rule in exchange for compensating preferential domestic industry access to a developed nation's market or other economic benefits granted in a bilateral trade arrangement.[12] In other instances the rule is used to encourage foreign IPR owners to serve its domestic market by preventing domestic revenue-reducing import competition from other lower-priced markets. Not only does that approach increase availability for domestic consumers (albeit at a higher price), it also generates inbound economic investment and technology transfer which help build a domestic industrial base.

The apparently anomalous behavior of a developed nation adopting a rule of international exhaustion is similarly explained by facts that affect its distributional situation. Some developed countries have high-priced domestic markets coupled with relatively low domestic IPR ownership making them a net IPR-consumer. Even when that is not the case, domestic consumer dissatisfaction with high prices can be a powerful political motivator. Either situation tips the domestic scales in favor of allowing international exhaustion-based competitive parallel imports from lower-priced markets.

These situations are visible in Japan, Germany, Finland, and Norway (pre-EU), which

---

[11] See Patent Related Flexibilities in the Multilateral Legal Framework and their Legislative Implementation at the National and Regional Levels, CDIP/5/4 Rev., Annex II, Categories of Different Positions on Specific Flexibilities, (2) Patent Exhaustion, available at www.wipo.int/edocs/mdocs/mdocs/en/cdip_5/cdip_5_4-annex2.pdf and WIPO, Report of the Standing Committee on the Law of Patents, Twenty-First Session, Geneva, November 3–7, 2014, Exceptions and Limitations to Patent Rights: Exhaustion of Patent Rights, available at www.wipo.int/edocs/mdocs/scp/en/scp_21/scp_21_7.pdf [hereinafter WIPO Report]. The same division is also apparent in the Trans-Pacific Partnership Agreement [hereinafter TPP], with the developing countries proposing the treaty encourage countries to adopt the international exhaustion position and the developed countries against that position. For the latest (leaked) version of the TPP, see https://wikileaks.org/tpp/#QQA12.

[12] The use of this approach in bilateral and regional treaties is discussed *infra* notes 22–23 and accompanying text.

favor international exhaustion. The best illustration, however, is the reaction of the U.S. when faced with the adverse domestic market effects of its favored non-exhaustion position. The first situation involved an unusual domestic market situation. The U.S. generally finds itself in the non-exhaustion sweet-spot of having many IPR owners engaged in international commerce and a highly competitive, low-priced domestic IPR-based goods market. But that is not true for pharmaceuticals. Unlike many countries, the U.S. does not impose price restrictions on pharmaceutical sales. As a result, its consumers generally pay significantly more than those in other markets.

Realizing that its consumers would benefit from, and politically demanded, parallel import competition from lower-priced, regulated foreign markets (most notably, Canada), the U.S. Congress passed two laws, one in 2000 and another in 2003, which would have applied international exhaustion to pharmaceutical sales.[13] Those statutory provisions were, however, conditioned on the Secretary of Health and Human Services taking certain actions designed to address possible safety concerns. When those actions did not occur, the pressure was sufficient to cause another effort by the 109th Congress to pass new legislation that would have created a self-executing statutory rule of international exhaustion.[14] Although that effort was unsuccessful, it shows how powerfully domestic market considerations affected even the most ardent proponent of non-exhaustion. The irony is deliciously inescapable. Had the U.S. succeeded in having its international non-exhaustion standard added to TRIPS, it would have found itself firmly aligned in Doha with the developing countries in support of a domestic health and welfare exception.[15]

The second situation involves the U.S. Supreme Court's *Kirtsaeng* decision discussed above. The majority opinion expressly supported its (highly) questionable holding that the U.S. Copyright Act adopted the rule of international exhaustion by noting that if it did not, then IPR owners could use their parallel rights portfolios to limit (or prevent) the importation of trillions of dollars of foreign-made goods, reducing their availability and price competition in a wide range of important domestic markets.[16] Faced with forcing the country to bear the distributional costs of the international non-exhaustion position the U.S. so ardently advocated in TRIPS, the Court's majority proved unready to find Congress had implemented that position in U.S. copyright law.

These examples demonstrate that resolving the exhaustion debate requires moving beyond arguing the doctrine's ability to maximize overall global market output. A workable rule must expressly acknowledge and address its distributional effects on all nations.

---

[13] See e.g. SUSAN THAUL & DONNA U. VOGT, CRS REPORT FOR CONGRESS: IMPORTATION OF PRESCRIPTION DRUGS PROVISIONS IN P.L. 108–173, THE MEDICARE PRESCRIPTION DRUG IMPROVEMENT, AND MODERNIZATION ACT OF 2003 (March 12, 2004), available at www.law.umaryland.edu/marshall/crsreports/crsdocuments/RL32271.pdf.

[14] See e.g. *Patent Rights and Pharmaceutical Reimportation: Is the New Law a Panacea or Pandora's Box?*, 25 GENETIC ENGINEERING & BIOTECHNOLOGY NEWS (November 1, 2005), available at www.genengnews.com/gen-articles/patent-rights-and-pharmaceutical-reimportation/882/.

[15] See Doha Ministerial 2001, *supra* note 6 (the desire to carve-out particular types of goods for domestic policy reasons goes beyond health and welfare concerns); see WIPO Report, *supra* note 11, paras. 29–30.

[16] See Kirtsaeng v. John Wiley & Sons, Inc., 133 S. Ct. 1351, 1364–67 (2013).

B. IPR Harmonization

If TRIPS truly represented an international accord regarding generally accepted IPR standards, then all nations should have quickly moved forward with their implementation despite the failure to agree on exhaustion. Clearly that has not happened. The conundrum disappears if the TRIPS failure to agree on exhaustion is viewed as a final "line in the sand" drawn by developing countries having profound concerns regarding the overall TRIPS harmonization enterprise, and not a mere open detail in a grand bargain.[17]

The same distributional issues that prevented an accord on exhaustion provide strong support for that interpretation. Considered at the national level, the benefits produced by an efficiency-based IPR system make the approach attractive to any country with a market economy. Harmonizing its implementation across the domestic market avoids the inefficiencies of fragmentation and variations among internal political subdivisions. The U.S. federal patent and copyright regimes provide a good example, but uniform national IP laws are the norm in virtually every country that has adopted the efficient-market IPR paradigm.

When that system is transplanted into the global marketplace, however, it produces the same distributional differences that drove the disagreement over exhaustion. Developed nations' domestic resources, capabilities, and infrastructure allow them to produce more intellectual property assets than they obtain from others. That makes internationally harmonized efficiency-based IPRs doubly attractive. The resulting ability of their innovators to capture global returns from adopting consuming nations simultaneously augments the incentives spurring increased domestic IP-related investment and the nation's share of the global IP-related market. Unsurprisingly, the developed nations proposed that TRIPS efficiency-based IPR system.

Less developed nations find themselves in the opposite situation. Their significantly lower production of intellectual property assets makes them net IPR-consumers who bear the costs of a harmonized IPR system. In addition, such IPRs limit access to others' IP assets impeding the inflow of the knowledge and skills necessary to developing their own innovation base. The only rational response was for them to resist the TRIPS standards, which they did. That raises the question of why, then, did the developing nations ultimately sign on?

The answer is the *realpolitik* of the parties' respective bargaining positions. To grow their domestic economies, the developing nations required access to the developed nations' markets. That made it essential they join the WTO. The developed nations used that leverage to add intellectual property to the global trade agenda, making agreeing to TRIPS harmonization the price of admission. With little alternative but to go along, the developing nations used their limited bargaining power to create some modest flexibility through ambiguities in the standards, to achieve a "tie" regarding exhaustion and to obtain a grace-period extension for compliance.

Two factual arguments support the above thesis. The first is how the grace-period has played out post-TRIPS. Its inclusion clearly signaled the developing countries were unready to move on to immediate implementation. The conventional explana-

---

[17] See generally Chiappetta, *IPR Exhaustion*, supra note 10.

tion for the grace-period was that the developing nations lacked the domestic expertise needed to enact the mandated laws and put the related institutions in place. That was accurate in part, but subsequent events demonstrate that as a complete explanation it was fanciful at best, delusional at worse. Not only has the original 2005 deadline long passed, but extensions have now pushed it back sixteen additional years. Surely twenty-five years far exceeds the time required for technical implementation by the willing.

For those who considered why the developed nations abandoned efficient market principles to advocate for international non-exhaustion and the developing nations proved so intractable in response, an alternative explanation for the grace-period is apparent: no country will rationally adopt an international efficiency-based system of harmonized IPRs unless it obtains net distributional benefits from doing so. For many (if not all) developing countries the TRIPS mandates make no sense. But absent sufficient power to effectively resist, the next best solution is to acquiesce, defer implementation, and then subsequently reopen the discussion using the developed nations' commitment to WTO success as leverage to renegotiate.

That explanation is supported by the post-TRIPS WTO negotiations. The ink was barely dry when the LDCs (and others) sought to readdress the distributional situation. Not only did they seek modifications of the TRIPS IPR agenda (e.g., the Doha Declaration exceptions and seeking to include traditional knowledge and folklore as protectable subject matter), but they expanded the post-TRIPS trade agenda to include topics enhancing their ability to capture a meaningful share of the global market—both short-term and through sustainable economic growth. These issues include favorable transnational trade rules governing agriculture, textiles, and clothing products (specifically, removing quotas, lowering customs duty rates, and even granting preferences to developing countries); development through technology transfer, technical cooperation, and capacity building; and extended deadlines for complying with trade-related investment and government subsidy restrictions.[18]

Yet more compelling is the WTO's express acknowledgment that overcoming delays in implementation requires more than just technical expertise. For harmonization to move forward, the mandated IPRs must serve all nations' development objectives, policy priorities, and domestic situations.[19] Although the most recent TRIPS grace-period extension explicitly incorporates that sentiment by tying the new deadline to a nation's transition out of LDC status, that is not sufficient. The crucial issue is distributional: the implementing nation must stand to at least break-even from implementation through either its inherent ability to capture a portion of the resulting increase in global economic output or other compensating concessions. Until that is true, there is every incentive to continue to drag one's legal feet.[20]

---

[18] See WTO, Understanding the WTO: The Doha Agenda, at www.wto.org/english/thewto_e/whatis_e/tif_e/doha1_e.htm: see also WTO, Understanding the WTO: Developing Countries, Some Issues Raised, available at www.wto.org/english/thewto_e/whatis_e/tif_e/dev4_e.htm.

[19] See *supra* note 8.

[20] The alternative is to encourage compliance through punitive sanctions. That "stick" approach is generally less efficacious than the "carrot" as there are many ways a targeted party can comply *de jure* while nonetheless producing *de facto* short-falls in implementation.

The second factual argument is found in the developed nations' own IP histories.[21] None of those now advocating efficiency-based IPRs started out as enthusiastic proponents of granting IP rights to foreign innovators. Such support only arose after they had developed a robustly competitive domestic market and innovation base. The U.S. experience is particularly instructive. At the time of its founding it was an unabashedly piratical nation, generating economic growth by withholding protection for, and overtly free riding on, foreign technological innovations and copyrightable works. Its increased advocacy for reciprocal, harmonized IP protection generally tracks the improvement of its domestic economic fortunes and its related transition from a net IPR-consumer to IPR-producer.

The evolving Chinese and Indian IPR views provide convincing contemporary evidence to the same effect. For many years developed nations have complained those countries' domestic IP regimes fail to prevent rampant "theft" of foreign-owned technologies. However, recent growth in China's and India's economies and innovation prowess have caused a notable increase in their enthusiasm for, and use of, transnational IP law. As the adage goes, much can be explained by following the money. In this case, that means looking at who stands to benefit from international efficiency-based IPR harmonization.

C. Addressing the Distributional Issue

The TRIPS exhaustion and implementation experiences make clear that until the underlying distributional concerns are resolved, true agreement on neither issue can be achieved. One solution, readily apparent in the expansion of the WTO trade negotiation agenda discussed above, is to make compensating economic adjustments. That approach is already being deployed in the bilateral and regional trade agreements put in place since TRIPS. These more limited contexts permit the parties to expressly negotiate *quid pro quo* economic benefits in return for IPR concessions ("TRIPS-plus" provisions).[22] For example, bilateral treaties between developed economic powers and countries having mid-level economies have granted the latter preferential access to the developed nation's market in exchange for domestic IP law adjustments, including, if not a rule of international non-exhaustion, an express agreement to limit the parallel importation of IPR-based goods.[23] Those seeking resolution on exhaustion and

---

[21] See Peter K. Yu, *The Rise of China and Other Middle Intellectual Property Powers*, 8 DRAKE U. OCCASIONAL PAPERS IN INTELL. PROP. L. 30–31 (2013).

[22] See e.g. Jean-Federic Morin, *Tripping Up: TRIPS Debates IP and Health in Bilateral Agreements*, 1 INT'L J. INTELL. PROP. MGT. 37 (2006); UNDP, UNAIDS ISSUE BRIEF: THE POTENTIAL IMPACT OF FREE TRADE AGREEMENTS ON PUBLIC HEALTH (2012), available at www.unaids.org/sites/default/files/media_asset/JC2349_Issue_Brief_Free-Trade-Agreements_en_0.pdf; Marco M. Aleman, *Topic 12: Patent-related Provisions in the Framework of Preferential Trade Agreements*, in WIPO SUB-REGIONAL WORKSHOP ON PATENT POLICY AND ITS LEGISLATIVE IMPLEMENTATION (April 2013), available at www.wipo.int/edocs/mdocs/patent_policy/en/wipo_ip_skb_13/wipo_ip_skb_13t12.pdf; Frederick M. Abbott, *Intellectual Property Provisions of Bilateral and Regional Trade Agreements in Light of U.S. Federal Law* (August 9, 2011), http://papers.ssrn.com/sol3/papers.cfm?abstract_id=1912621.

[23] Regional agreements similarly combine non-discriminatory market access throughout the group with specific TRIPS-plus harmonized IPR standards and an agreement to implement a rule of intra-region exhaustion. See e.g. Aleman, *supra* note 22.

progress on implementation would be well advised to take the developing countries' WTO trade requests noted above very seriously. They might even consider making additional concessions on their own.

Distributional concerns can also be addressed by changing the TRIPS substantive standards to adjust the benefits and costs to developing countries. On the benefits side, affirmative steps can be taken to improve their participation in the global IPR marketplace. In particular, it will help if the developed countries move beyond strictly market efficiency arguments when considering the developing countries requests for changes. For example, it is far more productive to approach the addition of traditional knowledge and folklore to protectable subject matter as an effort by those countries to ensure the TRIPS IPR system produces "fair and equal benefit sharing."[24] Professor Yu provides another useful example along the same lines.[25] He points out that the current TRIPS novelty and nonobvious requirements intentionally limit patent protection to "path-breaking" technological innovation. Although efficient market principles support that standard, it skews global patent returns heavily in favor of the developed nations.[26] While (perhaps) less efficient, utility model/petty patent regimes' less stringent standards "invite broader participation in inventive enterprises, especially by smaller collective enterprises and private citizens who are less likely to have resources devoted to invention patents." If TRIPS *also* required all WTO members to adopt such regimes, harmonization would enhance the developing countries ability to capture a greater share of the global IPR-based revenues. In addition, by giving such countries the ability to participate in the global IPR marketplace, those regimes would provide the exposure, information, and experience needed to move up the development curve. Again, such a concession by the developed nations would provide the benefits needed to convince the developing countries to move forward with implementation.

Specific cost mitigating adjustments can also help move the process forward. That approach was used in the post-TRIPS Doha Ministerial Declaration which addressed developing countries' IPR-related public health distributional concerns by creating exceptions limiting those domestic harms.[27] Identifying other specific, significant developing country cost concerns that can be dealt with in the same way will help achieve the more favorable distributional outcomes essential to actual agreement on standards and, ultimately, to their domestic implementation.

Regarding exhaustion, the distributional issues could, of course, be resolved if the developed nations would acknowledge that the efficiency paradigm calls (generally) for limiting their IPR holders' returns to the first sale and accept a baseline rule of international exhaustion.[28] But short of that unlikely prospect, the exceptions approach provides

---

[24] See WTO, Intellectual Property Briefing, *Current Issues in Intellectual Property* (2011), available at www.wto.org/english/tratop_e/trips_e/trips_issues_e.htm.
[25] See Yu, *supra* note 21, at 30 and 36.
[26] The view is visible in the U.S.'s recent limiting of its patentable subject matter requirement and tightening of its nonobviousness inquiry. See Alice Corp. v. CLS Bank Int'l, 134 S. Ct. 2347 (2014); KSR Int'l Co. v. Teleflex, Inc., 550 U.S. 398 (2007).
[27] See *supra* note 6.
[28] Although the abandonment of short-term economic self-interest asks a lot, it does merit consideration. In a globalized world we need to find ways to live together over the longer term. See

a practical alternative. Justice Ginsberg's dissent in *Kirtsaeng*[29] pointed out how it was used in the U.S. domestic context to produce a more balanced outcome. When granting copyright owners the right to prevent imports under section 602 of the Copyright Act,[30] the U.S. Congress dealt with that non-exhaustion rule's domestic cost concerns by adding specific mitigating exceptions.[31] In the international context, that technique can similarly eliminate the need to decide *between* exhaustion and non-exhaustion. It allows the parties to instead focus on creating a combination of baseline rule and exceptions dealing with specific national cost concerns that produces an acceptable distributional outcome on which all parties can agree.

IV. OTHER CONSIDERATIONS

A. Exhaustion

It is tempting to assume that if the distributional concerns are satisfactorily addressed the exhaustion debate can be easily resolved by applying international exhaustion across the IPR spectrum to make the largest aggregate global market output available for redistribution. However, that alluringly straightforward blanket, absolute "one-size-fits-all" approach ignores other important policy and normative considerations which must be reflected in an appropriate and internationally acceptable rule. And, once again, identifying and understanding those additional issues provide useful insights regarding the root causes of the current substantive IPR harmonization difficulties, as well as what can be done to resolve them.

Not without irony, one of the primary arguments against a blanket, absolute rule of international exhaustion comes from the market efficiency paradigm itself. Although within such a system all IP regimes share that baseline justification, they play very different roles in producing that outcome. Consequently, an appropriate rule must be sufficiently nuanced to reflect and advance each regime's specific objectives.

Patent law, as the purest market efficiency-based form of IPR, provides an excellent starting point for understanding the need for more nuance. The regime exists to address the underproduction of innovation that results if others can free ride on, and capture the returns from, an inventor's investments in time and resources. It does so by granting investor-inventors legal control over their invention's use. As discussed above, the single payment rationale justifies a blanket, absolute rule of international exhaustion. By controlling the terms of the first sale, the patent owner can capture what it deems to be the full value of the covered invention regarding the particular good. The regime's incentive thus produced, exhaustion should trigger, allowing secondary market competition to reduce market prices and increase access.

In the real world, however, one-size-fits-all international exhaustion is unlikely to

---

Vincent Chiappetta, *The Practical Meaning of Property*, 46 WILLAMETTE. L. REV. 297 (2009). The "generally" caveat in the sentence in the text is discussed at IV below.

[29] Kirtsaeng v. John Wiley & Sons, Inc., 133 S. Ct. 1351, 1373 (2013).
[30] 17 U.S.C. § 602.
[31] 17 U.S.C. § 602(a)(3).

produce an optimally efficient patent law result.[32] In response to secondary market competition, patent owners will increase the first sale price and reduce output to the point which maximizes their returns. That will reduce access which, in turn, reduces consumer welfare and causes economic deadweight loss. Modifying the exhaustion rule to treat otherwise legal contract restrictions on resale as enforceable under patent law resolves the problem. That exception would give patent owners the remedial certainty necessary to ensure effective secondary market control. That, in turn, allows them to sell to limited-use acquirers willing to forgo resale in exchange for a reduced purchase price, producing a more efficient overall market outcome.

When the other IPR regimes are considered, the inefficiencies of a blanket, absolute rule of international exhaustion becomes even more apparent. For example, trademark law also exists to enhance efficient market operation. It reduces wasteful consumer search costs by allowing producers to reliably identify and distinguish their goods from others' offerings in the marketplace. Given that objective, it makes no sense to use an exhaustion rule that optimizes the efficient outcome by properly balancing the incentive to invest produced by economic returns against post-sale interference with secondary market competition. The only relevant efficiency issue is the accuracy of the information conveyed by the mark's post-sale presence to consumers. For so long as the mark accurately describes the good's characteristics, the owner has no legitimate trademark interest in restricting its further conveyance. As trademark enforcement would create unjustified costs, the right should be exhausted. However, if at any point the mark's presence would mislead consumers, then downstream enforcement is appropriate and exhaustion should not (or no longer) apply. Applied to the international context, an efficient rule would only apply exhaustion when the mark's presence on goods moving between jurisdictions conveys accurate information to consumers in the import market, but only for so long as that continues to be true.

A one-size-fits-all, absolute rule of international IPR exhaustion is clearly a non-starter on efficiency grounds, not only across the IP spectrum but even within any single regime. But even making the necessary efficiency adjustments will not suffice. To garner broad-based international acceptance the rule must also address national normative policy differences regarding IP law. Copyright law raises the most significant issue in this regard.[33] Within the efficient-market IP paradigm, copyright law's justification parallels patent law, providing authors an incentive to invest in new works by giving them the legal right to prevent others from copying their original expression. The appropriate efficiency-based transnational rule on exhaustion would track patent law: generally applying international exhaustion but subject to contractual adjustments to permit tailoring of acquisition prices and increased access.

---

[32] See Chiappetta, *Patent Exhaustion*, *supra* note 9, at 1140–44 for the more detailed argument, including a few refinements, most particularly concerning downstream notice.

[33] Patent law and trademark law primarily raise the distributional and efficiency concerns already discussed. Undisclosed information (trade secret law) may, however, trigger other policy disagreements between nations which predicate protection on duties of confidence (which arguably should survive a first sale) and the U.S. view that it reduces the costs of preventing unauthorized third party appropriations (which might be exhausted when a sale by the holder of the information causes it to be disclosed).

But many nations also view the regime as providing protection to individual authors' natural rights, such as the right to attribution regarding works they have created and to insist the integrity of those works be maintained over time. To be acceptable to these countries, the rule of international exhaustion must address these non-efficiency policy concerns. However, unlike "internal" efficiency considerations, these issues require resolution of conflicting normative policy views. A nation that does not accept the natural rights view will find the inefficiencies created by post-first sale continuation of an author's personal copyright interests unacceptable. Similarly, no amount of efficiency-based calibration will satisfy a country which views natural rights as having paramount importance. Finding a workable solution requires adjusting the rule of international exhaustion to produce an acceptable compromise. For example, both groups might agree to a rule that limits exhaustion to a copyright owner's economic rights but continues any natural rights attaching to a particular copy unless expressly waived by the author.

B. IPR Harmonization

Understanding the need to address, and the means for resolving, non-distributional policy issues in the exhaustion debate sheds additional light on the sources of, and how to deal with, the difficulties plaguing substantive IPR harmonization. The connection is most clearly demonstrated through a few examples.

Patent law again provides the baseline illustration. The efficient market focus calls for an extremely broad-based application of its incentive so as to encourage investment over the full range of functional innovation. The U.S. approach to biological patenting exemplifies that implementation, treating all non-naturally occurring plants and animals, including those which have been genetically modified, as patentable subject matter.[34] Regarding human-related innovations, the U.S. Patent Act includes only a single (and enigmatic) exclusion—a recently added prohibition on claims "directed to or encompassing a human organism."[35] Beyond that, although the U.S. Supreme Court found claims to naturally occurring sequences of human DNA unpatentable, it has explicitly held artificially produced sequences (cDNA) do qualify for patent protection.[36]

In contrast, the EU takes a much more restrictive approach reflecting normative concerns over the patenting of life. EU Directive 98/44/EC[37] expressly excludes plants, animals, the essential biological processes for their reproduction, and parts of the human body which have not been isolated from the human body or are not produced by a technological process, including gene sequences. Also excluded are processes used for human cloning, to modify human germ-line genetic identity, and to modify the genetic identity of animals (and any animals resulting from such process) if likely to cause them suffering

---

[34] See 35 U.S.C. § 101; see also Diamond v. Chakrabarty, 447 U.S. 303 (1980).
[35] The exclusion is uncodified and can be found in s. 33(a) of the Leahy-Smith America Invents Act; see also Dennis Crouch, *Patents Directed to Human Organisms*, PATENTLYO (September 9, 2011), available at http://patentlyo.com/patent/2011/09/patents-directed-to-human-organisms.html; Dennis Crouch, *Patents Encompassing a Human Organism*, PATENTLYO (December 2, 2012), available at http://patentlyo.com/patent/2012/12/ex-parte-kamrava.html.
[36] See Association for Molecular Pathology v. Myriad Genetics, 133 S. Ct. 2107 (2013).
[37] Council Directive 98/44/EC, [1998] O.J. L213, 30.7.1998 (EU).

without any substantial medical benefit to humans or animals, as well as the use of human embryos for industrial and commercial purposes.

The EU certainly would have rejected a TRIPS mandate that it adopt the U.S. more "purist" efficiency approach. Equally clearly, those differences could not be resolved by pointing out that the latter approach maximizes overall economic output. As with copyright exhaustion, resolution requires a compromise standard. That is precisely how the issue was resolved in TRIPS. Article 27(1) sets out the efficient-market standard preferred by the U.S. Article 27(2) and (3), however, allow the EU (and others) to exclude normatively unacceptable subject matter on various *ordre public* and morality grounds.[38] That combination permitted the U.S. and the EU to agree on a patentability standard despite their normative differences regarding its appropriate scope. More importantly, by providing flexibility their disagreement ceased to be a barrier to domestic implementation.

While the major economic players had sufficient leverage to obtain standards compromises,[39] the developing nations did not. Normative disagreements with the adopted standards will impede the implementation process until they are addressed. Explicitly seeking workable compromise may prove especially productive regarding a particularly important unresolved issue at the heart of the current delays. Many developing nations have centralized economic and political systems. Because the TRIPS market-based IPR standards emphasize individual action and returns, they conflict directly with the communitarian ethos of personal abnegation in favor of joint purpose and enterprise that provides the core foundational premise for such systems. That social and, even more frequently, political disconnection creates substantial resistance to domestic implementation.

The U.S.-China IP relationship provides a good example of the problem as well as the utility of finding a compromise solution. The U.S. enthusiastically embraces the competitive market system as the appropriate normative framework for its economic interactions. Because its pre-TRIPS IP regimes expressly reflected that model and its related social ethos, compliance with the TRIPS efficiency-based standards was neither culturally nor politically problematic. China, in contrast, has a centralized economy and political structure justified (in part) by its communitarian social paradigm. Adopting market-based IPRs encouraging pursuit of individual rewards is considerably off message economically,

---

[38] See *ibid*. Unsurprisingly, the art. 27(2) and (3) exclusions closely track the exclusions in Council Directive 98/44/EC. The different views regarding patentability are, of course, more varied than those separating the U.S. and the EU. Other nations' patent laws also include exclusions reflecting their particular domestic policy priorities and domestic situations. See Denis Borges Barbosa & Karin Grau-Kuntz, WIPO, SCP/15/3, Annex III, 3. Exclusions from Patentable Subject Matter and Exceptions and Limitations to the Rights—Biotechnology (January 2010), available at www.wipo.int/edocs/mdocs/scp/en/scp_15/scp_15_3-annex3.pdf; WEIWEI HAN, COMPARATIVE ANALYSIS OF PATENTING BIOTECHNOLOGY INVENTIONS IN THE U.S., EUROPE, JAPAN AND CHINA (MIPLC, 2011/12), available at www.miplc.de/research/ (available at SSRN: http://ssrn.com/abstract=2225845).

[39] TRIPS contains other adjustments accommodating developed countries' policy preferences. For example, arts. 15.3 and 16.1 reconcile the difference between the U.S.'s use-based trademark law with much of the rest of the developed world's registration-based approach. Article 39.1 adopts the prevailing duty-based approach to undisclosed information/trade secret law, but Explanatory note 10 permits the U.S. to retain its more property-based regime.

culturally, and politically.[40] Although China did legislatively enact the mandated TRIPS IPR standards to move into *de jure* compliance, until very recently enforcement has been manifestly unenthusiastic. That combination represents *realpolitik*. The former action allowed China to gain admittance to the WTO, while the latter delay avoids the serious domestic problems of full implementation.[41]

The lack of rigorous enforcement produced strident U.S. claims that China was failing to comply with the spirit, if not the letter, of the TRIPS accord. Although accurate on the facts, insisting on China's immediate compliance has, unsurprisingly, not produced that result. A more productive approach would be to deal with the root causes of the delay. As discussed in section III above, distributional issues do play an important role and must be addressed. But that is too narrow a view. Other domestic considerations are also relevant; in particular the glaring inconsistency of the TRIPS standards with China's existing command and control economic policies and political structure.

But China's IP position has evolved over time. As its economy and domestic demand have grown, China has turned to market-based economic activity to increase output, including explicitly encouraging home-grown innovation and individual entrepreneurship. Those changes are making TRIPS' market-based IP incentives not only more acceptable, but affirmatively beneficial to its domestic economy which, in turn, is producing an increasingly TRIPS-like domestic IPR policy. But its position still retains "Chinese characteristics" which track its evolving domestic economic and political situations. Over time, those changes will continue to expand the common ground with the U.S. As past experience has amply demonstrated (both the failure of threats and the success of compromise regarding developed nations' normative policy differences in TRIPS), it will be more effective to put the gloves aside (or at least wield them less vigorously) and instead explicitly look for mutually acceptable standards that permit harmonization to the extent of normative overlap.

One point merits special attention regarding that process: the interaction between internal politics and particular IP regimes. Although there are sound reasons for a nation with a centralized economy to gradually hybridize its approach and phase-in efficiency-based IPRs, domestic political considerations will frequently play a countervailing role.

---

[40] Too much can be made of the market-communitarian conflict. Communitarian principles can be deployed to provide normative justification for free riding on other nations' investments in innovation, when the actual motivation is improving the domestic economic situation at outsiders' expense. The common enterprise argument can also be used to combat threats to an existing political regime's hegemony by framing dissents' demands for more individual autonomy as the greedy pursuit of personal gain at the expense of the whole. See Yu, *supra* note 21, at 3–12; see also Chiappetta, *IPR Exhaustion*, *supra* note 10, at 376.

[41] The developing nations are not the only ones who use the tactic. The U.S., once again, provides an excellent example. It has steadfastly resisted adopting copyright moral rights, which run counter to its current economic structures and politics. Although U.S. economic power allowed it to successfully exclude moral rights from TRIPS (see art. 9(1)), it was unable to sway the members of the Berne Convention. In order to gain admittance to Berne, it used China's TRIPS approach. It agreed to comply to gain admittance, but its implementation has fallen considerably short, if not *de jure*, certainly regarding the spirit of the treaty's requirements. (Interestingly, by excluding moral rights from TRIPS the U.S. also avoided the TRIPS enforcement mechanisms which might otherwise have been used to challenge its compliance with Berne.)

In particular the desire or need (perceived or actual) to maintain control over public discourse makes some IPRs more problematic than others. China is a case in point.[42] Despite having adopted both patent and copyright laws, implementation of the latter lags considerably behind the former. Its domestic political situation explains why. Patent law focuses on functional innovation which advances the economic development in a hybridizing economy. Although copyright law produces similar economic benefits, it also creates special political concerns. Its market-based incentive to individual expression can free authors from the need for public funding and with it, the related constraints on getting too far off message.[43]

Workable compromises must take such differences into account. For example, an "interim" harmonized copyright standard might reflect the same approach used to resolve the U.S.-EU normative differences over patentability: require domestic copyright law protect the IPR owner's economic interests but subject to domestic *ordre public* exceptions limiting public dissemination. The U.S. will find allowing such exemptions problematic on free speech and political democracy grounds, but must recognize that its disagreement constitutes the very essence of normative conflict. The shoe can easily be put on the other foot. The U.S. at one time barred importation and dissemination of material it deemed immoral through customs seizures and its obscenity censorship still turns on "community standards," both reflections of its domestic normative sensibilities. Although the reasons for censorship will vary, normative positions are strongly held and will have a very real effect on a nation's enthusiasm for domestic IPR adoption. At the very least refusals to compromise must, therefore, consider the consequences to IPR harmonization and related expectations regarding international agreement and compliance.

V. CONCLUSION

The inability of the TRIPS negotiators to reach consensus on IPR exhaustion can be traced to the doctrine's distributional consequences when transplanted into the global economic context. Because, unlike a national economy, the international community lacks the motivation and means to adjust for differences in individual competitive market outcomes, national positions reflect the doctrine's likely effect on its particular share of global IPR-based returns. Nations with developed economies, as net IPR-producers, generally favor a rule of international non-exhaustion which allows its IPR owners to segment the global market and maximize their returns. Developing nations, as net IPR-consumers, normally prefer international exhaustion and the resulting parallel import competition which lowers domestic market prices and increases local access to IPR-based goods.

Resolving the debate requires addressing these distributional effects. One approach is to offset the costs of international non-exhaustion borne by the developing, net IPR-consuming countries through compensating economic trade concessions, such as those they have proposed in the ongoing WTO negotiations. That solution could also use

---

[42] See Yu, *supra* note 21, at 51–53.
[43] See Eric Priest, *Copyright and Free Expression in China's Film Industry*, 26 FORDHAM INTELL. PROP., MEDIA & ENT. L.J. 1 (2015).

exceptions to address especially important national concerns. For example, a country might be allowed to apply international exhaustion if needed to ensure adequate domestic access to specific, locally-essential IPR-based products. Alternatively, albeit much less likely, the developed countries could acknowledge that under the efficiency rationale they advocate their continued insistence on non-exhaustion constitutes self-interested overreaching, thus producing agreement on a rule of international exhaustion. Again, to be workable that rule would require some "balancing" exceptions; for example, allowing net IPR-consuming nations to adopt international non-exhaustion in return for favorable trade concessions or to encourage domestic market entry by foreign IPR holders. In all events, bilateral and regional trade agreement negotiations provide a rich experimental laboratory for exploring these options and making incremental progress.

Although necessary, dealing with the exhaustion's distributional effects is not sufficient to reach agreement. An appropriate and acceptable international rule must also reflect other considerations, in particular, the different economic efficiency enhancing functions of each IPR regime; conflicting normative views regarding the proper objectives of IP law; and varying domestic economic and political situations.

These insights from the exhaustion debate also explain the slow progress toward substantive IPR harmonization under the TRIPS "agreement," as well as a way forward in that regard. It is fanciful to believe that the developing nations' failure to meet the now-many-times-extended implementation deadline(s) reflects their inadequate technical competence. It comes from a completely understandable lack of will. Not only do the accord's market efficiency-based IPR standards produce negative distributional effects, in many instances they fundamentally conflict with existing national normative, economic, and political paradigms. As with exhaustion, achieving harmonization in fact requires dealing with these root causes—ensuring developing nations can obtain adequate returns from the global market enterprise to justify their participation and that the TRIPS standards provide enough flexibility to accommodate differing normative, economic, and political situations. This compromise approach has the dual virtue of replacing the current ineffectual insistence on compliance with dialog and providing time for the developing nations' economies to evolve in ways that naturally increase the domestic benefits of implementing TRIPS-style market efficiency-based IPR regimes.

8. Parallel trade in pharmaceuticals: trade therapy for market distortions
Frederick M. Abbott*

I. OVERVIEW

A. Global Pharmaceutical Regulation

Pharmaceutical products are developed, approved, manufactured, traded, and used under complex and demanding regulatory schemes. While the intensity of regulation varies substantially among countries, lightly regulated markets are the exception, particularly from an economic standpoint. In this regard, pharmaceuticals are not generally traded in what might be described as a "free market" in the sense of absence of regulation, and this includes import restrictions which are generally consistent with the overall regulatory schemes. A drug that is not approved for marketing in a particular country does not become so because it is imported.

Parallel trade (i.e., imports and exports) in pharmaceuticals takes place in markets that are "distorted" by regulation. Probably the single most significant "distortion mechanism" is the patent. The patent allows its owner to price a pharmaceutical product in the absence of ordinary market competition in the sense that potential competitors may not freely copy the product. The ultimate price may depend on a variety of factors, including the uniqueness of therapeutic effect within a particular class. But, the price of patented pharmaceutical products generally does not represent the cost of reverse engineering plus production.

Substantially but not exclusively because of the effects of patents, many countries place controls on the prices of pharmaceutical products. Originator patented pharmaceutical products and generic products are often subject to controls. In addition, as a result of public health concerns regarding lower income countries, a number of pharmaceutical companies are voluntarily licensing patented products for manufacture and sale in developing countries at significantly lower prices than are charged in high income markets.

This is backdrop to addressing issues concerning parallel trade in pharmaceutical products. It is conducted in what typically are heavily regulated markets, and this may include price controls and voluntary discriminatory pricing. This adds a substantial layer of complexity to analysis of the "exhaustion question."

---

* Edward Ball Eminent Scholar Professor of International Law, Florida State University College of Law.

B. Some Historical Perspective

In reports prepared for the Committee on International Trade Law of the International Law Association in the 1990s, I analyzed the issues surrounding exhaustion of intellectual property rights and parallel trade, and made certain recommendations.[1] The basic finding was that international exhaustion would benefit consumers and the global economy as a whole, and that optimally, international exhaustion would be a mandatory rule for the international trading system.

In the mid to late 1990s, issues concerning access to medicines, particularly with respect to newly developed antiretroviral medicines to treat HIV-AIDS, became an important part of global public policy dialogue. The originator pharmaceutical industry sought to prevent the government of South Africa from authorizing parallel importation of patented medicines, contending that international exhaustion was precluded by the World Trade Organization (WTO) Agreement on Trade Related Aspects of Intellectual Property Rights (TRIPS Agreement).[2] This was transparently incorrect from a legal standpoint. The First Report made these incongruities plain substantially before the 1997 South African Medicines Amendment Act became an international issue.[3]

It has never been clear what motivated the originator pharmaceutical industry to pursue a manifestly incorrect legal claim, for which the industry paid a heavy price in terms of public perception. I served as legal advisor on TRIPS Agreement issues to the government of South Africa, defending the litigation initiated by the originator industry in the High Court of Pretoria; the case was ultimately abandoned by the industry, which ended up paying the South African government's legal expenses.[4]

The question in the Medicines Act case was not whether international exhaustion of patent rights was a good idea from a national or global policy standpoint. The question was simpler: did the TRIPS Agreement preclude South Africa from authorizing parallel importation? The answer was "no." The case received wide global attention not because parallel imports of antiretrovirals would significantly impact access to antiretroviral treatments

---

[1] Frederick M. Abbott, *First Report (Final) to the Committee on International Trade Law of the International Law Association on the Subject of Parallel Importation*, 1 J. INT'L ECON. L. 4, 607–36 (1998), available at http://ssrn.com/abstract=915046 [hereinafter First Report]; Frederick M. Abbott, *Second Report (Final) to the Committee on International Trade Law of the International Law Association on the Subject of the Exhaustion of Intellectual Property Rights and Parallel Importation*, 69TH CONFERENCE OF THE INTERNATIONAL LAW ASSOCIATION (2000), available at http://ssrn.com/abstract=1921856 [hereinafter Second Report].

[2] Agreement on Trade-Related Aspects of Intellectual Property Rights, April 15, 1994; Marrakesh Agreement Establishing the World Trade Organization, Annex 1C, 1869 U.N.T.S. 299 (1994) [hereinafter TRIPS Agreement].

[3] First Report, *supra* note 1, at 609. Among the legal experts closely associated with negotiation of the TRIPS Agreement, including the first Director of the World Trade Organization (WTO) TRIPS Division, this was the accepted view, as confirmed in meetings surrounding the Second Report. First Report, *supra* note 1.

[4] On behalf of the World Health Organization (WHO), the author served as legal advisor to the South African government during the court proceedings that arose, and were abandoned by the industry in 2001. See e.g. Frederick M. Abbott, *WTO TRIPS Agreement and its Implications for Access to Medicines in Developing Countries*, STUDY PAPER 2A, UNITED KINGDOM COMMISSION ON INTELLECTUAL PROPERTY RIGHTS (2002), available at http://ssrn.com/abstract=1924420.

in South Africa. Rather, because the originator industry was seeking to interfere with South Africa's determination regarding its approach to public health policy, and was seeking to deny the flexibilities clearly inherent in the WTO TRIPS Agreement. The European Union (EU) and United States (U.S.) had lined up to threaten South Africa with trade sanctions if it did not amend its legislation. The U.S. government eventually backed away.

The threats by the governments of the U.S. and EU, and the litigation initiated by the originator industry, were directly instrumental in giving rise to proposals at the WTO to reform its approach to public health, and ultimately to adoption of the Doha Declaration on the TRIPS Agreement and Public Health. This history is well-chronicled.[5]

South Africa went on to adopt and implement regulations authorizing parallel importation of medicines protected by patent and trademark.[6] Little (if any) actual use of these regulations has been made by importers.[7] The originator industry ultimately changed its approach regarding South Africa under pressure from competition authorities and provided voluntary licenses for its patented antiretrovirals.[8] More recently, through the efforts of the Medicines Patent Pool, companies such as Gilead have granted licenses to Indian and Chinese producers to produce and supply antiretroviral medicines.[9] Today virtually all of the antiretroviral medicines used in South Africa are procured at very low generic prices, and parallel importation of those medicines into South Africa for the time being is a moot point.[10]

II. COMPLEXITIES OF THE MEDICINES TRADE

There are very few industries subject to a more complex and demanding set of rules than the pharmaceutical industry.[11] Although medicines and their components form a

---

[5] See ELLEN 'T HOEN, THE GLOBAL POLITICS OF PHARMACEUTICAL MONOPOLY POWER 19–38 (2009); see also Frederick M. Abbott, *The Doha Declaration on the TRIPS Agreement and Public Health: Lighting a Dark Corner at the WTO*, 5 J. INT'L ECON. L. 469 (2002), available at http://ssrn.com/abstract=1493725.

[6] See BATTLING HIV/AIDS: A DECISION MAKER'S GUIDE TO THE PROCUREMENT OF MEDICINES AND RELATED SUPPLIES 117 (Yolanda Tayler ed., 2004).

[7] See Lynne Taylor, *S Africa Pledges Action on Compulsory Licenses, Parallel Imports*, PHARMATIMES, November 7, 2013, available at www.pharmatimes.com/article/13-1107/S_Africa_pledges_action_on_compulsory_licenses_parallel_imports.aspx.

[8] See Jonathan Berger, *Market Definition 119–22*, in UNDP, USING COMPETITION LAW TO PROMOTE ACCESS TO HEALTH TECHNOLOGIES: A GUIDEBOOK FOR LOW- AND MIDDLE-INCOME COUNTRIES (Frederick M. Abbott ed., 2014), available at http://ssrn.com/abstract=2439416 [hereinafter UNDP COMPETITION GUIDELINES].

[9] See e.g. Medicines Patent Pool, Licences in the MPP, www.medicinespatentpool.org/licensing/current-licences/. Regarding hepatitis C, see Gilead Press Release, *Gilead Announces Generic Licensing Agreements to Increase Access to Hepatitis C Treatments in Developing Countries* (September 14, 2014), available at www.gilead.com/news/press-releases/2014/9/gilead-announces-generic-licensing-agreements-to-increase-access-to-hepatitis-c-treatments-in-developing-countries.

[10] See e.g. Tamar Kahn, *SA Secures "World's Lowest Prices" for HIV Drugs*, BUSINESS DAY (SA) (2015), available at www.bdlive.co.za/national/health/2015/01/06/sa-secures-worlds-lowest-prices-for-hiv-drugs.

[11] See e.g. F. M. ABBOTT & G. DUKES, GLOBAL PHARMACEUTICAL POLICY (2009).

substantial component of the movement of goods among countries,[12] they do so in a heavily regulated way.

A. Manufacturing Side

Medicines can be divided roughly into three types. First are medicines derived from plant and other organic materials that are synthesized into medicinal products.[13] Second are medicines produced by synthetic organic chemistry largely from raw materials that usually are common to the basic chemicals industry.[14] The resulting products are small molecule compounds or drugs. Third are medicines produced by reproducing biological materials, typically after a modification of genetic code or instructions.[15] These are biological medicines or "biologics."

The raw materials for small molecule drugs are not subject to stringent regulation in trade, and they are unlikely to be protected by product patents. Regulators step in at the point where the raw materials and so-called "intermediates" (i.e., basic chemicals that have been synthesized into more complex compounds, but not yet drugs) are synthesized into active pharmaceutical ingredients (or APIs). APIs are the compounds that produce a drug's therapeutic effect. Because the quality of pharmaceutical products is difficult to assess following the synthesis of the APIs and their formulation, inspectors like the U.S. Food and Drug Administration (FDA) examine the manufacturing facilities for APIs to assess how the process is being carried out in terms of Good Manufacturing Practices (GMP).[16] There are stringent regulators (such as the FDA, the European Medicines Agency (EMA), and the World Health Organization (WHO) Prequalification Program) and non-stringent regulators across a spectrum. For the highly regulated markets like the U.S. and EU, imported drugs must have been produced using APIs from FDA and/or EMA approved facilities. GMP standards differ substantially among countries and producers.

APIs are "formulated" into finished pharmaceutical products (or FPPs).[17] The formulation process involves combining the API with so-called "excipients" which can be some form of sugar or other granulated digestible material so as to create a powder that can be

---

[12] See WORLD HEALTH ORGANIZATION (WHO), WORLD INTELLECTUAL PROPERTY ORGANIZATION (WIPO), AND WORLD TRADE ORGANIZATION (WTO), PROMOTING ACCESS TO MEDICAL TECHNOLOGIES AND INNOVATION: INTERSECTIONS PUBLIC HEALTH, INTELLECTUAL PROPERTY AND TRADE 191–95 (2012) [hereinafter TRILATERAL STUDY].

[13] See e.g. United States National Library of Medicine, Artemisinin Derivatives, http://livertox.nih.gov/ArtemisininDerivatives.htm.

[14] See generally J.M. Fortunak et al., *Active Pharmaceutical Ingredients for Antiretroviral Treatment in Low- and Middle-Income Countries: A Survey*, 19 ANTIVIRAL THERAPY 15 (2014 & 3 Supp.).

[15] See Guilbert Gates & Vu Nguyen, *Growing Biologic Drugs, From Vial to Vat*, N.Y. TIMES (June 11, 2007), available at www.nytimes.com/ref/business/20070611_VAT_GRAPHIC.html.

[16] See e.g. U.S. Food and Drug Administration, Facts about Good Manufacturing Practices (cGMPs), www.fda.gov/Drugs/DevelopmentApprovalProcess/Manufacturing/ucm169105.htm; WHO, Essential Medicines and Health Products: Production, www.who.int/medicines/areas/quality_safety/quality_assurance/production/en/.

[17] Fortunak et al., *supra* note 14.

compressed into a tablet, or placed in a capsule. APIs can also be formulated into injectable products, or for other delivery systems (such as transdermal patches). As with APIs, in order to import into the U.S., the EU, or any other stringently regulated market, the manufacturing facility (wherever located) must be inspected and approved by the FDA, EMA, or other relevant regulator. This is not the case for many other markets, although some developing countries (like Brazil) have contemplated requiring overseas inspections by its regulator (ANVISA) as well.[18] Medicinal products extracted and synthesized from plants and other organic materials are subject to the same type of inspection in order to be imported (although this differs from "herbal supplements," which may be the plant material itself).

Oversight of the production of biologics is stringent, particularly as the production process for biologic drugs involves very close attention to avoiding contamination and the reproduction environment of the biologic materials.[19] There is no "API" involved in a biologic. The biologic drug material is suspended in a liquid that is typically injected or infused into the bloodstream of the patient.

B. Drug Approval Side

For almost all countries, in order for a drug to be placed on the market, it must be approved and registered by the national drug regulatory authority (DRA).[20] The standards applied by DRAs vary widely. For approval of a "new" drug, the originator must typically submit details of clinical trials and manufacturing processes. The approval process can be quite elaborate, involving appointment of a committee of expert evaluators, etc. For approval of a generic version of a previously approved drug, the applicant may need only to provide information regarding "bioequivalence" of its chemical compound and information regarding manufacturing process. In less regulated markets, it may only be necessary to pay a registration fee in order to place a drug on the market, although this practice is no longer so common.[21] So-called "over-the-counter" drugs that are composed of well-known compounds in use for a substantial period of time are typically subject to minimum scrutiny in terms of DRA approvals.[22]

In the typical case, a drug product may not move from Country A to Country B without having been approved in some way from a regulatory standpoint, and the level of regulatory scrutiny may be quite intensive.

---

[18] See e.g. Food & Drug Law Institute, *International GMP Inspection Proposal Dropped by Anvisa* (March 2013), available at www.fdli.org/resources/resources-standard-detail-view/international-gmp-inspection-proposal-dropped-by-anvisa.

[19] U.S. Food and Drug Administration, General Biologics Guidances, www.fda.gov/BiologicsBloodVaccines/GuidanceComplianceRegulatoryInformation/Guidances/General/.

[20] See Frederick M. Abbott, Ryan Abbott, Wilbert Bannenberg, & Marianne Schürmann, *Regional Assessment of Patent and Related Issues and Access to Medicines: CARICOM Member States and the Dominican Republic (HERA)*, 1 HEALTH RESEARCH FOR ACTION FINAL REPORT: MAIN REPORT 28–30 (2009), available at http://ssrn.com/abstract=1909978.

[21] *Ibid.*

[22] See e.g. U.S. Food and Drug Administration, Over-the-Counter (OTC) Drug Monograph Process, www.fda.gov/Drugs/DevelopmentApprovalProcess/HowDrugsareDevelopedandApproved/ucm317137.htm.

150   *Research handbook on intellectual property exhaustion and parallel imports*

In addition, because drugs are subject to recall based on determinations of risk (e.g., manufacturing defects) by regulators, importers of drug products and/or their distributors must typically have procedures in place for undertaking recalls and provide assurance to regulatory authorities about that capacity.[23] The importers themselves are subject to regulation.

C. Price Controls

Many countries control the prices at which drugs are sold, whether through pharmacists, hospitals, retail outlets, etc.[24] There are a variety of approaches to how prices may be set, including reference pricing and cost plus pricing, and variations on those basic mechanisms. It is not uncommon for a country to set maximum prices on a defined basket of "essential" drugs, and to leave other prices to "market forces."[25] In some countries, prices are controlled only when a determination has been made that a particular price is "excessive."[26]

The net effect of this is that manufacturers place drugs on the market in different countries based often on the price that regulators have determined they may charge, not on a price determined by the manufacturer.

D. Import Controls

Pharmaceutical product imports are also affected by tariffs that are applied along the spectrum of the supply chain, including to raw materials, intermediates, APIs, and FPPs.[27] The imposition of tariffs on FPPs will affect pricing arbitrage opportunities.

In addition to regulatory controls generally affecting the local market, drug regulatory authorities may impose additional import controls on different grounds. For example, there is express legislation in the U.S. that precludes any party other than the U.S. manufacturer from re-importing that drug without the manufacturer's consent.[28] This is ostensibly done as a way to protect the integrity of the drug supply chain.

---

[23] See e.g. U.S. Food and Drug Administration, Industry Guidance Information on Recalls of FDA Regulated Products, www.fda.gov/Safety/Recalls/IndustryGuidance/.

[24] The United States is often referred to as an exception from the rule of price controls, though this is not entirely true. The U.S. Veterans Administration establishes price limits for its purchases of prescription drugs, and various States control drug prices by using formularies based on reimbursement costs. Statement, John E. Dicken, Director of Health Care, Committee on Finance, of the U.S. Senate, Prescription Drugs, An Overview of Approaches to Negotiate Drug Prices Used by Other Countries and U.S. Private Payers and Federal Programs, GAO-07-358T (January 11, 2007). For Organization for Economic Cooperation and Development (OECD) country practices, see U.S. Department of Commerce, *International Trade Administration, Pharmaceutical Price Controls in OECD Countries* (Washington, D.C., December 2004). With that said, the United States is among the least regulated markets globally in terms of pricing.

[25] See e.g. for India, Department of Pharmaceuticals, Drugs (Prices Control) Order (2013) (published in GAZETTE OF INDIA, Extraordinary, Part II, s. 3(ii), dated May 15, 2013).

[26] See e.g. for Canada, Frederick M. Abbott, *Anti-Competitive Behaviours and the Remedies Available for Redress*, UNDP COMPETITION GUIDELINES, *supra* note 8, at 78–79.

[27] For data, see TRILATERAL STUDY, *supra* note 12, at 195–97.

[28] As noted by the U.S. Food and Drug Administration (FDA): "Section 3 of the Prescription Drug Marketing Act of 1987 amends Section 801 of the Federal Food, Drug, and Cosmetic Act

III. FORMS OF INTELLECTUAL PROPERTY RELEVANT TO PHARMACEUTICAL TRADE[29]

A. Patents

From the standpoint of monetary value of pharmaceuticals in international trade, patents are the most important form of intellectual property, as they enable their holders to charge prices at substantial multiples of the prices of generic drugs. As of 2015, aggregate global revenues from sales of pharmaceutical products should exceed U.S.$1 trillion. Generic drugs will account for about U.S.$300–350 billion of that total. Yet, the volume of generic drugs in international trade far exceeds the volume of patented drugs.[30]

The level of conflict regarding pharmaceutical patents reflects their tremendous monetary value, providing a funding source for lawyers and litigation. It also reflects the importance of patented pharmaceutical products from a public health standpoint and how limitations on accessibility/affordability affect the public interest.

Patents are granted and enforced on a country by country basis.[31] A rule of international exhaustion eliminates the patent owner's control over resale of a pharmaceutical product once a sale takes place in any country. A rule of national exhaustion eliminates the patent owner's control with respect to the drug product only within the country where it is first sold. A rule of regional exhaustion eliminates the patent owner's control within the regional zone, but leaves it intact for countries outside the regional zone.

When a rule of international exhaustion is applied, the pharmaceutical patent holder does not determine the selling price of the product other than upon its initial sale. If the pharmaceutical patent holder elects to sell a drug at a low price in one country, the drug may be resold at that price in another country. This resale may deprive the patent holder

---

by creating new subsections 801(d)(1) and (2). New subsection 801(d)(1) prohibits the reimportation of human prescription drugs manufactured in a State (including the District of Columbia and Puerto Rico) except when the product is returned to the person who manufactured it. New Subsection 801(d)(2) provides an exception for the reimportation of prescription drugs when authorized by the Secretary in the case of a medical emergency." U.S. Food and Drug Administration, Import Alert 66–14, available at www.accessdata.fda.gov/cms_ia/importalert_177.html. It is unclear whether these rules are strictly enforced. The FDA no longer actively pursues personal importation of prescription medicines.

[29] For a general overview of the forms of intellectual property relevant to trade in medicines, see Frederick M. Abbott, *Intellectual Property Rights in World Trade*, in RESEARCH HANDBOOK IN INTERNATIONAL ECONOMIC LAW 444–84 (A. Guzman & A. Sykes eds., 2007). See also, TRILATERAL STUDY, *supra* note 12, at 53 *et seq.*

[30] The approximate 35 percent composition of generic revenues represents, in fact, a substantial increase over the past five years. INTERCONTINENTAL MARKETING SERVICES INSTITUTE FOR HEALTHCARE INFORMATICS, THE GLOBAL USE OF MEDICINES: OUTLOOK THROUGH 2016 (2012). In 2007, generic revenues accounted for approximately 15 percent of global revenues for the pharmaceutical sector. See ABBOTT AND DUKES, *supra* note 11, at 2.

[31] For a more detailed discussion of the principles of independence, territoriality, and the different geographical variants of exhaustion, see FREDERICK M. ABBOTT, THOMAS COTTIER, & FRANCIS GURRY, INTERNATIONAL INTELLECTUAL PROPERTY IN AN INTEGRATED WORLD ECONOMY 80–106, 239–52, 447–74, 644–62 (3rd ed., 2015).

of a higher price sale in that other country. Arbitrageurs may take advantage of the differences among prices and retain a portion of the differential on resale.

B. Trademarks

Each drug approved for commercial sale is given a generic name, also known as the INN (international nonproprietary name).[32] In addition to its generic name, a drug is typically given a "brand" name by the originator, and the selection of that brand name is subject to regulation. For example, the FDA approves the selection of brand names for the U.S. market, and originators are precluded from selecting brand names that describe or imply a unique therapeutic effect.[33] In addition to a brand name, a drug is typically associated with the trade name of the company that produces and/or markets it, which trade name may also be a trademark. For example, "Sovaldi" is the brand name for the generic/INN drug "sofosbuvir," which is sold and identified by the company "Gilead."

Trademarks are not limited to words or alphanumeric strings. The shape and/or coloring of a drug may be protected by "trade dress" which is a form of trademark, subject to functional limitations.

Consumers typically associate drug products with their brand names. For example, everyone is familiar with Pfizer's statin drug "Lipitor," but few are familiar with "atorvastatin calcium"; everyone is familiar with "Viagra," but few are familiar with "sildenafil citrate"; and so forth. While physicians presumably are sufficiently familiar with generic names to be able to prescribe in the absence of brand names, physicians often have a belief that a drug produced by the originator, e.g., Pfizer's Lipitor, is somehow better than the same drug produced by a generic company and are prepared to prescribe the brand name notwithstanding the availability of much lower priced generic versions. In fact, Pfizer has been surprised by the extent to which physicians and consumers continue to demand Lipitor notwithstanding the ready availability of generic substitutes since that drug has gone "off patent."[34]

Parallel traders are sensitive to the importance of trademarks. They know that the price a drug commands depends on consumer/physician identification of the originator brand

---

[32] WHO, GUIDELINES ON THE USE OF INTERNATIONAL NONPROPRIETARY NAMES (INNs) FOR PHARMACEUTICAL SUBSTANCES (1997), available at http://whqlibdoc.who.int/hq/1997/WHO_PHARM_S_NOM_1570.pdf?ua=1.

[33] U.S. FOOD AND DRUG ADMINISTRATION, GUIDANCE FOR INDUSTRY: CONTENTS OF A COMPLETE SUBMISSION FOR THE EVALUATION OF PROPRIETARY NAMES (2010), available at www.fda.gov/downloads/drugs/guidancecomplianceregulatoryinformation/guidances/ucm075068.pdf. The FDA summarizes in another document: "CDER's Division of Drug Marketing, Advertising, and Communications (DDMAC) evaluates proposed proprietary names to determine if they are overly fanciful, so as to misleadingly imply unique effectiveness or composition, as well as to assess whether they contribute to overstatement of product efficacy, minimization of risk, broadening of product indications, or making of unsubstantiated superiority claims." U.S. Food and Drug Administration, How FDA Reviews Proposed Drug Names, available at www.fda.gov/downloads/Drugs/DrugSafety/MedicationErrors/UCM080867.pdf.

[34] Sean O'Riordan, *Cholesterol Drug Demand Helps 136 Pfizer Workers Keep Jobs Until Year End*, IRISH EXAMINER (2015), available at www.irishexaminer.com/ireland/cholesterol-drug-demand-helps-136-pfizer-workers-keep-jobs-until-year-end-305989.html.

name on the box or other packaging. In principle, a wholesaler who buys a low-priced patented pharmaceutical product put on the market in Country A could repackage the product and sell it under its generic name or a different brand name in Country B, but this would reduce the value of the pharmaceutical product from the standpoint of consumers/ physicians. The parallel trader wants to retain the trademark that was initially placed on the product by the lawful owner of the trademark.

It is the combination of parallel trader interest in re-using the originator brand name, and the patient/doctor interest in using the originator product (and paying more), that impels originator/trademark owners to seek to block the use of trademarks in parallel trade. If a consumer or benefit plan is willing to pay more for the trademarked product, the originator/trademark owner wants to secure that producer surplus.

Trademark owners have for a long time argued that allowing parallel traders to reuse their trademarks poses some risk to public health, in part because parallel traders often repackage drugs so as to include new language labels, or different quantities of the product.[35]

C. Copyright

Copyright is not typically associated with the medicines trade, but it has a place. While information brochures accompanying pharmaceutical products may be limited in terms of expressive content, some may qualify for copyright protection. When the U.S. Supreme Court ruled in favor of international exhaustion for trademark for commonly controlled enterprises,[36] producers shifted to copyright to attempt to protect against parallel imports, claiming rights in package design, promotional material, etc.[37] The Supreme Court eliminated this possibility by ruling in favor of international exhaustion for copyright.[38] In this regard, if and when governments adopt international exhaustion to promote access to medicines, they must be careful to extend that to copyright (as well as patent and trademark) in order to avoid disputes with originators.

D. Data Exclusivity

Article 39.3 of the TRIPS Agreement requires that governments take steps to protect against unfair commercial use of regulatory data submitted in connection with approval of new chemical entities. In a number of countries, this requirement is implemented through the grant by the DRA of "marketing exclusivity" for some period of time. Like the patent, the grant of marketing exclusivity is a creature of national law within the country where exclusivity is granted, and covers only that territory (unless extended through a free trade agreement or other legal arrangement). So far, there has been little discussion concerning whether the placing of a drug on the market in one country where

---

[35] There is extensive European case law on this issue. For an overview, see Héctor Armengod & Laura Melusine Baudenbacher, *The Repackaging of Pharmaceutical Products and Parallel Trade in the EU*, RAJ PHARMA 783–86 (2009).
[36] Kmart v. Cartier, 486 U.S. 281, 108 S. Ct. 1811 (1988).
[37] See e.g. Quality King v. L'Anza, 523 U.S. 135, 118 S. Ct. 1125 (1998).
[38] Kirtsaeng v. John Wiley & Sons, Inc., 133 S. Ct. 1351, 131 S.E. 603 (2012).

there is marketing exclusivity "exhausts" a marketing exclusivity grant in another country (or region). For example, if the U.S. provides a five-year marketing exclusivity term and the EU provides a ten-year term, can a U.S.-based holder of marketing exclusivity in the EU prevent a third-party importer from marketing its drug after it has been lawfully placed on the market in the U.S.? Does the fact that it would be the third party placing it on the market in the EU give the marketing exclusivity holder a right to block the sale of its own U.S.-approved product if it is being sold by a third party? Or, does placing the product on the market in the U.S. exhaust the marketing exclusivity right for that product in the EU?

It may be that this issue has not surfaced in practice because the EU does not recognize international exhaustion of patent rights, and if patents (including extensions) run contemporaneously with marketing exclusivity, the originator holder of an EU parallel patent would be able to block the importation on patent grounds (and the marketing exclusivity would be superfluous).

IV. DIFFERENTIAL PRICING AND VOLUNTARY LICENSING

One long-standing issue regarding parallel trade in medicines concerns its relationship to differential pricing across countries to promote access to medicines. This issue surfaced as a substantial discussion point in the mid-1990s, was addressed in the First and Second Reports, and remains a front-burner issue today.

A patent-owning originator pharmaceutical company may decide to sell or authorize the sale of its product on the market of a developing country at a price substantially below that which it charges in a high income market.[39] As of this writing, for example, Gilead's Sovaldi (sofosbuvir) treatment for hepatitis C is lawfully sold in India pursuant to voluntary license at about U.S.$1,000 compared to US$84,000 for a course of treatment in the U.S.[40] The originator may price differentially for many reasons: altruistic motives (e.g., to promote access to medicines and public health); as a means to diffuse negative public attention to its business model; to discourage activists from challenging its patents; or based on a combination of these and other reasons. The motivation is not terribly relevant to the exhaustion analysis.

Going back to the 1990s, pharmaceutical originator companies argued that a rule of international exhaustion of patent rights would force them to refrain from selling products in developing country markets at lower differentiated prices.[41] They would be forced to charge the "world price" in developing countries. The world price would be the high income market price.

Back in the 1990s, there was little evidence that originator pharmaceutical companies

---

[39] See e.g. Medicines Patent Pool and Gilead Press Release, both *supra* note 9.

[40] Bloomberg, *Americans Want to Pop Made in India Sovaldi Drug for 1 Percent of the Cost*, ECONOMIC TIMES (INDIA), June 3, 2015, available at http://economictimes.indiatimes.com/industry/healthcare/biotech/pharmaceuticals/americans-want-to-pop-made-in-india-sovaldi-drug-for-1-per-cent-of-the-cost/articleshow/47521457.cms.

[41] Harvey E. Bale, Jr., *The Conflicts Between Parallel Trade and Product Access and Innovation: The Case of Pharmaceuticals*, 1 J. INT'L ECON. L. 637 (1999).

actually engaged in the behavior that underlies this issue. That is, there was little evidence of patented drugs being offered for sale at differential low prices in developing countries. But, that is not the case today.

Companies like Gilead, AbbVie and Merck license their patented products through the Medicines Patent Pool or directly to manufacturers in India and China (and most recently potentially to South Africa), allowing them to sell in a large number of developing countries. While the licensees typically may not use the originators' brand names in selling the products,[42] the originators are clearly authorizing the use of their patents, and in this sense the drugs are being placed on the market in the relevant developing countries with the consent of the patent owners. These voluntarily licensed drugs are typically sold at a price far lower than the price in the high income markets, presenting an obvious opportunity for arbitrageurs under a rule of international exhaustion to purchase the drugs in developing countries and move them for resale to high income markets.

In the First Report, I noted that there were at least two options to deal with the problem raised by the pharmaceutical originators. The first was a private market solution of entering into contractual arrangements with purchasers in the developing country markets that would preclude them from exporting the drugs or limiting exports to certain countries.[43] Such a solution would present the originators with an enforcement obligation. They might need to take legal action to block exports and for private operators, it might be difficult to identify, seize, and bar export shipments. Still, the originators could refuse to make subsequent sales to buyers who had previously violated the terms of their agreements, and this might be dissuasive.

The second option would be to transfer authority to block shipments to government authorities by legislating or regulating that pharmaceutical products identified as having been supplied under a specific program were prohibited from export.[44] Such legislation might prima facie be inconsistent with WTO rules against export quotas, but almost certainly would be justified under the General Agreement on Tariffs and Trade (GATT), Article XX(b) exception for measures necessary to protect public health.[45]

These solutions seem equally relevant today. Large quantity sales of low-price antiretroviral medicines to Africa, for example, are typically made to governmental authorities either directly, or through mechanisms like the President's Emergency Plan for AIDS Relief, or PEPFAR. Many of these drugs are generic, and issues of parallel trade may not arise. But, for some second line antiretrovirals, and more recently for drugs to treat hepatitis C, the products sold are under patent and there may be potential for profitable parallel trade. There is no reason why drugs sold under these programs, usually to governmental authorities, should not be contractually restricted to limited markets (e.g., markets specified under a voluntary licensing agreement). In addition, if contractual restraints are

---

[42] See e.g. MEDICINES PATENT POOL & GILEAD SCIENCES, APPENDIX 6D: SUBLICENSE AGREEMENT—NEW LICENSEES IN SOUTH AFRICA (FOR TAF, TDF, FTC, COBI, EVG AND THE QUAD) § 2.6(b) (2015), available at www.medicinespatentpool.org/licensing/current-licences/.
[43] First Report, *supra* note 1, at 635.
[44] *Ibid.*
[45] General Agreement on Tariffs and Trade 1994, April 15, 1994; Marrakesh Agreement Establishing the World Trade Organization, Annex 1A, art. XX(b), 1867 U.N.T.S. 187 (1994) [hereinafter GATT].

not effective, there is no reason why a government should not adopt legislation or regulation, as an exceptional measure, prohibiting exports of drugs supplied under specific differential pricing programs.

This is a potential "problem in fact" and requires a solution if voluntary differential pricing programs are going to be successful.

From the standpoint of access-oriented non-government organizations, it may well be preferable to eliminate the patents on the relevant drugs by challenging the grant of the patents. If there are no patents, there is no exhaustion or parallel trade problem. There is advocacy directed this way. That said, the successful challenge of a patent may entail years of litigation. Until that litigation is resolved, suppliers may not be willing to supply and procurement agencies may not be willing to purchase. This is one reason why a company successful at the initial stages of patent challenge litigation may be willing to accept a voluntary license in lieu of continuing the challenge, such as transpired in the case of Natco and Sovaldi.

V. COMPULSORY LICENSING

An important legal issue surrounding exhaustion of rights involves the definition of the event that may result in exhaustion. The question is whether the placement of pharmaceutical products on the market by a compulsory licensee exhausts the right of the patent holder in the same way as the placement of pharmaceutical products on the market by the patent holder or under its authority (e.g., by its voluntary licensee). This question has been addressed fairly extensively in legal literature and is the subject of some court decisions (e.g., in the European Union), but it is not one that is "resolved" at the international level.[46]

A. Consent and Reward

The jurisprudence of the U.S. Supreme Court and lower federal courts in the U.S. base exhaustion of patent rights on the consent to sell by the patent owner (or under its authority). From a philosophical standpoint, the U.S. federal courts have expressed the view that the patent gives its owner an exclusive right to "first sell" the patented product, and by doing so to recover the "reward" intended by the grant of the patent. This fulfills the intent of the patent law. The patent owner does not have a right to multiple recovery, so it does not control subsequent resales of the product. This would go beyond the intent of the patent law. This, in essence, explains the "first sale doctrine."

From the standpoint of national or international exhaustion as the proper rule, those favoring international exhaustion argue that the geographic location of the first sale is irrelevant to the patent owner's right to secure its reward. It is up to the patent owner to

---

[46] See discussion of the issue in Frederick M. Abbott, *The Doha Declaration on the TRIPS Agreement and Public Health: Lighting a Dark Corner at the WTO*, 5 J. INT'L ECON. L. 469, 494–97 (2002).

decide where to first sell the patented product, whether in the U.S. or outside it.[47] The argument of those favoring national exhaustion is that the reward is only recovered by a first sale in the U.S because of the territorial nature of patent law and because a sale outside the U.S. may not produce the same level of reward.[48]

The U.S. does not have a compulsory licensing provision in its Patent Act. However, courts may order compulsory licensing as a remedy for anticompetitive practices.[49] In addition, the U.S. government has blanket authority to use patented technologies without authorization from the patent owners, subject to the right of patent owners to make claims for the value of the usage before the Court of Claims.[50] While I am not aware of a judicial decision that specifically addresses the issue, it is very doubtful that a patent owner subject to a compulsory license for anticompetitive practices would be entitled to block subsequent resales of products by the compulsory licensees; to allow this practice would be inconsistent with the fundamental purpose of the license to further competition. In other words, the first sale rule under a compulsory license would apply from the standpoint of national exhaustion of rights. Whether the patent owner could continue to invoke its patent rights outside the U.S. would depend on the law of the other country(ies).

The Court of Justice of the European Union (CJEU) has decided that sales by compulsory licensees do not exhaust patent rights from the standpoint of free movement among the Member States.[51] Like the federal courts of the U.S., the CJEU has grounded its patent exhaustion rule on the placement of the product on the market by the patent owner, or with its consent. This appears also to be grounded in the "recovery of reward" theory employed by the U.S. federal courts.

Compulsory patent licensing is a feature of the patent law of the EU Member States, and the CJEU has not disapproved of the practice. The new EU patent system does not interfere with the right of the Member States to grant compulsory licenses, but limits their effect to the Member State granting the license.[52] While this "solution" has been criticized as inconsistent with the fundamental characteristics of a unitary patent, if applied consistently with prior CJEU jurisprudence, it would indicate that a compulsory license would not authorize "free movement" of the subject product among the EU Member States. Earlier versions of the draft EU Patent Regulation had made specific provision regarding compulsory licensing, but that was dropped.

---

[47] Lexmark Int'l v. Impression Products, Corrected Brief of Amicus Curiae Professors Barrett and Abbott in Support of Neither Party, 2015 WL 3645388 (Appellate Brief, C.A. Fed., 2015).

[48] Brief of Amicus Curiae American Intellectual Property Law Association in Support of Neither Party, 2015 WL 3645389 (Appellate Brief, C.A. Fed. 2015).

[49] See Makan Delrahim, Deputy Assistant Attorney General, Antitrust Division, U.S. Department of Justice, *Forcing Firms to Share the Sandbox: Compulsory Licensing of Intellectual Property Rights and Antitrust*, speech at the British Institute of International and Comparative Law, London, England, May 10, 2004.

[50] 28 U.S.C. § 1498 (1948).

[51] Case 19/84, Pharmon v. Hoechst, [1985] E.C.R. 2281. See Carri Ginter, *Free Movement of Goods and Parallel Imports in the Internal Market of the EU*, 7(3/4) EUROPEAN J. LAW REFORM 505, 511 (2006).

[52] See e.g. Clement Salung Petersen, Thomas Riis, & Jens Schovsbo, *The Unified Patent Court (UPC), Compulsory Licensing and Competition Law*, NORDISKT IMMATERIEELT RÄTTSKYDD (NIR) 8–9 (2014), available at http://ssrn.com/abstract=2489006.

B. Lawful Placement

An alternative theory of international exhaustion would recognize sales by compulsory licensees as exhausting patent rights because a sale under compulsory license is "lawful," i.e., authorized by governmental authority.[53] The government (including the courts) in a circumstance of compulsory licensing has decided that for one reason or another it is going to interfere with the right of the patent holder to determine its reward by setting its own price or other conditions of sale; it will usually determine a reward or royalty to be paid to the patent owner as an alternative. For remedy of competition abuse, that reward may be nonexistent or limited.[54]

As discussed above, in terms of an individual country, the decision by the government/courts to grant a compulsory license almost certainly constitutes a first sale that exhausts the patent owner's rights to control subsequent movement of the goods. The alternative would appear inconsistent with the reasons for granting compulsory licenses in the first place (i.e., to overcome patent-based limitations on access). From the standpoint of national exhaustion, sales by compulsory licensees almost certainly have the same effect as sales by patent owners.

The objection from the standpoint of international exhaustion is that under an international regime that recognizes compulsory licensing as a mechanism triggering a global first sale rule, any country could effectively deprive a patent owner of its right to determine its reward, and effectively, deprives the patent owner of its pricing power in every country that adopts a rule of international exhaustion. Absent some agreement among countries on the appropriate grounds under which such an action could be taken, the government/courts of any single country could effectively determine global pricing for any patent owner. To give an illustration of the concern, the courts of China could grant compulsory licenses on patents owned by U.S. companies, with those compulsory licensing decisions effectively authorizing Chinese companies to export "patent free" to any country that adopted international exhaustion. This is the same type of concern that underlies the rule of independence of patents in the Paris Convention. The ultimate concern is that the government of one country could determine the fate of patents in other members of the Paris Convention. Similar concerns underlay the inclusion of Article 31(f) of the TRIPS Agreement. This Article limits compulsory licensing to predominantly supplying the domestic market of the country in which the licenses are granted, subject now to the WTO August 30, 2003 Waiver Decision.[55] A rule of international exhaustion might circumvent this limitation if the exports are undertaken by third-party purchasers.

Commentators and non-governmental organizations (NGOs) supporting improved access to medicines support recognition of exhaustion based on compulsory licensing. The decision by any country to issue a compulsory license and substantially lower the

---

[53] See CARLOS CORREA, INTEGRATING PUBLIC HEALTH CONCERNS INTO PATENT LEGISLATION IN DEVELOPING COUNTRIES 71–80 (2000), available at http://apps.who.int/medicinedocs/pdf/h2963e/h2963e.pdf; see discussion in Abbott, *supra* note 5.

[54] See TRIPS Agreement, *supra* note 2, art. 31(k).

[55] See Frederick M. Abbott, *The WTO Medicines Decision: World Pharmaceutical Trade and the Protection of Public Health*, 99 AM. J. INT'L LAW 317 (2005), available at http://ssrn.com/abstract=763224.

price of a medicine could effectively make that pricing available for all other countries that recognize international exhaustion. This would be an easy solution to problems of access and affordability.

There is nothing in the TRIPS Agreement or the Doha Declaration that expressly limits exhaustion of rights to sales made by the patent owner (or with its consent) or that expressly denies exhaustion based on compulsory licensing. It can be argued that there is a limitation implied by Article 28 of the TRIPS Agreement regarding the rights of the patent owner to prohibit third parties from offering or selling goods without its consent.[56] The argument is that, because patent rights under the TRIPS Agreement are defined by the patent owner's consent, exhaustion is based on consent. The potential flaw in this argument is that from a national standpoint, there clearly are exceptions to the consent basis, e.g., for compulsory licensing and competition remedies. The potential rejoinder is that the TRIPS Agreement defines those exceptions and thereby limits them.

VI. PRICE CONTROLS AND OTHER MARKET REGULATIONS

Pharmaceuticals are not developed, sold, or traded on a "free market" in the sense of a commercial space subject to minimal regulation. Virtually every aspect of the pharmaceutical business is controlled in one manner or another, though the intensity of such control varies substantially among countries. The U.S., for example, makes it very difficult for the developer of a "new" drug to secure approval for commercial marketing because the FDA imposes stringent controls in terms of quality, safety, and efficacy. At the same time, the U.S. imposes modest controls regarding the prices that may be charged for medicines, leaving this comparatively unregulated from a global standpoint.

A. Price Controls

The consumers of medicines in the U.S., the purchasing arms of state health programs, and others have imported "prescription" drugs from Canada where prices are lower largely based on the Canadian price control mechanisms. Similarly, proposals have been introduced in the U.S. Congress to authorize importation from Europe in order to take advantage of lower European prices[57] which, again, are largely due to price controls of one form or another.

---

[56] Per the TRIPS Agreement, art. 28: "1. A patent shall confer on its owner the following exclusive rights: (a) where the subject matter of a patent is a product, to prevent third parties *not having the owner's consent* from the acts of: making, using, offering for sale, selling, or importing for these purposes that product." (Emphasis added.)

[57] Elliott A. Foote, *Prescription Drug Importation: An Expended FDA Personal Use Exemption and Qualified Regulators for Foreign-Produced Pharmaceuticals*, 27 Loy. Consumer L. Rev. 369 (2015), available at http://lawecommons.luc.edu/lclr/vol27/iss3/2. This legislative situation is rather complex. Congress has authorized the Department of Health and Human Services to promulgate rules allowing imports from Europe, but the Department has consistently refused to authorize such imports on grounds that it is unable to verify the safety of such products. If imports are to be authorized, this will probably require a more direct form of legislation from Congress that does not leave discretion to the Department.

It is obvious that authorizing parallel imports from Canada or the EU would benefit consumers in the U.S. by lowering prescription/patented drug prices. From the standpoint of the pharmaceutical originators the importation of price-controlled products interferes with the "free market" for pricing in the U.S. The originators are forced to compete with their own products, as to which prices have been set outside the U.S.; they view this as a form of unfair competition.

In the First Report, I expressed some sympathy for the argument by patent owner originators that parallel importation of price-controlled products interfered with their ability to set prices. I suggested first that as a "private market" solution the originators should sell only so much of their product on the price controlled market as was necessary to satisfy local demand and that resulting shortages based on parallel exports would be a subject for the national government to address. In fact, originator companies have sought to control parallel exports in this way, and the CJEU has refused to prohibit this practice as *per se* unlawful as a matter of competition law.[58] At the same time, up until now, the CJEU has refused to allow originator patent owners to block parallel imports on grounds that intra-union exports are being made from price-controlled EU markets,[59] although supplies destined for parallel trade may be limited under appropriate conditions (i.e., when reasonable and proportionate).[60]

To be clear, governments are allowed to adopt price controls of pharmaceutical products as a matter of WTO law. In all events, such measures are necessary to protect public health. There can be no suggestion that such controls nullify or impair benefits that WTO members or their companies expected to obtain when they entered into the WTO Agreements because price controls were ubiquitous when those agreements were negotiated, and there was no suggestion that the negotiations intended to eliminate those controls.[61] Price controls on pharmaceutical products serve a valuable public health function.

Government actions to promote pharmaceutical exports may constitute unfair trading practices, including unlawful subsidies and dumping. For example, if a country provides its pharmaceutical industry with below-market pricing for an input such as electricity, resulting exports may be considered unlawfully subsidized based on a bounty to a specific industry. Such subsidies are currently a subject of contention between India and China with respect to China's API sector.

A general program of price controls on pharmaceuticals is unlikely to be considered a prohibited subsidy or to involve dumping. While the price controls may be applicable to a specific industry, there is first a question of whether there is a benefit to the domestic industry. The domestic manufacturing sector is likely to become less profitable because of the price controls, so there is question whether there is a subsidy at all. Wholesalers

---

[58] *Ibid.*
[59] See e.g. Joined Cases C-267 and C-268/95, Merck v. Primecrown et al., [1996] E.C.R. I-06285.
[60] Cases C-468/06 to C-478/06, Sot Lélos kai Sia EE & ors. v. GlaxoSmithKline AEVE Farmakeftikon Proïonton1, [2008] E.C.R. I-07139.
[61] Frederick M. Abbott, *Non-Violation Nullification or Impairment Causes of Action Under the TRIPS Agreement and the Fifth Ministerial Conference: A Warning and Reminder*, QUAKER UNITED NATIONS OFFICE (GENEVA) (QUNO), OCCASIONAL PAPER NO. 1 (2003), available at http://ssrn.com/abstract=2364991.

(i.e., parallel traders) who purchase pharmaceuticals in the domestic market and export them to higher value markets may profit from the price controls. It is not clear from the beginning whether wholesalers are the type of enterprise to whom subsidies may be attributed under the WTO Subsidies Agreement. If they are, in order for a subsidy to be prohibited, it needs to cause material injury to the domestic industry of the importing country. Could parallel imports from a price controlled market materially injure the pharmaceutical industry of the U.S., for example?

Assuming for the sake of argument that a system of price controls could operate as a benefit in favor of an exporting industry (e.g., wholesalers) and injure a foreign industry (e.g., U.S. pharmaceutical producers), the remedy for the U.S. would be to impose countervailing duties on the imported products. That would offset the "subsidy." The exporting country is not obligated to withdraw the price control subsidy.[62]

With all that said, if the U.S. Congress decides to authorize parallel imports of patented pharmaceuticals from Canada, Europe, and other countries in comparable economic circumstances as a way to take advantage of price controls "through the back door," it can equally well legislate that there shall be no cause of action against such imports based on claims of unlawful subsidy or dumping.

This, however, brings us to a fundamental question. Why would the government of a country resort to parallel imports to take advantage of foreign government price controls when it can adopt price controls of its own? Does it make sense for the U.S. to rely on Canadian price control authorities to moderate pharmaceutical prices in the U.S.?

In the end, it is the unwillingness of the U.S. Congress to consider moderating prices in the U.S. that gives rise to these legal gyrations. It is possible to moderate prices through the "back door" using the mechanism of international exhaustion and parallel importation from price-controlled markets, but this is largely a matter of abdicating legislative responsibility. Almost certainly, the pharmaceutical originators would react to open parallel importation by limiting the quantities of products placed on foreign markets, the wholesalers would continue to arbitrage prices, and the foreign governments would need to step in to prevent drug shortages. For this reason, some of the legislative proposals to the U.S. Congress have included a statement that reducing supplies to foreign markets will be considered an anticompetitive practice within the U.S. While that might help to alleviate the potential supply problem, it merely adds another layer of illogic and obfuscation to attempting to address high prices by importing price controls. If Congress reaches the conclusion that U.S. prices need to be moderated, it should adopt measures to control those prices. It does not need to rely on the legislatures of Canada and France.

B. Other Regulatory Measures

Establishing access for parallel imported drugs is not only a matter of adopting a policy of international exhaustion of patent, trademark, and copyright. Whether a pharmaceutical product may be imported and sold is directly dependent upon compliance with local approval and registration requirements. A parallel trader in a country where the originator

---

[62] See e.g. Agreement on Subsidies and Countervailing Measures, April 15, 1994; Marrakesh Agreement Establishing the World Trade Organization, Annex 1A, 1867 U.N.T.S. 299 (1994).

does not market its product may find it difficult to register that product for importation for a potential variety of reasons, including (but not limited to) access to the originator's drug master file/dossier.

VII. TPP, ACTA, *ET AL.*

The most recently leaked draft of the Trans-Pacific Partnership Agreement (TPP) does not attempt to preclude prospective parties from adopting a rule of international exhaustion with respect to any intellectual property right.[63] However, as with the Anti-Counterfeiting Trade Agreement (ACTA)[64] before it, there is a proposal with respect to criminal trademark infringement that could have a serious adverse effect on parallel trade in pharmaceutical products. Specifically, from the May 16, 2014 Ho Chi Minh text,[65] it is proposed to criminalize willful importation and domestic use on a commercial scale of labels or packaging:

> to which a mark has been applied without authorization which is identical to a trademark registered in its territory; and . . . which are intended to be used in the course of trade on goods . . . which are identical to goods or services for which such trademark is registered.

There is case law in the U.S. holding that the re-use (e.g., through importation) by a parallel importer of a trademark without the consent of the trademark owner may constitute

---

[63] Trans-Pacific Partnership Negotiations, May 16, 2014, *Intellectual Property [Rights] Chapter, Ho Chi Minh, IP Group*, art. QQ.A.11: {Exhaustion of IP Rights}: "Nothing in this Chapter shall be construed to address the issue of the exhaustion of intellectual property rights." Available at https://wikileaks.org/tpp-ip2/.

[64] Office of the United State Trade Representative, Anti-Counterfeiting Trade Agreement (2011), available at www.mofa.go.jp/policy/economy/i_property/pdfs/acta1105_en.pdf.

[65] Trans-Pacific Partnership, *supra* note 63, art. QQ.H.7: "{Criminal Procedures and Remedies / Criminal Enforcement}[180] 3. Each Party shall provide for criminal [VN propose: or administrative] procedures and penalties to be applied in cases of willful importation[187] and domestic use, in the course of trade and on a commercial scale, of labels or packaging[188]: (a) to which a mark has been applied without authorization which is identical to, [PE oppose: or cannot be distinguished from][189], a trademark registered in its territory; and (b) which are intended to be used in the course of trade on goods or in relation to services which are identical to goods or services for which such trademark is registered.[190] 180 In conjunction with Article QQ.H.7, nothing prevents a Party from exercising any discretion that it may have to also provide for administrative enforcement procedures and penalties. [VN propose: A Party that provides for administrative procedures and penalties as an alternative to criminal procedures and penalties under [this Chapter]/[paragraphs QQ.G.10(a), QQ.G.13(a), QQ.H.7.3, QQ.H.7.4, QQ.H.8.2, QQ.H.9.1] shall ensure that: (i) such administrative penalties shall be [of sufficient severity to provide a deterrent]/[substantially equivalent to criminal penalties as required by this Chapter and may not include imprisonment]; and (ii) its administrative authorities may initiate a legal action without a formal complaint. 187 A Party may comply with its obligation relating to importation of labels or packaging through its measures concerning distribution. 188 A Party may comply with its obligation under this paragraph by providing for criminal procedures and penalties to be applied to attempts to commit a trademark offense. 189 Negotiator's Note: PE to confirm whether it can go along with this language. 190 Negotiator's Note: U.S. is prepared to drop illicit labels chausette ad ref pending outcome."

trademark infringement. In *Lever Brothers v. United States*,[66] the District of Columbia (DC) Circuit addressed the argument from the Treasury Department that a trademark placed on a good by the trademark owner was "genuine," so that use by a parallel importer did not unlawfully "copy or simulate" the owner's trademark, regardless whether the trademark owner's goods produced abroad were identical to its goods produced in the U.S. It held:

> Customs' main argument from the legislative history is that section 42 of the Lanham Act applies only to imports of goods bearing trademarks that "copy or simulate" a registered mark. Customs thus draws a distinction between "genuine" marks and marks that "copy or simulate." A mark applied by a foreign firm subject to ownership and control common to that of the domestic trademark owner is by definition "genuine," Customs urges, regardless of whether or not the goods are identical. Thus, any importation of goods manufactured by an affiliate of a U.S. trademark owner cannot "copy or simulate" a registered mark because those goods are *ipso facto* "genuine."

> This argument is fatally flawed. It rests on the false premise that foreign trademarks applied to foreign goods are "genuine" in the U.S. Trademarks applied to physically different foreign goods are not genuine from the viewpoint of the American consumer. As we stated in *Lever I*:

> On its face ... section [42] appears to aim at deceit and consumer confusion; when identical trademarks have acquired different meanings in different countries, one who imports the foreign version to sell it under that trademark will (in the absence of some specially differentiating feature) cause the confusion Congress sought to avoid. The fact of affiliation between the producers in no way reduces the probability of that confusion; it is certainly not a constructive consent to importation. 877 F.2d at 111.[67]

Although the *Lever II* decision is specifically directed at genuine parallel import goods that are materially different than the goods on the market in the U.S., the language used by the DC Circuit is broad. There is a "false premise" that "foreign trademarks" (i.e., parallel trademarks registered by U.S. companies abroad) are "'genuine' in the U.S.," even when placed on the goods by the original manufacturer/trademark owner.

The provision in the draft TPP refers to a mark that has been placed on goods without the authorization of the trademark owner. The DC Circuit has held that the trademark placed on the goods abroad is not "genuine" from the standpoint of U.S. law. It takes modest legal imagination to expect that U.S. courts may decide that virtually any act taken by a parallel trader with respect to a trademarked good will cause the mark not to be considered "genuine"; for example, repackaging or labeling of pharmaceutical products to include information required by the FDA.

The provision on criminal trademark infringement through packaging and labeling did not appear in the ACTA or draft TPP by accident. The potential implications for parallel traders are evident. Even assuming that there is some uncertainty as to whether U.S.

---

[66] Lever Brothers v. United States, 299 U.S. App. D.C. 128, 981 F.2d 1330 (D.C. Cir. 1993) ("*Lever II*").
[67] *Ibid.* at 136.

courts will continue to follow the line of reasoning of the DC Circuit in *Lever II*, it would almost certainly have a chilling effect on parallel trade in medicines.

VIII. CONCLUSION: THE FUTURE FOR PARALLEL TRADE IN MEDICINES

Pharmaceuticals do not trade in a freely competitive market. Pharmaceuticals markets are heavily regulated, particularly in the higher income countries. A combination of barriers to approval by drug regulatory authorities, import controls, and intellectual property protections can make it very difficult to penetrate markets. Not touched upon above, but nevertheless an important factor in terms of market penetration, is that in many countries procurement markets (private and public) are highly concentrated, with a few major distribution firms controlling the national supply chain.

In terms of pricing power, there is no greater distortion mechanism than the patent. Just in the past several years the pricing of new cancer treatments has become so high in the U.S. that leading oncologist groups have begun to protest the absence of correlation between cost and price, and legislation has been introduced to demand justification of pricing.[68]

Into this arena enters the relatively modest procompetitive trade mechanism of parallel trade. The producer chooses the market in which it places its drug product and then no longer controls future sales in terms of price or geography. That is the role of the parallel trader. Giving up this control does not mean an escape from further regulation. Parallel imports must comply with market entry and distribution regulations, but they are in new hands. Pharmaceuticals may move from low-priced markets to high-priced markets, taking advantage of spreads that may exist for any number of reasons, including fluctuations in currencies. They may take advantage of differences in price controls.

In light of the enormous pricing power of pharmaceutical originator patent owners, the price moderation mechanism of parallel trade is a modest step toward improving the situation of consumers/patients and government budgets.

This does not mean that there should not be exceptions to a general rule authorizing parallel trade in pharmaceutical products. If an originator company voluntarily licenses a patented product for distribution in low and middle income countries at prices substantially below the "market" price in the high income countries, it should be able to make contractual arrangements with the licensees that the resulting production and distribution will be limited to designated markets. Government programs that take advantage of such special discriminatory pricing may add the weight of government re-export restrictions on such specifically licensed products. In the absence of such arrangements, it is reasonable to assume that arbitrageurs will play their ordinary role and move specially priced products to higher income/higher-priced markets.

There is indeed the alternative of relying on the successful challenge of patents to

---

[68] See e.g. Andrew Pollack, *Drug Prices Soar, Prompting Calls for Justification*, N.Y. TIMES, July 23, 2015, available at www.nytimes.com/2015/07/23/business/drug-companies-pushed-from-far-and-wide-to-explain-high-prices.html?hp&action=click&pgtype=Homepage&module=first-column-region&region=top-news&WT.nav=top-news.

accomplish a similar end, but there are significant potential drawbacks to that approach as well. Patent challenges tend to be long drawn out affairs, winding their way through appeals processes, during which time producers face real risks of retroactive damages based on early market entry. Moreover, there are patents that will be upheld; patent challenges do not work in each case.

In the First Report, I was somewhat sympathetic to the complaints of the originators that price controls more generally took unfair advantage of them by forcing competition with government-directed lower-priced sales. Close to twenty years later, and with substantially more experience dealing in and with the pharmaceutical industry, I am far less sympathetic to originator complaints about government price controls distorting ordinary international trade mechanisms, if for no other reason than that pricing practices have shown no respect for consumers or public health budgets. The originator pharmaceutical industry is not a sympathetic group.

If a government's pricing control practices become sufficiently distortive such that the conduct is manifestly unfair, a pharmaceutical company may be justified in restricting the quantity of drugs delivered into that market. But, that is not ordinarily the case. A pharmaceutical company must justify restriction of supply on grounds that it is a reasonable and proportionate response, as suggested by the CJEU. Restriction of supply may otherwise constitute an anticompetitive practice.

As a general rule, international exhaustion of patent, trademark, and copyright should be a mandatory rule for the international trading system. Political reality may, for the time being, dictate otherwise. This still leaves each government with a choice to adopt international exhaustion. This should help to facilitate price reductions in the global market for pharmaceuticals. But, care must be exercised to police against cartelization among the originators. Cartelization is a "not atypical" response to pricing challenges.

PART III

INTELLECTUAL PROPERTY EXHAUSTION AND PARALLEL IMPORTS: REGIONAL AND NATIONAL APPROACHES

9. The European internal market: exhaustion plus
*Christopher M. Stothers**

I. INTRODUCTION

This chapter considers the extent to which the European Union (EU) and the European Economic Area (EEA) provide for intellectual property exhaustion principles going beyond those typically found in national laws.

Following the Agreement on Trade-Related Aspects to Intellectual Property Rights (TRIPS) of the World Trade Organization (WTO),[1] the term "TRIPS-plus" became commonly used to describe and propose international agreements providing for intellectual property protection beyond the TRIPS minimum requirements and was particularly adopted by those opposed to such extension.[2]

Most people regard TRIPS as neutral with relation to exhaustion. However, the term "exhaustion plus" is therefore used, by analogy, to describe the extent to which the Treaty on the Functioning of the European Union[3] (TFEU) and the Agreement on the European Economic Area (EEA Agreement)[4] provide for the principles of exhaustion that go beyond national norms.

II. EUROPEAN FRAMEWORK

The European framework is set out in the TFEU provisions regarding the free movement of goods. These provisions are found in Articles 34 and 36. Notably, Article 34 reads:

> Quantitative restrictions on imports and all measures having equivalent effect shall be prohibited between Member States.[5]

Article 36 reads:

---

*   Partner, Arnold & Porter (UK) LLP, London; Visiting Lecturer, University College London.
[1]   Agreement on Trade-Related Aspects of Intellectual Property Rights, April 15, 1994; Marrakesh Agreement Establishing the World Trade Organisation, Annex 1C, 1867 U.N.T.S. 154 (1995) [hereinafter TRIPS].
[2]   For some recent examples, see MOHAMMED EL SAID, PUBLIC HEALTH RELATED TRIPS-PLUS PROVISIONS IN BILATERAL TRADE AGREEMENTS: A POLICY GUIDE FOR NEGOTIATORS AND IMPLEMENTERS IN THE EASTERN MEDITERRANEAN REGION (2010); CYNTHIA HO, *An Overview of 'TRIPS-plus' Standards, in* ACCESS TO MEDICINES IN THE GLOBAL ECONOMY (2011).
[3]   Consolidated Version of the Treaty on the Functioning of the European Union, October 26, 2010, [2012] O.J. C326 [hereinafter TFEU].
[4]   Agreement on the European Economic Area, December 13, 1993, [1994] O.J. L1/3 [hereinafter EEA Agreement].
[5]   TFEU, art. 34.

The provisions of Articles 34 and 35 shall not preclude prohibitions or restrictions on imports, exports or goods in transit justified on grounds of public morality, public policy or public security; the protection of health and life of humans, animals or plants; the protection of national treasures possessing artistic, historic or archaeological value; or the protection of industrial and commercial property. Such prohibitions or restrictions shall not, however, constitute a means of arbitrary discrimination or a disguised restriction on trade between Member States.[6]

Provisions mirroring these are found in Articles 11[7] and 13[8] of the EEA Agreement. These provisions are therefore in effect in the 28 Member States of the EU[9] and also the three additional Contracting Parties of the EEA.[10]

Although these provisions do not explicitly mention exhaustion, the Court of Justice of the European Union (CJEU) quickly interpreted the provisions inclusively, beginning in *Deutsche Grammophon*[11] where the CJEU held:

12. If a right related to copyright is relied upon to prevent the marketing in a Member State of products distributed by the holder of the right or with his consent on the territory of another Member State on the sole ground that such distribution did not take place on the national territory, such a prohibition, which would legitimize the isolation of national markets, would be repugnant to the essential purpose of the Treaty, which is to unite national markets into a single market.

That purpose could not be attained if, under the various legal systems of the Member States, nationals of those states were able to partition the market and bring about arbitrary discrimination or disguised restrictions on trade between Member States.

13. Consequently, it would be in conflict with the provisions prescribing the free movement of products within the common market for a manufacturer of sound recordings to exercise the exclusive right to distribute the protected articles, conferred upon him by the legislation of a Member State, in such a way as to prohibit the sale in that state of products placed on the market by him or with his consent in another Member State solely because such distribution did not occur within the territory of the first Member State.

This language, which strongly supported parallel trade of goods between Member States, was subsequently adopted in the EU legislation harmonizing various intellectual property rights. For instance, Article 7 of the Trade Mark Directive, "Exhaustion of the rights conferred by a trade mark,"[12] reads:

---

[6] *Ibid.* art. 36.
[7] EEA Agreement, art. 11.
[8] *Ibid.* art. 13.
[9] The 28 Member States of the European Union (EU) are: Austria, Belgium, Bulgaria, Croatia, Cyprus, Czech Republic, Denmark, Estonia, Finland, France, Germany, Greece, Hungary, Ireland, Italy, Latvia, Lithuania, Luxembourg, Malta, Netherlands, Poland, Portugal, Romania, Slovakia, Slovenia, Spain, Sweden, and the U.K.
[10] The three contracting parties to the European Economic Area (EEA) in addition to the 28 EU Member States are: Iceland, Lichtenstein, and Norway.
[11] Case 78/70, Deutsche Grammophon v. Metro, [1971] E.C.R. 487, 500.
[12] Directive 2008/95/EC of the European Parliament and of the Council of October 22, 2008 to approximate the laws of the Member States relating to Trade Marks (codified version), [2008] O.J. L299/25, 29 [hereinafter Trade Mark Directive]. In 2015, a new Trade Mark Directive was adopted. See Directive (EU) 2015/2436 of the European Parliament and of the Council of December 16, 2015 to approximate the laws of the Member States relating to trademarks [2015] O.J. L336/1 (EU). According to Article 56, Article 15 will enter into force on January

1. The trade mark shall not entitle the proprietor to prohibit its use in relation to goods which have been put on the market in the Community under that trade mark by the proprietor or with his consent.

2. Paragraph 1 shall not apply where there exist legitimate reasons for the proprietor to oppose further commercialisation of the goods, especially where the condition of the goods is changed or impaired after they have been put on the market.

As a consequence, regional exhaustion applies across the EEA as it would within a single jurisdiction. However, the underlying policy goal to unite national markets into a single market in some cases has driven the CJEU to go further and require "exhaustion plus." Six specific examples of "exhaustion plus" are discussed in section III below: (a) goods whose condition has been changed—packaging; (b) goods which were put on the market under a different mark; (c) goods which were not put on the market by the proprietor or with his consent; (d) goods which were not put on the market in the EEA; (e) goods where the right holder did not object quickly enough; and (f) services.

III. EXAMPLES OF "EXHAUSTION PLUS"

A. Goods Whose Condition has been Changed—Packaging

Where a third party changes the condition of goods, the question arises whether the doctrine of exhaustion should still apply. This is the case not only in relation to the goods themselves, but also to their packaging. In *Hoffmann-La Roche v. Centrafarm*,[13] the CJEU recognized that the essential function of a trademark was "to guarantee the identity of the origin of the trade-marked product by the consumer or ultimate user" and so a trademark owner could justifiably have a right to oppose resale of repackaged goods. That right was then codified in Article 7(2) of the Trade Mark Directive.[14]

However, the CJEU also recognized that such a right could block parallel trade of goods, particularly where instructions had to be provided in a language the ultimate user understood, necessitating repackaging. Therefore, the CJEU held that the rights could not be exercised where various criteria were met, in particular that the repackaging did not adversely affect the original condition of the product and that the trademark owner receives prior notice of the marketing of the repackaged product.[15] This was extended in *Bristol-Myers Squibb v. Paranova*,[16] which laid down five conditions for repackaging in the following terms:

15, 2019 and repeal Article 7 of Directive 2008/95/EC (the current provision on trademark exhaustion).

[13] Case 102/77, Hoffmann-La Roche v. Centrafarm, [1978] E.C.R. 1139, 1164.
[14] Trade Mark Directive, art. 7(2).
[15] Hoffmann-La Roche v. Centrafarm, *supra* note 13, [1978] E.C.R. at 1166.
[16] Joined Cases 427, 429, & 436/93, Bristol-Myers Squibb v. Paranova, [1996] E.C.R. I-3457, and the related cases decided on the same day.

Article 7(2) of Directive 89/104 [now Directive 2008/95] must be interpreted as meaning that the trade mark owner may legitimately oppose the further marketing of a pharmaceutical product where the importer has repackaged the product and reaffixed the trade mark unless:

- it is established that reliance on trade mark rights by the owner in order to oppose the marketing of repackaged products under that trade mark would contribute to the artificial partitioning of the markets between Member States; such is the case, in particular, where the owner has put an identical pharmaceutical product on the market in several Member States in various forms of packaging, and the repackaging carried out by the importer is necessary in order to market the product in the Member State of importation, and is carried out in such conditions that the original condition of the product cannot be affected by it; that condition does not, however, imply that it must be established that the trade mark owner deliberately sought to partition the markets between Member States;
- it is shown that the repackaging cannot affect the original condition of the product inside the packaging; such is the case, in particular, where the importer has merely carried out operations involving no risk of the product being affected, such as, for example, the removal of blister packs, flasks, phials, ampoules or inhalers from their original external packaging and their replacement in new external packaging, the fixing of self-stick labels on the inner packaging of the product, the addition to the packaging of new user instructions or information, or the insertion of an extra article; it is for the national court to verify that the original condition of the product inside the packaging is not indirectly affected, for example, by the fact that the external or inner packaging of the repackaged product or new user instructions or information omits certain important information or gives inaccurate information, or the fact that an extra article inserted in the packaging by the importer and designed for the ingestion and dosage of the product does not comply with the method of use and the doses envisaged by the manufacturer;
- the new packaging clearly states who repackaged the product and the name of the manufacturer in print such that a person with normal eyesight, exercising a normal degree of attentiveness, would be in a position to understand; similarly, the origin of an extra article from a source other than the trade mark owner must be indicated in such a way as to dispel any impression that the trade mark owner is responsible for it; however, it is not necessary to indicate that the repackaging was carried out without the authorization of the trade mark owner;
- the presentation of the repackaged product is not such as to be liable to damage the reputation of the trade mark and of its owner; thus, the packaging must not be defective, of poor quality, or untidy; and
- the importer gives notice to the trade mark owner before the repackaged product is put on sale, and, on demand, supplies him with a specimen of the repackaged product.[17]

Thus, the CJEU requires, among other things, that the presentation of the repackaged product will not damage the reputation of the trademark or its owner, and that the importer not only gives notice, but supplies the trademark owner, on demand, with a specimen of the repackaged product.

There have been a slew of subsequent references in the CJEU regarding these "*BMS* conditions."[18] The main cases have been decided in favor of exhaustion and, therefore, the parallel importers, for instance, by indicating that fifteen working days' notice (just under a month) is likely to be reasonable. However, the obligation to provide advance notice is

---

[17] *Ibid.* at I-3541–42.
[18] See e.g. Case C-143/00, Boehinger Ingelheim v. Swingward, [2002] E.C.R. I-3759 ("*Dowelhurst I*"); Case C-348/04, Boehinger Ingelheim v. Swingward, [2002] E.C.R. I-3759 ("*Dowelhurst II*"), as applied by the English Court of Appeal in [2008] EWCA (Civ) 83; Joined Cases C-400/09 and C-207/10, Orifarm v. Merck Sharp & Dohme, [2011] E.C.R. I-7063.

a strong one. Failure to do will result in infringing goods and the importer will be liable for the normal remedies.[19] Similarly, the Danish Supreme Court has held that omitting the name of the trademark owner from the repackaged goods can be liable to damage its reputation and resulting infringement.[20]

However, regardless of the "*BMS* conditions," the first clear example of "exhaustion plus" is the fact that trademark owners have any limitations placed on their right to object to repackaging.

B. Goods Which Were Put on the Market Under a Different Mark

The second example of "exhaustion plus" is seen where parallel importers are permitted not only to repackage but even to use a different trademark. This is not permitted under the Trade Mark Directive but remains permitted under the TFEU itself. This example is perhaps the strongest illustration of "exhaustion plus" because the mark being used was never used on the particular goods for which it is now said to be exhausted. It would be unthinkable to allow a supermarket "own brand" product to be resold under a premium trademark on the basis that the trademark owner manufactured both products, even if there was no difference in quality.

However, the CJEU decided that this could be permissible in cases where the trademark owner deliberately used different marks in different countries seeking to partition the single market. The CJEU in *Centrafarm v. American Home Products*[21] held:

> 18. The proprietor of a trade-mark which is protected in one Member State is accordingly justified pursuant to the first sentence of Article 36 in preventing a product from being marketed by a third party in that Member State under the mark in question even if previously that product has been lawfully marketed in another Member State under another mark held in the latter state by the same proprietor.
>
> 19. Nevertheless it is still necessary to consider whether the exercise of that right may constitute a "disguised restriction on trade between Member States" within the meaning of the second sentence of Article 36.
>
> 20. In this connexion it should be observed that it may be lawful for the manufacturer of a product to use in different Member States different marks for the same product.
>
> 21. Nevertheless it is possible for such a practice to be followed by the proprietor of the marks as part of a system of marketing intended to partition the markets artificially.
>
> 22. In such a case the prohibition by the proprietor of the unauthorized affixing of the mark by a third party constitutes a disguised restriction on intra-Community trade for the purposes of the above-mentioned provision.
>
> 23. It is for the national court to settle in each particular case whether the proprietor has followed the practice of using different marks for the same product for the purpose of partitioning the markets.[22]

---

[19] See also Hollister v. Medik Ostomy Supplies, [2012] EWCA (Civ) 1419, [2012] W.L.R. 327 (Eng.).
[20] Case 286/2013, Merck Sharp & Dohme v. Orifarm (2015) (decided April 30, 2015, not yet reported).
[21] Case 3/78, Centrafarm B.V. v. American Home Prods. Co., [1978] E.C.R. 1823.
[22] *Ibid.* at 1841–42.

However, the need to prove the subjective intention of the trademark owner was removed in *Pharmacia & Upjohn v. Paranova*,[23] following the first of the "*BMS* conditions" for repackaging. The Court reasoned:

> 37. The view expressed by Paranova, by the Netherlands and United Kingdom Governments, and by the Commission, in this respect is correct: there is no objective difference between reaffixing a trade mark after repackaging and replacing the original trade mark by another which is capable of justifying the condition of artificial partitioning being applied differently in each of those cases.
>
> 38. In the first place, the practice of using different packaging and that of using different trade marks for the same product, in contributing similarly to the partitioning of the single market, adversely affect intracommunity trade in the same way; secondly, the reaffixing of the original trade mark on the repackaged product and its replacement by another trade mark both represent a use by the parallel importer of a trade mark which does not belong to him.
>
> 39. Consequently, where the trade-mark rights in the importing Member State allow the proprietor of the trade mark to prevent it being reaffixed after repackaging of the product or being replaced, and where the repackaging with reaffixing or the replacement of the trade mark is necessary to enable the products to be marketed by the parallel importer in the importing Member State, there are obstacles to intracommunity trade giving rise to artificial partitioning of the markets between Member States within the meaning of the case-law cited, whether or not the proprietor intended such partitioning.
>
> 40. The condition of artificial partitioning of the markets between Member States, as defined by the Court in *Bristol-Myers Squibb*, thus applies where a parallel importer replaces the original trade mark by that used by the proprietor in the Member State of import.
>
> 41. Furthermore, as the Advocate General notes in paragraphs 40 to 42 of his Opinion, this solution also has the practical advantage that it does not require national courts to assess evidence of intention, which is notoriously difficult to prove.
>
> 42. The view that the condition of market partitioning defined in *Bristol-Myers Squibb* applies to the case where a trade mark is replaced also implies, contrary to what Paranova argues, that this replacement of the trade mark must be objectively necessary within the meaning of that judgment if the proprietor is to be precluded from opposing it.
>
> 43. It follows that it is for the national courts to examine whether the circumstances prevailing at the time of marketing made it objectively necessary to replace the original trade mark by that of the importing Member State in order that the product in question could be placed on the market in that State by the parallel importer. This condition of necessity is satisfied if, in a specific case, the prohibition imposed on the importer against replacing the trade mark hinders effective access to the markets of the importing Member State. That would be the case if the rules or practices in the importing Member State prevent the product in question from being marketed in that State under its trade mark in the exporting Member State. This is so where a rule for the protection of consumers prohibits the use, in the importing Member State, of the trade mark used in the exporting Member State on the ground that it is liable to mislead consumers.
>
> 44. In contrast, the condition of necessity will not be satisfied if replacement of the trade mark is explicable solely by the parallel importer's attempt to secure a commercial advantage.
>
> 45. It is for the national courts to determine, in each specific case, whether it was objectively necessary for the parallel importer to use the trade mark used in the Member State of import in order to enable the imported products to be marketed.[24]

This distinction between a trademark being changed to avoid "hinder[ing] effective access to the market"[25] or it being "explicable solely by the parallel importer's attempt to secure a

---

[23] Case C-379/97, Pharmacia & Upjohn v. Paranova, [1999] E.C.R. I-6927.
[24] *Ibid.* at I-6967–69.
[25] *Ibid.* at I-6969.

commercial advantage"[26] has been rightly criticized and national courts have not found it easy to apply. For instance, the English Court of Appeal in *Speciality European Pharma v. Doncaster Pharmaceuticals*[27] held that this meant that changing the trademark could be permitted when 90 percent of the market was accessible regardless of brand name but less than 10 percent was prescribed by brand name.

Again, though, the fact that trademark owners cannot object to the use of another of their trademarks on goods, regardless of the precise limitations, is a second example of "exhaustion plus."

C. Goods Which Were Not Put on the Market by the Proprietor or With His Consent

The third example of "exhaustion plus" arises where different companies in different countries within the EEA own counterpart intellectual property rights. Are the first owner's rights in one country exhausted in relation to goods put on the market by the second owner in a second country?

To most intellectual property owners that sounds absurd, but during the 1970s and 1980s, the CJEU held that there would still be exhaustion in such cases, at least where the rights shared a common origin. This doctrine was adopted by the CJEU in *Hag I*,[28] which held that the owner of the trademark "HAG" in Luxembourg could not object to the sale of coffee legally produced in Germany by the owner of the trademark there (the marks having been divided as a result of government expropriation following the Second World War). The Commission indicated in the mid-1970s that the same approach should apply for the proposed European Patent, indicating that assignments to unrelated third parties should not prevent exhaustion.[29]

The doctrine was apparently then abolished in the 1990s with *Hag II*[30] and *Ideal Standard*.[31] In the first of these cases, this time it was the German owner of the HAG mark trying to oppose imports of Belgian HAG coffee. The CJEU remedied its previous decision and held that there was no consent and thus no exhaustion in this case—much to the delight of legal commentators, even if the infringer might have felt rather unfairly treated.[32] The reversal of the doctrine was completed in *Ideal Standard*, which confirmed that *Hag II* was not limited to marks separated involuntarily and also applied where the original right holder had chosen to sell off rights in one country.[33]

However, the English courts remain wary. In *Doncaster Pharmaceuticals v. Bolton*

---

[26] Ibid.
[27] Speciality European Pharma v. Doncaster Pharmaceuticals Ltd., [2015] EWCA (Civ) 54, para. 69, [2015] W.L.R. 55 (Eng.). Permission to appeal to the Supreme Court was refused. See also Flynn Pharma Ltd. v. Drugsrus Ltd., [2015] EWHC 2759 (Ch), paras. 87–95, appeal pending.
[28] Case 192/73, Van Zuylen Frèrese v. Hag, [1974] E.C.R. 731, 745 ("*Hag I*").
[29] Commission Opinion 75/597 of September 26, 1975 on the draft Convention for the European Patent for the common market, [1975] O.J. L261/26, 29 (EC).
[30] Case C-10/89, CNL-SUCAL N.V. v. Hag G.F. A.G., [1990] E.C.R. I-3711 ("*Hag II*").
[31] Case C-9/93, IHT Internationale Heiztechnik v. Ideal-Standard, [1994] E.C.R. I-2789 ("*Ideal Standard*").
[32] *Hag II*, supra note 30, [1990] E.C.R. at I-3758–61.
[33] *Ideal Standard*, supra note 31, [1994] E.C.R. at I-2792.

Pharmaceutical Company 100,[34] the Court of Appeal overturned a summary judgment of trademark infringement. The Court held that there was a "real prospect of success" in arguing that there was exhaustion where the trademark KALTEN had been assigned by AstraZeneca (AZ) to unrelated parties in Spain and in the United Kingdom (U.K.).[35] Curiously, the court noted that the "legal setting is the interface between EU competition law and UK trade mark law."[36] The Court explained its decision in the following terms:

> 74. I start from the position that prior to 2001 AZ owned the trade mark KALTEN in both Spain and UK. While that situation prevailed down to 2001 parallel imports into the UK of products, which had been circulated on the market in Spain with the consent of AZ, were lawful. They formed a substantial proportion of KALTEN sold on the UK market.
>
> 75. In 2001 AZ began to divest itself of ownership of the mark in favour of different entities in different member states. There has been no investigation of the reasons for this. I think that a proper investigation is called for, especially as it is contended by Bolton that the effect of the assignment of the Spanish mark in 2001 has been to reverse or revoke the effects of AZ's previous consent to circulation of the products in parts of the EU market, from which they were lawfully imported into the UK, and to make it unlawful in the future for Doncaster to do was previously lawful for it to do in relation to imports of KALTEN from Spain into the UK. Parallel imports had been conducted on such a scale that up to 70% of the KALTEN on sale in the UK had been parallel imports.
>
> 76. According to Bolton the assignments by AZ to Teofarma and Bolton have put Bolton, as assignee of the mark in UK, in a better and stronger position than AZ, the assignor, was in relation to the enforcement of the UK trade mark against Doncaster. This is difficult to square with the general rule that an assignee steps into the shoes of the assignor and, in law, is in no different position than the assignor was.
>
> 77. I do not think that it is sufficient for Bolton simply to rely on the judgment of the Court of Justice in *Ideal Standard* for the proposition that a voluntary assignment of a mark for a particular territory is a surrender of control in the territory in question and does not constitute a consent to the circulation of the goods for the purposes of the doctrine of exhaustion of rights.
>
> 78. I accept that there is no evidence here of conventional control by AZ continuing to manufacture KALTEN in Spain, or by the use of subsidiaries, or by the use of licensing, market sharing or franchising operations. I agree, however, with Mr Howe that the judgment in *Ideal Standard* probably does not comprehensively identify the variety of circumstances in which the doctrine of exhaustion of rights may be invoked as a defence to proceedings for infringement of trade mark. The limits of the doctrine of exhaustion of rights are less clear than Bolton asserts.
>
> 79. The assignment by AZ to Bolton may, for example, be part of a planned process for deliberately and artificially partitioning and manipulating the EU market for KALTEN so as to amount to a disguised restriction on trade between member states with respect to the product. I do not agree with Bolton's submission that the assignment to it should be looked at separately from the assignment to Teofarma. The assignments and related transactions and the circumstances in which they were made need to be analysed with care in order to see if there was present something behind the decision to split the ownership of the mark on a territorial basis and whether it was designed to conceal the reality of linkage and control so as to disguise a restriction on trade between member states.
>
> 80. This point is quite apart from the issues of economic links and the possibility of control via AZ over the products to which the mark is applied. This was not a case of bare out-and-out assignments of the mark. The assignments were accompanied by other transactions (know how

---

[34] Doncaster Pharmaceuticals v. Bolton Pharmaceutical Co. 100 Ltd., [2006] EWCA (Civ) 661, [2007] F.S.R. 3, [2006] E.T.M.R. 65 (Eng.).
[35] *Ibid.* at para. 69.
[36] *Ibid.* at para. 2.

licences, product agreement) which kept AZ in the frame. A trial preceded by disclosure of documents and exchange of witness statements is necessary in order to establish the facts relevant to the issue whether, in all the circumstances, there are also economic links or the possibility of control between AZ and its assignees, which might prevent the enforcement of the mark KALTEN by Bolton against Doncaster from being justified on the essential function principle.

81. Eventually, but not, I think, before the relevant facts have been ascertained at trial, it may even become necessary to refer the matter to the Court of Justice for a ruling on the interpretation of Article 30. Although this case may raise a point on exhaustion of rights not covered by the existing authorities, neither side suggested that a reference should be made under Article 234 at this stage.

There was no subsequent trial, as the parties settled. However, the ongoing legal uncertainty (and consequent inability to obtain summary judgment in such cases) makes this a third example of "exhaustion plus."

D. Goods Which Were Not Put on the Market in the EEA

Regional exhaustion in the EEA is limited to goods which are put on the market in the EEA. The TFEU provisions do not determine the position for goods put on the market outside the EEA, leaving it to national law of the Member States subject to any EU or EEA legislation.[37] In turn, that legislation, once adopted, has taken the policy decision to limit exhaustion to the region and to permit right holders to exercise their rights against parallel imports from outside the region (hence a prohibition of international exhaustion).[38] To that extent, therefore, regional exhaustion has not been extended beyond a standard national exhaustion rule.

However, that still leaves the question how to determine in what circumstances regional exhaustion is triggered. The CJEU adopted a broad approach in *Peak Holding*.[39] In that case, the right holder had imported clothing and accessories into the EEA and offered them for sale.[40] After a few seasons, it sold the remaining unsold stock to a French company, on the condition that 95 percent had to be resold outside the EEA (5 percent could be resold in France).[41] Inevitably, the stock reappeared for sale in the EEA (in shops in Sweden), the right holder sued, and the Swedish company claimed the rights had been exhausted. The CJEU rightly held that the earlier importation and offering for sale by the right holder had not triggered exhaustion since the goods were not in fact sold.[42] However, it went on to find that the sale to a third party in the EEA had exhausted the rights, regardless of the contractual restriction.[43]

This approach does not reflect any genuine consent to the goods being sold in the EEA

---

[37] Case 51/75, EMI Records v. CBS United Kingdom, [1976] E.C.R. 811, and the related cases decided on the same day.
[38] Case C-355/96, Silhouette Int'l Schmied v. Harlauer, [1998] E.C.R. I-4799 and subsequent cases. For a fuller discussion of this issue, see CHRISTOPHER STOTHERS, PARALLEL TRADE IN EUROPE: INTELLECTUAL PROPERTY, COMPETITION AND REGULATORY LAW 331–68 (2007).
[39] Case C-16/03, Peak Holdings v. Axolin-Elinor, [2004] E.C.R. I-11313.
[40] *Ibid.* at I-11336.
[41] *Ibid.*
[42] *Ibid.* at I-11348.
[43] *Ibid.*

and is highly impractical. The right holders themselves are effectively required to export goods that they wish to be put on the market outside the EEA (and possibly required to sell to a non-EEA entity). It appears to be a further example of the CJEU adopting a rather extreme approach, apparently driven by an underlying policy to ensure companies are unable to use contractual terms to avoid the consequences of regional exhaustion. It can therefore be regarded as a fourth example of "exhaustion plus."

E. Goods Where the Right Holder Did Not Object Quickly Enough

An intellectual property owner normally has no obligation to tell a potential infringer whether he/she intends to assert those rights. In some jurisdictions, the potential infringer may be able to commence an action itself (for instance, for revocation, a declaration of non-infringement or, in patent cases relating to standards, a declaration of non-essentiality to the standard). In addition, an intellectual property owner that fails to bring an action for a significant period of time can lose its rights by a wide range of doctrines, such as limitation, prescription, laches, and estoppel.

In some of these cases, failure to respond to a potential infringer will be a relevant factor. However, the CJEU has now held that intellectual property owners may need to respond if they later wish to assert their rights with respect to exhaustion.

The issue of "specific mechanism" arose when the EU expanded to countries in central and eastern Europe. These countries had introduced patent protection and supplementary protection certificates for pharmaceutical products relatively recently. This was originally set out in Annex IV.2 to the Act of Accession of April 16, 2003 as follows:[44]

> With regard to the Czech Republic, Estonia, Latvia, Lithuania, Hungary, Poland, Slovenia, or Slovakia, the holder or beneficiary, of a patent or supplementary protection certificate for a pharmaceutical product filed in a Member State at a time when such protection could not be obtained in one of the above-mentioned new Member States for that product, may rely on the rights granted by that patent or supplementary protection certificate in order to prevent the import and marketing of that product in the Member State or States where the product in question enjoys patent protection or supplementary protection, even if the product was put on the market in that new Member State for the first time by him or with his consent.
>
> Any person intending to import or market a pharmaceutical product covered by the above paragraph in a Member State where the product enjoys patent or supplementary protection shall demonstrate to the competent authorities in the application regarding that import that one month's prior notification has been given to the holder or beneficiary of such protection.

The relevant Acts of Accession extended this "specific mechanism" to Bulgaria, Romania, and Croatia.[45]

There has been very little litigation in relation to the "specific mechanism," despite large numbers of notifications, which may be a sign that the lines were drawn relatively clearly (or that there was insufficient value in litigating cases of doubt). However, the CJEU once again took a pro-exhaustion approach when finally given the opportunity to do so.

---

[44] Act of Accession of Cyprus, the Czech Republic, Estonia, Hungary, Latvia, Lithuania, Malta, Poland, Slovenia, and Slovakia, April 16, 2003, [2003] O.J. L236/33.

[45] Act of Accession of Bulgaria and Romania, [2005] O.J. L157/203, Annex V.1; Act of Accession of Croatia, [2012] O.J. L112/21, Annex IV.1.

In *Merck v. Sigma*,[46] Merck had a patent and Supplementary Protection Certificate (SPC) covering its product Singular (montelukast) in the U.K. Such protection could not have been obtained in Poland when it had been filed. Pharma XL provided advance notification of its intention to import and Merck accidentally did not respond.[47] Pharma XL proceeded to obtain parallel import licenses, under which Sigma (a company associated with Pharma XL) began to parallel import from Poland into the U.K.[48] Merck objected and Sigma ceased parallel imports.[49] Merck also sought damages for prior imports and destruction of stock remaining in the U.K.[50] This relief was granted at first instance but Sigma appealed, claiming Merck was not entitled to such relief due to its failure to respond to the notification.[51] The issue was referred to the CJEU.

On the face of the specific mechanism, there is no obligation on the holder or beneficiary of the patent or SPC protection to respond to a prior notification by raising objections.[52] Nor is there any obligation on the importer to respect that response by not filing an application to import, nor on the authorities to refuse any such application.[53] Nevertheless, the CJEU reasoned as follows:

> 23. In order for the reply to be given to the national court to be a useful one, it should be recalled that, under Article 2 of the 2003 Act of Accession, as from the date of accession, the provisions of the original Treaties and the acts adopted by the institutions and the European Central Bank before accession are binding on the new Member States and apply in those States under the conditions laid down in those Treaties and in that Act.
>
> 24. It follows that, as from the date of accession, the principles laid down by the Court on the basis of Treaty articles relating to the free movement of goods are applicable to trade between the new Member States and the other EU Member States. The Court has consistently held that the proprietor of an industrial or commercial property right protected by the legislation of a Member State cannot rely upon that legislation to prevent the importation of a product which has been lawfully marketed in another Member State by the proprietor himself or with his consent. The Court has inferred from that principle that an inventor, or someone deriving rights from him, cannot invoke the patent which he holds in one Member State to prevent the importation of a product freely marketed by him in another Member State where the product is not patentable (judgments in *Centrafarm and de Peijper*, 15/74, EU:C:1974:114, paragraphs 11 and 12; *Merck*, 187/80, EU:C:1981:180, paragraphs 12 and 13; and *Generics and Harris Pharmaceuticals*, C-191/90, EU:C:1992:407, paragraph 31).
>
> 25. However, the Specific Mechanism provides for a specific derogation from that principle. It is the Court's well established case-law that provisions in an Act of Accession which permit exceptions to or derogations from rules laid down by the Treaties must be interpreted restrictively with reference to the Treaty provisions in question and must be limited to what is absolutely necessary to attain the objective pursued (judgment in *Apostolides*, C-420/07, EU C/2009/271, paragraph 35 and the case-law cited). As the Advocate General observed at point 18 of his

---

[46] Case C-539/13, Merck Canada Inc. v. Sigma Pharmaceuticals plc (decided February 12, 2015, not yet reported). Available at http://curia.europa.eu/juris/document/document.jsf?text=&docid=162241&pageIndex=0&doclang=EN&mode=lst&dir=&occ=first&part=1&cid=46927.
[47] *Ibid.* para. 8.
[48] *Ibid.* paras. 9, 11.
[49] *Ibid.* para. 12.
[50] *Ibid.* para. 13.
[51] *Ibid.*
[52] *Ibid.* paras. 30–33.
[53] *Ibid.* para. 33.

Opinion, the Specific Mechanism seeks to achieve a balance between effective protection of patent or SPC rights and the free movement of goods.

. . .

28. The Specific Mechanism does not go so far so as to impose on a person intending to import a protected pharmaceutical product an obligation to obtain the express prior consent of the holder, or beneficiary, of a patent or SPC. However, any person contemplating importing a protected pharmaceutical product is required to comply with a number of obligations and formalities before he may import such a product.

29. First, such a person is required to give notification of his intention to the holder, or beneficiary, of the patent or SPC, so as to enable the latter, where appropriate, to invoke the rights conferred by the patent or SPC to prevent the importation and marketing of the product concerned, in accordance with the conditions which form the subject-matter of the third and fourth questions referred. Next, once such notice has been duly given, there is a waiting period of one month. Finally, it is only upon expiry of that period that the person in question may apply to the competent authorities for authorisation to import the protected pharmaceutical product. It follows from the above that the proposed import operation cannot go ahead without the prior authorisation of the competent national authorities, which cannot be sought before the expiry of the one-month waiting period following receipt of the notification by the person enjoying the protection conferred by the patent or SPC.

30. Accordingly, the Specific Mechanism added to national authorisation procedures for the importation of pharmaceutical products a requirement to give prior notification of the proposed operation to the holder, or beneficiary, of the patent or SPC, to which a one-month waiting period is attached. The purpose of that period is to enable the person enjoying the protection conferred by the patent or SPC to prevent any importation and the importer to be apprised of any such decision as soon as possible so that he may draw the relevant conclusions.

31. It is true that no provision in the Specific Mechanism expressly requires such a holder or beneficiary to communicate, before commencing any legal proceedings to that end, his intention to oppose a proposed importation of which he has been duly notified. However, if the holder, or beneficiary, of the patent or SPC fails to take advantage of that period in order to indicate his objection, the person proposing to import the pharmaceutical product in question may legitimately apply to the competent authorities for authorisation to import the product and, where appropriate, import and market it.

32. Nevertheless, in such a situation, the holder, or beneficiary, of the patent or SPC cannot be regarded as having forfeited the right to rely on the Specific Mechanism. Although he may not obtain compensation for the loss suffered as a result of the parallel imports which he failed to oppose in good time, such a holder or beneficiary remains, in principle, free to oppose future importation and marketing of the pharmaceutical product protected by the patent or SPC.[54]

The CJEU did moderate the impact of its ruling by mentioning that Pharma XL had only notified the holder of the marketing authorization, which had no rights in the patent or SPC. The Court then went on to hold that the notification must actually be given to "the holder, or beneficiary, of the patent or SPC, the latter term designating any person enjoying the rights conferred by law on the patent or SPC holder"[55] and that it cannot be given to another company in the same group on the basis they form with the holder or beneficiary "a single undertaking, or that, as a result of their conduct or status as holder of the marketing authorisation for the relevant pharmaceutical product, those persons give the appearance of being the holder's beneficiary."[56]

---

[54] *Ibid.* paras. 23–32.
[55] *Ibid.* para. 43.
[56] *Ibid.* para. 41.

Nevertheless, this is a quite remarkable extension of exhaustion on the basis of a failure to make timely objections, justified on the basis of the need to construe exceptions to exhaustion narrowly in the EU.

The extension of exhaustion could also have broader implications in relation to other notifications. As discussed above, parallel importers also have a separate obligation to notify the trademark owner of proposed repackaging within a reasonable time before commencing imports, with an indication that fifteen working days (just under a month) is likely to be reasonable where a sample is provided at the same time. It seems certain that parallel importers will seek to extend the judgment in *Merck v. Sigma* to any failure to object to repackaging within this timeframe, although it is submitted that any such extension should be rejected. Given the convoluted case law on repackaging, and the high threshold to show a breach, it would be entirely unreasonable to deprive the trademark owner of damages for past imports in such a case.

In any event, however, the above discussion and case law is clearly a fifth case of "exhaustion plus."

F. Services

Finally, we must consider services. These are subject to a separate provision in the TFEU on the freedom to provide services under Article 56, which reads:

> Within the framework of the provisions set out below, restrictions on freedom to provide services within the Union shall be prohibited in respect of nationals of Member States who are established in a Member State other than that of the person for whom the services are intended.
>
> The European Parliament and the Council, acting in accordance with the ordinary legislative procedure, may extend the provisions of the Chapter to nationals of a third country who provide services and who are established within the Union.[57]

Again, this is mirrored by the provisions in Article 36 of the EEA Agreement.

Services would not normally be the subject of exhaustion under national law and there is no similar line of case law in relation to services as there is to goods. Indeed, for many years the leading case was *Coditel I*, in which the CJEU held that the exclusive distributor in Belgium of the film *Le Boucher* was not prevented by Article 56 of the TFEU from enforcing its rights against Belgian cable television companies that relayed to their subscribers a channel showing the film in Germany (with the consent of the right holders).[58]

However, developments in recent years have led to increased digital distribution as a service rather than as a traditional good, including not only software but also music, television, and film. This had resulted in two major decisions of the CJEU, which extend exhaustion to cover services.

First, in *FAPL v. QC Leisure*,[59] the CJEU distinguished *Coditel I* and held that intellectual property rights could be exhausted when provided as services. Its extensive reasoning was as follows:

---

[57] TFEU, art. 56.
[58] Case 62/79, Coditel et al. v. Cine Vog Films et al., [1980] E.C.R. 881.
[59] Joined Cases C-403 & C-429/08, Football Assoc. Premier League v. QC Leisure, [2011] E.C.R. I-9083.

85. Article 56 TFEU requires the abolition of all restrictions on the freedom to provide services, even if those restrictions apply without distinction to national providers of services and to those from other Member States, when they are liable to prohibit, impede or render less advantageous the activities of a service provider established in another Member State where it lawfully provides similar services. Moreover, the freedom to provide services is for the benefit of both providers and recipients of services (see Case C-42/07 *Liga Portuguesa de Futebol Profissional and Bwin International* [2009] ECR I-7633, paragraph 51 and the case-law cited).

86. In the main proceedings, the national legislation prohibits foreign decoding devices—which give access to satellite broadcasting services from another Member State—from being imported into, and sold and used in, national territory.

87. Given that access to satellite transmission services such as those at issue in the main proceedings requires possession of such a device whose supply is subject to the contractual limitation that it may be used only in the Member State of broadcast, the national legislation concerned prevents those services from being received by persons resident outside the Member State of broadcast, in this instance those resident in the United Kingdom. Consequently, that legislation has the effect of preventing those persons from gaining access to those services.

88. It is true that the actual origin of the obstacle to the reception of such services is to be found in the contracts concluded between the broadcasters and their customers, which in turn reflect the territorial restriction clauses included in contracts concluded between those broadcasters and the holders of intellectual property rights. However, as the legislation confers legal protection on those restrictions and requires them to be complied with on pain of civil-law and pecuniary sanctions, it itself restricts the freedom to provide services.

89. Consequently, the legislation concerned constitutes a restriction on the freedom to provide services that is prohibited by Article 56 TFEU unless it can be objectively justified.

. . .

104. Therefore, if the national legislation concerned is designed to confer protection on sporting events—a matter which it is for the referring court to establish—European Union law does not preclude, in principle, that protection and such legislation is thus capable of justifying a restriction on the free movement of services such as that at issue in the main proceedings.

105. However, it is also necessary that such a restriction does not go beyond what is necessary in order to attain the objective of protecting the intellectual property at issue (see, to this effect, [Case C-222/07] *UTECA* [[2009] ECR I-1407], paragraphs 31 and 36).

106. In this regard, it should be pointed out that derogations from the principle of free movement can be allowed only to the extent to which they are justified for the purpose of safeguarding the rights which constitute the specific subject-matter of the intellectual property concerned (see, to this effect, Case C-115/02 *Rioglass and Transremar* [2003] ECR I-12705, paragraph 23 and the case-law cited).

107. It is clear from settled case-law that the specific subject-matter of the intellectual property is intended in particular to ensure for the right holders concerned protection of the right to exploit commercially the marketing or the making available of the protected subject-matter, by the grant of licences in return for payment of remuneration (see, to this effect, *Musik-Vertrieb membran and K-tel International*, paragraph 12, and Joined Cases C-92/92 and C-326/92 *Phil Collins and Others* [1993] ECR I-5145, paragraph 20).

108. However, the specific subject-matter of the intellectual property does not guarantee the right holders concerned the opportunity to demand the highest possible remuneration. Consistently with its specific subject-matter, they are ensured—as recital 10 in the preamble to the Copyright Directive and recital 5 in the preamble to the Related Rights Directive envisage—only appropriate remuneration for each use of the protected subject-matter.

109. In order to be appropriate, such remuneration must be reasonable in relation to the economic value of the service provided. In particular, it must be reasonable in relation to the actual or potential number of persons who enjoy or wish to enjoy the service (see, by analogy, Case C-61/97 *FDV* [1998] ECR I-5171, paragraph 15, and Case C-52/07 *Kanal 5 and TV 4* [2008] ECR I-9275, paragraphs 36 to 38).

110. Thus, with regard to television broadcasting, such remuneration must in particular—as recital 17 in the preamble to the Satellite Broadcasting Directive confirms—be reasonable in

relation to parameters of the broadcasts concerned, such as their actual audience, their potential audience and the language version (see, to this effect, Case C-192/04 *Lagardère Active Broadcast* [2005] ECR I-7199, paragraph 51).

111. In this context, it is to be noted, first of all, that the right holders at issue in the main proceedings are remunerated for the broadcasting of the protected subject-matter from the Member State of broadcast in which the act of broadcasting is deemed to take place, in accordance with Article 1(2)(b) of the Satellite Broadcasting Directive, and in which the appropriate remuneration is therefore payable.

112. Next, when such remuneration is agreed between the right holders concerned and the broadcasters in an auction, there is nothing to prevent the right holder from asking, at that time, for an amount which takes account of the actual audience and the potential audience both in the Member State of broadcast and in any other Member State in which the broadcasts including the protected subject-matter are also received.

113. In this regard, it should be borne in mind in particular that reception of a satellite broadcast, such as that at issue in the main proceedings, requires possession of a decoding device. Consequently, it is possible to determine with a very high degree of precision the total number of viewers who form part of the actual and potential audience of the broadcast concerned, hence of the viewers residing within and outside the Member State of broadcast.

114. Finally, as regards the premium paid by broadcasters in order to be granted territorial exclusivity, it admittedly cannot be ruled out that the amount of the appropriate remuneration also reflects the particular character of the broadcasts concerned, that is to say, their territorial exclusivity, so that a premium may be paid on that basis.

115. None the less, here such a premium is paid to the right holders concerned in order to guarantee absolute territorial exclusivity which is such as to result in artificial price differences between the partitioned national markets. Such partitioning and such an artificial price difference to which it gives rise are irreconcilable with the fundamental aim of the Treaty, which is completion of the internal market. In those circumstances, that premium cannot be regarded as forming part of the appropriate remuneration which the right holders concerned must be ensured.

116. Consequently, the payment of such a premium goes beyond what is necessary to ensure appropriate remuneration for those right holders.

117. Having regard to the foregoing, it is to be concluded that the restriction which consists in the prohibition on using foreign decoding devices cannot be justified in light of the objective of protecting intellectual property rights.

118. Doubt is not cast on this conclusion by the judgment in *Coditel I*, which has been relied upon by FAPL and others and by MPS in support of their arguments. It is true that, in paragraph 16 of that judgment, the Court held that the rules of the Treaty cannot in principle constitute an obstacle to the geographical limits which the parties to a contract of assignment of intellectual property rights have agreed upon in order to protect the author and his assigns and that the mere fact that the geographical limits in question coincide, in some circumstances, with the frontiers of the Member States does not require a different view.

119. However, those statements were made in a context which is not comparable to that of the main proceedings. In the case which led to the judgment in *Coditel I*, the cable television broadcasting companies communicated a work to the public without having, in the Member State of the place of origin of that communication, an authorisation from the right holders concerned and without having paid remuneration to them.

120. By contrast, in the main proceedings the broadcasters carry out acts of communication to the public while having in the Member State of broadcast, which is the Member State of the place of origin of that communication, an authorisation from the right holders concerned and by paying them remuneration—which can, moreover, take account of the actual and potential audience in the other Member States.[60]

---

[60] *Ibid.* at I-9210–19.

That decision was followed the next year in *UsedSoft*,[61] which concerned the permissibility of resale of licenses for computer software when that software would be downloaded. The CJEU concluded that rights would also be exhausted in such cases as follows:

> 1. Article 4(2) of Directive 2009/24/EC of the European Parliament and of the Council of 23 April 2009 on the legal protection of computer programs must be interpreted as meaning that the right of distribution of a copy of a computer program is exhausted if the copyright holder who has authorised, even free of charge, the downloading of that copy from the internet onto a data carrier has also conferred, in return for payment of a fee intended to enable him to obtain a remuneration corresponding to the economic value of the copy of the work of which he is the proprietor, a right to use that copy for an unlimited period.
>
> 2. Articles 4(2) and 5(1) of Directive 2009/24 must be interpreted as meaning that, in the event of the resale of a user licence entailing the resale of a copy of a computer program downloaded from the copyright holder's website, that licence having originally been granted by that rightholder to the first acquirer for an unlimited period in return for payment of a fee intended to enable the rightholder to obtain a remuneration corresponding to the economic value of that copy of his work, the second acquirer of the licence, as well as any subsequent acquirer of it, will be able to rely on the exhaustion of the distribution right under Article 4(2) of that directive, and hence be regarded as lawful acquirers of a copy of a computer program within the meaning of Article 5(1) of that directive and benefit from the right of reproduction provided for in that provision.[62]

These are recent decisions and their precise scope remains highly controversial. Nevertheless, by extending exhaustion into services the CJEU has provided a sixth example of "exhaustion plus," and one that could well end up being the most significant of all.

IV. CONCLUSION

There has been extensive criticism regarding the attempts to extend intellectual property protection through bilateral treaties beyond that required by TRIPS, often using the label "TRIPS-plus." Equally, there has been criticism by intellectual property owners that their rights are not fully respected in some jurisdictions. When it comes to the European systems, various issues have arisen over the years. This chapter has sought to draw some of these strands together to demonstrate that there has been a determined and extensive approach of extending the doctrine of exhaustion beyond national norms in order to integrate the European markets. This approach can be regarded as "exhaustion plus" which, regardless of its policy merits, should be distinguished from "exhaustion" as recognized in domestic intellectual property systems.

---

[61] Case C-128/11, UsedSoft v. Oracle Int'l, [2012] E.C.R. 1.
[62] *Ibid.* at 14.

10. The exhaustion doctrine in Singapore: different strokes for different IP folks
*Ng-Loy Wee Loon**

I. INTRODUCTION

The arguments for and against the doctrine of international exhaustion of intellectual property rights have been canvassed by many.[1] The reason probably most often cited in favor of international exhaustion is the benefit to the consumers in the country of importation because they can get access to genuine products at lower prices. Indeed, some studies have shown that this benefit is not merely a theoretical one. According to a study by Chen and Png on an international panel of changes in copyright law, legalisation of parallel imports was associated with a retail price reduction of 7.2–7.9 percent in the music CD market.[2] Another study by Ganslandt and Maskus found that drug prices in Sweden that were subject to competition from parallel imports fell relative to other drugs.[3]

As far as Singapore is concerned, this benefit to consumers has emerged as the overriding consideration in most debates on whether, and to what extent, intellectual property rights should be exhausted. Thus, in the late 1980s when Singapore was fashioning its own copyright law, it decided that parallel imports would be permitted under the new copyright law (Copyright Act 1987[4]) because:[5]

> [i]f dealings in parallel imports are prohibited, consumers may be denied the opportunity to purchase a lower-priced but legitimate edition of a work merely because the edition originates from some other country. The Select Committee [on the Copyright Bill] was particularly impressed by evidence presented to it of large price differentials of authorized editions of copyright materials, in particular books, originating from different countries.[6]

---

* Professor, Faculty of Law, National University of Singapore.
[1] See e.g. Frederick M. Abbott, *The First Report (Final) to the Committee on International Trade Law of the International Law Association on the Subject of Parallel Importation*, 1 J. INT'L ECON. L. 607 (1998); NATIONAL ECONOMIC RESEARCH ASSOCIATES, DGXV OF THE EUROPEAN COMMISSION, THE ECONOMIC CONSEQUENCES OF THE CHOICE OF REGIME OF EXHAUSTION IN THE AREA OF TRADEMARKS (1999) [hereinafter NERA REPORT]; Miranda Forsyth & Warwick Rothnie, *Parallel Imports*, in THE INTERFACE BETWEEN INTELLECTUAL PROPERTY RIGHTS AND COMPETITION POLICY (Steven D. Anderman ed., 2007).
[2] Yeh-ning Chen & Ivan Png, *Parallel Imports and Music CD Prices*, 5 KOREAN J. L. & ECON. 197 (2008).
[3] Mattias Ganslandt & Keith Markus, *The Price Impact of Parallel Imports in Pharmaceuticals: Evidence from the European Union*, 23 J. HEALTH ECON. 1035 (2004).
[4] Singapore Copyright Act (ch. 63), April 10, 1987, WIPO Lex. No. SG044 (Sing.). This new law came into force in April 1987.
[5] See Speech of the Minister for Law at the Third Reading of the Copyright Bill, 48 HANSARD col. 970 (January 26, 1987).
[6] *Ibid.*

For the same reason, when Singapore developed its own patents regime in the early 1990s, it decided to include a provision in the new law (Patents Act 1994[7]), which explicitly endorses international exhaustion. In the late 1990s, when it was time to revamp the trademarks regime, a provision endorsing international exhaustion was also included in the new law (Trade Marks Act 1998[8]). The same was done in the other pieces of intellectual property legislation promulgated around that period.[9] To a large extent, there is uniformity across the different intellectual property regimes in Singapore. This may be contrasted with the United States (U.S.) model where international exhaustion is adopted in the trademark[10] and the copyright[11] regimes, but not in the patent regime.[12]

At the same time, the treatment of parallel imports is not identical across all the intellectual property regimes in Singapore. For example, where the intellectual property right holder in Singapore is different from the intellectual property right holder in the country where the product was made or first marketed, the response of the trademark regime is different from that of the copyright and patent regimes. Another example lies within the patent regime itself, where there is some restriction on parallel importation, which applies to only one category of patented products, namely, pharmaceutical products. To this extent, the Singapore model is similar to the model of countries such as Hong Kong where international exhaustion is adopted in its copyright regime, but for only copyrighted computer programs.[13]

This chapter will focus on these differences in the exhaustion model in Singapore and explain why Singapore, a country which looks upon parallel importation so favorably, has chosen this "different strokes for different intellectual property (IP) folks" approach. As a starting point, it is necessary to provide more details on the concerted efforts that

---

[7] Singapore Patents Act (ch. 221, rev. edn. 2005), November 25, 1994, WIPO Lex. No. SG032 (Sing.). This new law came into effect on February 23, 1995.

[8] Singapore Trade Marks Act (Act No. 46 of 1998), November 26, 1998, WIPO Lex. No. SG 008 (Sing.). This new law came into effect on January 15, 1999.

[9] See Singapore Layout-Designs of Integrated Circuits Act (ch. 159A), January 26, 1999, s. 10(g), WIPO Lex. No. SG 017 (Sing.); see also Singapore Registered Designs Act (ch. 266) (rev. edn. 2005), November 13, 2000, s. 30(7), WIPO Lex. No. SG 028 (Sing.). Note that Singapore adopts the doctrine of national exhaustion in its plant varieties law: see Singapore Plant Varieties Protection Act (ch. 232A), July 1, 2004, s. 32, WIPO Lex. No. SG 039 (Sing.) This exception is due to the fact that, as a member of the International Union for the Protection of New Varieties of Plants (UPOV) established by the International Convention for the Protection of New Varieties of Plants, Singapore is obligated to adopt national exhaustion as laid out in art. 16 of the UPOV Convention.

[10] For a discussion of the U.S. trademark position, see Irene Calboli, *Market Integration and (the Limits of) the First Sale Rule in North American and European Trade Mark Law*, 51 SANTA CLARA L. REV. 1241 (2011); see also Mary LaFrance, *Wag The Dog: Using Incidental Intellectual Property Rights to Block Parallel Imports*, 20 MICH. TELECOM. & TECH. L. REV. 45 (2013).

[11] For a discussion of the U.S. copyright position, see Irene Calboli, *The (Avoidable) Effects of Territorially Different Approaches to Trademark and Copyright Exhaustion*, in TRADEMARK PROTECTION AND TERRITORIALITY CHALLENGES IN A GLOBAL ECONOMY 151 (Calboli & Lee eds., 2014).

[12] Jazz Photo Corp. v. Int'l Trade Comm'n, 264 F.3d 1094 (Fed Cir., 2001); Fuji Photo Film Co. v. Jazz Photo Corp., 394 F.3d 1368 (Fed. Cir. 2005).

[13] See Hong Kong Copyright Ordinance, No. 528, (1997) WIPO Lex. No. HK 001, ss. 35, 35A (H.K.).

Singapore has made to legalize parallel imports in its copyright, trademark, and patent regimes.

II. THE EXHAUSTION DOCTRINE IN SINGAPORE

A. Copyright Act 1987

Singapore became an independent nation in August 1965, but for twenty-two years after independence, the copyright law in Singapore was based on a piece of British colonial legislation, namely, the Imperial Copyright Act 1911. Case law decided under this legislation applied international exhaustion to copyrighted works.[14]

When Singapore enacted its own copyright law in the late 1980s, parallel importation was a "hot button" issue in the proceedings before the Select Committee on the Copyright Bill. It has earlier been mentioned that the Select Committee on the Copyright Bill was particularly impressed with evidence presented to it of large price differentials in the books sector.[15] In one example, the price differential was 31 percent.[16] The decision was taken to make an express provision in the new law to legalize parallel importation, rather than to leave this important issue to be dealt with by the courts (as was the position under the Imperial Copyright Act 1911). Thus, under the new law, the Copyright Act 1987, importation of an article into Singapore was permitted if the making of the article was carried out with the consent of the copyright owner.[17] There was no definition of who this copyright owner was, and the impact of this lacuna emerged in *PP v. Teoh Ai Nee*.[18]

The defendant in *Teoh Ai Nee* was charged under section 136 of the Copyright Act 1987, the criminal provision governing commercial exploitation of "infringing copies" of copyright works.[19] The goods of the defendant were copies of sound recordings imported from Japan and Europe.[20] Whether these imported copies were "infringing copies" depended on whether the making of the articles was carried out with or without the consent of the copyright owner.[21] There was disagreement as to who this copyright owner should be. The prosecution argued that the relevant copyright owner was the owner in Singapore, and led evidence to show that the imported copies in the defendant's

---

[14] See, in particular, C.B.S. United Kingdom Ltd. v. Charmdale Record Distribs. Ltd., [1980] F.S.R. 289 (Eng.), where it was held that there was no copyright infringement when the defendant imported into the U.K. sound recordings made in the U.S. by the plaintiff's parent company. However, the application of international exhaustion was limited to cases where the copyright owner in Singapore was the same as the copyright owner in the country where the product was made, or where they are companies within the same group.
[15] Speech of the Minister for Law, *supra* note 5.
[16] See GOVERNMENT OF SINGAPORE, REPORT OF THE SELECT COMMITTEE ON THE PATENTS BILL B70–B73 (1994). The comparison was between the U.K. edition of a book sold in Singapore through authorized channels and the U.S. edition of the book (the parallel import).
[17] See Singapore Copyright Act, s. 32.
[18] PP v. Teoh Ai Nee, [1993] 3 S.L.R.(R) 755 (Sing.).
[19] *Ibid.*
[20] *Ibid.*
[21] See the definition of "infringing copy" in Singapore Copyright Act, s. 7(1).

possession were not made with the consent of the copyright owner in Singapore.[22] The defendant, on the other hand, argued that the relevant copyright owner was the owner in the country of manufacture (Japan/Europe, in this case), and that the prosecution had no proof that the imported copies were not made with the consent of the copyright owner in Japan/Europe.[23]

The High Court interpreted the relevant provisions of the Copyright Act existing at the time the defendant was charged (i.e., 1992), and came to the conclusion that it was the copyright owner in Singapore whose consent was relevant for the purpose of determining if the imported copies were infringing copies.[24] This led to the conviction of the defendant under section 136.

The decision in *Teo Ai Nee* was delivered on December 4, 1993. Within nine months of this judgment, on August 25, 1994, Singapore amended the Copyright Act 1987. During the legislative process, the decision in *Teo Ai Nee* and its impact was discussed. Parliament was advised that, where the copyright owner in Singapore is different from the copyright owner in the country of manufacture, copyrighted products made by the latter were nevertheless "genuine" products. Once again, the benefit of allowing such "genuine" products into Singapore was repeated:[25]

> [T]he Government is mindful of the need to achieve a proper balance between ensuring cheaper prices for consumers and providing sufficient incentives for copyright industries to develop and remain competitive. The Government's policy on parallel imports is to prevent copyright owners and exclusive distributors here from carrying out price maintenance and discriminatory practices at the expense of consumers. Closing our markets to genuine products from other countries is also inconsistent with our advocacy of free and fair competition.[26]

To give effect to this policy of "free and fair competition," three amendments were enacted. The first amendment inserted a provision that unequivocally plugged the lacuna revealed by *Teo Ai Nee*. This provision specifies that, for the purposes of determining if an imported article was made with the consent of the copyright owner, the relevant party is the owner of the copyright *in the country of manufacture*.[27] There is an exception to this general rule, namely, where there is no copyright owner in the country of manufacture. In such a case, the relevant copyright owner would be the owner of the copyright in Singapore.[28] This is to deal with the situation where importers seek out countries that provide no copyright protection and get their supply of goods from these countries.

The second amendment inserted a provision which specifies as follows:[29]

> The making of the article shall be deemed to have been carried out with the consent of the owner [of the copyright] if, after disregarding all conditions as to the sale, distribution or other dealings

---

[22] PP v. Teoh Ai Nee, *supra* note 18.
[23] *Ibid.*
[24] *Ibid.*
[25] See Speech by the Parliamentary Secretary to the Minister for Law at the Third Reading of the Copyright (Amendment) Bill 1994, 63 HANSARD col. 415–16 (August 25, 1994).
[26] *Ibid.*
[27] See Singapore Copyright Act, s. 25(3)(a).
[28] See *ibid.* s. 25(3)(b).
[29] See *ibid.* s. 25(4).

in the article after its making, the article was made with his licence (other than a compulsory licence).[30]

The impact of this provision is clear: a copyright owner in the country of manufacture will not be able to rely on restrictions (contractual or otherwise) on the further movement of the article by, for example, restricting sale of the goods to a particular territory. Thus, it is legal to import into Singapore a product which bears a label stipulating that the product is "Not for Resale Outside Thailand."

The third amendment inserted new provisions specifying that the copyright in a work embodied in an "accessory" to an article (such as a label affixed to the article) is not infringed by the importation of the article, unless the article is an infringing copy.[31] The purpose of this amendment is to ensure that copyright in "product packaging" cannot be used as a ground to repel parallel imports.[32] Thus, for example, the importer of genuine *Baileys* liqueur has a clear-cut defense to a claim that he has infringed the copyright subsisting in the label by importing these products into Singapore.[33] Strictly speaking, these new provisions are not necessary. Even in the absence of these new provisions, the importation of genuine *Baileys* liqueur into Singapore would not constitute infringement of the copyright in the labels affixed to the bottles because it can be argued that the subject matter of the importation is the labels (and not the bottles), and the labels were made with the consent of the copyright owner in the country of manufacture.[34] Viewed

---

[30] *Ibid.*

[31] See *ibid.* s. 40A (which applies to authors' works); see also *ibid.* s. 116A (which applies to sound recordings, films, and published editions of works). The word "accessory" is defined in s. 2(1). *Ibid.* s. 2(1).

[32] See Speech by the Parliamentary Secretary, *supra* note 25.

[33] This example is derived from the facts of an Australian case, R & A Bailey & Co. Ltd. v. Boccaccio Pty. Ltd., [1986] 77 A.L.R. 177 (Austl.). This case was decided at the time when Australia adopted international exhaustion in its trademark regime and national exhaustion in its copyright regime. Accordingly, the court held that parallel importation of bottles of genuine BAILEYS liqueur sourced from the Netherlands was permitted under the Australian trademark law, but not under Australian copyright law. The use of copyright in labels to circumvent what trademark law permitted was perceived as a misuse of copyright law. Thus this case set in motion legislative reform activities, which resulted in the enactment of the "product packaging" defence in 1998: see Australia Copyright Act 1968, ss. 40C, 112C (Austl.). For a comparison between the Australian model and the Singapore model of the "product packaging" defence, see Irene Calboli & Mary LaFrance, *The Case for a Legislative Amendment Against 'Accessory Copyright' for Grey Market Products: What Can the U.S. Learn from Singapore and Australia?*, SINGAPORE J. LEGAL STUD. 253 (2013).

[34] This argument finds support in Société des Produits Nestlé S.A. v. Petra Foods Ltd., [2014] S.G.H.C. 252 (Sing.), the first case where s. 40A was invoked. The plaintiff was the trademark proprietor of KIT KAT chocolate biscuit product. The label on the plaintiff's products featured the KIT KAT logo as well as a drawing of a two-finger chocolate biscuit. The second defendant imported TAKE IT chocolate biscuit products which were packaged with a label which was similar to the label of the KIT KAT product. The main cause of action was trademark infringement. But there was also a copyright claim. The plaintiff claimed that artistic copyright subsisted in the label of the KIT KAT product, and that the second defendant's importation of the TAKE IT product bearing a similar label constituted copyright infringement. The second defendant resisted this copyright claim on the ground, *inter alia*, that the "product packaging" defense in s. 40A operated to exclude the plaintiff's copyright claim since the TAKE IT products were not infringing copies of

from this perspective, the new provisions in laying out the "product packaging" defence merely sought to clarify the law, demonstrating that the policy-makers in Singapore leave no stones unturned when it comes to legitimizing parallel imports.

There is one final piece of legislative amendment that illustrates Singapore's pro-parallel importation stance. This took place in 2004 when Singapore amended the Copyright Act 1987 to implement the obligations it had undertaken in the U.S.–Singapore Free Trade Agreement (2003).[35] One obligation was to provide civil remedies and criminal penalties for the circumvention of technological measures used by copyright owners in connection with the exercise of their copyright. When implementing this obligation, Singapore took the precaution to exempt from liability the following activity:[36]

> the import and sale of a device that does not render effective a technological measure whose sole purpose is to control market segmentation for access to cinematographic films, if the import or sale of the device does not otherwise contravene any written law including [the Copyright] Act.

The purpose of this exemption is obvious: it is intended to ensure that parallel importation of films would not be thwarted by the technological measures taken by the copyright owners to segment markets in the form of encrypting copies of films with different codes for different regions.

B. The Trade Marks Act 1998

When Singapore became an independent nation in 1965, it continued to use the Trade Marks Ordinance 1938, a piece of colonial legislation, as the basis of its trademark registration system for another thirty-four years. According to case law, parallel importation of trademarked products was non-infringing activity under this piece of legislation, provided that the quality of the imported products was not materially different from the quality of the products put on the Singapore market by the trademark proprietor.[37]

When revamping the trademark law in the late 1990s, it was decided that the principle of international exhaustion should be explicitly provided for in the new law, the Trade Marks Act 1998. Section 29 therein provides as follows:[38]

---

any copyright work. The High Court noted that s. 40A was enacted specifically to deal with parallel importation. Since the TAKE IT products were not parallel imports, the court concluded that the second defendant was not entitled to rely on s. 40A. In its analysis of s. 40A, the court opined that "in certain cases, the 'packaging' is in fact the relevant 'article' to be considered." (*Ibid.* at 298.) The copyright claim eventually failed because the plaintiff could not prove that it was the owner of the copyright subsisting in the artistic work in the label.

[35] United States-Singapore Free Trade Agreement (FTA) (May 2003), available at https://ustr.gov/sites/default/files/uploads/agreements/fta/singapore/asset_upload_file708_4036.pdf.

[36] See Singapore Copyright Act, s. 261C(10).

[37] See Revlon Inc. v. Cripps & Lee Ltd., [1980] F.S.R. 85 (Eng.) (where the difference in quality was not material) and Colgate-Palmolive Ltd. v. Markwell Finance Ltd., [1989] R.P.C. 497 (Eng.) (where the difference in quality was material).

[38] Singapore Trademark Act, s. 29. This provision is modelled on s. 12 of the U.K. Trade Marks Act 1994 (Trade Marks Act 1994, 42 Eliz. 2, c. 26 (Eng.)) and art. 7 of the EU Trade Marks Directive (Directive 2008/95/EC to approximate the laws of the Member States relating to trade marks, [2008] O.J. L299/25 (EC)). However, there are material differences between the Singapore

(1) Notwithstanding section 27 [the infringement provision], a registered trade mark is not infringed by the use of the trade mark in relation to goods which have been put on the market, whether in Singapore or outside Singapore, under that trade mark by the proprietor of the registered trade mark or with his express or implied consent (conditional or otherwise).
(2) Subsection (1) shall not apply where—
   (a) the condition of the goods has been changed or impaired after they have been put on the market; and
   (b) the use of the registered trade mark in relation to those goods has caused dilution in an unfair manner of the distinctive character of the registered trade mark.[39]

The extent to which Singapore embraces parallel imports is particularly evident in two aspects. The first relates to the phrase "conditional or otherwise" in section 29(1). This phrase creates a "deeming" effect: the proprietor is deemed to have given consent to the sale of the goods even when he has imposed conditions on the further movement of the goods. This is consistent with the approach taken in the copyright regime. It was mentioned earlier that it is legal under the Copyright Act 1987 to import into Singapore a product that bears a label stipulating that the product is "Not for Resale Outside Thailand." The importation of this product is also legal under the Trade Marks Act 1998.[40]

Second, the exception to the doctrine of international exhaustion envisaged by section 29(2) is arguably very narrow in scope. This exception envisages the scenario where "the condition of the goods has been changed or impaired after they have been put on the market."[41] If the phrase "condition of the goods" is interpreted to refer to the physical condition of the goods found inside the packaging,[42] it means that repackaging of the goods, which does not involve any change to the goods themselves (for example, where the parallel importer takes the goods out of their original packaging and puts them (intact) into a new box) would not qualify as a change to the "condition of the goods" for the purposes of section 29(2).[43]

However, the generous doctrine of international exhaustion laid down in section 29 is

---

provision and the English/European provision. For a detailed comparison between the two models, see Ng-Loy Wee Loon, *Exhaustion of Rights in Trade Mark Law: The English and Singapore Models Compared*, 22 EUR. INTELL. PROP. REV. 320 (2000).

[39] Singapore Trade Marks Act, s. 29.

[40] This approach under the Trade Marks Act 1998 is also consistent with the position taken at common law in the action for passing off. In Sin Heak Hin Pte. Ltd. v. Yuasa Battery Singapore Pte. Ltd., [1995] 3 S.L.R.(R) 123 (Sing.), the imported products were made in China by a licensee of the trademark proprietor subject to a term in the license agreement that the products were only to be sold within China. The High Court found that the licensee had probably breached this contractual term by selling the products to a party with knowledge that this party would export the products out of China. The High Court held that the import and sale of these China-made products in Singapore did not constitute passing off, even though the trademark proprietor had placed restrictions prohibiting export of these goods from China.

[41] Singapore Trade Marks Act, s. 29(2)(a).

[42] This interpretation finds support in the decision of the Court of Justice of the European Union in Bristol–Myers Squibb v. Paranova, [1997] F.S.R. 102 (Eng.), in the context of art. 7(2) of the EU Trade Marks Directive. See EU Trade Marks Directive, art. 7(2).

[43] This is to be contrasted with art. 7(2) of the EU Trade Marks Directive, where a change to "the condition of the goods" is only one of the scenarios which give rise to legitimate reasons for the proprietor of the trademark to oppose further sale and distribution of the goods.

subject to one major limitation. This limitation emerged in the case, *Pan-West (Pte.) Ltd. v. Grand Bigwin Pte. Ltd.*[44] The plaintiff was the registered proprietor of the mark KATANA GOLF in Singapore. In Japan, the trademark KATANA was registered in the name of a Japanese company that was unrelated to the plaintiff. The defendant imported into Singapore KATANA golf clubs made in Japan by this Japanese company. When sued for trademark infringement, the defendant invoked section 29(1), arguing that the imported golf clubs were parallel imports in that they were "genuine" goods in Japan since they were made by the trademark proprietor in Japan.[45] The High Court disagreed, pointing out that the Trade Marks Act 1998 was concerned with trademarks registered *in Singapore*, and, therefore, when determining infringement under this Act, it was the consent of the registered proprietor *in Singapore* that was relevant.[46] In the context of section 29(1), this means that the products can only be considered "parallel imports" if they have been put on the market by or with the consent of the *Singapore proprietor* under the *Singapore registered mark*. On the facts, the defendant's golf clubs were put on the market by the Japanese proprietor under the Japanese registered mark. The court concluded that the defendant was not entitled to rely on the exhaustion principle enshrined in section 29(1).[47]

It is important to note that the High Court's conclusion was premised on the fact that the plaintiff (the Singapore proprietor) and the Japanese proprietor were not related to each other.[48] Where the imported goods are made by a party that is related to the Singapore proprietor (for example, where the imported goods are made by the parent company or a subsidiary of the Singapore proprietor) it may be argued that the Singapore proprietor must be taken to have impliedly consented to the use of the goods being put on the market under the Singapore trademark.[49] There is a strong policy consideration in favor of this analysis: a trademark proprietor should not be allowed to get around the principle of international exhaustion of rights in section 29(1) by registering its mark in different countries in the names of different subsidiaries or associated companies. Whatever may be the corporate structure used by the trademark proprietor in its global marketing strategy, the fact remains that goods made by any one of the entities within the same corporate structure are made under the control of the trademark proprietor and, to this extent, these goods if imported into Singapore should be regarded as genuine goods for the purposes of section 29(1).

---

[44] Pan-West (Pte.) Ltd. v. Grand Bigwin Pte. Ltd., [2003] 4 S.L.R.(R) 755 (Sing.).
[45] *Ibid.*
[46] *Ibid.*
[47] *Ibid.*
[48] The High Court made specific mention that the Japanese company was not a "subsidiary or associated company" of the plaintiff. *Ibid.* at 35.
[49] The authority that supports this proposition is Revlon Inc. v. Cripps & Lee Ltd., [1980] F.S.R. 85 (Eng.). The imported products were shampoo bearing the trademark REVLON. This trademark was registered in the U.S. (country of first sale) in the name of the parent company, while the REVLON trademark in the U.K. (country of importation) was registered in the name of a subsidiary. The English Court of Appeal held that the U.K. registered proprietor (the subsidiary), being in no position to object to the use of the REVLON mark by the U.S. registered proprietor (its parent company), must be taken to have given implied consent to the use of the U.K. mark on the imported goods.

C. The Patents Act 1994

When Singapore became an independent nation in 1965, it continued for many years to apply a system of "re-registration" of U.K. patents that was put in place by the British under the United Kingdom Patents Ordinance 1937. In this system, patent protection was conferred on parents that were registered in the United Kingdom (U.K.) and then re-registered in Singapore within three years of the date of issue of the U.K. patent. Under this legislation, parallel importation of patented products was permitted where the products were made by the patentee, but not where the products were made by a licensee of the patentee.[50]

Steps were taken in the early 1990s to revamp the patent system. Consistent with the approach taken in the copyright and trademark regimes, the new patent law, the Patents Act 1994, made explicit provision for the doctrine of international exhaustion. According to the original version of section 66(2)(g), which applied to all patented products, it was not an infringement to import or sell a patented product if the product:

> is produced by or with the consent (conditional or otherwise) of the proprietor of the patent or any person licensed by him, and for this purpose "patent" includes a patent granted in any country outside Singapore in respect of the same or substantially the same invention as that for which a patent is granted under this Act and "patented product," "patented process" and "licensed" shall be construed accordingly.[51]

During the legislative process, this provision met with strong objections from the Singapore Association of Pharmaceutical Industries, which argued, *inter alia*, that parallel importation of pharmaceutical products raised issues of public health and safety because the patentee would have no control over the importers on matters such as storage conditions and expiration dates.[52] There was no basis for this concern because the safety aspect of all pharmaceutical products, regardless of whether they were sold by parallel importers or by the patentee, would be controlled and regulated by the Medicines Act. The policy-makers decided that international exhaustion in section 66(2)(g) would apply equally to pharmaceutical products.

This position changed in 2004 and once again in 2008 when amendments were made to prohibit the parallel importation of pharmaceutical products in certain circumstances. The amendments in 2004 were made to implement a provision in the U.S.–Singapore Free Trade Agreement (2003).[53] The amendments in 2008 were made to implement the World Trade Organization (WTO) Decision of August 30, 2003 ("WTO 2003 Decision").[54] With

---

[50] Betts v. Wilmott, (1871) L.R. 6 Ch. App. 239 (Eng.) (where the imported products were made by the patentee) and Sime Darby Singapore Ltd. v. Beecham Group Ltd., [1968–1970] S.L.R.(R) 209 (Sing.) (where the imported products were made by a licensee of the patentee).

[51] Singapore Patents Act, s. 66(2)(g).

[52] See GOVERNMENT OF SINGAPORE, REPORT OF THE SELECT COMMITTEE ON THE PATENTS BILL A14–A15, B14–B15 (1994) for the representations made by this association to the Select Committee on the Patents Bill, as well as the debates on this issue.

[53] See U.S. Singapore FTA, art. 16.7.2.

[54] World Trade Organization, Ministerial Decision of August 30, 2003, WT/L/540 (2003). See also World Trade Organization, Amendment to the TRIPS Agreement, WT/L/641, art. 31*bis* (2005).

these amendments, the current rules governing parallel importation of patented products vary, depending on the nature of the imported patented product.

Where the patented product is a "relevant health product," parallel importation of this product is prohibited.[55] This category of "relevant health products" comprises pharmaceutical products produced in another country under compulsory licence that are intended for an "eligible importing country," namely, a WTO country that is a least developed country or has given the Agreement on Trade-Related Aspects of Intellectual Property (TRIPS) Council the necessary notification under the WTO 2003 Decision.[56]

Where the patented product is a "pharmaceutical product"[57] other than a "relevant health product," parallel importation of this product is prohibited if:[58]

(a) the product has not previously been sold or distributed in Singapore by or with the consent (conditional or otherwise) of the proprietor of the patent or any person licensed by the proprietor of the patent to sell or distribute the product in Singapore;[59]
(b) the import of the product by the importer would result in the product being distributed in breach of a contract between the patentee and any person licensed by the proprietor of the patent to distribute the product outside Singapore; and
(c) the importer has actual or constructive knowledge of the matters referred to in paragraph (b).[60]

All other cases of parallel importation are dealt with by the provision mentioned earlier, section 66(2)(g). For the purposes of determining if the imported product was made with the consent of the patentee, the relevant party is the patentee in the country of manufacture.[61] The "deeming" effect of the phrase "conditional or otherwise" in this provision

---

[55] See Singapore Patents Act, s. 66(5A), which was inserted via the Patents (Amendment) Act 2008. Note, though, that the Government of Singapore is permitted to import "relevant health products" into Singapore for or during a national emergency or other circumstances of extreme urgency: see Singapore Patents Act, s. 56(1A), which was inserted via the Patents (Amendment) Act 2008.

[56] See the definition of "relevant health product" in s. 2(1) and the definition of "eligible importing country" in s. 66(6), both inserted via the Patents (Amendment) Act 2008.

[57] See the definition of "pharmaceutical product" in s. 2(1), which was inserted via the Patents (Amendment) Act 2004.

[58] See s. 66(3), which was inserted via the Patents (Amendment) Act 2004. *Ibid.* s. 66(3). Note that there is an exception to this prohibition. Under s. 66(2)(i), importation of a patented pharmaceutical product is permitted if this product is required for the use by or on a particular patient and the Health Sciences Authority in Singapore has granted approval specifically for the import of this product for this patient.

[59] The reason for imposing this condition is to give the patentee in Singapore only a "first mover advantage" in the Singapore market: see Speech of the Parliamentary Secretary to the Minister for Law at the Second Reading of the Patents (Amendment) Bill 2004, 78 HANSARD col. 118 (June 15, 2004). Once he has made his pharmaceutical product available in Singapore, he will have to compete with the parallel importers.

[60] Singapore Patents Act, s. 66(3)(g).

[61] This is the effect of the following words in s. 66(2)(g): "for this purpose, 'patent' includes a patent granted in any country outside Singapore in respect of the same or substantially the same invention as that for which a patent is granted under this Act."

means that, just like in the copyright and trademark regimes, restrictions imposed by the patentee (for example, by affixing a label "Not for Resale Outside Thailand" to the patented product) have no effect on the issue of consent.

III.   WHY DIFFERENT STROKES FOR DIFFERENT IP FOLKS?

The above overview shows that Singapore has made concerted efforts to harmonize the approaches taken towards parallel importation in the copyright, trademark, and patents regime. In spite of these efforts, the treatment of parallel imports is not identical across these regimes. Two forms of asymmetry have been highlighted in the overview.

The first, and most obvious, asymmetry lies in the fact that the Patents Act 1994 does not apply the international exhaustion principle uniformly across all industries: special exemptions are carved out for the pharmaceuticals sector. This is to fulfill Singapore's obligations under international law and the U.S.–Singapore Free Trade Agreement. Some may wonder why Singapore agreed to shield the pharmaceuticals sector from competition posed by parallel imports. The reason lies in Singapore's desire to build up this sector as part of its plans to become the biomedical hub in the region.[62] Another perspective is that Singapore's move is consistent with the calls made by some international organizations to higher-income countries to disallow parallel importation of patented pharmaceuticals products so that drug companies can be persuaded to sell essential medicine to poor countries without fear that the differentially priced drugs would leak into higher-income countries.[63]

The second asymmetry relates to the identification of the relevant intellectual property owner for the purposes of determining if the product is a genuine product. In the Copyright Act 1987, after the 1994 amendments following the *Teo Ai Nee* case, the relevant copyright owner is the copyright owner in the country of manufacture. In the Patents Act 1994, the relevant patent owner is also the patent owner in the country of manufacture. However, in the Trade Marks Act 1998, the High Court in the *Pan-West* case held that the relevant trademark owner is the party who is the registered proprietor in Singapore.

Some may doubt the correctness of the *Pan-West* decision, especially given the prompt reaction on the part of legislature to overrule the *Teo Ai Nee* case, which held that the relevant copyright owner was the Singapore copyright owner. The following scenario will be used to illustrate these critics' discomfort with the decision. ABC is a company selling machinery in the Association of Southeast Asian Nations (ASEAN) countries. ABC has registered its trademark, *inter alia*, in Thailand and Singapore. After some years of operating in Thailand, ABC decides to withdraw from the market in Thailand. ABC assigns the registered trademark in Thailand to XYZ, a party unrelated to ABC.[64] XYZ applies

---

[62] During parliamentary debates, the strengthening of the patent rights in pharmaceutical products was attributed to the need to "support the growth of the pharmaceutical and biomedical industries": see Speech of the Parliamentary Secretary, *supra* note 59.

[63] See WTO SECRETARIATS, REPORT OF THE WORKSHOP ON DIFFERENTIAL PRICING & FINANCING OF ESSENTIAL DRUGS (2001). This workshop was organized by the WTO and WTO Secretariats.

[64] If ABC and XYZ are related companies, the *Pan-West* case would not apply: Pan-West (Pte.) Ltd. v. Grand Bigwin Pte. Ltd., [2003] 4 S.L.R.(R) 755 (Sing.) and the accompanying main text.

this trademark to machinery it manufactures in Thailand, and sells this machinery in Thailand. Under the *Pan-West* analysis, the trademarked machinery made by XYZ in Thailand would not be regarded as "genuine" goods for the purposes of the Trade Marks Act 1998. ABC, the registered proprietor of the trademark in Singapore, would be able to stop importation of XYZ's machinery into Singapore. Yet, if the subject matter of ABC's assignment is a copyright or a patent, ABC would not be able to stop the importation of the copyrighted or patented products into Singapore. Is there something about trademarks that deserves this special treatment?

One response to the critics of the *Pan-West* case would be the following. There *is* something different about trademarks. The reason for protecting trademarks is different from the reason for protecting copyright and patents. Trademarks are protected so that they can function effectively as the badge of origin of a business. When machinery made by XYZ bearing a trademark that is identical with the trademark of ABC is allowed to circulate in Singapore, the public in Singapore will think that this machinery originates from ABC. Copyright and patents, on the other hand, are granted to reward creativity and innovation. When ABC assigned its copyright or patent in Thailand to XYZ, the fee paid by XYZ represents part of the ABC's reward for creating the copyright work or the patented invention. Thus, when copies of the copyright work or patented invention made by XYZ are sold in Singapore, they are copies for which ABC has already been duly compensated.

IV. CONCLUSION

The benefit to consumers may be foremost in the minds of Singapore's policy-makers, but it is not the only consideration. In the patents regime, the desire to become a biomedical hub has resulted in a restriction on parallel importation of patented pharmaceutical products. The statistics, as shown in Table 10.1, suggest that Singapore's economy has yet to reap the benefits of this move.

However, the economic success of this move becomes much less important if the restriction on parallel importation is viewed from the perspective that Singapore is playing a role in finding a solution to the public health problems in the less developed and low-income countries.

As for the special treatment given to trademark proprietors in Singapore, the justification lies in the very rationale for trademark protection. This move does not seem to have adverse effects where consumer benefits are concerned. In sectors that are heavily reliant on trademarks, the presence of parallel imports is very evident. For example, in the automobile sector, the price of a parallel imported MERCEDES BENZ model can cost

---

Note also that in Australia, the court has refused to allow sham assignments to be used to repel parallel imports: see Transport Tyre Sales Pty. Ltd. v. Montana Tyres Rims & Tubes Pty. Ltd., [1999] 93 F.C.R. 421 (Austl.). In this case, the foreign manufacturer of the product registered its trademark in Australia, and purportedly assigned this registration to its distributor in Australia. There was a condition in the assignment that when the distributorship came to an end, this trademark would be re-assigned to the foreign manufacturer. The assignment by the trademark owner (for the purpose of stopping parallel importation) could not be used to stop parallel importation.

Table 10.1 Economic contributions of the biomedical manufacturing sector

	2004	2006	2011	2014
Contribution to total output in manufacturing (%)	9.2	10	9.0	7.1
Contribution to employment in manufacturing (%)	2.6	2.8	3.7	4

Source: Economic Survey of Singapore (published by the Singapore Ministry of Trade and Industry).

as much as U.S.$9,100 less than the same model retailed by the local authorized distributor.[65] In the foodstuff and personal toiletries sectors, there are many "bargain stores" that have mushroomed in the suburbs where parallel imports are retailed at prices that can be 50 percent less than the prices found in the mainstream supermarkets.[66]

---

[65] See *Merc Buyers Snap Up Parallel Imports*, STRAITS TIMES, July 18, 1996. Parallel imported cars account for 15–25 percent of the market share in Singapore. See Godfrey Yeung & Vincent Mok, *Manufacturing and Distribution Strategies, Distribution Channels, and Transaction Costs: The Case of Parallel Imported Automobiles*, 34 MANAGERIAL & DECISION ECON. 44 (2013).

[66] See *Fancy a Drink of "ke kou ke le"? (Looks like Coke, Tastes like Coke . . . Because it is Coke—from China)*, STRAITS TIMES, June 22, 2008; see also *Stretch $ at Bargain Stores; Boom in Chains Offering Great Savings*, STRAITS TIMES, April 16, 2011.

11. Parallel imports and the principle of exhaustion of rights in Latin America
Carlos M. Correa* and Juan I. Correa**

I. INTRODUCTION

Based on the principle of exhaustion of rights in Article 6 of the Agreement on Trade-Related Aspects of Intellectual Property Rights (TRIPS),[1] members of the World Trade Organization (WTO) may admit parallel imports of products legitimately put on the market in a foreign market, thereby allowing consumers to get access to products protected under national intellectual property rights at prices lower than the products that are distributed locally by the right owners or licensees. Such imports may also be important when the local market is not adequately supplied by the right owners, for instance, when the quantity of the protected product is insufficient to meet the demand.

The very general provision of Article 6 of TRIPS, as examined elsewhere in this book,[2] leaves WTO members considerable policy space to define the geographical origin and source of parallel imports for all categories of intellectual property, as defined in Article 1.2 of TRIPS.[3] WTO members may determine whether such imports are admissible on an international basis, or only when originating from a country belonging to a particular grouping of countries, such as a regional common market, as in the case of the European Union (EU). In addition, national laws may decide whether the legality of parallel imports is conditional upon the right holder having consented to the commercialization of the protected products in the exporting country, or whether products commercialized without such consent by a person otherwise authorized (for instance, a compulsory licensee) may also be admissible under the principle of exhaustion.[4] Finally, parallel imports may be admitted for certain categories of intellectual property rights and not for others.

---

* Professor and Director of the Center for Interdisciplinary Studies on Industrial Property and Economics at the Faculty of Law, University of Buenos Aires; Advisor on Intellectual Property and Trade, South Centre.

** Candidate, Master in Intellectual Property, Facultad Latinoamericana de Ciencias Sociales (FLACSO); editor, Revista Temas de Derecho Industrial y de la Competencia; advisor to the Office of Policy Coordination of the Ministry of Agriculture and Fisheries of Argentina.

[1] AGREEMENT ON TRADE-RELATED ASPECTS OF INTELLECTUAL PROPERTY RIGHTS, April 15, 1994; Marrakesh Agreement Establishing the World Trade Organization, Annex 1C, Legal Instruments—Result of the Uruguay Rounds Vol. 31, 33 I.L.M. 83 (1994) [hereinafter TRIPS].

[2] See e.g. the various chapters in Part II of this volume.

[3] TRIPS, art. 1.2.

[4] See e.g. CARLOS CORREA, TRADE RELATED ASPECTS OF INTELLECTUAL PROPERTY RIGHTS, A COMMENTARY ON THE TRIPS AGREEMENT 85–86 (2007).

Latin American intellectual property legislation generally remained silent about this issue before a final draft of TRIPS became known in 1991 and the countries in the region were obliged to adapt their legislation to satisfy TRIPS' minimum standards.[5] Latin American legislation recognized, explicitly or implicitly, as part of the set of conferred exclusive rights, the legal power to control any commercialization made in the territory where protection was granted, whether based on the local production or the importation of the protected goods. The principle of exhaustion of rights was, thus, limited to the national jurisdiction. As examined below, a number of Latin American countries[6] have since provided for the principle of international exhaustion, thereby admitting parallel imports, although in some cases subject to certain limitations.

Interestingly, there is significant variation within national jurisdictions in Latin America regarding the treatment of parallel imports in respect to different categories of intellectual property rights. For instance, in several countries such imports are explicitly allowed for patents and/or trademarks and not in the area of copyright. This differentiation may be explained in some cases by the enactment date of the respective laws. The laws enacted prior to TRIPS did not address the issue and, unless amendments were subsequently introduced, still fail to specifically open the possibility to parallel imports. These laws either clearly exclude parallel imports (to the extent that the right owner is empowered to prevent imports) or leave the situation regarding parallel imports unclear, subject to the interpretation by national courts.[7] Some of the provisions adopted after TRIPS, however, prohibit parallel imports.

The dichotomy in allowing/prohibiting parallel imports within the same jurisdiction is illustrated by the case of the Andean Community.[8] As discussed below, the Andean Community has embraced the principle of international exhaustion of rights for patents and trademarks, while Decision 351 on copyright provides that the author "shall have the exclusive right to carry out, authorize or prohibit . . . the importation into the territory of any Member Country of copies made without the authorization of the owner of rights."[9]

Under the free trade agreements (FTAs) between the United States (U.S.) and, respectively, Australia, Morocco, and, Singapore, the patent owner is authorized to prevent parallel imports through the use of contract or other means.[10] This limitation

---

[5] Latin American countries benefited from the transitional periods provided for in art. 65 of TRIPS. See TRIPS, art. 65.

[6] The Table in the Annex is illustrative; it does not intend to cover all possible situations where parallel imports are admissible under Latin American laws and regulations.

[7] Case law addressing cases of parallel imports is scarce. In particular, no cases of parallel imports made to get access to cheaper medicines (one of the frequently mentioned possible uses of such imports) have been reported. See e.g. UNITED NATIONS DEVELOPMENT PROGRAMME, GOOD PRACTICE GUIDE: IMPROVING ACCESS TO TREATMENT BY UTILIZING PUBLIC HEALTH FLEXIBILITIES IN THE WTO TRIPS AGREEMENT 39 (January 19, 2011).

[8] The Andean Community is comprised of Bolivia, Colombia, Ecuador, and Peru. Andean Subregional Integration Agreement, May 26, 1969, WIPO Lex TRT/ASIACA/001 ("Cartagena Agreement").

[9] Decision No. 351 Establishing the Common Provisions on Copyright and Neighboring Rights, December 21, 1993, art. 13(d), WIPO Lex CAN010.

[10] Pedro Roffe & Christoph Spenemman have observed that these provisions do "not amount to a general exclusion of international patent right exhaustion . . . In the above FTAs, the parties keep in theory the freedom to maintain or introduce international patent right exhaustion. In case

was not, however, incorporated into the FTAs entered into between the U.S. and Latin American countries. In fact, such limitation found opposition within the U.S. Congress itself.[11] Section 631 of the U.S. Science, State, Justice, Commerce, and Related Agencies Appropriations Act[12] established that "[n]one of the funds made available in this Act may be used to include in any new bilateral or multilateral trade agreement" the texts of the provisions limiting parallel imports contained in those FTAs.

It is worth mentioning that the Latin American legislation reviewed here does not expressly refer in any case to the concepts of "exhaustion of rights" or "parallel imports." The provisions analyzed below have the effect of allowing what are generally known as "parallel imports" and, in many cases, their admissibility is based on conditions comparable to those applicable in the EU and other countries where the doctrine of exhaustion of rights has been introduced through legislation or case law. Under some laws, however, the admissibility of parallel imports does not seem to have been based on that doctrine, as they would be permitted when a product has been lawfully commercialized in the exporting country, potentially covering situations where no protection was available there (and, hence, no rights could have been "exhausted").

The right to parallel import, if admitted under the applicable national law, may not be sufficient in some cases to make the importation of protected products possible. Other regulations may prevent it, such as the need to comply with regulatory requirements for the marketing approval of pharmaceutical and agrochemical products. Of course, the doctrine of exhaustion of rights cannot be understood to eliminate or diminish the State regulatory powers in these and other fields.

This chapter first examines the treatment of parallel imports under the national laws of Latin American countries. The analysis focuses on patents and trademarks, while references to other categories of intellectual property (notably copyright) are also made in respect of some countries. Second, it considers the admissibility of such imports in the

---

the purchaser of a patented product does not agree on a territorial restriction for the resale of the products, he preserves his right to resell them anywhere in the world in parallel to the patent holder." Pedro Roffe & Christoph Spennemann, *The Impact of FTAs on Public Health Policies and TRIPS Flexibilities*, 1 INT'L J. INTELL. PROP. MGMT. 81 (2006).

[11] The Report of the United States House of Representatives to Rep. Henry Waxman warned against limitations on parallel imports in FTAs: "making this policy permanent in trade agreement prevents countries that do not currently restrict parallel importation from reconsidering their national policies. Even in the USA there is great support for a form of parallel importation: both the House and the Senate have measures that would allow the importation of lower-priced patented drugs from Canada. The trade agreement language would make it difficult for the USA or other nations with current restrictions on importation to revisit their national policies." UNITED STATES HOUSE OF REPRESENTATIVES, COMMITTEE ON GOVERNMENT REFORM, MINORITY STAFF SPECIAL INVESTIGATIONS DIVISION, TRADE AGREEMENTS AND ACCESS TO MEDICATIONS UNDER THE BUSH ADMINISTRATION 58 (June 2005), available at www.twn.my/title2/FTAs/Intellectual_Property/IP_and_Access_to_Medicines/TradeAgreementsandAccesstoMedicationsUnderTheBushAdmini.pdf.

[12] Science, State, Justice, Commerce, and Related Agencies Appropriations Act, H.R. 2862, 109th Cong. (2005).

context of the economic integration schemes (MERCOSUR and the Andean Community of Nations) established in the region.

II. PARALLEL IMPORTS UNDER NATIONAL LEGISLATION

A. Consent-based Approach

As illustrated by the provisions presented in the Annex to this chapter, many Latin American countries allow for parallel imports at least for some categories of intellectual property rights based on a consent approach, as developed under European law.[13] In general, those provisions have no geographical restrictions, that is, they incorporate an international principle of exhaustion of rights. Three types of provisions may be found in Latin America legislations.

A pure consent-based approach is found when the only requirement is that the commercialization in the exporting country has been made by the right holder or with his consent. In Chile, for instance, rules of this type apply to both patents and trademarks;[14] in Honduras, they apply to patents;[15] in Mexico, they apply to trademarks[16] while patents are subject to a principle of national exhaustion.[17]

In other cases where parallel imports are admitted, the pure consent-based approach is supplemented by considerations regarding whether the supplier is under the direct or indirect control of the right holder or whether both are under a common control. This type of provision requires engaging in an analysis of corporate structures and contractual situations (a subcontractor, for instance, may be deemed to act under the control of the contractor). In some cases, custom authorities or courts may need to pierce the corporate veil or apply other doctrines (such as the single economic unit). Examples of these provisions can be found in Cuba,[18] Guatemala,[19] and Dominican Republic[20] in relation to trademarked products.

An additional condition is established in many Latin American laws on trademarks with regard to the preservation of the original wrapping or packaging of parallel imported products. These imports will not be allowed if the products or their packaging have

---

[13] See e.g. CHRISTOPHER STOTHERS, PARALLEL TRADE IN EUROPE: INTELLECTUAL PROPERTY, COMPETITION AND REGULATORY LAW (2007).

[14] Law No. 19.039, January 24, 1991, arts. 19*bis*, 49.5, DIARIO OFICIAL [D.O.] (Chile).

[15] Industrial Property Law Decree No. 12-99-E, December 30, 1999, art. 18, WIPO HN002 (Hond.).

[16] Industrial Property Law, as amended, art. 91. Diario Oficial de la Federación [DOF], June 27, 1991 (Mex.), amended and published in DOF, April 9, 2012 [hereinafter Mexican Industrial Property Law].

[17] *Ibid.* art. 22.

[18] Decree-Law No. 203 on Trademarks and Other Distinctive Signs, December 24, 1999, art. 47.I, WIPO C001 (Cuba).

[19] Industrial Property Law Decree No. 57-2000, September 18, 2000, art. 37, WIPO GT001 (Guat.).

[20] Law No. 20-00 on Industrial Property, April 4, 2000, art. 88, WIPO DO001 (Dom. Rep.) [hereinafter DR Industrial Property Law].

been altered or deteriorated as provided for in the Dominican Republic,[21] Guatemala,[22] Panama,[23] Paraguay,[24] and Uruguay.[25]

In some cases, it is clarified that the condition regarding unaltered products or packaging is subject to the existence of a possible harm to the right holder. For instance, Costa Rica allows parallel imports in the case of legitimately marked goods, subject to the preservation of the original wrapping or packaging to the extent necessary to protect the right holders' interests.[26] The wording of this condition seems to leave open the possibility of arguing that changes in wrapping or packaging do not negatively affect such interests. A similar provision is contained in the Cuban law.[27]

B. Beyond Consent

There are several examples of legislation in Latin America which incorporated provisions allowing for parallel imports from any country where the protected products have been lawfully commercialized or put on the market by any authorized person. This means that parallel importation would be permitted even in cases where a product was commercialized in a foreign country without the consent of the right holder.

The first example concerns article 36(c) of Argentine Patent Law.[28] It limits the rights conferred by a patent in respect of a person who "imports or in any way deals in the product patented or obtained by the patented process once the said product has been lawfully placed on the market in any country."[29]

This provision applies to the importation of products that are patented in Argentina as well as to products that are off-patent there, but were "obtained" in a foreign country by a process patented in Argentina. Although no reference is made in article 36(c) to products obtained "directly" by the patented process, article 8 of the Patent Law, as amended by in 2003,[30] limits the right to prevent imports to situations where such condition is met.[31]

Importantly, article 36(c) allows for parallel imports in all cases where the product was "lawfully placed on the market" in any country.[32] This concept is reinforced by the second phrase of that article, which generically refers to situations where a product has been placed on the market in a foreign country "in accordance with" the TRIPS Agreement.

---

[21] Ibid.
[22] Industrial Property Law Decree No. 57-2000, September 18, 2000, art. 37, WIPO GT001 (Guat.).
[23] Law No. 35 on Industrial Property, May 10, 1996, art. 100, WIPO PA002 (Pan.).
[24] Law No. 1.294/1998 on Trademarks, August 6, 1998, art. 17, WIPO PY005 (Para.).
[25] Law No. 17.011 Establishing Provisions on Trademarks, September 25, 1998, art. 12, WIPO UY001 (Uru.).
[26] Law No. 7978 on Trademarks and Other Distinctive Signs, February 1, 2000, art. 27, WIPO CR003 (Costa Rica).
[27] Decree-Law No. 203 on Trademarks and Other Distinctive Signs, December 24, 1999, art. 47, WIPO C001 (Cuba).
[28] Law No. 24.481, October 23, 1995, art. 36(c), [LV-C] A.D.L.A. 2948 (as amended by Law No. 24.572) [LV-E] A.D.L.A. 5892, (1995) (Arg.) [hereinafter Argentine Patent Law].
[29] Ibid.
[30] Ibid. (as amended by Law No. 25.859 (2003)).
[31] This is consistent with art. 28.1(b) of the TRIPS Agreement. TRIPS, art. 28.1(b).
[32] Argentine Patent Law, art. 36(c).

Literally read, this provision would seem to open the door for the importation of products that are not protected in the country of exportation, since their commercialization would have been fully lawful under the rules of said Agreement. This reading would stretch the concept of exhaustion of rights beyond what is generally accepted (as there would be no rights that could have been "exhausted" in the exporting country). At a minimum, the wording of Article 36(c) seems to clearly include parallel imports of products commercialized by a compulsory licensee in a foreign country, since there is no doubt that in this situation the products have been "lawfully placed on the market."[33]

While the patent law clearly sets a broad standard for the admissibility of parallel imports, the implementing regulations[34] refer to the importation of the product by "the licensee authorized for its commercialization in the country."[35] It is unclear whether the intention of the regulations has been to suggest that parallel imports can only be made by a licensee, thereby limiting the scope of the rule established by the patent law.[36] The admissibility of parallel imports creates a limitation to the patent rights; hence, they may be performed by any third party without having negotiated a license. A possible interpretation of the regulations is that they only refer to a situation where parallel imports are made by a licensee of the patent holder. It may be further interpreted that they aim at overriding contractual provisions that may restrict parallel imports, that is, a licensee authorized to commercialize the product in Argentina could not be prevented from parallel importing it. Notably, the regulations refer to "a third party authorized to commercialize" the products, without limiting this condition to a voluntary licensee.[37] Hence, parallel imports could be deemed admissible even in cases where the supplier is a compulsory licensee.

In relation to the admissibility of parallel imports originating from a compulsory licensee, it is worth noting that although Article 31(f) of the TRIPS Agreement requires that a compulsory license be granted to "predominantly" supply the local market, it does not ban exports by the compulsory licensee if this condition is met. Moreover, the WTO in 2003 adopted a waiver,[38] which has been renewed so far,[39] in respect of Article 30(f) for the export of pharmaceutical products.[40]

The U.S. challenged the consistency of article 36(c) of the Argentine Patent Law with Articles 6 and 28.1 of the TRIPS Agreement, in a complaint submitted under the WTO

---

[33] *Ibid.*

[34] Argentine Patent Law (as amended by Law No. 24.572 (1995) and approved by Decree No. 260 (1996)) ("Argentine Regulations").

[35] *Ibid.*

[36] Whether this limitation is compatible with the hierarchy between laws and implementing regulations raises issues of constitutional law, which are not addressed here.

[37] See Argentine Regulations.

[38] World Trade Organization, Implementation of Paragraph 6 of the Doha Declaration on the TRIPS Agreement and Public Health, Decision of August 30 2003, WT/L/540 (September 2, 2003).

[39] The Decision will be in force until the date on which an amendment to the TRIPS Agreement replacing its provisions takes effect for a member state. *Ibid.* para. 11.

[40] An amendment to TRIPS that would incorporate the referred to Decision as a new article, 31*bis*, has been pending approval by WTO members since December 2005. World Trade Organization, Implementation of Paragraph 11 of the General Council Decision of August 30, 2003 on the Implementation of Paragraph 6 of the Doha Declaration on the TRIPS Agreement and Public Health, IP/C/41 (December 6, 2005).

204 *Research handbook on intellectual property exhaustion and parallel imports*

Dispute Settlement Understanding (DSU) in 2000.[41] Although the Argentine government could have invoked the policy space recognized under Article 6 of the TRIPS Agreement, it engaged in consultations with the U.S. government on the matter. After nearly two years of discussions, the parties reached an agreement and the issue was not submitted to a panel. In accordance with the "mutually agreed solution" reached by the parties:

> [t]he Governments of the United States and Argentina have analyzed article 36(c) of Law No. 24.481 and article 36 of Decree 260/96 in light of the provisions of Articles 6 and 28.1 of the TRIPS Agreement. Pursuant to this analysis, Argentina has confirmed that, according to its law and regulations, the owner of a patent granted in the Argentinean Republic shall have the right to prevent third parties not having the owner's consent from the acts of making, using, offering for sale, selling or importing the patented product in the territory of Argentina. However, a voluntary licensee in Argentina authorized by the Argentinean patent owner to import the patented product may import the product if he proves the product has been put on the market in a foreign country by the owner of the Argentinean patent or by a third party authorized for its commercialization. On this basis, Argentina and the United States agree that article 36(c) of Law No. 24.481, read in conjunction with article 36 of Decree 260/96, is consistent with Argentina's obligations under the TRIPS Agreement.[42]

The agreement relies on the concept of "licensee authorized" to import contained in the implementing regulations, who is described in the U.S.-Argentina "mutually agreed solution" as a "voluntary licensee."[43] If the situation described in the text were the only one where parallel imports would be admissible, the Argentine legislation would be considerably restrictive in this regard. However, neither the text of the legislation nor the "mutually agreed solution" excludes the possibility that a court considers admissible parallel imports more broadly, in conformity with article 36(c) of the Argentine Patent Law. Interestingly, the referred to solution alludes to "a third party authorized for its commercialization" which, as mentioned above, may include a compulsory licensee. In addition, if parallel imports were accepted under broader terms by Argentine courts or through an amendment to the regulations, other WTO members would be subject to the limitations imposed by Article 6 of the TRIPS Agreement, that is, they could not bring a complaint under the Dispute Settlement Understanding (DSU). This would also apply to the U.S., despite the interpretation that Argentina agreed to in the "mutually agreed solution."[44] Argentina, like any other WTO member, is free to change its legislation on parallel imports, and eventually expand the scope of admissible parallel imports.

Mexican trademark law contains a second example of a broadly conceived provision on parallel imports, which is based on the principle of international exhaustion of rights. In accordance with article 92(II) of the Industrial Property Law, the holder of a registered mark may not assert his rights against any person who commercializes, distributes, acquires, or uses imported "lawful products to which the mark is applied" pursuant "to

---

[41] Request for Consultations by the United States, *Argentina—Certain Measures on the Protection of Patents and Test Data*, WT/DS196/1/IP/D/22 (June 6, 2000).

[42] Notification of Mutually Agreed Solution According to the Conditions Set Forth in the Agreement, *Argentina—Certain Measures on the Protection of Patents and Test Data*, WT/DS196/4 (June 20, 2002).

[43] *Ibid.*

[44] *Ibid.*

the terms and conditions laid down in the Regulations under this Law."[45] A product is "lawful" if it has been "placed on the market by the owner of the trademark or the person who has been granted license."[46]

However, article 54 of the Implementing Regulations seems to narrow down the scope of the referred to provision. It stipulates, by way of a presumption, that the introduction of a product in the foreign market will be legitimate if: (I) it is made by the holder of the registered mark or its licensee; and (II) at the time the products are imported into the Mexican territory, the holders of the trademark in Mexico and the foreign country are the same person or are members of the same group of economic interest or their licensees or sublicensees.[47] Article 55 of the Regulations defines the conditions under which the holders of the trademark may be considered members of the same group of economic interest.[48] This condition, however, does not prevent a third party from parallel importing from any country. The possible sources of supply are limited to the holder of the registered mark or its licensee, but this does not affect the scope of the permission since compulsory licenses are banned in the area of trademarks,[49] and the licensee in this case can only be "voluntary."[50]

A third example of broad admissibility of parallel imports is provided by the Mexican Copyright Law of 1996. Article 27(IV) of this law spells out a first sale exception to the right of distribution of copyrighted works.[51] This exception is not applicable in the case of computer programs and databases whose right holders retain the right to authorize or prohibit the lending of copies thereof, even after the sale of the said copies, unless a computer program does not in itself constitute an essential element of the license for use.[52]

In the light of article 27(IV) and since the Copyright Law does not specifically grant to the holder a right to prevent importation of legitimate copies of protected works, it has been interpreted, *a contrario*, that parallel imports based on a principle of international exhaustion of rights are legally permitted.[53]

The Dominican Republic Industrial Property Law also provides for a broad admissibility of parallel imports in the case of patents. Parallel imports are permitted to the extent that the products have been put on the foreign market with the consent of the owner or

---

[45] Mexican Industrial Property Law, art. 92(II).
[46] *Ibid.*
[47] Regulation on the Industrial Property Law (consolidated text incorporating the amendments made in 2002, 2003, and 2011), art. 54, DOF, June 10, 2011, superseding Regulation on the Industrial Property Law (consolidated text) DOF, September 19, 2003, and Regulation on the Industrial Property Law of 1994, DOF, November 18, 1994, available at www.wipo.int/edocs/lexdocs/laws/es/mx/mx112es.pdf.
[48] *Ibid.*
[49] TRIPS, art. 21 ("Members may determine conditions on the licensing and assignment of trademarks, it being understood that the compulsory licensing of trademarks shall not be permitted.").
[50] *Ibid.*
[51] Federal Law on Copyright, art. 27(IV), Diario Oficial de la Federación [DO], December 5, 1996 (Mex.).
[52] *Ibid.* art. 104.
[53] See e.g. Sergio L. Olivares Jr, *How to Stop Parallel Imports in Mexico*, OLIVARES (July 26, 2010), available at www.olivares.com.mx/En/Knowledge/Articles/CopyrightArticles/HowtostopparallelimportsinMexico.

a licensee "or in any other legal manner."[54] The same provision further clarifies that the products shall not be considered legally placed on the market "if placed in violation to industrial property law."[55] This may be interpreted as allowing parallel imports whether the products are protected or not in the exporting country.

C. Exhaustion Within the National Market

The provisions listed in the Annex show that, in some cases, the exhaustion of rights is contemplated in situations where the protected product (or the product obtained with a protected process) is put on the market without clarifying whether it refers to the national market only or whether it may involve foreign markets as well. This may lead to an *implicit* rule of national exhaustion of rights. An example of this formulation can be found in Mexico regarding patents. The rights conferred by a patent cannot be asserted against "any person who markets, acquires or uses the patented product or the product obtained by means of the patented process, after said product has been lawfully placed on the market."[56] Given the territoriality of patents, an interpretation of "the market" as comprising any foreign market is unlikely to succeed in the courts.[57]

In a few cases, the principle of national exhaustion of rights is *explicitly* provided for in the reviewed legislation. For instance, the Copyright Law of Guatemala[58] provides that the right to control subsequent sales is extinguished only when the first sale of the original or copies of the work occurred within the Guatemalan territory.[59]

An explicit domestic exhaustion rule was also established in Brazil, where article 43.4 of Industrial Property Law No. 9.279 specifically refers, in relation to patents, to placing of a product into the domestic market.[60] However, the Brazilian legislation introduces a peculiar limitation to this rule. In cases where a compulsory license has been granted on grounds of abuse of economic power, the compulsory licensee and third parties may parallel import the protected products if placed on the market in a foreign country by the patent holder or with his consent. The practical applicability of this provision is likely to be limited, since parallel imports would only be legitimized when a compulsory license has been granted and on the basis of a consent approach.[61] Parallel imports from a compulsory licensee in a foreign country do not seem to be permissible.

Finally, some laws in force in Latin America subject imports to the exclusive rights granted to the right holders or contain a straightforward prohibition of imports of protected products, without any clarification regarding the source. Hence, imports made

---

[54] Industrial Property Law, art. 30.
[55] *Ibid.* art. 30(d).
[56] Mexican Industrial Property Law, art. 22.
[57] In the case of Mexico this is particularly so in view of the explicit provision on parallel imports contained in the same law in relation to trademarks.
[58] Law on Copyright and Related Rights, September 27, 2000, art. 21, WIPO GT002 (Guat.).
[59] *Ibid.*
[60] See also Law No. 9.279, May 14, 1996, art. 43.4, WIPO BR003 (Braz.). Article 132 of the Brazilian Industrial Property Law establishes a similar (explicit) national exhaustion principle with regard to trademarks. *Ibid.* art. 132.
[61] The Brazilian government has only issued so far one compulsory license, on the basis of public interest considerations, in respect of an anti-retroviral (efavirenz) in 2007.

by a third party may be deemed infringing on the respective intellectual property rights. This seems to be the case, for instance, in Cuba where Article 28 of TRIPS has been incorporated and has no apparent limitation.[62] This is also true in Brazil,[63] Venezuela,[64] and Paraguay.[65] Article 27 of the Copyright and Related Rights Law of Paraguay provides that parallel imports are not admissible "regardless of whether or not the holder of the right has authorized the making of the said copies in the country of origin" if the copies were not intended to be imported in Paraguay.[66] While article 5 of the Industrial Property Law of Venezuela deprives "patents of introduction"[67] from the exclusive right to prevent imports, *a contrario* regular patents may be deemed to confer such a right.

III. PARALLEL IMPORTS IN ECONOMIC INTEGRATION SCHEMES

The admissibility of parallel imports may be particularly important in the context of schemes of economic integration. In the absence of parallel imports, right holders can fragment the market despite the existence of a common market or free trade area. In fact, the Court of Justice of the European Union had a key role in developing the doctrine of exhaustion of rights as a tool to ensure the free flow of goods protected by intellectual property rights within the European Communities.[68] This section examines the extent to which this doctrine has been incorporated into intellectual property regulations adopted in economic integration schemes in Latin America.

A. MERCOSUR

The Common Market of the South (MERCOSUR) is an economic and political agreement established in 1991 by the Treaty of Asunción.[69] Current states parties include Argentina, Brazil, Paraguay, Uruguay, and Venezuela.[70] One of MERCOSUR's main goals is to promote the free movement of goods, services, and people among member states.

A Protocol for the Harmonization of Intellectual Property Provisions in MERCOSUR

---

[62] Decree-Law No. 290 on Inventions and Industrial Designs and Models, November 20, 2011, art. 65, WIPO CU080 (Cuba).

[63] Law No. 9.456 on Plant Variety Protection Law, April 25, 1997, art. 37, WIPO 005 (Braz.).

[64] Law on Copyright, August 14, 1993, art. 95, WIPO VE010 (Venez.).

[65] Law No. 1328/98 on Copyright and Related Rights, August 27, 1998, art. 27, WIPO PY001 (Para.).

[66] *Ibid.* art. 29.

[67] These patents, common in the legislation of the nineteenth century, are granted on the basis of the revalidation of a foreign patent regardless of the possible loss of novelty of the invention. Industrial Property Law, September 2, 1955, WIPO VE006 (Venez.).

[68] See e.g. Vladimír Týč & Radim Charvát, *European Court of Justice as Law-Maker: Example of Intellectual Property Protection on EU Internal Market*, in DNY PRÁVA – 2009 – DAYS OF LAW: THE CONFERENCE PROCEEDINGS (1st ed., 2009), available at www.law.muni.cz/sborniky/dny_prava_2009/files/prispevky/mezin_soud/Tyc_Charvat.pdf.

[69] Treaty of Asunción, March 26, 1991, 30 I.L.M. 1041.

[70] Bolivia will soon become a member of MERCOSUR (approval of its accession by the Parliaments of Paraguay and Brazil is pending).

on Trademarks, Indications of Source and Appellations of Origin was approved[71] and went into effect on August 6, 2000, but only in Paraguay and Uruguay as only Paraguay and Uruguay ratified it. In accordance with Article 13 of the Protocol:

> [the] registration of a trademark shall not prevent the free movement of marked goods, legitimately introduced into the market by the right holder or with his authorization. State Parties undertake to provide in their respective legislations measures providing for the Exhaustion of Rights conferred by the registration.[72]

This provision follows the consent-based approach ("introduced into the market by the right holder or with his authorization") incorporated into many national laws in Latin America, as discussed above, and elsewhere. It does not require that the trademarks in the exporting and importing countries belong to the same right holder, or to undertakings under common control. Hence, in principle, parallel imports would be allowed even if the trademarks belonged to different physical or juridical persons. There are also no requirements regarding the characteristics, quality, or packaging of the products, thereby leaving the MERCOSUR states parties significant leeway to admit parallel imports.

In addition, permissible parallel imports would not be limited to those originating within the common market (as is the case in the European Union), but suppliers may be located in any country. Thus, the Protocol enshrines a principle of international exhaustion of rights.

Another MERCOSUR Protocol was adopted in 1998 for the Harmonization of Norms on Industrial Designs,[73] which also addresses the issue of exhaustion of rights. In the absence of ratifications by MERCOSUR members, this Protocol has not become effective yet. Article 13 provides that the protection of an industrial design in a state party may not impede the free movement of articles bearing or embodying the same design after they have been legally introduced into commerce in any of the states parties to MERCOSUR, by the right holder or with his consent.[74]

To date, this Protocol has not been ratified by any MERCOSUR member state and, thus, has not yet become effective. Parallel imports would be admissible for industrial designs, if the Protocol is finally approved, under the same conditions established for trademarks and other signs referred to above, that is, they may originate in any country, but provided that the goods had been marketed by the right holder or with his consent.

While these Protocols provide for specific rules on exhaustion of rights to be enforced by MERCOSUR states parties, an additional Protocol on Basic Principles and General Rules on Intellectual Property adopted[75] in 2008, but not signed and not in effect yet,

---

[71] Protocol on Harmonization of Intellectual Property Norms in MERCOSUR in the Field of Trade Marks, Indications of Source and Appellations of Origin, MERCOSUR/CMC/DEC. No.8/95 (August 6, 2000).
[72] Ibid. art. 13.
[73] Protocol on Harmonization of Norms in the Field of Industrial Design, MERCOSUR/CMC/DEC. No.16/98 (December 10, 1998).
[74] Ibid. art. 13.
[75] Protocol on Basic Principles and General Rules on Intellectual Property in MERCOSUR, Annex V of Act No. 1/08 (adopted in Rio de Janeiro, September 24–26, 2008) [hereinafter MERCOSUR Protocol 2008].

followed a different approach regarding exhaustion of rights and parallel imports. In accordance with Article 4.1:

> [t]his Protocol shall not affect the right of each State Party to determine the conditions under which the exhaustion of rights related to products legitimately introduced into the market by their owner or by an authorized third party [will arise].[76]

Article 4.2 adds that "[i]n order to promote competition and remove barriers to trade, MERCOSUR States Parties shall endeavor to define the regime of exhaustion of rights in the respective specific thematic protocols."[77]

This Protocol would apply to *all* categories of intellectual property rights.[78] Unlike the thematic Protocols mentioned above, it leaves states parties the freedom to choose the scope of the exhaustion of rights. They may adopt a national, regional, or international principle, while in the previous Protocols the principle of international exhaustion was agreed upon. This difference in treatment may be explained by the fact that, as noted above, Brazil has adopted a principle of national exhaustion in the area of patents and trademarks and was probably reluctant to subscribe to regional rules that would require changing its national regime in this regard.

Another interesting difference between this general Protocol and those previously adopted by the MERCOSUR states parties lies in the determination of who would supply the parallel imports. While in the thematic Protocols a European-style consent theory has been incorporated, i.e., the goods must be put on the foreign market by the right holder or with his authorization or consent, the 2008 general Protocol refers to goods introduced into the foreign market "by their owner or by an authorized third party."[79] Since a third party may be "authorized" by the government under a compulsory license, this wording seems to suggest that the range of potential suppliers of parallel imports may include compulsory licensees. The adopted solution seems to accommodate the Argentine position on the matter, which, as discussed above, would seem open to parallel imports originating from such licensees.

The freedom recognized to the states parties to deal with the principle of exhaustion of rights at the national level indicates a low ambition of the states parties in terms of harmonizing the disciplines applicable to this issue within MERCOSUR. The only aspect that could be considered mandatory for all states parties, if this Protocol entered into force, would seem to be the latitude to admit parallel imports from any "authorized third party."

Article 4.2 of the commented Protocol suggests that more precise formulations on the principle of exhaustion of rights may be introduced into "specific thematic protocols" as is already the case, in fact, for trademarks, indications of source, appellations of origin, and industrial designs. Currently, however, there are no negotiations going on within MERCOSUR to adopt new thematic protocols. In particular, governments seem to be reluctant to enter into negotiations relating to the sensitive area of patents, since

---

[76] *Ibid.* art. 4.1.
[77] *Ibid.* art. 4.2.
[78] These categories are not limited to those covered by the TRIPS Agreement. They may include other modalities of intellectual property rights, such as utility models.
[79] See MERCOSUR Protocol 2008.

Table 11.1 Admissibility of parallel imports in MERCOSUR states parties

Country	Patents	Trademarks	Copyright
Argentina	International exhaustion	International exhaustion recognized by case law	National exhaustion
Brazil	National exhaustion	National exhaustion	National exhaustion
Paraguay	International exhaustion	International exhaustion	National exhaustion
Uruguay	International exhaustion	International exhaustion	National exhaustion
Venezuela	National exhaustion	International exhaustion	National exhaustion
Bolivia	International exhaustion	International exhaustion	National exhaustion

any attempt to reform the existing legislations is likely to trigger pressures by developed countries to increase the current levels of protection.

No attempt has been made so far to develop common rules in the area of copyright. In respect of plant varieties, MERCOSUR adopted in 2000 Resolution 1/00 that sets up criteria for the elaboration of standards for the production of certified propagating material with the aim of facilitating trade of seeds within member states.[80] For plant varieties, the member countries of MERCOSUR adopted a Decision approving an agreement of cooperation related to the protection of plant varieties.[81] The agreement defines rules on plant variety protection regarding equal treatment in Article 1; denomination of varieties in Article 2; harmonization of technical examinations in Article 3; exchange of information in Article 4; harmonization of administrative procedures in Article 5; and cooperation in Article 6. It does not contain any substantive provisions relating to the rights conferred to the breeders, including with regard to imports.

Given the limited success that MERCOSUR has reached in developing *regional* rules on parallel imports, trade flows within MERCOSUR are affected by the regulations on the subject adopted at the national level. The situation of some of the states parties has been examined above in more detail. Table 11.1 summarizes the current situation in the three main areas of intellectual property protection (patents, trademarks, and copyright).[82]

As indicated in Table 11.1, considerable differences in the treatment of parallel imports exist within MERCOSUR. The adoption of a national exhaustion principle by some states parties may frustrate the achievement of a regional market, as parallel trade can be blocked by right holders. It is particularly noticeable in the case of copyright law, an area where all states parties still seem to refuse the possibility of admitting parallel imports.

---

[80] Standard Criteria and Guidelines for the Preparation of Standards of Production Systems Propagation Materials Certificates, MERCOSUR/GMC/RES No.1/2000 (September 5, 2000).

[81] See Facilitation Agreement on Cooperation and Protection of Plant Varieties of States Parties in MERCOSUR, MERCOSUR/CMC/DEC No.1/99 (November 15, 1999).

[82] As regards trademarks in Argentina, see *La protección judicial de la marca*, Diario Judicial (July 5, 2000) (citing E. Aracama Zorraquín, *Las Marcas de Empresa en el Mercosur, Información Empresaria*, 261 Cámara de Sociedades Anónimas, Buenos Aires 24 (1995)), available at www.diariojudicial.com.ar/contenidos/2000/07/06/noticia_0011.html#_ftn18.

> **BOX 11.1 PARALLEL IMPORTS IN THE ANDEAN COMMUNITY: PATENTS**
>
> *Decision 85 (1974)*
> Article 28: ... The patent does not confer the exclusive right to import the patented product or that manufactured by the patented process.
>
> *Decision 311 (1991), Decision 313 (1992)*
> Article 35: The patent shall confer on its owner the right to prevent third parties from exploiting the patented invention without his consent. The owner may not exercise that right in any of the following cases:
> (a) In the case of the importation of the patented product that has been put on the market in any country, with the consent of the right owner or any other lawful manner...
>
> *Decision 344 (1994)*
> Article 35: The patent shall confer on its owner the right to prevent third parties from exploiting the patented invention without his consent. The owner may not exercise that right in any of the following cases:
> (a) when the case concerns the importation of the patented product that has been marketed in any country with the consent of the owner, a licensee or any other authorized person ...
>
> *Decision 486 (2000)*
> Article 54: The patent shall not give the right to prohibit a third party from engaging in commercial acts in relation to a product protected by the patent after that product has been brought on to the market in any country by the owner of the patent, or by another person who has obtained his consent or is economically associated with him.
> For the purposes of the foregoing paragraph, two persons shall be considered economically associated where one can directly or indirectly exercise a decisive influence on the other concerning the working of the patent, or where a third party can exercise such an influence on both.

(1) Andean Community

The Andean Community of Nations, previously known as the "Andean Pact," is a customs union originally established, in 1969, by the Cartagena Agreement signed by Bolivia, Chile,[83] Peru, Colombia, and Ecuador. Venezuela joined in 1973, but withdrew in 2006 in response to the signature by Colombia and Peru of FTAs with the U.S.[84]

The provision on exhaustion of rights relating to patents presents an interesting evolution in the Andean Community (see Box 11.1). The first common regime on industrial property adopted in 1974 explicitly excluded an exclusive right to import a patented products or a product manufactured by the patented process.[85] This rule was in line with

---

[83] Chile withdrew from the Andean Pact in 1976.
[84] See e.g. Carlos Malamud, *Venezuela's Withdrawal from the Andean Community of Nations and the Consequences for Regional Integration*, REAL INSTITUTO ELCANO, WORKING PAPER NO. 28/2006 (2006), available at www.realinstitutoelcano.org/documentos/273/273_Malamud_Venezuela_CAN.pdf. One of the reasons that precipitated Venezuela's withdrawal were the amendments to the Andean common industrial property regime introduced through Decision 689, 2008, to implement the obligations of the FTAs between the U.S., Colombia, and Peru.
[85] Decision No. 85, Regulation for the Application of Industrial Property Rules, WIPO CAN018 (June 5, 1974).

212 *Research handbook on intellectual property exhaustion and parallel imports*

the overall objective of the Andean patent regime to promote the local exploitation of patents and avoid the simple use of patents as a monopoly to import products manufactured abroad.[86]

Under Decisions 311 (1991) and 313 (1992), an exclusive right to import was introduced while parallel imports were broadly allowed when the imported product had been commercialized in the exporting market by the right owner, his consent, or in "any other lawful manner."[87] This wording could have been interpreted as allowing not only the importation of products put on the market by a compulsory licensee, but also by any third party in situations where the products were not protected in the exporting country.[88]

Decision 344 of 1994 amended one aspect of the referred to provision: it replaced "any other lawful manner" by "any other authorized person," thereby suggesting an intention to narrow down the scope of admissible imports to products commercialized by the right holder, a voluntary licensee, or another authorized person, such as a compulsory licensee.[89] However, an interpretation that "an authorized person" included a person who commercialized a product not protected in the exporting country could not be automatically ruled out.

The doctrine of exhaustion of rights, as developed in the European context, seems to have inspired the amendment introduced in 2000. Article 54 of Decision 486 incorporated the consent-based approach.[90] The previous wording referring to "any lawful manner" or "any authorized person" was replaced by a reference to a person who has obtained the patentee's consent or is economically associated with him.[91] Article 54, hence, would also cover situations where a formal consent (e.g., a voluntary license) has not been granted, but the supplier is "economically associated" with the patentee. The explanation of this concept makes it clear that parallel imports may be legitimate in cases where no formal relationship exists between the supplier and the patentee, if the latter exercises control over the former or both are subject to the common control of another party (e.g., subsidiaries within an economic group).

The Andean Community industrial property regime applies similar rules to those examined for patents to trademarks[92] and industrial designs.[93] In the case of trademarks, however, there is an additional condition for the admissibility of parallel imports: the

---

[86] In accordance with Decision 85, patents lasted for five years and this period could be extended for another five years only if the patent was exploited. *Ibid.* art. 29.

[87] Decision No. 311, Common Regime on Industrial Property, WIPO CAN023 (November 8, 1991); Decision No. 313, Common Regime on Industrial Property, WIPO CAN024 (February 6, 1992).

[88] It is worth recalling that in *Merck v. Primecrown* the Court of Justice of the European Union took into account the special situation of Spain and Portugal and admitted, under certain circumstances, the parallel importation of products commercialized there. Case C-267/95, Merck & Co. Inc. v. Primecrown Ltd. et al., [1996] E.C.R. I-06285.

[89] Decision No. 344, Establishing the Common Regime on Industrial Property, WIPO CAN013 (October 21, 1993).

[90] Decision No. 486, Establishing the Common Industrial Property Regime, WIPO CAN012 (September 14, 2000), art. 54.

[91] *Ibid.*

[92] *Ibid.* art. 158.

[93] *Ibid.* art. 131.

goods and the containers or packaging that are in direct contact with them must not have been subjected to any modification, alteration, or deterioration. This condition, which protects both the consumers and the right holders, was introduced by the phrase "in particular," suggesting that there may be other (undefined) situations where parallel imports could also be permitted.

In stark contrast to the admission of parallel imports for patents, trademarks, and industrial designs, the Andean Community regimes for copyright and plant varieties grant the right holders an unqualified right to prevent imports of protected subject matter. It is unclear why the states parties have introduced such a differentiation. The free circulation of copyrighted works within the common market may benefit consumers by preventing discriminatory treatment regarding pricing and other conditions for access to and use of such works. Many plant varieties are suitable for cultivation in more than one state party that share similar conditions for agriculture. To the extent that the requirements of seed certification and phytosanitary laws are complied with, the marketing of seeds at the regional level could benefit both farmers and breeders (who might exploit economies of scale). However, no parallel imports seem to be permitted in this area.

(2) Central American Integration System (SICA)

The Central American Integration System (SICA) (1991) includes Guatemala, El Salvador, Honduras, Nicaragua, Costa Rica, Panama, as well as Belize and the Dominican Republic. Among its objectives, SICA is aimed at the establishment of a common market.[94] It has developed a common external tariff and reached an almost complete customs union. Substantial advances in the area of free movement of persons, capitals, and services have also been made.[95] Although a directly elected parliamentary body (the Central American Parliament) and a judicial organ (the Central American Court of Justice) have been established, intellectual property regimes have not been harmonized. Most states parties to SICA (as shown in the Annex) have adopted a principle of international exhaustion. This would prevent right holders from blocking the circulation of protected goods within the SICA common market.

IV. CONCLUSION

The possibility of allowing for parallel imports originating from any country under a principle of international exhaustion of rights, is one of the important and often cited "flexibilities" of the TRIPS Agreement. The Latin American legislation reviewed in this chapter presents a very complex scenario. Some countries incorporated that principle for some categories of intellectual property rights and not for others. While international

---

[94] SICA members have set up a Settlement of Commercial Disputes Mechanism and signed a Central American Treaty on Investment and Trade in Services. They also agreed to coordinate common policies, such as agricultural policy and fisheries policy.

[95] See e.g. IOANNIS PAPAGEORGIOU, CENTRAL AMERICAN INTEGRATION SYSTEM, FIRST INTERNATIONAL DEMOCRACY REPORT 2011; CENTRE FOR STUDIES ON FEDERALISM (2011), available at www.internationaldemocracywatch.org/index.php/sica.

exhaustion has been adopted in many patent and trademark laws, national exhaustion prevails in the area of copyright. The rationale for this differentiation is unclear.

Most laws that allow parallel imports apply a consent-based approach. However, there are cases where compulsory licensees could be the legitimate source of such imports. There are also legal texts that leave open the possibility of allowing imports from countries where the respective subject matter is not protected (and, hence, strictly there would be no exhaustion of rights).

Despite some attempts to harmonize the disciplines on parallel imports within MERCOSUR, states parties still keep their own policies on the matter. While most of them have embraced an international principle of exhaustion for patents and trademarks that will avoid the fragmentation of the regional market, parallel imports originating from other states parties may be prevented in two of the largest economies of the group. The deeper level of integration reached by the Andean Community is reflected in the adoption of a common policy on the matter with a sharp contrast between the field of industrial property (where international exhaustion is the rule) and copyright (subject to national exhaustion). The states parties to SICA have not harmonized their intellectual property regimes, including the treatment of parallel imports. Most of them, however, recognize in some areas a principle of international exhaustion that may be instrumental for the consolidation of a regional market.

In summary, considerable legislative action will be necessary in many Latin American countries to fully benefit from the flexibility allowed by Article 6 of the TRIPS Agreement.

ANNEX: PROVISIONS IN LATIN AMERICAN LEGISLATION RELATING TO IMPORTS OF PRODUCTS PROTECTED BY INTELLECTUAL PROPERTY RIGHTS

Country	Legislation	Relevant provisions	Reference
Andean Community (Bolivia, Ecuador, Colombia, and Perú)	Decision No. 486 Establishing the Common Industrial Property Regime	**Article 54** The patent shall not give the right to prohibit a third party from engaging in commercial acts in relation to a product protected by the patent after that product has been brought on to the market in any country by the owner of the patent, or by another person who has obtained his consent or is economically associated with him. For the purposes of the foregoing paragraph, two persons shall be considered economically associated where one can directly or indirectly exercise a decisive influence on the other concerning the working of the patent, or where a third party can exercise such an influence on both.	Patent Law
		Article 158 Registration of a mark shall not give the right to prevent a third party from engaging in commercial acts in relation to a product protected by the said registration after the product has been brought on to the market in any country by the owner of the registration or by another person with the owner's consent or economically connected with him, in particular where the goods and the containers or packaging that are in direct contact with them have not been subjected to any modification, or alteration or deterioration. For the purposes of the foregoing paragraph, it shall be understood that two persons are economically connected when one is able to exert on the other a decisive direct or indirect influence regarding the exploitation of the rights in the mark, or where a third party is able to exercise such an influence on both persons.	Trademark Law
		Article 131 The registration of an industrial design shall not give the right to prohibit a third party from engaging in commercial acts in	Industrial designs

Country	Legislation	Relevant provisions	Reference
		relation to a product incorporating or reproducing that design after the product in question has been brought on to the market in any country by its owner or by another person with his consent or economically linked to him.	
		For the purposes of the foregoing paragraph, two persons shall be regarded as economically linked where one of them is able to exert a decisive direct or indirect influence on the other with respect to the exploitation of the industrial design, or where a third party is able to exert such an influence on both persons.	
	Decision 345, Common Provisions on the Protection of the Rights of Breeders of New Plant Varieties	Article 24 The grant of a breeder's certificate shall confer on the owner thereof the right to prevent third parties from engaging without his consent in the following acts in respect of reproductive, propagating or multiplication material of the protected variety: . . . . (f) importation.	Plant varieties
	Decision 451 Establishing the Common Provisions on Copyright and Neighboring Rights	Article 13 The author or his successors in title where applicable, shall have the exclusive right to carry out, authorize or prohibit: . . . . (d) the importation into the territory of any Member Country of copies made without the authorization of the owner of rights.	Copyright Law
Argentina	Patents and Utility Models Law No. 24,481	Article 36 The right conferred by a patent shall not take effect against: . . . (c) Any person who acquires, uses, imports or in any way deals in the product patented or obtained by the patented process once the said product has been lawfully placed on the market in any country. It will be understood that placing on the market is legal when it is done in accordance with the Agreement on Trade-Related Intellectual Property Rights. Part III Section IV of TRIPS-GATT Agreement.	Patent Law

	Decree 260/96 Regulations Implementing the Patent Law	Article 36 For the purposes of subsection (c) of article 36 of the Act, the holder of the patent in Argentina will have the right to prevent third parties, without his consent, from acts of making, using, offering for sale or importing into the territory the product object of the patent, as long as the product has not been placed lawfully on the market in any country. It will be deemed to have been lawfully placed on the market when the licensee authorized for its commercialization in the country proved that the products has been placed on the market by the patent holder in the country of purchase, or by a third party authorized to commercialize it. The commercialization of the imported product shall be subject to the provisions of article 98 of the Law and this regulation.	
Brazil	Plant Variety Protection Law No. 9,456	Article 37 Any person who sells, offers for sale, reproduces, imports or exports, or who packs or holds in storage for such purposes, or for any purpose supplies the propagating material of a protected plant variety, under the correct designation or any other, without being authorized to do so by the holder thereof, shall be bound to indemnify the said holder, in amounts to be specified by regulation, in addition to having the material seized, shall also pay a fine in an amount equivalent to 20 per cent of the commercial value of the seized material, and shall be deemed guilty of the crime of infringement of the rights of the breeder, without prejudice to whatever other legal penalties may be applicable.	Plant variety protection
	Industrial Property Law No. 9,279	Article 43.4 [The provision of article 42 about the rights conferred on its titleholder does not apply] . . . to a product manufactured in accordance with a process or product patent that has been introduced onto the domestic market directly by the patent holder or with his consent;	Patent Law
		Article 68.II (3) In the case that a compulsory license is granted on the grounds of abuse of economic power, the licensee who proposes local manufacture shall be assured a period, limited to the	Patent Law

Country	Legislation	Relevant provisions	Reference
		provisions of Article 74, to import the object of the license, provided that it was introduced onto the market directly by the titleholder or with his consent. (4) In the case of importation to exploit a patent and in the case of importation as provided for in the preceding paragraph, third parties shall also be allowed to import a product manufactured according to a process or product patent, provided that it has been introduced onto the market by the titleholder or with his consent.	
		Section II Article 132 The titleholder of a mark may not: III prevent free circulation of the product placed on the internal market either by itself or by a third party with his consent, except with regard to the provisions of 3 and 4 of article 68.	Trademark Law
Chile	Industrial Property Law No. 19,039	Article 19*bis* The right conferred by the trademark does not entitle the holder to prohibit third parties from using it on products lawfully marketed in any country with that mark by that proprietor or with his consent.	Trademark Law
		Article 49.5 The patent does not confer the right to prevent others from commercializing the product covered by the patent, which they have legitimately acquired after that product has been lawfully introduced into the market in any country by the right holder or a third party, with his consent.	Patent Law
Costa Rica	Law on Trademarks and Other Distinctive Signs, Law No. 7978	Article 27 Exhaustion of rights. Trademark registration shall not give owners the right to prevent a third party from using the mark for legitimately marked goods which have been introduced into trade, in the country or abroad, provided that those goods and the wrappings or packaging in immediate contact with them have not been changed, altered or damaged in any way that could harm the interests of the owners or their rightful claimants.	Trademark Law

Cuba	Law on Invention Patents, Industrial Designs and Utility Models Law No. 6867	Article 16 Rights conferred by patents. Limitations. Provided that the following exceptions do not unjustifiably affect the normal working of the patent or result in unreasonable prejudice to the legitimate interests of the owner or his licensee, the rights conferred by the patent shall not extend to: . . . . (d) the act of selling, offering for sale, use, usufruct, import or any means of marketing a product protected by the patent or obtained via a patented process, once the product has been traded by any country, with the consent of the owner or a licensee.	Patent Law
	Decree-Law No. 203 on Trademarks and Other Distinctive Signs	Article 47 I. The registration of a trademark does not grant to its owner the right to prevent a third party from using it in relation to products legitimately labeled, having been lawfully placed on any market with that mark by him, or by another person with his consent or economically linked to it, provided that the products and the containers which were in immediate contact with them have not been modified, altered or damaged, or other legitimate reason that justifies the holder to oppose further commercialization of the goods. II. For the purposes of the preceding paragraph, it is understood that two persons are economically related where one person can exercise directly over the other a decisive influence with regard to the exploitation of the trademark, or where a third party can exert such influence directly on such persons.	Trademark Law
	Decree-Law No. 290 of November 20, 2011 on Inventions and Industrial Designs and Models	Article 65 The patent confers to its owner the right to prevent third parties, without his consent, realizing the following acts: I. When subject matter of the patent is a product, the making, using, selling, offering for sale or importing the patented product. II. When the subject matter of the patent is a process, the utilization of that process and from using, selling, offering for sale or importing the product obtained directly by that process.	Patent Law

Country	Legislation	Relevant provisions	Reference
Dominican Republic	Industrial Property Law No. 20-00 modified by Law 424-06 on Implementation of the Dominican Republic-Central America-United States Free Trade Agreement (CAFTA-DR)	Article 30 Limitation and exhaustion of patent rights The patent does not give the right to prevent: …. (d) The sale, leasing, use, usufruct, importation or any means of marketing a product protected by patent or obtained by a patented process, once the product has been placed on the market in any country with the consent of the owner or of a licensee or in any other lawful manner. Products and procedures that infringe industrial property law shall be considered to be on the market unlawfully.	Patent Law
		Article 88 Limitation of rights exhaustion (1) The trademark registration does not confer on its owner the right to prohibit a third party from using the mark in relation to legitimately marked products that the owner or other person with his consent or economically linked to him had been introduced in the trade, in the country or abroad, provided that such products and containers which were in immediate contact with such products have not been modified, altered, or deteriorated. (2) It is understood that two persons are economically related where one person can exercise directly or indirectly on the other a decisive influence over the exploitation of the trademark, or where a third party can exert such influence over both persons.	Trademark Law
Guatemala	Industrial Property Law Decree No. 57-2000	Article 37 The trade mark confers on its owner the right to prohibit the free movement of products that carry legitimately and had been introduced commercially in the country or abroad, by such holder or another person with consent of the owner or economically connected to it, provided that these products and containers which were in immediate contact with them have not been modified, altered, or deteriorated. For the purposes of the preceding paragraph, it is understood that two persons are economically related where one person can exercise directly or indirectly on the other a decisive influence over the exploitation of rights in the mark, or where a third party can exert such influence over both people.	

Article 131

The patent does not give the right to prevent third parties from making commercial business in respect of a product protected by the patent or obtained by a patented process, after the product had been introduced in the market in any country by the holder of the patent or other person with the consent of the holder or economically linked to him. For purposes of the preceding paragraph, it is understood that two persons are economically related where one person can exercise directly or indirectly on the other a decisive influence regarding the exploitation of the patent, or where a third party can exert such influence over both persons. When the patent protects biological material capable of reproduction, the patent shall not extend to material obtained by multiplication or propagation of the material introduced into the market under the first paragraph, provided that the multiplication or propagation is a necessary consequence of the use of the material according to the purposes for which it was introduced into commerce, and that material derived from such use is not used for multiplication or propagation purposes.

Copyright Law Decree No. 33-9

Copyright Law

Article 21

Pecuniary or economic right, gives the copyright holder the authority to use the work directly and personally to transfer all or part of its rights on it and to allow its use or exploitation by third parties. . . .

(e) The public distribution of the original or copies of his work, whether by sale, lease, rent, loan or otherwise. When duly authorized by the right holder distribution by sale, the right to control subsequent sales is extinguished only when the first sale of the original or copies of the work occurred within the Guatemalan territory, except in cases provided for in article 38 of this law and any other legal exceptions. It is not extinguished by the authorized distribution by sale, reproduction rights, lease, rent, loan, modification, adaptation, arrangement, transformation, translation, import or communication to the public.

Country	Legislation	Relevant provisions	Reference
Honduras	Industrial Property Law Decree No. 12-99-E	Article 18 The rights conferred by the patent may not be asserted against any person who acquires or uses the patented product or obtained by the patented process after the said product has been lawfully placed on the commerce national or international by the holder of the patent or his licensees.	Patent Law
Honduras	Copyright and Neighboring Rights Law Decree No. 4-99-E	The authors have the exclusive right to authorize or prohibit the use of their works by any means, form or process. Therefore, may make or authorize especially any of the following acts: . . . 8. Authorize or prohibit the import of legally made copies of his work, and to prevent the importation of copies made without your authorization.	Copyright Law
Mexico	Industrial Property Law of June 27, 1991 (as last amended in 2012)	Article 22 The right conferred by a patent shall not have any effect against: . . . II. any person who markets, acquires or uses the patented product or the product obtained by means of the patented process, after said product has been lawfully placed on the market.	Patent Law
		Article 92 Registration of a mark shall not be effective against: . . . II. Any person who comercializes, distributes, acquires or uses the product to which the trademark is applied after the said product has been lawfully placed on the market by the owner of the trademark or the person who has been granted license. This case shall include the import of lawful products to which the mark is applied, carried out by any person for their use, distribution or marketing in Mexico, pursuant to the terms and conditions laid down in the Regulations under this Law.	Trademark Law

222

Panama	Copyright Law of December 1996 (as last amended in 2014)		**Article 27** The owners of the economic rights may authorize or prohibit: ... IV. The distribution of the work, including sale or other forms of transfer of the ownership of the physical material in which it is embodied, and also any form of transfer of the use of exploitation thereof; where distribution is effected by means of sale, the right of opposition shall be considered exhausted on the first sale, except in the case expressly provided for in article 104 of this Law. V. The importation into the country of copies of the work made without their authorization. **Article 104** As an exception to the provisions of article 27(IV), the owner of the copyright in a computer program or database shall retain the right to authorize or prohibit the lending of copies thereof, even after the sale of the said copies. This principle shall not apply where the copy of the computer program does not in itself constitute an essential element of the license for use.
	Industrial Property Law No. 35 of May 1996 (as amended in 2012 by Law No. 61)	Patents	**Article 9.** The article 19 of the Law 35 is as follows: The right that confers a patent will produce no effect against: ... 2. Any person who commercializes, acquires or uses the patented product or a product obtained by a patented process, after the product has been legally introduced in the market in any country.
	Industrial Property Law No. 35	Trademark Law	**Article 100** The registration of a trademark does not grant the right to prohibit a third party from: 1. Performing acts of commerce in relation to the products legally marked, the owner himself, his licensee or any other person thereby authorized, had sold or otherwise lawfully introduced in the commerce bearing such trademark, upon the condition that those products and the containers or packages which were in immediate contact with such products, would not have undergone any modifications or alteration.

Country	Legislation	Relevant provisions	Reference
Paraguay	Patent Law No. 1630/2000	Article 34 Limitations on the patent right and exhaustion of rights. The patent does not give the right to prevent: c) Acts of commerce done by a third party with respect to a product protected by the patent after it had lawfully placed on the market in any country by the patent owner or other person with the consent of the owner or legally authorized;	Patent Law
	Trademarks Law No. 1294	Article 17 Free circulation of products bearing marks, lawfully introduced into the market in any country by the owner or with his authorization, based on registration of the mark, may not be prevented, provided that the products, together with their containers and packaging, have not been altered, modified or damaged.	Trademark Law
	Copyright and Related Rights Law No. 1328/98	Article 29 Importation shall include the exclusive right to authorize or prohibit the entry into the national territory of copies of the work that have not been expressly authorized for the country of importation, regardless of whether or not the holder of the right has authorized the making of the said copies in the country of origin. The right of importation shall extend to the electronic transmission of works. It shall suspend the free circulation of the said copies at the border, but shall have no effect on a single copy for individual use carried in personal baggage.	Copyright Law
	Seeds and Protection of Plant Varieties Law No. 385/94	Article 63 May be imported seeds, in addition to those enrolled in the National Register of Seed Traders, traders, farmers individually or partners. The quantity being imported by farmers may not be greater than necessary to cover the sowing area programmed by the casual importer. The regulations establish requirements to be met by these people for importation.	Plant variety protection

Uruguay	Law Regulating Rights and Obligations Relating to Patents, Utility Models and Industrial Designs, Law No. 17.164	Article 40 Owners of patents may not prevent a person from using, importing or commercializing a patented product in any way after it has lawfully been put on sale within Uruguay or abroad by the patent owner or by a third person with the owner's consent or lawfully authorized to do so. Products or processes which infringe intellectual property rights shall not be considered as having been lawfully put on sale (Part III, Section 4, of the TRIPS Agreement of the WTO).	Patent Law
	Trademarks Law No. 17.011	Article 12 The registration of a trademark shall not afford the right to prevent the free circulation of products bearing the trademark that have been lawfully placed on the market by the owner or with his authorization, on condition that those products and their presentation, together with the packaging and get-up that is in immediate contact with them, have not undergone any significant alteration, modification or deterioration.	Trademark Law
Venezuela	Copyright Law 1993	Article 95 Producers of phonograms shall have the exclusive right to authorize or prohibit the reproduction of their phonograms, and also the importation, distribution to the public, rental or other use, in whatever form and by whatever means, of copies of their phonograms.	Copyright Law
	Industrial Property Law No. 25.227	Article 5 Patents of invention or improvement patents, industrial models or designs and the patents of introduction of an invention or improvement, give their holders the privilege to exploit exclusively the industrial production or process object of the patent, under the terms and conditions established in this Act. The patents of introduction do not entitle their holders to prevent others from importing into the country products similar to those covered by these patents.	Patent Law

Note: The provisions included in this table are illustrative. When no official translations of the quoted text were available, translation was made by the author.

12. Exhaustion of intellectual property rights and the principle of territoriality in the United States
*John A. Rothchild**

I. INTRODUCTION

The geographical scope of exhaustion is one of the most controversial issues in all of intellectual property law. Exhaustion occurs when the owner of an intellectual property right transfers ownership of a particular embodiment of that right, such as by selling a book or a DVD embodying a copyrighted literary work or movie, a machine with a patented design, or a consumer product sold under a trademark. Geographical scope refers to the geographical limits, if any, within which the sale must take place, or the article must be manufactured, in order to trigger exhaustion. The two principal variants are national exhaustion and international exhaustion.[1] With the former, intellectual property rights to a particular article are exhausted only if it is sold or manufactured within the country whose intellectual property laws the rights owner has invoked. In the case of the latter, the location of sale or manufacture is irrelevant, and any authorized transfer of ownership results in exhaustion.

Which exhaustion regime applies can have enormous consequences for rights owners. Under a national exhaustion regime, a rights owner can control or prohibit a secondary market in those products that are manufactured or first sold abroad, and can prevent parallel importation, thereby making segmentation of national markets possible. International exhaustion inhibits or curtails the possibility of achieving these goals. The choice of regime has equally significant implications for consumers of these goods, as it may determine whether a consumer can find a used or refurbished article on the secondary market, or a cheaper version that was manufactured in another country and aimed at a lower-income market.

The geographical scope of exhaustion has been litigated in the United States (U.S.) since the republic's early years. Remarkably, one of the most basic issues pertaining to

---

* Associate Professor, Wayne State University Law School.
[1] There is also a third version, known as regional exhaustion. Under this variant, exhaustion is triggered by a sale or manufacture occurring either within the territory of the nation whose intellectual property protection is at issue, or in the territory of some defined group of foreign nations. Regional exhaustion is most frequently referenced in connection with the European Union (EU) which has implemented a regime of regional exhaustion of patent, copyright, and trademark rights. See SHUBHA GHOSH, INTERNATIONAL CENTRE FOR TRADE AND SUSTAINABLE DEVELOPMENT, THE IMPLEMENTATION OF EXHAUSTION POLICIES: LESSONS FROM NATIONAL EXPERIENCES 36–38 (2013), available at www10.iadb.org/intal/intalcdi/PE/2014/13661.pdf. For present purposes, regional exhaustion may be assimilated to national exhaustion, with the regional agreement treating a group of nations like a single federal nation for purposes of exhaustion. For specific analysis of EU-wide exhaustion see the various chapters in this volume addressing the topic.

the geographical scope of copyright exhaustion was not fully resolved until 2013, and the key issue in patent law has, as this book goes to press, just been reconsidered by the U.S. Court of Appeals for the Federal Circuit, sitting *en banc*.

One reason for this lack of clarity is the tangled relationship between the geographical scope of exhaustion and the territorial limits on the effectiveness of intellectual property laws. Under U.S. law, it is undisputed that copyright and patent laws are territorially limited in the sense that conduct taking place outside the U.S. cannot constitute an infringement. What has not been so clear is how to apply this principle to situations in which some relevant conduct occurs within the U.S. and other conduct occurs abroad. Some courts adopted the view that allowing exhaustion of copyright rights to be triggered by the sale of an article embodying a copyrighted work that was manufactured outside the U.S. violates the principle of territoriality, and that the principle therefore implies a regime of national exhaustion. That view has now been definitively rejected by the Supreme Court. An analogous view underlies the Federal Circuit's case law holding that exhaustion of patent rights is not triggered by sale of an article embodying a patent if the sale occurs outside the U.S.

Territoriality also comes into play through the system of treaties that governs international aspects of intellectual property protection among most of the world's countries, under the rubric of national treatment.

In this chapter, I seek to clarify the relationship between the geographical scope of exhaustion of patent and copyright rights[2] and the principle of territoriality under U.S. law. I hope to demonstrate that (1) courts have invoked the principle of territoriality to hold that the U.S. copyright and patent laws are subject to a regime of national exhaustion; (2) that principle, however, is a red herring in this context, as the U.S. Supreme Court recognized in a 2013 decision; and (3) the Federal Circuit, in its recent reconsideration of the geographical scope of patent exhaustion, appropriately declined to base its decision on the territoriality principle.

Section II introduces the doctrine of exhaustion. Section III addresses the principle of national treatment, and explains why this principle does not determine the geographical scope of exhaustion. Section IV examines the impact of the principle of territoriality. It

---

[2] The geographical scope of the U.S. trademark laws is treated very differently from that of the patent and copyright laws. Unlike the patent and copyright laws, the Lanham Act has been interpreted to have extra-territorial reach. See Steele v. Bulova Watch Co., 344 U.S. 280 (1952) (holding that the Lanham Act's provision making it applicable to "all commerce which may lawfully be regulated by Congress" demonstrates a congressional intention that the Act's geographical scope is not limited to the U.S.). This does not mean that *every* extra-territorial act is within the scope of the Lanham Act; this is determined case by case, and the various circuits have propounded differing approaches for making this determination. See e.g. Vanity Fair Mills, Inc. v. T. Eaton Co., 234 F.2d 633 (2d Cir. 1956); Reebok Int'l, Ltd. v. Marnatech Enterprises, Inc., 970 F.2d 552 (9th Cir. 1992); McBee v. Delica Co., 417 F.3d 107 (1st Cir. 2005). For a critical examination of the extra-territorial scope of the Lanham Act, see Curtis A. Bradley, *Territorial Intellectual Property Rights in an Age of Globalism*, 37 Va. J. Int'l L. 505, 531–69 (1997). Because the reach of the trademark laws is not subject to the territoriality principle, the geographical scope of trademark exhaustion does not depend upon this principle. U.S. law generally implements a regime of international exhaustion with respect to trademarks. See Gamut Trading Co. v. U.S. Int'l Trade Comm'n, 200 F.3d 775 (Fed. Cir. 1999) (holding that an authorized foreign sale exhausts the trademark as long as there are no "material differences" between the foreign-made and a domestically produced article).

reviews the courts' decisions holding that the territoriality principle implies a regime of national exhaustion, the Supreme Court's recent rejection of that line of reasoning in the copyright area, and the Federal Circuit's recent reconsideration of its previous holdings in the patent area. Section V briefly concludes.

II. EXHAUSTION OF INTELLECTUAL PROPERTY RIGHTS

Exhaustion is a curtailment of the intellectual property rights pertaining to a particular article embodying protected intellectual property that arises when there is an authorized transfer of ownership of that article. Each of the three principal heads of intellectual property protection grants rights holders the authority to control distribution of an article embodying a protected right, and it is this right that is curtailed when exhaustion applies. Thus, the copyright laws grant the owner the exclusive right to publicly distribute material objects containing copyrighted works of authorship—books, music CDs, movie DVDs, works of visual art, etc.[3] Once the copyright owner has authorized the making of such a material object, the owner of that object is free to sell, lease, lend, or otherwise dispose of its possession without any need for the copyright owner's permission.[4] But the copyright owner retains all of the remaining exclusive rights with respect to that article, including the right to make copies of it, to make derivative works based on it, to perform it publicly, and (to a limited extent) to display it publicly.[5]

Under the Patent Act, exhaustion frees the owner of an article embodying a protected invention from the patent owner's right to control its sale and use.[6] The owner can therefore resell the patented article, including by importation, and can use it as he likes, without seeking the patent owner's permission. But the patent holder can still exclude others from making additional articles embodying the invention.[7]

Trademark law differs from the copyright and patent laws in that it does not create

---

[3] 17 U.S.C. § 106(3).

[4] 17 U.S.C. § 109(a). In copyright law, exhaustion is often referred to as the "first sale" rule, and it is sometimes characterized as arising once the copyright owner has made or authorized an initial sale of a copy. See e.g. Kirtsaeng v. John Wiley & Sons, Inc., 133 S. Ct. 1351, 1355 (2013) (stating that the public distribution right is exhausted once a copy "has been lawfully sold (or its ownership otherwise lawfully transferred)"). However, the statute requires no transfer of ownership: it nullifies the public distribution right with respect to the "owner" of a copy, providing only that the copy is "lawfully made under" the Copyright Act. *Ibid.* The Copyright Act's implementation of exhaustion includes some intricacies, such as a limitation on exhaustion for copies of software and phonorecords of sound recordings, which (with some exceptions from the exception) results in the copyright owner's retention of the right to control commercial rental, lease, or lending of material objects containing these categories of copyrighted works. *Ibid.* § 109(b)(1)(A), (B). These complications may be ignored for present purposes.

[5] *Ibid.* § 106(1), (2), (4). Exhaustion limits but does not eliminate the copyright owner's public display right. *Ibid.* § 109(c).

[6] The patent exhaustion doctrine is not codified in the Patent Act but derives from judicial interpretation. See Quanta Computer, Inc. v. LG Elecs., Inc., 553 U.S. 617, 625 (2008) (tracing "[t]he longstanding doctrine of patent exhaustion" back to the Supreme Court's nineteenth-century cases).

[7] 35 U.S.C. § 271(a).

exclusive rights. The trademark owner instead receives the more limited right to prevent uses of a mark that are likely to cause confusion.[8] Once the trademark owner has authorized the sale of an article bearing the mark, its authority to control resale of that article is exhausted.[9]

To summarize, under all three principal heads of intellectual property law the effect of exhaustion is to curtail the right owner's authority to control sale, use, or other disposition of an article embodying or (in the case of trademarks) displaying the protected intellectual property once that article is in the hands of another party.

III. NATIONAL TREATMENT AND THE GEOGRAPHIC SCOPE OF EXHAUSTION

The system of treaties governing international aspects of intellectual property rights is based on a principle called "national treatment," which is premised on a limitation of the geographic scope of intellectual property laws. It is clear, however, that national treatment does not dictate any particular regime of exhaustion.

Under the rule of national treatment, states that are signatories to the principal intellectual property treaties agree that they will not discriminate against non-nationals in the enforcement of intellectual property rights. The Agreement on Trade-Related Aspects of Intellectual Property Rights (TRIPS), the premier global intellectual property treaty, formulates the rule as:

> Each Member shall accord to the nationals of other Members treatment no less favourable than that it accords to its own nationals with regard to the protection of intellectual property, subject to [certain limited exceptions].[10]

What this means is that a rights holder whose rights under the intellectual property law of a signatory state are infringed by conduct occurring within the territorial limits of that state, and who is not a national of that state, may bring an action for enforcement of his

---

[8] 15 U.S.C. §§ 1114(1), 1125(a)(1)(A). This is a slight simplification. In the case of "famous" marks, the mark owner may receive an exclusive-like right to prevent uses that dilute, even in the absence of confusion. § 1125(c). In addition, a mark owner may prevent another from registering a domain name with a "bad faith intent to profit" from the mark, likewise without a showing of confusion. § 1125(d).

[9] See e.g. Sebastian Int'l, Inc. v. Longs Drug Stores Corp., 53 F.3d 1073, 1074 (9th Cir. 1995) ("[T]he right of a producer to control distribution of its trademarked product does not extend beyond the first sale of the product. Resale by the first purchaser of the original article under the producer's trademark is neither trademark infringement nor unfair competition.").

[10] Agreement on Trade-Related Aspects of Intellectual Property Rights, April 15, 1994, art. 3(1); Marrakesh Agreement Establishing the World Trade Organization, Annex 1C, 1869 U.N.T.S. 299. The TRIPS version of the principle echoes statements of the principle appearing in the two nineteenth-century treaties that provide TRIPS with most of its content: the Berne Convention for the Protection of Literary and Artistic Works, September 9, 1886, art. 5(1), 828 U.N.T.S. 221 (last revised at Paris, July 24, 1971) (protecting copyright), and the Paris Convention for the Protection of Industrial Property, March 20, 1883, art. 2(1), 21 U.S.T. 1630 (last revised July 14, 1967) (protecting trademark and patent rights).

rights in the courts of that state and will be accorded treatment at least as favorable[11] as that which the state would apply to its own nationals similarly situated. Thus, consider a hypothetical person who is a citizen and resident of Italy, and owns a patent issued by the U.S. Patent and Trademark Office. If her patent is infringed by conduct occurring within the U.S., and she brings a patent infringement action in a U.S. court, the national treatment principle means that U.S. law must treat her at least as favorably as it would if she were a U.S. citizen.

The principle of national treatment is closely related to the territoriality principle. The result of national treatment is that each member state applies its laws to all conduct occurring within its borders, and is able to rely on all other member states' doing the same. Therefore, a member state's nationals are in principle protected with respect to their intellectual property rights regardless of where the infringing conduct takes place, without the need for any state to apply its laws extra-territorially: each state applies its own laws to conduct occurring within its borders. In fact, it is sometimes said that national treatment *implies* a rule of territoriality.[12]

However, the principle of national treatment neither implies a regime of national exhaustion nor excludes the possibility of international exhaustion. National treatment requires only that a member state make its intellectual property laws available to non-nationals on a non-discriminatory basis. The principle will come into play when conduct occurring within the nation's borders allegedly infringes intellectual property rights claimed by a non-national. In such a situation, the defendant might invoke exhaustion as a defense: he might argue, as the case may be, that the plaintiff's claimed exclusive right to publicly distribute a particular copy of a copyrighted work, or the exclusive right to sell or use an article that embodies a patent, has been exhausted by the plaintiff's authorized first sale[13] of the article. Under a regime of national exhaustion, such a defense will succeed only if the first sale occurred within the territory of the state whose laws are invoked; under a regime of international exhaustion, the location of the first sale is irrelevant. Either regime is consistent with national treatment as long as the same rule is applied to non-nationals as to nationals of the forum state. The principle of national treatment is a nondiscrimination rule; it is not one that requires application of any particular substantive rule.

If there were any doubt about the matter, TRIPS makes it clear that national treatment may coexist with either national or international exhaustion. While TRIPS requires national treatment, it is explicitly agnostic on exhaustion: "nothing in this

---

[11] The TRIPS national treatment provision allows a member state to treat non-nationals *more* favorably than its own citizens. An example of such a provision is 17 U.S.C. § 104A, which restores copyright in certain works owned by foreign nationals but does not extend the same benefit to U.S. citizens.

[12] See Subafilms, Ltd. v. MGM-Pathe Commc'ns Co., 24 F.3d 1088, 1097 (9th Cir. 1994) (*en banc*) ("it is commonly acknowledged that the national treatment principle implicates a rule of territoriality").

[13] I use the term "first sale" to reference whatever conduct by the rights owner gives rise to exhaustion, recognizing that neither a sale, nor even a change in ownership, is necessarily required. See *supra* note 4.

Agreement shall be used to address the issue of the exhaustion of intellectual property rights."[14]

IV. TERRITORIALITY AND THE GEOGRAPHICAL SCOPE OF EXHAUSTION

It is clear that the Copyright Act and the Patent Act have no extra-territorial reach. Some courts have interpreted that fact as implying a regime of national exhaustion, according to which copyright rights are not exhausted by the sale of an article manufactured outside the U.S. (unless, perhaps, there is an authorized sale of the article within the U.S.), and patent rights are not exhausted by the sale of an article occurring outside the U.S.

In this section, I will address court decisions applying the two statutory regimes in situations involving conduct some of which occurs within, and some outside, the U.S. In the realm of copyright, most courts held that the territoriality principle meant that there could be no exhaustion of rights with respect to an article that was manufactured abroad, until a 2013 decision by the U.S. Supreme Court rejected that analysis. In the domain of patent, the Federal Circuit invoked the same principle to hold that there was no exhaustion of rights with respect to an article that was first sold abroad.

A. Copyright Act

Courts have consistently held that the Copyright Act does not apply extra-territorially. In the leading case of *Subafilms, Ltd. v. MGM-Pathe Communications Co.*, the Ninth Circuit reviewed what it called "over eighty years of consistent jurisprudence" in support of the proposition that the Copyright Act has no "extraterritorial reach."[15] In arriving at this conclusion, courts have applied a generally applicable presumption that federal statutes do not have extra-territorial effect. The presumption, as expressed by the Supreme Court in *American Banana Co. v. United Fruit Co.*,[16] is that a statute is "intended to be confined in its operation and effect to the territorial limits over which the lawmaker has general and legitimate power."[17] Congress is free to enact a statute that does apply extra-territorially,[18]

---

[14] TRIPS, art. 6. The treaty's neutral position on this point was a compromise of the strong opposing views held by various negotiating states. See Daniel Gervais, The TRIPS Agreement: Drafting History and Analysis 198–99 (3d ed., 2008). The North American Free Trade Agreement avoids addressing exhaustion of intellectual property rights altogether. See Carsten Fink, *Entering the Jungle of Intellectual Property Rights: Exhaustion and Parallel Importation*, in Intellectual Property Protection: Effects on Market Structure, Trade and Foreign Direct Investment (Carsten Fink & Keith Maskus eds., 2004).

[15] Subafilms, Ltd. v. MGM-Pathe Commc'ns Co., 24 F.3d 1088, 1095 (9th Cir. 1994) (*en banc*).

[16] American Banana Co. v. United Fruit Co., 213 U.S. 347 (1909). See also E.E.O.C. v. Arabian Am. Oil Co., 499 U.S. 244, 248 (1991) ("It is a longstanding principle of American law 'that legislation of Congress, unless a contrary intent appears, is meant to apply only within the territorial jurisdiction of the United States.'") (quoting Foley Bros. v. Filardo, 336 U.S. 281, 285 (1949)).

[17] *American Banana*, *supra* note 16, 213 U.S. at 347.

[18] Under both U.S. and international law, "Congress has the authority to enforce its laws beyond the territorial boundaries of the United States." E.E.O.C. v. Arabian Am. Oil Co., *supra*

but the presumption means that unless Congress does so explicitly it is presumed not to intend extra-territorial application. Since the Copyright Act lacks any declaration that it *does* apply to conduct occurring outside the territorial limits of the U.S., it is universally held not to have extra-territorial reach.[19]

(1) Extra-territoriality and multi-territorial conduct under the Copyright Act

There is little difficulty applying the rule that the Copyright Act has no extra-territorial effect when all of the relevant conduct takes place either domestically or abroad. But matters are not so straightforward when some of the relevant conduct occurs within the U.S. and some of it abroad.

One scenario with this feature is that in which some act of infringement occurs within the U.S., additional acts occur abroad, and the plaintiff seeks damages flowing from the latter. In *Los Angeles News Service v. Reuters*,[20] the defendants, newsgathering organizations, committed four acts of infringement in the U.S., by making two unauthorized copies of each of two news videotapes. They then transmitted the contents of the tapes, via satellite, to news organization subscribers in Europe and Africa, which presumably broadcast the contents to viewers.[21] The plaintiff copyright owner of the material sought damages based not only on the four domestic acts of infringement, but also on the unauthorized showing of the material overseas as a result of the transmission of the taped content. The district court held that defendants were not liable "for damages arising extraterritorially,"[22] and awarded only U.S.$60,000 in statutory damages based on the four domestic acts of infringement.[23] The Ninth Circuit viewed the matter differently. It applied the rule, which had previously been established in several Second Circuit cases,[24] that a plaintiff "is entitled to recover damages flowing from exploitation abroad of the

---

note 16, 499 U.S. at 248. And courts regularly apply U.S. law to conduct occurring abroad on the basis of the "effects test." See RESTATEMENT (THIRD) OF FOREIGN RELATIONS LAW § 402(1)(c) (1987) ("[A] state has jurisdiction to prescribe law with respect to . . . conduct outside its territory that has or is intended to have substantial effect within its territory.").

[19] See e.g. Palmer v. Braun, 376 F.3d 1254, 1258 (11th Cir. 2004) ("[F]ederal copyright law has no extraterritorial effect, and cannot be invoked to secure relief for acts of infringement occurring outside the United States."); Update Art, Inc. v. Modiin Pub., Ltd., 843 F.2d 67, 73 (2d Cir. 1988) ("It is well established that copyright laws generally do not have extraterritorial application."); 7 WILLIAM F. PATRY, PATRY ON COPYRIGHT § 25:86 (2015) ("*Every* court to have examined the issue has held that Congress did not intend the Copyright Act to be applied extraterritorially, beginning with the Supreme Court in 1908.").

[20] Los Angeles News Serv. v. Reuters Television Int'l, Ltd., 149 F.3d 987 (9th Cir. 1998).

[21] *Ibid.* at 990.

[22] Los Angeles News Serv. v. Reuters Television Int'l, Ltd., 942 F. Supp. 1265, 1269 (C.D. Cal. 1996), *aff'd in part, rev'd in part*, 149 F.3d 987 (9th Cir. 1998).

[23] Los Angeles News Serv. v. Reuters Television Int'l, Ltd., 942 F. Supp. 1275, 1283–84 (C.D. Cal. 1996), *vacated*, 149 F.3d 987 (9th Cir. 1998).

[24] Update Art, Inc. v. Modiin Pub., Ltd., 843 F.2d 67, 73 (2d Cir. 1988) (finding an "exception" to the rule against extra-territorial application of the Copyright Act "when the type of infringement permits further reproduction abroad"); Sheldon v. Metro-Goldwyn Pictures Corp., 106 F.2d 45, 52 (2d Cir. 1939), *aff'd*, 309 U.S. 390 (1940) (holding that plaintiffs acquired a "constructive trust" over profits generated by overseas infringement that flowed from infringing copies made in the U.S.).

domestic acts of infringement committed by defendants."[25] In doing so it did not view itself as departing from the rule of *Subafilms*, which held only "that the United States copyright laws do not reach acts of infringement that take place *entirely* abroad."[26] Thus, the court's resolution of the issue endorsed the proposition that taking cognizance of conduct occurring abroad in assessing liability for copyright infringement does not necessarily amount to a forbidden extra-territorial application of the law, as long as the infringing conduct does not take place "*entirely* abroad."[27]

A second scenario is where the challenged conduct is an act within the U.S. authorizing another to engage in uses of the copyrighted work abroad that are not permitted by the copyright owner. Thus, in *Subafilms*, the Ninth Circuit held that the action of a person, located in the U.S., directing a person located outside the U.S. to engage in copying that is not authorized by the copyright owner does not constitute infringement, because (1) the domestic party's action, not being direct infringement, could be infringing only as contributory infringement; (2) there can be "no liability for contributory infringement unless the authorized or otherwise encouraged activity itself could amount to infringement"; (3) the purported direct infringement is by hypothesis extra-territorial; (4) therefore, to find the domestic actor contributorily liable would amount to an extra-territorial application of the Act to the conduct occurring abroad.[28]

Other courts, however, hold that a domestic act of authorizing conduct abroad that would be infringing if it occurred within the U.S. is itself infringing. In *Curb v. MCA Records*, a district court found that the language "to do and to authorize" appearing in section 106 of the Copyright Act created an independent right that a copyright owner could invoke against one who authorizes extra-territorial conduct interfering with his exclusive rights, disagreeing with the Ninth Circuit's holding in *Subafilms* that this language merely established the scope of liability for contributory infringement.[29] Since *Curb* accepted the premise that the Copyright Act does not have extra-territorial effect, its holding must be understood as disputing the characterization of the application of the

---

[25] Los Angeles News Serv. v. Reuters Television Int'l, Ltd., 149 F.3d at 992.
[26] Subafilms, Ltd. v. MGM-Pathe Commc'ns Co., 24 F.3d 1088, 1098 (9th Cir. 1994) (*en banc*) (emphasis added).
[27] The Copyright Act generally allows the prevailing plaintiff a monetary award consisting of both actual damages and infringer's profits, as long as the two measures are not duplicative. 17 U.S.C. § 504(b). In a subsequent opinion, a differently composed panel of the Ninth Circuit, addressing issues arising on an appeal after remand from the initial panel's decision, held in a split decision that the plaintiff could only claim damages based on the infringer's profits, and not actual damages. The majority's rationale was that it was necessary to narrowly construe the initial panel's decision so as to "preserve consistency with Congress's decision to keep the copyright laws ... territorially confined." Los Angeles News Serv. v. Reuters Television Int'l (USA) Ltd., 340 F.3d 926, 931 (9th Cir. 2003). The difference between a domestic and an extra-territorial application of the Act could hardly be sliced any more thinly.
[28] *Subafilms, supra* note 26, 24 F.3d at 1090–95. Accord Illustro Sys. Int'l, LLC v. Int'l Bus. Machs. Corp., No. 3:06-CV-1969-L, 2007 WL 1321825, at *13 (N.D. Tex. May 4, 2007).
[29] Curb v. MCA Records, Inc., 898 F. Supp. 586, 595 (M.D. Tenn. 1995) ("The Ninth Circuit rejected the argument that the 1978 addition of the words 'to authorize' in § 106 created an independent right, just as the words 'to do' do. Instead, *Subafilms* holds that 'to authorize' merely codifies the doctrine of contributory infringement."). Accord Expediters Int'l of Washington, Inc. v. Direct Line Cargo Mgmt. Servs., Inc., 995 F. Supp. 468, 476 (D.N.J. 1998).

Act in this situation as an extra-territorial application. Its determination that the domestic conduct was actionable infringement took cognizance of conduct occurring overseas, but the decision did not find that overseas conduct itself to be infringing.

(2) Copyright exhaustion in the context of multi-territorial conduct

Just such a disagreement on whether a particular application of the Copyright Act amounts to an extra-territorial application clouded the law on the territorial scope of exhaustion until the Supreme Court's 2013 decision in *Kirtsaeng v. John Wiley & Sons, Inc.*[30] The issue is whether the sale of an article embodying a copyrighted work triggers exhaustion when the article (the tangible copy, not the intangible work of authorship) was manufactured outside the U.S. The issue arises because of some ambiguous language in the Copyright Act. Section 109(a) provides that the copyright owner's exclusive right to control public distribution of copies embodying the copyrighted work is exhausted with respect to the owner of a copy that is "lawfully made under this title." For three decades courts struggled to determine how this phrase applied to a situation in which the copy was manufactured outside the U.S.: was such a copy "lawfully made under this title," that is, under Title 17 of the U.S. Code, which contains the Copyright Act? And for three decades the courts uniformly answered the question in the negative.

The earliest such case was *Columbia Broadcasting System, Inc. v. Scorpio Music Distributors, Inc.*[31] The articles at issue were phonorecords (probably vinyl records or cassette tapes) containing recorded music to which the plaintiff held the copyright. The phonorecords were manufactured in the Philippines, and defendant imported them into the U.S. against the wishes of the copyright owner. The defendant invoked the exhaustion defense—after all, the phonorecords had been manufactured and placed on the market with the copyright owner's blessing, and in a domestic context this would have been enough to trigger exhaustion. But the court held that the phonorecords did not qualify for the defense, because they were not "lawfully made under this title." The court's logic ran like this: (1) the Copyright Act does not apply to conduct occurring outside the U.S.; (2) these phonorecords were manufactured outside the U.S.; (3) therefore the phonorecords cannot have been "lawfully made under" the Act.[32] In other words, the court reasoned that making exhaustion applicable to an article manufactured outside the U.S. would amount to extra-territorial application of the Copyright Act, which would be contrary to Congress's intent that the statute have only domestic effect.

Subsequent decisions from other courts generally reached the same result: sale of an article does not result in exhaustion if the article was manufactured overseas.[33] The doc-

---

[30] Kirtsaeng v. John Wiley & Sons, Inc., 133 S. Ct. 1351 (2013).
[31] Columbia Broadcasting System, Inc. v. Scorpio Music Distributors, Inc., 569 F. Supp. 47 (E.D. Pa. 1983), *aff'd mem.*, 738 F.2d 424 (3d Cir. 1984). *Scorpio* was decided less than six years after the January 1, 1978 effective date of the current Copyright Act. The version of the first-sale rule codified in the predecessor statute, the 1909 Act, contained no geographical limitation. *Kirtsaeng, supra* note 30, 133 S. Ct. at 1351, 1360.
[32] *Columbia Broadcasting System, supra* n. 31, at 49.
[33] A 1988 decision by the Third Circuit expressed doubt on this point, noting that it felt "some uneasiness" with *Scorpio*'s interpretation of "lawfully made under this title" as meaning made with the copyright owner's approval in the U.S. The statement was dictum, as the case involved articles

trine was further developed in a series of Ninth Circuit decisions. That court relied on *Scorpio* in holding that "[t]he words 'lawfully made under this title' in § 109(a) grant first sale protection only to copies legally made and sold in the United States."[34] But the court later recognized that this construction of the statute led to an unanticipated oddity: it allowed a copyright owner to completely evade the effect of the first-sale rule simply by shifting its manufacturing operations overseas. If it manufactured books, music CDs, or movie DVDs abroad, and then imported and sold them in the U.S., the public distribution right as to those articles would never be exhausted, since they would never be "lawfully made under this title." This would allow the copyright owner to invoke its public distribution right to shut down resale of its products in used book and record stores, rental of movie videos, lending by libraries, etc. Deeming such an outcome "untenable,"[35] the Ninth Circuit invented a rule, lacking any support in the text of the Copyright Act, that exhaustion *does* apply to an article manufactured abroad once it has been sold in the U.S. with the copyright owner's authorization.[36] In a 2008 decision, the Ninth Circuit reiterated the rationale for the rule, first stated in *Scorpio* and modified to avoid the "untenable" result of completely eviscerating the first-sale doctrine, that there is no exhaustion as to an article that is manufactured and sold abroad:

> [T]he application of § 109(a) to foreign-made copies would impermissibly apply the Copyright Act extraterritorially ... To characterize the making of copies overseas as "lawful ... under [Title 17]" would be to ascribe legality under the Copyright Act to conduct that occurs entirely outside the United States, notwithstanding the absence of a clear expression of congressional intent in favor of extraterritoriality.[37]

Meanwhile, in *Quality King Distributors, Inc. v. L'anza Research International, Inc.*,[38] the Supreme Court weighed in on the geographical scope of exhaustion under a slightly different scenario: what happens when an article is manufactured in the U.S., exported, and then reimported without the copyright owner's authorization? The Court determined that exhaustion applies in this situation, holding that the first-sale rule of section 109(a) functioned as a limitation on the copyright owner's section 602(a) right to control imports.[39]

---

manufactured in the U.S. Sebastian Int'l, Inc. v. Consumer Contacts (PTY) Ltd., 847 F.2d 1093, 1098 n.1 (3d Cir. 1988).

[34] BMG Music v. Perez, 952 F.2d 318, 319 (9th Cir. 1991).

[35] Parfums Givenchy, Inc. v. Drug Emporium, Inc., 38 F.3d 477, 482 n.8 (9th Cir. 1994).

[36] Denbicare U.S.A. Inc. v. Toys R Us, Inc., 84 F.3d 1143, 1150 (9th Cir. 1996) (declaring that "§ 109 applies to copies made abroad only if the copies have been sold in the United States by the copyright owner or with its authority").

[37] Omega S.A. v. Costco Wholesale Corp., 541 F.3d 982, 988 (9th Cir. 2008), *aff'd by an equally divided Court*, 562 U.S. 40 (2010).

[38] Quality King Distributors, Inc. v. L'anza Research Int'l, Inc., 523 U.S. 135 (1998).

[39] *Ibid.* at 145 (reasoning that "since § 602(a) merely provides that unauthorized importation is an infringement of an exclusive right 'under section 106,' and since that limited right does not encompass resales by lawful owners, the literal text of § 602(a) is simply inapplicable to both domestic and foreign owners ... who decide to import them and resell them in the United States."). Section 602(a)(1) provides: "Importation into the United States, without the authority of the owner of copyright under this title, of copies or phonorecords of a work that have been acquired outside the United States is an infringement of the exclusive right to distribute copies or phonorecords under section 106."

Along the way, it dropped an *obiter dictum* that appeared to endorse the view, introduced in *Scorpio* and adopted by the Ninth Circuit cases, that finding exhaustion with respect to an article manufactured outside the U.S. would amount to a forbidden extra-territorial application of the Copyright Act:

> If the author of the work gave the exclusive United States distribution rights . . . to the publisher of the United States edition and the exclusive British distribution rights to the publisher of the British edition . . . presumably only those made by the publisher of the United States edition would be "lawfully made under this title" within the meaning of § 109(a).[40]

By contrast, the Court noted, finding exhaustion when the article was manufactured in the U.S., but first sold abroad, "does not require the extraterritorial application of the Act."[41]

That *dictum* turned out to have legs: several lower courts cited and relied on it in concluding that exhaustion cannot apply to articles manufactured abroad.[42]

The *Quality King dictum* stood as the Supreme Court's most authoritative statement on the matter until it reversed course in *Kirtsaeng v. John Wiley & Sons*.[43] In that case the Court was squarely confronted[44] with the issue first addressed in *Scorpio*: whether "lawfully made under" the Copyright Act means (1) manufactured under the authority of the copyright owner or otherwise lawfully;[45] or (2) manufactured under such authority *within the territory of the U.S.* The Court resolved the issue in accordance with the first alternative, announcing unequivocally: "We hold that the 'first sale' doctrine applies to copies of a copyrighted work lawfully made abroad."[46] As the copies in question were also first sold abroad, the decision necessarily also holds exhaustion may be triggered by a sale occurring outside the U.S.

In arriving at this conclusion, the Court put a stake through the heart of the hobgoblin of extra-territoriality that had haunted courts addressing the issue from *Scorpio* through *Costco*. First, it repented its fecklessness in penning the *Quality King dictum*: "Is the Court

---

[40] Ibid. at 148.
[41] Ibid. at 145, n.14.
[42] See e.g. Pearson Educ., Inc. v. Kumar, 721 F. Supp. 2d 166, 178 (S.D.N.Y. 2010) ("[W]hen the Supreme Court directly addresses that question in unanimous language, albeit *dicta*, deference must be paid by district courts."), *judgment vacated sub nom.* Kumar v. Pearson Educ., Inc., 133 S. Ct. 1631 (2013); John Wiley & Sons, Inc. v. Kirtsaeng, 2009 WL 3364037, at *9 (S.D.N.Y. 2009) ("Ultimately, the court is persuaded by the dicta in *Quality King*, which would limit section 109(a)'s coverage to U.S.-manufactured goods."), *aff'd*, 654 F.3d 210 (2d Cir. 2011), *rev'd and remanded*, 133 S. Ct. 1351 (2013); Pearson Educ., Inc. v. Liu, 656 F. Supp. 2d 407, 416 (S.D.N.Y. 2009) ("When the Supreme Court addresses an unsettled question of federal law in unanimous dicta, respect for the Supreme Court as an institution and the dedicated jurists who serve on it mandates deference in all but the most exceptional circumstances.").
[43] Kirtsaeng v. John Wiley & Sons, Inc., 133 S. Ct. 1351 (2013).
[44] It was also squarely confronted with the issue when it granted certiorari in Omega v. Costco, but deadlocked 4–4 when Justice Kagan recused herself. Costco Wholesale Corp. v. Omega, S.A., 562 U.S. 40 (2010).
[45] "Otherwise lawfully" refers to situations in which the copyright owner does not authorize the making of the copy but it is lawful nonetheless, such as when a copy is made pursuant to the compulsory license of 17 U.S.C. § 115.
[46] *Kirtsaeng, supra* n. 43, 133 S. Ct. at 1355–56.

having once written dicta calling a tomato a vegetable bound to deny that it is a fruit forever after?"[47] Second, although it did not say so explicitly, the holding amounts to a decisive rejection of the notion that finding exhaustion with respect to an article manufactured overseas would be a forbidden extra-territorial application of the Copyright Act. Justice Ginsburg's dissent in *Kirtsaeng* (joined by Justices Kennedy and Scalia) relied on this notion:

> The Copyright Act, it has been observed time and again, does not apply extraterritorially... The textbooks thus were not "lawfully made under [Title 17]," the crucial precondition for application of § 109(a).[48]

But the Court rejected this reasoning, recognizing that applying a U.S. law so that it *takes account* of conduct occurring outside the U.S. in order to ascertain the legal status of *conduct occurring within the U.S.* does not amount to an extra-territorial application of the law, as long as the regulated conduct is that occurring within the U.S.

As I have pointed out elsewhere,[49] this understanding of what it means for a U.S. law to apply extra-territorially is consistent with the courts' determinations in other contexts. The point was well expressed by the D.C. Circuit in *Environmental Defense Fund, Inc. v. Massey*,[50] which held that interpreting the National Environmental Policy Act to require federal officials *in the U.S.* to produce an environmental impact statement before taking action to incinerate waste *in Antarctica* was not an extra-territorial application of the statute:

> By definition, an extraterritorial application of a statute involves the regulation of conduct beyond U.S. borders. Even where the significant effects of the regulated conduct are felt outside U.S. borders, the statute itself does not present a problem of extraterritoriality, so long as the conduct which Congress seeks to regulate occurs largely within the United States.[51]

That describes the situation addressed in *Kirtsaeng*: the regulated conduct consisted of the domestic acts of importing into[52] and selling textbooks within the U.S. It is true that

---

[47] *Ibid.* at 1368.
[48] *Ibid.* at 1376.
[49] See John A. Rothchild, *Exhausting Extraterritoriality*, 51 SANTA CLARA L. REV. 1187, 1233–38 (2011).
[50] Envtl. Def. Fund, Inc. v. Massey, 986 F.2d 528 (D.C. Cir. 1993).
[51] *Ibid.* at 531. See also Laker Airways Ltd. v. Sabena, Belgian World Airlines, 731 F.2d 909, 921 (D.C. Cir. 1984) ("Territoriality-based jurisdiction... allows states to regulate the conduct or status of individuals or property physically situated within the territory, even if the effects of the conduct are felt outside the territory."); Larry Kramer, *Vestiges of Beale: Extraterritorial Application of American Law*, SUP. CT. REV. 179, 181 (1991) ("The presumption against extraterritoriality... refers to a presumption that laws regulate only acts occurring within the United States.").
[52] Although importation by definition involves conduct both within and outside the U.S., the conduct that was claimed to be infringing was Kirtsaeng's domestic actions, not the actions of persons in Thailand who purchased the textbooks and shipped them to Kirtsaeng. Kirtsaeng v. John Wiley & Sons, Inc., 133 S. Ct. 1351, 1356 (2013) ("While he was studying in the United States, Kirtsaeng asked his friends and family in Thailand to buy copies of foreign edition English-language textbooks at Thai book shops, where they sold at low prices, and mail them to him in the United States."). See Palmer v. Braun, 376 F.3d 1254, 1258 (11th Cir. 2004) (holding that

regulating that domestic conduct might have effects overseas. In the *Kirtsaeng* scenario, for example, holding that the publisher's copyright was exhausted by its first sale, in Thailand, of books manufactured abroad makes it more likely that residents of Thailand will purchase copyrighted materials and send them to the U.S. for distribution via the gray market. But the mere presence of "extraterritorial spillovers"[53] does not make application of the law to domestic conduct an extra-territorial application.

In summary, for thirty years a string of court decisions held that there can be no exhaustion of distribution rights with respect to an article manufactured overseas[54] because that would amount to a forbidden extra-territorial application of the Copyright Act. In *Kirtsaeng*, the Supreme Court decisively rejected that view, holding that taking account of conduct occurring overseas (manufacture and possibly sale of an article embodying a copyrighted work) to determine the domestic effect of the Act does not amount to extra-territorial application of it.

B. Patent Act

The Patent Act explicitly provides that its reach is limited to conduct occurring within the U.S.: section 271(a) provides that one infringes a patent if he "makes," "uses," or "sells" a patented invention "within the United States."[55] Judicial statements to this effect are legion.[56]

(1) Extra-territoriality and multi-territorial conduct under the Patent Act

As with copyright law, in patent law the principle that the law does not reach extra-territorial conduct gives rise to controversy when applied to conduct that occurs partly in the U.S. and partly abroad. The most familiar example of this arose in a scenario where the components of a patented machine are manufactured in the U.S. but assembled abroad. *Deepsouth Packing Co. v. Laitram Corp.*[57] involved a shrimp deveining machine that was protected by a combination patent, but whose components were not themselves patented. The defendant manufactured the components in the U.S., and then shipped

---

application of the Copyright Act to importation of copyrighted materials is not an extra-territorial application of the Act).

[53] Alexander Peukert, *Territoriality and Extra-Territoriality in Intellectual Property Law, in* BEYOND TERRITORIALITY: TRANSNATIONAL LEGAL AUTHORITY IN AN AGE OF GLOBALIZATION 189, 201 (Günther Handl et al. eds., 2012).

[54] Or, in the weaker form adopted by later Ninth Circuit decisions, see *supra* text accompanying notes 35–36, unless and until the article is subject to an authorized first sale within the U.S.

[55] 35 U.S.C. § 271(a). Liability also applies to one who "imports" a patented invention "into the United States." *Ibid.* See also *ibid.* § 154(a) (a patent grants the patentee the right to exclude "throughout the United States").

[56] See e.g. Dowagiac Mfg. Co. v. Minn. Moline Plow Co., 235 U.S. 641, 650 (1915) ("The right conferred by a patent under our law is confined to the United States and its Territories . . . and infringement of this right cannot be predicated of acts wholly done in a foreign country."); NTP, Inc. v. Research In Motion, Ltd., 418 F.3d 1282, 1313 (Fed. Cir. 2005) ("The territorial reach of section 271 is limited. Section 271(a) is only actionable against patent infringement that occurs within the United States.").

[57] Deepsouth Packing Co. v. Laitram Corp., 406 U.S. 518 (1972).

them to buyers abroad as a kit that could be assembled in "less than one hour."[58] The Fifth Circuit held that the resulting machines were "made" in the U.S., and therefore infringed the patentee's exclusive right to "make" the invention "within the United States."[59] The Supreme Court disagreed, unwilling to accept the view that a machine that is assembled abroad from components that are manufactured in the U.S. is "made" in the U.S. for purposes of section 271(a). This conviction was premised on inferred congressional intent: several cases had held, prior to Congress's 1952 enactment of the present Patent Act, "that unassembled export of the elements of an invention did not infringe the patent."[60] The Court bolstered its conclusion by observing that the patent system "makes no claim to extraterritorial effect."[61] Despite the fact that the components were "made" in the U.S., the machine composed of them was "made" abroad, and therefore beyond the reach of the Patent Act. The defendant therefore did not directly infringe the patent. Justice Blackmun, writing for a four-justice dissent, would have held that holding the defendant directly liable would *not* amount to an extra-territorial application of the Act, since "I do not see how one can escape the conclusion that the Deepsouth machine was made in the United States."[62]

The Court further held that the defendant's conduct could not constitute contributory infringement, because "there can be no contributory infringement without the fact or intention of a direct infringement."[63] The assembly and use of the machines within the U.S. would be infringing, but the same conduct by the defendant's customers occurring outside the U.S. could not be direct infringement, since "it is not an infringement to make or use a patented product outside of the United States."[64] This scenario thus stands as a close analogy to that presented under the Copyright Act in *Subafilms*:[65] in both cases, an action that the defendant took in the U.S., which brought about conduct abroad that would be infringing *if it occurred within the U.S.*, was found not to be actionable as contributory infringement because the statute did not reach the extra-territorial conduct.

Congress subsequently legislatively overruled the outcome in *Deepsouth Packing*. The legislation, which was explicitly aimed at overcoming *Deepsouth Packing*,[66] amended the Patent Act by adding section 271(f), which provides:

> Whoever without authority supplies or causes to be supplied in or from the United States all or a substantial portion of the components of a patented invention, where such components are uncombined in whole or in part, in such manner as to actively induce the combination of such components outside of the United States in a manner that would infringe the patent if such combination occurred within the United States, shall be liable as an infringer.[67]

---

[58] *Ibid.* at 524.
[59] 35 U.S.C. § 271(a).
[60] *Deepsouth Packing*, *supra* note 57, 406 U.S. at 529.
[61] *Ibid.* at 531.
[62] *Ibid.* at 533.
[63] *Ibid.* at 526.
[64] *Ibid.* at 527.
[65] See *supra* text accompanying note 28.
[66] See S. Rep. No. 98-663, at 2–3 (1984) ("This provision is a response to the Supreme Court's 1972 *Deepsouth* decision.").
[67] Patent Law Amendments Act of 1984, Pub. L. No. 98-622, § 101, 98 Stat. 3383, 3383 (1984) (adding 35 U.S.C. § 271(f)(1)). The amendment also added a second provision that similarly

Under this provision, specified conduct occurring within the U.S., namely, supplying "in or from the United States" components for a machine that will be "made" and "used" abroad, is deemed infringing. Although liability is *premised* partly on conduct occurring outside the U.S., the conduct that is made actionable is only that occurring within the U.S. Where, as will typically be the case, the person doing the supplying is different from the person who assembles and uses the machine, only the supplier, who acts within the U.S., is made liable.

Does section 271(f) amount to a legislative exception from the general rule that the Patent Act has no extra-territorial reach? The Supreme Court so characterized it, but I believe this characterization reflects a misunderstanding of what it means for a law to have extra-territorial effect. In *Microsoft v. AT & T*,[68] the Court addressed the question whether Microsoft violated section 271(f) when it sent a CD-ROM disk containing Windows software to computer manufacturers located outside the U.S., who then installed the software on the computers they made and sold abroad. AT & T held a patent on an apparatus for speech processing, and the parties agreed that the patent was infringed not by the production of Windows alone, but "only when a computer is loaded with Windows and is thereby rendered capable of performing as the patented speech processor."[69] The Court held that there was no violation of section 271(f), because (1) the Windows "software in the abstract" is not a "component" for purposes of the statutory provision—only the CD-ROM disk qualifies as a "component";[70] (2) the foreign manufacturers did not install the CD-ROM that Microsoft supplied; rather, the manufacturers made copies of the CD-ROM that Microsoft supplied, and "[t]hose copies, not the master sent by Microsoft, are installed on the foreign manufacturers' computers";[71] (3) therefore, the manufacturers did not "combin[e]" any component supplied from the U.S. into their infringing machines.[72] To bolster its analysis, the Court observed that section 271(f) "is an exception to the general rule that our patent law does not apply extraterritorially," and accordingly, "[a]ny doubt that Microsoft's conduct falls outside § 271(f)'s compass would be resolved by the presumption against extraterritoriality."[73]

In just what respect section 271(f) is an extra-territorial application of the law, however, the Court does not say. To so characterize it conflicts with the understanding, discussed above,[74] that the application of a statute "does not present a problem of extraterritoriality,

---

imposes liability for supplying "any component" (not necessarily constituting "a substantial portion of the components" of the invention) if it is "especially made or especially adapted for use in the invention and not a staple article or commodity of commerce." 35 U.S.C. § 271(f)(2).

[68] Microsoft Corp. v. AT & T Corp., 550 U.S. 437 (2007).
[69] *Ibid.* at 441.
[70] *Ibid.* at 449.
[71] *Ibid.* at 445.
[72] This reasoning is internally inconsistent in its reliance on step (2) of the analysis. As the concurrence correctly recognizes, if only a tangible object can qualify as a "component" then the same result should follow even if the manufacturers installed Windows directly from the CD-ROM that Microsoft supplied, since in neither case does the tangible object (the CD-ROM) remain attached to the computer after installation. *Ibid.* at 462 (opinion of Justice Alito, concurring as to all but n. 14).
[73] *Ibid.* at 441, 454.
[74] See *supra* text accompanying note 51.

so long as the conduct which Congress seeks to regulate occurs largely within the United States."[75] The characterization is in any event inconsistent with the Court's resolution of *Kirtsaeng*. Both situations involve applying a statute to regulate conduct occurring within the U.S. (importing and selling books, in the one case; exporting machine parts, in the other) while taking account of conduct occurring abroad (the foreign manufacture of the books, in the one case; the assembly of a particular machine, in the other). If the former is not an extra-territorial application of the law, neither is the latter.

The courts have treated other claims of patent infringement involving conduct both within and outside the U.S. in ad hoc ways.[76] Thus, for example, an accused global positioning system, consisting of two transmitters in the U.S. and one in Norway, with receivers placed on airplanes and ships that might be anywhere in the world, was deemed to be located in the U.S. and therefore within the reach of the Patent Act, based on multiple considerations "with particular emphasis on the ownership of the equipment by the United States, the control of the equipment from the United States and on the actual beneficial use of the system within the United States."[77] And the email system used in BlackBerry mobile phones, which included a critical component located in Canada, was found to be "used" in the U.S., on the ground that "RIM's United States customers send and receive messages by manipulating the handheld devices in their possession in the United States," and therefore "the location of the use of the communication system as a whole occurs in the United States."[78]

(2) Patent exhaustion in the context of multi-territorial conduct

The history of cases treating exhaustion of patents where relevant conduct occurs in more than one country is much longer than that of cases treating the issue in the copyright context (which, as discussed above,[79] date only from 1983). The earliest case dealing with the issue, *Holiday v. Mattheson*[80] in 1885, held without much discussion that the sale, in England, of an article embodying an invention protected by a U.S. patent, with the authorization of the patentee, resulted in exhaustion of the patent as to that article, so that the patentee could not invoke the patent to prevent the defendant from using or selling the article in the U.S. The opinion gave no indication that the court considered the location of the sale outside the U.S. to be relevant to the question of exhaustion. Five years later, in *Boesch v. Graff*,[81] the Supreme Court held that sale of an article in Germany,

---

[75] Envtl. Def. Fund, Inc. v. Massey, 986 F.2d 528, 531 (D.C. Cir. 1993).

[76] See Katherine E. White, *The Recent Expansion of Extraterritoriality in Patent Infringement Cases*, UCLA J.L. & TECH. 2 (2007).

[77] Decca Ltd. v. United States, 544 F.2d 1070, 1083 (Ct. Cl. 1976). The court did not arrive at any definite conclusion as to whether the accused invention was "made" in the U.S., but did conclude that it was "used" domestically. *Ibid.* at 1082.

[78] NTP, Inc. v. Research In Motion, Ltd., 418 F.3d 1282, 1317 (Fed. Cir. 2005). The court went on to apply a different analysis to the method claims. Applying the rule that "a process cannot be used 'within' the United States . . . unless each of the steps is performed within this country," the court held that since one of the steps was performed in Canada application of the Patent Act to those claims would be impermissibly extra-territorial. *Ibid.* at 1318.

[79] See *supra* text accompanying note 31.

[80] Holiday v. Mattheson, 24 F. 185 (C.C.S.D.N.Y. 1885).

[81] Boesch v. Graff, 133 U.S. 697 (1890).

under circumstances that did not yield any compensation to the plaintiff owner of the U.S. patent,[82] did not exhaust the U.S. patent. While I have argued elsewhere that the case does not stand for the proposition that a U.S. patent is not exhausted by sale of an article taking place outside the U.S.,[83] several later courts did derive that rule from the case.

Most significantly for present purpose, the Federal Circuit invoked that reading of *Boesch v. Graff* to hold, in a series of cases decided in the 2000s, that sale of an article outside the U.S. does not exhaust the patent it embodies. In the first of the cases, *Jazz Photo Corp. v. International Trade Commission*,[84] the court held that an authorized sale of disposable cameras outside the U.S. did not exhaust the U.S. patent on them, with the result that the patentee could prevent defendants from refurbishing cameras and reselling them in the U.S.: "To invoke the protection of the first sale doctrine," the court held, "the authorized first sale must have occurred under the United States patent," that is, through a "first sale in the United States."[85] The court gave no indication of its reasoning, beyond its citation of *Boesch v. Graff*. In a later related case (an appeal after the remand ordered by the *Jazz Photo* decision), the Federal Circuit was more forthcoming in explaining its rationale: "foreign sales can never occur under a United States patent," and can never result in exhaustion, "because the United States patent system does not provide for extra-territorial effect."[86] Thus, as with the copyright cases discussed above, the unavailability of international exhaustion was laid at the door of the rule against extra-territorial application of the intellectual property laws.

Several subsequent cases disagreed on the question whether the Supreme Court's 2008 decision in *Quanta Computer, Inc. v. LG Electronics, Inc.*,[87] had undermined the *Jazz Photo* rule that no exhaustion results from an overseas sale of a patented article. *Quantum Computer* addressed the issue whether the authorized sale of computer microprocessor and memory chips exhausted the patents on those chips, where the patents could not be fully practiced until the chips were used in combination with certain other components. The Court held that the sale did result in exhaustion, finding that there was "no reasonable use" for the chips other than in such a combination, and that therefore the chips sufficiently embodied the patents.[88] One district court concluded that *Quantum Computer* effectively abrogated the *Jazz Photo* rule, inasmuch as some of the chips involved in that case had apparently been sold overseas and the Court made no distinction in its exhaustion analysis based on the location of the sale.[89] But in a 2010 decision the Federal Circuit adhered to the *Jazz Photo* rule.[90]

The Supreme Court's 2013 decision in *Kirtsaeng* that copyright may be exhausted by a first sale outside the U.S. gave defendants in patent infringement cases another avenue for

---

[82] The sale was authorized by a German law protecting the rights of prior users of the patented invention. *Ibid.* at 701.
[83] See Rothchild, *supra* note 49, at 1200–201.
[84] Jazz Photo Corp. v. Int'l Trade Commission, 264 F.3d 1094 (Fed. Cir. 2001).
[85] *Ibid.* at 1105.
[86] Fuji Photo Film Co., Ltd. v. Jazz Photo Corp., 394 F.3d 1368, 1376 (Fed. Cir. 2005).
[87] Quanta Computer, Inc. v. LG Electronics, Inc., 553 U.S. 617 (2008).
[88] *Ibid.* at 630–35.
[89] LG Electronics, Inc. v. Hitachi, Ltd., 655 F. Supp. 2d 1036, 1044–47 (N.D. Cal. 2009).
[90] Fujifilm Corp. v. Benun, 605 F.3d 1366, 1371 (Fed. Cir. 2010) ("*Quanta Computer, Inc. v. LG Electronics, Inc.* did not eliminate the first sale rule's territoriality requirement.").

arguing that the *Jazz Photo* rule was no longer good law. In *Lexmark International v. Ink Technologies Printer Supplies*,[91] a district court addressed at length whether the *Kirtsaeng* decision implied that patents, like copyrights, could be exhausted by a foreign sale. It concluded that *Kirtsaeng* could not be read as overturning *Jazz Photo* by implication:

> [A]n appellate court decision should not be overturned unless it is plainly inconsistent with the Supreme Court precedent . . . In this instance, the balance of considerations weighs in favor of finding that *Kirtsaeng* is not plainly inconsistent with *Jazz Photo*.[92]

That decision was appealed to the Federal Circuit, which heard argument in March 2015. However, the panel did not issue a decision, as the full court acting *sua sponte* decided to hear the case *en banc*.[93] The first issue that the court ordered the parties to address in the rehearing was:

> In light of *Kirtsaeng v. John Wiley & Sons, Inc.*, . . . should this court overrule *Jazz Photo Corp. v. International Trade Commission* . . . to the extent it ruled that a sale of a patented item outside the United States never gives rise to United States patent exhaustion.[94]

In its February 2016 *Lexmark International, Inc. v. Impression Products, Inc.* decision, the Federal Circuit adhered to its prior holdings in the *Jazz Photo* cases that sale of a patented article outside the U.S. does not exhaust the U.S. patent.[95] The court found that the Supreme Court's decision in *Kirtsaeng* did not undermine those earlier decisions, inasmuch as, among other things, the analysis in *Kirtsaeng* focused on specific language of the Copyright Act ("lawfully made under this title") that does not appear in the Patent Act.[96]

In seeking to justify the distinction it had made in *Jazz Photo* between sales occurring in the U.S. (which result in exhaustion) and those made outside the U.S. (which do not), the court focused on the notion of "reward": that the policy of the patent exhaustion doctrine is to reserve for the patent holder the right to seek, in exchange for a particular article embodying the patent, and free from competition by other sellers of that article, whatever reward the market will grant. The fact that the patentee has obtained a reward for the article in a non-U.S. market does not exhaust its right to seek a domestic reward, since the rewards offered in the two markets are not necessarily congruent:

> The combined logic of the statutory grant of patent rights and the long-recognized basis for exhaustion leads naturally to rejecting exhaustion based on a foreign sale. The statute gives patentees the reward available from American markets. A patentee cannot reasonably be treated

---

[91] Lexmark Int'l, Inc. v. Ink Technologies Printer Supplies, LLC, 9 F. Supp. 3d 830 (S.D. Ohio 2014), *aff'd sub nom.* Lexmark Int'l, Inc. v. Impression Prod., Inc., 816 F.3d 721 (Fed. Cir. 2016) (*en banc*).
[92] *Ibid.* at 835. Another district court found it harder to reconcile *Kirtsaeng* with *Jazz Photo*. San Disk Corp. v. Round Rock Research LLC, No. C 11-5243 RS, 2014 WL 2700583, at *4 (N.D. Cal. June 13, 2014) ("*Kirtsaeng* provides at least some additional support for the notion that it would be inconsistent with the theoretical underpinnings of the exhaustion doctrine to apply a territorial limitation.").
[93] Lexmark Int'l, Inc. v. Impression Prod., Inc., 785 F.3d 565, 565 (Fed. Cir. 2015).
[94] *Ibid.* at 566.
[95] Lexmark Int'l, Inc. v. Impression Prod., Inc., 816 F.3d 721 (Fed. Cir. 2016) (*en banc*).
[96] *Ibid.* at 756–60.

as receiving that reward from sales in foreign markets, and exhaustion has long been keyed to the idea that the patentee has received its U.S. reward.[97]

Differences between the U.S. market and non-U.S. markets that may affect the price at which the patentee may sell an article include the comparative availability of a patent, the patent's strength, economics of the markets, and government regulations.

The court also invoked the principle of territoriality, but only obliquely. It explained that the rule against international exhaustion "has a mirror-image counterpart in the territoriality principle of U.S. patent law that broadly denies projection of U.S. patent rights to cover foreign conduct."[98] This observation served as additional support for its reward-based justification. The court explained that the fact that "[p]atent law is especially territorial, and laws vary considerably from country to country, ... reinforces our conclusion that foreign markets are not the predictable equivalent of the American markets in which the U.S. patentee is given a right to exclude and the rewards from that exclusivity."[99]

Two judges dissented. In their view, a foreign sale should exhaust a U.S. patent unless the patentee has "notified the buyer of its retention of the U.S. patent rights."[100] The dissent's view that a patentee should be able to avoid international exhaustion by making such a reservation of rights was based on an agreement with the majority's exposition of the reward principle, and its recognition of differences between U.S. and foreign markets when it comes to determining the size of the reward. The dissent, however, rejected any notion that this outcome was required by the principle of extra-territoriality, declaring "the doctrine of extraterritoriality" to be "inapposite."[101]

The *en banc* Federal Circuit thus retained its rule against international exhaustion, but offered a noticeably different justification from the one it had advanced in the *Jazz Photo* cases. Instead of being compelled by the Patent Act's acknowledged absence of any extra-territorial reach, the rule followed from the principle that a patentee is entitled to a market-based reward for the sale of each patented article, and the market in which the patentee is entitled to seek that reward is the U.S. market, even if the patentee has already received a reward from the sale of that article outside the U.S.

V. CONCLUSION

The geographical scope of exhaustion of the intellectual property laws is a topic that has long vexed courts, legislatures, and litigants. On the international stage, it has proven such a divisive topic that the parties negotiating TRIPS agreed to disagree, excluding the topic from the treaty's framework.

The geographical scope of exhaustion of the U.S. patent and copyright laws has been left principally to courts for its development: Congress is silent on the subject in the Patent Act, and the Copyright Act's pronouncement that exhaustion depends on whether the

---

[97] *Ibid.* at 760.
[98] *Ibid.* at 764.
[99] *Ibid.* at 765.
[100] *Ibid.* at 788 (Dyk, J., dissenting).
[101] *Ibid.* at 784.

article in question was "lawfully made under" the Act has engendered much confusion. The Supreme Court's decision in *Kirtsaeng v. John Wiley & Sons* has done much to dispel the confusion. The rationale that some courts applied to hold that the Copyright Act demands a regime of national exhaustion—that finding exhaustion with respect to an article that was manufactured and sold abroad would constitute an extra-territorial application of the law—has now been swept away. The Federal Circuit's analogous reasoning in the patent arena—that finding exhaustion with respect to an article based on its sale abroad is an extra-territorial application of the law—has now been discarded, in favor of an analysis predicated on the nature of the "reward" to which a patentee is entitled by virtue of its U.S. patent.

PART IV

SELECTED ISSUES (AND CHALLENGES) ON PATENT EXHAUSTION

13. Patent exhaustion and free transit at the interface of public health and innovation policies: lessons to be learned from EU competition law practice
*Josef Drexl**

I. INTRODUCTION

Patent protection for pharmaceuticals has become a major topic for international trade negotiations. Under the multilateral Agreement on Trade-Related Aspects of Intellectual Property Rights (TRIPS), World Trade Organization (WTO) members are, in principle, required to provide for such protection.[1] A large number of recent bilateral agreements have put a particular emphasis on that issue.[2] For a rather naïve observer, this movement towards enhanced patent protection must come as a surprise, since patents are exclusive

---

* Director, Max Planck Institute for Innovation and Competition, Munich; Honorary Professor, Faculty of Law, University of Munich.

[1] Agreement on Trade-Related Aspects of Intellectual Property Rights, April 15, 1994; Marrakesh Agreement Establishing the World Trade Organization, Annex 1C, 1869 U.N.T.S. 299 (1994) [hereinafter TRIPS]. Art. 27(1) of TRIPS obliges WTO members to make patent protection available in "all fields of technology" and to guarantee that patent protection be enjoyable without discrimination to the fields of technology. The transition period of least developed countries (LDCs) under Art. 66(1) of TRIPS to comply, *inter alia*, with Art. 27 of TRIPS has been extended to July 1, 2021. See Council for Trade-Related Aspects of Intellectual Property Rights, *Extension of the Transition Period under Article 66.1 for Least Developed Country Members*, IP/C/64, (June 11, 2013), available at www.wto.org/english/news_e/news13_e/trip_11jun13_e.htm#decision.

[2] Many bilateral Free Trade Agreements (FTAs), especially from the United States (U.S.), the European Union (EU), and European Free Trade Area (EFTA) provide for the introduction of test data exclusivity rights. More interestingly for this chapter are FTAs that oblige the parties to provide for some kind of patent term extension for pharmaceuticals. This is the case, for instance, under the Comprehensive Economic and Trade Agreement (CETA) recently negotiated between the EU and Canada, which would oblige Canada to introduce a patent restoration system equal to the European system of supplementary protection certificates (SPCs). See Art. 9.2 of the Intellectual Property Chapter of CETA, available at http://trade.ec.europa.eu/doclib/html/152806.htm (not yet in force). An important impact of CETA on Canada will therefore be to make access to medicine more expensive. See Joel Lexchin & Marc-André Gagnon, *CETA and Pharmaceuticals: Impact of the Trade Agreement Between Europea and Canada on the Costs of Patented Drugs*, CANADIAN CENTRE FOR POLICY ALTERNATIVES (2013), available at www.policyalternatives.ca/sites/default/files/uploads/publications/National%20Office/2013/10/CETA_and_Pharmaceuticals.pdf. Most far-reaching and comprehensive are the patent rules that were incorporated in the Trans-Pacific Partnership (TPP) Agreement between the U.S. and 11 other Pacific Rim countries. These rules, as supported by the U.S. and Japan, include patent term "adjustment," test data exclusivity, and a particular form of patent linkage that provides patent protection prior to the grant of any marketing authorization for generic drugs that are covered by patents. See Arts. 18.48 through 18.54 of the TPP Agreement, signed February 4, 2016, available at https://ustr.gov/trade-agreements/free-trade-agreements/trans-pacific-partnership/tpp-full-text.

rights under national law that have the potential of restricting rather than promoting parallel trade.

The reasons for this are obvious. The interest in promoting global protection seems to trump free-trade principles. Originator pharmaceutical companies argue that they need to recoup their research and development (R&D) investment within the international markets in which their drugs are sold in order to maintain incentives for innovation. Against the backdrop of a globalized economy, pharmaceutical companies may have a point in claiming that especially the newly rich living in emerging economies that are rapidly catching up with the old industrialized countries should participate in the financing of the innovation brought to them through better and more effective drugs.

Yet there is a price to be paid for strong international patent protection. Pharmaceutical patents exclude price competition from generics until the expiry of the patents and thereby restrict access to affordable drugs. This is not only a problem for poorer countries that cannot afford to provide for general healthcare for all of their citizens. The welfare states of this world, with their aging societies, are also encountering increasing difficulties in financing a full supply of patented, and often very expensive, drugs to patients. Thus, practically all countries of the world entertain some policies to control drug prices for patented drugs in particular.

However, such policies differ considerably and may be more or less interventionist. Poorer countries, and those countries that do not have to take account of the interest of major domestic originator companies, may especially try to control drug prices directly. A more market-oriented instrument of keeping prices low exists in the application of the principle of international exhaustion. Whereas the sale of generics leads to "interbrand" price competition, parallel trade leads to "intrabrand" price competition. It is the parallel trader who competes with the originator company by importing original drugs from abroad and selling them at lower prices. For such competition to emerge, two requirements, an economic one and a legal one, need to be fulfilled. From an economic perspective, there has to be a considerable difference in price of the drugs sold by the originator company in the exporting and the importing countries. There may be two reasons why such a difference in price exists. Either it is the originator company itself that decides to set low prices in the exporting country, especially if the buying power in that country is considerably lower than in the importing country, or the exporting country implements a policy of strict price control. From a legal perspective, parallel imports depend on the recognition of the principle of international exhaustion, which prevents the originator company from prohibiting parallel imports based on patent law.

Regarding international exhaustion, international trade law has the advantage of giving states considerable flexibility. In a rather obscure way, Article 6 of TRIPS stipulates that:

> [f]or the purposes of dispute settlement under this Agreement, subject to the provisions of Articles 3 and 4 nothing in this Agreement shall be used to address the issue of the exhaustion of intellectual property rights.[3]

---

[3] TRIPS, art.6.

Indeed, Article 6 of TRIPS is the result of a compromise of the WTO members on the issue of exhaustion.[4] Although exhaustion could be considered as one of the clearest candidates for being qualified as a "trade-related" aspect of intellectual property rights (IPRs), during the Uruguay Round negotiations, the Contracting Parties of the General Agreement on Tariffs and Trade (GATT) were not able to reach an agreement on a uniform approach to dealing with exhaustion. Article 6 of TRIPS is therefore usually understood in the sense of leaving the decision to WTO members whether to implement a principle of national or international exhaustion for the different IPR regimes.[5]

This chapter aims to promote a better understanding of the appropriate way to read the link between parallel trade and exhaustion on the international level by relying on more recent experience from the European Union (EU). This experience is particularly relevant since exhaustion of intellectual property rights, including patents, in trade between the Member States (so-called "European exhaustion") is recognized as a fundamental principle of EU law for the regulation of the internal market. Yet more recent case law on the application of EU competition law regarding restrictions on parallel trade of pharmaceuticals sheds doubts on the soundness of such principle in light of the public interest in promoting innovation. Based on this analysis, this chapter will also look beyond the topic of exhaustion to address the issue of whether states should be allowed to seize pharmaceuticals in transit that are protected in the transit country but neither in the exporting nor the importing countries.

In the following, this chapter will dig deeper into the economics of parallel trade (section II) and sketch the recent development of the abovementioned European case law (section III). Then this chapter will reconsider the issue of exhaustion from a global perspective with a particular focus on Article 6 of TRIPS (section IV) and finally address the scenario of pharmaceuticals in transit (section V).

II. THE ECONOMICS OF PARALLEL TRADE

In recent years, economic theory on parallel trade has evolved considerably. Most economists nowadays argue in favor of a more lenient approach towards restraints on parallel trade than in the past. The reasons for this are basically twofold: first, restraints on parallel trade only reduce "intrabrand" competition between dealers, but may be capable of promoting "interbrand" competition between manufacturers. Second, restraints on parallel trade allow for geographical price discrimination.

---

[4] On the negotiating history, see UNITED NATIONS CONFERENCE ON TRADE AND DEVELOPMENT & INTERNATIONAL CENTRE FOR TRADE AND SUSTAINABLE DEVELOPMENT, RESOURCE BOOK ON TRIPS AND DEVELOPMENT 97–104 (2005) [hereinafter UNCTAD-ICTSD].

[5] *Ibid.* at 105. This interpretation has been confirmed by World Trade Organization, Ministerial Conference, Fourth Session, Doha Declaration on the TRIPS Agreement and Public Health of November 20, 2001, WT/MIN(01)/DEC/2 (2001), available at www.wto.org/english/thewto_e/minist_e/min01_e/mindecl_trips_e.htm. Paragraph 5(a) of the Declaration reads: "The effect of the provisions in the TRIPS Agreement that are relevant to the exhaustion of intellectual property rights is to leave each member free to establish its own regime for such exhaustion without challenge, subject to the MFN and national treatment provisions of Articles 3 and 4."

Modern economics argues that price discrimination can be efficient and, therefore, procompetitive in many instances.

Restraints on parallel trade are restraints that relate to the distribution of goods. Modern economics advocates a lenient approach to such vertical restraints concerning the distribution of goods in general.[6] It is held that a manufacturer who faces fierce competition with other manufacturers ("interbrand" competition) will not be able to harm competition by vertically restricting the freedom of dealers to compete. Quite the contrary, it is assumed that such manufacturers will structure their distribution systems in such a way that their ability to compete with other manufacturers will be enhanced. Vertical restraints are, therefore, held to be efficient and procompetitive, at least if the manufacturer is not market-dominant. This is why some authors even recommend giving up the ban on vertical market partitioning along the borders of the EU Member States.[7]

The second evolution relates to the link between parallel trade and the manufacturer's ability to price discriminate geographically. Parallel trade makes it harder for manufacturers to charge different prices to consumers in different countries. Therefore, parallel trade serves the interest of consumers in the importing countries, where the ability to pay is higher, by bringing down prices.[8] At the same time, parallel trade puts pressure on manufacturers to raise prices in countries where the buying power is considerably lower in order to reduce the potential of parallel trade. In the EU, parallel trade therefore has a tendency to harmonize the level of consumer prices. It may drive prices down in richer countries and put economic pressure on poorer countries to adjust to higher prices.[9]

Whether parallel trade has overall positive welfare effects is less clear. What is obvious in the first place is that consumers in the exporting countries will be harmed, while consumers in the importing countries will benefit. Based on a global welfare analysis, economists therefore argue that positive welfare effects are more likely to arise where two countries are rather heterogeneous in relation to their market size.[10] If parallel trade takes place from a rather small country to a country with a huge number of consumers, the welfare benefits of bringing down prices in the importing country will outweigh the welfare losses in the exporting country.

---

[6] A recent and most prominent manifestation of this is the judgment in Leegin Creative Leather Prods., Inc. v. PSKS, Inc. et al., 551 U.S. 877 (2007), in which the US Supreme Court switched from *per se* illegality to a rule-of-reason approach on resale price maintenance. For a critical view on this case, see e.g. Marina Lao, *Resale Price Maintenance: A Reassessment of Its Competitive Harms and Benefits*, in MORE COMMON GROUND FOR INTERNATIONAL COMPETITION LAW? 59 (Josef Drexl et al. eds., 2011).

[7] See e.g. Denis Waelbroeck, *Vertical Agreements: 4 Years Of Liberalisation By Regulation No. 2790/90 After 40 Years of Legal (Block) Exemption*, in THE EVOLUTION OF EUROPEAN COMPETITION LAW 85, 99–105 (Hanns Ullrich ed., 2006).

[8] According to Patricia M. Danzon, *The Economics of Parallel Trade*, 13 PHARMACOECONOMICS 293, 294 (1998), parallel trade is exporting low prices.

[9] On the pricing of pharmaceuticals in the EU market see generally, *ibid*.

[10] See Frank Müller-Langer, *An Analysis of the Welfare Effects of Parallel Trade Freedom*, MAX PLANCK INSTITUTE FOR INTELLECTUAL PROPERTY, COMPETITION & TAX LAW RESEARCH PAPER SERIES 10.3 (2010), available at http://works.bepress.com/frank_mueller_langer/5/.

With regard to competition law, the question is whether the law should prohibit price discrimination in the first place. Indeed, it seems that EU competition law is very critical of discrimination in general. Discriminatory practices are listed as a competition law violation by both Article 101(1)(d) and Article 102(2)(c) of the Treaty on the Functioning of the European Union (TFEU).[11] Yet modern economics, which is supported on this point by most of today's competition lawyers,[12] does not view price discrimination as *per se* anticompetitive. Territorial price discrimination is no exception to this. Economists advocate a more sophisticated assessment: price discrimination may be efficient in some cases and anticompetitive in others.[13] Most importantly, it is held that charging different prices to different groups of consumers may lead to more efficient pricing in areas where producers have to cover high fixed costs like those caused by R&D expenditure in the pharmaceutical industry (so-called "Ramsey pricing").[14]

In a competitive market, the reasons for price discrimination may be manifold indeed. Designing tailor-made price policies may much better serve the interests of specific consumer groups. In particular, if manufacturers are able to charge consumers in poorer countries less, this will facilitate access to the specific goods for poorer consumers. As a consequence, price discrimination leads to cross-subsidization. In the drug market, where originator companies have to recoup high investments in R&D in world markets, price discrimination allows them to keep prices low in poorer countries, yet above the level of variable costs, while consumers in the richer countries will finance R&D in the interest of patients of the whole world.

III. EU COMPETITION LAW ON RESTRAINTS ON PARALLEL TRADE

A. The Link Between the Principle of European Exhaustion and EU Competition Law

The principle of European exhaustion is among the most fundamental principles of European intellectual property (IP) law. Its development goes back to the period prior to the adoption of the Single European Act of 1986,[15] when the former European Court of Justice (ECJ, now Court of Justice of the European Union, CJEU) promoted market integration by limiting the application of national laws, including IP laws that created barriers to trade between the Member States. In doing so, the Court relied upon the principle of free movement of goods and former Article 36 of the Treaty Establishing the European

---

[11] Consolidated Version of the Treaty on the Functioning of the European Union, arts. 101(1)(d), 102(2)(c), [2012] O.J. C326/47 at 88–89 [hereinafter TFEU].
[12] See e.g. Peter Behrens, *Parallelhandelsbeschränkungen und Konsumentenwohlfahrt – Zur neueren Rechtsprechung von EuG und EuGH*, ZEITSCHRIFT FÜR WETTBEWERBSRECHT 20 (2008).
[13] See e.g. FEMI ALESI, FEDERAL ANTITRUST AND EC COMPETITION LAW 374–75 (2008); Wolfgang Kerber & Ullrich Schwalbe, *Economic Principles of Competition Law*, in COMPETITION LAW: EUROPEAN COMMUNITY PRACTICE AND PROCEDURE: ARTICLE-BY-ARTICLE COMMENTARY 202, paras. 1454–55 (Günter Hirsch *et al*. eds., 2008).
[14] Danzon, *supra* note 8, at 295.
[15] Treaties Establishing the European Communities, Single European Act (1987).

Economy Community[16] (now Article 36 of the TFEU) to prevent Member States from applying a principle of national exhaustion.[17]

However, it is to be recalled that even prior to the recognition of the principle of European exhaustion, the ECJ, in its ground-breaking *Consten and Grundig* judgment, had held that parties to a trademark licensing agreement violate the prohibition on restrictive agreements that is part of European competition law if the licensee is prevented from exporting branded goods to other Member States.[18] Hence, historically, the European competition law prohibition of private restraints on parallel trade preceded, and paved the way for, the principle of European exhaustion, which in turn protects parallel trade against the application of national exhaustion under domestic IP laws.[19]

The close link between the exhaustion principle and EU competition law characterized European law from the very beginning. In the EU legal order, the fundamental freedoms, including the principle of free movement of goods, and competition law are complementary legal instruments that pursue the identical goal of establishing and maintaining the internal market. The fundamental freedoms are addressed to the Member States and prevent them from applying legal rules that collide with the internal market principle. Competition law, in turn, guarantees that private undertakings do not replace state-initiated barriers to trade by private restraints of competition. This is why territorial restrictions have always been a particular focus of EU competition law.

Since the 1960s and 1970s, when these principles were developed, EU law and EU intellectual property law has moved ahead. The CJEU is no longer the only or principal "engine of market integration." The Single European Act has facilitated internal market legislation and, thereby, laid the foundation for harmonizing IP law in the Member States. In addition, since the 1990s, the European legislature has also created some unitary rights systems such as the Community trademark system and, more recently, the unitary patent system in particular. In this shift from "negative integration" under the free movement principles to "positive integration" through legislation, the principle of European exhaustion also made it to secondary IP law.[20]

---

[16] Treaty Establishing the European Economic Community, March 25, 1957, 298 U.N.T.S 11 [hereinafter EEC Treaty].

[17] The first case related to copyright; see Case 78/70, Deutsche Grammophon v. Metro-SB-Großmärkte, [1971] E.C.R. 487. In later cases the principle was extended to other IP rights. See Case 15/74, Centrafarm v. Sterling Drug, [1974] E.C.R. 1147 (on patents); Case 119/75, Terrapin v. Terranova, [1976] E.C.R. 1039 (on trademarks).

[18] Joined Cases 56 & 58/64, Etablissements Consten SARL and Grundig-Verkaufs-GmbH v. Comm'n, [1966] E.C.R. 299.

[19] In *Deutsche Grammophon*, the German court referred the case to the ECJ with the question of whether application of the national exhaustion rule under German copyright law violated competition law. The ECJ rephrased the question in the sense of whether German law breached the European principle of free movement of goods. See *Deutsche Grammophon*, supra note 17, paras. 2–10.

[20] See First Council Directive 89/104 to approximate the laws of the Member States relating to trademarks, art. 7, [1989] O.J. L40/1 (EEC); Directive 98/71 of the European Parliament and the Council of October 13, 1998 on the legal protection of designs, art. 15, [1998] O.J. L289/28 (EC); Directive 2001/29 of the European Parliament and the Council of May 22, 2001 on the harmonization of certain aspects of copyright and related rights in the information society, art. 4(2), [2001] O.J. L167/10 (EC).

European IP legislation has had its impact on the way the CJEU views the role of IP in the internal market. Whilst IPRs were largely considered by the Court as obstacles to free trade in the 1970s and 1980s, the Court now recognizes a positive role of IP with regard to market transparency (trademarks) and enhancing innovation and creativity (patents and copyright) in the internal market. Yet this development did not affect the principle of freedom of parallel trade, which apparently is deeply enshrined in the European legal order.

However, most recent competition cases on trade in pharmaceuticals seem to be modifying the law on parallel trade within the EU. In three cases, which all involved restraints on parallel trade initiated by GlaxoSmithKline (GSK), the issue arose whether restraints on parallel trade between Member States should always, or practically always, be held illegal under EU competition law or whether the argument of innovation should justify a more lenient approach to restraints on parallel trade in pharmaceuticals. While, in the first case, the referral was held inadmissible,[21] and the ECJ avoided the innovation argument in the second case,[22] in the last case, the ECJ accepted the innovation argument in principle and held that, under former Article 81 of the Treaty establishing the European Community Treaty (EC, now Article 101 of the TFEU), this argument can justify a restraint of parallel trade implemented in the framework of a restrictive agreement.[23]

In none of these cases was the ECJ requested to go into reviewing its earlier case law on the European exhaustion principle. Yet given the complementarity of the two legal instruments, the question may well be asked whether European law on free movement of goods relating to trademarks for pharmaceuticals and pharmaceutical patents needs to be reviewed.[24]

B. EU Competition Law and Parallel Trade in Pharmaceuticals

Traditionally, EU law does not distinguish between the legal regimes governing parallel trade in pharmaceuticals and parallel trade in other products. The most obvious manifestation of this is provided by the ECJ judgment in *Merck v. Stephar*, in which the Court confirmed the application of the principle of European exhaustion where the holder of a pharmaceutical patent was denied the ability to rely on the principle of national exhaustion even in a case where the exporting country, at the time when the case arose, did not even provide for the possibility of pharmaceutical patents.[25]

---

[21] Case C-53/03, Syfait v. GlaxoSmithKline, [2005] E.C.R. I-4609, however, remains important because of the most interesting and influential opinion delivered by Advocate General Jacobs.

[22] Joined Cases C-468/06–C-478/06, Sot. Lélos kai Sia v. GlaxoSmithKline, [2008] E.C.R. I-7139. See also Josef Drexl, *Healing with Bananas: How Should Community Competition Law Deal with Restraints on Parallel Trade in Pharmaceuticals?*, in TECHNOLOGY AND COMPETITION, CONTRIBUTIONS IN HONOUR OF HANNS ULLRICH 571 (Josef Drexl et al. eds., 2009).

[23] Joined Cases C-501, C-513, C-515, & C-519/06 P, GlaxoSmithKline v. Comm'n, [2009] E.C.R. I-9291.

[24] In this regard, see JOHANNA MÜLLER-GRAFF, DER PARALLELHANDEL MIT ARZNEIMITTELN IM EUROPÄISCHEN BINNENMARKTRECHT 361–484 (2014) (concluding that the abovementioned competition law cases do not advocate a general departure from the principle of European exhaustion where trade in pharmaceuticals is concerned).

[25] Case 187/80, Merck v. Stephar, [1981] E.C.R. 2063 (no patent protection for pharmaceuticals in Italy).

(1) The Greek and Spanish GlaxoSmithKline cases

Equal treatment of parallel trade in pharmaceuticals with parallel trade in any other product, however, was questioned by Advocate General Jacobs in his opinion in *Syfait v. GlaxoSmithKline*.[26] Based on three particularities of the pharmaceutical market, namely (i) the high level of regulation of this market in the different Member States; (ii) the importance of R&D expenditure as a competition parameter in the pharmaceutical industry; and (iii) the doubtful beneficial effects on consumers of parallel trade in pharmaceuticals, he held restraints of trade in pharmaceuticals to be capable of a justification under former Article 82 of the EC Treaty (now Article 102 of the TFEU).[27] Yet he also made clear that he considered his conclusions "highly specific to the pharmaceutical industry."[28]

Advocate General Jacobs's opinion was without any influence on the proceedings concerned. Indeed, he had to provide his opinion on a referral for preliminary judgment initiated by the Greek Competition Commission, which had to decide whether the unilateral refusal of GSK to deliver drugs to Greek wholesalers beyond demand in Greece violated former Article 82 of the EC Treaty (now Article 102 of the TFEU). This case raised the preliminary question of whether the Greek Competition Commission was to be considered a court or a tribunal of a Member State in the sense of former Article 235 of the EC Treaty (now Article 267 of the TFEU). This question, against the position of Advocate General Jacobs, was answered in the negative by the ECJ and, therefore, the referral was rejected as inadmissible without the Court having addressed the substantive issues of the case.

Yet Advocate General Jacobs's questioning of the illegality of restraints on parallel trade had by then launched an intensive debate on how to deal with parallel trade in the future. Most importantly, in October 2006, two years after Jacobs had rendered his opinion in *Syfait*, it was for the Court of First Instance (CFI, now General Court) to take up some of his ideas in the Spanish *GSK* case.[29] In Spain, GSK intended to apply a slightly different approach to prevent domestic wholesalers from exporting GSK products to other EU Member States. Instead of simply reducing the volume of sales in Spain, GSK attempted to implement a dual-pricing scheme that would have obliged Spanish wholesalers to pay higher prices for such drugs that they resold to customers outside of Spain. With regard to this practice, the question was whether it violated the prohibition of restrictive agreements according to former Article 81 of the EC Treaty (now Article 101 of the TFEU). In order to avoid competition law liability, GSK decided to apply to the European Commission for an individual exemption.[30] Simultaneously,

---

[26] Opinion of Advocate General Jacobs in Case C-53/03, Syfait v. GlaxoSmithKline, [2005] E.C.R. I-4609.
[27] *Ibid.* para. 100.
[28] *Ibid.*
[29] Case T-168/01, GlaxoSmithKline v. Commission, [2006] E.C.R. II-2969.
[30] When the case developed, the former Implementation Directive 17/62 (First Regulation Implementing Articles 85 and 86 of the Treaty), [1962] O.J. 13/204, was still applicable. Outside of the scope of so-called block exemption regulations, Regulation 17/62 required an individual decision by the European Commission for restrictive agreements to be exempted according to former art. 81(3) of the EC Treaty (now art. 101(3) of the TFEU). This system of individual exemption was replaced by Council Regulation (EC) 1/2003 of December 16, 2002 on the implementation of the rules on competition laid down in Articles 81 and 82 of the Treaty, [2003] O.J. L1/1 (EC),

Spanish wholesalers had brought complaints to the European Commission against GSK for having violated EU competition law. While the Commission denied the individual exemption,[31] the CFI seemed to adopt the earlier position of Advocate General Jacobs by annulling the Commission decision for not having sufficiently reasoned the rejection of GSK's argument according to which the agreement would promote investment by GSK in R&D and, thereby, contribute to technological and economic progress in the sense of former Article 81(3) of the EC Treaty. This was a clear sign that at least the CFI was now willing to accept a more lenient approach to parallel trade in pharmaceuticals.

Later, the ECJ had to decide on the substance of both the Greek and the Spanish cases. After the *Syfait* decision, the Greek *GSK* case was again referred to the ECJ by Greek courts that had to decide on private actions for violation of competition law brought by Greek wholesalers.[32] This time, there was no doubt as to the admissibility of the referral. Most interestingly, the competent Advocate General Ruiz-Jarabo Colomer explicitly disagreed with his colleague Jacobs, especially on the question of whether the company's need of high income in order to invest in R&D could be accepted as a justification for a restraint of parallel trade.[33] In such circumstances, it would have been most interesting to see how the ECJ reacted to this open conflict between two Advocates General and how it balanced the freedom of parallel trade with the interest in promoting investment in R&D in the pharmaceutical industry. However, the ECJ explicitly left the "innovation issue" undecided, holding that there is no abuse on the part of a dominant pharmaceutical company in the role of GSK in Greece as long as the company is willing to fulfill orders that are not out of the ordinary.[34]

A year later, in the autumn of 2009, the ECJ finally had to decide on the appeal against the CFI judgment concerning the Spanish *GSK* case.[35] This time, given the clear statements of the CFI on the recognition of the innovation argument put forward by GSK, the ECJ could not avoid providing its say on how to achieve an appropriate balance between the interest in promoting free parallel trade and the interest in promoting innovation. While the ECJ rejected the test developed by the CFI for identifying a restraint

---

which made art. 81(3) of the EC Treaty directly applicable as of the date of entry into force of the Regulation on May 1, 2004.

[31] Commission Decision of May 8, 2001 relating to a proceeding pursuant to art. 81 of the EC Treaty, [2001] O.J. L302/1 (EC) [hereinafter Commission Decision of May 8, 2001].

[32] *Sot. Lélos kai Sia*, supra note 22.

[33] Opinion of Advocate General Ruiz-Jarabo Colomer, *Sot. Lélos kai Sia*, supra note 22, [2008] E.C.R. I-7139, para. 123 (who explicitly professes "taking a different view from that taken by Advocate General Jacobs in *Syfait*").

[34] *Sot. Lélos kai Sia*, supra note 22, [2008] E.C.R. I-7139, para. 70 (The Court rendered its judgment "without it being necessary to examine the arguments raised by GSK AEVE that it is necessary for pharmaceutical companies to limit parallel exports in order to avoid the risk of a reduction in their investments in the research and development of medicines"). In substance, the Court relied upon its earlier decision in *United Brands*, in which it had held that a dominant supplier may not refuse to fulfill ordinary orders. See Case 27/76, United Brands & United Brands Continental v. Commission, [1978] E.C.R. 207, para. 182. In this regard, the Court seemed to ignore the fact that the *United Brands* case, which related to bananas, was different from the Greek *GSK* case in so far as *United Brands* did not involve issues of innovation in the first place. For a more extensive critique on that decision, see Drexl, *supra* note 22.

[35] *GlaxoSmithKline*, supra note 23.

of competition in the sense of former Article 81(1) of the EC Treaty,[36] it confirmed the CFI judgment with regard to the standard for an exemption under former Article 81(3) of the EC Treaty (now Article 101(3) of the TFEU). The ECJ stated that the CFI was correct "in holding that the Commission's approach may entail ascertaining whether, in the light of the factual arguments and the evidence provided, it seems more likely either that the agreement in question must make it possible to obtain appreciable advantages or that it will not."[37]

In the light of the foregoing analysis of the history of the *GSK* cases, the opinion of Advocate General Jacobs in *Syfait* and the decision of the ECJ in the Spanish *GSK* case appear as the most important documents for a better understanding of the current EU regime on restraints of parallel trade in pharmaceuticals.

As indicated,[38] Advocate General Jacobs relied on three reasons for advocating a special regime for parallel trade in pharmaceuticals. The European Courts rejected two of them, namely, the level of regulation of pharmaceutical markets in the EU Member States and the lack of economic benefits accruing to consumers from parallel trade, while the third argument on innovation was finally taken into consideration by the CFI and the ECJ in the Spanish *GSK* case.

(2) Regulation of pharmaceutical markets in the Member States

With regard to existing regulation in the EU Member States, Advocate General Jacobs had argued that distortions of competition between the Member States did not primarily arise from GSK's unilateral refusal to supply to Greek wholesalers but from "pervasive and diverse" national regulation of the markets for pharmaceuticals, which led to considerable price differentials between the EU Member States.[39] Under EU medicinal law, the EU Member States are indeed allowed to control prices and to impose a public service duty on pharmaceutical companies to fulfill domestic demand.[40] Jacobs concluded:

> When pharmaceutical undertakings attempt to block parallel trade, they are not thereby seeking to entrench price differentials of their own making, but rather to avoid the consequences which

---

[36] The CFI, for the first, and so far only time, had relied upon a consumer-harm approach according to which a showing of consumer harm would be required for an agreement to be considered restrictive in the sense of former art. 81(1) of the EC Treaty. See the CFI in *GlaxoSmithKline*, *supra* note 29, para. 119. This argument was rejected by the ECJ, which defended the earlier case law, according to which former art. 81(1) of the EC Treaty (now art. 101(1) of the TFEU) "aims to protect not only the interests of competitors or of consumers, but also the structure of the market and, in so doing, competition as such. Consequently, for a finding that an agreement has an anti-competitive object, it is not necessary that final consumers be deprived of the advantages of effective competition in terms of supply or price." See the ECJ in *GlaxoSmithKline*, *supra* note 23, para. 63 (relying on the previous Case C-8/08, T-Mobile Netherlands v. Raad van bestuur van de Nederlandse Mededingingsautoriteit, [2009] E.C.R. I-4529, paras. 38–39).

[37] *GlaxoSmithKline*, *supra* note 23, para. 94.

[38] See argument and discussion, *supra* notes 26–28.

[39] Opinion of Advocate General Jacobs, *supra* note 26, paras. 77–78.

[40] See Council Directive 89/105 of December 21, 1988 relating to the transparency of measures regulating the prices of medicinal products for human use and their inclusion in the scope of national health insurance systems, [1989] O.J. L 40/8 (EEC).

would follow if the very low prices imposed upon them in some Member States were generalised across the Community.[41]

These arguments were rejected by the ECJ in its decision in *Sot. Lélos kai Sia*, the second ECJ preliminary ruling on the Greek *GSK* case. In response to the respective arguments advanced by GSK, the Court stressed that national regulation "does not entirely remove the prices of those products from the law of supply and demand."[42] It also relied on the Commission's and Advocate General Ruiz-Jarabo Colomer's argument according to which even in countries such as Greece, where price controls are strictest, the sales prices are negotiated between the health authorities and the pharmaceutical companies.[43] Or to put it differently: as long as there is some room for free economic action, EU competition law has to be applied against business conduct that may restrict remaining competition.[44]

(3) No benefits for consumers created by parallel trade?

With regard to the benefits of parallel trade, Advocate General Jacobs argued that special features of the pharmaceutical market made it doubtful that parallel trade would actually bring down prices to the benefit of consumers in the importing countries. Given that the national healthcare systems often guarantee fixed prices to pharmacists, he concluded that parallel traders would simply take advantage of the price differentials and thereby free ride on the investment of the pharmaceutical companies in R&D and marketing.[45]

In *Sot. Lélos kai Sia*, the ECJ rejected Jacobs's concerns in this regard as well. The Court held that price differentials "open up in principle an alternative source of supply to buyers of the medicinal products in [the importing] States, which necessarily brings some benefits to the final consumer of those products."[46] Thereby, the Court clearly realized that parallel trade in pharmaceuticals will also create price pressure in the importing country. The healthcare systems will be able to adjust their policies, for instance, with regard to refunding the price of drugs to patients, and large buyers of drugs such as hospitals could take parallel trade in pharmaceuticals into account in the framework of their procurement policies.[47]

It was along the same lines that the CFI had already argued, in its earlier judgment in the Spanish *GSK* case, that GSK's dual-pricing scheme restricted competition in the

---

[41] Opinion of Advocate General Jacobs, *supra* note 26, para. 84.
[42] *Sot. Lélos kai Sia*, *supra* note 22, para. 61.
[43] *Ibid.* para. 63.
[44] The Court also argued that protecting parallel trade in pharmaceuticals was most important, since, in the case of pharmaceuticals protected by patents, parallel trade would be the "only form of competition which can be envisaged." *Ibid.* para. 64. This, however, is to be criticized, since different drugs, which may all be patent-protected, may well be substitutes for the treatment of the same disease and, therefore, belong to the same market. That IPRs do not confer market dominance as such has long been accepted by the ECJ. See, in particular, Joined Cases C-241 & 242/91 P, RTE & ITP v. Comm'n ("*Magill*"), [1995] E.C.R. I-743, para. 46 ("So far as dominant position is concerned, it is remembered at the outset that mere ownership of an intellectual property right cannot confer such a position.").
[45] Opinion of Advocate General Jacobs, *supra* note 26, paras. 96–99.
[46] *Sot. Lélos kai Sia*, *supra* note 22, para. 53.
[47] *Ibid.* para. 56.

sense of former Article 81(1) of the EC Treaty (now Article 101(1) of the TFEU), after requiring a showing of concrete harm to consumers for an agreement to be restrictive.[48]

(4) Innovation versus parallel trade in pharmaceuticals

This brings us to the most influential innovation argument by Advocate General Jacobs, which was finally held to be relevant by the ECJ for accepting a rather lenient approach to assessing restraints on parallel trade in pharmaceuticals. Thereby, the Court rejected both the opinion of the Commission in the Spanish *GSK* case and the opinion of Advocate General Ruiz-Jarabo Colomer in the Greek referral case of *Sot. Lélos kai Sia*.

At the outset, it has to be stressed that the two Advocates General and the Courts all agreed to the extent that restraints of parallel trade should not be considered illegal *per se*. Even Advocate General Ruiz-Jarabo Colomer conceded that former Article 82 of the EC Treaty (Article 102 of the TFEU) was not suited for holding that any particular conduct, including a restraint on parallel trade, could be considered illegal *per se*.[49] The ECJ confirmed this in *Sot. Lélos kai Sia*, holding that the refusal to supply does not constitute an abuse in the sense of former Article 82 of the EC Treaty so long as the dominant undertaking does not refuse to fulfill ordinary orders.[50] The same holds true for the application of Article 101 of the TFEU, since, from a legal point of view, there is no form of restrictive agreement that, from the outset, would be excluded from the possibility of obtaining an exemption under Article 101(3) of the TFEU. Thereby, EU law takes account of the economic insight that price discrimination implemented through a restraint of competition can be procompetitive.[51]

Advocate General Jacobs also relied upon the second economic insight that parallel trade only affects intrabrand competition and, by restricting this form of competition, has the potential of enhancing interbrand competition. In identifying the procompetitive effects of the restraint of parallel trade, he therefore referred to competition among pharmaceutical companies that do not compete so much by price as by investment in R&D. Accordingly, he argued: "Innovation is an important parameter of competition in the pharmaceuticals sector. Substantial investment is typically required in the research and development of a new pharmaceutical product."[52]

However, he presented this idea in the context of a more general debate on the role of innovation in the pharmaceutical sector without putting it in a more analytical scheme for assessing the pro- and anticompetitive effects of restraints on parallel trade. Yet such an analysis is possible. To rephrase Jacobs, it would have to be argued that if pharmaceutical companies are allowed to restrain parallel trade and price discriminate they will be better able to charge a price for the high fixed costs of R&D. The intrabrand reduction of price competition will then be outweighed by the dynamic efficiency gains accruing from the enhanced ability of the pharmaceutical companies to invest in R&D in interbrand competition for better future products with other pharmaceutical companies.

---

[48] See the Court of First Instance in *GlaxoSmithKline*, *supra* note 29, paras. 182–90.
[49] Opinion of Advocate General Ruiz-Jarabo Colomer, *supra* note 33, para. 76 (this is why he then considered the possibility of an economic justification).
[50] *Sot. Lélos kai Sia*, *supra* note 22, para. 71.
[51] See discussion *supra* II.
[52] Opinion of Advocate General Jacobs, *supra* note 26, para. 89.

In order to justify a decision in favor of a restraint on parallel trade, however, Jacobs would also have to explain that pharmaceutical companies would actually reinvest higher profits generated from restraints of parallel trade in R&D. Indeed, this is the point on which both the Commission in the Spanish *GSK* case and Advocate General Ruiz-Jarabo Colomer most disagreed with Jacobs. The Commission, in rejecting GSK's application for an individual exemption, stated that GSK had failed to demonstrate a causal link between parallel trade and a reduction of GSK's investment in R&D.[53] Similarly, Advocate General Ruiz-Jarabo Colomer had very harsh words to say about GSK's allegations on the innovation-reducing effect of parallel trade:

> [A]part from the description of the "horrors" caused by parallel trade, GSK does not indicate any positive aspect resulting from its restriction of supplies of medicinal products to the wholesalers, except that its profit margins recover, which is irrelevant for the purposes of classifying the conduct as an abuse, or for the purposes of justifying it.[54]

Advocate General Ruiz-Jarabo Colomer thereby hinted at the problem that higher profits are, first of all, the result of the restrictive effect on price competition, and that making higher profits can therefore not be used as an argument for justifying a competition law defence.

However, Jacobs's view could still be supported based on the argument that competitive pressure from other pharmaceutical companies that engage in R&D will guarantee that higher income from restraints of parallel trade will be reinvested in R&D. In the Spanish *GSK* case, the CFI and the ECJ finally seem to have adopted this view by, first, obliging the Commission to take GSK's innovation argument seriously and, second, by obliging the Commission to assess whether the alleged efficiency gains are more likely to occur than not.[55]

While this may seem a theoretically sound approach, there are yet two problems linked to it: first, competition agencies also have to take into consideration that investment in innovation is not the only form by which originator pharmaceutical companies compete with each other. When patents are about to expire, investment in evergreening strategies, including the filing of secondary patents, may turn out to be more successful and profitable in view of maintaining the market position. Originator companies have also started to become more diversified firms; therefore, it cannot be ruled out that higher income from restraints on parallel trade will be invested in mergers with generic companies or the building up of generics departments. Second, the ECJ requires the Commission to make most uncertain predictions about future dynamic processes of innovation. It is not only highly uncertain whether and how much of the higher income will be reinvested in R&D. It is also practically impossible to predict whether enhanced research efforts will be successful, to which forms of innovation such efforts will lead, and whether new drugs in the future will provide medical benefits that can outweigh the disadvantage of higher prices arising from restraints on parallel trade for existing drugs.[56]

---

[53] Commission Decision of May 8, 2001, *supra* note 31, paras. 154–55.
[54] Opinion of Advocate Genereal Ruiz-Jarabo Colomer, *supra* note 33, para. 118.
[55] *GlaxoSmithKline*, *supra* note 23, para. 94.
[56] On these critical points, see also Drexl, *supra* note 22, at 591–94. See also Josef Drexl, *Real Knowledge is to Know the Extent of One's Own Ignorance: On the Consumer Harm Approach in Innovation-Related Competition Cases*, 76 ANTITRUST L.J. 677 (2010) (highlighting the problem of

(5) Summary of the GlaxoSmithKline cases

With the *GlaxoSmithKline* decisions, EU competition law has reached a more balanced approach to the application of competition law to restraints of competition on parallel trade in pharmaceuticals. The argument is that such restraints may enhance the ability of R&D-oriented pharmaceutical companies to compete with each other in innovation. The problem remains that, in individual cases, it will be extremely difficult or even practically impossible to draw the line between procompetitive restraints that overall enhance innovation, on the one hand, and anticompetitive conduct, on the other hand.

The question to be asked in the following two subsections is what lessons can be learned from this EU debate as to how to deal with trade in pharmaceuticals protected by IPRs (patents and trademarks) on the global level. In the following, the chapter therefore turns to the issues of international exhaustion and the seizure of transit goods.

IV. HOW TO DEAL WITH PARALLEL TRADE IN PHARMACEUTICALS INTERNATIONALLY

Right at the beginning, it has to be pointed out that an analysis from an international perspective has to take into account the fundamental differences between the legal orders of the EU and the WTO. With regard to the EU, it is certainly easier to base the analysis and policy recommendations on a global-welfare approach, although such an analysis may lead to the conclusion that, with regard to the regulation of trade in pharmaceuticals, some EU Member States will be on the winning side, while others will lose. The EU legal order includes other legal instruments that can guarantee that the negative distributional effects on the losing countries will be balanced out.

In contrast, on the global level, the debate is characterized by a conflict between roughly two groups of states. On the one hand, there are those states that advocate strong IP protection in the interest of pharmaceutical companies and in view of maintaining high levels of investment in R&D, and on the other hand, there are the predominantly poorer states that are more interested in keeping prices low in order to facilitate access of their citizens to essential medicine. Although WTO law is based on the principle of "mutual advantages" and, therefore, obligations in one field may be balanced by concessions in another field, WTO law does not create a "social" community of states that would adequately respond to negative distributional effects of its legal regimes.

As pointed out in the Introduction, Article 6 of TRIPS leaves it to the WTO members to decide on international exhaustion. In the light of the economics of parallel trade,[57] Article 6 of TRIPS should not be considered a rule in need of reform. While it may seem that the authorization of WTO members to maintain a rule of purely national exhaustion conflicts with the principle of trade liberalization deeply enshrined in the legal regime

---

predicting future effects on dynamic efficiency in innovation-oriented competition cases, including the European *GlaxoSmithKline* cases).

[57] See *supra* II.

of GATT in particular, it is also clear that the interests of individual WTO members are highly diverse.

Recognition of a principle of international exhaustion as an obligation of WTO law would produce highly undesirable effects in the field of trade in pharmaceuticals in particular.

As indicated above,[58] international exhaustion may make it more difficult for pharmaceutical companies to price discriminate between different countries. Such an effect would contradict the interests of countries that want to support the economic interests of their pharmaceutical companies and the interest in promoting R&D in the pharmaceutical industry as well as the interest of poorer nations. First, international exhaustion would make it more difficult for pharmaceutical companies to charge a price for the high fixed costs caused by the development of new drugs. Second, international exhaustion would drive prices up in the poorer countries and hamper access to essential drugs even more for the most economically disadvantaged peoples of the world.

The only group of people who are harmed by Article 6 of TRIPS are consumers in the richer countries, where governments are usually against a principle of international exhaustion for guaranteeing higher returns for pharmaceutical companies, who will be able to rely on their IPRs to prevent parallel imports. These consumers cross-subsidize access to medicine in the poorer countries of the world. Since, however, Article 6 of TRIPS leaves the choice between national and international exhaustion to the individual WTO members, this is not a concern that needs to be addressed on the level of the WTO. It should be left to the political process in the richer countries as potential beneficiaries of parallel imports to balance the current financial interests of their consumers and patients with the interest of the local pharmaceutical industry and the public interest in promoting innovation.[59]

It is to be noted that having a choice between national and international exhaustion is of little meaning for poorer countries. Since parallel trade depends on the existence of considerable price differentials, poorer countries can hardly enhance parallel imports by switching to international exhaustion, given the overall low ability to pay in such countries.[60] Rather, poorer countries should have an interest in their richer trading partners applying a principle of national exhaustion that would enable pharmaceutical companies to sell their drugs at lower prices in the poorer countries.[61]

---

[58] See *supra* II.
[59] The pharmaceutical industry in particular has tried to rely on art. 28.1 lit.(a) of TRIPS, according to which the patent includes an exclusive right of importation, to argue that WTO members may not apply a principle of international exhaustion to patents. However, footnote 6 to this provision clarifies that art. 6 of TRIPS will prevail and that art. 28.1 lit.(a) of TRIPS cannot be used to address the issue of exhaustion. Hence, under art. 6 of TRIPS, members cannot be challenged for having adopted a rule of international patent exhaustion before WTO dispute settlement bodies. See UNCTAD-ICTSD, *supra* note 4, at 105–6.
[60] However, adoption of a principle of international exhaustion may still be beneficial for poorer countries for another reason. In a situation in which the originator company has acquired patent protection in that country but still refrains from distributing the drug there, parallel trade based on international exhaustion will be the only route through which patients can legally gain access to the patented drugs.
[61] In this context, see also the interesting analysis by PATRICIA BOHN, PARALLELIMPORTREGELUNGEN IM PATENT – UND MARKENRECHT IN LATEINAMERIKA (2010) (analysing the policy reasons for having

As a matter of clarification, it is also important to understand that these arguments on exhaustion only refer to trade in patented and not in generic drugs, although the latter may be, and regularly are, also protected by trademarks. With regard to generic drugs, there is no argument of innovation that would count against a principle of international exhaustion.

V. HOW TO DEAL WITH TRANSIT OF PHARMACEUTICALS

A recent, more intensely discussed issue concerning international trade in pharmaceuticals is whether customs authorities can legally seize pharmaceuticals that are in transit, although patent protection is neither available in the country of origin nor in the country of destination.[62]

A. The Legal Situation in the European Union

This issue arose in the EU when, in December 2008, Dutch customs authorities seized drugs in transit from India to Brazil at Schiphol airport. The seizure was initiated by the pharmaceutical company Merck, which relied upon patent protection in the Netherlands, while the drug did not enjoy any patent protection in India or Brazil.[63] In February 2009, the customs authorities at Schiphol airport even stopped the transit of HIV medicine, produced by the Indian generics company Aurobindo, which was about to be shipped to Nigeria as part of a programme of the Clinton Foundation and UNITAID.[64]

Such transit cases raise legal and moral issues both on the EU and the global WTO level. As regards EU law, the question at that time was whether the 2003 Border Measures Regulation provided a legal basis for temporary detention or permanent seizure.[65] Article 2(1)(c)(i) of the Regulation required that the goods seized infringe a patent "under that Member State's law." Strictly speaking, however, transit as such does not violate any

---

a principle of national or international exhaustion in Latin American countries with regard to patents and trademarks).

[62] See e.g. Frederick M. Abbott, *Seizure of Generic Pharmaceuticals in Transit Based on Allegations of Patent Infringement: A Threat to International Trade, Development and Public Welfare*, 1 WIPO JOURNAL 43 (2009), available at www.wipo.int/freepublications/en/intproperty/wipo_journal/wipo_journal_1_1.pdf; Shashank P. Kumar, *Border Enforcement of IP Rights Against In-Transit Generic Pharmaceuticals: An Analysis of Character and Consistency* (2009), available at http://papers.ssrn.com/sol3/papers.cfm?abstract_id=1383067; Marius Schneider, *Counterfeiting Counter-Fight*, 5 J. INTELL. PROP. L. & PRAC. 285 (2010); Xavier Seuba, *Free Trade of Pharmaceutical Products: The Limits of Intellectual Property Enforcement at the Border*, INTERNATIONAL CENTER FOR TRADE AND SUSTAINABLE DEVELOPMENT (ICTSD), ISSUE PAPER NO. 27 (2010).

[63] See Abbott, *supra* note 62, at 47.

[64] See UNITAID, UNITAID Statement on Dutch Confiscation of Medicines Shipment (July 29, 2015), available at www.unitaid.eu/en/Resources/News/156-Unitaid-Statement-On-Dutch-Confiscation-Of-Medicines-Shipment (arguing that the drugs were not counterfeit products and did not infringe IP rights).

[65] See Council Regulation 1383/2003 of July 22, 2003 concerning customs action taken against goods suspected of infringing certain intellectual property rights and the measures to be taken against goods found to have infringed such rights, [2003] O.J. L196/7 (EC).

rights of the patent holder, since the goods are not produced, imported, or sold in the country of transit. Nevertheless, the Dutch Court of The Hague sustained detention of transit goods by relying upon Recital 8 to the Regulation and applying a so-called "manufacturing fiction," according to which the question needs to be asked whether the goods would infringe the patent if they were manufactured in the country of transit.[66] Recital 8 reads as follows:

> Proceedings initiated to determine whether an intellectual property right has been infringed under national law will be conducted with reference to the criteria used to establish whether goods produced in that Member State infringe intellectual property rights.

However, the wording of this recital does not have to be understood in the sense of a manufacturing fiction. Rather, with regard to patents in particular, Article 2(1)(c)(i) of the Regulation is clear about its character as a pure choice-of-law rule, which provides that infringement has to be assessed according to the domestic patent law of the Member State where the seizure takes place. Such a rule is needed because EU law does not offer uniform standards for the rights conferred to a patent owner and the concept of patent infringement. It would then be for this national law alone to identify the rights conferred to the patent owner. If that law does not protect against transit, the customs authorities will not be empowered to stop shipment of the goods. Reading Recital 8 as a legal basis for a manufacturing fiction would have extended Article 2(1)(c)(i) of the Regulation from a choice-of-law rule to a rule on harmonization of substantive patent law in the Member States, falling outside the wording of this provision and the overall purpose of the Regulation.

In the *Nokia* case, the High Court of Justice for England and Wales seemed to be of a similar opinion when it explicitly rejected a reading of Recital 8 as a sufficient legal basis for a "manufacturing fiction."[67] The question of how to interpret the Border Measures Regulation was then decided by the CJEU.[68] The Court concluded that, in line with the view of the English High Court, the EU Border Control Regulation did not support a "manufacturing fiction."[69] However, the *Philips and Nokia* case decided by the CJEU only related to trademarks and not patents. Yet, since the referrals were about the same legal terminology used for trademarks and patents in the Border Measures Regulation, it can be assumed that the CJEU judgment is also relevant for patents.[70]

---

[66] Sisvel v. Sosecal (Court of The Hague, July 18, 2008, on the transit of MP4 players). See Catherine Dounis, *Enforcing Intellectual Property Rights via EU Border Regulations: Inhibiting Access to Medicine or Preventing Counterfeit Medicine?*, 36 BROOKLYN J. INT'L L. 717, 745–46 (2011).

[67] Nokia Corp. v. Her Majesty's Commissioners of Revenue & Customs, 2009 EWHC 1903 (Ch) (decision of July 27, 2009) (dealing with trademark infringement).

[68] Joined Cases C-446/09 & C-495/09, Koninklijke Philips Elecs. v. Lucheng Meijing Indus. Co. & Nokia Corp. v. Her Majesty's Commissioners of Revenue and Customs, [2011] E.C.R. I-12435. The second case was actually referred to the CJEU by the English Court of Appeal, which was asked to decide on the appeal of the cited *Nokia* decision of the Chancery Division of the High Court.

[69] *Ibid.* paras. 69–70.

[70] Doubts may arise from the fact that trademark cases are often discussed in the light of the *Rioglass* and *Montex* decisions, in which the CJEU held that national trademark laws prohibiting

As to WTO law, the question is whether such border seizure violates the principle of freedom of transit pursuant to Article V of the General Agreement on Tariffs and Trade 1994[71] in particular. The seizures effectuated by the Dutch authorities caused India and Brazil to start WTO dispute resolution procedures against the EU and the Netherlands.[72] Yet, after consultations with India and Brazil, the European Commission, in 2012, solved the conflict by adopting guidelines on the application of the 2003 Border Measures Regulation. These guidelines explicitly state that the:

> mere fact that medicines are in transit through the EU territory, and there is a patent right applicable to such medicines in the EU territory, does not in itself constitute enough grounds for customs authorities in any Member State to suspect that the medicines at stake infringe patent rights.[73]

On January 1, 2014, the 2003 Border Measures Regulation was replaced by the new Regulation (EU) 608/2013.[74] Given the importance of the transit issue, it is very surprising that this Regulation does not contain a clear statement regarding the transit of goods.[75] Still, the text of the Regulation sufficiently clarifies that right holders cannot rely on patent rights to stop the transit of pharmaceuticals in the EU. While Article 2(7)(a), which defines "goods suspected of infringing an intellectual property right" as "goods which are the subject of an act infringing an intellectual property right in that Member State,"[76] seems to follow the wording of the former provision of Article 2(1)(c)(i) of the 2003 Regulation, the new Regulation does not contain any text that equals Recital 8 to the 2003 Regulation. Quite the contrary, the new Recital 11, which nevertheless could have been phrased more explicitly, confirms the Union's international commitments, thereby mentioning the Doha WTO Ministerial Conference and the need to interpret and implement

---

the transit of branded goods may not be applied as a matter of the EU guarantee of free movement of goods and in the light of the Trade Mark Directive, which, for an infringement, requires an "act in the course of trade." See Case C-115/02, Administration des douanes et droits indirects v. Rioglass & Transremar, [2003] E.C.R. I-12705; Case C-281/05, Montex Holdings Ltd v. Diesel SpA, [2006] E.C.R. I-10881.

[71] General Agreement on Tariffs and Trade 1994, April 15, 1994; Marrakesh Agreement Establishing the World Trade Organization, Annex 1A, 1867 U.N.T.S. 187 (1994) [hereinafter GATT 1994].

[72] Request for Consultations by India, European Union and a Member State—Seizure of Generic Drugs in Transit, WT/DS408/1, IP/D/28, G/L/921 (May 12, 2010); Request for Consultations by Brazil, WT/DS/409/1, IP/D/29, G/L/922 (May 19, 2010). On these complaints, see Henning Grosse Ruse-Khan, *A Trade Agreement Creating Barriers to International Trade? ACTA Border Measures and Goods in* Transit, 26 AM. U. INT'L L. REV. 645, 650–59 (2011).

[73] Guidelines of the European Commission Concerning the Enforcement by EU Customs Authorities of Intellectual Property Rights with Regard to Goods, in Particular Medicines, in Transit Through the EU, February 1, 2012, available at http://ec.europa.eu/taxation_customs/resources/documents/customs/customs_controls/counterfeit_piracy/legislation/guidelines_on_transit_en.pdf.

[74] Regulation 608/2013 of the European Parliament and of the Council of June 12, 2013 Concerning Customs Enforcement of Intellectual Property Rights and Repealing Council Regulation (EC) 1383/2003, [2013] O.J. L171/15 [hereinafter Regulation 608/2013].

[75] See also Trevor Cook, *Revision of the European Union Regime on Customs Enforcement of Intellectual Property Rights*, 18 J. INTELL. PROP. RIGHTS 485 (2013).

[76] Regulation 608/2013, at 20.

the TRIPS Agreement in a manner supportive of WTO members' right to protect public health and to promote access to medicines. Consequently, this recital states that:

> [W]ith regard to medicine, the passage of which across the customs territory of the Union, with or without transhipment, warehousing, breaking bulk, or changes in the mode or means of transport, is only a portion of a complete journey beginning and terminating beyond the territory of the Union, customs authorities should, when assessing a risk of infringement of intellectual property rights, take account of any substantial likelihood of diversion of such medicines onto the market of the Union.[77]

This should make clear that, in a case where there is no likelihood of the goods being diverted onto the internal market, pharmaceuticals in transit cannot be seized under the new Border Measures Regulation.

Yet the European Union is now on its way to making pure transit of goods an infringement in the framework of the ongoing reform of European trademark law.[78] This reform was indeed triggered by discontent on the part of trademark owners with the rejection of the "manufacturing fiction" by the CJEU in *Philips and Nokia*.[79] Such change should in principle not affect the free transit of generics across the EU.[80] Of course, pharmaceuticals are also protected by trademarks. But generics can be marketed without bearing the trademark of the originator drug, although there might be cases of similarity.[81] In addition, it is to be pointed out that the 2013 Border Measures Regulation does not apply to parallel trade either.[82] Hence, it will not be possible to stop the transit of goods where the right holder has consented to the first sale in the country of origin and where the country of destination applies the principle of international exhaustion.

B. On the Appropriate Legal Regime for Pharmaceuticals in Transit

However, the legal situation in the EU does not answer the question of what the most appropriate legal regime for dealing with pharmaceuticals in transit should be. In the light of recent European experience in the field of restraints on parallel trade within the EU, the question could be asked whether the interest in promoting innovation does not argue in favor of seizures of patent-protected pharmaceuticals in transit.

In answering this question, it first seems important to distinguish clearly between the

---

[77] *Ibid.* at 16.

[78] See Proposal of March 27, 2013 for a Directive of the European Parliament and of the Council to Approximate the Laws of the Member States Relating to Trade Marks, art. 10(5), COM(2013)162 final, and Proposal of March 27, 2013 for a Regulation of the European Parliament and of the Council Amending Council Regulation (EC) 207/2009 on the Community Trade Mark, art. 9(5), COM(2013)161 final.

[79] See the Explanatory Memorandum of the Proposal for a New Trademark Directive, *supra* note 78, para. 5.1.6.

[80] In the same sense, see Cook, *supra* note 75, at 488–89.

[81] The latter is stressed by Daniel Opoku Acquah, *Balancing or Lobbying? On Access to Medicines, Border Measures and the European Parliament's Amendments to the Proposed EU Trademark Rules*, 19 J. INTELL. PROP. RIGHTS 404, 407 (2014).

[82] See Regulation (EU) 608/2013, art. 2(5)(a). According to this rule, the Regulation only applies where goods bear the trademark "without authorization" of the trademark owner.

issue of exhaustion and parallel trade, on the one hand, and transit cases, on the other hand. Parallel trade is limited to cases in which the right holder has at least consented to the first sale in the country of exportation. In contrast, cases of pharmaceuticals in transit concern generic drugs produced and sold without the consent of the right holder.

On the other hand, trade in generic drugs and parallel trade share the common feature of generating price competition for the originator drug. Hence, all the pro-innovation arguments developed above in favor of the legality of restraints on parallel trade could also be relied upon for the transit cases. The fact that the right holders have not even consented to the first sale in the transit cases seems to support the position of the patent owner even more.

Yet the fact that consent by the right holder is missing in the transit cases should not be taken as an argument to justify seizure of generic pharmaceuticals in transit. Experience with European competition law also teaches us that the appropriate solution has to rely on a balance between the incentives to innovate and the interest in access to medicine at lower prices. This balance can be assessed by EU competition law with reference to the global welfare within the EU, while, as was pointed out above,[83] a global welfare approach would risk harming patients in poorer countries, since the WTO law has no legal and social mechanism in place that would compensate poorer patients for the losses they incur due to higher levels of patent protection. This argues in favor of pursuing a balance between the conflicting interests based on the different laws of the WTO members. This is why, from a legal perspective, transit of pharmaceutical products predominantly presents an issue on which national law should decide on infringement.[84]

To clarify this a bit further, it is helpful to have a closer look at the reasons why patent protection may only exist in the country of transit and not in the countries of origin and destination. In this regard, Abbott identifies at least four different scenarios: (1) the inventor has never sought patent protection; (2) the patent has expired; (3) the patent application was rejected for not meeting the criteria for patentability; and (4) the invention is not deemed to constitute patentable subject matter.[85]

In the first scenario, it is clear that the inventor himself did not deem it economically profitable to even seek patent protection in the respective countries. Accordingly, it may be argued that patent protection in these countries is not important enough to raise incentives for innovation significantly. Similarly, there is no economic basis for justifying a seizure of such pharmaceuticals in transit.

In the second scenario, where patent protection has already expired, the inventor has sufficiently benefited from the protection of its patents before they expire according to the law of the countries of origin and destination. Such scenarios may in particular arise where the countries of origin and destination do not dispose of any form of patent term extension. In such cases, the invention may still be protected in the EU for some years based on a supplementary protection certificate (SPC) or, in the United States (U.S.), due

---

[83] See supra beginning of IV.
[84] Note that, technically speaking, it would go too far to call this an issue of conflict of laws. Under private international law, states remain free to define the scope of protection under their IP laws.
[85] Abbott, supra note 62, at 46. With regard to the fourth case, Abbott mentions the example of the denial of patent protection for computer software in Europe.

to the patent-term extension rule, while patent protection has expired in other countries. In such instances, domestic legislatures seem to disagree considerably with regard to the appropriate term of protection. Allowing a seizure in the country of transit in this case would export the transit country's balancing of the interests to third countries. Since the interests of the patients in the country of importation in having access to medicine will not be taken into account by the substantive patent law of the transit country, it should be for the country of importation alone to decide on the term of protection.

Similarly, also in the third and fourth case, the reasons for lack of protection in the exporting and importing countries are to be explained by differences in the weighing of interests according to different national laws. If some countries deny patent protection because the invention does not meet the patentability requirements or the invention is not considered to be patentable subject matter, this is so because the grant of a patent would be deemed to lead to overprotection against the public interest of these countries.

In the *Philips and Nokia* case, Advocate General Cruz Villalón seemed to argue in a similar sense. He makes the point that application of a "manufacturing fiction" would conflict with the territoriality principle as a fundamental principle of international IP law.[86]

VI. CONCLUSION

European competition law has produced considerable case law on how to deal with restraints on parallel trade in pharmaceuticals between the Member States. Thereby, the ECJ (now CJEU) has recognized that, under certain conditions, the argument of enhancing innovation by higher profits may justify a restraint on parallel trade.

However, in accepting the innovation argument, policy-makers risk committing a number of fallacies. In competition law, higher profits are first of all a sign of a restraint of competition. The argument in favor of creating incentives for innovation, if driven too far, would risk creating a sectorial exemption from competition law for the originator pharmaceutical industry. Therefore, the innovation argument should not be accepted without a factual basis that justifies the expectation that higher income will indeed be reinvested in R&D. Since there are also other ways to compete with originator pharmaceutical companies than by innovation, mere existence of competitive pressure by other originator pharmaceutical companies will not guarantee such reinvestment in innovation. Also, the CJEU recognizes that innovation comes with a price for those consumers who depend on affordable access to already existing medicine. For an exemption or a justification under competition law, it therefore requires evidence that the alleged benefits regarding the development of new drugs are more likely to materialize and that these benefits at least outweigh the losses of the consumers who have to pay higher prices for existing drugs. A major problem arises from the difficulties in making reliable predictions about future dynamic processes in applying this test defined by the Court of Justice.

---

[86] Opinion of Advocate General Cruz Villalón on Joined Cases C-446 & C-495/09, Koninklijke Philips Electronics v. Lucheng Meijing Indus. Co. & Nokia Corp. v. Her Majesty's Commissioners of Revenue and Customs, [2011] E.C.R. I-12435, para. 65.

From this EU case law, a few lessons can be learned for the international debate on exhaustion and the seizure of patented goods in transit. As to the exhaustion issue, Article 6 of TRIPS applies the correct approach by leaving it to the WTO members to choose between national and international exhaustion. This rule enables the pharmaceutical companies to price discriminate between richer and poorer countries and to recoup high investments in their R&D efforts, while keeping prices low in poorer countries.

With regard to the issue of pharmaceuticals in transit, there is an imminent risk of overstretching the innovation argument supporting strong patent protection if the national laws allow seizure in the transit countries. It is most important in this regard to assess the adequate balance of the interest in innovation with the interest in access to affordable drugs under the law of the country of destination rather than under the law of the transit country. Hence, there is no justification for seizure of pharmaceuticals in transit. The EU has at least confirmed this understanding in the most recent revision of the Boarder Measures Regulation. Yet, without sufficient justification, the proposal of the Commission to make pure transit an infringement of trademark law moves in the opposite direction, which, however, could affect transit of generic drugs only under certain, limited, circumstances. In addition, trading nations should abstain from entering into bilateral or plurilateral agreements that promote seizure of goods in transit with a view to protecting intellectual property rights.[87]

---

[87] On the ambiguous approach of the Anti-Counterfeiting Trade Agreement (ACTA) to seizure of goods in transit, see Grosse Ruse-Khan, *supra* note 72.

14. Regulatory responses to international patent exhaustion
*Sarah R. Wasserman Rajec**

I. INTRODUCTION

Modern international trade law seeks to increase global welfare by lowering barriers to trade and encouraging competition. Multilateral treaties such as the 1947 General Agreement on Tariffs and Trade (GATT)[1] have significantly lowered tariffs and led to increased trade. Additionally, the theories underlying modern trade law have been applied to non-tariff barriers to trade, so that the World Trade Organization (WTO) includes agreements addressing subjects as diverse as telecommunication, industrial and product safety standards, and intellectual property. While the overriding purpose of the WTO is to encourage free trade, this principle has not been fully applied to patent law, placing the two fields in tension. Currently, patent law grants rights that are fortified by national borders while trade law aims to diminish the relevance of borders.

In one very important respect patent law remains at odds with modern trade theory in most countries. Under current United States (U.S.) law, for example, a U.S. patent holder may block the importation, use, or sale of patented goods purchased abroad, even if purchased from a seller licensed under a foreign patent. In contrast, an unconditional purchase of a patented good within the U.S. exhausts the patent holder's rights with respect to that good. The doctrine of exhaustion (also called the first sale doctrine) advances consumer interests by limiting restraints on alienation and fosters efficient use of goods by lowering transaction costs in resale markets while limiting the patent holder to a single reward for each sale. However, because most countries do not adhere to a doctrine of international exhaustion for patents, there is no free trade in patented goods. Moreover, the current rule undermines the purposes of exhaustion in the domestic context, because the information costs associated with determining the origin and history of goods in the resale market will apply to goods first sold domestically when they are identical to imported goods first sold abroad. The current rule also adds transaction costs to the manufacture of goods, such as consumer electronic goods, that contain multiple, patented components and are sourced from multiple countries.

In the U.S., the scope of the exhaustion doctrine has been the subject of recent judicial scrutiny, and the issue of international patent exhaustion may soon come before the Supreme Court. Following a Supreme Court decision interpreting the Copyright statute

---

* Assistant Professor of Law, William & Mary Marshall-Wythe School of Law. This chapter has been adapted from a previously-published article, *Free Trade in Patented Goods: International Exhaustion for Patents*, 28 BERKELEY TECH. L.J. 317 (2014).

[1] General Agreement on Tariffs and Trade, *opened for signature* October 30, 1947, 61 Stat. A-3, 55 U.N.T.S. 187 [hereinafter GATT].

to provide for international exhaustion,[2] the Court of Appeals for the Federal Circuit—the appellate court with national jurisdiction over patent law—recently issued an *en banc* decision affirming its precedent and declining to apply a rule of exhaustion to foreign sales of patented goods.[3] While Court-watchers await the inevitable petitions for certiorari, it is a good time to take stock of the doctrine, address criticism, and explore potential means of implementation.

One criticism of international patent exhaustion relates to the general economic benefits of price discrimination; the second is the specific potential impact of such a rule in the pharmaceutical industry. These consequentialist arguments do not directly address the single-reward theory underlying national exhaustion, nor can they find support in patent statutes. There is no express right to geographic price discrimination. The standard economic argument against international exhaustion draws on the potential gains to patent holders and to consumers in low-income countries from geographic price discrimination. This argument describes the current rule as allowing patent holders to market goods worldwide, adjusting prices for countries with lower purchasing power while continuing to reap rewards in high-income countries. An international exhaustion regime, according to this view, will push patent holders either to restrict sales to high-income markets or to offer goods at a globally uniform price, to the detriment of consumers in low-income countries. However, geographic price discrimination is but one of many options for identifying and marketing to populations with differing abilities to pay; many goods, regardless of patent protection, are available in different versions at different prices worldwide. Geographic price discrimination is desirable to firms because of its effectiveness at preventing arbitrage and because enforcement costs are shared by states through customs enforcement. It may not be the most desirable form of price discrimination for consumers, however, because it is imprecise in identifying differing demand curves. This is particularly true for countries with large or growing income disparities. A shift to international exhaustion would likely result in changes in how firms market goods, but would not necessarily entail the wholesale welfare losses that the standard argument suggests, because that argument compares geographic price discrimination with no price discrimination at all. Although price discrimination may be desirable, there is no reason that it must be based on geographic boundaries.

The industry that is often used as an example of the potentially devastating effects of a rule of international exhaustion is the pharmaceutical industry. The global welfare effects of an international exhaustion rule are more complex for the drug industry, given the heavy involvement of other regulatory regimes and a number of patent law measures that currently serve to remove the industry from typical market forces. In particular, geographic price discrimination may be more desirable in the drug industry because current price differentials reflect regulatory choices rather than demand differences, other forms of price discrimination may not be ethical, and access concerns tend

---

[2] Kirtsaeng v. John Wiley & Sons, Inc., 133 S. Ct. 1351, 1355–56 (2013).

[3] Lexmark Int'l, Inc. v. Impression Products, Inc., No. 2014-1617, 2016 WL 559042 (Fed. Cir. Feb. 12, 2016). The case has garnered attention, attracting briefs from *amici* in academia and industry groups, including medical device manufacturers, pharmaceutical researchers and manufacturers, the biotechnology industry, and telecommunications companies such as Nokia and Qualcomm. The United States (U.S.) also filed an *amicus* brief in support of neither party.

to be more pressing in that industry. While these concerns are valid, they are better met through the regulatory regimes that already control market access in the industry or through trade mechanisms, rather than through maintenance of a patent law rule that no longer makes sense for other industries. The very measures that govern the development, approval, and distribution of medicines worldwide result in a heavily-regulated market less likely to respond to the incentives and efficiencies that free trade is meant to encourage. The exceptional pharmaceutical sector of the market should not drive exhaustion policy—and it need not. The very same agencies that govern the availability of drugs may, with relatively modest adaptations, be able to regulate and stop parallel imports of pharmaceuticals.

This chapter first summarizes the argument for international exhaustion. Next it describes the doctrinal landscape in the U.S., showing how the limits of exhaustion doctrine are shaped by concerns about the proper control accompanying a patent right in future market transactions, not about the geographic scope of control. This chapter addresses both the economic argument against international patent exhaustion and the industry-specific example of pharmaceutical patents. Arguments that rely on the benefits of geographic price discrimination fail to account for other types of price discrimination that are potentially more desirable. In terms of access to medicine, an international exhaustion rule would be superimposed upon a heavily-regulated field. This chapter concludes by exploring how already-existent regulatory regimes might counteract a rule of international exhaustion in the industry in which its gains are least apparent and its losses potentially gravest.

II. THE ARGUMENT FOR INTERNATIONAL PATENT EXHAUSTION

The doctrine of exhaustion is a limit on patent holders' exclusive rights, freeing from infringement claims downstream sales and uses of inventions initially sold with the patent holder's authorization.[4] As a result, the patent holder need not "authorize" each and every sale for subsequent sales and uses to be non-infringing, and would-be purchasers need not research and understand myriad restrictions attached to all the goods they purchase.[5] The exhaustion doctrine thus reduces transaction costs of disposing of purchased goods while vindicating ideas of consumer rights in the goods they own. It also limits a patent holder's control over sales and uses that may compete with her own sales, thereby fostering competition in resale markets. Another explanation for exhaustion puts it in terms of what the inventor deserves, namely, a single reward for each product she sells, and no more. Exhaustion has developed as a common law doctrine in the U.S., and is consistent

---

[4] See Quanta Comput., Inc. v. LG Elecs., Inc., 533 U.S. 617, 625 (2008); see also Amelia Smith Rinehart, *Contracting Patents: A Modern Patent Exhaustion Doctrine*, 23 HARV. J.L. & TECH. 483, 484 (2010).

[5] Molly Shaffer Van Houweling, *The New Servitudes*, 96 GEO. L.J. 885, 914 (2008).

with property law's aversion to restrictive servitudes[6] and restraints on alienation,[7] in addition to economic ideas about reducing transaction costs.[8] Typically called simply "exhaustion," the doctrine has generally been applied only to goods sold domestically, and this chapter refers to it as "national exhaustion" to distinguish it from international exhaustion.

International patent exhaustion would extend the current rule to patented goods first sold abroad, so that the first unconditional, authorized sale anywhere in the world would exhaust a patent holder's rights in the U.S. patent. Currently, foreign sales do not exhaust domestic patent rights and unauthorized importation, subsequent sales, and use constitute infringement. This position appears consistent with a traditional understanding of patents as territorial exclusion rights. A strictly national rule of exhaustion allows a patent holder to control the first sale of patented goods in the domestic market without competition from unauthorized imports, thus securing the market and allowing her to reap whatever reward the national market will bear. In contrast, international exhaustion permits those who have bought patented goods abroad to use and sell them domestically without authorization from the patent holder, diminishing the patent holder's control of the domestic market. Just as a rule of national exhaustion reduces rewards to a patent holder who cannot use her patent to carve up the country into smaller markets, so would a move from a rule of national exhaustion to one of international exhaustion.

However, the same purposes underlying a national exhaustion rule also apply to goods purchased abroad. The nature of manufacturing, sales, and personal life are ever more globalized, making the information and transaction cost arguments from national exhaustion applicable to international transactions as well. Moreover, in complex technologies with multinational supply chains, it is difficult to ascertain whether a component was made or sold "under" a U.S. patent.[9] From a trade viewpoint, a national exhaustion rule may be characterized as a trading cost that hinders efficient downstream sales and uses of products because of the requirement to seek authorization for each contemplated resale market. In this sense, national exhaustion is a barrier to efficient trade. The Agreement on Trade-Related Aspects of Intellectual Property Rights (TRIPS) that forms part of the WTO characterizes variations in the protection of intellectual property rights generally as a non-tariff barrier to trade, and seeks to minimize such variations through minimum

---

[6] See Michael J. Madison, *Law as Design: Objects, Concepts, and Digital Things*, 56 Case W. Res. L. Rev. 381, 430–34 (2005).

[7] See e.g. Herbert Hovenkamp, *Post-Sale Restraints and Competitive Harm: The First Sale Doctrine in Perspective*, 66 N.Y.U. Ann. Surv. Am. L. 487, 493 (2011) (noting that national exhaustion reflects "the common law's strong policy against restraints on alienation").

[8] See Van Houweling, *supra* note 5, at 915.

[9] See e.g. Cornell Research Found., Inc. v. Hewlett–Packard Co., No. 5:01-CV-1974 (NAM/DEP), 2007 WL 4349135, *50–52 (N.D.N.Y. January 31, 2007) (denying summary judgment on the issue of where the sales occurred for purposes of an exhaustion determination, following an intensive discussion of the evidence); see also Laserdynamics, Inc. v. Quanta Storage Am., Inc., No. 2:06-CV-348-TJW-CE, 2009 WL 3763444, at *1 (E.D. Tex. June 29, 2009); Minebea Co. v. Papst, 444 F. Supp. 2d 68, 140–41 (D.D.C. 2006); Minebea Co. v. Papst, 374 F. Supp. 2d 202, 215–16 (D.D.C. 2005).

requirements for protection of intellectual property rights.[10] The removal of these various trading restrictions has fostered the growth of multinational companies and transnational supply chains.[11] A rule of international exhaustion would limit the patent right after an authorized sale in any country, paving the way for subsequent importation to—and resale in—all WTO member countries. This would result in more efficient manufacture and distribution by reducing transaction costs and increasing competition in resale markets.[12]

On the other hand, because even international exhaustion allows monopoly control over initial market placement, the trade literature demonstrates concern over a possible loss in global welfare if international exhaustion leads lower-income markets to be unserved or underserved. In other words, unlike the typical comparative advantage story, patent holders can choose not to compete with imports by choosing not to sell abroad, thus undermining, rather than enhancing, the benefits of trade. The starkest example of the possible effects of such a rule is in the pharmaceutical industry. The real world effects of an international exhaustion rule are of particular interest in the U.S., where the courts have taken up the question of international exhaustion in intellectual property. The Court of Appeals for the Federal Circuit and, likely, the Supreme Court will face arguments about the benefits of geographic price discrimination and warnings about the potential impact of access to pharmaceuticals that would result from a regime of international patent exhaustion. This chapter addresses each in turn.

III. EXHAUSTION IN U.S. COURTS

The Supreme Court has not recently weighed in on the question of international patent exhaustion, declining opportunities in 2002 and 2013 to hear cases that presented the issue, but the doctrine is getting more attention by U.S. courts now.[13] Early cases do not preclude application of exhaustion to foreign sales. In contrast, the recent decision of the Federal Circuit to reaffirm its stance *en banc* signals its awareness of likely Supreme Court review. In other contexts, the exhaustion doctrine has been the subject of a number of recent Supreme Court decisions. These cases show the Court weighing the same concerns in the domestic context that underlie the debate surrounding international patent exhaustion: weighing the freedom to contract against the single reward theory and the drag of transaction costs in downstream markets. In the context of copyright law, the Court weighed the territorial nature of copyright protection against the global reach and

---

[10] Agreement on Trade-Related Aspects of Intellectual Property Rights, April 15, 1994; Marrakesh Agreement Establishing the World Trade Organization, Annex 1C, 1869 U.N.T.S. 299 [hereinafter TRIPS].

[11] DOUGLAS A. IRWIN, *International Trade Agreements*, in THE CONCISE ENCYCLOPEDIA OF ECONOMICS 298 (David R. Henderson ed., 2008), available at www.econlib.org/library/Enc/InternationalTradeAgreements.html.

[12] See e.g. Frederick M. Abbott, *Parallel Importation: Economic and Social Welfare Dimensions*, INT'L INSTITUTE FOR SUSTAINABLE DEVELOPMENT (2007), available at www.iisd.org/pdf/2007/parallel_importation.pdf.

[13] Jazz Photo Corp. v. Int'l Trade Comm'n, 536 U.S. 950 (2002), *denying cert.* to 264 F.3d 1094 (Fed. Cir. 2001); Ninestar Tech. Co. v. Int'l Trade Comm'n, 133 S. Ct. 1656 (2013), *denying cert.* to 667 F.3d 1373 (Fed. Cir. 2012).

globalized nature of modern industry in extending exhaustion to international sales of copyrighted works. The Federal Circuit held that the Supreme Court's ruling in *Kirtsaeng* was not controlling for patent law.

Nevertheless, the Supreme Court's decision that lawful foreign sales exhaust U.S. copyright in *Kirtsaeng v. John Wiley & Sons, Inc.* was supported by policy considerations that apply *mutatis mutandis* to patent law, although the statutory basis of the decision leaves the possibility open for a different ruling in patent law.[14] The Court framed the question as whether there was a geographic component to the exhaustion rule codified as an exception to infringement for otherwise-infringing activities by owners of copies "lawfully made under this title," and determined there was not.[15] The Court was concerned that a different interpretation would allow publishers to control all downstream sales of books initially published abroad, creating incentives for publishers to move operations abroad and allowing for restraints on future sales that are at odds with a functioning market.

In patent law, the Court ruled on a patent holder's ability to condition patent rights on contractual limitations on downstream use in *L.G. Electronics v. Quanta*, ruling that L.G. Electronics' patent rights were exhausted when Intel sold chipsets it manufactured pursuant to the parties' license agreement.[16] A separate agreement requiring Intel to notify its customers that Intel's license did not extend to combining Intel chipsets with non-Intel products did not allow L.G. to recover for patent infringement from downstream customers who combined the goods. The Court situated its decision with other cases disallowing downstream price-fixing and thwarting attempts to expand patent rights beyond their proper scope.

The Supreme Court also followed a tradition of exhibiting more leniency toward restrictions that travel with goods when those goods are long-lasting and easy to replicate perfectly in *Bowman v. Monsanto*.[17] The Court held that the farmer who bought patented seeds from a grain elevator that had lawfully purchased them and, without permission, planted the seeds and harvested the newly-grown seed crop had infringed Monsanto's patents. The Supreme Court held that while Bowman could have consumed the seed, fed it to animals, or sold it to others, planting the patented seeds to "make" new, patented seeds was infringement. This case cabined exhaustion and showed the Court to be sensitive to a patent holder's right to her single reward, even as other cases limit rights that go beyond that single reward.

These recent Supreme Court cases on exhaustion fit into a long history. Early cases did not allow geographic restrictions (subdividing the national market) on downstream sales based on the single reward theory.[18] In 1890, the Supreme Court held that a lawful-but-unauthorized sale in Germany did not exhaust U.S. patent rights in *Boesch v. Graff*.[19] The patent holders, who held patents in both the U.S. and Germany, did not authorize the German sale, which was lawful there under a right held by prior users of technol-

---

[14] See generally Sarah R. Wasserman Rajec, *Free Trade in Patented Goods*, 29 BERKELEY TECH. L.J. 317 (2014).
[15] Kirtsaeng v. John Wiley & Sons, Inc., 133 S. Ct. 1351, 1355 (2013); *ibid.* at 1357–60.
[16] Quanta Computer, Inc. v. LG Elecs., 553 U.S. 617 (2008).
[17] Bowman v. Monsanto, 133 S. Ct. 1761 (2013).
[18] Adams v. Burke, 84 U.S. 453, 456 (1873).
[19] Boesch v. Graff, 133 U.S. 697, 703 (1890).

ogy. The case did not settle the question of international exhaustion of rights through authorized sales, though Second Circuit cases that followed *Boesch* indicated that authorization was the appropriate measure of exhaustion, rather than geographic location of a sale. In *Dickerson v. Matheson*, the Second Circuit Court of Appeals explained that if a foreign purchase was from the owner (or licensee) of *both* the foreign and U.S. patents, then U.S. patent rights were exhausted, but held that a purchase from a licensee of *only* the foreign patent did not exhaust U.S. patent rights.[20] The 1909 case *Daimler Manufacturing Co. v. Conklin* also granted an injunction to an exclusive licensee of a U.S. patent against someone who purchased a car (with patented components) while in Germany, from the company authorized to sell the patented goods there, and later imported it to the U.S. for personal use.[21] Soon after, the court in *Curtiss Aeroplane & Motor Corp. v. United Aircraft Engineering Corp.* found international exhaustion and distinguished *Daimler*, basing its decision on the patent holder's ownership of all relevant rights.[22] Ultimately, the impression given by *Boesch* and the cases decided soon after it is that the owner of patents in multiple countries exhausts rights in them all through his first, unrestricted sale. The cases rely on the agency of the patent owner in deciding to sell the patented product and on the reward he is due to collect for it—but only once.

More recent cases at the Federal Circuit have taken a different direction. The appellate court's precedent holds that there is no international patent exhaustion. In a 2001 decision, *Jazz Photo Corp. v. International Trade Commission* ("*Jazz Photo I*"), the Federal Circuit first held that there was no rule of international exhaustion of patents,[23] a position it strengthened in later cases. In that case, Fuji Photo Film sued a number of importers who sold disposable cameras, primarily from Chinese firms that bought used disposable camera cartridges and reloaded them for resale in various markets, including the U.S. The Federal Circuit found that reloading the cameras constituted repair, a non-infringing use of goods bought pursuant to authorized sales.[24] However, the court held that because many of the initial, authorized sales had been in foreign countries, the sales did not exhaust rights in the U.S. patents. As a result, the repaired cameras were excludable and only cameras that had been the subject of an authorized first sale in the U.S. were non-infringing. In *Fuji Photo Film Co. v. Jazz Photo Corp.* ("*Jazz Photo II*"), the Federal Circuit again refused to apply exhaustion to authorized foreign sales, holding that "[t]he patentee's authorization of an international first sale does not affect exhaustion of that patentee's right in the United States."[25] The court reasoned that the foreign sales did not occur "under" a U.S. patent and that a contrary ruling would contravene the rule against the extra-territorial application of U.S. law.

---

[20] Dickerson v. Matheson, 57 F. 524, 527 (2d Cir. 1893).
[21] Daimler Mfg. Co. v. Conklin, 170 F. 70, 72 (2d Cir. 1909).
[22] Curtiss Aeroplane & Motor Corp. v. United Aircraft Eng'g Corp., 266 F. 71 (2d Cir. 1920).
[23] Jazz Photo Corp. v. Int'l Trade Comm'n ("*Jazz Photo I*"), 264 F.3d 1094, 1105 (Fed. Cir. 2001) ("United States patent rights are not exhausted by products of foreign provenance. To invoke the protection of the first sale doctrine, the authorized first sale must have occurred under the United States patent.") (citing Boesch v. Graff, 133 U.S. 697, 701–3 (1890)).
[24] *Ibid.* at 1107. This contrasts with reconstruction of patented goods, which is considered the "making" of a new good rather than use of an existing good; reconstruction is considered infringing activity.
[25] *Ibid.* at 1376.

With these cases, the groundwork has been laid to address international patent exhaustion. And the Court will soon be presented with the opportunity in *Lexmark International v. Impression Products*. The Federal Circuit has now upheld its *Jazz Photo* decisions on international exhaustion and reaffirmed its case law on restricted use licenses. Lexmark sold print cartridges abroad and pursuant to restricted use licenses domestically. Impression Products refilled the spent cartridges and sold them in the U.S. The *en banc* opinion emphasizes that patent rights vary more among countries than copyrights, in particular because of the process, cost, and formalities associated with obtaining a patent. As a result, the court suggests that patent rights are more territorial than copyright and a different rule is appropriate. The court also dismisses the single reward theory for patents in an international context, suggesting that sales in a foreign market cannot be understood to bestow upon patentees "the reward available from American markets" that is granted by U.S. patent law.[26] An international exhaustion rule for patents might have seemed highly unlikely in the years since *Jazz Photo I* and *II* were decided—and particularly in the context of the U.S. position in trade negotiations. However, the Supreme Court's recent decision in *Kirtsaeng* signals a willingness to reconsider exhaustion in the copyright context, supported by policy considerations that apply to patent law, and the *Lexmark* opinion shows that the Federal Circuit is aware of the likelihood of Supreme Court review of this topic. Indeed, most of the reasoning in *Kirtsaeng* is consistent with the justification for the rule of national patent exhaustion and, given the global nature of commerce and consumption, their application to a global market provides a natural next step.

It appears that U.S. courts are receptive to the idea that the same arguments underlying exhaustion in the national context apply internationally. Nonetheless, strong objections remain.[27] These objections emphasize the benefits associated with the geographic price discrimination allowed by the current rule and the potential access concerns, particularly in the pharmaceutical industry, that might accompany a change. These arguments are best responded to separately. Although the access to medicine problem is often held up as the strongest example of the benefits of geographic price discrimination, the approval and distribution of medicine is subject to a complex regime, of which patent law is only a small part. I turn first to geographic price discrimination and claims that without it, rights holders will suffer huge losses and/or consumers will lose access to patented goods.

A. Questioning the Benefits of Geographic Price Discrimination

The economic argument against international exhaustion posits that the geographic price discrimination currently possible carries benefits that would be lost in a move to international exhaustion. According to this view, the social welfare effects of international exhaustion would result in less innovation and less access for consumers in low-income

---

[26] Lexmark Int'l, Inc. v. Impression Products, Inc., No. 2014-1617, 2016 WL 559042, at *34 (Fed. Cir. Feb. 12, 2016).

[27] In addition to the concerns addressed in this chapter, an international patent exhaustion rule would make more salient concerns already raised by national rules of exhaustion, such as the appropriate treatment of restrictive licensing and the need—or potential—for differential treatment for single-use versus self-replicating technologies. The proper response to restrictive licensing and treatment of easily-replicated or self-replicating technologies is beyond the scope of this chapter.

countries, so that the otherwise outdated distinction between foreign and domestic sales is justified as best suited to meet the objectives of the patent system. There are insufficient data for an empirical conclusion either way. However, the traditional argument against international exhaustion fails to recognize the costs of geographic price discrimination—costs that are exacerbated by growing income disparity. These include access costs for poorer consumers in otherwise high-income countries, and recognition that even with geographic price discrimination, poor consumers in low-income countries also have limited access. In addition, the models fail to account for substitute price discrimination measures firms would likely undertake to limit the contemplated ill effects. These substitute measures could result in more access as firms find other ways to target broad and diverse markets.

Price discrimination occurs when a seller, particularly a monopolist, charges different prices to different buyers, based on some measure of their willingness to pay.[28] Perfect (or "first-degree") price discrimination describes the situation of a monopolist who sells to each consumer at the highest price she is willing to pay. It is, however, a "never-attained theoretical limit."[29] If such a thing were possible, it would result in the greatest gain to the seller who could make more sales, extracting the highest possible price for each one. It would also theoretically result in greater consumer access to goods, because everyone willing to pay more than the marginal price of production of a good would be able to obtain it. However, there would be no consumer surplus; that is, no one would be able to buy the good for less than the highest price they were willing to pay. Instead, the consumer surplus that would have existed without discriminatory pricing would all accrue to the monopolist. This explains why both rights holders and consumer advocates might (theoretically) prefer a regime that allowed geographic price discrimination.

In reality, companies find many ways to engage in price discrimination, sometimes through volume discounts or "versioning" methods that differentiate consumers according to their willingness to pay—both types of second-degree price discrimination.[30] One example of versioning is the different amounts of memory or processing power that come with tablet computers and the regular introduction of newer models.[31] Third-degree price discrimination occurs when sellers "separate [buyers] into groups that correspond roughly to their wealth or eagerness."[32] The classic example is using demographic generalizations

---

[28] See ROBERT H. FRANK, MICROECONOMICS AND BEHAVIOR 389–95 (8th ed. 2010).

[29] *Ibid.* at 394 (explaining that imperfect knowledge of consumer preferences make first-degree price discrimination impossible).

[30] *Ibid.* at 395–96. Volume discounts are one type of second-degree price discrimination, in which the seller induces the buyer to reveal her preferences. One example of a volume discount is the pricing structure utilities companies use, charging less per kilowatt-hour after a certain limit has been reached. Companies can also try to differentiate consumers who are willing to pay more from those willing to pay less by setting "hurdles," such as mail-in rebates, that only some customers will undertake the nuisance of completing. "Versioning" refers to selling slightly different products, possibly introduced at slightly different times, such as hardcover, paperback, and electronic books. See *ibid.*; William W. Fisher III, *When Should We Permit Differential Pricing of Information?*, 55 UCLA L. REV. 1, 3–4 (2007).

[31] This differentiates consumers willing to pay more for greater computing capacity or for the newest version of electronics.

[32] Fisher, *supra* note 31, at 4.

to grant discounts to certain groups, such as student or senior discounts in movie theaters. All of these methods are imperfect,[33] but allow sellers to reach consumers they might otherwise not reach while maintaining higher prices for a large portion of the market. The success of such methods from the seller's viewpoint depends in part on how well the division differentiates markets. For example, versioning is successful if high-income buyers do not see a cheaper version of a product as a sufficient substitute for the more expensive one. It also requires that arbitrage be limited, so that low-cost buyers are unable to resell goods to high-cost buyers.[34]

The description and requirements of third-degree price discrimination apply to patents and a rule of national exhaustion.[35] A rule of national exhaustion allows patent holders to engage in geographic price discrimination, offering goods at lower prices in lower-income markets while preserving their ability to sell at higher prices in higher-income markets. This theoretically results in higher returns to the patent holder,[36] higher costs to consumers in high-income markets, and lower costs (and therefore greater access to goods) in lower-income markets. It follows that elimination of geographic price discrimination would result in lower returns to patent holders, lower prices in high-income markets, and less access for those in lower-income countries. This is because the threat of competition from goods bought abroad and imported for sale—parallel imports—would cause patent holders either to raise prices abroad or to decline to sell in low-income markets.[37] David Malueg and Marius Schwartz suggest, in this vein, that when there are great income disparities between countries, international exhaustion (and the uniform pricing that resulted) would lead to lower welfare than a system of national exhaustion.[38] Mattias Ganslandt and Keith Maskus also critique international exhaustion, disagreeing that it necessarily results in lower prices in high-income locations because of changes in distribu-

---

[33] For example, some students and retirees are quite wealthy.
[34] David A. Malueg & Marius Schwartz, *Parallel Imports, Demand Dispersion, and International Price Discrimination*, 37 J. INT'L ECON. 167, 170–71 (1994).
[35] The welfare effects of third-degree price discrimination are generally considered to be ambiguous. Hal R. Varian, *Price Discrimination and Social Welfare*, 75 AM. ECON. REV. 870 (1985) (generalizing results that price discrimination only increases welfare when it results in increased output).
[36] Alan O. Sykes, *TRIPS, Pharmaceuticals, Developing Countries, and the Doha "Solution,"* 3 CHI. J. INT'L L. 47, 64 (2002) ("Parallel importation invariably reduces the rents that are earned by pharmaceutical patent holders. To the degree that those rents are important to inducing worthwhile R&D investments, as suggested above, this effect is unfortunate."). But see Peter Yu, *The International Enclosure Movement*, 82 IND. L.J. 827, 844–45 (2007) (suggesting that Sykes "overstate[s] the practical impact of [parallel] importation").
[37] Malueg and Schwartz, *supra* note 34, at 171; see also Pinelopi Koujianou Goldberg, *Intellectual Property Rights Protection in Developing Countries: The Case of Pharmaceuticals*, 8 J. EUR. ECON. ASS'N. 326, 329–30 (2010) (arguing that pharmaceutical companies might not serve low-income countries or may raise prices there if there is parallel importing).
[38] *Ibid.* If patent holders continue to place goods on separate markets at vastly different prices, then it is true that consumers in high-income markets benefit from parallel trade. However, because the patent holder controls market entry of the patented goods worldwide, we can expect that her behavior *ex ante* will change. One way it might change is that she stops selling goods at different prices and introduces a worldwide price (with some variation to account for transportation and other distribution cost differences among regions). Another option is for the patent holder to choose not to make goods available in some low-income markets in order to preserve high returns in the high-income market.

tional structure that would result.[39] Kamal Saggi discusses the interests and motivations of different countries and companies, suggesting that the combination of intellectual property rights protection now mandated by TRIPS with an international exhaustion policy by high-income countries would result in welfare gains to companies and consumers in those countries at the expense of consumers in low-income countries.[40] This argument conflicts with the previous two with respect to patent holders, but the conclusion that national exhaustion allows for greater welfare is the same.

The economic arguments in favor of geographic price discrimination are not without caveats or critics. The caveats are that these theoretical models, while useful, make assumptions that are not necessarily borne out in reality or fail to account for reactions other than those modeled.[41] Gene Grossman and Edwin Lai suggest that international exhaustion may provide more support for innovation than national exhaustion by encouraging countries that use price controls to raise their prices, thus providing greater remuneration to patent holders.[42] Peter Yu raises a question about the extent to which firms currently engage in price discrimination that permits access to low-income markets.[43] In particular, Yu suggests that concerns about parallel imports in the pharmaceutical industry are overblown, both because many pharmaceutical companies have chosen not to enter lower-income markets even with a rule of national exhaustion and because the vast wealth disparities *within* some countries lead companies to target only the high-income market instead of selling at lower prices.[44] If the opportunity for geographic price discrimination

---

[39] Mattias Ganslandt & Keith E. Maskus, *Vertical Distribution, Parallel Trade, and Price Divergence in Integrated Markets*, 51 EUROPEAN ECON. REV. 943, 944 (2007) (suggesting that the conclusion that "permitting [parallel imports] unambiguously brings down retail prices in expensive locations is misleading"). Ganslandt and Maskus argue that in response to an international exhaustion regime, intellectual property rights holders may consolidate distributors and change wholesale pricing in ways that would obviate perceived benefits to consumers. *Ibid.* at 945.

[40] Kamal Saggi, *Market Power in the Global Economy: The Exhaustion and Protection of Intellectual Property*, 123 ECON. J. 131, 135 (2013). However, these results would change if strong intellectual property rights were necessary to induce importation of technology, for industries where there is a quality gap between innovator companies and imitators. *Ibid.*

[41] See e.g. Frederick M. Abbott, *Second Report (Final) to the Committee on International Trade Law of the International Law Association on the Subject of the Exhaustion of Intellectual Property Rights and Parallel Importation* (September 6, 2000), in 69TH CONFERENCE OF THE INT'L LAW ASSOC. 11 (July 2000) (noting Maskus's reminder that current static game theory models were incomplete and pointing to later work that shows how the reduction of trade barriers will result in increasing benefits from parallel trade).

[42] Gene M. Grossman & Edwin L.-C. Lai, *Parallel Imports and Price Controls*, 39 RAND J. ECON. 378, 380 (2008) (arguing that worldwide international exhaustion leads to more innovation than national exhaustion for industries with price controls because countries face the possibility that innovator companies will choose not to sell to them). Grossman and Lai base their argument on the idea that governments with price controls will tend to raise their price caps under a scheme of international exhaustion to ensure that producers will continue to serve their market. However, in the drug industry, many countries with price caps also require companies to fulfill demand and are able to threaten compulsory licensing when the demand is not met.

[43] Yu, *supra* note 36, at 844–45.

[44] *Ibid.*; see also Keith E. Maskus, *Ensuring Access to Essential Medicines: Some Economic Considerations*, 20 WIS. INT'L L.J. 563, 566 (2002) (explaining that sometimes "pharmaceutical firms and their distributors in poor countries may find it more profitable to sell drugs in low

is not resulting in greater access, the argument for keeping it gets weaker. Although Yu discusses the pharmaceutical market, this critique highlights the problem with using geographic markets as demand indicators. As discussed above, price discrimination works best when it successfully differentiates markets and arbitrage is limited. A rule against international exhaustion limits arbitrage, as discussed below, but its success at differentiating markets is questionable. For example, even developed countries have increasingly large levels of wealth disparity,[45] and therefore increasingly diverse levels of demand. The social welfare argument for geographic price discrimination becomes weaker when it does not result in greater access for low-income countries and simultaneously results in high prices for poorer members of developed countries. With regard to limitation of arbitrage: one reason that geographic price discrimination is so attractive to patent holders is that enforcement costs are relatively low. However, this is a benefit that only accrues to the patent holders. Borders are relatively easy to patrol for infringing goods,[46] and a hefty portion of the cost is borne by the government through its deployment of customs officials rather than through the efforts by the patent holder. This makes a national exhaustion rule more attractive to rights holders than other means of price discrimination, even when national markets are not an ideal basis for distinguishing among variable levels of demand.

Another critique is that geographic price discrimination should be compared with a regime in which sellers engage in other forms of price discrimination, rather than a world with uniform pricing. Patent holders in an international exhaustion regime will be unable to sell to large portions of foreign markets if they engage in uniform pricing (or choose not to sell abroad at all).[47] If their only choices are whether to sell and how to set the price, the arguments suggesting there will be a worldwide, uniform price or abandonment of foreign markets may be correct. However, patent holders may well choose to offer more versions of patented products and engage in second-degree price discrimination mechanisms to capture more of the market. This reaction would mitigate access concerns for consumers in low-income countries. In fact, if companies faced additional pressure to develop multiple versions of a good, we could expect increased access in both low- and high-income countries (where income disparity may already omit a number of people from the market).

---

volumes and high prices to wealthier patients with price-inelastic demand rather than in high volumes at low prices to poorer patients").

[45] See e.g. *An Overview of Growing Income Inequalities in OECD Countries: Main Findings*, in DIVIDED WE STAND: WHY INEQUALITY KEEPS RISING 21, 22 (OECD, 2011), available at www.oecd.org/els/soc/49499779.pdf. In the U.S., the GINI coefficient, a measure of income inequality that is 0 under conditions of perfect equality and 1 under complete inequality, has steadily risen from 0.399 in 1967 to 0.466 in 2001, according to information from the U.S. Census Bureau. See *Historical Income Tables-Income Equality*, http://web.archive.org/web/20070208142023/http://www.census.gov/hhes/www/income/histinc/ie6.html.

[46] Based on laws that require importers to declare goods and have them inspected, as opposed to domestic market transactions that may be conducted entirely privately and may therefore be difficult for patent holders to detect. 19 U.S.C. § 1484 (2012) (requiring that importers use reasonable care in making entries and classifying the imported merchandise).

[47] But see Ganslandt and Maskus, *supra* note 39, at 4 ("It is conceivable that wholesale prices may be set in a way that offsets or even counteracts the anticipated impacts of an open [parallel importation] regime.").

In sum, geographic price discrimination likely results in higher returns to patent holders. However, some of these higher returns are due to enforcement burdens taken on by customs officials. In addition, while geographic price discrimination theoretically allows for greater access by residents of low-income countries, in practice these populations are often underserved even in our current regime. Last, proponents of geographic price discrimination fail to account for the likely move of firms to other forms of price discrimination that might better segment and identify groups with differing demand curves. A rule of international exhaustion would not end price discrimination; it would likely encourage *better* price discrimination.

B. The Pharmaceutical Industry: Role of Regulation in Access

The pharmaceutical industry is often used in studies on the effects of parallel imports on industry and is often held up as an example of why geographic price discrimination is so desirable for patents. In part this is because access to medicine and healthcare plays a strong role in global notions of human rights. The very thing that sets the pharmaceutical industry apart for many who study patent law, however, has also resulted in heavy regulation of medicines by myriad national agencies. As a result of this regulation, the pharmaceutical industry operates outside normal markets in many ways, meaning that "free trade" is not an option and that geographic price differentials in the pharmaceutical industry are often dictated by these regulatory regimes, rather than by current rules against international exhaustion. Potential administration might focus on distribution and access to medicine, through the Food and Drug Administration (FDA), or on pricing differentials and market distortions, through the Department of Commerce.

Concerns about the availability of patented drugs in low-income countries are not merely academic.[48] The importance of access to medicines has spurred disagreement over the requirements of minimum levels of patent protection throughout the history of TRIPS.[49] One of the main points of contention between the global north and the global south during negotiations was the treatment of patents for pharmaceutical products. Many developing and least developed countries did not allow them, and there was great concern that implementing such regimes would lead to a crisis in access to medicine for poor countries.[50] Since the passage of TRIPS, advocates of access to medicine have pushed for flexibility in interpretation and application of the agreement, and India, for example, has chosen to make full use of flexibilities rather than simply adopting versions of other members' patent laws.[51]

---

[48] See Ellen t'Hoen, *TRIPS, Pharmaceutical Patents, and Access to Essential Medicines: A Long Way from Seattle to Doha*, 3 CHI. J. INT'L L. 27 (2002) (describing that 90 percent of those killed by infectious diseases each year are in the developing world and suggesting that "[t]he reasons for the lack of access to essential medicines are manifold, but in many cases the high prices of drugs are a barrier to needed treatments").

[49] See e.g. Amy Kapczynski, *Harmonization and Its Discontents: A Case Study of TRIPS Implementation in India's Pharmaceutical Sector*, 97 CALIF. L. REV. 1571, 1571–72 (2009).

[50] See CYNTHIA M. HO, ACCESS TO MEDICINE IN THE GLOBAL ECONOMY: INT'L AGREEMENTS ON PATENTS AND RELATED RIGHTS 91 (2011).

[51] Kapczynski, *supra* note 50, at 1573–74.

Some who oppose international patent exhaustion suggest it will result in less access for patients in lower-income countries and in insufficient rewards to companies engaged in expensive research and development in the industries. Whereas nongeographic forms of price discrimination may be effective for many consumer goods, these methods do not lend themselves easily to use in the pharmaceutical industry. For example, providing less effective versions of drugs for lower prices (versioning) is conceptually and ethically problematic. In practical terms, drugs belong to a type of technology that is not susceptible to the alternate forms of price discrimination that I suggest will generally replace geographic price discrimination. This is because drugs are relatively simple, and designed for optimal treatment efficacy and safety, not to meet other consumer interests. In ethical terms, the goal of access to medicine is not achieved if the medicine accessed is of such inferior quality that it would be undesirable as a parallel import. To return to the example of consumer electronics, there is no equivalent to adding or taking away memory for different models of electronics without changing the product's ability to perform its function.

As a result of these distinguishing characteristics, one of the strongest counter-arguments to a regime of international patent exhaustion focuses on the effects such a regime would have on patient populations in poor countries. The argument follows the general economic argument in favor of geographic price discrimination, discussed above. The first part of the argument is that major pharmaceutical companies will either sell globally for a high price, or refuse to sell at all in low-income markets because of the potential for parallel imports to erode the very large profits they glean in high-income markets. As a result, patient populations in least developed and developing countries will suffer. The second part of the argument against international exhaustion centers on the high cost of research and development for drugs and the importance patents have in funding future research.[52] Under this argument, the lower gains to pharmaceutical companies under an international exhaustion regime would lower incentives to innovate significantly. Thus, in addition to a lack of access to drugs today, there will be a dearth of new drugs in the future. From either perspective, drugs are special. Access is of great importance in the area of health, and profits derived from patents are valued more by innovators in this area.

The drug industry might provide a compelling thought experiment into the problems that would accompany a rule of international exhaustion, but the same access concerns that lead to opposition to the strong patent protection required by TRIPS also motivate special treatment of drugs by most countries in ways that make international patent exhaustion less relevant and simultaneously offer means of minimizing any ill effects that would accompany an international exhaustion regime. This special treatment takes the form of domestic regulation of drug sales and medical treatment in addition to provisions in TRIPS and the subsequent Doha Declaration that are meant to ensure access to medicine.

Many countries have an agency equivalent to the U.S. FDA that ensures the safety, efficacy, and quality of medicines placed on their national markets. These agencies

---

[52] See e.g. Henry Grabowski, *Patents and New Product Development in the Pharmaceutical and Biotechnology Industries*, in THE PROCESS OF NEW DRUG DISCOVERY AND DEVELOPMENT 533, 535 (Charles G. Smith & James T. O'Donnell eds., 2d ed. 2002).

require the submission of test results proving that drugs for which approval is sought are safe and effective, in addition to showing that they are manufactured in ways that ensure their quality. In addition to FDA-equivalent agencies, many countries have centralized healthcare and single-payer insurance. In these countries, prices for drugs are negotiated with representatives from the government, which serves as another gatekeeper to the market. An additional control on drug prices may be implemented at the national level through compulsory licensing, allowed by TRIPS in some circumstances. In the U.S., the Commerce Department and the International Trade Commission (ITC) work together with Customs and Border Patrol to keep out imports that result in unfair competition. These agencies (and perhaps others) all control access to their respective markets in different ways.

If the economic argument were right, a patent holder could respond to the introduction of international exhaustion by not selling drugs in low-income markets at all. This would be undesirable if it resulted in a lack of access to life-saving medicines. Alternatively, countries faced without access could engage in compulsory licensing to produce generic versions of life-saving drugs.[53] This result would still insulate the pioneer drug makers from parallel imports because drugs produced pursuant to a compulsory license would not be interpreted as authorized sales.[54] However, this result imposes costs (lost sales to the otherwise willing drug company, procedural costs of procuring a license, and, although relatively small, the costs to generic drug companies of reverse engineering). With a small margin for profits in least developed countries to start with, these inefficiencies could be problematic to the access cause. A better policy would encourage patent holders to manufacture and sell drugs to low-income markets and reserve compulsory licenses for situations where patent holders are unwilling to do so. The position of the FDA as a market gatekeeper means that drugs sold to certain countries, or under certain conditions, could be exempted from international exhaustion, thus encouraging drug companies to sell drugs at the cost of production (or below) without concerns about parallel imports.

The strong control of market entry exercised by the FDA (and equivalent agencies in other developed countries) could be expanded to exempt drugs sold to least developed countries from international exhaustion.[55] Drugs must go through an approval process

---

[53] See TRIPS, art. 31 (allowing and setting parameters for compulsory licensing).

[54] In addition, the compulsory licensing provisions of TRIPS require that goods produced pursuant to such a license be primarily for the domestic market, although manufacturers in a given country can also do so for a particular foreign market that does not have manufacturing capabilities. TRIPS, art. 31. Similarly, for countries in which inventors have chosen not to seek patents, manufacture and sales of those products would not be infringing, but they would also not be "authorized," and thus sale would not exhaust the patent holder's rights in other countries.

[55] A rule against unauthorized reimportation is already part of the FDA's governing statute. See Federal Food, Drug, and Cosmetic Act, 21 U.S.C. § 381(d)(1) (2012) (providing that "no [prescription] drug ... which is manufactured in a State and exported may be imported into the United States unless the drug is imported by the manufacturer of the drug."). Kevin Outterson explains how that law has been used to limit the reimportation of drugs produced in the U.S. and sent to Canada. Kevin Outterson, *Pharmaceutical Arbitrage: Balancing Access and Innovation in International Prescription Drug Markets*, 5 YALE J. HEALTH POL'Y L. & ETHICS 193, 213–14 (2005) ("The law was ostensibly intended to address safety concerns for the U.S. pharmaceutical supply

before they may be marketed. In the U.S., the FDA has a complex process for companies wishing to sell drugs—patented or not—to patients that aims to ensure the drugs are both safe and effective.[56] The registration of drugs and approval of processes mean that the FDA serves as a gatekeeper for all who wish to sell drugs in the U.S. market, and an expansion in this role to exclude drugs first sold in least developed countries would not exceed the scope of the agency's current expertise.

The complicated effects of international exhaustion in the drug industry do not only concern questions of access for least developed countries. The drug industry is appropriate for special treatment in large part because it is subject to such strong price controls in so many countries.[57] These market conditions mean that in many places, patent holders have little control over the price at which they introduce products to the market, making the single reward justification for international exhaustion less compelling. Under a regime of price control, the autonomy of the patent holder in choosing to place goods on the market at a given price is no longer so clear. While patent holders may retain the choice of *whether* to sell, they no longer decide a price. And, as discussed above, the threat of compulsory licensing means that companies have less bargaining power when setting prices. For developed or developing countries that engage in price controls, patented medicines are bought at prices much lower than in countries (like the U.S.) that do not engage in such measures. And unlike the case of compulsory licensing, such sales are authorized. A regime of international exhaustion could be devastating to patent holding companies facing competition from imports in countries that engage in such pricing.

The potential for lower prices of imported goods would not be a consequence of comparative advantage in manufacturing or the benefits of increased competition, but a result of disparate regulatory control. Europe provides an interesting example. It has seen an increase in parallel trade in pharmaceutical products because the European Union (EU) practices regional exhaustion. The combination of regional exhaustion with strong price controls has proved problematic, as parallel traders engage in arbitrage that does not bring down the cost of medicines in countries that pay more for them, but serves only to appropriate profits that would otherwise go to patent holding pharmaceutical companies. In particular, pharmaceutical wholesalers in Greece ordered a surplus of medicines at the negotiated price there and then sold the drugs in Germany, at the higher, negotiated price there, to the benefit of neither consumers nor the patent holder. As a result, courts have become sympathetic to companies that limit their supply in accordance with the demand of a given market.[58]

One possible solution would be to exempt pharmaceuticals from parallel importation

---

chain, but its effect is to prevent international pharmaceutical arbitrage or parallel trade." (citations omitted)).

[56] See 21 U.S.C. § 393(b)(2)(B) (establishing the FDA and giving its mission as "protect[ing] the public health by ensuring that . . . drugs are safe and effective"); see also Ho, *supra* note 50, at 13–16, 94 (describing similar agencies in other countries).

[57] John A. Vernon *et al.*, *The Economics of Pharmaceutical Price Regulation and Importation: Refocusing the Debate*, 32 AM. J.L. & MED. 175, 176 (2006).

[58] See e.g. Case C-53/03, Synetairismos Farmakopoion Aitolias & Akarnanias (Syfait) v. GlaxoSmithKline AEVE, [2005] E.C.R. I-4609, 4637 (opining that GlaxoSmithKline AEVE was justified in refusing to meet in full orders it received from Greek pharmaceutical wholesalers in order to limit parallel trade "where the price differential giving rise to the parallel trade is a result

entirely. Such a move would recognize that although similar levels of patent protection exist in all WTO member countries, other market forces intervene to alter the benefits a patent confers. In this sense, it is the unequal protection afforded to pharmaceutical products by patents that creates barriers to trade in patented goods. However, as with any rule targeting a particular technology area, this could result in line-drawing problems. The scope of the exemption from international exhaustion could extend to all pharmaceutical products or methods of treating diseases using chemical compounds, but it could also cover treatment with biosimilars. Implementing legislation would have to describe a category that itself is growing due to innovation.

While implementation of a wide-scale exemption could be delegated to the FDA, another possibility for treatment of drugs sold subject to price regulations would draw upon trade mechanisms and the expertise of the agencies that implement them. Under this potential scheme, imports of patented pharmaceuticals from countries engaged in price controls could be treated as potentially dumped goods under trade law, sold in a non-market industry (akin to non-market economies in trade).[59] Under our trade law, foreign manufacturers and importers cannot sell goods in the U.S. at less than fair value; that is, they cannot "dump" their goods on the U.S. market, because of the harm that would do to domestic industry.[60] If such dumping is found, the Department of Commerce calculates the amount by which the sale is lower than normal value and taxes imports accordingly, raising the prices of the imported goods on the U.S. market so that they are in "fair" competition with domestically produced goods. In the drug industry, drugs imported from single-payer system countries would surely sell for less than domestically produced drugs, but because their U.S. prices would be comparable to those of the home market, they would not usually qualify as dumped. However, there is special treatment of goods that come from a non-market economy, defined as a foreign country that does "not operate on market principles of cost or pricing structures, so that sales of merchandise in such country do not reflect the fair value of the merchandise."[61] Drugs don't function according to market principles of pricing.[62] Therefore, the Department of Commerce would be free to compare their prices in the U.S. with a "constructed fair market value," which would likely be the market value in the U.S. The treatment of imports of drugs from single-payer systems as dumped merchandise is one possibility for controlling the potential downsides of a system of international exhaustion.

---

of State intervention in the Member State of export to fix the price there at a level lower than that which prevails elsewhere in the Community").

[59] Dumping refers to selling goods in a foreign market at lower than "fair value." Most often, this is manifested in selling goods for a lower price in a foreign market than in the producer's home market. Luke P. Bellocchi, *The Effects of and Trends in Executive Policy and Court of International Trade (CIT) Decisions Concerning Antidumping and the Non-Market Economy (NME) of the People's Republic of China*, 10 N.Y. INT'L L. REV. 177, 179–80 (1997).

[60] JOHN H. JACKSON, *Dumping in International Trade: Its Meaning and Context*, in ANTIDUMPING LAW AND PRACTICE 4–5, 11 (1990).

[61] 19 U.S.C. § 1677(18)(A) (2012).

[62] See Vernon *et al.*, *supra* note 57, at 176.

IV. CONCLUSION

Courts in the U.S. are grappling with whether to adopt a rule of international exhaustion in patent law. Such a move would bring the law in line with copyright law and vindicate the practical goals of the *Kirtsaeng* opinion. But more importantly, applying the theories that justify national exhaustion to international sales and movements of goods will increase competition and lower barriers to trade. Modern trade law operates under a recognition that greater global welfare comes from increased competition and freedom for downstream innovators, retailers, and consumers. This change would involve increased costs to patent holders, but it is unlikely that those increases will be as drastic as some argue. In addition, the change may encourage other forms of price discrimination that better track differences in consumer preferences. Some opponents of international patent exhaustion suggest that it would adversely affect pharmaceutical research and access to medicine worldwide. However, this concern can be addressed through one or more of the regulatory bodies governing approval and distribution of drugs in any given country. The strong regulation of medicines make the area particularly unsuited to the arguments underlying international patent exhaustion because there is not a "free" market in drugs that would benefit from greater cross-border trade. However, these regulatory bodies are also well-suited to counteract any potential ill effects from an international regime. This chapter has suggested a number of possibilities for regulatory maintenance of geographic price discrimination through the regulatory structure of the U.S. These suggestions have the advantage that they allow expert agencies to explicitly pursue the goals of access to medicine while maintaining incentives to innovate in this important industry.

15. Patent exhaustion rules and self-replicating technologies
*Christopher Heath**

I. INTRODUCTION

The theories on patent exhaustion, be it the theory of implied license[1] or the theory of first marketing,[2] are unanimous in that exhaustion applies to a specific product that has been put into the market. These theories apply to a given product that has been put on the market by its lawful owner or with his consent, yet cannot have an effect on the marketing of other products that fall under the claims of the same patent. Under the theories supporting patent exhaustion, it is not the "patent right" that exhausts, but the right to use the patent to prohibit the further commercial use of the specific product that has been first marketed. In other words, the exhaustion of the patent right to exclude others from making, marketing, or further selling the patented products applies only, and is limited to, the specific product at issue.

One may wonder, however, what should happen in the cases where the product for which the patent right has exhausted is capable of self-replicating, i.e., of multiplying itself, thereby producing progeny that also falls under the patent claim. This issue is of particular relevancy for patents over genetically modified seeds or animals. If, say, a claim reads "[a] glyphosate-tolerant plant cell comprising a DNA-molecule [with the following specifications],"[3] or "[a] transgenic human animal that carries in the genome of its somatic or germ cells a nucleic acid sequence,"[4] then the most common (if not the only) way of obtaining such patented product would be by natural breeding of those products already on the market. Ordinarily, the sale of patented seeds or animals carries with it the (implied or explicit) license to use the product for breeding purposes and, therefore, produce first-generation offspring, but does not extend to the production of a further generation. If exhaustion rules were to apply to all further offspring, this would amount to a license for the production of otherwise infringing products in direct competition with those marketed by the patentee (at least to the extent that third and further generation products would be stable enough to still possess the advantageous characteristics of the first-generation product).

---

* Member of the Boards of Appeal, European Patent Office; former Head of the Asia Department, Max-Planck Institute for Innovation and Competition.

[1] Betts v. Willmott, [1871] 6 L.R.Ch. 239, 245; Nat'l Phonograph Co. of Australia v. Menck, [1911] 28 R.P.C. 229; Roussel Uclaf S.A. v. Hockley Int'l Ltd., [1996] 113 R.P.C. 441. See *infra* II.

[2] Josef Kohler, Handbuch des Deutschen Patentrechts 452 (1900). An English translation of Josef Kohler's passages on exhaustion can be found in Christopher Heath, *Exhaustion and Patent Rights*, in Patent Law in Global Perspective 419, 424 (Margo Bagley & Ruth Okediji eds., 2014). See *infra* II.

[3] EP Patent No. 0546090 (filed August 28, 1991) for glyphosate tolerant plants.

[4] EP Publication No. 1170994 (filed April 20, 2000) (concerning "Enviro Pig").

In the United States (U.S.), most cases related to modified seeds were decided on the basis of contractual restrictions on the buyer.[5] Yet, in the first case that was heard by the U.S. Supreme Court, *Bowman v. Monsanto*,[6] there was no contractual restriction due to the fact that Mr. Bowman had purchased the seed from a so-called "grain elevator" that had obtained a variety of different seeds without any contractual obligations or limitations as to the use of such seeds. In its decision, the Court of Appeals for the Federal Circuit had affirmed that there were no specific exhaustion rules for self-replicating technologies.[7] It is indeed difficult to see why the (purposeful) reconstruction of a patented machine would amount to infringement (as reconstruction can never be placed under the rules of exhaustion), while the (mostly purposeful) plantation of patented seeds with the aim of obtaining progeny would not. In both instances, the aim is to obtain a product that undoubtedly falls under the patent claim and that would be in direct competition with those products sold by the patentee under the monopolistic right.

In Europe, the case that the Court of Justice of the European Union (CJEU) has decided in this area, also on a claim brought forward by the Monsanto Corporation, was *Monsanto v. Cefetra*,[8] which concerned the reverse question: not the issue as to whether the patent right extended to progeny, but whether the patent right was limited to products where the genetically modified material could still "perform its function." After all, for the product that was sold (soya flour), this was clearly not the case.

In this chapter, I analyze the decisions of the U.S. Supreme Court and the CJEU in this area and offer some critical consideration on the challenges that apply to self-replicating technologies with respect to the applicability of the traditional theories of intellectual property exhaustion. This chapter proceeds as follows. In section II, I briefly elaborate on the theories of intellectual property exhaustion. In section III, I review the basic principles of the type of technology under consideration in the cases decided, respectively, by the U.S. Supreme Court and the CJEU. In sections IV and V, I address, respectively, the U.S. and the European Union (EU) decision and offer a critical analysis of both decisions. In section VI, I briefly conclude the chapter with some critical considerations over the tension between traditional concepts of patent law and so called "self-replicating" technologies.

II. THEORIES OF PATENT EXHAUSTION: IMPLIED LICENSE AND REMUNERATION BY FIRST MARKETING

To date, two primary theories have shaped the interpretation and application of the principle of patent exhaustion. In this section, I briefly summarize these theories.

First, the theory of implied license was developed by the English High Court in *Betts v. Willmott*[9] and subsequently elaborated by the Privy Council in *Nat'l Phonograph*

---

[5] Monsanto v. McFarling, 302 F.3d 1291 (Fed. Cir. 2002); see also Monsanto v. Scruggs, 459 F.3d 1328 (Fed. Cir. 2006).
[6] Bowman v. Monsanto Co., 133 S. Ct. 1761 (2013).
[7] Monsanto v. Bowman, 657 F.3d 1341 (Fed. Cir. 2011).
[8] Case C-428/09, Monsanto v. Cefetra, [2010] E.C.R. I-09961.
[9] Betts v. Willmott, [1871] 6 L.R.Ch. 239, 245.

Co. of Australia v. Menck.[10] This case is still good law in the United Kingdom.[11] The gist of this rule is that the patentee can only invoke restrictive conditions for goods that have been lawfully marketed if these restrictions have been brought home with the purchaser. The license to freely deal with a product is thus "implied" unless there is an express limitation that is made known to the purchaser. The rationale of this doctrine is the freedom of commerce: there should not be limitations to the free circulation of goods unless such limitations are apparent to any subsequent buyer of the goods.

Second, the theory of remuneration by first marketing was first advocated by the Germany academic Josef Kohler, in his book on patent law published in 1900.[12] In particular, taking an approach that was different from the doctrine of implied license, Kohler found it unsatisfactory that the seller of protected goods should be in a position to limit their subsequent commercial distribution at all.[13] To Kohler, the free flow of goods required a notion of absolute, inherent limits of patent law.[14] Kohler, thus, came up with two theses and one conclusion. His first thesis concerned the rationale of patent protection. Kohler elaborated the theory that patent protection was meant to grant the patentee a reward for his inventive efforts by the allocation of a monopolistic right that allowed the exclusion of all others from the commercial exploitation of the patented invention.[15] Kohler's second thesis related to the connection between the forms of commercial use of a patented product. According to him, the different forms of patent use (production, advertisement, offer for sale, sale, rental, lending, export, import) could not be viewed in isolation, but were intrinsically linked with each other.[16] In fact, these forms of use could be viewed as different expressions of one common right. Based on these two theses, Kohler's conclusion was the following: to the extent that the patent gave the patentee the opportunity for a reward by excluding others, this reward could be obtained once for each product.[17] Yet, once the patentee himself had used the patented invention with respect to a certain product, he could no longer exercise his patent right for this specific product.[18] This limitation was not confined to the form of use the patentee had chosen, but, since the different forms of use flowed from each other, had an effect for all subsequent acts of commercial use of this product. Accordingly, if the patentee had sold (or leased or distributed for free) a patented article, he could no longer exclude third parties from making any sort of commercial use of this product, e.g., by its subsequent sale, rental, or export. This connection between the forms of use was justified by Kohler's underlying thesis of the patent's function: if the patentee was granted one chance of obtaining a reward for each patented product, the first act of commercial use satisfied this requirement, and the patentee was subsequently not entitled to exercise his patent

---

[10] Nat'l Phonograph Co. of Australia v. Menck, [1911] 28 R.P.C. 229.
[11] Roussel Uclaf S.A. v. Hockley Int'l Ltd., [1996] 113 R.P.C. 441.
[12] See generally KOHLER, *supra* note 2.
[13] *Ibid.* at 454.
[14] *Ibid.* at 453.
[15] *Ibid.* at 427, 454.
[16] *Ibid.* at 452.
[17] *Ibid.* at 454.
[18] *Ibid.*

right with respect to this product, whatever form of use was made. The rationale of this theory is the just reward of the patentee and the proper balancing of interests between patentee and society.

In this respect, it is important to note that the U.S. principle of "first sale" is different from Kohler's doctrine in two respects. First, according to Kohler it is not only the first *sale* that can trigger exhaustion, but rather the first act of *commercial marketing*. Second, that exhaustion as a principle of public order cannot be limited by contract.

III. THE SELF-REPLICATING TECHNOLOGY AS PATENTED BY MONSANTO

The cases analyzed in sections IV and V of this chapter both concern patents owned by the company Monsanto, respectively in the U.S. and in Europe. These patents, which essentially relate to the same products, are based on the same U.S. priority patent application No. 576537 of August 31, 1990, "Glyphosate tolerant 5-enolpyruvyshikimate-3-phosphate synthases." The corresponding patents are, in the U.S., USRE 39247E,[19] and in the EU, EP 0546090.[20] Due to a different history or examination / opposition /reissue of the respective patents, the claims of the U.S. Patent and European Patent are somewhat different. However, both patents contain claims directed to a DNA sequence: a glyphosate-tolerant plant cell and a glyphosate-tolerant plant.

In particular, the claims of the U.S. Patent read as follows. Claim 1 reads, "An isolated DNA molecule which encodes an EPSPS enzyme having the sequence of SEQ ID NO:3."[21]

Claim 7 covers "a DNA molecule of claim 6 in which the structural DNA sequence encodes an EPSPS,"[22] and claim 15 covers "a method of producing genetically transformed plants which are tolerant toward glyphosate herbicide, comprising the steps of . . ."[23] Further, claim 27 is directed towards a glyphosate-tolerant plant.[24]

On the other hand, the claims of the European Patent read as follows. Claim 1 reads, "An isolated DNA sequence encoding a Class II EPSPS enzyme, said enzyme being an EPSPS enzyme having a Km for phosphoenolpyruvate (PEP) between 1–150µM and a Ki (glyphosate)/Km(PEP) ratio between 3–500, which enzyme is . . ."[25]

Claim 6 of the European Patent is directed to "[a] DNA sequence encoding a Class II EPSPS enzyme selected from the group of SEQ ID No:3 and SEQ ID No:5."[26] Claim 14 is directed to "[a] method of producing genetically transformed plants which are tolerant toward glyphosate herbicide, comprising the steps of . . ."[27] Claim 20 is directed to "[a]

---

[19] U.S. Patent No. 05633435 (filed September 13, 1994).
[20] European Patent No. 0546090 B1 (filed August 28, 1991).
[21] U.S. Patent No. 05633435, claim 1 (filed September 13, 1994).
[22] *Ibid.* claim 7.
[23] *Ibid.* claim 15.
[24] *Ibid.* claim 27.
[25] EP Patent No. 0546090 B1, claim 1 (filed August 28, 1991).
[26] *Ibid.* claim 6.
[27] *Ibid.* claim 14.

glyphosate tolerant plant cell comprising a DNA molecule of claims 8, 9, 12 or 13,"[28] and Claim 24 to "A glyphosate tolerant plant comprising cells of Claim 20."[29]

In simpler words, both the U.S. and the European Patents concern a new class of EPSPS genes (to be) inserted into plant cells in order to enhance the glyphosate (basis of a herbicide) tolerance of a plant cell transformed with said DNA molecule, and a corresponding method to this end, as well as the plants comprising said plant cells. The plants so modified show a resistance towards glyphosate herbicides that in ordinary plants inhibit the endogenous enzyme EPSPS, which is essential for the growth of the plant. As the members of the new class of EPSPS are less sensitive to inhibition, the said plants display tolerance to glyphosate. Thus, when a field is sprayed with a glyphosate herbicide, all plants die with the exception of those plants genetically modified by introduction of said genes. The glyphosate herbicide sold by Monsanto is called Roundup Ready, and the plants genetically modified according to the patent are resistant to this herbicide, while everything else is essentially not.

The patentee (Monsanto) has developed a number of plants with the patented modification, namely, soya, cotton, maize, and canola (oilseed rape). Seeds are sold to farmers together with the herbicide, and to the extent that the seeds are patented, Monsanto is able to control (and, thus, prohibit) the propagation of harvested seed. Patent law, unlike the law of plant varieties, does not contain an exception for farmers to propagate material obtained from the propagation of first-generation seed, for that reason the protection of propagation material under patent law has always been regarded as a difficult issue.[30] No less problematic seem to be Monsanto's strategies to "persuade" farmers to plant genetically modified seed,[31] or to enforce its patent rights over genetically modified seed against those farmers who do not comply with the terms and conditions of use.[32] An issue

---

[28] *Ibid.* claim 20.
[29] *Ibid.* claim 24.
[30] Margaret Llewellyn, *Perspectives on Patenting Biological Material, in* INDUSTRIAL PROPERTY IN THE BIO-MEDICAL AGE 73 (Christopher Heath & Anselm Kamperman Sanders eds., 2003).
[31] Françoise Gérard, *Agricultura Patenteada*, LE MONDE DIPLOMATIQUE (February 2009), available at www.diplomatique.org.br/artigo.php?id=327. She describes the case of Burkina Faso and Monsanto's methods of spreading the use of genetically modified cotton. An overview of Monsanto's methods is given in MARIE-MONIQUE ROBIN, LE MONDE SELON MONSANTO: DE LA DIOXINE AUX OGM, UNE MULTINATIONALE QUI VOUS VEUT DU BIEN (2008). See also MARIE-MONIQUE ROBIN, MIT GIFT UND GENEN – WIE DER BIOTECH-KONZERN MONSANTO UNSERE WELT VERÄNDERT (Dagmar Mallet trans., 2d ed. 2009); *O Mundo Segundo a Monsanto*, RADICALLIVROS (July 10, 2012), available at www.radicallivros.com.br/livros/o-mundo-segundo-a-monsanto/. Interestingly enough, no English translation seems to have been published yet. Subsequent citations of this book refer to the German version. In general, the technology in the patent at issue seems to be problematic for two reasons: first, an increasing resistance to Roundup Ready (RR) over time may require higher doses of the herbicide; and, second, a switch to non-modified seeds is not immediately possible due to contamination of the soil with RR. Other technologies used by Monsanto, e.g., maize genetically modified with the bacterium thuringiensis, do not have these disadvantages.
[32] A case that has come to wider attention is Monsanto v. Schmeisser, argued before the Canadian courts and ultimately decided by the Canadian Supreme Court: Monsanto v. Schmeisser, [2004] 1 S.C.R. 902, 2004 SCC 34. In this case, the defendant's field of canola was found to contain more than 95 percent of the variety as modified by Monsanto, although it could not be proven that he had purchased any seed from the plaintiff, or that he had used the herbicide Roundup Ready in

of future litigation may be the liability for contamination of fields without genetically modified seeds where such contamination leads to the loss of a certification, or no longer allows the harvested material to be sold with certain characteristics.

IV. THE UNITED STATES SUPREME COURT DECISION IN *BOWMAN V. MONSANTO*

A. Case History

Monsanto usually determines the conditions of use for its genetically modified (GM) seeds by contract. The contract allows the purchasers to use the seeds as first-generation propagating material, while the harvested second-generation cannot be used for this purpose. Seeds for the purposes of propagation can normally be obtained only under contract.

The plaintiff, Mr. Bowman, obtained part of his GM seeds from a grain elevator, a place where seeds of different origin are sold for human or animal consumption. Most of these seeds were in fact Monsanto's GM seeds, and Mr. Bowman used them as propagating material in the same way as those directly purchased from Monsanto, also in combination with the herbicide Roundup Ready. Different from the above-mentioned *Schmeisser* case, Mr. Bowman made actual use of the glyphosate tolerance of the plants, and did so for several seasons. Sued by Monsanto, Mr. Bowman contended that there was no contract that prevented him from replanting the seeds, and that the patent exhaustion doctrine permitted an unfettered use of the purchased seeds, as these had been lawfully sold by Monsanto. The first and second instance courts did not agree. The Federal Circuit reasoned that patent exhaustion did not protect Mr. Bowman because he had "created a newly infringing article."[33] The "right to use" a patented article "does not include the right to construct an essentially new article on the template of the original, for the right to make the article remains with the patentee."[34]

B. The Decision

The most relevant part of the U.S. Supreme Court decision with respect to the issue of the applicability of the doctrine of exhaustion to self-replicating technologies is reproduced below. Notably, the Court stated:

---

order to spray his plants. In a 5:4 decision, the court affirmed infringement, yet denied damages, as the defendant had not gained any commercial advantage by use of the modified variety. The minority denied infringement, as the infringement claim was directed towards the use of plants and a certain plant variety, although the patent had specifically disclaimed plants and plant varieties. For details, see Brad Sherman, *Biological Inventions and the Problem of Passive Infringement*, in INDUSTRIAL PROPERTY IN THE BIO-MEDICAL AGE 105 (Christopher Heath & Anselm Kamperman Sanders eds., 2003).

[33] Monsanto v. Bowman, 657 F.3d 1341, 1348 (Fed. Cir. 2011).
[34] *Ibid.*

Under the patent exhaustion doctrine, Bowman could resell the patented soybeans he purchased from the grain elevator; so too he could consume the beans himself or feed them to his animals. Monsanto, although the patent holder, would have no business interfering in those uses of Roundup Ready beans. But the exhaustion doctrine does not enable Bowman to make *additional* patented soybeans without Monsanto's permission (either express or implied). And that is precisely what Bowman did.[35]

In other words, the Court highlighted the distinction between the actual "use" of an article, which is permissible once that article has been lawfully marketed, and the "making" or "reproducing" of an identical article, which is not permissible also after the article has been lawfully marketed. The Court also added that:

[b]ecause Bowman thus reproduced Monsanto's patented invention, the exhaustion doctrine does not protect him. Were the matter otherwise, Monsanto's patent would provide scant benefit. After inventing the Roundup Ready trait, Monsanto would, to be sure, "receiv[e] [its] reward" for the first seeds it sells. *Univis*, 316 U.S., at 251. But in short order, other seed companies could reproduce the product and market it to growers, thus depriving Monsanto of its monopoly. And farmers themselves need only buy the seed once, whether from Monsanto, a competitor, or (as here) a grain elevator. The grower could multiply his initial purchase, and then multiply that new creation, *ad infinitum*—each time profiting from the patented seed without compensating its inventor . . . The exhaustion doctrine is limited to the "particular item" sold to avoid just such a mismatch between invention and reward.[36]

Here, the court applied Josef Kohler's "remuneration doctrine" as the rationale for the exhaustion doctrine.[37] Under the traditional English common law doctrine of implied licenses, the Court would have had more difficulties in reaching and explaining this result, as no such restriction on the seeds had been "brought home" with the buyer as part of sale of the seeds.[38] This is why the English courts, as highlighted below, generally need to distinguish between the act of "repair" (fixing an article and thereby maintaining its identity) and "reconstruction" (making an article from scratch, or replacing so many parts of an existing article that it is equivalent to a new one) and limit the implied license doctrine to the former. An interesting point not touched upon in the Court's decision, however, is the exhaustion of the method embodied in claim 15 where the "method" equals natural propagation: method patents do not relate to products, and it is not *a priori* clear if the exhaustion doctrine can be applied to method patents in the same way as product patents. After all, by replicating seeds, also the patented method is used, suggesting an infringement of the latter.

---

[35] *Ibid.*
[36] *Ibid.*
[37] See the explanations *supra* under II. The patent monopoly allows the patentee to obtain a one-time reward for each patented product. Due to the connection between the forms of use, exhaustion can only refer to a product that has been marketed by the patentee.
[38] Obviously, a seed obtained from replication cannot carry any limitation as to its use, and contractual limitations can only bind the parties to the contract.

C. Analysis

(1) General exhaustion rules and biological material

As I noted above, it should first be highlighted that the decision of the Supreme Court follows the traditional distinction that was originally elaborated by Josef Kohler between the *acts of use* of a patented product (which are exhausted after the first marketing of the products) and the *acts of manufacture* of the products (that can never exhaust). In particular, as stated by Kohler:

> The use and distribution of patented products, be it that the product or the manufacture is patented, is always in connection with the manufacture, it is a continuation of the latter, it is a further economic development of the patent exploitation that lies in the manufacture.[39]

The decision also follows the principle established by the United Kingdom (U.K.) House of Lords in *United Wire Ltd. v. Screen Repair Services (Scotland) et al.* in 2000: "The sale of a patented article cannot confer an implied licence to make another or exhaust the right of the patentee to prevent others from being made."[40]

Different from what was argued by the plaintiff in *Bowman v. Monsanto* in the U.S., it is not necessary to create special exhaustion rules for self-replicating material in order to arrive at this solution (but see the observations below). The economic rationale for the exhaustion doctrine as developed by Josef Kohler—the one-time remuneration for each patented article put on the market—implies that a remuneration can be obtained by the patentee for each item marketed by the patentee within the scope of the patent right.[41] If there was exhaustion for self-replicating technologies, no remuneration could be obtained for further generation seeds although these fall within the patented monopoly. This is a bit like arguing that a copyright owner cannot prevent further digital copies being made from one copy that has been lawfully sold.

Still, a number of jurisdictions have introduced specific legislation in order to clarify the boundaries between exhaustion and self-replication technologies. For example, the EU Biotechnology Directive stipulates in Articles 8 and 10 the following:

> Article 8
> 1. The protection conferred by a patent on a biological material possessing specific characteristics as a result of the invention shall extend to any biological material derived from that biological material through propagation or multiplication in an identical or divergent form and possessing those same characteristics.[42]

---

[39] KOHLER, *supra* note 2, at 453. For Josef Kohler, this already follows from the connection between the forms of use and the fact that exhaustion is triggered by the manufacture rather than the first marketing.

[40] United Wire Ltd. v. Screen Repair Servs. (Scotland), [2000] 4 All E.R. 535 (H.L.).

[41] For Kohler, contractual arrangements could not extend the limits of patent exhaustion. This part of his doctrine seems to have got lost in the U.S. discussion on exhaustion. But see the critical remarks by Daryl Lim, *Living with Monsanto*, 2015 MICH. ST. L. REV. 1 (2015).

[42] Directive 98/44/EC of the European Parliament and of the Council of July 6, 1998 on the Legal Protection of Biotechnological Inventions, [1998] O.J. L213/13, 14 [hereinafter Biotechnology Directive].

Article 10
The protection referred to in Articles 8 and 9 shall not extend to biological material obtained from the propagation or multiplication of biological material placed on the market in the territory of a Member State by the holder of the patent or with his consent, where the multiplication or propagation necessarily results from the application for which the biological material was marketed, provided that the material obtained is not subsequently used for other propagation or multiplication.[43]

Interestingly, the EU legislation is the only law applicable in industrialized countries on this matter, although other jurisdictions include equally relevant provisions. For example, the Intellectual Property Code of Brazil, in Article 43, contains specific rules on the limits of patent rights.[44] Following the general exhaustion rule under Article 43, subsections IV, V, and VI of the same provision explicitly concern living matter. Subsection V, in particular, allows patented products over living subject matter to be used as propagation material, only if such use is without profit-making purposes—a provision that applies to second-generation material and corresponds to the farmer's privilege envisaged under the International Union for the Protection of Plant Varieties (UPOV).[45] Subsection VI additionally clarifies that when undertaken for profit, second-generation material may not be sold for propagation purposes.[46] This is, strictly speaking, an act of indirect or contributory infringement (as only the propagation as such would be an act of manufacture prohibited by Article 42 I).[47]

In the absence of similar provisions under U.S. patent law, it should thus be noted that the U.S. Supreme Court essentially sought to reach a similar solution, and, thus, clarify the boundaries between exhaustion and self-replication technologies, with its decision in *Bowman v. Monsanto*. More specifically, the Court sought to clarify that the first-generation material can be used for propagating purposes, be it under an explicit or implicit license, while further generations can be used for propagating purposes only with the consent of the patentee.

---

[43] *Ibid.*
[44] Law No. 9.279, May 14, 1996, art. 43, WIPO Lex. No. BR003 (Brazil) [hereinafter Brazil IP Code].
[45] *Ibid.* art. 43(V); See UPOV, *The UPOV System of Plant Variety Protection* (2011), available at www.upov.int/about/en/upov_system.html; see also *infra* IV.C(3).
[46] Brazil IP Code, art. 43(VI).
[47] *Ibid.* art. 42(I). It is disputed, however, whether this provision itself is subject to the provisions of the Plant Protection Act (Law No. 9.456, April 25, 1997, art. 10, WIPO Lex. No. BR005 (Brazil)) which in art. 10 prohibits any restrictions on the further use of seeds for reproductive purposes. This was affirmed by a first instance decision of the Civil Court of Porto Alegre, April 4, 2012, in Monsanto v. Sindicato Rural de Passo Fundo et al., but denied on appeal by the Appeal Court of Rio Grande do Sul, T.J.-R.S., Ap. No. 70049447253, Relator: Maria Claudia Cachapuz, 09.24.2014, Diário da Justiça [D.J.], 02.10.2014. This case is commented by Charlene de Ávila, *Apontamentos Sobre a Cobrança de Royalties da Soja RR1 e Outras Questoes Emblemáticas em Propriedade Intectual*, 134 REVISTA DA ASSOC. BRAS.PRPRIEDADE INTELECTUAL 3 (Jan/Feb 2015). A similar argument was made in the U.S., but ultimately failed in the U.S. Federal Circuit, Monsanto v. McFarling, 302 F.3d 1291 (Fed. Cir. 2001).

(2) "Making" and self-replication

While I do not take issue with the reasoning of the U.S. Supreme Court regarding the issue of exhaustion, a further analysis of the act of infringement might have been desirable on the part of the Court. Mr. Bowman had argued that he did not infringe because the seeds were self-replicating, to which the Supreme Court replied that Mr. Bowman was not a passive observer and controlled the replication of the seeds. This is certainly so, but it is not the same as saying that Mr. Bowman made or manufactured new seeds. He did not. He could not. Instead, what Mr. Bowman did, and could do, was to create the conditions under which the seeds would replicate.

Accordingly, it seems clear that the terminology used in the U.S. Patent Act, namely, in sections 154 and 271 of the Act, which refer to "making" (the same language used in Article 28 of the Agreement on Trade-Related Aspects of Intellectual Property Rights)[48] to define an act of infringement, is unsuitable when it refers to self-replicating organisms.[49] Because of this, the Supreme Court could have further developed its analysis on the case and specified in greater detail the definition of patent infringement with respect to self-replicating technologies.

In this respect, the U.S. Supreme Court could have followed the example of Canada over a decade ago. In particular, the definition of infringement in the context of self-replicating technologies featured prominently in the Canadian Supreme Court case concerning the patentability of the famous "Harvard Oncomouse."[50] In that case, the majority held that such invention could not qualify as a "manufacture," as it was, *inter alia*, capable of self-replication.[51] Notably the Canadian Court stated:

> With respect to the meaning of the word "manufacture" (*fabrication*), although it may be attributed a very broad meaning, I am of the opinion that the word would commonly be understood to denote a non-living mechanistic product or process. For example, the *Oxford English Dictionary* (2nd ed. 1989), vol. IX, at p. 341, defines the noun "manufacture" as the following: "The action or process of making by hand . . . The action or process of making articles or material (in modern use, on a large scale) by the application of physical labour or mechanical power."[52]

The Canadian Court further held that:

> the patenting of higher life forms raises special concerns that do not arise in respect of non-living inventions. Unlike other inventions, biologically based inventions are living and self-replicating. In addition, the products of biotechnology are incredibly complex, incapable of full description, and can contain important characteristics that have nothing to do with the invention.[53]

Building on these observations, the Court by majority drew the conclusion:

---

[48] Agreement on Trade-Related Aspects of Intellectual Property Rights, April 15, 1994; Marrakesh Agreement Establishing the World Trade Organization, Annex 1C, art. 28, Legal Instruments—Result of the Uruguay Rounds Vol. 31, 33 I.L.M. 83, 1869 U.N.T.S. 299 (1994) [hereinafter TRIPS Agreement].
[49] 35 U.S.C. §§ 154, 271 (2015).
[50] Harvard College v. Canada (Commissioner of Patents), [2002] 4 S.C.R. 45 (Can.).
[51] Ibid.
[52] Ibid.
[53] Ibid.

that the Patent Act in its current state is ill-equipped to deal appropriately with higher life forms as patentable subject matter is an indication that Parliament never intended the definition of "invention" to extend to this type of subject matter.[54]

A couple of years later, however, the same Supreme Court of Canada partially reversed itself and affirmed infringement for self-reproducing seeds in the *Schmeisser* decision.[55] Still, it remains true that the term "manufacture," be it as a requirement for defining patentable subject matter or as a definition of infringement, is unsuitable for self-replicating technologies and calls for specific legislation.

(3) Plant variety protection and saving seeds

In this context, it should also be noted that doubts about the patentability of living subject matter[56] led to a *sui generis* protection system for plant varieties: the UPOV. The UPOV Convention was initially signed in 1961 by a number of European countries and entered into force in 1968.[57] The Convention was revised in 1972, 1978, and 1991.[58] Plant variety protection under the UPOV Convention bestows the same kind of protection to plant breeders as patents, yet contains significant limitations for breeders and farmers. Thereby, the UPOV Convention with its finely balanced system of rights and exceptions has tried to accommodate the special requirements not only of plant variety development, but also of traditional agricultural structures.[59] Different from the rules under patent law, the notion that harvested seed may be used again for propagation purposes (so-called farmer's privilege) is one of the cornerstones of the UPOV system and takes care of the specific needs of subsistence farming.[60]

---

[54] *Ibid.*

[55] Monsanto v. Schmeisser, [2004] 1 S.C.R. 902 (Can.). The minority opinion justly pointed out that this position was inconsistent with the previous *Harvard* decision.

[56] See e.g. Am. Fruit Growers v. Brogdex, 51 S. Ct. 328 (1931); [German Federal Supreme Court,] July 6, 1962, 1962 GRUR 577 (Ger.).

[57] International Convention for the Protection of New Varieties of Plants, December 2, 1961, WIPO Lex. No. TRT/UPOV/003.

[58] International Convention for the Protection of New Varieties of Plants (UPOV), WIPO, available at www.wipo.int/wipolex/en/other_treaties/details.jsp?group_id=22&treaty_id=27.

[59] For further details, see Mark Janis, *Patenting Plants: A Comparative Synthesis*, in PATENT LAW IN GLOBAL PERSPECTIVE 213 (Ruth Okediji & Margo Bagley eds., 2014); Margarat Llewellyn, *Perspectives on Patenting Biological Material*, in INDUSTRIAL PROPERTY IN THE BIOMEDICAL AGE 73 (Christopher Heath & Anselm Kamperman Sanders eds., 2003); Christopher Heath, *Plant Varieties, Biotechnology and Biodiversity*, in INDUSTRIAL PROPERTY IN THE BIOMEDICAL AGE 3 (Christopher Heath & Anselm Kamperman Sanders eds., 2003).

[60] The farmer's privilege is one of the reasons why patent protection is more popular than protection as a plant variety. Hans Kast, CEO of BASF Plant Science, in an interview in reply to the question if it was not the traditional right of farmers to save part of the harvest for future use as propagation material stated, "We invest a lot of money to develop solutions to agricultural problems. Thereby, unique products are developed that we are going to protect so that our investment is worth its while. Our customers simply have to respect this." "Genfood-Manager: 'Wir brauchen neue Werkzeuge für die Pflanzenzüchtung'," SPIEGELONLINE, April 29, 2009 www.spiegel.de/wirtschaft/0,1518,621695,00.html. Art. 11 of the Biotechnology Directive provides for a farmer's privilege also for plant patents, yet is of limited assistance due to the small number of plants which are covered by the famer's privilege. See Biotechnology Directive, *supra* note 42.

Many jurisdictions in fact exclude plant varieties from patent protection. In Europe, this is stipulated in Article 53 of the European Patent Convention (EPC) that mentions "plant varieties" as excluded subject matter.[61] The reason for enacting this provision was that under the original UPOV Convention 1961, there could not be dual protection both under UPOV and patent law for a plant variety. UPOV was concluded at a time when plants and plant varieties were developed by natural selection and cross-breeding rather than artificial genetic modification. The latter type of modification can often be applied to a multitude of plant varieties, begging the question whether in such case, the exception should still apply. The Enlarged Board of Appeal, highest judicial authority of the European Patent Office (EPO), denied this according to Decision G 1/98: "a claim wherein specific plant cells are not individually claimed is not excluded from patentability under Art. 53(b) EPC even though it may embrace plant varieties."[62]

The reasoning of the Enlarged Board is consistent when trying to delineate the borderline between plant variety and patent protection: what cannot be protected under plant variety protection should be open to patent protection, even if such claim also encompasses plant varieties.[63] The reasoning is more problematic when looking at the rationale for enacting specific legislation for plant variety protection, namely, to find a balance between the developers of new plants, the users, and the general public.[64] In this respect, it is of no concern to farmers whether an invention covers one variety, or may be used for several varieties. The distinction drawn by the Enlarged Board is a bit like prohibiting monogamy, but allowing polygamy.

Thus, while genetic modifications in the food sector and the corresponding expectation to obtain patent protection for the modified products may have done a lot to stimulate development in this area,[65] the balance between users and developers has notably shifted towards the latter.[66]

Ultimately, as the above analysis has shown, the tension between patent rights and the practice of seed-saving can be addressed from various angles: it can call into account the principle of intellectual property exhaustion or refer to *sui generis* rules on plant variety protection,[67] which can carve limitation by excluding patent protection inventions that are

---

[61] European Patent Convention (15th edn.), October 5, 1973, WIPO Lex. No. TRT/EP001/001.
[62] Decision of the Enlarged Board of Appeal G 1/98, [2000] O.J. 111, headnote 1 (December 20, 1999).
[63] *Ibid.*
[64] The Court stated that, "One significant concern arising out of the increased scope of patent protection is the impact that it will have on Canada's agricultural industry. The CBAC recommends that a farmers' privilege provision be included in the Act. The privilege would permit farmers to collect and reuse seeds harvested from patented plants and to breed patented animals for their own use, so long as these were not sold for commercial breeding purposes. Although the CBAC puts forward suggestions pertaining to the general nature of such a provision, it nonetheless recognizes that more work would need to be done to identify the extent of the privilege in relation to plants and animals." Harvard College v. Canada (Commissioner of Patents), [2002] 4 S.C.R. 45, para. 171 (Can.).
[65] This is argued by Eva Willnegger, Patents in the Food Sector 75–90 (2008).
[66] In his critical comment on the *Monsanto* decision, Darryl Lim focuses on yet another angle and argues that also the patent misuse doctrine might have been invoked here. Lim, *supra* note 41.
[67] This issue was argued not only in Brazil (see *supra*), but also in the U.S. in connection with Roundup Ready seeds. Monsanto v. McFarling, 302 F.3d 1291 (Fed. Cir. 2001).

(also) covered as plant varieties. Nevertheless, until further clarification in the U.S., this tension is likely destined to resurface in the courts.

V. THE EUROPEAN COURT OF JUSTICE DECISION IN *MONSANTO V. CEFETRA ET AL.*

A. Case History

The European case that went up to the CJEU was a bit more complicated than the one decided by the U.S. Supreme Court discussed in section IV. The starting point was genetically modified soya beans that had been planted in Argentina where no corresponding patent could be taken out by Monsanto, because the subject matter was considered unpatentable in Argentina at that point in time.[68] The genetically modified soya beans were processed in Argentina into soya flour and exported as follows: three-quarters to China, and the remainder to some European countries.[69] The imports to Europe then became problematic, as Monsanto wanted the Argentinean exporters to pay U.S.$3 per tonne on exportation and U.S.$15 per tonne for import to Europe, which they refused.[70] While processed flour would normally only contain starch rather than any DNA containing nuclei of cells, impurities in the material and improved methods of detection allowed traces of DNA sequences as specified in the claims to be found in the imported product.[71] According to Monsanto, existence of these traces constituted an infringement of the European patent as mentioned above. Monsanto, thus, raised lawsuits in those countries where the soya flour (or soya meal) was imported. The infringement suits against the importation were dismissed in the United Kingdom (U.K.)[72] and in Spain,[73] while the

---

[68] Argentinian Patent Act, art. 6g excludes "all living matter and substances already present in nature" from the realm of patents, which in art. 6 of the Implementing Decree 260/96 is understood as "plants, animals and essentially biological processes for their reproduction." See Law No. 24.481, March 30, 1995, WIPO Lex. No. AR092 (Arg.); Decree No. 260/1996, March 20, 1996, WIPO Lex. No. AR092 (Arg.). Arguably, this interpretation is incorrect and, some would argue, unconstitutional. Monica Witthaus, *Propriedad Industrial Sobre Plantas Transgénicas, in* Derechos Intelectuales 131 (2001); Monica Witthaus & Miguel Angel Rapela, *Vacíos de Protección en la Legislación Argentina Sobre Derechos del Obtentor y de Patentes, in* Inovación y propriedad intelectual en mejoramiento vegetal y biotecnología agrícola 269, 273 (Miguel Á. Rapela & Gustavo J. Schötz eds., 2006).
[69] Importation of Monsanto's variety of genetically modified soy flour to Europe is permissible for animal consumption under Council Directive 90/220/EC of April 23, 1990 on the deliberate release into the environment of genetically modified organisms, [1990] O.J. L117/15.
[70] Robin, Mit Gift und Genen – Wie der Biotech-Konzern Monsanto unsere Welt Verändert, *supra* note 31, at 373.
[71] The processing of the soya beans involves ten steps including heating, cracking, flaking, and defatting.
[72] Monsanto Technology L.L.C. v. Cargill Int'l, [2008] F.S.R. 7 (Eng.).
[73] Commercial Court Madrid, July 27, 2007 – Case No. 488/07 (Monsanto Technology LLC v. Sesotris S.A.E., "Roundup Ready Spain," 40 Int'l Rev. Intel. Prop. & Comp. L. 233 (2009). Apparently, two further proceedings were instigated by Monsanto against other importers. Both suits were dismissed at first instance.

Hague District Court of the Netherlands[74] referred certain questions on the interpretation of the EU Biotechnology Directive to the CJEU.

Although issues of patent infringement are mostly decided on the basis of domestic law, the Hague District Court took the view that infringement should be determined on the basis of the EU Biotechnology Directive, interpretation of which was a matter for the CJEU.[75] The Hague District Court affirmed an infringement under the traditional concept of absolute product protection in this respect.[76] Article 9 of the EU Biotechnology Directive[77] provides for a specific rule on the scope of gene patents. Notably, according to the provision:

> The protection conferred by a patent on a product containing or consisting of genetic information shall extend to all material, save as provided in Article 5(1), in which the product is incorporated and in which the genetic information is contained and performs its function.[78]

B. The Decision

In his opinion, Advocate General Mengozzi[79] made some interesting comments on the relationship between the rationale of the patent system, and the scope of DNA patents. He stated that:

> The great importance attached by Directive 98/44 to the function performed by a DNA sequence is naturally intended to permit a distinction to be drawn between "discovery" and "invention." The isolation of a DNA sequence without any indication of a function constitutes a mere discovery and as such is not patentable. Conversely, the sequence is transformed into an invention, which can then enjoy patent protection, through the indication of a function that it performs. However, to maintain that a DNA sequence enjoys "traditional" patent protection—that is to say, protection extending to *all the possible functions of the sequence itself*, including those not identified at the time when the patent is applied for—would mean that patents would be recognised as covering functions as yet unknown at the time of the patent application. In other words, lodging an application for a patent for a *single function* of a DNA sequence is all it would take to obtain protection for *all the other possible functions* of the same sequence. In my view, such an interpretation would ultimately, in practice, make a mere discovery patentable, in breach of the basic principles on patents.
>
> Nor should it be forgotten that, as a matter of principle, the essential nature of a patent consists in a genuine exchange. On the one hand, the inventor makes public his own invention, thereby enabling the general public to benefit from it. In exchange, the inventor enjoys exclusive property rights over the invention itself for a limited period of time. It seems to me that to grant absolute protection to an invention consisting in a DNA sequence, thereby conferring on the patent holder exclusive rights over that sequence, extending to all its possible uses, including those unspecified or unknown at the time when the application was lodged, would be in breach

---

[74] Decision of the Hague District Court, March 19 and September 24, 2008, "Roundup Ready Netherlands," 40 INT'L REV. INTEL. PROP. & COMP. L. 228 (2009).
[75] Ibid.
[76] Ibid.
[77] Biotechnology Directive, art. 9.
[78] Ibid.
[79] Opinion of Advocate General Mengozzi delivered on March 9, 2010 in Case C-428/08, Monsanto Tech. L.L.C. v. Cefetra B.V., [2010] E.C.R. I-06765.

of that fundamental principle, in so far as it would confer on the patent holder a disproportionate level of protection.[80]

As is further explained below, this is a fundamental criticism of the current patent system that goes far beyond gene patents. As a matter of fact, granting absolute protection to inventions consisting in a chemical formula and thereby conferring exclusive rights over that sequence, extending to all possible uses, is one of the cornerstones of modern patent law for pharmaceutical and chemical inventions. The above statements thereby gave rise to concern in interested circles, and the CJEU[81] avoided this rather fundamental point by departing from the Advocate General's statements and focusing on the wording of the above-mentioned Article 9 of the EU Biotechnology Directive. In particular, the Court stated that:

> In that regard, it must be noted that Article 9 of the Directive makes the protection for which it provides subject to the condition that the genetic information contained in the patented product or constituting that product "performs" its function in the "material . . . in which" that information is contained.
> The usual meaning of the present tense used by the Community legislature and of the phrase "material . . . in which" implies that the function is being performed at the present time and in the actual material in which the DNA sequence containing the genetic information is found.
> In the case of genetic information such as that at issue in the main proceedings, the function of the invention is performed when the genetic information protects the biological material in which it is incorporated against the effect, or the foreseeable possibility of the effect, of a product which can cause that material to die.
> The use of a herbicide on soy meal is not, however, foreseeable, or even normally conceivable. Moreover, even if it was used in that way, a patented product intended to protect the life of biological material containing it could not perform its function, since the genetic information can be found only in a residual state in the soy meal, which is a dead material obtained after the soy has undergone several treatment processes.
> It follows from the foregoing that the protection provided for in Article 9 of the Directive is not available when the genetic information has ceased to perform the function it performed in the initial material from which the material in question is derived.
> It also follows that that protection cannot be relied on in relation to the material in question on the sole ground that the DNA sequence containing the genetic information could be extracted from it and perform its function in a cell of a living organism into which it has been transferred. In such a scenario, the function would be performed in a material which is both different and biological. It could therefore give rise to a right to protection only in relation to that material.[82]

Building on these considerations, the Court thus focused on the specific provision of Article 9 that limits the scope of protection to material in which the product is incorporated "and performs its function."[83] In particular, the Court determined that herbicide resistance is the function of the material, and that this function is not foreseeably or possibly performed in the soy meal. Therefore, the Court stated that the use of the products as soy meal existed outside the scope of protection of the patent at issue.

---

[80] *Ibid.* (emphasis added).
[81] *Ibid.*
[82] *Ibid*; see also Biotechnology Directive, art. 9.
[83] Monsanto Tech. L.L.C. v. Cefetra B.V., *supra* note 79.

C. Analysis

(1) "Function" of genetic material

The CJEU decision was essentially based on an interpretation of Article 9 of the EU Biotechnology Directive, specifically the wording "performs its function." In this respect, the CJEU clarified that the "function" of genetic material is first of all to carry information.[84] The position that genetic material serves such function of carrying information seems to be addressed by Article 9, which explicitly requires that the DNA ("genetic material" in the wording of Article 9) be "contained" in the product.[85] The additional mention of a "function" in the provision should therefore mean something beyond the mere presence of the information.[86] This interpretation is also confirmed by Recital 23 of the EU Biotechnology Directive, whereby a "mere DNA sequence without indication of a function" is not patentable.[87]

Accordingly, in light of the CJEU decision, it seems that the term "function" should rather refer to what the DNA sequence will actually do. In this case, the function of the DNA sequence is that of "encoding a Class II EPSPS enzyme," the expression of which results in glyphosate tolerance in plants. This is, precisely, the function of the DNA sequence as described in the patent at issue. According to the patent abstract "Genes encoding class II EPSPS enzymes . . . are useful in producing transformed bacteria and plants which are tolerant to glyphosate herbicide . . . The Class II EPSPS enzymes are characterized by being more kinetically efficient than Class I EPSPSs in the presence of glyphosate."[88]

And, according to the description of the patent, "[0008] A DNA molecule comprising DNA encoding a kinetically efficient, glyphosate tolerant EPSP synthase is presented. The EPSP synthases of the present invention reduce the amount of overproduction of the EPSPS enzyme in a transgenic plant."[89]

In this respect, it is also interesting to note that the Spanish courts understood the word "function" in this manner when dismissing the claim brought by Monsanto in Spain.[90] Ultimately, it appears difficult to give "function" any meaning other than the indication of what the patented invention is meant to do.[91] Accordingly, the interpretation of the

---

[84] Ibid.
[85] Ibid.
[86] Ibid.
[87] Ibid; Biotechnology Directive, art. 23.
[88] European Patent No. 0546090 B1 (filed August 28, 1991).
[89] Ibid.
[90] Commercial Court Madrid, July 27, 2007, *supra* note 73; Provincial Court Madrid, March 10, 2009, 40 INT'L REV. INTEL. PROP. & COMP. L. 971 (2009).
[91] According to RUDOLF KRASSER & WOLFGANG BERNHARDT, PATENTRECHT: EIN LEHR- UND HANDBUCH ZUM DEUTSCHEN PATENT – UND GEBRAUCHSMUSTERRECHT, EUROPÄISCHEN UND INTERNATIONALEN PATENTRECHT, 231 (5th ed. 2004): "the scope of protection in this case requires not only the use of the patented product, but also a use of the genetical information expressed thereby, in other words that the product is used for a certain function. This only makes sense if not just any function is used that can be fulfilled by the genetic information, but rather the very function that according to Art. 5(3) Biotech Directive and the corresponding provision in domestic law has been disclosed with the application and has been made the basis for the patent grant." (228) "As the function that has to be indicated in the application also determines the scope of the patent once

CJEU would seem to fall squarely within Recital 24 of the EU Biotechnology Directive, according to which "in cases where a sequence or partial sequence of a gene is used to produce a protein or part of a protein, to specify which protein or part of a protein is produced or what function it performs."[92]

Ultimately, it is clear from the facts in the case that the DNA of the claim at issue is meant to encode glyphosate tolerant EPSP, and when contained in the soy flour, the DNA cannot do this. This interpretation would also seem appropriate based on the traditional interpretation of the scope of patent protection and the general rules of patent law. In particular, the inventive merit of the DNA sequence does not lie in providing the sequence as such (otherwise it would not be patentable if no further function had been disclosed), but rather in the sequence encoding glyphosate tolerant EPSPS. This, in turn, excludes a patent infringement where this function is not activated.

(2) Possible scope of protection outside Europe

Following the CJEU decision in the *Monsanto* case, one of the interesting questions that remains is whether countries outside Europe and without specific legislation on self-replicating technologies would have decided a similar case along the same lines as the CJEU, or whether they would follow an approach similar to the decision adopted by the Dutch court ruling on the case that affirmed infringement under the traditional rules of patent protection for products.[93] If the answer to this question would be the latter, then similar cases could arise for the importation of cotton, namely, the Roundup Ready variety that Monsanto has started selling in India without corresponding patent protection. In this instance, any trace of the protected DNA in, say, imported jeans or t-shirts could thus allow Monsanto to request seizure of these products at the border, or to raid the premises of any manufacturer of these products, or any shop commercially distributing these goods—an interesting, but somewhat worrying scenario.

In fact, the English court denied the infringement of claim 6 of the patent owned by Monsanto for reasons unrelated to the interpretation of the EU Biotechnology Directive or the corresponding provisions under U.K. law.[94] In particular, the English court interpreted claim 6 as referring to the DNA sequence of claim 1, thus encoding an enzyme "capable of reacting with antibodies raised against a Class II EPSPS enzyme selected from the group consisting of the enzymes of SEQ ID No:3 and SEQ ID No:5."[95] According to the court, these enzymes could be distinguished from Class I EPSPSs by their "inability to react with polyclonal antibodies prepared from Class I EPSPS enzymes under conditions where other Class I EPSPS enzymes would readily react with the Class I antibodies."[96] As Monsanto had not proven that the DNA contained in the flour displayed this difference

---

granted, it will not be sufficient that the function whose discovery and use determines the inventive merit will only be mentioned in the description. Rather, the function must also find its way into the patent claim . . . Art[icle]s 5(3) and 9 Biotech Directive consequently leave no room for an 'absolute product protection' of genetic sequences, partial sequences or the proteins expressed thereby."
[92] Monsanto Tech. L.L.C. v. Cefetra B.V., *supra* note 79; Biotechnology Directive, art. 24.
[93] Decision of the Hague District Court, March 19 and September 24, 2008, *supra* note 74.
[94] Monsanto Tech. L.L.C. v. Cargill Int'l, [2008] F.S.R. 7 (Eng.).
[95] *Ibid.*
[96] *Ibid.*

(which distinguished the patented product from prior art), the court thus dismissed its claim. This may simply mean that Monsanto had not sufficiently proven that the DNA fragments imported in the flour, had they still been intact, would not have reacted with the antibodies prepared for Class I EPSPS. In turn, this would mean that there was no proof that the DNA found in the imported soya was in practice DNA that would perform the function that was claimed in claim 6 of the patent at issue. This could also mean that the imported traces of DNA could no longer react in the same way as described in the patent. The latter interpretation would simply be an alternative way of saying that the imported soya no longer performed its function, a reasoning that the Spanish courts adopted in their decisions dismissing the claims brought by Monsanto in Spain (see above).

Determining infringement would thus, for a good part, depend on how the patent claim is written, and whether the inventive concept that distinguishes the invention from prior art is expressed in a manner that would allow a court to deny infringement if the inventive concept was absent in the allegedly infringing embodiment. Here again, one can observe the advantage of the approach taken by the Canadian Supreme Court in the *Harvard Oncomouse* case to deny product claims over genetic material, but allow claims for the process of manufacture: the latter would, in fact, be found infringing only in the event of actual multiplication (if considered to be an act of "manufacturing").[97]

(3) Scope of protection and contribution to society

Finally, it should be noted that not the CJEU, but the Advocate General touched on a far more fundamental issue in the case at issue in the EU: the relationship between the invention's contribution to the state of the art and the scope of the patent monopoly.

Notably, Articles 8 and 9 of the EU Biotechnology Directive are to a certain extent purpose-bound in that protection under these provisions requires not only the presence of the biotechnological material or the genetic information as such, but also the presence of characteristics of the product or the function of the information. To the contrary, where the patent (or the respective claim of the patent) falls within the ambit of Article 8 or 9, while the allegedly infringing product does not, the EU Biotechnology Directive does not allow a recourse to "traditional" principles of absolute product protection; that is, to find for infringement merely because the DNA has been discovered in the imported soy flour, although it does not show the corresponding characteristics of the invention.[98] Yet, it is interesting to note that these traditional principles, to the extent that they allow the patenting of a new chemical compound (and gene sequences are also chemical compounds) without an indication of its function(s), are still (and will perhaps always be) questioned for the reason that patent protection should be limited to the contribution the patent makes to the state of the art, as the Advocate General has rightly pointed out.[99]

---

[97] See *supra* IV.
[98] Biotechnology Directive, arts. 8, 9.
[99] Horst-Peter Götting, *Kritische Bemerkungen zum absoluten Stoffschutz*, GRUR 256, 259 (2009). According to Rudolf Kraßer: "the argument that the inventor of the compound was the first to make it available must be contradicted in that the inventive merit of providing a compound only finds its justification in the compound's surprising qualities, and in this respect it is not enough to allow others to discover such qualities by way of providing the compound, but rather to actually discover them." Krasser & Bernhardt, *supra* note 91, at 134.

According to a German Supreme Court judge:

> There is a certain tension between absolute product protection and the view repeatedly taken by the EPO, and adopted by the jurisprudence in the Netherlands and the UK—but as of yet not consistent with the jurisprudence by the [German] Federal Supreme Court—that the protection claimed must be limited to the contribution that the invention as disclosed makes to the state of the art.[100]

In other words, a purpose-bound protection for gene sequences is more in line with the fundamental principles of patent law than the absolute product protection currently applied to product inventions.

VI. CONCLUSION

Self-replicating technologies have called a number of traditional concepts of patent law into question: patentability, infringement, scope of protection, and exhaustion of patent rights. While exhaustion may be the least controversial of these concepts, the analysis of exhaustion with respect to self-replicating technologies still gives rise to revisit some basic economic equations underlying the exhaustion doctrine, namely, appropriate remuneration and scope of protection commensurate to the contribution to society—concepts originally elaborated by Josef Kohler in 1900. In this respect, both decisions addressed in this chapter—the U.S. and EU decisions on the respective disputes brought forward by Monsanto—touch upon basic questions of patent law. Notably, the U.S. Supreme Court's decision concerned the appropriate balance between monopolistic rights and society. In other words, the decision addressed the following question: is it desirable and appropriate to have patent monopolies encroach on traditional behavioral patterns of agriculture, namely, the saving of seed for replantation? On the other hand, the CJEU's decision concerned the relationship between contribution to society and scope of protection and addressed the following questions: should protection extend to acts that do not and cannot use the advantages for which the patent was granted? Should the function of patents over genetic modifications be written in the claims so as to achieve a purpose-limited protection? Should patents for chemical formula be granted a scope of protection that is limited to the function as disclosed in the patent, or is it appropriate to grant a scope of protection that goes beyond the actual contribution to society? To date, neither court has offered a fully satisfactory answer to these questions. Accordingly, it is likely that more litigation in this area will ensue until the boundaries between self-replicating technologies and exhaustion will be further clarified.

---

[100] Alfred Keukenschrijver, *Stoffschutz und Beschreibungserfordernis – Legt Art. 5(3) der Biotechnologie-Richtlinie eine Neubewertung nahe?*, in FESTSCHRIFT FÜR TILMANN 475, 485 (Erhard Keller ed., 2003). An international comparison is provided by Doris Walter, *Harmonisierung und angemessene Anspruchsbreite bei der Gensequenzpatentierung*, GRUR INT'L 284 (2007), and Dieter Schneider & Doris Walter, *Ist der absolute Stoffschutz noch zu retten?*, GRUR INT'L 831, 838 (2007).

16. Development of patent exhaustion in Mainland China
Xiang Yu* and Conghui Yin**

I. INTRODUCTION

There are currently three different approaches regarding parallel importation throughout the world. One approach permits parallel imports, another prohibits them, and a third approach places conditional restricts on parallel importation. Theoretically speaking, these different approaches reflect the differing principles on exhaustion of intellectual property in the different countries and regions, i.e., national exhaustion, international exhaustion, and regional exhaustion (in the European Economic Area, for example). In fact, the attitudes taken by the different countries and regions on the principle of exhaustion directly relate to the applicable intellectual property laws of those countries, which generally reflects economic and even political considerations. While at the same time these laws have to comply with international agreements like the Agreement on Trade-Related Aspects of Intellectual Property Rights (TRIPS) under the World Trade Organization (WTO).[1]

As a developing country, the cost of labor in China is still relatively low compared to developed countries, thus, Chinese enterprises are typically exporters of intellectual property goods, especially patented goods, in international trade practice. Cases involving the parallel importation of patented goods into China are scarce and this problem will inevitably become prominent with the increasing labor cost in China. Additionally, China must also bring its intellectual property laws into harmony with its international trade partners regarding trade-related intellectual property rights. Based on the current Chinese Patent Law, which has been amended three times and went into effect in 2009, this chapter examines the laws and practices related to parallel imports of patented goods in China. This chapter also analyzes the effects and problems with regard to economic considerations, and, based on previous research, offers suggestions on how to apply the principle of exhaustion and parallel imports in China.

---

* Professor and director of Chinese-German Institute for Intellectual Property, School of Management, Huazhong University of Science and Technology, Wuhan, China. This research was supported by the National Nature Science Foundation of China (NSFC), Project Number: 71072033.

** Doctoral candidate, Chinese-German Institute for Intellectual Property, School of Management, Huazhong University of Science and Technology, Wuhan, China.

[1] Xiang Yu, *An Inquiry into the Issue of Exhaustion of Patent Right under WTO Legal System*, 64–67 CHINA PATENTS & TRADEMARKS 15–28 (2001).

II. LEGAL FRAMEWORK

A. Changes Before and After the Third Amendment to the Chinese Patent Law

(1) State of patent law in China before the Third Amendment to the current Chinese Patent Law

The first Patent Law was passed by the Standing Committee of the People's Congress on March 12, 1984 and became effective on April 1, 1985.[2] The first Patent Law was successively amended in 1992, 2000, and 2008, respectively.[3] Prior to the Third Amendment to China's Patent Law in 2008, there was no clear regulation in the Chinese laws regarding exhaustion and parallel imports of patented goods.

The 1984 Patent Law did not include any definite provisions concerning parallel imports of patented products.[4] In the 1992 Patent Law, a paragraph was added to Article 11,[5] which stated:

> After the grant of the patent right, except as otherwise provided for in the law, the patentee has the right to prevent any other person from importing, without its or his authorization, the patented product, or the product directly obtained by its or his patented process, for the uses mentioned in the preceding two paragraphs.[6]

According to the literal meaning of the provision, this paragraph may be understood as providing that patentees have the right to prevent parallel imports of patented products.[7]

On November 12, 2001, China became a member of the WTO.[8] Before that, China passed the Second Amendment to the Patent Law on August 25, 2000, and the amendment became effective on July 1, 2001.[9]

However, the 2000 Patent Law did not include a substantive amendment regarding the rights concerning importation. Article 11[10] of the 2000 Patent Law states:

---

[2] Patent Law of the People's Republic of China (promulgated by the Standing Comm. Nat'l People's Cong., March 12, 1984, effective April 1, 1985) 1984 P.R.C. 529 (China) [hereinafter 1984 Patent Law].

[3] Patent Law of the People's Republic of China (promulgated by the Standing Comm. Nat'l People's Cong., December 27, 2008, effective October 1, 2009) CN028 (China) [hereinafter 2008 Patent Law].

[4] See 1984 Patent Law, *supra* note 2.

[5] Patent Law of the People's Republic of China (promulgated by the Standing Comm. Nat'l People's Cong., September 4, 1992, effective January 1, 1993) 1992 P.R.C. 69, art. 11 (China) [hereinafter 1992 Patent Law].

[6] *Ibid.*

[7] See generally WANG AIMIN, PARALLEL IMPORTS OF PATENTED PRODUCTS (2011).

[8] World Trade Organization, *Accession of the People's Republic of China*, WT/L/432 (November 10, 2001).

[9] Patent Law of the People's Republic of China (promulgated by the Standing Comm. Nat'l People's Cong., August 25, 2000, effective July 1, 2001) CN022 (China) [hereinafter 2000 Patent Law].

[10] *Ibid.* art. 11.

> After the patent right is granted for an invention or a utility model, unless otherwise provided for in this Law, no unit or individual may exploit the patent without permission of the patentee, i.e., it or he may not, for production or business purposes, manufacture, use, offer to sell, sell, or import the patented products, use the patented method, or use, offer to sell, sell or import the products that are developed directly through the use of the patented method.
>
> After a design patent right is granted, no unit or individual may exploit the patent without permission of the patentee, i.e., it or he may not, for production or business purposes, manufacture, offer to sell, sell or import the design patent products.[11]

In particular, the meaning of the wording "otherwise provided for" in the provision remained unclear, both in light of other provisions in the Patent Law itself and any related laws.

Furthermore, Article 11 did not explicitly prescribe whether parallel imports should be prohibited.[12] If one wanted to interpret the provision as supporting the principle of national exhaustion of patents, the provision could be interpreted as follows: as long as an imported product is a patented product of China, or a product directly obtained by use of a patented process of China, no matter how the importer obtained the product in another country (legal or illegal), the importation of the product into China will infringe the Chinese patent right.

On the other hand, if one wanted to interpret the provision as supporting the principle of international exhaustion, the provision could be interpreted as follows: the purpose of the importation right is to prevent the importation of a product made in a foreign country without the permission of the patentee, or made in a country where the product has no patent protection, i.e., the importation right is used for preventing an infringing product or a product made without the consent of the patentee from being imported.[13]

Obviously, in the absence of a provision regarding importation rights that explicitly prohibits parallel imports, a patent holder (patentee or his exclusive licensee) can initiate infringement proceedings only for the purpose of production and business in China. In contrast, a clear provision prohibiting parallel imports makes it possible for the patent holder to prohibit the importation of the infringing product or the product made without his consent as soon as possible, so that the patent holder can prevent the damage of infringement from occurring or extending.[14]

The language of Article 11 of the 2000 Patent Law can be compared with the provision of Article 28(1) of TRIPS, especially the footnote concerning the word "importing,"[15] which refers to the language of Article 6 of TRIPS, "nothing in this Agreement shall be used to address the issue of exhaustion of intellectual property rights."[16] In this respect,

---

[11] Ibid.

[12] Ibid.

[13] See also Christopher Heath, *Parallel Imports and International Trade*, 28 INT'L REV. INTELL. PROP. & COMPETITION L. 623 (1997).

[14] Xiang Yu, *The Regime of Exhaustion and Parallel Imports in China: A Study Based on the Newly Amended Chinese Laws and Related Cases*, 3 EUR. INTELL. PROP. REV. 105–12 (2004).

[15] *Compare* 2000 Patent Law, *supra* note 9 and Agreement on Trade-Related Aspects of Intellectual Property Rights, April 15, 1994; Marrakesh Agreement Establishing the World Trade Organization, Annex 1C, art. 28(1), Legal Instruments—Result of the Uruguay Rounds Vol. 31, 33 I.L.M. 83 (1994) [hereinafter TRIPS].

[16] TRIPS, art. 6.

from the analysis of the background to the amendment of the Patent Law, it seems that the main objective of the Law, at the time at which the Law was enacted, was to comply with the minimum standard of TRIPS regarding the importation right. Thus, Article 11 of the Patent Law did not have any clear provision prohibiting parallel imports.

(2) Current Patent Law of 2008 and current regulation of parallel imports

As mentioned above, there were no regulations regarding parallel imports before the 2008 Patent Law. Those advocating in favor of the doctrine of "international exhaustion" argued that the patent owners' rights are exhausted internationally when their products are sold in an overseas market; therefore, patent owners should no longer be entitled to protection under the Chinese Patent Law.[17] On the other hand, those advocating in favor of the "national exhaustion" doctrine argued that patent owners' rights only exhaust in the foreign countries where they sell their products, but not in China;[18] thus, parallel importers' importation of patented products constituted infringement of patent owners' rights in China.

The current Chinese Patent Law was amended in 2008 and became effective in 2009.[19] The Third Amendment revised a substantial number of provisions in the Patent Law and also added some completely new articles to the previous revisions of the Law. Differing from the previous revisions, the Third Amendment was not only designed to align Chinese law with international patent standards (most notably, by shifting to an "absolute novelty" standard for granting patents), but also to accommodate the growing national demand for patent protection. The Chinese legislative body believed that by strengthening the country's patent protection system, China would also strengthen the innovative economy in the long term.[20]

The 2008 Patent Law ("Patent Law") adopts the doctrine of "international exhaustion" and allows parallel imports from foreign countries. The most pertinent legislative provision is contained in Article 69(1) of the Patent Law,[21] which states:

> the following shall not be deemed to be patent infringement:
> (1) After a patented product or a product directly obtained by using the patented method is sold by the patentee or sold by any unit or individual with the permission of the patentee, any other person uses, offers to sell, sells or imports that product;[22]

Article 69(1) of the Patent Law clearly provides that when a patented product or a product directly obtained by using a patented process is sold by a patentee or with the permission of the patentee, the successive acts of using, offering to sell, selling, or importing that

---

[17] Chen Lijuan, *The Legitimacy of Parallel Importation of Patented Goods and its Regulations*, 2 J. FUJIAN INST. POL. SCI. & L. (April 2002).
[18] ZHENG CHENGSI, THE THEORY OF INTELLECTUAL PROPERTY RIGHTS 342 (1996); Lan Guizhen, *Parallel Imports of Patented Goods*, ZHONGGUO ZHUANLIBOA, April 16, 1999.
[19] See 2008 Patent Law, *supra* note 3.
[20] King & Wood Mallesons, *Comments on Judicial Protection of Intellectual Property in Chinese Courts in 2014* (2014), available at www.kwm.com/en/knowledge/insights/comments-on-judicial-protection-of-intellectual-property-in-chinese-courts-in-2014-20150514.
[21] 2008 Patent Law, art. 69(1).
[22] *Ibid.*

product, by any other person, shall not be deemed as infringing the patent.[23] This provision has confirmed the legality of parallel imports and, thus, has introduced the regime of international exhaustion of patent rights. No doubt, such international exhaustion system restricts the ability of patentees to charge higher prices in China than in other jurisdictions for the same patented product, as they will be vulnerable to being undercut by parallel importers.[24]

The Patent Law allows parallel import to ensure a balance of interest between patentees and the public. As soon as a patented product or a product obtained directly by a patented process has been put in a foreign market by the patentee or his licensee, other entities or individuals are then allowed to import the product and put it in the Chinese market, without any additional authorization of the patentee in China. Such amendment to the Patent Law is in line with TRIPS, taking into consideration the flexibility provided by Article 6 of TRIPS, which allows WTO members to make their own decision on the exhaustion of rights in their respective countries.[25]

(3) Legislation background: balance of advantages

China is still a developing country and, although the economy has been quickly developing in the past two decades, there is still a large gap between China and other developed countries with respect to economic strength and technology level. The development of industry to a certain extent still relies on importing technology from developed countries.

Table 16.1[26] and Figure 16.1 show relevant data about applications and grants of invention patents for the State Intellectual Property Office (SIPO).

From these figures, it is clear that the number of patent applications from Chinese applicants has grown dramatically from 2001 to 2014. Notably, from 2001 to 2008,[27] 58.38 percent of the total number of the invention patents granted by the SIPO, which contains more technical contents and are more important to the development of industry and economy, were granted to foreign applicants.[28] In particular, foreign applicants held most patents granted by the SIPO in high tech fields, such as medicines and microelectronic

---

[23] Ibid.

[24] Marks & Clerk China, *The Third Amendment to the Chinese Patent Law*, REMARKS 1 (October 2009), available at www.marks-clerk.com/MarksClerk/media/MCMediaLib/PDF's/Remarks%20PDFs/Marks-Clerk-ReMark-China-Autumn-2009.pdf?ext=.pdf.

[25] Xiang Yu & Shuijing Hu, *The Third Amendment of the Chinese Patent Act and the Comparison Between the New Patent Act and TRIPS*, 24 INTELL. PROP. L. & POL'Y J. 213–28 (2009); see also State Intellectual Property Office, General Introduction to the Third Revision of the Patent Law of the People's Republic of China and Its Implementing Regulations (December 10, 2010), available at http://english.sipo.gov.cn/laws/lawsregulations/201012/t20101210_553631.html.

[26] Based on Annals of the State Intellectual Property Office of China. See STATE INTELLECTUAL PROPERTY ORGANIZATION, DOMESTIC AND FOREIGN PATENT APPLICATIONS OF THREE RECEIVING ANNUAL STATUS (2008), available at www.sipo.gov.cn/ghfzs/zltjjb/jianbao/year2008/a/a2.html.

[27] The Third Amendment to the Chinese Patent Law was published at the end of 2008 and became effective in 2009, while the Second Amendment to the Chinese Patent Law was published in 2000 and became effective in 2001. See generally 2008 Patent Law, *supra* note 3; see generally 2000 Patent Law, *supra* note 9. See also Table 16.1; Figure 16.1.

[28] See Table 16.1; Figure 16.1.

Table 16.1 Applications and grants for invention patents received from China and abroad from 2001 to 2014 at SIPO (unit: piece)

Year	Domestic Applications from Chinese applicants	Domestic Grants to Chinese applicants	Foreign Applications from foreign applicants	Foreign Grants to foreign applicants
2001	30,038	5395	33,166	10,901
2002	39,806	5868	40,426	15,605
2003	56,769	11,404	48,549	25,750
2004	65,786	18,241	64,347	31,119
2005	93,485	20,705	79,842	32,600
2006	122,318	25,077	88,172	32,709
2007	153,060	31,945	92,101	36,003
2008	194,579	46,590	95,259	47,116
2009	229,096	65,391	85,477	63,098
2010	293,066	79,767	98,111	55,343
2011	415,829	112,347	110,583	59,766
2012	535,313	143,847	117,464	73,258
2013	704,936	143,535	120,200	64,153
2014	801,135	162,680	127,042	70,548
Total	3,735,216	872,792	1,200,739	617,969

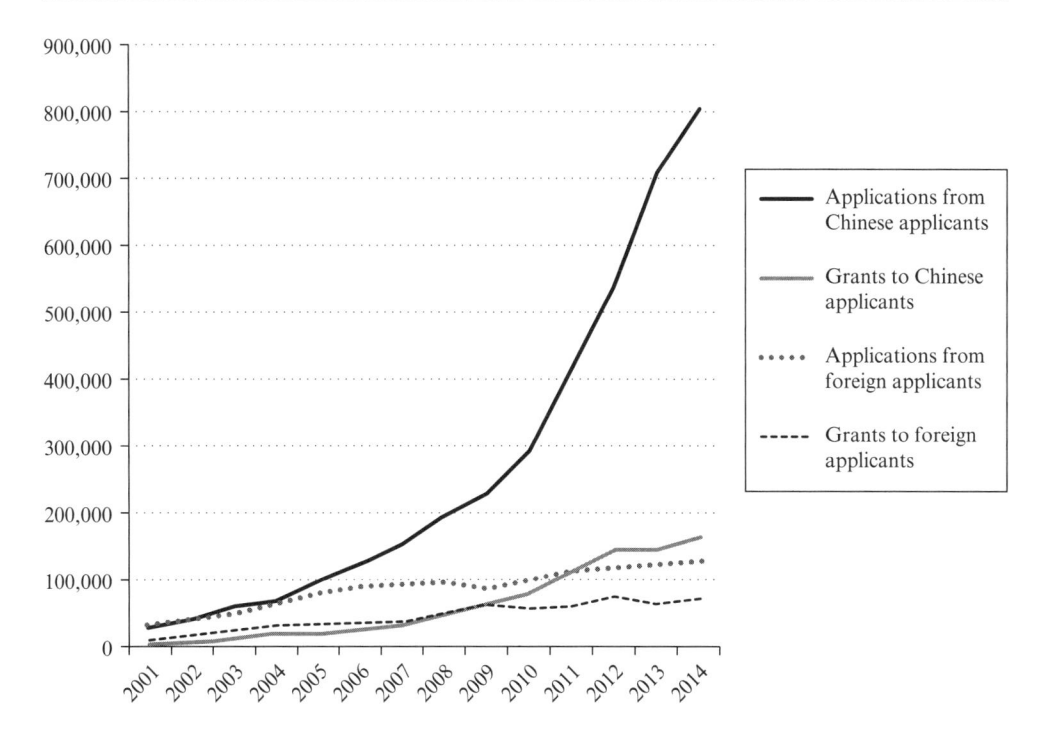

Figure 16.1 Comparison of patents applications and grants for inventions received from China and abroad from 2001 to 2014 at SIPO

techniques.[29] However, starting in 2009, the grant of invention patents to Chinese applicants began to exceed the grants to foreign applicants.[30] In 2014, the number of invention patents obtained by Chinese applicants was more than twice as many as foreign applicants,[31] even though the granting rate for foreign applications was much higher than Chinese domestic applications.

This data is important and indicates how the economic, and political, considerations to be weighed while adopting specific patent provisions in technology importing countries are not necessarily the same considerations applicable to technology exporting countries. Naturally, the latter group of countries grant and support more protections to the patentees, which are mostly domestic citizens or enterprises in technology exporting countries. When governments provide patentees with stronger protections, they do so to encourage their citizens to engage in more inventive activities, hence promoting the development of domestic industry.

In technology importing countries, however, important patents are generally held by foreigners. Thus, if governments provide patentees with overly-strong protections, including the right of prohibiting the importation of genuine products, domestic enterprises would be restricted from exploiting related patented technology and the development of domestic industries would be hampered. This, in turn, would be counter to the original purpose of patent legislation. So, it seems critical for China to find a proper equilibrium between protecting the interest of the patentee and promoting the development of industry.

At the same time, it is important to note that, when it comes to technology transfers and investment decisions in foreign countries, foreign enterprises may also weigh other aspects as equally, if not more, important than the existence of a strong patent system. These other aspects include investment climate, economic, political, and so forth.[32] It is also important to keep in mind that lower costs of production in developing countries have traditionally motivated multinational enterprises to move their production facilities to these countries and take advantage of the international division of labor, which has made these less developed countries more competitive than the local firms in the developed countries.[33]

Ultimately, international patent exhaustion could promote further development of the economy and foreign trade in China. The possibility of obtaining genuine products through parallel imports would also benefit consumers in China. Generally, parallel imports can benefit consumers everywhere, including in developed countries. Most relevant, a system of free trade cannot be supported without a generalized rule of international exhaustion. Corporations in developed countries support free trade because

---

[29] Based on Annals of the State Intellectual Property Office of China. See STATE INTELLECTUAL PROPERTY ORGANIZATION, TABLES OF THE GRANTS OF INVENTION PATENTS AND UTILITY MODELS ACCORDING TO IPC CLASSIFICATION (2001–2008), available at www.sipo.gov.cn/tjxx/.
[30] See Figure 16.1; Table 16.1.
[31] See Table 16.1.
[32] See S.K. Verma, *TRIPs-Development and Transfer of Technology*, 27 INT'L REV. INTELL. PROP. & COMPETITION L. 342 (1996).
[33] See S.K. Verma, *Exhaustion of IPRs and Free Trade*, 29 INT'L REV. INTELL. PROP. & COMPETITION L. 564 (1998).

developed countries have expensive labor resources and these corporations want to be able to export technology and invest in developing countries and manufacture products there. Developing countries welcome this foreign investment because it helps the industries of developing countries develop more quickly. Yet, the same corporations that advocate free trade for manufacturing their products at lower costs often oppose international exhaustion and parallel imports because it can affect their pricing strategies in different countries. Thus, only under a global system that permits parallel imports can a sound circle of international free trade be truly formed. Such a system would better use the complementary resources from developed and developing countries, which is consistent with the essential purpose of the WTO.

(4) Legislation basis (without prejudice to international agreements)
Article 6 of TRIPS is the central provision regarding exhaustion in the WTO legal framework. As highlighted before, the provision adopts an open approach to the issue and states:

> For the purpose of the dispute settlement under this agreement, subject to the provisions of Articles 3 and 4 nothing in this Agreement shall be used to address the issue of the exhaustion of intellectual property rights.[34]

More specifically, TRIPS does not set forth any mandatory provisions regarding whether or not the principle of international exhaustion of patent rights is to be adopted in each member state.[35] This becomes clearer when combined with footnote 6 of TRIPS, which is a clear explanation to the right of "importation" conferred by Article 28 of TRIPs.[36] Article 28 states:

> This right, like all other rights conferred under this Agreement in respect of the use, sale, importation or other distribution of goods, is subject to the provisions of Article 6 above.[37]

Because no agreement could be reached during the negotiations, it is still impossible to address the issue of exhaustion of rights through the WTO dispute resolution mechanism. In fact, Article 6 represents an "agreement based on disagreement,"[38] meaning that each WTO member is entitled to make its own policy on the exhaustion of intellectual property rights[39] provided that it meets the non-discrimination principle set out in Articles 3 and 4 of TRIPS. Neither TRIPS nor the provisions of any other WTO laws set forth any principle governing the exhaustion of patent rights.

Moreover, within the legal framework of the WTO, the discussion on the principle of the exhaustion of patent rights is completely open. With regard to issues relating to the exhaustion of patent rights, the WTO members need to harmonize their views expressed

---

[34] TRIPS, art. 6.
[35] See Xiang Yu, *supra* note 14.
[36] TRIPS, art. 28.
[37] *Ibid.*
[38] See generally *ibid.* art. 6; see Xiang Yu, *supra* note 1.
[39] See H.P. Kunz-Hallstein, *Zur Frage der Parallelimporte im internationalen gewerblichen Rechtsschutz-Neuer Wein in alten schlauchen?*, INTELL. PROP. RTS. INT'L REV. 268, 270–71 (1998).

in their policies, but not in their laws.[40] If the members want to reach different principles on the exhaustion of rights with respect to patent rights and trademark rights through negotiations, there is no evidence from any WTO law that this is prohibited. Since TRIPS is the only agreement in the WTO regime that exclusively governs intellectual property matters, all new agreements relating to the exhaustion of intellectual property rights will be incorporated into TRIPS.

In addition, in analyzing the "principle of independence of patent" in Article 4(2) of the Paris Convention for the Protection of Industrial Property (Paris Convention),[41] it should be understood that the examination and approval of patent applications, the duration of patent rights, the reason for invalidation, and forfeiture of patent rights are independent in every member country. However, this provision does not directly involve the problem of exhaustion of rights or parallel imports.

B. Anti-Unfair Competition Law

After parallel imports of patented products became legal in China following the amendment to the 2008 Patent Law, some problems have nonetheless emerged with respect to products imported by parallel importers. For example, parallel imported goods have, in some instances, a worse after-sales service compared with products distributed by the patent holders or with their consent in China. The lower quality of after-sales service for these products could, in turn, damage the interests of consumers. In addition, parallel importers of patented products can take advantage of the market reputation established by the authorized local dealers who have invested a significant amount of effort in establishing their business, who have obtained the license to distribute the product at issue, and who also ensure the quality of the products in the market. This problem is also known as "free rider behavior," and may lead to acts of unfair competition.

Under the Chinese Anti-Unfair Competition Law, however, there is no provision that directly relates to parallel imports.[42] Article 5 lists four kinds of unfair means in trade, but parallel imports are not included as one of these four kinds of unfair acts.[43] Instead, it could be supported that the general principles of the Anti-Unfair Competition Law could be used to regulate acts of unfair competition related to parallel importers in order to protect the legitimate rights of patent holders, their licensees, and the interests of consumers.[44] For example, article 9[45] of the Anti-Unfair Competition Law states that:

---

[40] See Xiang Yu, *supra* note 1.
[41] Paris Convention for the Protection of Industrial Property, opened for signature March 20, 1883, 21 U.S.T. 1583, 828 U.N.T.S. 305, art. 4(2) (revised 1967).
[42] Law of September 2, 1993, of the People's Republic of China Against Unfair Competition (promulgated by the Standing Comm. Nat'l People's Cong., September 2, 1993, effective December 1, 1993) (China) [hereinafter Anti-Competition Law].
[43] *Ibid.* art. 5.
[44] *Ibid.*
[45] *Ibid.* art. 9.

business operators are prohibited from making misleading or false representations regarding the quality, manufacturing components, functions, uses, manufacturers, period of validity, place of origin and other aspects of merchandise.[46]

Consequently, a parallel importer may be in violation of article 9 if he makes a misrepresentation (such as, that the sale of his parallel imported goods was authorized by the original patentee when in actuality it was not).

C. Customs Regulation on Intellectual Property Rights

The China Customs Office has the duty to protect the rights of intellectual property owners under the Regulations of the People's Republic of China on Customs Protection of Intellectual Property Rights ("Regulations") promulgated in 1995.[47] On November 26, 2003, the State Council amended the Regulations.[48] However, the 2003 Regulations and the Implementing Measures to the 2003 Regulations remain silent on their applicability to parallel import cases.[49]

The State Council promulgated and amended the Regulations again in 2010.[50] The revisions affected articles 11, 23, 24, 27, and 28 of the 2003 Regulations.[51] In the 2010 Regulations, the protection of patent rights related to import or export goods is clearly stipulated in the article 2,[52] which reads:

> Customs protection of intellectual property rights in these Regulations means the protection provided by the Customs for the exclusive rights to use a trademark, copyrights and their related rights, and patent rights (hereinafter referred to as intellectual property rights) related to import or export goods and protected under the laws and administrative regulations of the People's Republic of China.[53]

The protection of patent rights is included in the China Customs Office's protection of intellectual property rights in China. However, the 2010 Regulations still did not address the issue of parallel importation. This is unfortunate, especially because in the past Customs officers have exceeded their authority by imposing administrative sanctions on

---

[46] *Ibid.*

[47] Regulations of the People's Republic of China on Customs Protection of Intellectual Property Rights (promulgated by the State Council of the People's Republic of China, July 5, 1995) WIPO CN013 (China).

[48] Regulations of the People's Republic of China on Customs Protection of Intellectual Property Rights (promulgated by the State Council of the People's Republic of China, November 26, 2003) WIPO CN025 (China).

[49] Xiang Yu, *The New Regulations Regarding Customs Protection of Intellectual Property Rights in the People's Republic of China*, 7 INT'L REV. INTELL. PROP. & COMPETITION L. 835–41 (2005).

[50] Regulations of the People's Republic of China on Customs Protection of Intellectual Property Rights (promulgated by the State Council of the People's Republic of China, March 27, 2010, effective April 1, 2010) art. 2, WIPO CN032 (China) [hereinafter 2010 Customs Regulation].

[51] See also State Council Decision on Amending the Regulations of the People's Republic of China on Customs Protection of Intellectual Property Rights (Decree No. 572).

[52] 2010 Customs Regulation, art. 2.

[53] *Ibid.*

parallel importers without a legal foundation.[54] Also, as analyzed in detail above, since 2009, under the rule of the 2008 Chinese Patent Law, the parallel imports of patented goods are clearly permitted into China.

Article 3 of the 2010 Regulations[55] states:

> Import or export of goods that infringe intellectual property rights protected by the laws and administrative regulations of the People's Republic of China is forbidden.[56]

But what are "infringing goods?" Does this include parallel imported goods? The answer to these questions remain unclear because, as we also noted above, neither TRIPS nor other Chinese intellectual property laws give a definitive answer to the problem of intellectual property exhaustion and parallel imports.[57]

III. ECONOMIC EFFECTS

The issue of parallel imports is not only a legal issue, but it is also an economic issue, one that has a significant impact on economic and trade policies.

As we stressed above, since the cost of labor in China remains relatively low, production costs are also relatively low. This is a primary reason why China has become the manufacturing base for many multinational enterprises in the modern global economy. For now, China's low labor costs and the (generally) good quality of the goods produced by its skilled and industrious workforce are factors that make it unlikely that patented goods produced in other countries would be purchased at a lower price and imported into China and cases of parallel imports into China are still rare. But, labor costs in China have risen in the past few decades, and will certainly continue to rise along with the further development of the economy and Chinese overseas investments. In turn, multinational enterprises have partially shifted (some of) their international manufacturing to countries with even lower labor costs than China, such as Vietnam, Thailand, and other countries in Southeast Asia or other regions of the world. As China's journey from developing country to a more developed economy will continue in future years, cases involving parallel imports from other countries into China may arise with greater frequency.[58] Thus, the impact of parallel imports into the Chinese economy will no doubt increase. For this reason, taking a clear position on parallel imports is necessary for China at the present stage.

---

[54] In October 2002, for example, the Tianjin Customs detected "mini cups" bearing the FIFA sign, which were imported from South Korea. Even though they were identified as genuine at the request of customs, the FIFA organization successfully requested their detention, arguing that the manufacturer was only authorized to produce and sell the cups in South Korea (Information of the Tianjin Customs 2002, No. 23).
[55] 2010 Customs Regulation, art. 3.
[56] Ibid.
[57] Xiang Yu, *Exhaustion and Parallel Imports in China*, in PARALLEL IMPORTS IN ASIA 25–38 (Christopher Heath ed., 2004).
[58] Daniel Chow, *Exhaustion of Trademarks and Parallel Imports in China*, 51 SANTA CLARA L. REV. 4 (2011).

A. The Economic Effects of Permitting Parallel Imports in China

The economic rationale in China for allowing parallel imports and adopting a rule of international exhaustion is to create more choices for consumers and lower prices for the same or similar products.[59] Distributors import patented goods from other countries because these goods are cheaper than the same patented goods produced or distributed by authorized parties in China. Some commentators in China believe that allowing the importation of parallel imported patented goods will also increase employment.[60] These commentators argue that lower priced parallel imported goods will force the manufacturers or the distributors of genuine goods in China to reduce their prices, and that lower prices will stimulate consumer demand.[61] If the manufacturer of the goods in question has excess capacity, that is, additional capacity to produce more goods, then the increased output may lead the manufacturer to hire additional workers, resulting in increased employment for China.

(1) Impact on authorized importers or distributors

Although most products are produced in China today, China still relies on imports for several types of products in several different industries. This is the case, for example, in some key industry fields, such as precision instruments, aircraft engines, special materials, large-scale integrated circuit chips, where Chinese producers are importing the necessary products from foreign countries.[62]

For the authorized importers of these products into China, the fact that interested Chinese producers can lawfully purchase these products from parallel importers instead of the authorized importers naturally results in a financial loss from the loss of sales or reduced profits. As parallel imported goods are generally less expensive than authorized imports, national dealers in China would need to reduce the price of their products to compete with the parallel imported goods.

Still, in the long run, allowing parallel imports can contribute to effectively reducing the abuse of patent rights by patent holders and their licensees, prevent the creation of market monopolies by patentees or their licensees, and promote market competition and free trade. Additionally, the competition created by parallel imports can energize the importer market and stimulate the domestic consumption demand of imported products. Therefore, parallel imports can have positive economic benefits.

(2) Impact on consumers

Those who generally benefit the most from parallel imports are consumers. Chinese consumers will be able to buy patented products at a lesser cost, a cost that may better match their income levels. At the same time, since the products are genuine, they will benefit from the guaranteed quality of the imported products. In addition, allowing parallel imports also provides consumers with more choices, which increase the instances of legal and

---

[59] See Xiang Yu & Shuijing Hu, *supra* note 25.
[60] See Chow, *supra* note 58.
[61] *Ibid*.
[62] Based on NATIONAL BUREAU OF STATISTICS OF THE PEOPLE'S REPUBLIC OF CHINA, CHINA STATISTICAL Yearbook (2015), available at www.stats.gov.cn/tjsj/ndsj/.

foreign patented products in the Chinese market. Again, as parallel importers engage in a competitive relationship with the authorized importers or distributors, this eliminates the price monopoly and the pricing controls on the (still patented) products.

(3) Impact on patentees in China

Naturally, allowing parallel imports of patented products has mostly negative effects on patentees' rights, such as limiting the patentee's right to control the importation of patented products; reducing the ability for the patentee to issue licenses, because foreign patented products can legally enter the Chinese market; and reducing royalties for patent licensing, because the Chinese licensees should consider the possible shrunken future market space induced by the parallel imported goods.

B. Parallel Imported Cars in the Shanghai Free-Trade Zone

Approved by the State Council of China, the Shanghai Free-Trade Zone ("Shanghai FTZ" or SFTZ, officially China (Shanghai) Pilot Free-Trade Zone) was officially established in Shanghai, China, on September 29, 2013.[63] SFTZ is the first free-trade zone in Mainland China.[64] Since its establishment, the SFTZ has carried out institutional reform and innovation in areas of investment, foreign trade, finance, and post-filing supervision to form a legal framework for investment and trade within the zone.[65] In particular, it has outlined prohibited conduct for investment management, simplified foreign trade supervision procedures, promoted financial system reform to realize RMB capital account convertibility, and advocated post-filing supervision as a way to transform government functions.[66]

The creation of the SFTZ is the latest major initiative of the Chinese government in adapting to global economic development trends and furthering the cooperation between China and other countries and regions worldwide. The SFTZ is being used as a testing ground for a number of economic and social reforms, for example, the parallel import of cars.[67]

On January 7, 2015, the Shanghai Municipal Commission of Commerce[68] released

---

[63] Shanghai Free Trade Zone (promulgated by the State Council of China, August 22, 2013, effective September 29, 2013).
[64] *Shanghai Free-Trade Zone Launched*, BBC News, September 29, 2013.
[65] *Introduction*, in CHINA (SHANGHAI) PILOT FREE TRADE ZONE-INTRODUCTION (2014), available at http://en.shftz.gov.cn/About-FTZ/Introduction/.
[66] *Ibid.*; China Briefing, *Shanghai Releases "Negative List" for Foreign Investment in Shanghai Free Trade Zone*, CHINA BRIEFING NEWS (September 30, 2013), available at www.china-briefing.com/news/2013/09/30/shanghai-releases-negative-list-for-foreign-investment-in-shanghai-free-trade-zone.html.
[67] *The Notice on Parallel Imported Vehicles Piloted in China (Shanghai) Free Trade Zone of the Test Notification*, SHANGHAI MUNICIPAL COMMISSION OF COMMERCE (January 7, 2015), available at www.scofcom.gov.cn/zxxxgk/237471.htm; Samuel Shen & Kazunori Takada, *China Launches Pilot "Parallel Import" for Foreign Cars*, REUTERS (January 7, 2015), available at www.reuters.com/article/2015/01/08/china-carimport-idUSL3N0UN16A20150108.
[68] Shanghai Municipal Commission of Commerce is a department under Shanghai Government, national superior competent department is the Ministry of Commerce of China.

"Notice about carrying out the parallel imported cars pilot in China (Shanghai) free trade zone."[69] This notice officially launched the pilot program for parallel import of cars in the SFTZ.[70] As a result, parallel importation of cars finally received official permission, from being a gray area in which much uncertainty had dominated for an extended period of time.

Before the adoption of this program, it was unclear whether national policies supported parallel imports of cars. In 2001, importation of cars was included in China Compulsory Certification((3C))Regulations,[71] which included, as part of the implementation of 3C, rules on windshields and some other components of cars that were imported into China.[72] However, the Regulations did not address, nor include, the importation of a whole vehicle.[73] In the past decade, however, parallel imports of cars in China grew. Since 2011, certain price advantages and the relatively stable quality of the imported cars led to a stable-growth phase in the market for imported cars, even though the share of imported cars could not be too large. Still, from a legal standpoint, the lawfulness of these imports was still in a "gray area." Regardless, parallel imports continued. In 2013, more than 80,000 parallel imported cars were imported into China, accounting for 8 percent of total sales volume and 12 percent of the total value of imported cars.[74] In 2014, the number increased to more than 100,000, accounting for 7 percent of total sales volume of imported cars.[75]

Since the implementation of the program, the SFTZ has become the first place in China where dealers are officially authorized to sell parallel imported cars.[76] Still, the Shanghai Municipal Commission of Commerce and the SFTZ Administrative Committee have set several strict restrictions for dealers who operate under the new system. It is also estimated that parallel imported cars will mainly cater to the special needs of a small group of customers in China and remains a niche market.[77] Analysts have also said that such niche market will not make a significant difference for the Chinese automobile market as a whole,[78] but it will better meet the demands of China's increasingly diversified auto market.

As noted above, low quality after-sales service has been a recurring problem for the

---

[69] Ibid.; Shanghai Municipality, *Circular on Launching a Pilot Project for the Parallel Import of Motor Vehicles in the China (Shanghai) Pilot Free Trade Zone*, CHINA LAW & PRACTICE (January 7, 2015), available at www.chinalawandpractice.com/Article/3433165/Shanghai-Municipality-Circular-on-Launching-a-Pilot-Project-for-the-Parallel-Import-of-Motor-Vehicles.html.

[70] CHINA LAW & PRACTICE, *supra* note 69.

[71] China Compulsory Certification (CCC Mark) (promulgated by the General Administration of Quality Supervision, Inspection and Quarantine of the People's Republic of China (AQSIQ) and Certification and Accreditation Administration of the People's Republic of China (CNCA), May 1, 2002, effective May 1, 2003) (China).

[72] Ibid.

[73] Ibid.

[74] Wang Lijiao. *Parallel Imported Cars Still Go Forward Against the Wind*, CNAUTONEWS.COM (June 26, 2015), available at www.cnautonews.com/tebd/201506/t20150624_413550.htm.

[75] Ibid.

[76] Zhu Shiyun, *Shanghai FTZ Starts Pilot Allowing Parallel Imports of Vehicles*, CAIXIN ONLINE (January 9, 2015), available at http://english.caixin.com/2015-01-09/100772896.html.

[77] Du Xiaoying, *Shanghai Starts its "Parallel Import" Pilot for Foreign Cars*, CHINADAILY USA (January 12, 2015), available at http://usa.chinadaily.com.cn/2015-01/12/content_19300923.htm.

[78] Ibid.

owners of these vehicles, which have previously been imported through some coastal harbor cities in China. Several of these problems will be resolved, or reduced, thanks to the creation of the pilot program in the SFTZ. Notably, in order to resolve the after-sales service problem, the SFTZ Administrative Commission will implement a quality control system for the parallel-imported vehicles.[79] It will also impose "the same warranty, recall, and investigation policies as for vehicles sold by authorized dealers."[80]

At present, the legalization of parallel importation of cars into China once again shows that China is moving to support parallel importation, and gradually to adopt the international exhaustion principle of intellectual property rights. Therefore, it is essential for China to make efforts to balance the interests between patentees and the public.

IV. CONCLUSION

The 2008 Patent Law adopts the doctrine of "international exhaustion of patent rights" and allows parallel imports of patented goods. The 2008 Law has clarified, for the first time, the legality of parallel importation of patented goods in China. This development represents a significant action taken by China to encourage free trade, and at the same time attempts to strike a balance between patentees' and consumers' interests. Such amendment in the Patent Law is in line with the TRIPS Agreement, taking into consideration the flexibility provided by Article 6 and the footnote in Article 28 of TRIPS, which allows WTO members to make their own decisions on the exhaustion of patent rights.

The 2008 Patent Law also has an economic effect on China. For example, the parallel importation of cars in the SFTZ has been legalized, and SFTZ became the first place in China where dealers can be officially authorized for so-called parallel imports of cars direct from overseas' manufacturers. Permitting parallel imported cars is conducive to the development of domestic and foreign enterprises and balances the interests of the patentees and the public.

However, although the current Chinese Patent Law confirmed the legal status of parallel imports of patent goods, there are still no clear regulations regarding the parallel imports of products covered by national trademarks and copyrights in China. The absence of such regulations also clearly impacts the parallel imports of patented products, since most products today are protected not only by patent law, but also under trademark and/or copyright laws.

Accordingly, based on the analysis of the related rules under the WTO's legal system, the laws, case law, and practices of some other countries and areas[81] in China, the authors

---

[79] Shiyun, *supra* note 76.
[80] Du Xiaoying, *Cut-Price Parallel-Imported Vehicles Could Curb Hefty Price*, CHINA DAILY (February 16, 2015), available at www.chinadaily.com.cn/business/motoring/2015-02/16/content_19602356.htm.
[81] See Xiang Yu, *supra* note 14; see also Xiang Yu, *Exhaustion of Patent Rights and Parallel Imports: Analyses on Laws, Practices and Theories in EU*, 9 TAIWAN LAW REVIEW 115–27 (2000); Xiang Yu, *Exhaustion of Patent Rights and Parallel Imports in the USA: Analysis on Legislation and Cases*, 12 GUOJI MAOYI INTERNATIONAL TRADE 36–38 (2000); Xiang Yu, *Study on the Development of Exhaustion of Trademark Rights and Its Tendency in the EU*, 3 TAIWAN LAW REVIEW 141–50

would like to conclude this chapter by making the following recommendations for future legislative amendments in China.[82]

With respect to trademark law, the authors suggest that the Chinese legislature adopt the principle of international exhaustion of trademark rights, thus permitting parallel imports of trademarked goods. Parallel imports should be prohibited, and the principle of national exhaustion should be adopted, in the following exceptional situations: (1) if there are substantial differences between the parallel imported goods and the goods marketed in China with the same trademark; and (2) if there is no obvious notice on the goods or its package or container to indicate the difference. Whether a difference is substantial or not depends on whether this kind of difference would affect consumer choice. That should be decided by the courts. In addition, according to the provision of article 57(5) of the 2013 Chinese Trademark Law, parallel imports of trademarked goods would be prohibited in the case of "rebranding."

With respect to copyright law, the authors also suggest that the Chinese legislature adopt the principle of international exhaustion of copyright, thus permitting parallel imports of copyrighted goods.

Ultimately, the legislature in China should strive for the adoption of the following principles with respect to intellectual property exhaustion and parallel imports: (a) compliance with international rules; (b) harmonization of domestic law with the practice of China's trading partners so as to foster reciprocity in trade; and (c) development of the domestic economy, science and technology, industry, and trade.

(2001); Xiang Yu, *Laws, Cases, Theories and Rules of Practice: Exhaustion of Trademark Rights and Parallel Imports in the USA*, 6 SCI. & TECH. L. REV. 31–42 (2001). Christopher Heath, *From "Parker" to "BBS": The Treatment of Parallel Imports in Japan*, 24 INT'L REV. INTELL. PROP. & COMPETITION L. 179, 180 (1993); see also Abraham Van Melle, *Parallel Importing in New Zealand: Historical Origins, Recent Developments, and Future Directions*, 21 EUR. INTELL. PROP. REV. 63 (1999).

[82] See generally Xiang Yu, *Study on the Principle of Exhaustion of Patent Right and Parallel Imports in China*, 6 GUOJI MAOYI 43–46 (2001).

17. The hermeneutics of the patent exhaustion doctrine in India
Yogesh Pai*

I. INTRODUCTION

The law on exhaustion of rights (or "first sale" doctrine) is a highly contested area of intellectual property. In many ways, the development of this doctrine that traditionally only applied to property (land and chattels), has had a checkered history in the context of intellectual property. This is due, in part, to the changes regarding the law on servitudes governing tangibles over the last several centuries. With the growth of intellectual property-based markets, there are questions concerning the application of such doctrine in a distinct market for intellectual property due to the limited nature and scope of intellectual property rights.[1] For the most part, the law on intellectual property exhaustion has developed in adversarial proceedings in different courts across various jurisdictions.[2] Hence, there is rich jurisprudence for countries to look to and it continues to grow in different jurisdictions through legislative measures, executive guidance, and caselaw jurisprudence where new questions pertaining to the extent and scope of the law, policy, and its doctrinal aspects are addressed. India is not untouched by these developments.

The doctrine of exhaustion in India has developed through several judicial decisions and legislative amendments that have shaped the evolving legal and policy landscape. However, unlike in other jurisdictions where exhaustion issues have moved beyond definitional ambiguities to those cases questioning the limits of the law and doctrine in new situations, cases on exhaustion in India have primarily revolved around the nature of the exhaustion regime: whether exhaustion is national or international.[3] Very few judicial cases have tested the limits of exhaustion in dealing with different kinds of intellectual property

---

* Assistant Professor of Law, National Law University, Delhi, India.

[1] Amelia Rinehart, *Contracting Patents: A Modern Patent Exhaustion Doctrine*, 22 HARV. J.L. & TECH. 484 (September 11, 2009). Rinehart notes that the inherent tension between patent owners and users could be reduced by: "a modern interpretation of the exhaustion doctrine where an authorized sale of a patented good, even when restricted, triggers a shift from property rule protection to liability rule protection . . . a pliability rule . . . is sometimes superior to a property rule after a patented good has been sold . . . The advantages of the initial property rule protection are retained, and the flexibility of the changed rule allows the patented good to end up in the hands of the user who values the good most." *Ibid.* at 514.

[2] SHUBHA GHOSH, THE IMPLEMENTATION OF EXHAUSTION POLICIES: LESSONS FROM NATIONAL EXPERIENCES (unpublished Legal Studies Research Paper, University of Wisconsin, February 3, 2014), available at http://ssrn.com/abstract=2390232.

[3] India does not have any regime for regional exhaustion within the regional economic block called South-Asia Association for Regional Cooperation (SAARC). Shamnad Basheer & Mrinalini Kochupillai, *TRIPS, Patents and Parallel Imports in India: A Proposal for Amendment*, 2 INDIAN J. INTELL. PROP. L. 63 (2009).

protected works.[4] It may be noted that the question of intellectual property exhaustion is no longer viewed as a pure policy issue. Although policy-makers are divided over which regime to adopt, it is generally accepted that an international exhaustion regime that allows parallel imports benefits consumers (despite the question of whether or not firms adopt global price discrimination). An international exhaustion regime facilitates trade and leads to competitive pricing. In fact, some have suggested that it must be "imposed" on all World Trade Organization (WTO) members.[5] Contrastingly, it is also argued that it is because of international exhaustion that firms are not incentivized enough to follow global price discrimination.[6]

This chapter does not address in detail the policy debates surrounding intellectual property exhaustion. Instead, it focuses on the hermeneutics that form the current legal landscape of patent exhaustion law in India. There are several reasons why this chapter has chosen to focus on the legal hermeneutics of the doctrine of patent exhaustion in India. First, the policy debates on patent exhaustion are very polarized and have had little impact on the legal content. Thus, it is the content of law that informs the policy today. Second, many jurisdictions, including India, have already undertaken several legislative measures, including failed measures, to legislate the contours of the patent exhaustion doctrine. Hence the debate has shifted back to how the law is interpreted. Third, the policy debate is less relevant today since there is a clear deference to WTO members to enact their own regime of exhaustion. The Agreement on Trade-Related Aspects of Intellectual Property Rights (TRIPS) does not prescribe or proscribe a regime of exhaustion, which is otherwise consistent with the agreement. Hence, exhaustion is totally dependent on what WTO members have chosen to enact. Lastly, legal hermeneutics as a field of study routinely challenges one to think how law is "interpreted" or "constructed," which has led to a distinct discourse on how the law informs policy.

With respect to legal hermeneutics, scholars have noted that modern views have made a distinction between "legal interpretation" and "legal construction."[7] Drawing from early

---

[4] See Agreement on Trade-Related Aspects of Intellectual Property Rights, art. 12, April 15, 1994; Marrakesh Agreement Establishing the World Trade Organization, Annex 1C, Legal Instruments—Result of the Uruguay Rounds Vol. 31, 33 I.L.M. 83 (1994) [hereinafter TRIPS]. India allows rental rights in case of films, music, and computer programs largely owing to the mandate in Article 12 of TRIPS. Because of this connection, courts have taken note of the fact that rental rights effectively operate as a limitation on the doctrine of first sale. Warner Bros. v. V.G. Santosh, (2009) CS(OS) No. 1692/2006 (India).

[5] Enrico Bonadio, *Parallel Imports in a Global Market: Should a Generalised International Exhaustion be the Next Step?*, 33 EUR. INTELL. PROP. REV. 153 (2011). A study commissioned by the Government of India on the issue of exhaustion of copyright has found in favor of international exhaustion, pointing to the consumer benefits. See NATIONAL COUNCIL FOR APPLIED ECONOMIC RESEARCH, THE IMPACT OF PARALLEL IMPORTS OF BOOKS, FILM/MUSIC AND SOFTWARE OF THE INDIAN ECONOMY WITH SPECIAL REFERENCE TO STUDENTS (2014), available at http://copyright.gov.in/documents/parallel_imports_report.pdf.

[6] S. Zubin Gautam, *The Murky Waters of First Sale: Price Discrimination and Downstream Control in the Wake of Kirtsaeng v. John Wiley & Sons, Inc.*, 29 BERKELEY TECH. L.J. 717 (2014). International Trademarks Association, *Position Paper on Parallel Imports* (2007), available at www.inta.org/Advocacy/Documents/INTAParallelImports2007.pdf.

[7] Ralph Poscher, *Hermeneutics, Jurisprudence and Law*, in THE ROUTLEDGE COMPANION TO HERMENEUTICS 451 (Jeff Malpas & Hans-Helmuth Gander eds., 2015).

works of Dworkin, Savigny, and Lieber, it was noted that interpretation must locate the "meaning the legal authority was desirous of expressing, even if it does not correspond to the standard meaning of the expression."[8] Contrastingly, legal construction has an important role to play in the development of the law since "the intentions an authority connected with a legal utterance might simply not include an intention applicable to the case at hand."[9] It is impossible to understand the communicative intention of the law in all cases. This is especially true in cases involving intellectual property rights where the legislature may not even be aware about technical concepts like exhaustion of rights. It is often a laborious task to determine what the legislature actually intended even if the law is expressly stated, when the law on the point is ambiguous or leads to a contrary interpretation. The relevance of legal hermeneutics in determining the patent exhaustion regime is unique. Giving meaning and content to such a law is an interpretative task, which must take into account the pitfalls about which hermeneutics scholars have repeatedly warned. As we will see in this chapter, while the outcomes sought by the legislature are clear, the law on the point is plainly ambiguous.

II. LEGISLATIVE AMENDMENTS AND THE LACK OF JUDICIAL GUIDANCE: AMBIGUITIES IN THE DOCTRINE OF PATENT EXHAUSTION IN INDIA

The Indian Patents Act of 1970 ("1970 Act") was enacted with a vision to balance patent law with access to patented products. Although India has had a long history of patent protection beginning in the colonial era,[10] the reforms envisaged in the 1970 Act primarily targeted creation of a domestic industry from a self-sufficiency perspective in order to allow cheaper access to products. The crucial provisions enacted in the 1970 Act were largely based on recommendations of the Rajagopal Ayyangar Report commissioned by the Government of India, which extensively relied upon past experiences in dealing with the patent system in the post-independence era, when prices for medicines were among the highest in the world.[11] The report stressed the need to withdraw product patents for chemical substances, food, and medicines.[12] And, thus, the 1970 Act was born with several layers of public interest provisions aimed at ensuring access to patented products.

It is interesting to note that the 1970 Act did not have any provision regarding exhaustion of rights by first sale, let alone international exhaustion. Similarly, section 48 of the 1970 Act did not explicitly provide a right to importation. Consequently, any act of

---

[8] *Ibid.* at 454.
[9] *Ibid.* at 454.
[10] A brief historical overview of the Indian patent system is available at *History of Indian Patent System*, CONTROLLER GENERAL OF PATENTS DESIGNS AND TRADEMARKS, GOVERNMENT OF INDIA, available at http://ipindia.nic.in/ipr/PatentHistory.htm.
[11] The report suggested that the patent law enacted during the colonial period had not worked in the interests of the Indian public. JUSTICE N. RAJAGOPALAAYYANAR, REPORT ON THE REVISION OF THE PATENTS LAW (1959).
[12] *Ibid.* Section 5 of the 1970 Act restricted product patent by excluding chemical substances, food, and medicines. This provision was subsequently repealed by the 2005 Amendment as an obligation under the TRIPS Agreement.

distribution without the permission of the patent holder could be treated as an infringement. The absence of a first sale provision may be largely due to the fact that product patents were not allowed in critical areas, which negated the need for having explicit provisions on exhaustion of rights. However, patents were available on products in other fields of technology and also on processes in all fields of technology. It is quite intriguing to note that without a provision on exhaustion by first sale, it is difficult to impute "use" of a patented product ("use" being a specific right), unless we invoke a concept of implied license[13] or a common law principle of peaceful enjoyment of property.[14] It is also noteworthy that the 1970 Act failed to include a provision allowing for parallel imports until legislation was passed in 2002. Some commentators are of the opinion that such a doctrine of first sale (territorial or national exhaustion) is recognized by other laws governing the sale of goods by virtue of sale of a product embodying the patent, which holds strong even before a concept akin to exhaustion was recognized by the 2002 Amendment to the 1970 Act.

The 2002 Amendment to the 1970 Act enacted a new section 107A that provided for Bolar exemption and a regime for exhaustion of rights that allowed imports. As originally enacted section 107A(b) read:

> importation of patented products by any person from a person *who is duly authorized by the patentee to sell or distribute the product*, shall not be considered as an infringement of patent rights.[15]

As per the Statement of Objects and Reasons of the 2002 Amendment, this provision was introduced to "ensure availability of the patented product in the Indian market at minimum international market price."[16] It is evident that unless there is authorization by the patentee to sell or distribute the product, a subsequent act by the purchaser to import the patented good into India can be infringing. This is assuming that the patent holder may refuse to sell or impose post-sale restraints on her licensee and, hence, such a licensee may not be authorized to sell the product to anyone importing such patented products into India. One commentator has argued that the authorization by the *patentee* makes it difficult to import a product into India even while it is placed in the market by the patent holder in other jurisdictions.[17] In other words, if a patented product is imported into India that was lawfully purchased in any other jurisdiction after first sale, such a product may be infringing in India if the seller in such other jurisdiction was barred by the patentee or the licensee from selling it to someone importing it into India. This creates a logical fallacy because, although exhaustion occurs upon first sale of the product in another jurisdiction, Indian law would require the consent of the patent holder in such other jurisdictions to constitute non-infringing imports into India. However, if challenged in a court of law,

---

[13] Some scholars have argued that it is difficult to import implied license for "use" in the context of Indian law, which holds true for the 1970 Act and also post Amendments of 2002 and 2005, which recognize parallel imports. Basheer & Kochupillai, *supra* note 3, at 63.

[14] Jens Schovsbo, *Exhaustion of Rights and Common Principles of European Intellectual Property Law*, in COMMON PRINCIPLES OF EUROPEAN INTELLECTUAL PROPERTY 169 (Ashgar Ohly et al. eds., 2010).

[15] Patents (Amendment) Act, 2002, No. 38, Acts of Parliament, 2002 (India) (emphasis added).

[16] *Ibid.*

[17] Basheer & Kochupillai, *supra* note 3.

such a strict interpretation may not find favor in light of the objectives of enacting a provision that allows parallel imports.

Another way to interpret this provision would have been to simply consider that once the patent holder sold the patented product through first sale in the other jurisdiction, there was an implied exhaustion by first sale, irrespective of whether or not the consent of the patentee was granted. Such an interpretation is consistent with the conceptual basis for international exhaustion, which should only determine whether or not the patented product flowed from the patentee or the licensee, and not if there was any kind of authorization to sell. This would be too much of an interpretive exercise that relies more on the doctrinal basis rather than the pure expression of law. Hence, the 2002 Amendment that introduced section 107A(b) was considered restrictive because it required express or implied authorization of the patentee.[18]

The 2005 Amendment to the 1970 Act attempted to provide clarity by broadening the scope, but has created new problems in conceptualizing whether or not the amendment allows international exhaustion. The 2005 Amendment to section 107A(b) states:

> importation of patented products by any person from a person *who is duly authorised under the law to produce and sell or distribute the product*, shall not be considered as an infringement of patent rights.[19]

This provision was enacted to remove ambiguities surrounding the 2002 Act by adding two critical clarifications on the concept of non-infringing importation (section 107A(b) does not use the word exhaustion or first sale). The earlier requirement of consent of the patent holder is now replaced with "a person who is duly authorised under the law" and now includes the word "to produce."[20] These two changes have led to intense confusion in conceptualizing the nature of the exhaustion regime that India's patent law imagined. The confusion stems from the fact that exhaustion is now determined not by first sale by the patentee, but by anyone duly authorized under the law. In such a situation, import of products that are not covered by patents in other jurisdictions, those under price controls, or those under a compulsory license in such other jurisdictions (where clearly there is no first sale by the patentee for exhaustion to occur) is validly covered by section 107A(b). In other words, the addition of "duly authorised under the law to produce and sell or distribute the product" creates a broad scope of non-infringing imports, clearly moving beyond the traditional scope of exhaustion.

Unfortunately, there is no clear judicial guidance on this issue. In *Strix Ltd. v. Maharaja Appliances Ltd.* (2009),[21] a single bench of the Delhi High Court refused to accept the defense under section 107A(b) pleaded by the defendants. In this case, the plaintiffs owned a patent in India on kettle heaters with sensors. The defendants initially purchased products from the plaintiffs and sold them in India. However, the defendants found that Chinese kettles of the same variety, but with improved quality, could

---

[18] Ibid.
[19] Patents (Amendment) Act, 2005, No. 15, Acts of Parliament, 2005 (India) (emphasis added).
[20] Ibid. s. 107A(b).
[21] Strix Ltd. v. Maharaja Appliances Ltd., (2008) I.A. No.7441 of 2008 in C.S. (OS) No.1206 of 2008 (India).

be imported. The defendant contended that the Chinese supplier held valid patents on the imported product and, hence, the plaintiff could not initiate an infringement action. The defendant also counterclaimed invalidity of patents held by the plaintiff in India. The defendants' argument under section 107A(b) was that since it was importing products for which patents were held by the Chinese supplier, it was not liable for infringing similar patents in India. It appears conceptually difficult to imagine a situation where patents similar to those belonging to the plaintiff in India could also be held by Chinese suppliers or *vice versa*, since novelty is a requirement to attain a valid patent and the novelty of both products would be brought into question (presuming that the Chinese supplier was not a licensee of the Indian plaintiff or *vice versa*). Moreover, the defendant could not produce the relevant Chinese patent number to establish a defense of exhaustion at the interim stage. The Delhi High Court went on to presume that there was no such valid patent held by the Chinese supplier and, thus, awarded injunction in favor of the plaintiff.[22] It is clear that the Delhi High Court failed to look into the scope of section 107A(b) and an opportunity to clarify the provision was, thus, missed by the court. However, section 107A(b) does not appear to require exhaustion by first sale by the patent holder, but instead by a person *who is duly authorized under the law to produce and sell or distribute the product*. Going by the pure legal requirement of section 107A(b), the prerequisite of showing proof of the patent number held by the Chinese supplier was not critical, notwithstanding the negative consequences that such a decision may have had on the rights of patent holders in India.

A division bench of the Delhi High Court refused to entertain a public interest litigation filed by a public-spirited lawyer to interpret the contours of section 107A(b) purely on grounds of locus of the petitioner, rather than on the merits of the interpretation advanced by the petitioner.[23] The petitioner advanced several arguments in his submissions on why section 107A(b) refers to national/territorial exhaustion of rights, which are critically discussed *infra*. Other scholars and commentators have offered different interpretations, which include some arguments justifying the wider ambit of the current provision to connote a "new breed" of international exhaustion, some suggesting amendments so that it could be properly construed as international exhaustion, and some others advocating that section 107A(b) clearly points to national exhaustion.

---

[22] *Ibid.*
[23] J Sai Deepak v. Central Board of Excise & Customs & anor., (2012) WP(C) No. 3165 of 2012 (India). In this case the petitioner challenged Circular No. 13/2012, Customs (also numbered as F.No. 528/21039/08- Cus/ICD) titled "Enforcement of Intellectual Property Rights on Imported Goods: Clarification on the Issue of Parallel Imports, Regarding," dated May 8, 2012, issued by the Central Board of Excise and Customs, as illegal since it was violative of ss. 48 and 107A(b) of the Patents Act of 1970 and s. 11 of the Customs Act of 1962.

III. TELEOLOGICAL INTERPRETATION: POLICY STYLE REASONING OF THE EXHAUSTION LAW

Arguments in favor of the wider interpretation of section 107A(b) place a significant amount of emphasis on policy justifications and also on a purposive construction of text based on what the legislature intended. Hence, these commentators favor a teleological interpretation, which leads to maximum effectiveness.[24]

These commentators have relied on the arguments that follow. First, Article 6 of TRIPS provides wide latitude for countries to interpret the term exhaustion without being subjected to dispute settlement since it acknowledges diminution of the right to importation granted under Article 28 of TRIPS.[25] It is also argued that such an exhaustion regime cannot be tested for compliance with Article 30 of TRIPS (limited exceptions) since it is already explicitly recognized as causing diminution of the right of the patent holder under Article 28 of TRIPS, and under the issue of exhaustion featured in Part I of TRIPS dealing with "general provisions."[26] Second, "duly authorized under the law" allows importation of the patented product into India from any manufacturer (not necessarily a patent holder for first sale to occur) since it is a non-infringing product in such other country. Thirdly, the much broader scope (i.e., duly authorized under the law) is necessary to "capture more instances" that "permits importation of patented products even from countries not recognizing patent for that invention as even in such cases the importing person or the person from whom he buys it is acting legally."[27] They argue that such an outcome would require an interpretation where the word

> "Patented product," used in this section, only means the product patented in India, and not in the country from where the product is imported, as the exclusion from infringement is evidently of the patent granted in India. Similarly the word "law" used in this section is the law applicable in the country from where the product is imported and not the Indian law.[28]

Fourthly, that provisions like section 107A(b) are structured to allow "public interest" that would include "not only the availability of the product but also transfer of technology to countries that lack manufacturing capacity."[29] Such a teleological interpretation, the commentators argue, is necessary in order to force the patent owners to obtain patents in such other jurisdictions and invest in manufacturing, so that the patent holder's competitors cannot invest in such jurisdictions (primarily, in the least developed countries (LDCs) in transition) due to the non-existence of patents.[30]

Certainly, the above view does not answer how such importation is valid in India, notwithstanding several policy benefits to other countries and public interest arguments that favor Indian consumers. First, such a broad interpretation is clearly beyond the scope of

---

[24] N.S. Gopalakrishnan & T.G. Agitha, *Indian Patent System: The Road Ahead*, in THE FUTURE OF THE PATENT SYSTEM 229 (Ryo Shimanami ed., 2012).
[25] *Ibid.* at 246–47 and TRIPS, arts. 6, 28.
[26] Gopalakrishnan & Agitha, *supra* note 24, at 246–47 and TRIPS, arts. 6, 30, 28.
[27] Gopalakrishnan & Agitha, *supra* note 24, at 246–47.
[28] *Ibid.*
[29] *Ibid.*
[30] *Ibid.*

exhaustion, although the term is not defined in Article 6 of TRIPS. It does not violate Article 6, but may violate Articles 28, 41, and 44 of TRIPS.[31] The key to exhaustion lies in first sale made by the patent holder, otherwise footnote 6 to Article 28 of TRIPS will render no help since it does not touch on the rights of the patent holder (as there are no such rights to exhaust) and that importation is otherwise a specific right.[32] Furthermore, if a wider interpretation as above is imputed to section 107A(b), the solution under paragraph 6 of the Doha Declaration of TRIPS and Public Health, including the lengthy provisions in Article 31*bis* set out in the August 2003 Waiver Decision, would not have been required.[33] In such a situation, any country with "insufficient manufacturing capacity" could simply import the drug from a person who is duly authorized under the law to produce, sell, or distribute the product without recourse to the complicated mechanism established under the August 2003 Waiver Decision. Such importation would constitute valid grounds for importation of otherwise infringing drugs into several WTO members. Moreover, the question becomes whether Indian law should be interpreted in a way to promote broader technology transfer objectives that benefit other jurisdictions? The flexibilities available today are largely for the benefit of WTO members, except in expressly mentioned situations like export license.

Also "capturing more instances" of import may not be legally tenable since it is in contrast to the concept of exhaustion, especially where rights are not exhausted. Apart from the instances where someone other than the patentee who is "duly authorised under the law" manufactures the product (patented in India) in such other countries, which is completely out of the question, there are a few other tricky situations that might arise where the imported product may be duly authorized under law of the exporting destination. For example: (A) importation of a product into India from a jurisdiction where no patent exists (either due to non-existence of patent law or due to a decision by the putative patentee not to provide patent protection), but the product is put into market by the putative patent holder; (B) importation from a jurisdiction where the product is manufactured under a compulsory license by some manufacturer or is available under price control; and (C) where a product is produced by any person other than a patentee under a court granted remedy of continuing infringement or where a compulsory license has been granted to remedy an anticompetitive practice.

In situation A, it is difficult to argue that there was a first sale since there is no patent granted and no patent law exists (as in some LDCs in transition). At least one case in the European context has argued that such situations are covered by the doctrine of

---

[31] Article 6 of TRIPS does not excuse WTO members from violation of other provisions of the law. While WTO members are free to have any regime of exhaustion, it must be consistent with rights of the patent holders under art. 28 and also consistent with arts. 41 and 44, which deal with enforcement, including other provisions of GATT. See TRIPS, art. 6. See also Nuno Pires De Carvalho, The TRIPS Regime of Patents Rights 173 (2010).

[32] Footnote 6 to the word "importing" appearing in art. 28 reads, "this right, like all other rights conferred under this Agreement in respect of the use, sale, importation or other distribution of goods, is subject to the provisions of Article 6." TRIPS, art. 28, fn. 6.

[33] Ministerial Declaration, WTO doc. WT/MIN(01)/DEC/1, adopted at Doha, Qatar, November 14, 2001, available atwww.wto.org/english/thewto_e/minist_e/min01_e/mindecl_trips_e.htm.

exhaustion.[34] However, this is not a general rule of exhaustion since there is a "fictitious" presumption that the person is a putative patent holder and, hence, exhaustion applies. Although section 107A(b) covers such a situation, it leads to the unintended results of allowing importation of infringing goods into India.

In situation B, where there is a compulsory license, although it is a license, such a license is obtained not by virtue of the patent holder exercising a right (voluntary license), but through government enforced contracts.[35] In such a situation, although the manufacturer is duly authorized under the law, the manufacturer is not acting under the influence of a sale made by the patent holder. Also, since compulsory licenses are predominantly for the supply of domestic markets, the patented product can only be imported into countries where it is non-infringing. In situations of government enforced price controls on patented drugs (not voluntary price discrimination by the patent holder), there is some argument that there is exhaustion of rights since such patented products were put into the market at the option of the patent holder. Perhaps this is the only situation where section 107A(b) can be validly interpreted to provide the option for anyone to import products that have been placed under price controls after first sale in other jurisdictions.

In situation C, although section 107A(b) clearly applies because the manufacturer is continuing infringement by manufacturing a patented product under a compulsory license as a remedy to anticompetitive practice as a person duly authorized under the law, it is doubtful that these instances actually capture the meaning of exhaustion of rights. Article 31(k) of TRIPS clearly allows total exports of products that are under compulsory license granted to remedy an anticompetitive practice.[36] It is highly unlikely that when exports are valid it will automatically amount to an infringement in the importing country. Similarly, since injunction is a remedy in equity, an injunction may not be granted in many situations where monetary damages will suffice. In such a situation, it leads to bizarre results if such products were not allowed to be imported into other jurisdictions. In fact, since there is flow of such goods produced and sold under a continuing infringement rule in some jurisdictions, India has questioned the consistency of such exports of patented product under a *de facto* compulsory license (continuing infringement) in the context of TRIPS.[37] Of course, it can be argued that "more instances," although allowed

---

[34] Case 187/80, Merck & Co. v. Stephar B.V. & Petrus Stephanus Exler., [1981] E.C.R. I-02063.
[35] For a contrary view see INTERNATIONAL CENTRE FOR TRADE AND SUSTAINABLE DEVELOPMENT, RESOURCE BOOK ON TRIPS AND DEVELOPMENT 107 (2005), available at www.iprsonline.org/unctadictsd/docs/RB_Part1_Nov_1.4_update.pdf. The commentators note that "although allowing international exhaustion based on compulsory licensing does place power in the hands of the granting Member, since TRIPS permits each Member to determine its own policy and rules on the exhaustion issue, it is not clear why there is a threat to importing Members. They are not required to recognize compulsory licensing as the basis for exhaustion, but they may do so."
[36] TRIPS, art. 31(k).
[37] India's question to the United States delegation stated: "[w]e understand that there have been several such cases in the United States following the landmark Supreme Court judgment in eBay vs MercExchange in the issuance of all compulsory licences. We would request the US delegation to explain to the Members how these cases are not bound by the restrictions on exports under a compulsory license granted under Article 31 of the TRIPS." *WTO TRIPS Council: India Questions the United States on eBay v. MercExchange Precedent as Alternative to Paragraph 6*, KNOWLEDGE ECOLOGY INT'L (October 26, 2011), available at http://keionline.org/node/1299.

by section 107A(b), are legally contentious since it does not answer the question of validity of such goods in importing destinations in light of how exhaustion must be conceptually understood.

IV. REWORKING SECTION 107A(b): FIXING THE PATENT LAW ON "INTERNATIONAL EXHAUSTION"

Other scholars have emphasized that although section 107A(b) provides for international exhaustion, it does not expressly provide for national exhaustion.[38] Comparing section 30(3) of the Trade Marks Act of 1999, which is able to subsume both territorial first sale and international exhaustion, scholars argue that section 107A(b) is vastly different and it restricts itself to import. Thus, the scholars argue that the relevant provisions in the Sale of Goods Act of 1930[39] would automatically create a rule on territorial exhaustion by first sale. It is also argued that first sale of a physical product exhausts the patent holder's rights in the patent and, hence, the possessor cannot be sued distinctly for infringement of a patent, if the sale is otherwise not defective.[40] Relying on a United Kingdom (U.K.) House of Lords decision,[41] it is argued that exhaustion by first sale may also be created by virtue of an implied license.[42]

There are certain problems with this proposition. First, if territorial exhaustion by first sale could be broadly interpreted through sale of a physical product, it would mean that the Sale of Goods Act of 1930 recognizes diminution in the specific property, and distinct rights pertaining to the offer of sale or in actually selling different kinds of intellectual property embodying the sale of a product.[43] What constitutes a market for a general good or landed property is different from the market for an intellectual property protected

---

[38] Basheer & Kochupillai, *supra* note 3.
[39] *Ibid*. Relying on ss. 14, 19(1) and (2), the authors argue, that "when a patent-holder is selling a patented product, in the absence of any indication to the contrary in course of the sale, the property and hence the associated rights with respect to that specific product is transferred to the buyer, who then has the right to resell that product if she so desires." Sale of Goods Act, 1930, No. 3 of 1930, INDIA CODE (1930).
[40] Basheer & Kochupillai, *supra* note 3, at 70. Here the decision of Microbeads A.C. & anor. v. Vinhurst Road Markings Ltd., [1975] 1 All E.R. 529 (H.L.) is relied on by the authors. In a case where buyer of a patent-infringing product was sued by the patent holder (who was not the seller of the patented product herself), the court has noted that "it may be the seller is innocent himself, but when one or other must suffer, the loss should fall on the seller; because, after all, he sold the goods and if it turns out that they infringe a patent, he should bear the loss."
[41] Basheer & Kochupillai, *supra* note 3, at 70. The authors note that in United Wire Ltd. v. Screen Repair Services (Scotland) Ltd., [2000] 4 All E.R. 353 (H.L.), Lord Hoffman distinguished the doctrine of exhaustion from the theory of implied license and stated that "the difference in the two theories is that an implied licence may be excluded by express contrary agreement or made subject to conditions while the exhaustion doctrine leaves no patent rights to be enforced."
[42] It is argued that without such an interpretation even "use" of a patented product may be challenged since it is a specific right granted under s. 48. It is also argued that since such license must be in writing and registered in the Indian context (s. 68), the theory of implied license may not hold good and that the court may fall back on provisions in the Sale of Goods Act of 1930.
[43] See Sale of Goods Act, *supra* note 39.

good.[44] The second problem is that it is difficult to conceive why section 30(3) of the Trade Marks Act of 1999 and section 14 (a)(ii) of the Copyright Act, 1957 would either explicitly or implicitly provide for territorial exhaustion. The only way to resolve this dichotomy is to rely on a traditional common law rule that disfavors limitations on the alienation of private property.[45] In that sense, the intellectual property exhaustion through the first sale doctrine draws its strength from tangible property.[46] Thus, statutory recognition of the common law first sale doctrine is inherent in any transaction of sale, whether real property or intellectual property.[47]

These scholars have argued for amendments to section 107A(b) because of the expansive scope of the provision, due to the fact that the conceptual dichotomy presented by the notion of "duly authorized under the law to produce and sell or distribute the product"[48] is in direct conflict with section 48 of the 1970 Act that expressly provides for the exclusive rights of the patent holder.[49] First, these scholars note the missing word "sale" in section 107A(b) and that the provision restricts only imports, but does refer to a provision on exhaustion of rights by first sale.[50] However, it is unlikely that any court will restrict section 107A(b) only to imports since sale is a necessary occurrence. Notwithstanding, the authors conclude that the current expansive scope, if plainly interpreted, will hit the right to "import" granted under section 48 of the 1970 Act. Secondly, these scholars argue that it is incompatible with TRIPS since the rights to import and sell granted under Article 28 of TRIPS are impaired, and because Article 6 would not apply as there would be no case of exhaustion of rights, which is indeed excused by Article 6 of TRIPS.[51] The authors hope that the courts will construe the provision consistently with TRIPS to avoid potential conflict with international law. In any case, the authors seek an amendment to put to rest the controversies relating to section 107A(b) by amending it to limit parallel imports to situations where patent rights are actually exhausted, but not in

---

[44] Ariel Katz, *What Antitrust Law Can (and Cannot) Teach About the First Sale Doctrine* (January 23, 2012), available at http://dx.doi.org/10.2139/ssrn.1845842. Noting that: "the economics of efficient land use and the economics of efficient distribution (and use) of goods embedding IP differ substantially. Although both land use restraints and post-sale restraints may solve organizational problems and foster more efficient asset use, the organizational problems are different and the negative effects of enforceable restraints are different. Consequently, the costs and benefits of various instruments for enforcing the restraints (e.g., contract vs. property rules) are not the same, and it would be an unfortunate error to apply uncritically lessons from one area to another."

[45] See Schovsbo, *supra* note 14.

[46] Brilliance Audio, Inc. v. Haights Cross Commc'ns, Inc., 474 F.3d 365, 373 (6th Cir. 2007). The court stated: "this bargain, first developed in the common law, and later codified in the first sale doctrine, provides that once a copyright owner consents to release a copy of a work to an individual (by sale, gift, or otherwise), the copyright owner relinquishes all rights to that particular copy ... The first sale doctrine ensures that the copyright monopoly does not intrude on the personal property rights of the individual owner, given that the law generally disfavours restraints of trade and restraints on alienation."

[47] Bobbs-Merrill v. Straus, 210 U.S. 339 (1908) (proposing that "in view of the language of the statute, read in the light of its main purpose," there is "the right to impose ... a limitation at which the [good] shall be sold at retail by future purchasers.").

[48] Patents (Amendment) Act, 2005, No. 15, Acts of Parliament, 2005, s. 107A(b) (India).

[49] Basheer & Kochupillai, *supra* note 3, at 77–78.

[50] *Ibid.*

[51] *Ibid.*

all cases of "duly authorised under the law."[52] Such an amendment, the authors argue, should provide clarity so as to include national/territorial exhaustion, cover exhaustion of process/methods patents, and also to preclude instances of conditional sales that restrict the scope of exhaustion and subsequent resale and redistribution.[53]

However, it is doubtful if we need further amendments to section 107A(b) to achieve a robust and yet balanced regime of national and international exhaustion. It may be noted that the court may import the common law doctrine of first sale by simply reading the rights outlined in section 48 of the 1970 Act in a manner that allows "use," "sale," etc. as incidental to enjoyment of property in patented goods. This applies to rights that flow with reference to both products and process patents. Although section 107A(b) allows for a wide variety of imports duly authorized under the law, it is possible to interpret it in agreement with the importation right under section 48. Hence, the court has to make a conceptual argument of what amounts to "infringing copy," interpreting the phrase duly authorized under the law to mean duly authorized through rights that flow from patent law and not any other law. The court could look to recent attempts by the Indian legislature to enact a definition of international exhaustion in the area of copyright law to fix the contours of what conceptually amounts to international exhaustion in patent law. In doing so, the court should also be aware that any definition set forth by the courts must be in accordance with TRIPS.

V. STRICT LEGAL CONSTRUCTION: DOES SECTION 107A(b) REFER TO NATIONAL EXHAUSTION?

Is there a possibility that section 107A(b) is limited exclusively to territorial/national exhaustion and certain duly authorized import situations? At least one commentator has argued it is.[54] Relying on internal and external aids of interpretation, he concludes that those assuming that section 107A(b) unquestionably refers to international exhaustion are basing their views on "politico-economic arguments" and that "biases dictate the course of law and logic."[55] The author emphasizes that the concept of territoriality strongly suggests that section 107A(b) refers to "conditional import of patented products" and not international exhaustion as such.[56] The author argues that "duly authorized under the law" cannot be a foreign law because established rules of legislative drafting require such reference to a "foreign law" must be crystal clear from the plain reading of the provision.[57] The author refutes that even an interpretation that leads one to conclude that

---

[52] *Ibid.* at 84.
[53] *Ibid.* at 84.
[54] Such an interpretation was advanced in a public interest litigation in the matter of J. Sai Deepak v. Central Board of Excise & Customs & anor., (2012) WP(C) No. 3165 of 2012 (India). The petitioner's arguments were subsequently published as J. Sai Deepak, *Section 107A(b) of the Patents Act: Why it May Not Refer to or Endorse Doctrine of International Exhaustion?*, 4 INDIAN J. INTELL. PROP. L. 121 (2011).
[55] *Ibid.* at 138.
[56] *Ibid.* at 122.
[57] *Ibid.* at 127.

336   *Research handbook on intellectual property exhaustion and parallel imports*

international exhaustion in the most restricted sense is envisaged under section 107A(b) is plainly beyond the scope of the law. He argues for an interpretation that construes "duly authorised under law" to mean Indian law only, thus restricting it to territorial exhaustion and certain acts of "conditional import of patented products."[58]

There are a few claims made by the author that favor such a restricted interpretation of section 107A(b). First, the author suggests that section 84(7)(e) of the 1970 Act calls for a compulsory license to be issued when reasonable requirements of the public are not met.[59] This compulsory license should also include situations where the working of the patented invention commercially in India on a commercial scale is being prevented or hindered by the importation from abroad by the patentee or his licensee, including any party whom the patentee acquiesces infringement.[60] The author also refers to section 90(2), which provides restrictions on importation as a condition on the compulsory licensee.[61] Briefly, the argument is that the legislature could not have allowed a *carte blanche* import exception by way of an international exhaustion rule since such imports by the patent holder, the licensee, or even the compulsory licensee are not otherwise allowed.[62] The author argues that since the statute must be read as a whole, it is important that due attention be paid to such internal aids of interpretation.[63] There are certain problems with such an interpretation. First, the "persons" who are entitled to use the defense of section 107A(b) cannot be a patentee or his licensee since his right to import is already covered by section 48 of the 1970 Act. Hence, the "persons" referred to in section 107A(b) stand on a different footing than the patentee whose activity is sought to be restricted under section 84(7)(e) of the 1970 Act (by introducing a ground for compulsory license based on lack of working on a commercial scale). Irrespective of obligations on the patent holder (which is *quid pro quo*), any person other than the patent holder can always take recourse to section 107A(b). Secondly, the reason why there is a bar on importation figures as a condition to the compulsory license in section 90(2) of the 1970 Act is in order to get the compulsory licensee to use the patented invention on a commercial scale in India, which is also clear from section 89(a) of the 1970 Act, where there is an obligation on the Controller to secure it.[64]

It should be noted that, although a compulsory license operates as if it were a deed executed by the patentee, the compulsory licensee does not stand on a different footing than the "person" referred to in section 107A(b). This is because the rights of the patent holder survive even after a grant of a compulsory license, including against the compulsory licensee for violations of the terms of the compulsory license that are beyond the scope of such license, but within the scope of patentee's rights under section 48

---

[58]   *Ibid.* at 128–30.
[59]   *Ibid.* at 129.
[60]   *Ibid.*
[61]   Indian Patents Act, 1970, No. 39 of 1970, INDIAN CODE §90(2) (1970). See Deepak, *supra* note 54, at 129–30.
[62]   Deepak, *supra* note 54, at 129–30.
[63]   *Ibid.* at 129–30.
[64]   Indian Patents Act, 1970, No. 39 of 1970, INDIAN CODE § 89(a) (1970): "The powers of the Controller upon an application made under section 84 shall be exercised with a view to securing the following general purposes, that is to say,—(a) that patented inventions are worked on a commercial scale in the territory of India without undue delay and to the fullest extent that is reasonably practicable." *Ibid.*

of the 1970 Act. Section 90(2) of the 1970 Act restricts such importation only to the extent that it would be a violation of the patentee's rights under section 48 of the 1970 Act, and does not have anything to do with an act of importation allowed under section 107A(b). In other words, a compulsory license holder is allowed to import as long as it is covered by section 107A(b). In fact, section 90(2) of the 1970 Act plainly makes this distinction since it allows importation, which would otherwise not constitute infringement under the Act. It is inconceivable to imagine that there is a total prohibition on imports that are otherwise allowed. Section 107A(a), for example, *inter alia*, allows "importation" solely for the purposes of regulatory review, which also applies *qua* the compulsory licensee.[65]

Furthermore, such importation by a patentee by taking advantage of section 107(A)(b) is only a theoretical possibility if parallel imports are advantageous because the patentee would then not have applied for a compulsory license in the first place. Section 90(2) of the 1970 Act covers additional situations where importation may be in direct conflict with the rights of the patent holder, i.e., imports that are otherwise infringing under section 48 of the 1970 Act. What section 90(2) makes clear is that the exclusive importation right of the patent holder does not naturally flow as part of the terms of the license to the compulsory license holder. Such an interpretation is evident since section 90(3) of the 1970 Act speaks in terms of allowing importation in the "public interest," but based on certain terms and conditions, which include matters relating to royalties. Why would a compulsory licensee be liable to pay royalties to the Indian patent holder for what otherwise constitute valid imports under section 107A(a) or (b)? This leaves us with the only interpretation: that defenses to parallel imports asserted under section 107A(a) or (b) have to be construed independently of section 90(2).

It is further argued that by use of several external aids of interpretation, section 107A(b) ought to be narrowly construed.[66] Four arguments are proposed. The first argument is that by comparing the language adopted in the then proposed amendment for international exhaustion in the Copyright (Amendment) Bill of 2010 and the language in section 30(3) of the Trade Marks Act of 1999, which refers to international exhaustion, there is an appealing conclusion that if section 107A(b) seeks to allow parallel imports, the provision needs to be more clearly, and expressly, worded.[67] The second argument relies on India's submissions during the Uruguay Round, which clarified that the principle of international exhaustion of rights should apply to trademarks.[68] The author notes that similar submission on international exhaustion for patents was not made during the Uruguay Round.[69] It is also noted that India's submissions clearly advocated for government use of patents, wherein the government or any third party authorized by the government could also import patented products. The author suggests that section 107A(b) is precisely meant to cater to these situations where such importation would be

---

[65] Indian Patents Act, 1970, No. 39 of 1970, INDIAN CODE § 107A(b) (1970). Section 107A(a) allows "imports" within the regulatory review exemption.
[66] Deepak, *supra* note 54, at 130.
[67] Ibid.
[68] Ibid. at 131.
[69] Ibid.

required to be "duly authorised [sic] by law."[70] In other words, without Section 107A(b) persons who are otherwise authorized to import under limited exceptions, government use, or a compulsory license would infringe the rights of the patent holder. The author's third argument relies upon on a statement made by the Minister of Parliamentary Affairs during the introduction of the Patents (Amendment) Bill in 2005 wherein, in the context of section 107A(b), it was stated:

> [o]n import of patented commodity from anywhere in the world, the Government reserves the right. Despite the fact that a particular medicine may be patented here by any other company, we have the right to import that patented commodity from anywhere in the world, where it is cheaper, even though it is patented here.[71]

The author concludes that section 107A(b) can refer only to those situations where government or any third party authorized by the government may import.[72] Finally, the author envisages this as a ground for price control in addition to compulsory licenses, particularly in situations where compulsory licenses fail to bring down the prices and the government has to wait for two years after the grant of first compulsory license for revoking the patent under section 85 on grounds of non-working.[73]

Considering the arguments made *supra*, each of them will be addressed *infra*. First, it is true that the language proposed in Copyright (Amendment) Bill of 2010 and section 30(3) of the Trade Marks Act of 1999 both provide a significant amount of clarity regarding international exhaustion. However, there are different histories of how such provisions came about. As discussed in the introduction, it is wrong to presume that both copyright law and trademark law clearly provide for international exhaustion.

Second, it may be noted that India did not have any provision on parallel imports in the 1970 Act until it was introduced in 2002 and amended in 2005. It is also incorrect to infer from India's submission during the Uruguay Round negotiations regarding international exhaustion a pro-government approach, or pro-government authorized import for patented products. It should be noted that paragraph 28 of the Uruguay Communication typically refers to a case of government use and third party authorized government use. This provision existed in the 1970 Act even during the Uruguay Round. Section 100(4), *inter alia*, includes "import" among acts that the central government can exercise on its own behalf or may authorize any person other than the patent holder.[74] Since importation is already duly authorized by law under section 100(4), it is futile to impute that the Uruguay Round Communication intended to give a restricted meaning to section 107A(b) at a time when it did not exist in the statute book! Furthermore, since the grant of a patent is subject to conditions under section 47(1) and (4) of the 1970 Act, which also allow for

---

[70] Ibid.
[71] Patents (Amendment) Act, 2005, No. 15, Acts of Parliament, 2005, INDIA CODE (India) (statement of Minister of State for Parliamentary Affairs, Mr. Pawan Kumar Bansal).
[72] Deepak, *supra* note 54, at 135.
[73] Ibid. at 135.
[74] Indian Patents Act, 1970, No. 39 of 1970, INDIAN CODE § 100(4) (1970). Section 100(4) states, "the authorisation by the Central Government in respect of an invention may be given under this section . . . to make, use, exercise or vend the invention or import the machine, apparatus or other article or medicine or drug covered by such patent."

several limited exceptions, *inter alia*, for "import" by or on behalf of the government for the purpose merely of its own use (a provision distinct from government use based on compensation),[75] any interpretation narrowing the language of section 107A(b) is an artificial construction.[76] It is also possible that the Uruguay Round Communication mentioned "importation" for government use primarily to distinguish it from other possible (and TRIPS consistent) acts, like exhaustion, since they are already allowed under Article 6 of TRIPS.

Third, it is clear from the statement made by the Minister in the Indian Parliament that section 107A(b) intended to cover "parallel imports."[77] This particular intent to allow parallel imports may not be overlooked, particularly when instances of importation other than by the patentee stand independent of section 107A(b). Also, what cannot be missed is that the Minister's statement makes it clear that the "law" referred to in section 107A(b) is the foreign law that applies to the foreign exporter.[78] Section 107A(b) was clearly not enacted to include acts already duly authorized under Indian law.

Finally, it is reasonable to view section 107A(b) as a mechanism of price control since it is primarily a tool used to benefit from global price discrimination. It is difficult then to imagine that section 107A(b) is limited to a particular instance when only a person otherwise duly authorized under the 1970 Act can exercise the defense of parallel importation. This is particularly true when the government has several other methods in addition to compulsory licenses for price controls, both under the 1970 Act and several other external regulatory mechanisms, such as the National Pharmaceutical Pricing Authority, to engage in price controls.[79] Effectively, the government need not wait for three years from grant of patent for someone to apply for a compulsory license and another two years from the grant of a compulsory license to revoke a patent under section 85. Patents can be revoked in the public interest under section 66 of the 1970 Act and several measures, like limited exceptions under section 47 and government use under section 100, allow for imports even without taking recourse to a compulsory license.[80] To interpret a provision on parallel importation strictly as a policy lever for government authorized imports is not a legal construction permitted within the framework of the 1970 Act.

---

[75] Section 99(3) clarifies that Chapter XVII's use of inventions for purposes of government and acquisition of inventions by central government are not mutually exclusive, with limited exceptions provided in s. 47. Indian Patents Act, 1970, No. 39 of 1970, INDIAN CODE § 99(3) (1970).

[76] Interestingly, s. 107 allows limited exceptions under s. 47 as defenses. No such mention is made of s. 100, precisely because they are already authorized acts under Chapter XVII. Indian Patents Act, 1970, No. 39 of 1970, INDIAN CODE § 107 (1970).

[77] Combined Discussion on the Statutory Resolution Regarding Disapproval of Patents (Amendment) Ordinance, 2004 (No. 7 of 2004) and the Patents (Amendment) Bill, 2005 (March 22, 2005) (Lok Sabha Debates), available at http://indiankanoon.org/doc/1704755/.

[78] *Ibid*. The Minister noted that "the position now would be that 'the *foreign exporter* be authorised under the law, thus making the parallel imports easier.'"

[79] GOVERNMENT OF INDIA, REPORT OF THE COMMITTEE ON PRICE NEGOTIATION ON PATENTED DRUGS (2013), available at www.jetro.go.jp/ext_images/world/asia/in/ip/pdf/price_negotiation_en.pdf. Furthermore, price controls by way of an external regulation are possible, particularly when TRIPS does not place any bar on price controls by way of an external regulation.

[80] Indian Patents Act, 1970, No. 39 of 1970, INDIAN CODE §§ 66, 47, 100 (1970).

VI. CONCLUSION

This chapter has highlighted the distinct hermeneutic methods employed by scholars and commentators to discern the meaning, scope, and content of the patent exhaustion doctrine in India. It is noted that since section 107A(b) was enacted to provide for parallel imports, it has led to ambiguity on the question of territorial first sale. In any event, it is possible to imply the doctrine of first sale through common law restraints on alienation of property (codified through the Sale of Goods Act of 1930) and distinct developments in the common law of intellectual property exhaustion which has evolved over a period of time. This chapter has contested the use of teleological interpretation which attempts to provide purposive construction so as to take maximum advantage of the ostensible flexibilities in the international intellectual property landscape. Such a construction to "capture more instances" of import moving beyond the classic doctrine of international exhaustion presents a good many conceptual challenges, although teleological interpretations may be a good hermeneutic tool at the disposal of the court. And yet, this chapter has argued that there may be a few instances where section 107A(b) may be of some help to cover certain situations of valid imports.

While there is a need to construe section 107A(b) as allowing international exhaustion, it is doubtful if an amendment is needed to achieve such an outcome. As noted, the courts may import the common law doctrine of first sale as a condition precedent to alienation of property and, thus, bring in the concept of territorial first sale. In interpreting section 107A(b), the court could articulate the conceptual basis of international exhaustion and limit it to genuine instances of parallel imports. In doing so, the court could look to the language and conceptualization of parallel imports in comparative jurisdictions and the constraints imposed by section 48 of the Patents Act of 1970 dealing with rights of the patentee.

This chapter has contested the view that section 107A(b) is restricted to certain instances of imports that are duly authorized under Indian law, thus limiting it to national exhaustion. In discerning the use of both external and internal aids to interpretation, it is noted that the legislative intent to give effect to parallel imports was clear, although section 107A(b) could have been better worded. It places reliance on several instances where a wholesome reading of the 1970 Act, along with India's position during the Uruguay Round, will offer an answer that authorization required under the law is not Indian law.

PART V

SELECTED ISSUES (AND CHALLENGES) ON TRADEMARK EXHAUSTION

…

18. Trademark exhaustion and its interface with EU competition law
Apostolos G. Chronopoulos* and Spyros M. Maniatis**

I. INTRODUCTION

The exhaustion doctrine moulds trademarks into legal rights of exclusion, which are, in principle, solely pertaining to the initial commercialization of the trademarked good.[1] Mirroring the common law principle against the imposition of restrictions on the alienation of chattels, the doctrine of exhaustion creates alternative commercial sources for commodities outside the trademark proprietor's control and opens up collateral markets, all to the benefit of consumers. For the rights holder, there remains a single opportunity to devise a strategy for extracting revenue from the commercialization of the trademarked good when setting the price for the initial sale.

This legal construct reflects the archetypical form of the doctrine. A more functional approach was dictated by the need to promote the proper functioning of the common market. Territorial trademark exhaustion has been qualified so that it may only be triggered by sales within the European Union (EU) or European Economic Area (EEA) market.[2] Therein lies a decision of economic policy to protect the integration of the single market and incentivize European undertakings to exploit rent-seeking opportunities through price discrimination in international markets. The exhaustion doctrine is further mandated by EU primary law forbidding the partitioning of the internal market, in particular Articles 34 and 36 of the Treaty on the Functioning of the European Union (TFEU),[3] which is a goal shared by EU competition law.

Additional qualifications were then prompted by the necessity to implement a single market, characterized by free trade and operating under conditions of fair and effective competition. The aim of this chapter is to track down the evolutionary patterns of the rules on the exhaustion of trademark rights in the EU/EEA and to indicate how the principles of competition law shape the doctrine of trademark exhaustion.

---

* Lecturer in Trade Mark Law, Centre of Commercial Law Studies, Queen Mary University of London.
** Professor of Intellectual Property Law and Director, Centre of Commercial Law Studies, Queen Mary University of London.
[1] For an introduction, see Shubha Ghosh, *The Implementation of Exhaustion Policies: Lessons from National Experiences*, Issue Paper 40, ICTSD Programme on Innovation, Technology and Intellectual Property, available at www.ictsd.org/downloads/2014/01/the-implementation-of-exhaustion-policies.pdf.
[2] Case C-355/96, Silhouette Int'l v. Hartlauer, [1998] E.C.R. I-4799.
[3] Consolidated Version of the Treaty on the Functioning of the European Union, October 26, 2012, [2012] O.J. C326/49, 61 [hereinafter TFEU].

II. THE INTERFACE BETWEEN TRADEMARK EXHAUSTION, FREE MOVEMENT OF GOODS, AND COMPETITION POLICY AT ITS EARLY STAGE OF DEVELOPMENT

In *Consten and Grundig*,[4] the European Court of Justice (ECJ), as the Court of Justice for the European Union (CJEU) then was, ruled that an agreement between a German manufacturer of electronic products and its French exclusive distributor contravened European competition law because it compartmentalized the common market by providing absolute territorial protection against parallel imports into France. For the implementation of the agreement, the parties relied on the enforcement of Grundig's trademarks in France by its exclusive distributor, to whom these rights had been assigned. The Court noted that the parties could not invoke the exception to the principle of the free movement of goods for the purpose of protecting national property rights, now provided in Article 36 of the TFEU. The free movement of goods, a cornerstone for the internal market's effectiveness, was held to be an overarching policy promoted by European competition law. The application of this principle did not interfere, in the view of the court, with the grant of property rights, but only limited their exercise to the extent necessary for giving way to a precompetitive goal.[5]

After linking the free movement of goods with competition as a principle capable of restricting the exercise of intellectual property (IP) rights in the name of the proper functioning of the common market, the ECJ consistently fell back on the same value judgments to interpret provisions related to the free movement of goods. By dint of the distinction between the existence and the exercise of an IP right, the primacy was accorded to the free trade and free competition mandate. In the light of these considerations, the ECJ held that Deutsche Grammophon could not assert its copyright in order to forestall the importation of records from France into Germany that it had itself supplied to its French subsidiary.[6]

This notion was projected to the field of trademarks through a holding of the ECJ in *Hag I*, according to which the proprietor of a national trademark could not prevent the importation of goods bearing an identical mark that were lawfully marketed in the country of origin by virtue of its exclusive right.[7] The factual context of the case was rather exceptional involving the confiscation of a German business and its assets in Belgium as a consequence of the end of the Second World War. The clash arose when the Belgian company, a former subsidiary of HAG AG, sought to import its goods into Germany.[8] Considering the potentially perpetual nature of trademark rights, the ECJ saw a threat to the free movement of goods and the competitive process within the common market.[9] While the ECJ acknowledged the interests of consumers relying on trademarks to reach a conclusion regarding the commercial origin of goods, the Court was adamant

---

[4] Joined Cases 56 & 58/64, Etablissements Consten, S.A.R.L. & Grundig-Verkaufs GmbH v. Commission, [1966] E.C.R. 299 ("*Consten and Grundig*").
[5] *Ibid.* at 345.
[6] Case 78/70, Deutsche Grammophon v. Metro, [1971] E.C.R. 487.
[7] Case 192/73, Van Zuylen Freres v. Hag A.G., [1974] E.C.R. 731, 744 ("*Hag I*").
[8] *Ibid.* at 733.
[9] *Ibid.* at 744.

that the public interest against confusion should be served through other means that do not interfere with the free movement of goods.[10]

Driven by functional considerations to accomplish an effective regional market characterized by a system of undistorted competition, the exhaustion doctrine was meant to eradicate any possible restraints in the free flow of trade and competition raised by the exercise of national IP rights. It was a maximalist approach essentially seeking to preserve the freedom of trade and competition to the greatest extent possible. This framework describes, broadly speaking, the interface between the principles of free movement of goods, competition law, and the doctrine of exhaustion at the time when the latter was making its way into European trademark law.

III. THE ESSENTIAL FUNCTION AND THE SPECIFIC SUBJECT MATTER OF TRADEMARKS

It eventually turned out that the absence of any IP restraints in the free movement of goods was not the right approach for achieving a proper balance between the policies underlying the various IP rights and the competitive mandate. As the tension between the free movement of goods and the territorial nature of rights in trademarks increasingly attracted judicial scrutiny, more specific rules emerged.

Without an inviolable core of legal exclusivity, IP rights could not possibly fulfill their role in a market economy. In respect to trademarks, the ECJ defined this particular zone of legal exclusivity by reference to their essential function, after balancing the competing policies mentioned above. The ECJ eventually determined the so-called specific subject matter of a trademark, whose protection could not be denied as an impediment to the free movement of goods pursuant to Articles 28 and 30 of the Treaty Establishing the European Community (TEC)[11] (now Articles 34 and 36 of the TFEU). In particular the rights holder should enjoy "the exclusive right to use his trademark for the purpose of putting a product into circulation for the first time and therefore his protection against competitors wishing to take advantage of the status and reputation of the mark by selling products illegally bearing that trademark."[12] The legal construct of the specific subject matter of an IP right could be metaphorically perceived as a coin with two sides.[13] One side circumscribes the breadth of the trademark proprietor's exclusive authority: the right to control the initial sale of the trademarked good. The other side describes the policy consideration for granting protection to trademarks in a competitive economy. One may disagree with the ECJ's delimitation of the trademark monopoly and its substantive evaluation on the policy behind trademark protection. However, from the perspective of legal methodology, the specific subject matter theory has been a paradigmatic legal con-

---

[10] *Ibid.*
[11] Consolidated Versions of the Treaty on European Union and of the Treaty Establishing the European Community, December 24, 2002, [2002] O.J. C345/1 (EC) [hereinafter TEC].
[12] Case 3/78, Centrafarm B.V. v. Am. Home Prods. Corp., [1978] E.C.R. 1823, 1840.
[13] On this particular point, see DAVID T. KEELING, INTELLECTUAL PROPERTY RIGHTS IN EU LAW, Vol. I, FREE MOVEMENT AND COMPETITION LAW 65 (2004) (citing Valentine Korah, *National Patents and the Free Movement of Goods Within the Common Market*, 38 MODERN L. REV. 333, 335 (1975)).

struct that sought to optimally design[14] the scope of IP rights in order to attend the legal necessity of conforming these rights within the broader system of norms to which they belonged:[15] the rules governing the functioning of the internal market.[16] Main point, the principle of exhaustion was expressly articulated.

Revisiting *Hag I*, the Court held that the German trademark proprietor could eventually oppose the importation of Belgian HAG coffee into Germany by virtue of his exclusive right.[17] Pivotal to this direction shift was the consideration of the specific subject matter of trademarks as determined by their essential function. The latter would be impaired if an identical trademark was permitted to coexist in the same territory. Equally determinative of the outcome was the absence of any element of consent on behalf of the trademark proprietor, which translates into lost opportunities to generate revenue by marketing coffee bearing the HAG mark in Germany.[18] Using other means to protect consumers from being misled, as suggested by the Court in *Hag I*, cannot effectively serve the goals of trademark policy for two main reasons: first, these other means would not always eliminate consumer confusion; and secondly, trademarks could only fulfill their role as credible indicators of origin and quality if they are subjected to rights of exclusivity.[19]

In other words, the imposition of competition restraints through exceptions to the free movement of goods principle was deemed necessary to promote other policy goals that contribute to the effectiveness of competition. These policy goals included the

---

[14] This is actually what we still strive to do today. See generally Josef Drexl, *Intellectual Property Rights as Constituent Elements of a Competition-Based Market Economy*, in INTELLECTUAL PROPERTY AND MARKET POWER, ATRIP PAPERS 2006–2007, 167–78 (Gustavo Ghidini & Luis Mariano Genovesi eds., 2008).

[15] On this point, see the observations of HANNS ULLRICH, GEWERBLICHER RECHTSSCHUTZ UND URHEBERRECHT IM BINNENMARKT, EU-WETTBEWERBSRECHT para. 53 (Ulrich Immenga & Joachim Mestmäcker eds., 5th ed. 2012) (reviewing English and German literature adopting a critical stance towards the concept of the specific subject matter and noting that the criticism has been "unfair" at least with regard to claims that this concept is foreign to IP theory and that it inappropriately subsumes IP rights under the principle of free movement of goods). See also KEELING, *supra* note 13, at 62 (arguing that criticism has been "a little harsh").

[16] Perhaps the most constructive criticism that could be directed against the concept of the specific subject matter at a policy level is that it is not apt for balancing the diverse interests that collide in the background of a context where IP, competition, and trade policy intersect. As we shall see later on, the analysis of vertical restraints under competition laws commands more nuanced approaches to the application of the exhaustion doctrine. Hence, it has been considered more pertinent to distinguish between proper (competitive) and improper (anticompetitive) exercise of a trademark right. See generally, Friedrich-Karl Beier, *Industrial Property and the Free Movement of Goods in the Internal European Market*, 21 INT'L REV. INTELL. PROP. & COMPETITION L. 131 (1990) (critically evaluating subsequent decisions of the Court that adopted a more flexible approach).

[17] Case C-10/89, S.A. CNL-Sucal v. Hag Gf AG, [1990] E.C.R. I-3711.

[18] *Ibid.* at I-3758–59; the same principles were held applicable to voluntary assignments: see Case C-9/93, IHT Internationale Heiztechnik GmbH v. Ideal-Standard GmbH, [1994] E.C.R. I-2789 ("*Ideal Standard*"). Adhering to the principle laid out in *Consten and Grundig* the Court sought in para. 59 of its ruling in *Ideal Standard* to make trademark proprietors aware that these assignments *might* run afoul of Article 85 of the EEC Treaty (Article 101 of the TFEU).

[19] See generally, Friedrich-Karl Beier, *Trademark Conflicts in the Common Market: Can They Be Solved by Means of Distinguishing Additions?*, 9 INT'L REV. INTELL. PROP. & COMPETITION L. 221 (1978).

precompetitive virtues of trademarks[20] and the legitimate interests of traders,[21] including the interest in making informed decisions when calculating the profits deriving from the commercialization of their IP rights. Upon the latter point, the CJEU has widely elaborated in the meantime through a series of cases that concretized the requirement of consent.

At this stage, trademark exhaustion becomes subjected to a "rule of reason" analysis directed at balancing all the interests involved in cases of parallel importation, much like a theory of unfair competition.[22] This became even more evident in the *Hoffmann-La Roche* case where the ECJ had to rule on the trademark proprietor's authority to prevent the importation of repackaged goods that were initially marketed with his consent in the common market.[23] As the Court opined, repackaged pharmaceuticals may well be parallel-imported into the Member States provided that the essential function of the respective trademarks is not affected.[24] The trademark proprietor should also prevail, according to the Court, when the original condition of the product is affected.[25]

Notably, both trader interests in maintaining a good reputation and consumer interests in getting the pharmaceutical they actually wish to buy are simultaneously protected under these two rules. In the latter case, concerning the effect of repackaging on the goods' condition, the Court made a rather implicit reference to the quality function. Concessions to the rights holder are more easily made when the protection granted would promote some consumer interest in corollary manner. *Hoffmann-La Roche* imposed a duty on the parallel importer to provide notice of importation of repackaged goods to the trademark proprietor and clearly state on the new packaging that the product has been repackaged by him,[26] which again promotes both trader and consumer interests. The interests involved are balanced by reference to a measure of social welfare, namely, the social benefits flowing out of the free movement of goods within the internal market. Of course, the assertion of trademark rights to prevent the importation of repackaged goods should never constitute a "disguised restriction on trade" between the Member States as provided in Article 30 of the TEC, now Article 36 of the TFEU.[27]

In sum, soon after the sweeping proposition of *Hag I* that sought to deny the trademark proprietor any possibility of interfering with the free movement of goods, trademark exhaustion developed into a doctrine requiring a more nuanced analysis under the rule of reason of trademark law, which traditionally entails a value judgment on whether and to what extent the law should protect a certain function of trademarks. The ECJ, as it then

---

[20] Case 119-75, Terrapin (Overseas) Ltd. v Terranova Industrie C.A. Kapferer & Co., [1976] E.C.R. 1039, 1061–62.
[21] Rene Joliet & David T. Keeling, *Trade Mark Law and the Free Movement of Goods: The Overruling of the Judgment in Hag I*, 22 INT'L REV. INTELL. PROP. AND COMPETITION L. 303, 310–12 (1991).
[22] In regard to the unfair competition impulse in the judgments of the CJEU, see generally, Spyros Maniatis, *Whither European Trade Mark Law—Arsenal and Davidoff: The Creative Disorder Stage*, 7 MARQ. INTELL. PROP. L. REV. 99 (2003).
[23] Case 102/77, Hoffmann-La Roche & Co. A.G. v. Centrafarm, [1978] E.C.R. 1139.
[24] *Ibid.* at 1164.
[25] *Ibid.* at 1165.
[26] *Ibid.*
[27] *Ibid.* at 1164–65.

was, sought to balance the interests involved in parallel importation disputes by concretizing Articles 28 and 30 of the TEC (now Articles 34 and 36 of the TFEU) into specific rules that resembled unfair competition norms.[28]

IV. EXHAUSTION AND THE SYSTEM OF THE TRADE MARK DIRECTIVE

As evidenced by *Consten and Grundig*, the nexus to competition was already an essential feature of the exhaustion doctrine from the early stages of its development, with the free movement of goods being the crucial precompetitive aspect. However, that case concerned an agreement between private parties whose legality had to be ascertained under Article 81 of the TEC (now Article 101 of the TFEU). As a consequence of the application of this provision, the anticompetitive enforcement of trademark rights could be avoided. But in legal terms, the assertion of trademark rights constitutes a state, and not a private, restraint on trade because these rights are actually enforced by the Member States. It was for this reason that the doctrine of exhaustion had to develop within the legal framework of the rules governing the free movement of goods. Since the avoidance of the partitioning of the internal market is a goal shared by the European rules on competition and the free movement of goods, this shift in the legal foundation should not be taken to suggest that the normative link between the exhaustion doctrine and competition law was intentionally broken. Nevertheless, Articles 34 and 36 of the TFEU cannot cover the wide range of competition issues regulated through Articles 101 and 102 of the TFEU,[29] many of which are directly related to the exhaustion doctrine.

In the course of the legal developments, the exhaustion rule was codified in European secondary legislation.[30] Still, as the CJEU noted in *Bristol Myers*, Article 7 of the European Trade Mark Directive (TMD)—which will be replaced by Article 15 of Directive (EU) 2015/2436 with effect from 15 January 2019 (2015 Trade Mark Directive)—has to be interpreted in the light of Articles 34 and 36 of the TFEU (then Articles 28 and 30 of

---

[28] Alexander Von Mühlendahl, Dimitris Botis, Spyros Maniatis & Imogen Wiseman, Trade Mark Law in Europe, 722 (3rd ed. 2016).

[29] Valentine Korah, *Dividing the Common Market Through National Industrial Property Rights*, 35 Modern L. Rev. 634, 643 (1972).

[30] Directive 2008/95/EC of the European Parliament and of the Council of October 22, 2008 to approximate the laws of the Member States relating to trade marks (codified version), [2008] O.J. L299/25 (EC) [hereinafter TMD]. This Directive codified the First Council Directive 89/104/EEC of December 21, 1988 to approximate the laws of the Member States relating to trade marks, [1989] O.J. L040/1 (EC). The TMD is repealed with effect from January 15, 2019 by Directive (EU) 2015/2436 of the European Parliament and of the Council of December 16, 2015 to approximate the laws of the Member States relating to trade marks [2015] O.J. L336/1 (EU) [hereinafter 2015 Trade Mark Directive], which entered into force on January 12, 2016 (see Articles 55–56 of the Trade Mark Directive). Article 7 TMD is titled "Exhaustion of the rights conferred by a trade mark" and reads: "1. The trade mark shall not entitle the proprietor to prohibit its use in relation to goods which have been put on the market in the Community under that trade mark by the proprietor or with his consent. 2. Paragraph 1 shall not apply where there exist legitimate reasons for the proprietor to oppose further commercialisation of the goods, especially where the condition of the goods is changed or impaired after they have been put on the market."

the TEC).[31] The core of the argument was basically that secondary legislation may not run afoul of primary legislation. As a result, the development of trademark exhaustion as a limiting doctrine was confined to a narrow horizon of principles relevant to the free movement of goods.

With a consistent line of cases, the CJEU has further developed the principles emerging from the jurisprudence on Articles 28 and 30 of the TEC. In particular, the CJEU has further concretized the legitimate interest of the rights holder that the doctrine of exhaustion protects. Apart from the legitimate interest in deciding whether the trademarked goods will be commercialized in the first place, the trademark proprietor is also entitled to oppose the commercialization of such goods that were indeed distributed to the public but did not actually enter the market as items of commerce. In *eBay*, for example, it was held that by distributing testers and samples of perfumes, the respective trademark rights were not exhausted.[32] The trademarked goods had been gratuitously distributed to retailers and, as a consequence thereof, the goods had not been placed on the market with the consent of the trademark proprietor, as Article 7(1) TMD (Article 15(1) of the 2015 Trade Mark Directive) requires.[33] The circumstances surrounding the gratuitous distribution of such items may reveal a lack of consent to their commercialization. Such intent was evident in *Coty*, where the trademark proprietor had formally retained the property of the bottles that had additionally been marked with the words "demonstration" and "not for sale."[34]

The principles surrounding the adverse effect on the trademarked good's original condition as a legitimate reason for the rights holder to oppose its further commercialization evolved further with the ruling of the ECJ in *Bristol-Myers*, a case that involved the parallel importation of repackaged pharmaceuticals into Denmark.[35] Balancing the public interest in the freedom of trade within the common market and the interest position of the rights holder, the ECJ emphasized that only a real risk of an adverse effect on the product's original condition would prevent the exhaustion of the respective trademark rights.[36] As a rule, when repackaging is carried out in a manner that the product remains intact, parallel importation would be permissible, such as when the repackager affects only the external layer of double packaging.[37] Depending on the nature of the goods in question their sensitivity to repackaging may vary.[38]

To cut a long descriptive story of case law short, detailed contextual inquiries are necessary so as to give effect to the balance of interests required under Article 7 TMD (Article 15 of the 2015 Trade Mark Directive). The essence is that the jurisprudence of the CJEU has sought to conduct a meticulous analysis of the interests involved. *Bristol-Myers* is an

---

[31] Joined Cases C-427, C-429, & C-436/93, Bristol Myers Squibb v. Paranova A/S, C.H. Boehringer Sohn, Boehringer Ingelheim K.G. & Boehringer Ingelheim A/S v. Paranova A/S, & Bayer Aktiengesellschaft and Bayer Danmark A/S v. Paranova A/S, [1996] E.C.R. I-3457, I-3527. *Cf.* recital 28 of the 2015 Trade Mark Directive.
[32] Case C-324/09, L'Oréal S.A. v. eBay International A.G., [2011] E.C.R. I-6011.
[33] *Ibid.* at I-6105–6.
[34] Case C-127/09, Coty Prestige Lancaster Group GmbH v. Simex Trading A.G., [2010] E.C.R. I-4965, I-4981–82.
[35] *Bristol-Myers*, *supra* note 31, [1996] E.C.R. at I-3520 *et seq.*
[36] *Ibid.* at I-3537.
[37] *Ibid.* at I-3536–37.
[38] *Ibid.* at I-3536.

illustrative example of the Court's efforts, noting that repackaged goods may be indirectly affected when the parallel importer omits to disclose important information regarding the nature, functionality, or maintenance of the parallel-imported goods.[39]

Since the integrity of the internal market remains the main competition related aspect of the teleology underlying Article 7 TMD (Article 15 of the 2015 Trade Mark Directive), the Court had to further elaborate on the circumstances under which the enforcement of trademark rights would give rise to an artificial partitioning of that market. For instance, to the extent that repacking is necessary for importing a product into a particular Member State due to regulations on the marketing of alcohol or pharmaceuticals ("necessity requirement"), it will not constitute a legitimate reason upon which the trademark proprietor may oppose the further commercialization of the goods.[40] Repackaging is not necessary in the legal sense when it is solely driven by an attempt of the parallel importer to secure a commercial advantage over the trademark proprietor.[41] That could be the case when the parallel importer's repackaging is directed at appropriating the marketing efforts of the proprietor of the national trademark (free rider problem). Consumer aversion to repackaged or relabeled products, which may exist in respect to pharmaceuticals, is relevant to the inquiry of whether the parallel importer is guaranteed an effective access to the national market. However, this consumer aversion must be particularly strong to prevent the exhaustion of trademark rights.[42] Apparently, the CJEU has further inquired into the interests of the parallel importer that seem to be corollary to the public interest in promoting the free movement of goods, just as the interests of the trademark proprietor are corollary to the public interest against confusion as to source.

At the same time, as already indicated, the Court has sought to balance the interests of the trademark proprietor, the parallel importer, and consumers in the light of the mandate in favor of free trade pursuant to Articles 28 and 30 of the TEC (now Articles 34 and 36 of the TFEU). It effectively did so by imposing various requirements on the latter, such as giving proper notice of the importation and providing detailed, as well as clearly visible, information on the package about the manufacturer, as well as the re-packager.[43] These obligations of the parallel importer allow the trademark proprietor to timely prepare his legal and business reaction to the parallel importation.[44] Developing the principles established in *Hoffmann-La Roche*, the CJEU strengthened the interest position of the rights holder by holding that notice taken through sources other than the parallel importer, such

---

[39] *Ibid.* at I-3538.
[40] *Ibid.* at I-3535; see also Case C-143/00, Boehringer Ingelheim K.G. v. Swingward Ltd., [2002] E.C.R. I-3759, I-3783 ("*Boehringer I*"); Case C-379/97, Pharmacia & Upjohn S.A. v. Paranova A/S, [1999] E.C.R. I-6927, I-6969; Case C-349/95, Frits Loendersloot v. George Ballantine, [1997] E.C.R. I-6227, I-6259–60.
[41] Case C-348/04, Boehringer Ingelheim K.G. & ors. v. Swingward Ltd. & Dowelhurst Ltd., [2007] E.C.R. I-3391, I-3457 ("*Boehringer II*"); *Upjohn*, *supra* note 40, [1999] E.C.R. at I-6969.
[42] *Bristol Myers*, *supra* note 31, [1996] E.C.R. at I-3540–41; *Boehringer I*, *supra* note 40, [2002] E.C.R. at I-3784.
[43] *Bristol-Myers*, *supra* note 31, [1996] E.C.R. at I-3539–41 (citing Hoffmann-La Roche & Co. A.G. v. Centrafarm, [1978] E.C.R. 1139); see also Nicholas Shea, *Parallel Importers' Use of Trade Marks: The European Court of Justice Confers Rights but also Imposes Responsibilities*, 19 EUR. INTELL. PROP. L. REV. 103 (1997).
[44] *Boehringer I*, *supra* note 40, [2002] E.C.R. at I-3787.

as public authorities, does not relieve the latter from the respective duty.[45] In similar vein, the mere failure to comply with the notice obligation would qualify as an infringement of trademark rights.[46] Resembling the regulation of the competitive process through general obligations to refrain from unfair competition, the Court imposed on both the trademark proprietor and the parallel importer a reciprocal duty "to make sincere efforts to respect each other's legitimate interests."[47]

A series of eloquent decisions emerged at this stage of the exhaustion doctrine's development, including the well celebrated case of *Dior v. Evora*.[48] One important principle set by this case is that once trademark exhaustion has occurred, the rights holder may not fetter the free movement of goods through the assertion of other IP rights such as copyrights.[49] A chain of chemists' shops in the Netherlands, Evora, sold parallel-imported luxury cosmetics manufactured by Dior.[50] Evora's offers had been advertised in leaflets depicting pictures of containers and packaging that were protected by copyright.[51] As the Court noted, the enforcement of copyright should not limit the legal consequences of trademark exhaustion in such a context.[52]

Perhaps the most significant aspect of *Dior v. Evora* is the recognition that the damage to the trademarked good's luxurious aura constitutes a legitimate interest of the rights holder within the meaning of Article 7 TMD (Article 15 of the 2015 Trade Mark Directive), which allows him to oppose the further commercialization of goods already placed on the market with his consent.[53] The ruling of the ECJ gave the strong impression of a concession to the advertising function, perceiving that function as the capacity of a trademark to generate sales through the appeal of the brand image encapsulated in it, although there was no explicit reference to that effect.[54] Evaluating the decision in hindsight, one could well claim that it was a rather hesitant recognition of the legal significance of the other so-called "economic functions" of trademarks. The decision could be seen as a pre-feast to *Arsenal*'s qualified statement focusing on the essential function,[55] *Opel*'s invitation to trademark proprietors to raise arguments entailing the impairment of other functions,[56] and the unequivocal recognition of their relevance to the application of the "double identity" rule in *L'Oreal*.[57] Elements of a similar analysis are also present in *Bristol-Myers*, where it was held that repackaging should not adversely affect the legitimate interests of

---

[45] *Ibid.* at I-3788.
[46] *Ibid.* On the issue of financial remedies as a measure of deterring failure to comply with the notice requirement, see *Boehringer II, supra* note 41, [2007] E.C.R. at I-3466–68.
[47] *Boehringer I, supra* note 40, [2002] E.C.R. at I-3787.
[48] Case C-337/95, Parfums Christian Dior S.A. v. Evora B.V., [1997] E.C.R. I-6013.
[49] *Ibid.* at I-6053.
[50] *Ibid.* at I-6036–37.
[51] *Ibid.* at I-6038.
[52] *Ibid.* at I-6053.
[53] *Ibid.*
[54] Gert-Jan Van De Kamp, *Protection of Trade Marks: The New Regime—Beyond Origin?*, 20 EUR. INTELL. PROP L. REV. 364, 367 (1998); Helen Norman, *Perfume, Whisky and Leaping Cats of Prey: A U.K. Perspective on Three Recent Trade Mark Cases Before the European Court of Justice*, 20 EUR. INTELL. PROP. L. REV. 306, 307 (1998).
[55] Case C-206/01, Arsenal Football Club v. Matthew Reed, [2002] E.C.R. I-10273, I-10317–19.
[56] Case C-48/05, Adam Opel v. Autec, [2007] E.C.R. I-1017, I-1045.
[57] Case C-487/07, L'Oréal v. Bellure, [2009] E.C.R. I-5185, I-5253.

the trademark proprietor in the maintenance of a particular brand image when the repute of the mark influences the consumers' purchasing decisions, as the case may well be with pharmaceuticals.[58] An explanation for the indirect reference to functions other than the essential function could be found in the prevailing theory of trademark protection at the time *Dior* was decided. The overwhelming majority of legal and scholarly opinions favored a trademark system oriented at the protection of the origin function.

To sum up, the CJEU has shaped the exhaustion doctrine by balancing the diverse interests involved in the light of a normatively binding measure of social welfare: the free movement of goods. The exhaustion doctrine was analyzed through the lens of the functional approach inquiring on the protectability of each trademark function. Consistent with the analysis made under Article 5(1)(a) TMD (Article 10(2)(a) of the 2015 Trade Mark Directive), the CJEU adopted the notion of the impairment of a trademark function as a limiting principle. Obviously, trademark exhaustion implicates the whole bunch of theoretical problems surrounding trademark law, including the rights holder's level of reward, the protectability of the various trademark functions, and the market effects of trademarks.

Concluding, while the doctrine of exhaustion was initially linked to value judgments related to antitrust analysis it was later on cabined into the teleology flowing out of the EU primary law provisions governing the free movement of goods and subjected to the functional analysis of trademark law.

V. TOWARDS A WIDER INTEGRATION OF COMPETITION CONCERNS IN THE EXHAUSTION DOCTRINE

Another underlying doctrinal question, which can only be briefly sketched here, is actually whether the principle of free movement of goods as a cornerstone of the internal market could encompass considerations derived from competition law analysis. Arguably, a distinction existed under the TEC between the normative concept of the internal market, which mandated the strict implementation of the four freedoms, and the normative concept of the common market, which traversed the rules on free movement of goods to encompass further policies, including the effectiveness of competition (Articles 81 and 82 of the TEC).[59] According to this argument, which basically rested on the TEC using the

---

[58] *Bristol Myers*, *supra* note 31, [1996] E.C.R. at I-3540: "Even if the person who carried out the repackaging is indicated on the packaging of the product, there remains the possibility that *the reputation of the trade mark, and thus of its owner*, may nevertheless suffer from an *inappropriate presentation of the repackaged product*. In such a case, the trade mark owner has *a legitimate interest, related to the specific subject-matter of the trade mark right*, in being able to oppose the marketing of the product." *Ibid.* (emphasis added). See also *Boehringer II*, *supra* note 41, [2007] E.C.R. at I-3457–58; neither the requirement of necessity (*Boehringer II*, *supra* note 41, [2007] E.C.R. at I-3457) nor a principle of minimum intervention (Case C-276/05, Wellcome v. Paranova, [2008] E.C.R. I-10511) could justify an exception to the protectability of a proprietor's interest in avoiding harm to the reputation of his trademark through repackaging that is inappropriate in manner and style. In that regard, the protection of the interests of the trademark proprietor is particularly strong.

[59] Laurence W. Gormley, *Competition and Free Movement: Is the Internal Market the Same as a Common Market?*, 13 Eur. Bus. L. Rev. 517 (2002) (highlighting succinctly the issue).

two concepts in a seemingly non-interchangeable manner,[60] there could be no limitation to the principle of free movement of goods, and consequently, to trademark exhaustion in the form of a rule derived from Articles 28 and 30 of the TEC that would take into consideration the effectiveness of competition. However, the CJEU never drew such a distinction in its case law, adopting contextual interpretations in the light of the TEC's objectives and paving the way to a gradual convergence of the two principles.[61] Eventually, the references to the common market in the Treaties were replaced with those to the internal market as the Lisbon Treaty[62] entered into force. The Lisbon Treaty's internal market references thereby deprived the proponents of an isolated reading of Articles 34 and 36 of the TFEU from a strong foothold in the letter of the law. Competition and free movement rules complementarily operate to promote the proper functioning of the internal market. Therefore, the differences in their addressees, their legal consequences and their enforcement could not support an argument for their isolated application.

Antitrust considerations resurfaced with the changes in trademark enforcement that followed the expansion of these rights both in subject matter and scope. Trademark law has in the meantime accommodated legitimate business interests of the rights holders getting to grips with the market effects of trademarks. Since almost anything can now be protected as a trademark, there is plenty of elbow-room available to the proprietors for obtaining a competitive advantage through the assertion of their exclusive rights. With the new possibilities for strategic procurement and enforcement of trademarks, the danger of proprietors abusing their rights to stifle competition arose. Some of the competition considerations were internalized into trademark doctrine while others called for a direct application of competition law to the exercise of trademark rights.[63]

An illustrious example is the *Kosan Gas*[64] case. There, the trademark rights were invoked to foreclose a downstream market where gas was sold as a staple article for an innovative composite bottle, the shape of which was protected as a three-dimensional mark.[65] Kosan was in the business of selling gas in Denmark as an exclusive licensee and distributor of the Norwegian producer of the bottle.[66] Kosan had also affixed its own trademarked name and logo to the bottle.[67] When a third party, Viking, started to sell its own gas by refilling used composite bottles already sold by Kosan, the latter sought to assert its trademark rights in the bottle.[68]

Viking neither removed nor covered the marks of Kosan that were affixed to the

---

[60] TEC, Articles 2, 3(c), 14(2), 94, 95.
[61] See generally, Kamiel Mortelmans, *Towards Convergence in the Application of the Rules on Free Movement and on Competition?*, 38 COMMON MARKET L. REV. 613 (2001).
[62] Treaty of Lisbon amending the Treaty on European Union and the Treaty Establishing the European Community, December 13, 2007, [2007] O.J. C305/1 (EC).
[63] VON MÜHLENDAHL, BOTIS, MANIATIS & WISEMAN, *supra* note 28, at 296–97 and 773 (concluding their analysis of the relevant CJEU jurisprudence); Vlotina Liakatou & Spyros Maniatis, *Red Soles, Gas Bottles and Ethereal Market Places: Competition, Context and Trade Mark Law*, 34 EUR. INTELL. PROP. L. REV. 1 (2012).
[64] Case C-46/10, Viking Gas A/S v. Kosan Gas A/S, [2011] E.C.R. I-6161.
[65] *Ibid.* at I-6186.
[66] *Ibid.*
[67] *Ibid.* at I-6187.
[68] *Ibid.*

bottle.[69] Therefore, Kosan made an argument that Viking's practice entailed the danger of false attributions of product quality by consumers. While that argument was somehow weak, as consumers going directly to Viking for refilling their bottles could not possibly err in attributing the quality of the staple article to the right trader, it becomes apparent that once argued successfully, the exceptions to the exhaustion doctrine have a significant potential to allow for the monopolization of a downstream market. This potential increases when the rights holder would seek to rely on an argument that the refilling process affects the original condition of the product or somehow damages the repute of the trademark. That was not the case in *Kosan*, actually.

A significant aspect of *Kosan* is the emphasis put on the fact that trademarks are part of a system of undistorted competition.[70] While this point is commonly raised when justifying legal protection for the essential function of trademarks to designate commercial source,[71] the CJEU has also referred to the concept of undistorted competition whenever it needed to prevent an anticompetitive enforcement of trademark rights.[72] This teleological interpretation coexists with and, at times, overshadows the analysis based on the trademark functions.[73]

In the context of *AdWords*, for instance, the outcome was decisively determined by the welfare enhancing virtues of (comparative) advertising on the Internet.[74] Seeking to strike a balance of the interests at stake, the CJEU therefore noted that the rights holder has to tolerate some "repercussions" on the advertising use of the mark and his commercial strategy.[75] To give effect to that value judgment, the Court adopted narrow definitions

---

[69] Ibid.

[70] Ibid. at I-6195.

[71] See e.g. S.A. CNL-Sucal v. Hag Gf A.G., [1990] E.C.R. I-3711, I-3758–59; *Arsenal, supra* note 55, [2002] E.C.R. at I-10316; Case C-299/99, Koninklijke Philips Elecs. v. Remington Consumer Prods., [2002] E.C.R. 1-5475, I-5504; Case C-412/05P, Alcon v. OHIM, [2007] E.C.R. I-3569, I-3613. In Case C-48/09P, Lego Juris A/S v. OHIM, [2010] E.C.R. I-8403, I-8456 and Joined Cases C-337-C-340/12P, Pi-Design/Bodum v. Yoshida Metal Industry/OHIM, ECLI:EU:C:2014:129, para. 42, the Court uses a different formulation. The term "undistorted" is not mentioned and the Court simply refers to "trademark law" as "an essential element in the system of competition in the European Union" and then links it to the essential function. The formulation adopted in these cases gives an impression of factoring out the diverse market effects that trademarks have. In any event, both *Lego* and *Pi-Design* cite the preceding cases for their proposition. It should also be noted that the substantive content of Article 3(g) of the TEC resides now in Protocol 27 to the TEU and the TFEU, which considers the system of undistorted competition as a *sine qua non* element of the internal market. Since the Protocols constitute, pursuant to Article 51 of the TEU, an integral part of the Treaties, the reforming Treaty of Lisbon could not be taken as discarding some old competition policy paradigm in the EU.

[72] Case C-46/10, Viking Gas A/S v. Kosan Gas A/S, [2011] E.C.R. I-6161; Case C-323/09, Interflora Inc. v. Marks & Spencer, [2011] E.C.R. I–8625, I-8686.

[73] Apostolos Chronopoulos, *Determining the Scope of Trademark Rights by Recourse to Value Judgements Related to the Effectiveness of Competition: The Demise of the Trademark-Use Requirement and the Functional Analysis of Trademark Law*, 42 INT'L REV. INTELL. PROP. & COMPETITION L. 535 (2011).

[74] Joined Cases C-236/08, C-237/08, & C-238/08, Google France, Google Inc. v. Louis Vuitton Malletier; Google France v. Viaticum Luteciel; Google France v. CNRRH Pierre Alexis Thonet Bruno Raboi Tiger, a franchisee of Unicis, [2010] E.C.R. I-2417, I-2506–7.

[75] *Google, supra* note 74, [2010] E.C.R. at I-2506; *Interflora, supra* note 72, [2011] E.C.R. at I-8685–86.

of the trademark functions. The advertising function, to which the Court referred as the proprietor's capacity to use the mark as a factor in sales promotion or as an instrument of his commercial strategy, would not be impaired simply because the junior use forces the trademark proprietor to intensify his efforts to improve his access to consumers conducting Internet searches.[76] Nor does the junior use in this case interfere with the right holder's opportunity of using his mark effectively to inform and win over consumers.[77] As for the investment function, namely, the proprietor's capacity to preserve a reputation capable of attracting consumers and retaining their loyalty, it could not, in the view of the Court, possibly be impaired by a non-confusing junior use of the mark as an AdWord.[78] Competitive pressure on the proprietor may indeed increase as a result of exempting such junior uses of his own mark from liability but the Court considered this to be an aspect of healthy competition as long as third parties do not cause consumers to be misled as to the commercial source.[79] A broader legal definition of the advertising and investment functions that would lead to the internalization of all economic benefits generated by reputation/brand image was avoided.

As we saw in *Dior*, the CJEU is hesitant to explicitly refer to the trademark functions in the context of exhaustion, even though the legitimate reasons allowing the rights holder to prevent the further commercialization of the goods clearly point to circumstances where the functions of the trademark are impaired. A similar pattern was repeated in *Kosan* where the Court restricted its analysis to the origin function and focused on the adverse effects on competition that would accrue if the trademark proprietor were successful in enforcing his rights. In these two cases, the analysis of the (unfair) competition dimension of the dispute set aside the analysis based on the trademark functions.

Seemingly, the teleology of trademark exhaustion gradually broadens its horizon, leaving behind the functional analysis to encompass value judgments derived from competition law beyond the free movement of goods. As already indicated, this development is an affluent of the sensible expansion of trademark rights and the (at times anticompetitive) rent-seeking business strategies of rights holders. On the other hand, the normative link to competition law calls for a more nuanced approach to the legal evaluation of such disputes. In a case like *Kosan*, one could not axiomatically assume that the restraint imposed to competition in the downstream market is anticompetitive *per se*. It is legitimate, for instance, that a trader seeks to obtain the reward for marketing an item of commerce not in the primary, but in the secondary market for staple articles meant for use with the basic product. "Tying arrangements" usually constitute the means to facilitate the financing of such a purchase. They would survive the scrutiny under competition laws quite often.[80] Bearing in mind that the doctrine of exhaustion attends to the legitimate interests of the trademark proprietor in making strategic decisions regarding profit generation based upon the commercialization of the trademarked good, an analysis of trademark exhaustion in

---

[76] *Google, supra* note 74, [2010] E.C.R. at I-2506-07; *Interflora, supra* note 72, [2011] E.C.R. at I-8686.
[77] *Google, supra* note 74, [2010] E.C.R. at I-2507; *Interflora, supra* note 72, [2011] E.C.R. at I-8686.
[78] *Interflora, supra* note 72, [2011] E.C.R. at I-8687–88.
[79] *Ibid.*
[80] European Commission: Guidelines on Vertical Restraints, [2010] O.J. C130/1, 43–44.

the light of competition law might highlight circumstances under which the relativization of the exhaustion principle would be justified. However, the main problem in cases like *Kosan* is that there are no such agreements in place. The consumers suddenly find themselves in a lock-in situation whereby they are vulnerable to the seller's pricing policy and only come to realize it at the stage of trademark enforcement. That particular point was raised by the CJEU in *Kosan* as an aspect militating in favor of trademark exhaustion.

But if the enforcement of a trademark is meant to serve the implementation of a business scheme that competition law deems precompetitive, then its proprietor may well claim that there is a legitimate reason for the exhaustion of his rights to be prevented.[81] *Consten and Grundig* may well be taken as the initial authority for the broad proposition that the enforcement of trademark rights should not contradict the application of competition law. To narrow down and further concretize that principle, it is necessary to evaluate the relevant set of facts through the norms regulating the competitive process. Competition concerns would often bar the anticompetitive enforcement of trademark rights just as in *Kosan*. However, a rule of reason analysis balancing the pre- and anticompetitive effects of a business scheme might reveal that under a given set of circumstances, there is a legitimate reason for the rights holder to oppose the further commercialization of the trademarked good. The doctrine of exhaustion as an absolute and rigid rule that forbids any after-sales impediments to the commercialization of commodities emerged in an era when antitrust theory had not yet come to fully appreciate the effects of vertical restraints on competition.

Copad v. Dior[82] points exactly to that path of argumentation.[83] Dior marketed luxury

---

[81] On this particular point see C.W.F. Baden Fuller, *Economic Issues Relating to Property Rights in Trademarks: Export Bans, Differential Pricing Restrictions on Resale and Repackaging*, 6 EUR. L. REV. 162, 179 (1981) (commenting on *Hoffman La-Roche* and *American Home Products*); Nancy T. Gallini & Aidan Hollis, *A Contractual Approach to the Gray Market*, INT'L REV. L. & ECON. 19 (1999); Guido Westkamp, *Intellectual Property, Competition Rules, and the Emerging Internal Market: Some Thoughts on the European Exhaustion Doctrine*, 11 MARQ. INTELL. PROP. L. REV. 291 (2007) (linking the European doctrine of exhaustion with the analysis of vertical restraints under competition law); Yuka Aoyagi, *Free Movement Rules and Competition Law: Regulating the Restriction on Parallel Importation of Trade Marked Goods*, INSTITUTE OF INTELLECTUAL PROPERTY BULL. (2007), available at www.iip.or.jp/e/e_summary/pdf/detail2006/e18_23.pdf; Ole-Andreas Rongstad, *The Exhaustion/Competition Interface in EC Law: Is There Room for a Holistic Approach?*, in RESEARCH HANDBOOK ON INTELLECTUAL PROPERTY AND COMPETITION LAW 427–50 (Josef Drexl ed., 2008) (arguing that the principle of exhaustion and the competition rules must always be read in close context); Herbert Hovenkamp, *Post-Sale Restraints and Competitive Harm: The First Sale Doctrine in Perspective*, 66 N.Y.U. ANN. SURV. AM. L. 487 (2011); APOSTOLOS CHRONOPOULOS, DAS MARKENRECHT ALS TEIL DER WETTBERBSORDNUNG 301–13 (2013) (for an analysis specific to trademarks).

[82] Case C-59/08, Copad v. Christian Dior, [2009] E.C.R. I–3421; cf. Kamen Troller, *The Parallel Importation of Trade-Marked Goods and the Protection of Selective Distribution Systems*, 10 EUR. INTELL. PROP. L. REV. 67 (1988); Case C-439/09, Pierre Fabre Dermo-Cosmétique S.A.S. v. Président de l'Autorité de la concurrence, Ministre de l'Économie, de l'Industrie et de l'Emploi, [2011] E.C.R. I-9419 should be distinguished on the grounds that it involved an absolute ban on Internet sales. Cf. Press Release, European Commission, IP/02/916, Commission clears B&W Loudspeakers distribution system after company deletes hard-core violations; Case 107/82, AEG-Telefunken v. Commission, [1983] ECR 3151, 3194.

[83] For a critical view, see Irene Calboli, *Reviewing the (Shrinking) Principle of Trademark*

goods including clothes, cosmetics, accessories, and the like through a system of selective distribution in France. At some point the distributor, Societe Industriel Lingerie (SIL), violated its contractual obligations by selling contract goods to discount suppliers that were not part of Dior's selective distribution network.[84] In order to protect the integrity of its distribution system, Dior sought to turn against SIL on the basis of the French rule implementing Article 8(2)(e) TMD (Article 25(2)(e) of the 2015 Trade Mark Directive).[85] According to this provision, the trademark proprietor may invoke his rights against a licensee who contravenes a provision with regard to, *inter alia*, the quality of the goods manufactured or of the services provided by that licensee. In reply to the request for guidance on the interpretation of Article 8(2)(e) TMD (Article 25(2)(e) of the 2015 Trade Mark Directive), the CJEU opined that the term "quality" refers also to the aura of luxury emanating from the goods.[86] The rights of the trademark proprietor are not exhausted against the licensee who markets the goods in violation of such a term.[87]

Whether the same rationale could be relevant to the application of Article 7(2) TMD (Article 15(2) of the 2015 Trade Mark Directive) by means of a purposive interpretation is another, even more intriguing, question. The Court relied on *Bristol-Myers* and *Dior* for the proposition that damage to reputation of the trademark constitutes a legitimate reason within the meaning of that provision.[88] Hence, such a legitimate reason would only exist when a particular channel of trade is likely to damage the reputation of the trademark by tarnishing the luxury aura of the goods.[89] That approach would mirror the concept of an impairment of a trademark function as a limiting principle to the "double identity" rule. In any event, difficult questions of proof would arise. It is also arguable whether recognizing the impairment of the luxury image of a trademarked good as a legitimate ground for denying exhaustion would do justice to the interests of the rights holder. The trademark proprietor has a broader valid business interest in protecting the smooth operation of his distribution system.

Linking the exhaustion doctrine to the rule of reason analysis deployed by competition law is a more fruitful approach. Selective distribution systems generate many efficiencies and are, generally speaking, precompetitive.[90] In the course of time, the criteria for the conformity of qualitative and quantitative selective distribution agreements with European competition law have been radically loosened. A detailed analysis

---

Exhaustion in the European Union (Ten Years Later), 16 MARQ. INTELL. PROP. L. REV. 257–81 (2012).

[84] Case C-59/08, Copad v. Christian Dior, [2009] E.C.R. I-3421, I-3444.
[85] *Ibid.* at I-3445.
[86] *Ibid.* at I-3451.
[87] *Ibid.* at I-3454.
[88] *Ibid.* at I-3455–56.
[89] *Ibid.* Furthermore, unlike *Dior*, *supra* note 84, [2009] E.C.R. at I-6050, *Copad* does not impose any quantitative requirement of the trademark's reputation being "seriously damaged." Commentators who are skeptical of the recognition of exceptions to the exhaustion principle criticize this aspect of the decision. See DAVID KEELING, DAVID LLEWELYN, JAMES MELLOR, TOM MOODY-STUART, & IONA BERKELEY, KERLY'S LAW OF TRADE MARKS AND TRADE NAMES paras. 16-131/132 (2014). For more detailed rules on parallel importations of perfumes see Case C-324/09, L'Oréal S.A. v. eBay Int'l A.G., [2011] E.C.R. I-6011, I-6106–9.
[90] European Commission: Guidelines on Vertical Restraints, *supra* note 80, at 36–39.

of selective distribution systems is outside of the scope of this chapter. However, it could indicatively be stressed that if the following requirements are cumulatively met, these agreements would even lie outside of the application field of Article 101 of the TFEU:[91] (a) selective distribution is necessary in the light of the nature of the goods involved; (b) participation to the system is made dependent on objective criteria; and (c) the restraints must not exceed the level necessary to achieve the goals of the distribution system.

Trademark rights have a great role to play in serving the maintenance of the integrity of selective distribution systems as an additional means to discipline distributors not complying with qualitative requirements, primarily because they allow the rights holder to prohibit the further commercialization of the goods when they are not in the hands of market operators bound by contract. Accordingly, the legitimate reason for imposing restraints on further sales of a trademarked good within the meaning of Article 7(2) TMD (Article 15(2) of the 2015 Trade Mark Directive) refers to the protection of a lawful selective distribution system as a business scheme that promotes the effectiveness of competition. Neither the principles founded in *Hoffmann La-Roche* nor the concept of the impairment of a trademark function developed under Article 5(1)(a) TMD (Article 10(2)(a) of the 2015 Trade Mark Directive) are effective in balancing the diverse interests involved in such disputes.

Trademark rights might also support the functioning of vertical price control systems to the extent they survive antitrust scrutiny. Resale price maintenance is a rather controversial issue. Vertical price control systems are subjected to a rule of reason analysis according to the U.S. Supreme Court in *Leegin*[92] and do not qualify for a block exemption, but they could theoretically be exempted under Article 101(3) of the TFEU.[93] This actually remains an open issue for competition law.

It becomes evident that the law of vertical restraints is highly relevant to the legal assessment made when trademark exhaustion issues are examined. This is definitely a point that deserves further research and reflection. Competition law developments in this field have implications for trademark law and policy.

In the meantime, the CJEU has further scrutinized the legality of limitations to parallel trade under EU competition law. The CJEU had to rule on the legality of price discrimination schemes administered by pharmaceutical companies in the internal market.[94] National legislations often eliminate price competition in the market for pharmaceuticals through legislation. In an industry characterized by races to innovate, it is vital for manufacturers to be able to capture the full market value of their patents. That would only be possible if manufacturers are allowed to adjust their prices to accommodate the differences in demand elasticity within the internal market. If, for example, there is price regulation for pharmaceuticals in Spain, the patent holder would normally seek higher rents in other markets to the extent that consumers can afford

---

[91] *Ibid.* at 36.
[92] Leegin Creative Leather Prods., Inc. v. PSKS, Inc., 551 U.S. 877, 890–91 (2007).
[93] European Commission: Guidelines on Vertical Restraints, *supra* note 80, at 12.
[94] Case T-168/01, GlaxoSmithKline v. Commission, [2006] E.C.R. II-2969.

them. A restriction on the freedom of parallel trade is necessary for implementing that pricing model.

According to the General Court of the European Union (the first instance of jurisdiction within the CJEU),[95] such agreements do not have the restriction of competition as their object. Even in the absence of restraints on parallel trade, the benefit of a lower price would not be passed on to consumers because parallel traders would seek to appropriate the price difference as a profit for themselves.[96] It could not be excluded, though, that the price discrimination schemes had an adverse effect on competition since national insurance providers may rely on parallel-imported pharmaceuticals to minimize their costs, in which case the benefits from parallel trade would be passable to consumers.[97] Importantly, the General Court of the European Union noted that such restrictions to parallel imports of pharmaceuticals may be exempted by virtue of Article 101(3) of the TFEU when they entail redeeming precompetitive effects.[98] They actually generate revenue that is indispensable for pharmaceutical companies to innovate, as they need to heavily invest capital in research and development (R&D) for that purpose. Exempting these agreements from the prohibition of Article 101 of the TFEU would intensify dynamic competition at interbrand level, which is tough. The CJEU opined, though, that these price discrimination schemes did have the restriction of competition as their object since they are aiming at restricting parallel imports.[99] It rejected the General Court's arguments in their abstract form. Nevertheless, it did not exclude the possibility of an undertaking providing concrete arguments in a specific market context to exempt a similar business scheme under Article 101(3) of the TFEU.

The question whether restrictions to parallel trade imposed by unilateral actions may be justified by competition policy arguments was revisited in *Sot. Lelos kai Sia/ GlaxoSmithKline*.[100] The pharmaceutical company decided to implement its pricing strategy by delivering national suppliers with only enough volumes to cover the demand for their markets, thereby leaving no room for parallel trade on the products they placed in the internal market.[101] In an attempt to provide a justification for the abuse of its dominant position through a refusal to supply, GlaxoSmithKline argued that its practices were dictated by the particularities of the competition process in the pharmaceutical industry described above.[102] Advocate General Ruiz-Jarabo Colomer considered the freedom of parallel trade as an overriding principle and was, in any event, skeptical of the justifications put forward by the pharmaceutical company.[103] In his view, the capital needed for

---

[95] For information about the General Court of the European Union, see Eur-Lex, Rules of Procedure of the General Court, available at http://eur-lex.europa.eu/legal-content/EN/TXT/HTML/?uri=URISERV:ai0047&from=EN.
[96] Case T-168/01, GlaxoSmithKline v. Commission, [2006] E.C.R. II-2969, II-3016, II-3019, II-3022–23.
[97] *Ibid.* at II-3035 *et seq.*
[98] *Ibid.* at II-3063.
[99] Joined Cases C-501, C-513, C-515, & C-519/06P, GlaxoSmithKline v. Commission, [2009] E.C.R. I-9291, I-9400 *et seq.*
[100] Joined Cases C-468–C-478/06, Sot. Lelos kai Sia v. GlaxoSmithKline, [2008] E.C.R. I-7139.
[101] *Ibid.* at I-7181.
[102] *Ibid.* at I-7184.
[103] Opinion of Advocate General Ruiz-Jarabo Colomer, [2008] E.C.R. I-7139, I-7171–72.

R&D should be generated through the continuous marketing of innovative products and not through restrictions to parallel trade.[104] Unfortunately, the CJEU did not get into this discussion. The Court ruled that an entity occupying a dominant position lawfully takes measures to protect its economic interests in avoiding the distribution of a large volume of its products in a Member State, when the purchase by a wholesaler is made with the intention of deriving profit from parallel trade.[105] Hence, the CJEU advised the national court to examine whether the orders placed by the wholesaler were proportional to the demand of the national market or whether they could be deemed reasonable in the light of previous dealings.[106] Competition in the pharmaceutical sector poses additional questions that cannot be addressed here.

Rebranding poses some interesting questions as well. When the trademark proprietor markets different branded versions of the same commodity in different parts of the internal market, it is likely that the parallel importation of these relabeled products would undermine his branding strategies. A parallel importer could relabel a product bought in state A to market it in state B as the branded good was originally meant for this market by basically reaffixing the trademark used by the proprietor in the state of import. That could reduce the incentives of firms to differentiate their brands and match the diverse consumer preferences within the internal market.[107] The precompetitive aspects of these branding activities must be balanced against the lower prices offered by competition from parallel-imported goods. By treating such relabeling as a repackaging in the sense of *Bristol-Myers* and rendering its legality dependent on a requirement of necessity, as the ECJ effectively did in *Upjohn*,[108] the law has provided the trademark proprietor with a legal basis to support his branding strategy that is also flexible enough to accommodate the interests of third parties and the public.

The parallel importer could not avail himself of the necessity requirement when the replacement of the trademark has the sole purpose of gaining a commercial advantage over the trademark proprietor. This approach builds upon the ruling in *American Home Products*[109] where the ECJ emphasized that the use of different marks for the same product in different Member States is not unlawful *per se* but the exercise of trademark rights should not constitute a disguised restriction on the free flow of trade within the internal market. The use of different labels allows price discrimination that is not deemed to be *per se* anticompetitive as unilateral conduct in competition.[110] Finally, this brand differentiation strategy limits the possibilities of parallel importers to free ride upon the promotional efforts of national distributors without barring parallel imports at the same

---

[104] *Ibid.* at I-7170.
[105] *Sot. Lelos kai Sia, supra* note 100, [2008] E.C.R. I-7139, I-7198.
[106] *Ibid.*
[107] On these issues see Fuller, *supra* note 81, at 177–79 (arguing further that limiting the availability of marketing strategies would lead to various inefficient outcomes, such as unexhausted economies of scale, by way of a chain reaction).
[108] Case C-379/97, Pharmacia & Upjohn S.A. v. Paranova A/S, [1999] E.C.R. I-6927, I-6967–69.
[109] Case 3/78, Centrafarm B.V. v. Am. Home Prods. Corp., [1978] E.C.R. 1823, 1841.
[110] Taking into account the legitimacy of a certain scheme of geographically discriminatory prices that allows profit-maximization makes sense since the exhaustion doctrine addresses the interest of the trademark proprietor in obtaining a reward from the commercialization of his goods.

time.[111] The legality of trademark enforcement should depend on the evaluation of the said business practices in each individual case under competition law.[112]

Due to the particularities of the competitive process in the pharmaceutical industry, the legal assessment of rebranding necessarily touches upon questions of policy that are controversial and to a large extent unsettled. Problematic situations may arise when a pharmaceutical company markets the same drug under different brand names within the internal market. At times, competition from parallel-imported products that the originator has already marketed in other Member States under different brand names (let's say X, Y, Z) might not be effective, when the parallel importer faces barriers to entry into a substantial part of the market that is occupied by the originator's brand (Z) in the country of importation.

For parallel importers, barriers to entry into such a market segment may arise when that national brand is preferred in the doctors' prescriptions, who in view of their professional reputation being at stake might distrust a parallel importer as a source of supply, or when pharmacists fill generic prescriptions with the branded product to increase their own profit. Barriers to entry may increase when state regulation requires the drug to be branded.

While other economic operators such as generic manufacturers or sellers of competing brands may well compete with the originator's brand in the country of importation, the same does not equally apply to the case of the parallel importer. To win over the buyers situated in the respective market segment, the parallel importer must devise his own branding strategy and incur the necessary investment costs. However, the parallel importer would normally lack the continuous stream of revenue derived from the sales of a given drug that would render the introduction of his own brand commercially viable. In addition, placing additional burdens to the access of national markets would undermine the role of the parallel importer in facilitating the functioning of the internal market. For these reasons the U.K. Court of Appeal held that the requirement of necessity was fulfilled under a similar set of circumstances.[113]

Notably, even though the defendant could compete for a large part of the broader market corresponding to the generic prescriptions, the court held that the necessity requirement should be deemed fulfilled when the assertion of trademark rights would foreclose the parallel importer from a substantial part the market. This is consistent with the CJEU's case law that considers partial impediments to market access as illegitimate restrictions of parallel trade. An interesting underlying issue is the relevance of the market definition methodology for the purpose of determining the scope of an IP right. Markets

---

[111] For the free-riding aspect of parallel imports, see generally, John C. Hilke, *Free Trading or Free-Riding: An Examination of the Theories and Available Empirical Evidence on Gray Market Imports*, 31 WORLD COMPETITION L. & ECON. REV. 75 (1988); Andrade M. Richard, *Parallel Importation of Unauthorized Genuine Goods: Analysis and Observations of the Gray Market*, 14 U. PA. J. INT'L BUS. L. 409, 428–29 (1993–94).

[112] Thomas Heide, *Trade Marks and Competition Law After Davidoff*, 25 EUR. INTELL. PROP. L. REV. 163–68 (2003).

[113] Speciality European Pharma Ltd. v. Doncaster Pharmaceuticals Group Ltd. & Madaus GmbH, [2015] EWCA Civ 54. We think that the trial decision of Asplin, J., in Speciality European Pharma Ltd. v. Doncaster Pharmaceuticals Group Ltd. & Madaus GmbH, [2013] EWHC 3624 (Ch) addressed the competition dimension of the dispute more effectively.

would often be narrowly defined in the light of competition policy considerations.[114] Some scholars have indicated that positions of economic power attributed to product differentiation may undermine consumer welfare especially in respect to the pricing of pharmaceuticals and, thus, argued that legal norms should encourage possibilities to expose them to intense competition on the price.[115] Rebranding by parallel importers constitutes a measure that could serve this policy goal. On the other hand, other scholars highlight the need for a more cautious approach, noting that in industries with high fixed costs and large expenditures on R&D the revenue generated by price premiums resulting from brand differentiation strategies is indispensible to socially beneficial market performance.[116]

Moreover, rebranding may well entail free riding upon the promotional efforts of the trademark proprietor, who has in the meantime diligently built up the quality assurance attached to the mark in the country of importation. If the trademark proprietor is an exclusive licensee of a pharmaceutical company marketing a drug under different marks within the EU territory, the possibility of parallel imports through rebranding might undermine the incentives to enter into exclusive distributorship agreements. It is also arguable whether raising the partial impediment to market access, namely, allowing the parallel importer to enter into the aforementioned market segment, would be beneficial to the effectiveness of competition. The parallel importer's rebranding may serve the purpose of capitalizing the higher premiums that the branded drug attracts in the country of importation. One could also argue that excluding the parallel importer from that particular market segment might provide incentives for him to lower the price of the parallel-imported goods further. Last but not least, the parallel importer may in that latter case avail himself of the promotional materials that facilitated the marketing of the drug in the country of exportation and, thus, legally capitalize upon the originator's reputation as a manufacturer of the parallel-imported drug.

A partial impediment to access a national market may indeed justify rebranding. Administrating the exhaustion doctrine in the light of competition considerations calls, however, for a more nuanced approach balancing the pre- and anticompetitive effects of a partial impediment to access the market in order to assess the legality of rebranding.

Finally, a strict requirement of consent makes it possible for the rights holder to avoid the need to contractually impose after-sales restrictions on the commercialization of the trademarked good and, as a consequence thereof, to avoid the application of Article 101 of the TFEU. Whether the exercise of the rights in a trademark is anticompetitive should then be determined according to the principles governing unilateral conduct in competition. This approach expands the scope of trademark rights to include additional exclusive authorities to oppose parallel imports, which could only be deemed anticompetitive when exercised by a dominant firm under exceptional circumstances.[117] Strengthening the legal

---

[114] See the discussion in Mark A. Lemley & Mark P. McKenna, *Is Pepsi Really a Substitute for Coke? Market Definition in Antitrust and IP*, 100 GEO. L.J. 2055 (2012).
[115] *Ibid.*
[116] Herbert Hovenkamp, *Response: Markets in IP and Antitrust*, 100 GEO. L.J. 2133, 2145–48 (2012).
[117] On the applicability of competition rules to the exercise of trademark rights with the purpose of fettering parallel trade, see Christopher Stothers, *Article 36 TFEU: Intellectual*

position of the trademark proprietor would support the effectiveness of precompetitive branding strategies without excluding the possibility of screening out those practices that are anticompetitive overall.

The extent to which competition law permits exceptions to the principle of free parallel trade is a legal issue in constant development. Without doubt, the likelihood that such restraints would be occasionally exempted from competition law liability for the sake of their precompetitive effects is strong. The precompetitive virtues of such restraints would provide the trademark proprietor with legitimate reasons to oppose the further commercialization of goods already placed in the market within the meaning of Article 7(2) TMD (Article 15(2) of the 2015 Trade Mark Directive). Not only prohibition contained in Article 101 of the TFEU, but also the rules governing unilateral conduct in competition are relevant to the purposive interpretation of Article 7(2) TMD (Article 15(2) of the 2015 Trade Mark Directive).[118] In many cases, however, there would be no direct relationship between the assertion of trademark rights and an anticompetitive outcome.[119]

VI. EXCEPTIONS TO THE RULE OF REGIONAL EXHAUSTION FOR REASONS RELATED TO COMPETITION?

It is clear from the wording of the Trade Mark Directive that the European legislator opted for a rule of European exhaustion. Placing a product into a market outside the EEA does not exhaust the right of the trademark proprietor to oppose the importation of that product into the EEA. The Court had the opportunity to stress this point in *Silhouette*.[120] Moreover, in order to protect the trademark proprietor's freedom of strategic choice regarding the generation of revenue from the commercialization of his goods, the CJEU has interpreted the consent requirement to mean that it would take an equivocal renouncement of the right to oppose the importation of goods marketed outside the EEA to trigger trademark exhaustion pursuant to Article 7(1) TMD (Article 15(1) of the 2015 Trade Mark Directive).[121] Furthermore, trademark rights are only exhausted in respect to specific individual items of commerce that had been put on the market in the EEA with the consent of the proprietor.[122]

Property, in OLIVER ON FREE MOVEMENT OF GOODS IN THE EUROPEAN UNION 313, 323 (Peter Oliver ed., 5th ed. 2010) (briefly commenting on Case 51-75, EMI Records Ltd. v. CBS United Kingdom Ltd., [1976] E.C.R. 811).

[118] Case 102/77, Hoffmann-La Roche & Co. A.G. v. Centrafarm, [1978] E.C.R. 1139, 1167; Ulrich Löwenheim, *Trademarks and European Community Law*, 9 INT'L REV. INTELL. PROP. & COMPETITION L. 422, 423 (1978).

[119] Hoffmann-La Roche, *supra* note 118, [1978] E.C.R. at 1167.

[120] Silhouette Int'l v. Hartlauer, *supra* note 2, [1998] E.C.R. at I-4834–35; see generally, Irene Calboli, *Trademark Exhaustion in the European Union: Community-Wide or International? The Saga Continues*, 6 MARQ. INTELL. PROP. L. REV. 47 (2002).

[121] Joined Cases C-414–C-416/99, Zino Davidoff v. A & G Imports; Levi Strauss & Co v. Tesco Stores & Costco Wholesale, [2001] E.C.R. I-8691, I-8751; Case C-324/08, Makro Zelfbedieningsgroothandel C.V. v. Diesel SpA., [2009] E.C.R. I-10019, I-10030.

[122] Case C-173/98, Sebago Inc. & Antienne Maison Dubois & Fils S.A. v. G-B Unic S.A., [1999] E.C.R I-4103, I-4110–11.

With the doctrine of international exhaustion stably anchored in the system of the Trade Mark Directive, it remains unresolved whether EU competition law might, under particular circumstances, justify an exception. Where distributors in non-Member States are obliged by contract to refrain from importing trademarked goods into the EEA, the rights holder would be entitled to oppose the importation of the goods by virtue of his exclusive right, if the underlying agreement is void pursuant to Article 101 of the TFEU. This is the implication of *Javico v. YSL*,[123] a case concerning the distribution of articles of a famous fashion brand in Russia and Ukraine through an exclusive distributor. Some of these articles were spotted in the internal market despite contractual stipulations to the contrary.[124] After enumerating the precompetitive advantages of such agreements, the ECJ opined that it is possible for them to be held void in a specific case as running afoul of the prohibition contained in Article 101 of the TFEU.[125] In any event, it seems that the circumstances under which an agreement like the one implicated in *Javico* would be deemed as violating Article 101 of the TFEU are rather extreme. They would have to involve an appreciable effect on trade between the Member States. The gist is that the enforcement of trademark rights should not be exercised to implement violations of competition law.

The rights holder may strategically avoid the application of Article 101 of the TFEU by excluding the incorporation into the distribution agreement of an explicit contractual term prohibiting the importation of the trademarked goods into the EEA. As already seen, the requirement of consent is interpreted in a purposive manner that allows the trademark proprietor to achieve the same effect without an express stipulation in the contract.[126] When the rights holder is deemed as acting unilaterally, the application of competition laws to reverse the rule of regional exhaustion becomes even more problematic. Thus, it is only under exceptional circumstances that competition law would render the regional exhaustion rule inapplicable to a specific case.

An interesting case is *Honda Giken v. Maria Patmanidi*.[127] The defendant imported spare parts into Greece that were manufactured in Thailand and were meant for distribution in Asia.[128] Relying on *Silhouette*, Honda argued that its national and EU trademark rights entitled it to prevent the distribution of these products in Greece since exhaustion had not been triggered pursuant to Article 7(1) TMD (Article 15(1) of the 2015 Trade Mark Directive). The national court inquired whether the CJEU would be willing to craft exceptions to the rigid rule confirmed in *Silhouette* after taking into account Articles 101 and 102 of the TFEU. According to the national court, the case at hand could potentially be distinguished since it concerned products (i.e., spare parts for motor vehicles) with a large profit margin and price squeezing, which was evidenced by large fluctuations in pricing policy. Permitting parallel imports would eventually promote competition in the

---

[123] Case C-306/96, Javico Int'l & Javico A.G. v. Yves Saint Laurent Parfums S.A., [1998] E.C.R. I-1983.
[124] *Ibid.* at I-2000–1.
[125] *Ibid.* at I-2006–7.
[126] Case C-535/13, Honda Giken Kogyo Kabushiki Kaisha v. Maria Patmanidi AE, ECLI:EU:C:2014:2123, para. 25; LIONEL BENTLY & BRAD SHERMAN, INTELLECTUAL PROPERTY 1092 (4th ed. 2014).
[127] Honda Giken Kogyo Kabushiki Kaisha v. Maria Patmanidi AE, *supra* note 126.
[128] *Ibid.* para. 12.

relevant market and lower prices to the benefit of consumers. The CJEU answered that Articles 101 and 102 of the TFEU do not affect the normative content of Article 7(1) TMD (Article 15(1) of the Trade Mark Directive) in any way because the exercise of trademark rights neither constitutes an agreement nor amounts to an abuse of a dominant position.[129]

One could be critical of both opinions. The CJEU failed to read the exhaustion doctrine in close context with Articles 101 and 102 of the TFEU. Even in the absence of an agreement, a theoretical situation could not be excluded, whereby the enforcement of the regional exhaustion rule constitutes an instrument for implementing a unilateral scheme that violates Article 102 of the TFEU.[130] Following the spirit of *Consten and Grundig*, as well as *Javico*, one could expect the exercise of trademark rights to be barred in such a theoretical case.[131] Perhaps the national court did not frame the question properly. Deciding whether a general rule of international exhaustion, or maybe a limited exception in respect of particular goods for the purpose of lowering their price in the internal market (as the national court suggested in *Honda Giken*) would be an optimal rule, constitutes rather a *de lege ferenda* question that the European Commission has already considered once in the past.[132] Cases related to the supply of spare parts may involve an abuse of a dominant position in terms of excessive pricing or discriminatory refusals to supply independent service providers.[133] In addition, Article 5(b) of Regulation 461/10[134] provides that the block exemption does not cover agreements between manufacturers and suppliers imposing restrictions on the sales of spare parts to independent distributors, repairers, or end users. In general, trademark rights may be asserted with the purpose of giving effect to a manufacturer's anticompetitive strategy within the EU. It is arguable, though, whether the exercise of the right to prevent the importation of goods placed in the market outside the EU/EEA, derived from the principle of regional exhaustion, would be the direct and immediate instrument for the implementation of the respective anticompetitive scheme.[135]

VII. CONCLUSION

From a rigid rule not allowing the trademark proprietor to control the further commercialization of a trademarked good after its initial sale, the exhaustion doctrine in the EU has gradually developed into a complex set of sub-rules balancing the diverse interests of traders, parallel importers, and the consuming public in a manner that resembles market regulation through unfair competition norms. Trademark rights are frequently asserted to

---

[129] *Ibid.* para. 25.
[130] *Cf.* LAZAROS G. GRIGORIADIS, TRADE MARKS AND FREE TRADE – A GLOBAL ANALYSIS 317–18 (2014); VALENTINE KORAH, INTELLECTUAL PROPERTY RIGHTS AND THE EC COMPETITION RULES 16–18 (2006).
[131] Opinion of Advocate General Jacobs in *Silhouette, supra* note 2, [1998] E.C.R. I-4799, I-4815–16; see also, Case T–198/98, Micro Leader Bus. v. Commission, [1999] E.C.R. II–3989.
[132] Communiqué from Commissioner Bolkestein on the issue of exhaustion of trademark rights, June 7, 2000, available at http://ec.europa.eu/internal_market/indprop/docs/tm/comexhaust_en.pdf.
[133] Case 238/87, AB Volvo v. Erik Veng (UK) Ltd., [1988] E.C.R. 6211, 6223.
[134] Commission Regulation (EU) 461/2010, [2010] O.J. L129/52, 56.
[135] *Cf.* Oracle America Inc. v. M-Tech Data Ltd., [2012] UKSC 27.

implement business schemes of vertical integration, such as selective distribution systems, or to support unilateral conduct in competition, such as geographical price discrimination and brand differentiation strategies. To the extent that trademark rights are asserted in pursuit of a precompetitive aim, the trademark proprietor should be deemed to have legitimate reasons for imposing post-sale restrictions on the commercialization of the trademarked good within the meaning of Article 7(2) TMD (Article 15(2) of the 2015 Trade Mark Directive).

19. Trademark exhaustion and free movement of goods: a comparative analysis of the EU/EEA, NAFTA and ASEAN
*Irene Calboli**

I. INTRODUCTION

In this chapter, I address the relationship between the principle of trademark exhaustion and the free movement of goods in free trade areas. In particular, I analyze the existing approaches to trademark exhaustion and parallel imports in the following free trade areas: the European Union (EU), or rather the European Economic Area (EEA); the North American Free Trade Area (NAFTA); and the Association of Southeast Asian Nations (ASEAN). The results of this analysis highlight the different approaches that countries that are members of a free trade area may choose regarding national policies on trademark exhaustion—i.e., national, international, or regional trademark exhaustion as I explain below—and how these policies directly impact the free movement of goods within the free trade area. In particular, I note that it is only when all countries that are members of a free trade area consistently adopt a principle of international or regional trademark exhaustion that goods can freely move amongst these countries. Still, as the case of the EU/EEA demonstrates, the approach that countries adopt with respect to trademark exhaustion can also evolve over time and lead to a unified approach only at a second stage, particularly when the members of a free trade area agree to achieve a higher level of economic integration. In these instances, members of free trade areas are more likely to adopt a unified approach on trademark exhaustion that facilitates the free movement of goods within the free trade area.

Other contributions in this volume comprehensively address the alternative approaches to intellectual property exhaustion. Building on these contributions, in section II, I elaborate on the principle of trademark exhaustion in the EU/EEA. In this section, I note that market integration has historically been a priority in the EU, thus EU law explicitly imposes a consistent approach on exhaustion to all EU/EEA Member States in order to promote free movement of goods and the internal market. In section III, I analyze

---

* Lee Kong Chian Fellow, Visiting Professor, and Deputy Director, Applied Research Centre for Intellectual Assets and the Law in Asia, Singapore Management University School of Law; Professor of Law, Texas A&M University School of Law. This chapter builds upon my research in this area. In particular, portions of this chapter update and adapt my previous article, Irene Calboli, *Market Integration and (the Limits of) the First Sale Rule in North American and European Trademark Law*, 51 Santa Clara L. Rev. 1241 (2011). I thank the participants of the Roundtable on Exhaustion and Intellectual Property, Singapore Management University School Law, November 19, 2015, for their feedback. I also thank Yanbing Li and Jia Wang for their excellent research assistance and comments. All mistakes and omissions are my own.

the rules on trademark exhaustion in NAFTA. In this section, I note that, unlike in the EU/EEA, NAFTA members never intended to create a NAFTA internal market, thus, each NAFTA member follows its own system of choice on trademark exhaustion. Still, all NAFTA members have adopted the principle of international trademark exhaustion, which in turn permits the free movement of trademarked goods within NAFTA. Last, in section IV, I elaborate on the approach(es) adopted by the countries that are members of ASEAN. In this section, I stress that ASEAN members adopt a principle of non-interference with respect to national exhaustion policies (ASEAN members generally follow the principles of consensus and non-interference, referred to as the "ASEAN way," as a general principle, not only with respect to intellectual property-related issues). In this section, I also note that, to date, ASEAN members follow different approaches on trademark exhaustion. Notably, several ASEAN members follow international exhaustion, while other members are silent on the issue or adopt the principle of national exhaustion. Differently than the situation in the EU/EEA and NAFTA, however, the approach adopted by ASEAN members ultimately results in preventing an effective free movement of trademarked goods within ASEAN.

In section V, I conclude the chapter and compare the experiences of the EU/EEA, NAFTA, and ASEAN. In particular, I conclude that countries that are members of free trade areas do not necessarily seek a full-scale market integration and free movement of goods. Accordingly, different countries may adopt different positions on trademark exhaustion due to specific regional economic, political, and social conditions. I also conclude that countries' economic conditions may change over time, which may lead to changes in their domestic approaches to trademark exhaustion. Still, in my conclusion, I argue that the very purpose of free trade areas remains to promote free trade, and thus to eliminate *any* restriction to legitimate trade. In this respect, adopting a consistent position of trademark exhaustion—international or at least regional exhaustion—remains a crucial component in order to reach the purpose for which free trade areas are (at least theoretically) built.

II. ONE RULE FOR ALL: TRADEMARK EXHAUSTION IN THE EUROPEAN UNION/EUROPEAN ECONOMIC AREA

Since the signing of the Treaty Establishing the European Economic Community (EEC or Community) in 1957, the primary objective of the Member States of the EEC (now the EU) was the creation of an integrated European market where goods, services, people, and capital could move without restrictions.[1] Since then, the European Parliament, the European Commission (EC), and Court of Justice of the European Union (CJEU) (or the European Court of Justice (ECJ) as it was previously known) have carefully balanced

---

[1] Consolidated Version of the Treaty on the Functioning of the European Union, March 30, 2010, [2010] O.J. C83 [hereinafter TFEU] as amended following the entering into force of the Treaty of Lisbon on December 1, 2009. Treaty of Lisbon, December 13, 2007, [2007] O.J. C306. A complete list of the various amendments to the original Treaty Establishing the European Economic Community (now the European Union) is available at EUR-Lex, http://eur-lex.europa.eu/legal-content/EN/TXT/?uri=CELEX:12006E/TXT.

the protection of intellectual property rights among Member States with the primary objective of promoting the free movement of goods in the European market.[2] As I have illustrated in my previous scholarship, this has resulted in the development of a system of region-wide exhaustion where intellectual property rights, including trademark rights, are exhausted with respect to the territory of the EU after the first sale of a product, or a batch of products, in the EU; thereafter, those products can freely circulate within the European market.[3] Still, the harmonization of national laws on trademark exhaustion has been a lengthy process. Before the adoption of and entry into force of the First Council Directive 89/104/EEC, later replaced by Directive 2008/95 ("Trademark Directive") and more recently replaced by Directive 2015/2436 ("2015 Directive"),[4] EU Member States followed different approaches—international and national exhaustion. And even though the ECJ promoted free movement of goods and in fact overruled national laws providing for national exhaustion, the EU/EEA rule on exhaustion did not reach full harmonization until over three decades after the creation of the EEC.

Originally, the ECJ turned to the competition law provisions of the Treaty on the Functioning of the European Union (TFEU) (then the Treaty Establishing the European Economic Community (EEC Treaty) to declare "incompatible with the common market" attempts to block the free movement of goods across Member States.[5] Starting in the 1970s, the ECJ relied on the principle of free movement of goods in Articles 34 and 36 of the EEC Treaty to permit the free movement of goods within the EU and to resolve the interpretative tension between the exercise of intellectual property rights (which remained territorially anchored to national trademark laws) and the need to integrate the European

---

[2] On the historical tension between the protection of intellectual property and the free movement of goods in the EU, see Friedrich-Karl Beier, *Industrial Property and the Free Movement of Goods in the Internal European Market*, 21(4) INT'L REV. INTELL. PROP. & COMP. L. 131 (1990) [hereinafter Beier, *Industrial Property*]; Friedrich-Karl Beier, *The Doctrine of Exhaustion in EEC Trademark Law—Scope and Limits*, 10 INT'L REV. INTELL. PROP. & COMP. L. 20 (1979); Herman Cohen Jehoram, *Harmonising Intellectual Property Law Within the European Community*, 23 INT'L REV. INTELL. PROP. & COMP. L. 622 (1992).

[3] For a detailed analysis see Irene Calboli, *Trademark Exhaustion in the European Union: Community-Wide or International? The Saga Continues*, 6 MARQ. INTELL. PROP. L. REV. 47, 53–59 (2002) [hereinafter Calboli, *Trademark Exhaustion in the EU*]; Irene Calboli, *Reviewing the (Shrinking) Principle of Trademark Exhaustion in the European Union (Ten Years Later)*, 16 MARQ. INTELL. PROP. L. REV. 257 (2012) [hereinafter Calboli, *Reviewing Trademark Exhaustion*]. The creation of the European internal market imposed the acceptance of the principle of Community-wide exhaustion with respect to patents and copyrights.

[4] Council Directive 89/104, [1989] O.J. L40/1 (EEC). This Directive codified the First Council Directive 89/104/EEC of December 21, 1988 to approximate the laws of the Member States relating to trade marks, [1989] O.J. L040/1 (EC) hereinafter Trademark Directive]. The Trademark Directive is repealed with effect from January 15, 2019 by Directive (EU) 2015/2436 of the European Parliament and of the Council of December 16, 2015 to approximate the laws of the Member States relating to trade marks [2015] O.J. L336/1 (EU) [hereinafter 2015 Directive], which entered into force on January 12, 2016.

[5] Articles 101 and 102 are the antitrust provisions of the TFEU. See TFEU, arts. 101–102. The Court of Justice of the European Union (CJEU), then still the European Court of Justice (ECJ), applied these provisions in Joined Cases 56/64 & 58/64, Costen & Grunding v. EC Commission, [1966] E.C.R. 299; Case 24/67, Parke Davis v. Centrafarm, [1968] E.C.R. 55; Case 40/70, Sirena v. Eda, [1971] E.C.R. 69.

market. Article 34 of the EEC Treaty, today Article 34 of the TFEU, prohibits quantitative restrictions on importation between Member States and other measures having an "equivalent effect,"[6] whereas Article 36 states that domestic laws should not provide a means of "arbitrary discrimination or a disguised restriction of trade between Member States."[7] In a series of leading cases, the ECJ clarified that the primary purpose of trademark protection was to indicate the products' commercial origin; thus, no reason subsisted to prevent the free circulation across Member States of genuine goods identified by marks controlled by the same companies in each Member State.[8] Only when the marks did not share a common origin would it be possible to block the parallel imports of products carrying a similar or identical mark to prevent consumer confusion in the importing Member States.[9]

Still, the ECJ conceded that the imports of products that have been altered without the trademark owners' consent could be prohibited.[10] However, this prohibition related to cases where products had been materially altered by the importers—for example, repackaged or relabeled—and not to cases where the products were genuine (originally manufactured), and the quality was materially different only because of production choices or market differentiation strategies directly originating with trademark owners.[11] Moreover, the ECJ developed the principle of "mutual recognition" to prevent product discrimination and disguised restrictions to trade. Notably, Member States could not "prohibit the sale in [their] territory of a product lawfully produced and marketed in another Member . . . even if the product is produced according to technical or quality

---

[6] Article 34 of the TFEU states that "[q]uantitative restriction on imports and all measures having equivalent effect shall be prohibited between Member States." TFEU, art. 34.

[7] *Ibid.* art. 36. Article 36 states that European Union (EU) members can prohibit or restrict "imports, exports or goods in transit" based upon "public morality, public policy or public security; the protection of health and life of humans, animals or plants; the protection of national treasures possessing artistic, historic or archaeological value; or the protection of industrial and commercial property." *Ibid.* These prohibitions "shall not, however, constitute a means of arbitrary discrimination or a disguised restriction on trade between Member States." *Ibid.*

[8] In Case 78/70, Deutsche Grammophon Gesellschaft mbH v. Metro-SB-Grossmarket GmbH, [1971] E.C.R. 487, the ECJ distinguished between the "existence" and the "exercise" of intellectual property rights and stated that the "exercise" should be consistent with the TFEU and protect only the "specific subject matter" of the right. The ECJ clarified the interpretation of "specific subject matter" in Case 16/74, Centrafarm B.V. v. Winthrop B.V., [1974] E.C.R. 1183, 1194 and confirmed its view in Case 3/78, Centrafarm B.V. v. Am. Home Prods. Corp., [1978] E.C.R. 183 and Case 1/81, Pfizer Inc. v. Eurim-Pharm GmbH, [1981] E.C.R. 2913.

[9] On the principle of "common origin," *compare* Case 192/73, Van Zuylen Freres v. Hag A.G., [1974] E.C.R. 731 (controversially stating that common origin included the case of companies "sharing the same origin" even if the marks were not owned by the same entities), with Case 119/75, Terrapin Ltd. v. Terranova Industrie C.A. Kapferer & Co., [1976] E.C.R. 1039 (stating that the "common origin" doctrine was applied to a special case in *Hag I*); Case C-10/89, CNL-Sucal v. Hag A.G., [1990] E.C.R. I-3711 (reversing the ECJ's position in *Hag I*); and Case C-9/93, IHT Internationale Heiztechnik GmbH v. Ideal-Standard GmbH, [1994] E.C.R. I-2782 (holding that the principle of "common origin" does not apply when marks have been voluntarily assigned).

[10] See Case 102/77, Hoffmann-La Roche & Co. v. Centrafarm Vertriebsgesellschaft Pharmazeutischer Erzeugnisse mbH, [1978] E.C.R. 1139, 1164–65; see also Ansgar Only, *Trade Marks and Parallel Importation: Recent Developments in European Law*, 30 INT'L REV. INTELL. PROP. & COMP. L. 521, 516 (1999) (surveying the cases where genuine products have been repackaged, rebranded, and relabeled).

[11] For additional analysis, see Chapter 9 in this volume.

requirements which differ from those imposed on its domestic products."[12] Differences in product ingredients, presentation, or even technical standards would thus not qualify as a legitimate reason to prevent parallel imports within the European market except in very limited and specific circumstances.[13] European legislators also harmonized an increasing number of technical standards. In 1985, the European Council adopted the *New Approach to Technical Harmonization and Standards*,[14] according to which EU legislators were responsible for indicating products' "essential requirements" whereas independent European Standards Organizations would develop the actual technical standards complying with these requirements.[15]

The principle of Community-wide exhaustion of trademark rights was ultimately codified in the Directive 89/104/EEC, later replaced by the 2008 Trademark Directive, and in turn by the 2015 Directive,[16] and repeated verbatim in Council Regulation (EC) 40/94, now replaced by Council Regulation 207/2009 ("Community Trademark Regulation").[17] The adoption of the Agreement for the European Economic Area of May 2, 1992 extended this principle to the European Free Trade Agreement (EFTA) countries joining the EEA (Norway, Iceland, and Liechtenstein).[18] Notably, Article 7(1) of the Trademark Directive (which will be replaced by Article 15(1) of the 2015 Directive) states that trademark rights "shall not entitle the proprietor to prohibit its use in relation to goods which have been put on the market in the Community under that trade mark by the proprietor or with his consent."[19] Because Article 7(1) did not explicitly say that Community-wide exhaustion is the *only* principle applicable within the EU (and now within the EEA),[20] several Member

---

[12] Commission Communication No. C256/2, Communication from the Commission concerning the consequences of the judgment given by the Court of Justice on February 20, 1979 in Case 120/78 ("Cassis de Dijon"), [1980] O.J. C256/2, 2–3 (EC). The ECJ developed the principle of "mutual recognition" in Case 120/78, Rewe-Zentral A.G. v. Bundesmonopolverwaltung fur Branntwein, [1979] E.C.R. 649 (*Cassis de Dijon*). In *Cassis de Dijon*, the ECJ stated that there was no valid reason why "provided that [the goods] have been lawfully produced and marketed in one of the Member States, [they] should not be introduced into any other Member State." *Ibid.* para. 14.

[13] In *Cassis de Dijon*, the ECJ limited those instances to the measures "being necessary to satisfy mandatory requirements relating in particular to the effectiveness of fiscal supervision, the protection of public health, the fairness of commercial transactions and the defense of the consumer." *Ibid.*

[14] Council Resolution of May 7, 1985 on a new approach to technical harmonization and standards, [1985] O.J. C136/1 (EC).

[15] On the process of harmonization of technical standards and *The New Approach to Technical Harmonization and Standards*, see EUROPEAN COMMISSION, ENTERPRISE DIRECTORATE GENERAL, VADEMECUM ON EUROPEAN STANDARDISATION (2004), available at http://ec.europa.eu/DocsRoom/documents/10449/attachments/8/translations/en/renditions/pdf.

[16] See Trademark Directive and 2015 Directive.

[17] Council Regulation 40/94 of December 20, 1993 on the Community Trade Mark, [1994] O.J. L11/1 (EC), now replaced by Council Regulation 207/2009, [2009] O.J. L78/1 (EC).

[18] Protocol to the Agreement on the European Economic Area, January 3, 1994, [1994] O.J. L1, Annex XVII, art. 2(1) extended the effect of art. 7 of the Trademark Directive to the EEA from January 1, 1994.

[19] Trademark Directive, art. 7(1). Article 7 of the Trademark Directive will be replaced by Article 15 of the 2015 Directive starting on January 2019. See 2015 Directive, arts. 15 and 56.

[20] See e.g. Nicholas Shea, *Does the First Trade Marks Directive Allow International Exhaustion of Rights?*, 10 E.I.P.R. 463, 463 (1995).

States favoring international exhaustion argued that this principle was simply a minimum standard.[21] Against this position, however, the ECJ clarified that EEA-wide exhaustion is the *only* applicable criterion within the European market and that national rules providing different exhaustion regimes needed to be amended.[22] Accordingly, even though Member States adopted a broader regime (i.e., international exhaustion) before the adoption of the Trademark Directive, Community-wide exhaustion successively became the general rule for all EU Member States.[23]

Finally, Article 7(2) of the Trademark Directive (which will be replaced by Article 15(1) of the 2015 Directive) states that trademark rights are not exhausted where "there exist legitimate reasons for the proprietor to oppose further commercialization of the goods, especially where the condition of the goods is changed or impaired after they have been put on the market."[24] In the years following the adoption of the Trademark Directive, the ECJ, later renamed CJEU, clarified that Article 7(2) does not apply to the imports of genuine goods of materially different quality when these differences are the result of marketing strategies and the importers have not modified the products.[25] However, the unauthorized repackaging and relabeling of genuine products may constitute "legitimate reasons" against parallel trade within the EEA when this may lead to consumer confusion or provoke unfair detriment to the reputation of a mark.[26] The CJEU additionally held that a licensee's breach of a contract clause prohibiting selling the products in discount stores may be a "legitimate reason" if sales in discount stores

---

[21] For a detailed reconstruction of the debates on this issue following the adoption of the Trademark Directive, see Calboli, *Trademark Exhaustion in the EU*, supra note 3, at 60–66.

[22] See Case C-335/96, Silhouette Int'l Schmied v. Hartlauer Handelsgesellschaft, 30 INT'L REV. INTELL. PROP. & COMP. L. 920 (1998). In *Silhouette*, the ECJ explicitly stated that "[n]ational rules providing for exhaustion of trade-mark rights in respect of products put on the market outside the EEA under that mark by the proprietor or with its consent are contrary to Article 7(1)." *Ibid.* para. 31. See C-173/98, Sebago Inc. & Ancienne Maison Dubois et Fils A.S. v. GB- Unic S.A., [1999] C.M.L.R. 1317; see also Joined Cases C-414/99–C-416/99, Zino Davidoff S.A. v. A & G Imports Ltd.; Levi Strauss & Co. v. Tesco Stores Ltd.; Levi Strauss & Co. v. Costco Wholesale UK Ltd., [2001] E.C.R. I-8691; see also C-324/08, Makro Zelfbedieningsgroothandel C.V., Metro Cash & Carry B.V., Remo Zaandam B.V. v. Diesel SpA, [2009] E.C.R. I-10019. But see Case C-306/96, Javico Int'l & Javico A.G. v. Yves Saint Laurent Parfums S.A., [1998] E.C.R. I-1983 (where the ECJ adopted a different position based upon the antitrust provisions of the TFEU); but see Mag Instrument Inc. v. California Trading Co., 29 INT'L REV. INTELL. PROP. & COMP. L. 316 (EFTA 1998) (where the EFTA court stressed that courts or legislators in EFTA states should decide on the admissibility of products imported from outside the EEA).

[23] See Calboli, *Trademark Exhaustion in the EU*, supra note 3, at 60–66.

[24] Trademark Directive, art. 7(2); 2015 Directive, art. 15.

[25] In Case C-349/95, Loendersloot v. Ballantine & Son Ltd., [1997] E.C.R. I-6227, the ECJ also said that importers could remove labels when these labels had been placed by trademark owners simply to control distribution and prevent parallel imports. In Case C-337/95, Parfums Christian Dior S.A. v. Evora B.V., [1997] E.C.R. I-6013, the ECJ went even further and applied trademark exhaustion to the use of trademarks in advertising. More recently, however, in Case C-59/08, Copad S.A. v. Christian Dior Couture S.A. & ors., [2009] E.C.R. I-3421, the now CJEU stated that a trademark owner may oppose the unauthorized sale of luxury goods to discount stores by a licensee if the sale could damage the reputation of the mark.

[26] Calboli, *Reviewing Trademark Exhaustion*, supra note 3, at 261–62.

could affect the image and reputation of the marks.[27] Despite these exceptions, however, the CJEU and the EU legislators remain committed to protect the free movement of goods, which include the application of EU/EEA-wide trademark exhaustion. Likewise, Member States continue to be subject to the principle of mutual recognition.[28] Last, but not least, the commitment to free movement of goods is reflected in the fact that a *New Legislative Framework* has replaced the *New Approach to Technical Harmonization*.[29] This requires that EU/EEA Member States take on an even larger role in increasing compliance with European standards to promote product uniformity within the EU, and thus intra-EU/EEA trade.

III. THE *LAISSEZ FAIRE* APPROACH (THEN AND NOW): TRADEMARK EXHAUSTION IN NAFTA

The adoption of NAFTA in 1994 marked the creation of a free trade area covering Canada, the United States (U.S.), and Mexico,[30] the purpose of which was, in theory, to eliminate all barriers to trade and facilitate free movement of goods across NAFTA members.[31] In practice, NAFTA members had different objectives in mind: the U.S. and Canada looked at Mexico primarily as a lower-cost country for manufacturing their products (to be later reimported at a lower tariff rate), while Mexico joined the agreement particularly because of the foreign direct investment (FDI) that it would receive from U.S. and Canadian firms. Adopted two years prior to the implementation of the Agreement on Trade-Related Aspects of Intellectual Property Rights (TRIPS), NAFTA was also the first free trade agreement to impose detailed obligations to protect intellectual property rights.[32] Specifically, Article 1701 of NAFTA requires that NAFTA member countries

---

[27] See *Copad*, [2009] E.C.R. I-3421; Case C-558/08, Portakabin Ltd., Portakabin B.V. v. Primakabin B.V., [2010] E.C.R. I-0000; Case C-127/09, Coty Prestige Lancaster Group GmbH v. Simex Trading A.G., [2010] E.C.R. I-0000.

[28] See Council Resolution of October 28, 1999 on mutual recognition, [2000] O.J. C141/2 (incorporated into the Agreement on the European Economic Area, [1994] O.J. L1/3 [hereinafter EEA Agreement]); see Decision of the EEA Joint Committee 15/2002 of March 1, 2002 amending Annex II (technical regulations, standards, testing, and certifications) to the EEA Agreement, [2002] O.J. L110/9.

[29] European Parliament and Council Regulation (EC) 765/2008 of July 9, 2008, [2008] O.J. L218/30.

[30] North American Free Trade Agreement, U.S.-Can.-Mex., art. 1701(1), December 17, 1992, 32 I.L.M. 289 (1993) [hereinafter NAFTA].

[31] *Ibid.* art. 102 ("The objectives of this Agreement . . . are to . . . eliminate barriers to trade in, and facilitate the cross-border movement of, goods and services between the territories of the Parties, . . . promote conditions of fair competition in the free trade area."). *Ibid.*

[32] *Ibid.* ch. 17. NAFTA was negotiated alongside the negotiations that led to the creation of the World Trade Organization (WTO) and the adoption of the Agreement on Trade-Related Aspects of Intellectual Property Rights (TRIPS). Thus, NAFTA provisions are largely modeled after TRIPS. See Agreement on Trade-Related Aspects of Intellectual Property Rights, April 15, 1994; Marrakesh Agreement Establishing the World Trade Organization, Annex 1C, Legal Instruments—Result of the Uruguay Rounds Vol. 31, 33 I.L.M. 83 (1994); see also Laurinda L. Hicks & James R. Holbein, *Convergence of National Intellectual Property Norms in International Trading Agreements*, 12 AM. U. J. INT'L L. & POL'Y 769, 791 (1997).

provide "adequate and effective protection and enforcement of intellectual property rights" in each party's territory,[33] even though these measures should not "become barriers to legitimate trade."[34] According to Article 1704, NAFTA members can also specify licensing practices or conditions in their domestic law that may have an adverse effect on market competition and they can also adopt measures to prevent and control these practices or conditions subject to the general principles of the agreement.[35]

Despite this commitment to promote free trade and integrate the markets of NAFTA members, NAFTA does not address the issue of exhaustion of intellectual property rights, including trademark exhaustion.[36] Instead, similar to TRIPS, NAFTA leaves its members free to adopt their preferred position with respect to the geographical extent of their national rules on trademark first sale and the importation of gray market goods into their territories.[37] In the absence of any guidance or harmonization in this area, NAFTA members, thus, continue to adopt their pre-NAFTA national policies. Nevertheless, even without an ad hoc harmonization of national rules, the three NAFTA members adopt consistent national positions with respect to trademark first sale and the importation of genuine, but materially different, goods into their territories. Notably, NAFTA members individually practice the principle of international trademark exhaustion within their respective territories and allow, although with some variations, the importation of materially different gray market goods from other NAFTA members as well as from other foreign jurisdictions.

In particular, international exhaustion of trademark rights has been the general rule in Canada since the late 1880s.[38] Canadian law has long established that once products have entered the stream of trade anywhere in the world, their importation into the national territory is permitted and does not constitute trademark infringement when the same or affiliated owners control the marks both inside and outside Canada (common origin marks).[39] Based upon the general principles of trademark protection, Canadian law only prohibits as trademark infringement the importation of products bearing marks identical or similar to marks already in use in the national territory when these marks are not owned or controlled by the same entity and the imported goods could create consumer confusion.[40] Still, Canadian courts have occasionally objected to the importation of imported

---

[33] NAFTA, art. 1701(1).
[34] Ibid.; see also, e.g., George Y. Gonzalez, *An Analysis of the Legal Implications of the Intellectual Property Provisions of the North American Free Trade Agreement*, 34 HARV. INT'L L.J. 305, 306 (1993) (discussing NAFTA treatment of intellectual property rights).
[35] NAFTA, art. 1704.
[36] See Gonzalez, *supra* note 34, at 308.
[37] Ibid.; see also Theodore H. Davis Jr., *Territoriality and Exhaustion of Trademark Rights Under the Laws of the North Atlantic Nations*, 89 TRADEMARK REP. 657 (1999) (describing the approach adopted by Canada and the United States with respect to parallel imports).
[38] Condy v. Taylor, [1887] 56 L.T.R. 891 (Can.) (stating that no trademark infringement occurs when the goods are genuine goods manufactured by trademark owners).
[39] See Wilkinson Sword (Can.) Ltd. v. Juda, [1966] 51 C.P.R. 55 (Can.); Wella Canada Inc. v. Pearlon Products Ltd., [1984] 4 C.P.R. 3d 287 (Can. Ont. H.C.J.); Coca-Cola Ltd. v. Pardham, [1999] 85 C.P.R. 3d 489 (Can. F.C.A.).
[40] See Consumers Distributing Co. v. Seiko Time Canada Ltd., [1984] 1 C.P.R. 3d 1, 13–14 (Can. S.C.C.). This decision was codified in the Canadian Trade-marks Act of 1985, SC 1952–53, c. 49, *as amended*, RSC 1985, c. T-10 (Can). Section 7(b) provides that "[n]o person shall . . . direct

goods carrying common origin marks when these goods were materially different from the products authorized in the Canadian market and when these differences could harm consumers or the public good[41]—for example, when the goods had been damaged and the distributor had replaced the original labels placed on the goods;[42] or when the formulation of the imported goods was different than the products sold nationally.[43] Canadian courts have also carefully scrutinized the importation of products that required compliance with technical standards and only allowed their sale if importers disclosed to the public any differences with respect to product standards.[44] Generally, however, Canadian courts have been sympathetic toward unauthorized parallel importers. In particular, it seems that courts rarely prohibit the importation of genuine products when the importers use labels to disclaim the fact that the products are imported and may be of different quality in order to prevent consumer confusion as to the products' quality.[45]

Similar to Canada, the U.S. follows a system of international exhaustion,[46] and prohibits parallel imports only for products that carry marks identical or similar to marks already in use in the U.S. by third parties.[47] U.S. law explicitly allows parallel imports when "both

---

public attention to his wares, services or business in such a way as to cause or be likely to cause confusion in Canada . . . between his wares, services or business and the wares, services and business of another." Canadian Trade-marks Act, R.S.C. 1985, c. T-13, s. 7(b). Section 19 states that a national registration "gives to the owner of the trade-mark the exclusive right to the use throughout Canada of the trade-mark in respect of those wares or services." *Ibid.* s. 19. Section 20 provides that "[t]he right of the owner of a registered trade-mark to its exclusive use shall be deemed to be infringed by a person not entitled to its use under this Act who sells, distributes or advertises wares or services in association with a confusing trade-mark or trade-name." *Ibid.* s. 20.

[41] But see Davis, *supra* note 37, at 730 ("The significance of material differences in goods sought to be imported to the exhaustion of trademark rights has been the subject of inconsistent decisions under Canadian law.").

[42] Dupont of Canada Ltd. v. Nomad Trading Co., [1968] 55 C.P.R. 97 (Can. Que. S.C.).

[43] See H.J. Heinz Co. of Canada Ltd. v. Edan Foods Sales Inc., [1991] 35 C.P.R. 3d 213 (Can. F.C.T.D.) (finding potential consumer confusion between the formulation of ketchup in Canada and the U.S. because of the different tomatoes used in the respective products).

[44] *Consumers Distributing*, *supra* note 40, 1 C.P.R. 3d 1. But see Sharp Electronic of Canada Ltd. v. Continental Electronic Info. Inc., [1988] 23 C.P.R. 3d 330 (Can. B.C.S.C.) (enjoining the further importation of facsimile machines because the goods were "inherently different in quality" from those sold by the plaintiff in Canada).

[45] *Consumers Distributing*, *supra* note 40, 1 C.P.R. 3d at 24–25 (noting that the notice affixed to the products neutralized the significance of any difference in the products' warranties). See also Nestle Enterprises Ltd. v. Edan Sales Inc., [1991] 37 C.P.R. 3d 480 (Can. F.C.A.) (stating that "[t]he evidence does not satisfy . . . that Mountain Blend is an 'inferior' product. It is simply different from the plaintiff's pure coffee blends and that difference is adequately stated on the label.").

[46] Originally, U.S. courts allowed parallel imports based on the principle of "universality" of trademark rights. See Hunyadi Janos Corp. v. Steger, 285 F. 861 (2d Cir. 1922); Fred Gretsch Mfg. Co. v. Schoening, 238 F. 780 (2d Cir. 1916); Apollinaris Co. v. Scherer, 27 F. 18 (C.C.N.Y. 1886). In A. Bourjois & Co. v. Katzel, 275 F. 539 (2d Cir. 1921), *rev'd*, 260 U.S. 689 (1923), the Supreme Court affirmed that marks have separate existence in separate national territories. See also American Circuit Breaker Corp. v. Oregon Breakers Inc., 406 F.3d 577 (9th Cir. 2005) (noting that in *Katzel* the Supreme Court "marked a dramatic change in trademark law by adopting the principle of 'territoriality' of trademarks and moving away from the rule of 'universality'").

[47] The U.S. Tariff Act prohibits the importation of a product "that bears a trademark owned by a citizen of . . . the United States and is registered in the U.S. Patent and Trademark Office." See Tariff Act of 1930 § 526(a), 19 U.S.C.S. § 1526(a) (2006). The U.S. Trademark Act (Lanham Act)

the foreign and the U.S. trademark are owned by the same person or business entity" or the owners of these marks are "parent and subsidiary companies or otherwise subjected to common ownership and control."[48] Nevertheless, again similar to Canada, U.S. courts have prohibited the importation of products when they "differ materially" from the goods authorized for sale in the domestic market even if the marks share a common ownership or control inside and outside the U.S. This rule was adopted in the *Lever Brothers* case and seeks to prevent the product quality-related confusion that could otherwise exist if two seemingly identical products of different quality are sold in the U.S. market under the same marks.[49] As an exception to this rule, however, the U.S. Customs Service Regulations provide that materially different products can be lawfully imported when importers properly label the goods with the notice: "This product is not authorized by the United States trademark owner for importation and is materially different from the authorized products."[50] In other words, under the U.S. Customs Service Regulations, it seems that proper labeling can guarantee that marks continue to serve the traditional trademark functions—indicating to consumers that the marked products are the same goods, in terms of commercial origin and quality, which were first distributed in the market by trademark owners.[51]

Finally, like Canada and the U.S., Mexico adopted a system of international trademark exhaustion.[52] According to Article 92(II) of the Mexican Industrial Property Law,[53] the reg-

---

bars the importation of goods with a mark that will "copy or simulate" a registered trademark. Lanham Act § 42, 15 U.S.C. § 1124 (2006). The Lanham Act also applies the traditional provisions against infringement to confusingly similar products. Lanham Act §§ 32(a) (registered marks), 43(b) (unregistered marks), 15 U.S.C. §§ 1114(a), 1125(b).

[48] K-Mart Corp. v. Cartier, Inc., 486 U.S. 281, 289 (1988) (indicating that the "extraordinary protection" afforded by the Tariff Act § 526 is exclusively for domestic U.S. trademark owners that have no corporate affiliation with the foreign manufacturer).

[49] See Lever Bros. Co. v. United States, 877 F.2d 101 (D.C. Cir. 1989) and Lever Bros. Co. v. United States, 981 F.2d 1330 (D.C. Cir. 1993). The court ruled that when a mark is applied to physically different goods, the mark is not "genuine" for the American consumer and the affiliation between the producers does not reduce the confusion that could result from those differences. *Lever Bros.*, 877 F.2d 101; *Lever Bros.*, 981 F.2d 1330. See also Société des Produits Nestle, S.A. v. Casa Helvetia, Inc., 982 F.2d 633, 639 (1st Cir. 1992) (stating that "under section 42, as under section 32, the question of whether [defendant] infringed the PERUGINA mark hinges on whether physical or like material differences exist between the Italian-made and Venezuelan-made products").

[50] 19 C.F.R. § 133.23(b). "Goods determined by the Customs Service to be physically and materially different . . . shall not be detained . . . where the merchandise or its packaging bears a conspicuous and legible label designed to remain on the product until the first point of sale." *Ibid.* "The label must be in close proximity to the trademark as it appears in its most prominent location on the article itself or the retail package or container. Other information designed to dispel consumer confusion may also be added." *Ibid.* Mark S. Sommers & Louis J. Levy, *US Customs Amends Gray Market Import Rule*, 117 TRADEMARK WORLD 32, 33 (1999).

[51] But see Chapter 20 in this volume (in which Mary LaFrance supports that trademark law could still serve to prevent parallel imports in some instances of materially different quality).

[52] See generally, Gonzalez, *supra* note 34, at 305–6 (analyzing parallel imports under Mexican law); Bill F. Kryzda & Shaun F. Downey, *Overview of Recent Changes in Mexican Industrial Property Law and the Enforcement of Rights by the Relevant Government Authorities*, 21 CAN.-U.S. L.J. 99, 101 (1995) (considering the changes to the Mexican Industrial Property Law in 1994 as a result of Mexico's signing of NAFTA).

[53] Ley de Fomento y Protección de la Propiedad Industrial [Mexican Industrial Property Law], Diario Oficial de la federación [DO], 4, June 27, 1991, *as amended* Diario Oficial de la federación

istration of a mark cannot be used against "any person who markets, distributes, acquires or uses the product to which the trademark is applied for after the said product has been lawfully introduced on the market by the owner of the registered mark or his licensee."[54] Specifically, "[t]his case shall include the import of legitimate products to which the registered mark is applied, carried out by any person for their use, distribution or marketing in Mexico."[55] Parallel imports are considered "legitimate" under the Mexican Industrial Property Law Regulations based upon two conditions: (a) that the products are introduced into the market of the country from which they are imported by the "owner or licensee of the registered mark;" and (b) that the owner of the mark inside and outside Mexico are "the same person or members of the same joint economic interest group, or their licensees or sublicensees."[56] Similar to Canada and the U.S., Mexican law prohibits as trademark infringement the circulation of marked products when their quality has been altered by unauthorized third-party importers,[57] or when the mark has been altered or removed altogether.[58] Still, the Mexican Industrial Property Regulations do not prevent the importation of materially different genuine gray market goods and do not require special labeling for those goods to be admitted and lawfully circulate in the Mexican territory.[59] Moreover, to date, Mexican courts do not seem to have halted or expressed concern as to the importation of materially different parallel imports into Mexico because of potential consumer confusion.[60]

IV. THE *LAISSEZ FAIRE* APPROACH (FOR NOW): TRADEMARK EXHAUSTION IN ASEAN

ASEAN was established in 1967 with the signing of the ASEAN Declaration[61] (the Bangkok Declaration). ASEAN's five founding members were: Indonesia, Malaysia,

---

[DO], August 2, 1994 (Mex.) [hereinafter Mexican Industrial Property Law].

[54] *Ibid.* art. 92(II).

[55] *Ibid.* This provision is applicable "pursuant to the terms and conditions laid down in the Regulations under this law." *Ibid.*

[56] Article 54 of the Mexican Industrial Property Regulations provides that: "it shall be presumed ... that imported goods are legitimate where they meet the following requirements: I. the introduction of the goods to the market of the country from which importation takes place must be done by the person who in that country is the owner or licensee of the registered mark; II. the owners of the mark registered in Mexico and in the foreign country must, on the date on which the importation of the goods takes place, be the same person or members of the same joint economic interest group, or their licensees or sub licensees." *Ibid.* art. 54. Reglamento de la Ley de la Propiedad Industrial [Regulation on the Industrial Property Law], Diario Oficial de la federación [DO], November 18, 1994, art. 54 (Mex.) [hereinafter Mexican Industrial Property Regulations].

[57] Mexican Industrial Property Law, art. 213(XX).

[58] *Ibid.* art. 213(XXI).

[59] Mexican Industrial Property Regulations, art. 54. The Mexican Industrial Property Regulations are also silent as to the case of imports concerning repackaged or relabeled goods. *Ibid.*

[60] Although courts have not considered the repackaging or relabeling of gray market products, these instances could likely fall under the prohibition of art. 213 of the Mexican Industrial Property Law. Mexican Industrial Property Law, art. 213(XX), (XXI).

[61] The ASEAN Declaration (Bangkok Declaration), Bangkok, Thailand, ASEAN, August 8, 1967, available at www.asean.org/news/item/the-asean-declaration-bangkok-declaration. The 1967 ASEAN Declaration set forth the aims and purpose of ASEAN, *inter alia*, "to accelerate the eco-

378 *Research handbook on intellectual property exhaustion and parallel imports*

Philippines, Singapore, and Thailand. Within the next three decades, the number of members doubled to ten and today include: Brunei Darussalam, Vietnam, Lao People's Democratic Republic (PDR), Myanmar, and Cambodia.[62] All ASEAN members are currently also members of the World Trade Organization (WTO).[63] As declared in the Treaty of Amity and Cooperation in Southeast Asia of 1976, ASEAN members adopt, as fundamental principles, the principles of consensus and non-interference with national policies.[64] This approach is different from the approach adopted by EU Member States, and it has been defined as the "ASEAN Way." Also different from the EU, ASEAN members did not create any regional institution comparable with EU institutions. Still, in 2003, the ASEAN members resolved to establish an ASEAN Community and, in 2007, adopted the ASEAN Charter.[65] One of the pillars of the ASEAN Community was the creation of the ASEAN Economic Community (AEC), which was launched in December 2015.[66] The AEC aims at integrating ASEAN members' markets into a single market that, similar to the EU internal market, comprises the free movement of goods, services, investment, capital, and skilled labor.[67] The foundation of the ASEAN market can also be traced to the Declaration on the ASEAN Economic Community Blueprint.[68] Additionally, ASEAN members signed an Agreement on the Common Effective Preferential Tariff Scheme for

---

nomic growth, social progress and cultural development in the region" and to promote "the rule of law in the relationship among countries of the region."

[62] *ASEAN Member States* (ASEAN 2014), available at www.asean.org/asean/asean-member-states. *Ibid.*

[63] The list of WTO Members and Observers is available at *Understanding the WTO: The Organization, Members and Observers* (WTO 2015), available at www.wto.org/english/thewto_e/whatis_e/tif_e/org6_e.htm.

[64] Treaty of Amity and Cooperation in Southeast Asia, Indonesia, ASEAN, February 24, 1976, [2012] O.J. L154/6. The 1976 Treaty of Amity and Cooperation contained, *inter alia*, the following fundamental principles: "a. mutual respect for the independence, sovereignty, equality, territorial integrity and national identity of all nations; b. the right of every State to lead its national existence free from external interference, subversion or coercion [*sic*]; c. non-interference in the internal affairs of one another." ASEAN has been described as a "weakly formalized intergovernmental regime with limited effectiveness due to the member states' deeply-felt concern with the preservation of internal and external sovereignty." Morten F. Greve, *ASEAN Down the "EU Way"?*, 39 COOPERATION & CONFLICT—J. NORDIC INT'L STUD. ASS'N 207, 210 (2004).

[65] Declaration of ASEAN Concord II (Bali Concord II), ASEAN, October 7, 2003, available at www.asean.org/news/asean-statement-communiques/item/declaration-of-asean-concord-ii-bali-concord-ii-3; the ASEAN Charter, ASEAN, November 20, 2007, available at www.asean.org/archive/publications/ASEAN-Charter.pdf.

[66] The ASEAN members committed to accelerate the establishment of the ASEAN Economic Community in the Cebu Declaration on the Acceleration of the Establishment of an ASEAN Community by 2015. ASEAN, Cebu Declaration on the Acceleration of the Establishment of an ASEAN Community by 2015 (January 13, 2007), available at www.asean.org/component/zoo/item/about-asean-overview-cebu-declaration-on-the-acceleration-of-the-establishment-of-an-asean-community-by-2015?Itemid=185. The ASEAN Community consists of three pillars of the ASEAN Security Community, ASEAN Economic Community (AEC), and ASEAN Socio-Cultural Community and these form the Roadmap for an ASEAN Community 2009–2015.

[67] ASEAN, Declaration on the ASEAN Economic Community Blueprint, para. 9 (2008), available at www.asean.org/archive/5187-10.pdf. For a detailed analysis of the creation of the AEC, see STEFANO INAMA & EDMUND W. SIM, AN INSTITUTIONAL AND LEGAL PROFILE (2015).

[68] *Ibid.* paras. 11, 13, & 14.

the ASEAN Free Trade Area[69] (AFTA) in order to foster regional economic integration and eliminate tariff and non-tariff barriers.[70]

With respect to intellectual property, ASEAN members adopted the ASEAN Framework Agreement on Intellectual Property Cooperation[71] ("Framework Agreement") in 1995. The Framework Agreement aims at establishing cooperation among ASEAN members in several areas, including copyright and related rights, patents, trademarks, industrial designs, geographical indications, trade secrets, and lay-out designs of integrated circuits.[72] Still, to date, the ASEAN cooperation regarding trademarks has focused primarily on administrative matters. In particular, the following initiatives have been established: (a) the creation of a trademark online database,[73] which facilitates information on trademark registrations and applications in ASEAN members; and (b) the adoption of Common Guidelines for the Substantive Examination of Trademarks[74] to enhance the transparency and consistency of the decisions in the substantive examination of trademark applications in ASEAN. So far, however, no harmonized substantive trademark rules have been adopted, including the adoption of a regional common position on trademark exhaustion.[75]

In the absence of any specific guideline, ASEAN members thus remains free to decide their preferred system of trademark exhaustion to be adopted domestically. In particular, the exhaustion rules followed by ASEAN members can be divided into three separate groups: countries without a specific rule on exhaustion; countries following

---

[69] Agreement on the Common Effective Preferential Tariff (CEPT) Scheme for the ASEAN Free Trade Area (AFTA), January 28, 1992, art. 5, WIPO Lex. No. TRT/AFTA/001 [hereinafter CEPT-AFTA].

[70] But art. 8(d) of the ASEAN Trade in Goods Agreement (ATIGA) stipulates that the protection and enforcement of trademark rights (IPRs) may constitute a general exception to the prohibition to non-tariff barriers within ASEAN. ATIGA, February 26, 2009, WIPO Lex. No. TRT/ASEAN/001. ATIGA replaced the earlier CEPT-AFTA scheme signed in 1992.

[71] ASEAN Framework Agreement on Intellectual Property Cooperation, December 15, 1995, WIPO Lex. No. TRT/ASEAN-IP/001.

[72] *Ibid*. art. 3(1).

[73] The ASEAN TMview was developed by the Intellectual Property Offices of the ASEAN member states with the support of the EU-ASEAN Project on the Protection of Intellectual Property Rights (ECAP III Phase II) administered by the EU Office for Harmonization in the Internal Market (OHIM), ASEAN TMVIEW, available at www.asean-tmview.org/tmview/welcome.html?language=en.

[74] Common Guidelines for the Substantive Examination of Trademarks were prepared by a group of experts in the ASEAN Intellectual Property Offices concerning the substantive examination of trademark applications with the assistance of ECAP, the program is available at *Guidelines for the Substantive Examination of Trademarks*, ECAP III, www.ecap3.org/activities/guidelines-substantive-examination-trademarks.

[75] See Siraprapha Rungpry & Oliver Knox, *The ASEAN Economic Community: Good News for Trademark Owners?*, WORLD TRADEMARK REVIEW 55, 58 (2012), even though all ASEAN members are members of TRIPS, the Paris Convention for the Protection of Industrial Property, and the Berne Convention for the Protection of Literary and Artistic Works, and in turn are mandated to harmonize their national standards pursuant to these agreements. Paris Convention for the Protection of Industrial Property, opened for signature March 20, 1883, 21 U.S.T. 1583, 828 U.N.T.S. 305 (revised 1967); Berne Convention for the Protection of Literary and Artistic Works, September 9, 1886, WIPO Lex. No. TRT/BERNE/001.

national exhaustion; and countries following international exhaustion. Among the ASEAN members in the latter group, similar to the U.S. and Canada, some countries do not follow international exhaustion when the products at issue are of materially different quality. Furthermore, ASEAN members do not adopt a principle similar to the EU principle of mutual recognition and so far have not developed a system of integrated standardization for products manufactured in other ASEAN members similar to the system that has been adopted in the EU.

Notably, Indonesia[76] and Brunei Darussalam[77] have not yet adopted any relevant statutory provision on trademark exhaustion and no judicial decision on the issue can be found so far in either country. In the absence of any specific provision, it could thus be supported that these countries would admit parallel imports from other ASEAN members, and in general from foreign jurisdictions. Still, this remains, for the time being, an assumption based on the lack of any rules in this respect. In addition to Indonesia and Brunei, Myanmar also has not adopted any provision on trademark exhaustion to date, as Myanmar does not currently have a law on trademarks. However, a trademark law draft has been approved by the Myanmar Attorney General's Office and has been under review in the Parliament of Myanmar since 2014.[78] As reported by the International Trademark Association (INTA), Article 41 of the Myanmar Draft Trademark Law adopts the principle of international exhaustion while Article 42 "prevents the importation of goods which have been altered after their initial sale."[79]

On the other hand, Cambodia and Lao PDR have adopted national trademark exhaustion, even though neither country's laws specify that parallel imports are forbidden. In particular, Article 11(c) of the Cambodian Law concerning Marks, Trade Names and Acts of Unfair Competition[80] provides that "the rights conferred by registration of a mark shall not extend to acts in respect of articles which have been put on the market in the Kingdom of Cambodia by the registered owner or with his consent."[81] Similarly, Article 57(3) lit.1 of Lao PDR's Law on Intellectual Property 2011 states that "no indi-

---

[76] Indonesia Law No. 15 of August 1, 2001, regarding Marks, art. 1(13), WIPO Lex. No. ID046 (Indon).

[77] Trade Marks Act (ch. 98, Laws of Brunei Darussalam, rev. edn. 2000) (BN008) WIPO Lex. No. BN008 (Brunei).

[78] Nick Redfearn, *The Never Ending Delay in Myanmar's Trademarks Law*, ROSE MAG. (January 13, 2015), available at www.rouse.com/magazine/articles/ip-komodo-blog/the-never-ending-delay-in-myanmars-trademarks-law.

[79] International Trademark Association, Comments by the International Trademark Association on the Myanmar Draft Trademark Law, ss. 41, 42, available at www.inta.org/advocacy/documents/january82013comments.pdf [hereinafter INTA]. The INTA suggested "national exhaustion in relation to parallel imports" and in case international exhaustion remain unchanged, art. 42 should introduce the rule of "material difference" as "notwithstanding anything contained in Section 41, the owner of the registered mark may, when the goods are materially different from those put on the national market by the owner himself or by a third party with his consent, or when the condition of the goods has been changed or impaired after they have been put on the national or international market, prohibit the sale of the said goods in conformity with the existing law." *Ibid.* s. 42.

[80] Law Concerning Marks, Trade Names and Acts of Unfair Competition of the Kingdom of Cambodia, NS/RKM/0202/006, February 7, 2002, WIPO Lex. No. KH001 (Cambodia).

[81] LAZAROS G. GRIGORIADIS, TRADE MARKS AND FREE TRADE: A GLOBAL ANALYSIS 488 (2014).

vidual or organization . . . [other] than the trademark owner" is entitled to enter into any activity or act as described in paragraph 1 of the Law of Lao PDR without the authorization of the trademark owner, "except as otherwise provided in this Law." To the contrary, "any such acts without authorization shall be considered to be an act of infringement."[82] Based on the language of these provisions, parallel imports seem to be forbidden as the importation of genuine goods is not explicitly allowed as a statutory exception to trademark infringement.

Still, the rest of ASEAN members, which is the majority of countries, follow the principle of international trademark exhaustion, either as a statutory provision or under the rule of leading case law. These countries include Singapore and Vietnam, which have adopted specific provisions establishing the principle of international trademark exhaustion as their respective domestic rule. The Philippines is also included in this majority. In particular, the interpretation of the existing law tilts toward the argument that the Philippines follows international trademark exhaustion *de facto*, even though the Philippines has not included a specific provision in this sense. Finally, Malaysia and Thailand have also adopted international exhaustion following national case law rulings in this respect.

Notably, Article 29(1) of the Singapore Trade Mark Act excludes trademark infringement for products that have been distributed in the market "whether in Singapore or outside Singapore" with the "express or implied consent (conditional or otherwise)" of the trademark owners.[83] The exception to this rule applies when "the condition of the goods has been changed or impaired after they have been put on the market" or "the use of the registered trade mark in relation to those goods has caused dilution in an unfair manner of the distinctive character of the registered trade mark."[84] Similarly, Article 125(2)(b) of the Vietnam Intellectual Property Law of 2009[85] introduced the principle of international exhaustion.[86] However, the provision does not address the issue of products or goods of different quality, but states that the following does not constitute infringement: "circulating, importing, exploiting utilities of products having been lawfully put on the market, including overseas markets, except for products put on the overseas markets not by the mark owners or their licensees."[87] Prior to 2009, Vietnam adopted national exhaustion without written regulation, although the National Office of Industrial

---

[82] Law No. 01/NA, December 20, 2011, on Intellectual Property (as amended), art. 57(3) lit 1, WIPO Lex. No. LA025 (Lao).

[83] Singapore Trade Marks Act (ch. 332, 2005 rev. edn.), art. 29(1), WIPO Lex. No. SG035 (Sing.).

[84] *Ibid.* s. 29. See also Ng-Loy Wee Loon, *Exhaustion of Rights in Trademark Law: The English and Singapore Models Compared*, 22 E.I.P.R. 320 (2000).

[85] Law No. 50/2005/QH11, November 29, 2005, on Intellectual Property Law (promulgated by Order No. 28/2005/L-CTN, December 12, 2005, of the President of the Socialist Republic of Vietnam), WIPO Lex. No. VN003 (Viet.). This law was amended in 2009 by Law No. 36/2009/QH12, June 19, 2009, amending and supplementing a Number of Articles of the Law on Intellectual Property (promulgated by Order No. 12/2009/L-CTN, June 29, 2009 of the President of the Socialist Republic of Vietnam), WIPO Lex. No. VN047 (Viet.). However, the trademark exhaustion provision, art. 125, remains unchanged.

[86] *Ibid.* art. 125(2)(b).

[87] *Ibid.*

Property of Vietnam "occasionally" permitted the import of products manufactured by third countries as "an ad hoc policy," such as the import of motorbikes from China under the trademark licensing agreements.[88]

To the contrary, the Intellectual Property Code of the Philippines of 2013 does not explicitly provide for a provision on exhaustion. Still, Article 166[89] considers as infringing an article that is imported into the Philippines that copies or simulates a mark registered in the Philippines.[90] Since parallel importation involves genuine products—while the provision refers to counterfeits or infringing products[91]—it is, thus, supported that the principle of international exhaustion applies to the importation of genuine goods. In addition, neither the Intellectual Property Code of the Philippines nor the Philippine courts have addressed the issues relating to goods of materially different qualities for different markets thus far.[92] Here again, the general wisdom on the issue could be that, in the absence of an explicit prohibition, these products should be considered as legitimate imports into the Philippines.

Similar to the Philippines, Article 70D of the Malaysia Trademark Act of 1976[93] allows the proprietor of a registered trademark to submit an application for border measures to prohibit the importation of "counterfeit trademark goods"[94] into Malaysia. Here again, it remained unclear whether importation of "genuine goods" into Malaysia constitutes trademark infringement. However, the judiciary in Malaysia explicitly embraced the principle of international trademark exhaustion in the *Panadol* case.[95] In this case, the court held that the parallel imports of goods sharing the common origin should be allowed.[96] Still, the *Panadol*

---

[88] See Pham Duy Nghia, *Exhaustion and Parallel Imports in Vietnam*, in PARALLEL IMPORTS IN ASIA 88 (Christopher Heath ed., 2004).

[89] Intellectual Property Code of the Philippines (Republic Act No. 8293), June 6, 1997, WIPO Lex. No. PH001 (Phil.) *as amended* Implementing Rules and Regulations of the Republic Act No. 9502 of 2008, July 4, 2008, WIPO Lex. No. PH048 (Phil.) *as amended* Republic Act No. 10372, entitled "An Act Amending Certain Provisions of Republic Act No. 8293, otherwise known as the Intellectual Property Code of the Philippines, and for other purposes," February 28, 2013, WIPO Lex. No. PH100 (Phil.).

[90] *Ibid.* art. 166. Article 166 of the Intellectual Property Code of the Philippines 2013 provides: "no article of imported merchandise which shall copy or simulate the name of any domestic product, or manufacturer, or dealer, or which shall copy or simulate a mark registered in accordance with the provisions of this Act, or shall bear a mark or trade name calculated to induce the public to believe that the article is manufactured in the Philippines, or that it is manufactured in any foreign country or locality other than the country or locality where it is in fact manufactured, shall be admitted to entry at any customhouse of the Philippines." *Ibid.*

[91] Alex Ferdinand S. Fider, *Exhaustion and Parallel Imports in the Philippines*, in PARALLEL IMPORTS IN ASIA 115 (Christopher Heath ed., 2004).

[92] *Ibid.*

[93] Trademark Act (Act 175 of 1976, as last amended by Act A1138 of 2002), June 21, 1976, WIPO Lex. No. MY044 (Malay).

[94] The definition of "counterfeit trademark goods" is set out in art. 70C of the Trademark Act 1976. *Ibid.* art. 70C.

[95] Winthrop Products Inc. & anor v. Sun Ocean (M) Sdn Bhd & anor, [1988] 2 M.L.J. 317 [hereinafter *Panadol* case]. For the case summary and analysis, see John Chong, *Exhaustion and Parallel Imports in Malaysia*, in PARALLEL IMPORTS IN ASIA 127–30 (Christopher Heath ed., 2004).

[96] *Panadol* case, *supra* note 95. Therefore, "they can be said to have *impliedly consented* to their doing so so that the holder from time to time of the goods acquires the absolute ownership of the

case is the only case dealing with the issue of trademark exhaustion in Malaysia[97] to date, and the decision in that case left many questions unanswered. In particular, the court did not address the issue concerning the parallel imports of goods of different origin or with materially different qualities. Finally, similar to Malaysia, Thailand also has no express legislation regarding the exhaustion of trademark rights.[98] Nevertheless, the Thai Central Intellectual Property and International Trade Court[99] and the Thai Supreme Court[100] have all embraced international trademark exhaustion.[101] In particular, in a 1999 decision, the Thai Central Intellectual Property and International Trade Court allowed the parallel import of genuine goods bearing the same mark from Singapore to Thailand, stating that trademark rights are internationally exhausted because trademark owners have already fairly received rewards from the first sale of the goods.[102] This decision was affirmed by the Supreme People's Court of Thailand in 2000.[103]

V. COMPARING THE EU/EEA, NAFTA, AND ASEAN: WHAT IS THE SUCCESSFUL RECIPE TO PROMOTE FREE MOVEMENT OF GOODS IN FREE TRADE AREAS? SHOULD THERE BE ONE?

As I have observed in previous writings, the principle of trademark exhaustion is based on the premise that trademark rights should not be used to control the distribution of a product, or a batch of products, after their first release into the market. With respect to international trade, however, the key inquiry remains whether trademark rights exhaust only with respect to products that have been distributed in the national market or also in foreign markets as long as the products are genuine products. In particular, the adoption of one type of exhaustion versus another—national vs. international or regional exhaustion—translates into accepting parallel imports or, instead, raising national barriers to international legitimate trade carried out by third parties. Hence, effective free trade in free trade areas can be secured only by limiting, amongst other trade-related barriers, the domestic enforcement of national trademark rights when this enforcement can represent a barrier to legitimate trade.[104]

---

goods including the right to *sell* the goods in any part of the world *in the same condition in which they were disposed of.*" Ibid. (emphasis added).

[97] GRIGORIADIS, *supra* note 81, at 483.
[98] For an overview of the history of the exhaustion rule in Thailand, see Vichai Ariyanuntaka, *Exhaustion and Parallel Imports in Thailand*, in PARALLEL IMPORTS IN ASIA 98–100 (Christopher Heath ed., 2004).
[99] Thailand Central Intellectual Property and International Trade Court Decision No. 16/2542 (1999).
[100] Thailand Supreme Court Decision No. 2817/2543 (2000).
[101] GRIGORIADIS, *supra* note 81, at 495.
[102] Ariyanuntaka, *supra* note 98, at 99.
[103] Thailand Supreme Court Decision affirmed Decision No. 16/2542 (1999) in Decision No. 2817/2543 (2000).
[104] See e.g. Irene Calboli, *Market Integration and (the Limits of) the First Sale Rule in North American and European Trademark Law*, 51 SANTA CLARA L. REV. 1241 (2011).

Still, as the above described approaches adopted by the EU/EEA, NAFTA, and ASEAN members reflect, not all members of free trade areas necessarily desire to achieve a full-scale market integration as part of their commitment to a free trade area. This may be due to several reasons. For example, not all members of free trade areas may desire, or may be ready for, a full-scale market integration within the free trade area due to national levels of development, national interests, or national politics. In particular, some of the members of a free trade area may need to protect their national markets from foreign imports, including from imports from other countries in the free trade area (and thus adopt national exhaustion). To the contrary, other members may need to open their markets to as many foreign products as possible in certain sectors (and adopt international exhaustion) because these countries do not manufacture these products domestically, and parallel imports may increase choices and decrease prices for national consumers. In short, choosing a domestic policy on exhaustion (whether in favor of national, regional, or international exhaustion) remains a sensitive topic and not all members of a free trade area may be interested in reaching an agreement on the topic as it happened (not without controversy) in the EU/EEA.[105]

In particular, the process of market integration in the EU/EEA required that EU/EEA Member States abandon their national policies and harmonize national laws on trademark exhaustion, adopt similar standards to remove any disguised barriers to effective intra-EU/EEA trade, and accept the principle of mutual recognition of other Members' standards when the standards remain different. Only very serious concerns relating to health, security, or public policy in member countries can supersede free movement of goods in EU/EEA trade.[106] Yet, as noted above, this process of integration and legal harmonization was met with resistance by several Member States. Several leading cases by the ECJ (and later CJEU) contributed to clarify the extent of this legal harmonization, and further proved that the Court was willing to prioritize free movement of goods versus the exercise of trademark rights, including in instances of materially different quality. Moreover, the Court stated that trademark rights can also be exhausted with respect to products that have been repackaged by the importers as long as the products remain genuine. Nevertheless, this full-force integration of markets does not extend beyond the territory of the EU/EE. Instead, EU/EEA Member States are bound to adopt regional exhaustion, and genuine products coming from outside "fortress Europe" can be legally stopped at the will of trademark owners as trademark infringement.[107] Ultimately, as much as the EU/EEA solution certainly constitutes a stronger and more definite approach to facilitate trade among members of a free trade area, this solution permits (and safeguards) market partitioning outside the EU/EEA.[108]

---

[105] See SUSY FRANKEL, TEST TUBES FOR GLOBAL INTELLECTUAL PROPERTY ISSUES 159–84 (2015) (analyzing in detail the national policies on parallel imports of small market economies, namely, Israel, New Zealand, and Singapore). See also Chapter 5 in this volume by Susy Frankel and Daniel Gervais.
[106] See discussion *supra* II.
[107] See e.g. Carl Steele, *"Fortresse Europe" for Trademark Owners*, 1998 TRADEMARK WORLD 14 (August 1998) (summarizing the relevance of the ECJ's decision in *Silhouette* in creating a closed trading block among Member States).
[108] Critically, on this aspect of the principle of the EEA-wide exhaustion, see Calboli, *Trademark Exhaustion in the EU, supra* note 3, at 87–90.

Quite differently from the EU/EEA, NAFTA members never intended to build a NAFTA internal market. Instead, the U.S. and Canada joined NAFTA primarily to produce at lower costs in Mexico (and import back or sell internationally products manufactured at lower costs) while Mexico joined NAFTA primarily as a source of foreign direct investment from the U.S. and Canada. Thus, NAFTA members harmonize several intellectual property standards, but not their national rules on exhaustion.[109] Still, as a fortuitous coincidence perhaps, all NAFTA members practice international trademark exhaustion, which permits parallel imports within their respective territories. Yet, NAFTA members never attempted to discuss the approach to be adopted at the national level with respect to the importation of genuine products of materially different quality.[110] Here again, it thus remains a fortuitous circumstance that each of the three NAFTA members has developed, via the courts or legislators, specific provisions that permit the importation of genuine products that are of materially different quality.[111] Specifically, appropriate labeling can cure material product differences and allow the importation of qualitatively different gray market goods into Canada and the U.S. In Mexico, the national trademark law does not seem to prevent the admissibility of any products into Mexico, even those that are materially different, as long as the importers have not altered the products.[112] Hence, nothing may prevent a change in national policies, which would effectively operate as a barrier to legitimate trade and free movement of goods across NAFTA. Lastly, NAFTA members do not follow a principle equivalent to the EU principle of mutual recognition[113] nor are they pursuing a full scale harmonization of national standards.[114]

Again different from both the EU/EEA and NAFTA, ASEAN members have adopted a position that is a mid-way between the full-scale EU/EEA integration and the NAFTA *laissez faire* approach. Notably, ASEAN members certainly intend to integrate their national markets and have already taken important steps toward creating an internal market through AFTA and the ASEAN Blue Print.[115] In particular, the latter specifically

---

[109] See Kenneth W. Abbott & Gregory W. Bowman, *Economic Integration in the Americas: A Work in Progress*, 14 Nw. J. INT'L L. & BUS. 493, 493–96 (1994) (discussing the 1990 initiation of NAFTA negotiations between the U.S. and Mexico); Richard Bernal, *Regional Trade Arrangements in the Western Hemisphere*, 8 AM. U. J. INT'L L. & POL'Y 683, 697 (1993) (discussing the proposal of NAFTA in the 1990s); Frank J. Garcia, *Protection of Intellectual Property Rights in the North American Free Trade Agreement: A Successful Case of Regional Trade Regulation*, 8 AM. U. J. INT'L L. & POL'Y 817, 821 (1993) (noting Mexico's desire to be a part of the NAFTA).

[110] For a similar conclusion, see Gonzalez, *supra* note 34, at 329 (comparing the NAFTA and EU trading blocks).

[111] See discussion *supra* III.

[112] *Ibid.*

[113] See NAFTA, art. 714; see also Maureen Irish, *Regulatory Convergence, Security and Global Administrative Law in Canada-United States Trade*, 12 J. INT'L ECON. L. 333, 339–40 (2009). "Both SPS and TBT provisions in NAFTA contain explicit obligations to recognize measures of other NAFTA Parties as equivalent." *Ibid.* at 339. For a position in favor of creating a full NAFTA common market, see Wendy Dobson, *Shaping the Future of the North American Economic Space*, 162 C.D. HOWE INST., THE BORDER PAPERS 1 (2002), available at www.cdhowe.org/pdf/commentary_162.pdf.

[114] See NAFTA, ch. 7B on sanitary and phytosanitary measures (SPS), and ch. 9 on technical barriers to trade (TBT). See also Irish, *supra* note 113, at 339 (providing a detailed analysis of these and other provisions related to NAFTA SPS and TBT measures).

[115] See discussion *supra* IV.

states that the "[f]ree flow of goods is one of the principal means by which the aims of a single market and production base can be achieved."[116] Still, the level of economic integration currently achieved, and perhaps possible at this time, in ASEAN has not yet reached the same level that can be seen in the EU/EEA market. Instead, even though AFTA has gone a long way to reduce intra-ASEAN tariffs on most products, some tariffs still exist with respect to the most relevant products for national economies, such as rice or sugar.[117] However, it should not be judged against ASEAN members' desire to effectively integrate their markets in the long term that national laws on trademark exhaustion still diverge. As noted above, the domestic approach of EU Member States also diverged for several decades after the launch of the EEC in 1957, and it was harmonized only with the enactment of the Trademark Directive in 1988.[118] Nevertheless, it remains surprising that two of the least developed countries in ASEAN, Cambodia and Lao PDR, have opted for a system of national trademark exhaustion, whereas both countries would certainly benefit from parallel imports. Instead, their current system of national exhaustion allows trademark owners—primarily foreign entities with national registrations in these countries and in other ASEAN members—to block parallel imports of trademarked products (from Coca-Cola beverages, to Apple iPhones, etc.) into Cambodia and Lao PDR. In turn, citizens of these countries may not benefit from the possible economic benefits of parallel imported products.[119]

Ultimately, the comparative analysis of the EU/EEA, NAFTA, and ASEAN demonstrates that the adoption of uniform rules on either international or regional trademark exhaustion remains a necessary condition for creating a system of effective free move-

---

[116] In 2007, a Protocol to provide special consideration for rice and sugar was signed in Makati City, Philippines. Protocol to Provide Special Consideration for Rice and Sugar, ASEAN, August 23, 2007, available at www.asean.org/images/2012/Economic/AFTA/Common_Effective_Preferential_Tariff/Protocol%20to%20Provide%20Special%20Consideration%20for.pdf. In 2010, following the signing and entry into force of ATIGA, a revision to the Protocol was adopted that refers to "the need to amend the Protocol to take into account the entry into force of the ASEAN Trade in Goods Agreement." See Protocol to Amend the Protocol to Provide Special Consideration for Rice and Sugar, ASEAN, October 28, 2010, available at http://investasean.asean.org/files/upload/00%20Protocol%20Amendment%20Protocol%20Rice%20and%20Sugar%20(2010)(1).pdf.

[117] *ASEAN Free Trade Area (AFTA Council)* (ASEAN 2014), available at www.asean.org/communities/asean-economic-community/category/asean-free-trade-area-afta-council; see also *ASEAN Free Trade Area (AFTA): An Update* (ASEAN 2014), available at www.asean.org/communities/asean-economic-community/item/asean-free-trade-area-afta-an-update.

[118] See discussion *supra* II.

[119] In practice, however, it is unclear to what extent cross-border enforcement or claims of trademark infringement have effectively prevented parallel imports into Cambodia and Lao PDR to date. In the absence of any data or court decision in this respect, the author thinks that the current level of practical enforcement is very low. Moreover, due to the low per-capita GDP in Cambodia and Lao PDR, it is unlikely that these countries represent today a market suitable for pricing arbitrage. Still parallel imports can be very beneficial for these countries, as parallel importers may make available in these countries products otherwise not available. Thus, it would be important for these countries to move to a system of international exhaustion, so as to avoid possible cross-border enforcement in the future and to permit the imports of products not marketed national, but for which perhaps a mark has been registered based on intent to use and not actual use, or simply use in advertising or the Internet.

ment of products across the territory of the members of a free trade area. In contrast, when some of the members of a free trade area adopt domestic rules in favor of national exhaustion (as is the case currently in Cambodia and Lao PDR) this disparity of national regimes can necessarily result in blocking the free movement of goods within the free trade area. The same applies when the members of a free trade area practice a non-uniform regime of international and regional exhaustion (as was the case in the EU/EEA immediately after the enactment of the Trademark Directive).

Hence, the analysis above also indicates that requiring the adoption of the same rules on trademark exhaustion is not sufficient, *per se*, to guarantee the effective free movement of goods in free trade areas. In particular, under the current law of several countries practicing international trademark exhaustion, trademark owners can successfully block parallel imports when the products are genuine, yet are of materially different quality. As I have extensively elaborated in my previous scholarship, these differences are often strategically planned, and later enforced, by trademark owners precisely in order to partition the international market as a means to combat product arbitrage by parallel importers.

Accordingly, securing an effective free movement of goods in free trade areas also requires the additional condition of eliminating these additional barriers to otherwise legitimate trade through specific mechanisms. Based on the different experiences analyzed above, this result could be achieved in several ways: (a) by harmonizing product standards, or by enforcing a principle of mutual recognition of national standards amongst members of free trade areas as has been done in the EU/EEA; or (b) by adopting laws and regulations according to which parallel importers could "cure" the different quality of the paralleled imported products through proper labels and disclaimers on the products so consumers would not be confused as to the products' actual quality or origin, as is currently the case in NAFTA members and some ASEAN members.

In this respect, it could be supported that only the adoption of uniform products standards across members of free trade areas would eliminate the possibility of using any qualitative product difference as a reason to prevent parallel trade in the long term.[120] Still, obtaining a full-scale standard harmonization is a close to impossible objective, at least in the early stages of the functioning of a free trade area. Moreover, even where members of a free trade area would be willing to engage in this harmonization, as has been the case in the EU, standard harmonization is a lengthy process.[121] And not all product standards may be harmonized, as national differences relate to national tastes, available raw materials and ingredients, and consumer preferences. Thus, some product differences may continue to exist even when technical standards are harmonized, and in turn these differences could still be used to segment the regional markets within free trade areas. Accordingly, adopting a principle of mutual recognition of product standards as it was done in the EU/EEA may also become necessary in addition to product standardization, at least until most standards have been harmonized. More generally, adopting

---

[120] See e.g. Lori M. Wallach, *Accountable Governance in the Era of Globalization: The WTO, NAFTA, and International Harmonization of Standards*, 50 U. KAN. L. REV. 823, 823–24 (2002) (arguing in this context with respect to NAFTA and the WTO that "decades of popular political movements . . . have struggled to ensure that those who will live with the results are able to control the process and outcomes of important policy decisions").

[121] See discussion *supra* II.

this principle could be a viable alternative to the harmonization of product standards altogether. Still, adopting the principle of mutual recognition results in the acceptance of products of different standards within a national market and leads to discriminating between foreign and national products in national markets, which is also controversial.[122] In addition, some authors have noted that adopting this principle may run against the non-discrimination and most-favored-nation principles that all WTO members are supposed to follow as part of their WTO and TRIPS obligations.[123]

Perhaps less controversial, but equally effective, may be the use of labels and disclaimers by the parallel importers. As noted above, this approach is currently applied in several countries, including the U.S. and Canada.[124] In particular, unauthorized importers can use labels to disclose the quality of the imported products, and the fact that the product is imported by a third party. Thanks to these disclaimers, consumers can purchase products based on an informed judgment about the product's quality and trademark owners can no longer claim that consumers may be confused by qualitative differences, which trademark owners implement often simply in order to control international trade.

In summary, although generally opposed by trademark owners because of the additional pressure that parallel imports create for their business, the exercise of national trademark law should not entail the creation of barriers to the free movement of legitimate genuine products. Accordingly, when blocks of countries create free trade areas in order to take advantage of the benefits of free trade, they should not permit that the national exercise of trademark rights interfere with the free movement of goods across the free trade area so long as the products at issue are genuine. Likewise, trademark owners should not be allowed to object to the free movement of products by relying on differences in quality, particularly when labels or other notices can properly inform consumers about these product differences. To the contrary, the proper functioning of free trade in free trade areas would be jeopardized and trademark protection would wrongfully exceed its scope to the detriment of competition and consumers.

VI. CONCLUSION

Different trade areas in the world have adopted different solutions with respect to the application of the principle of trademark exhaustion to promote free trade areas

---

[122] See generally, Irish, *supra* note 113, at 350 (stating that "[f]or [mutual recognition] to work effectively, regulators from the involved countries must trust each other and accept that they have obligations extending beyond responsibilities to their own citizenries"). The tension between mutual recognition and national standards "is especially significant for mutual recognition of conformity assessments in which testing, inspection, verification or monitoring of compliance is done in one country and recognized in others." *Ibid*.

[123] Generally, it has been affirmed that the EU principle of mutual recognition is compatible with WTO principles, although some doubts in this respect have been raised during the recent enlargement of the EU. See Lorand Bartels, *The Legality of the EC Mutual Recognition Clause Under WTO Law*, 8 J. INT'L ECON. L. 691 (2005); Kalypso Nicolaidis, *Non-Discriminatory Mutual Recognition: An Oxymoron in the New WTO Lexicon?*, in REGULATORY BARRIERS AND THE PRINCIPLE OF NON-DISCRIMINATION IN WORLD TRADE LAW 267 (2000).

[124] See discussion *supra* III and IV.

and regional market integration. To a large extent, the remaining differences in these approaches depend on several factors, which include: the degree of integration that the members of different free trade areas effectively desire to, and realistically can, achieve; the size of their markets, and their respective level of development of the countries; their historical approaches in this area, and so forth. Moreover, as the development of the EU (from the EEC in 1957 to the creation of the internal market in the late 1980s) has demonstrated, the process of market integration in free trade areas is a lengthy process and national policies on trademark exhaustion can shift over time.

Still, from the analysis of the market integration achieved to date by, respectively, the EU/EEA, NAFTA, and ASEAN members, the following conclusions can be derived. First, regional market integration requires, at a minimum, the adoption of uniform national rules providing for the exhaustion of trademark rights internationally or, at least, within the territory of members of a free trade area. Second, effective integration in free trade areas may be jeopardized when material differences in product quality operate as barriers to trade among members, even if members uniformly practice international or regional trademark exhaustion. Third, these barriers could nonetheless be overcome by adopting national laws accepting the importation of materially different products with appropriate labels disclosing these differences. And finally, at a more comprehensive level, these barriers could be overcome by harmonizing, or approximating, national product standards or at least by adoption of a principle of mutual recognition.

Ultimately, despite the fact that the members of some free trade areas perhaps never intended to create a full-fledged "free market" for the circulation of trademarked products, it is undeniable that invoking trademark protection to segment the market against the parallel trade of genuine goods does undermine the very purpose of free trade. Free trade areas are, at least in principle, created specifically in order to eliminate any barriers to legitimate trade between their members, including the exercise of trademark protection with respect to parallel imports both when the products are the same or in the case of material products differences, particularly when the products carry labels dispelling the likelihood of consumer confusion.

20. Using trademark law to override copyright's first sale rule for imported copies in the United States
*Mary LaFrance**

I. INTRODUCTION

Can copyright owners use trademark law to circumvent the first sale rule of copyright law in the United States (U.S.)? In the case of parallel imports, the answer appears to be "yes."

In both trademark and copyright law, non-counterfeit goods that are imported without the consent of the owner of the domestic intellectual property rights are referred to as parallel imports, or "gray market goods."[1] Legal restrictions on parallel imports benefit domestic intellectual property owners by enabling them to maintain separate markets in different territories. In some cases, this benefits consumers by enabling merchants to tailor their offerings to meet the needs and preferences of consumers in different territories.[2] However, it also allows merchants to engage in price discrimination, by offering their goods at higher prices in the U.S. than in foreign markets without facing competition from imports of the cheaper foreign goods or from domestic secondhand sales of the imported goods. Because secondhand sales by third parties generate no royalties for copyright owners, any strategy that reduces the number of secondhand copies on the market can increase revenues for copyright owners by enabling them (1) to sell more new copies; and (2) to charge higher prices for those new copies due to the absence of price competition from secondhand sales.[3]

---

* IGT Professor of Intellectual Property Law, William S. Boyd School of Law, University of Nevada, Las Vegas. This chapter is adapted from *A Material World: Using Trademark Law to Override Copyright's First Sale Rule for Imported Copies*, 21 MICH. TEL. & TECH. L. REV. 43 (2014).

[1] Ferrero U.S.A., Inc. v. Ozak Trading, Inc., 952 F.2d 44, 45 n.1 (3d Cir. 1991); K Mart Corp. v. Cartier, Inc., 486 U.S. 281 (1988); 5 J. THOMAS MCCARTHY, MCCARTHY ON TRADEMARKS AND UNFAIR COMPETITION § 29:46 (4th ed. 2013).

[2] There are many justifications for territorial price discrimination. For example, the economic conditions of the foreign country may require setting a lower price in order to be competitive. Local law may impose price controls. The manufacturer may not provide the same level of advertising and marketing support to retailers in the foreign country, or it may not provide the same kind of customer service or warranty support in that country. The manufacturer may also face greater economic risks under product liability laws in the U.S. than in other markets. See ROSE ANN MACGILLIVRAY, PARALLEL IMPORTATION 19–21, 26–28 (2010); Pernilla Larsson, *Parallel Imports: Effects of the Silhouette Ruling*, SWEDISH COMPETITION AUTH. 28–29 (1999), available at http://www.konkurrensverket.se/globalassets/english/publications-and-decisions/parallel-imports-effects-of-the-silhouette-ruling.pdf; Mary LaFrance, *Wag the Dog: Using Incidental Intellectual Property Rights to Block Parallel Imports*, 20 MICH. TELECOMM. & TECH. L. REV. 45, 47 (2013); Jacqueline Nolan-Haley, *The Competitive Process and Gray Market Goods*, 6 N.Y.L. SCH. J. INT'L & COMP. L. 231, 233 (1983).

[3] See R. Anthony Reese, *The First Sale Doctrine in the Era of Digital Networks*, 44 B.C. L.

In *Kirtsaeng v. John Wiley & Sons, Inc.*,[4] the U.S. Supreme Court announced for the first time that federal copyright law incorporates a rule of international exhaustion. This decision was a major defeat for copyright owners, who can no longer rely on copyright law to divide their domestic and foreign markets. However, copyright owners have an alternative remedy in trademark law, because *Kirtsaeng* addressed only copyright exhaustion, not trademark exhaustion. Under federal trademark law, a domestic trademark owner can prevent the unauthorized importation and domestic sale of trademarked goods that are "materially different" from the goods that the trademark owner has authorized for domestic sale under the same trademark. In addition, some trademark owners can prevent importation of foreign-made goods even in the absence of material differences. Applying trademark law to their copyrighted goods will allow many U.S. copyright owners to continue to control the importation of lawfully made copies of their works. This end-run around *Kirtsaeng*'s rule of international copyright exhaustion raises serious policy concerns.

II. THE LIBERALIZED COPYRIGHT RULES ON PARALLEL IMPORTS

In *Kirtsaeng*, the Supreme Court held that copyright's first sale rule—embodied in section 109(a) of the Copyright Act of 1976[5]—applies to all lawfully made copies, regardless of their country of manufacture.[6] As a result, domestic copyright owners cannot invoke copyright law to prevent the unauthorized importation and domestic sale of lawfully made foreign copies of their works, notwithstanding their exclusive importation rights under sections 106(3)[7] and 602(a)[8] of the Copyright Act.

Prior to *Kirtsaeng*, copyright owners had reason to believe that they could prevent the importation and domestic resale of foreign-made copies of their works even if those copies had been made with their consent—that is, even if they were non-pirated copies. Case law from several federal courts indicated that the first sale rule did not apply to foreign-made copies.[9] This interpretation was reinforced by the Supreme Court's 1998 decision in *Quality King Distributors, Inc. v. L'anza Research International*,[10] which held

---

REV. 577, 585–86, 591 (2003); Aaron Perzanowski & Jason Schultz, *Digital Exhaustion*, 58 UCLA L. REV. 889, 894–95 (2011).
 [4] Kirtsaeng v. John Wiley & Sons, Inc., 133 S. Ct. 1351 (2013).
 [5] 17 U.S.C. § 109(a) (2012).
 [6] *Kirtsaeng*, *supra* note 4, 133 S. Ct. at 1355–56.
 [7] 17 U.S.C. § 106(3) (2012).
 [8] *Ibid.* § 602(a).
 [9] See BMG Music v. Perez, 952 F.2d 318 (9th Cir. 1991) (records); T.B. Harms Co. v. Jem Records, Inc., 655 F. Supp. 1575 (D.N.J. 1987) (records); Hearst Corp. v. Stark, 639 F. Supp. 970, 976–77 (N.D. Cal. 1986) (books); Columbia Broad. Sys. v. Scorpio Music Distrib., 569 F. Supp. 47, 49 (E.D. Pa. 1983) (records), *aff'd mem.*, 738 F.2d 421 (3d Cir. 1984); Nintendo of America, Inc. v. Elcon Indus., 564 F. Supp. 937 (E.D. Mich. 1982) (videogames); see also Denbicare USA, Inc. v. Toys R Us, Inc., 84 F.3d 1143, 1149–50 (9th Cir. 1996) (first sale rule applies to imported copies only after U.S. copyright owner consents to their initial sale in the U.S.).
 [10] Quality King Distributors, Inc. v. L'anza Research Int'l, 523 U.S. 135, 145 (1998).

that the first sale rule permitted the re-importation of copies that had been lawfully made in the U.S.,[11] but strongly implied that this rule did not apply to foreign-made copies.[12] Under the latter approach, if copyright owners arranged for copies to be manufactured overseas, they could authorize those copies to be sold exclusively in foreign markets and could use copyright law to prevent their importation for domestic sale. Although this implied holding was dictum, lower federal courts generally adopted this interpretation, allowing trademark owners to use copyright claims to prevent unauthorized importation of their foreign-made goods that were intended solely for foreign distribution (typically at lower-than-domestic prices).[13] In some cases, merchants added copyrightable elements (such as minor ornamentation) to their merchandise precisely for this purpose.[14]

In *Kirtsaeng*,[15] the Supreme Court finally addressed the scope of international exhaustion under domestic copyright law. The plaintiff, publisher John Wiley & Sons, was printing its college textbooks in Thailand, where it sold them at lower prices than they commanded in the U.S. The accused infringer acquired copies of the books in Thailand, then imported and resold them domestically for a profit, albeit at a price lower than the publisher's authorized domestic price. To prevent such arbitrage from undermining its domestic price structure, the publisher sued for copyright infringement, arguing that the first sale rule did not apply to foreign-made copies.

The *Kirtsaeng* majority expressly rejected this argument, as well as the *Quality King* dictum that supported it, holding squarely that copyright's first sale rule permits the importation and domestic sale of lawfully made copies without regard to their place of manufacture. This decision was a major defeat to copyright owners that distribute their works through tangible copies, including books, CDs, home videos,[16] videogames, art

---

[11] The copyrighted works in question were the labels on hair care products. There was little inherent value in these copyrighted works; rather, the plaintiffs were attempting to use copyright law to prevent parallel imports of their trademarked but uncopyrightable merchandise. Trademark relief was probably unavailable because L'anza itself (rather than a licensee) had directly authorized the use of its trademark on the goods, and the goods were not materially different from the goods authorized for domestic sale. See Trademarks, Trade Names, and Copyrights, 19 C.F.R. § 133.23 (2014) (restricting importation of genuine goods only when (a) the trademark was attached by someone other than the trademark owner or an affiliate under common ownership or control; or (b) the goods are materially and physically different from those authorized for domestic sale).

[12] *Kirtsaeng, supra* note 4, 523 U.S. at 147–48; see also *ibid.* at 154 (Ginsburg, J., concurring).

[13] Omega S.A. v. Costco Wholesale Corp., 541 F.3d 982, 988–90 (9th Cir. 2008), *aff'd by an equally divided court*, 131 S. Ct. 565 (2010) (per curiam) (watches); Pearson Educ., Inc. v. Kumar, 721 F. Supp. 2d 166, 176–78 (S.D.N.Y. 2010); Microsoft Corp. v. Cietdirect.com LLC, No. 08-60668-CIV, 2008 WL 3162535 (S.D. Fla. August 5, 2008) (software); UMG Recordings, Inc. v. Norwalk Distribs., Inc., No. SACV 02-1188, 2003 WL 22722410 (C.D. Cal. March 13, 2003) (records).

[14] Watchmaker Omega engraved a copyrighted design on the back of its Swiss-made watches for this reason alone. Omega S.A. v. Costco Wholesale Corp., No. CV 04-05443, 2011 WL 8492716, at *1 (C.D. Cal. November 9, 2011).

[15] *Kirtsaeng, supra* note 4, 133 S. Ct. at 1355–56.

[16] *Kirtsaeng* was less of a setback for movie studios than for other copyright owners, because most DVDs and many Blu-ray discs contain region codes that make them compatible only with players in the regions where they are sold. See Peter K. Yu, *Region Codes and the Territorial Mess*, 30 Cardozo Arts & Ent. L.J. 187, 194–95 (2012). Like many technological protection measures, however, the region codes can be circumvented.

reproductions, and textiles. After *Kirtsaeng*, content owners can no longer invoke copyright law to prevent importation and domestic resales of lawful foreign-made goods.

In the absence of a digital first sale rule, shifting from hard copy distribution to digital deliveries will help many content owners maintain the separation of domestic and foreign markets, at least for now.[17] However, because consumer demand for hard copies is likely to remain strong for certain categories of works,[18] content owners will still seek out ways to prevent parallel imports of tangible copies.

III. TRADEMARK LAW AS A COPYRIGHT ALTERNATIVE

Although *Kirtsaeng* extended the first sale rule of copyright law to foreign-made copies, it does not control the first sale rule of *trademark* law.[19] Most owners of commercially valuable copyrighted works, such as books, motion pictures, sound recordings, software, and videogames, also use one or more trademarks associated with those works. As discussed below, many of these copyright owners can avoid the consequences of *Kirtsaeng* by using trademark law instead of copyright law to block unauthorized imports.

In particular, the fact that a work is protected by copyright does not foreclose the use of trademark law to prevent false designations of the origin of that work.[20] Like other merchants, most domestic publishers and producers of copyrighted works use at least

---

[17] As publishers transition to digital delivery of content, some of the copyright questions surrounding imported copies may change. Section 109(a) in its current form may not permit the transfer of a digital file unless the tangible medium embodying the file (for example, an iPod) is also transferred. See Capitol Records, LLC v. ReDigi Inc., 934 F. Supp. 2d 640, 651 (S.D.N.Y. 2013); Clark D. Asay, *Kirtsaeng and the First-Sale Doctrine's Digital Problem*, 66 STAN. L. REV. ONLINE 17 (May 7, 2013), available at http://www.stanfordlawreview.org/online/kirtsaeng-and-first-sale-doctrines-digital-problem; John Villasenor, *Rethinking a Digital First Sale Doctrine in a Post-Kirtsaeng World: The Case for Caution*, 2 CPI ANTITRUST CHRON. (May 28, 2013), available at http://papers.ssrn.com/sol3/papers.cfm?abstract_id=2273022. Also, many digital copies are not "sold" but "licensed," and s. 109(a) may not apply to licensed copies. See e.g. Vernor v. Autodesk, 621 F.3d 1102 (9th Cir. 2010).

[18] Textbooks, the subject of the price discrimination in *Kirtsaeng*, are a good example. Research indicates that many students continue to prefer hard copies over e-books. William Douglas Woody et al., *E-books or Textbooks: Students Prefer Textbooks*, 55 COMPUTERS & EDUC. 945, 947 (2010). In addition, while the market for music downloads is steadily increasing, CD sales still constitute roughly half the market. Keith Caulfield, *CD Album Sales Fall Behind Album Downloads, Is 2014 the Year Digital Takes Over?*, BILLBOARD (February 11, 2014, 9:30 AM), http://www.billboard.com/biz/articles/news/digital-and-mobile/5901188/cd-album-sales-fall-behind-album-downloads-is-2014-the. Children's books, art reproductions, and textiles illustrate additional markets where most consumers will still purchase hard copies.

[19] One commentator suggests that trademark protection against parallel imports is so robust that *Kirtsaeng* will have little practical impact. Charles E. Colman, *Post-Kirtsaeng, "Material Differences" Between Copyright and Trademark Law's Treatment of Gray Goods Persist*, N.Y.U. SCH. OF LAW PUB. LAW & LEGAL THEORY RESEARCH PAPER SERIES, WORKING PAPER NO. 13-40 (2013).

[20] "Books are 'sold in the commercial marketplace like other more utilitarian products, making the danger of consumer deception a legitimate concern that warrants some government regulation.'" Cliff's Notes, Inc. v. Bantam Doubleday Dell Pub. Group, Inc., 886 F.2d 490, 493 (2d Cir. 1989) (quoting Rogers v. Grimaldi, 875 F.2d 994, 997 (2d Cir. 1989)).

one trademark to identify the source of their publications. Book publishers' trademarks, for example, include any indications of origin displayed on or in the book—the name of the publisher, the name of any specialized imprint, a logo, or a particular design or color scheme that is used consistently on books distributed by that publisher. Motion picture producers and distributors, record companies, and makers of software and videogames typically display their brand names and/or logos on the packaging of their physical products. Even distributors of poster art typically display their name and/or logo somewhere on the poster or its packaging. All of these trademarks can be protected whether or not they are federally registered. However, publishers and producers typically register some or all of their eligible marks, which enables them to receive the strongest degree of protection against parallel imports.

As discussed below, with appropriate planning a copyright owner can utilize a variety of trademark remedies, including monetary damages, injunctions, and seizure of goods by agents of U.S. Customs and Border Protection (CBP), in order to prevent the importation and/or domestic sale of copies that are completely lawful under copyright law.

IV. TRADEMARK REMEDIES AGAINST PARALLEL IMPORTS

Under several provisions of the Lanham Act,[21] as well as section 526 of the Tariff Act of 1930,[22] trademark owners enjoy multiple avenues for relief against unauthorized imports even when the goods in question are lawfully made rather than counterfeit. Judicial interpretations of these laws have strongly favored trademark owners.

A. Trademark Infringement

A trademark owner can bring an infringement claim under the Lanham Act against any party (whether a seller or an importer) that uses the mark in a way that is likely to confuse or mislead consumers about the origin of particular goods or services. This principle, derived from common law, is reflected in several provisions of the Lanham Act: section 32(1),[23] addressing infringement of federally registered marks; section 43(a)(1)(A),[24] addressing infringement of unregistered marks; section 43(b),[25] allowing civil actions to enjoin importation of any goods likely to infringe registered or unregistered trademarks;[26] and section 42,[27] which authorizes CBP to prevent the importation of goods that infringe registered or unregistered trademarks.

Although these provisions enable trademark owners to prevent the importation and domestic sale of counterfeit goods—that is, goods to which a trademark has been affixed

---

[21] 15 U.S.C. §§ 1114, 1125 (2012).
[22] 19 U.S.C. § 1526 (2012).
[23] 15 U.S.C. § 1114(1) (2012).
[24] Ibid. § 1125(a)(1)(A).
[25] Ibid. § 1125(b).
[26] Regulations under s. 43(b) allow infringing imports to be seized and forfeited. 19 C.F.R. § 11.13 (2014).
[27] 15 U.S.C. § 1124.

without the consent of the trademark owner—they can also apply to non-counterfeit goods. As discussed below, Lanham Act remedies can, in many cases, prevent the importation and domestic sale of goods to which the trademark was affixed *with the consent* of the trademark owner (or a licensee), if the trademark owner has not also consented to their importation. The key requirement is that the unauthorized imports must be "materially different" from the products authorized for domestic sale.

(1) First sale rule and material differences

Under the first sale rule of trademark law, also known as trademark exhaustion, a trademark owner generally cannot prevent the distribution of goods on which it has authorized the use of its mark.[28] The rationale is that "when a retailer merely resells a genuine, unaltered good under the trademark of the producer, the use of the producer's trademark by the reseller will not deceive or confuse the public as to the nature, qualities, and origin of the good."[29]

Despite this rule, a trademark owner that authorizes the use of its mark on goods intended for sale only *outside* the U.S. can often use the Lanham Act to prevent those specific goods from being imported and/or sold domestically. If the goods authorized for foreign sale are "materially different" from the goods authorized for domestic sale, domestic consumers may be confused or misled about the nature or quality of the unauthorized imports, and may assume that the trademark owner authorized the goods for domestic sale.[30] If the goods do not possess the same characteristics as the authorized domestic goods, consumers will blame the trademark owner for the discrepancy.[31] Thus, the consumer's confusion can undermine the goodwill associated with the trademark.[32] Accordingly, the first sale rule of trademark law does not apply to materially different goods that are imported without the trademark owner's consent; the material differences render the unauthorized imports "non-genuine" for purposes of trademark law.[33]

---

[28] See e.g. Matrix Essentials, Inc. v. Emporium Drug Mart, Inc., 988 F.2d 587, 590 (5th Cir. 1993); Polymer Tech. Corp. v. Mimran, 975 F.2d 58, 61 (2d Cir. 1992). See generally, RESTATEMENT (THIRD) OF UNFAIR COMPETITION § 24 cmt. b (1995); 4 MCCARTHY, *supra* note 1, § 25:41.

[29] Tumblebus, Inc. v. Cranmer, 399 F.3d 754, 766 (6th Cir. 2005); see also NEC Elecs. v. CAL Circuit Abco, 810 F.2d 1506, 1509 (9th Cir. 1987); RESTATEMENT (THIRD) OF UNFAIR COMPETITION § 24 cmt. B.

[30] See e.g. Original Appalachian Artworks, Inc. v. Granada Elecs., Inc., 816 F.2d 68 (2d Cir. 1987); Philip Morris, Inc. v. Cigarettes for Less, 69 F. Supp. 2d 1181, 1184 (N.D. Cal. 1999), *aff'd*, 215 F.3d 1333 (9th Cir. 2000); Société des Produits Nestle, S.A. v. Casa Helvetia, Inc., 982 F.2d 633, 641 (1st Cir. 1992); see generally, 5 MCCARTHY, *supra* note 1, § 29:51.75.

[31] See Martin's Herend Imports, Inc. v. Diamond & Gem Trading USA, Co., 112 F.3d 1296, 1302 (5th Cir. 1997); Weil Ceramics & Glass, Inc. v. Dash, 878 F.2d 659, 671 (3d Cir. 1989).

[32] Davidoff & Cie, S.A. v. PLD Int'l Corp., 263 F.3d 1297, 1301–2 (11th Cir. 2001); *Weil Ceramics*, *supra* note 31, 878 F.2d at 671; Mishawaka Rubber & Woolen Mfg. Co. v. S.S. Kresge Co., 316 U.S. 203, 205 (1942).

[33] Beltronics USA, Inc. v. Midwest Inventory Distrib., LLC, 562 F.3d 1067 (10th Cir. 2009); Brilliance Audio, Inc. v. Haights Cross Commc'ns, Inc., 474 F.3d 365 (6th Cir. 2007); *Davidoff*, *supra* note 32, 263 F.3d at 1302; Iberia Foods Corp. v. Romeo, 150 F.3d 298, 302–3 (3d Cir. 1998); *Martin's Herend Imports*, *supra* note 31, 112 F.3d at 1301–2; *Société des Produits Nestle*, *supra* note 30, 982 F.2d at 635; *Original Appalachian Artworks*, *supra* note 30, 816 F.2d at 73; *Phillip Morris*, *supra* note 30, 69 F. Supp. 2d at 1184.

A trademark owner can therefore bring a trademark infringement claim against an importer or seller of unauthorized imports that are materially different from the goods authorized for domestic sale. This Lanham Act remedy is available for both federally registered marks (under section 32(1)) and common law marks (under section 43(a)). However, trademark relief may be limited in one important respect: while remedies under sections 32(1) and 43(a) apply to gray market goods lawfully manufactured by third-party licensees,[34] courts disagree on whether they also apply to materially different goods manufactured by the U.S. trademark owner itself or by a corporate affiliate.[35] Therefore, to bring an infringement claim based on material differences, it is better for the trademark owner to have the goods manufactured by a foreign licensee.

(2) Importation and the *Lever* rule
In addition to section 32(1) and 43(a) infringement actions, section 42 of the Lanham Act[36] permits trademark owners to enlist CBP to block the importation of materially different goods bearing a mark that copies or simulates a federally registered mark.[37] In contrast to infringement actions, CBP enforcement under section 42 is available even if the U.S. trademark owner is affiliated with the foreign manufacturer. Specifically, the existence of common ownership or control does not preclude CBP enforcement provided that (1) the mark is federally registered; (2) the trademark owner records the mark with CBP; and (3) the imported goods are *physically and materially different* from those authorized for domestic sale.[38]

To obtain CBP enforcement, the trademark owner must notify CBP of the specific "physical and material differences between the specific articles authorized for importation or sale in the United States and those not so authorized,"[39] and must provide supporting documentation.[40] If these requirements are met, then CBP will prohibit importation

---

[34] *Original Appalachian Artworks*, supra note 30, 816 F.2d at 70.
[35] *Compare* NEC Elecs. v. CAL Circuit Abco, 810 F.2d 1506, 1510 (9th Cir. 1987) and *Phillip Morris*, supra note 30, 69 F. Supp. 2d at 1187, with R.J. Reynolds Tobacco Co. v. Cigarettes Cheaper!, 462 F.3d 690 (7th Cir. 2006) and Phillip Morris, Inc. v. Allen Distributors, Inc., 48 F. Supp. 2d 844, 852–53 (S.D. Ind. 1999).
[36] 15 U.S.C. § 1124 (2012). Section 43(b) extends similar protection to unregistered marks, *ibid.* § 1125(b), with implementing regulations under 19 C.F.R. § 11.13 (2014), but owners of such marks do not appear to be utilizing this provision. See 5 MCCARTHY, *supra* note 1, § 29:53.
[37] 15 U.S.C. § 1124. Although early case law held that s. 42 did not apply to parallel imports, see *Weil Ceramics*, supra note 31, 878 F.2d at 666; Olympus Corp. v. United States, 792 F.2d 315 (2d Cir. 1986), later cases established that s. 42 applies when the imported goods are materially different, see *Société des Produits Nestle*, supra note 30, 982 F.2d at 639; Lever Bros. Co. v. United States, 981 F.2d 1330, 1338 (D.C. Cir. 1993).
[38] Trademark, Trade Names, and Copyrights, 19 C.F.R. §§ 133.2–133.3(a)(1) (2014). In 1998, the D.C. Circuit held in the *Lever Bros.* case that s. 42 applies to "physically, materially different goods" even if they are made by a corporate affiliate of the U.S. trademark owner. 981 F.2d at 1338. That decision was implemented in the 1999 Customs regulations. See *K Mart*, supra note 1.
[39] 19 C.F.R. § 133.2(e).
[40] The CBP regulations include a non-exhaustive list of differences which may qualify as physical and material:

"(1) The specific composition of both the authorized and gray market product(s) (including chemical composition);

of the goods, under what has become known as the "*Lever* rule."[41] However, under an exception to this rule, CBP must permit the importation of gray market goods if they bear a conspicuous label indicating that they are physically and materially different from the genuine goods.[42] The regulations even prescribe the specific language that must appear on the label.[43]

(3) Uncertain impact of *Lever* disclaimers on trademark infringement claims

The impact of a *Lever* disclaimer on trademark infringement claims under sections 32(1) and 43(a) is unsettled. While a *Lever* label may preclude CBP from blocking gray market goods, it does not immunize the importer or domestic reseller of the goods from liability for trademark infringement. In analyzing infringement claims, courts determine for themselves whether, under all of the facts and circumstances, a particular disclaimer is sufficient to eliminate the likelihood of confusion.[44] In recent years, courts have increasingly expressed doubt about the ability of disclaimers to alleviate consumer confusion, and have frequently found a likelihood of confusion despite the presence of a disclaimer, both in the specific context of parallel imports[45] and also with respect to other claims of trademark infringement.[46]

---

(2) Formulation, product construction, structure, or composite product components, of both the authorized and gray market product;
(3) Performance and/operational characteristics of both the authorized and gray market product;
(4) Differences resulting from legal or regulatory requirements, certification, etc.;
(5) Other distinguishing and explicitly defined factors that would likely result in consumer deception or confusion as proscribed under applicable law." *Ibid.*

[41] 19 C.F.R. § 133.23(a)(3) (2014).
[42] *Ibid.* § 133.23(b).
[43] *Ibid.*
[44] Those facts and circumstances are usually explored by analyzing a non-exhaustive list of factors considered relevant to the likelihood of consumer confusion. See e.g. AMF Inc. v. Sleekcraft Boats, 599 F.2d 341, 348–49 (9th Cir. 1979); Polaroid Corp. v. Polarad Elecs. Corp., 287 F.2d 492, 495 (2d Cir. 1961).
[45] See e.g. *Société des Produits Nestle*, *supra* note 30, 982 F.2d at 641; Premier Dental Prods. Co. v. Darby Dental Supply Co., 794 F.2d 850, 859 (3d Cir. 1986); Hyundai Constr. Equip. USA, Inc. v. Chris Johnson Equip., Inc., No. 06-C-3238, 2008 U.S. Dist. LEXIS 84687, at *8 (N.D. Ill. September 10, 2008); Certain Cigarettes and Packaging Thereof, Inv. No. 337-TA-424, USITC Pub. 3366 (November 3, 2000) (Final); Certain Agricultural Tractors Under 50 Power Take-Off Horsepower, Inv. No. 337-TA-380, USITC Pub. 3227 (August 1999) (Final), *aff'd*, Gamut Trading Co. v. U.S. Int'l Trade Comm'n, 200 F.3d 775 (Fed. Cir. 1999).
[46] See e.g. First Nat'l Bank in Sioux Falls v. First Nat'l Bank in S.D., 679 F.3d 763, 769–70 (8th Cir. 2012); Nat'l Bus. Forms & Printing v. Ford Motor Co., 671 F.3d 526, 533 (5th Cir. 2012); Au-Tomotive Gold Inc. v. Volkswagen of Am., Inc., 603 F.3d 1133, 1138 (9th Cir. 2010); Au-Tomotive Gold, Inc. v. Volkswagen of Am., Inc., 457 F.3d 1062, 1078 (9th Cir. 2006); Weight Watchers Int'l, Inc. v. Luigino's, Inc., 423 F.3d 137, 143–44 (2d Cir. 2005); Int'l Kennel Club of Chi., Inc. v. Mighty Star, Inc., 846 F.2d 1079, 1093 (7th Cir. 1988); Home Box Office, Inc. v. Showtime/Movie Channel Inc., 832 F.2d 1311, 1315–17 (2d Cir. 1987); Univ. of Ga. v. Laite, 756 F.2d 1535, 1547 (11th Cir. 1985); Gilliam v. Am. Broad. Cos., Inc., 538 F.2d 14, 25 n.13 (2d Cir. 1976); Bos. Prof'l Hockey Ass'n v. Dall. Cap & Emblem Mfg., 510 F.2d 1004, 1013 (5th Cir. 1975); Freeway Ford, Inc. v. Freeway Motors, Inc., 512 F. Supp. 2d 1353 (M.D. Ga. 2007); Ty, Inc. v. Publ'ns Int'l, Ltd., No. 99-C-5565, 2005 WL 464688, at *1 (N.D. Ill. February 25, 2005); 1-800 Contacts, Inc. v. WhenU.com,

In analyzing trademark infringement claims against parallel imports, courts have good reason to give limited weight to *Lever* labels. Substantively, the requirements a *Lever* label must satisfy are too nondescript to protect consumers from unwittingly purchasing materially different goods.[47] The disclaimer must state: "This product is not a product authorized by the United States trademark owner for importation and is physically and materially different from the authorized product."[48] No other disclosures are required.[49] Consumers are left to guess what "physically and materially different" means, whether these differences will affect their experience with the product, and whether it matters that the product is not "authorized." Moreover, a consumer who has never purchased the product before will have no basis for comparing the unauthorized import with its domestic counterpart. In the case of copyrighted works, this problem is particularly acute, because consumers tend to purchase a single copy of a copyrighted work, rather than making repeat purchases over time. A consumer that purchases gray market PERUGINA chocolates or L'ANZA hair care products may already have experience with the domestic version of the same product due to prior purchases (or receipt of gifts), and thus, once alerted by the *Lever* label, might be able to evaluate differences in packaging or ingredients before deciding whether to make the purchase. In contrast, a consumer purchasing a book or CD has probably never owned any version of that specific product. Once the consumer reads a book or listens to a CD, he or she typically has little reason to purchase the same item again (except as a gift). At the point of purchase, therefore, the buyer of a copyrighted item may have greater difficulty identifying the material and physical differences that distinguish the gray market version from the authorized version.[50] Simply telling the consumer that this version of the product is "different" from the authorized version gives no indication of what the differences are. A purchaser unfamiliar with the book or CD would have to make an affirmative effort to seek out the authorized version for compari-

---

309 F. Supp. 2d 467, 494 (S.D.N.Y. 2003), *rev'd on other grounds*, 414 F.3d 400 (2d Cir. 2005); E. & J. Gallo Winery v. Gallo Cattle Co., No. CV-F-86-183 REC, 1989 U.S. Dist. LEXIS 7950, at *77 (E.D. Cal. June 19, 1989); Marquis Who's Who, Inc. v. N. Am. Adver. Assocs., Inc., 426 F. Supp. 139, 143 n.5 (D.D.C. 1976), *aff'd*, 574 F.2d 637 (D.C. Cir. 1978); Edgar Rice Burroughs, Inc. v. Manns Theatres, No. 76-3612, 1976 U.S. Dist. LEXIS 11754, at *8–9 (C.D. Cal. December 20, 1976); Volkswagenwerk Aktiengesellschaft v. Karadizian, No. 70-2244 JWC, 170 U.S.P.Q. 565, 567 (C.D. Cal. 1971); see also McCarthy, *supra* note 1, § 23.51.

[47] See Margo A. Bagley, *Using Section 337 of the Tariff Act of 1930 to Block Materially Different Gray Market Goods in the Common Control Context: Are Reports of Its Death Greatly Exaggerated?*, 44 Emory L.J. 1541, 1573–74 (1995) (presenting a skeptical view of the effectiveness of disclaimers on gray market goods).

[48] Trademark, Trade Names, and Copyrights, 19 C.F.R. § 133.23(b) (2014).

[49] In contrast, some State statutes impose more specific disclosure requirements on parallel imports. See e.g. Cal. Civ. Code § 1797.81 (West 2014); N.Y. Gen. Bus. § 218-aa (McKinney 2014); Conn. Gen. Stat. § 42-210 (2014).

[50] The same reasoning has led courts to be skeptical as to the value of disclaimers in other scenarios. In concluding that a disclaimer would not alleviate consumer confusion where a television network edited a program without the consent of its creators, the Second Circuit stated: "We are doubtful that a few words could erase the indelible impression that is made by a television broadcast, especially since the viewer has no means of comparing the truncated version with the complete work in order to determine for himself the talents of the plaintiffs." *Gilliam*, *supra* note 46, 538 F.2d at 25 n.13.

son. The authorized version of the book or CD may not be readily available at a local store, and the merchandise offered by online merchants generally cannot be inspected before purchase. Thus, the purchaser evaluating a gray market purchase of copyrighted goods will typically have to guess at the nature and materiality of the differences.

The *Lever* label may be ineffective for another reason. The regulations do not specify how the label must be attached to the product, and do not require that it remain attached throughout the useful life of the product, including resales. The label must be "conspicuous and legible," placed "in close proximity to the trademark as it appears in its most prominent location on the article itself or the retail package or container," and "designed to remain on the product until the first point of sale to a retail customer."[51] The label might, therefore, appear on a sticker or wrapper that can be easily removed. Despite the vague requirement that the label be "designed to remain on the product until the first point of sale," there is no way to ensure that the disclaimer will still be visible when the article is first sold to a consumer. Even if the label persists through the initial sale, the law does not require that it remain visible through subsequent resales. Once again, the problem is particularly acute with respect to copyrighted works. There is a lively secondhand market for books, CDs, videogames, and similar works—unlike chocolates. The secondhand purchaser of a copyrighted work may never see the label that enabled the imported copy to enter the U.S. in the first place.

B. Tariff Act Remedies

Under some circumstances, a U.S. trademark owner can block the importation of genuine but foreign-made goods even when the imported goods are *identical* to those authorized for domestic sale. Section 526 of the 1930 Tariff Act allows the owner of a federally registered mark to block parallel imports of foreign-made goods only if (1) the domestic trademark owner is a U.S. person;[52] (2) the gray market copies are manufactured overseas;[53] and (3) the trademark is applied under the authority of a foreign trademark owner that is neither the U.S. trademark owner nor a corporate affiliate thereof.[54]

No showing of material differences or likelihood of confusion is required for this avenue of relief, and trademark owners can obtain trademark infringement remedies (both injunctions and damages) even if CPB does not exclude the goods.[55] The original purpose of section 526 was to protect domestic companies that purchase U.S. trademark

---

[51] 19 C.F.R. § 133.23(b) (2014).
[52] *Ibid.* § 1526(a).
[53] *Ibid.*
[54] *K Mart*, *supra* note 1, 486 U.S. at 292–93; *Weil Ceramics*, *supra* note 31, 878 F.2d at 664, 673; Trademark, Trade Names, and Copyrights, 19 C.F.R. § 133.23(a)(2) (2013).
[55] *Original Appalachian Artworks*, *supra* note 30, 816 F.2d at 71; Olympus Corp. v. United States, 792 F.2d 315, 320 (2d Cir. 1986); Vivitar Corp. v. United States, 761 F.2d 1552, 1570 (Fed. Cir. 1985); Philip Morris USA Inc. v. Lee, 481 F. Supp. 2d 742 (W.D. Tex. 2006); PepsiCo, Inc. v. Torres, 1993 U.S. Dist. LEXIS 17588 (C.D. Cal. February 18, 1993); Dial Corp. v. Encina Corp., 643 F. Supp. 951 (S.D. Fla. 1986); Osawa & Co. v. B & H Photo, 589 F. Supp. 1163 (S.D.N.Y. 1984). See also Vittoria N. Am. LLC v. Euro-Asia Imports, Inc., 278 F.3d 1076 (10th Cir. 2001); Philip Morris USA Inc. v. C.H. Rhodes, Inc., 2010 U.S. Dist. LEXIS 39114 (E.D.N.Y. April 19, 2010); Ahava (USA) Inc. v. J.W.G., Ltd., 250 F. Supp. 2d 366 (S.D.N.Y. 2003).

rights from foreign manufacturers against the possibility that the foreign manufacturer's identical goods—bearing the identical trademark—would find their way into the U.S. market.[56]

The major disadvantage of using the Tariff Act as a remedy against parallel imports is the requirement that the U.S. trademark owner cannot also own the trademark (directly or through an affiliate) in the country of manufacture. Most U.S. trademark owners would find it disadvantageous to assign the foreign rights in a valuable trademark; thus, the Tariff Act is better suited for protecting U.S. parties that have acquired domestic rights from foreign trademark owners—the parties that Congress intended section 526 to protect.[57] Due to the relative ease of introducing material differences in their products, most trademark owners will find the Lanham Act a more elegant and cost-effective solution.

V. APPLYING LANHAM ACT REMEDIES TO COPYRIGHTED WORKS

To maximize their ability to use the Lanham Act to segregate their domestic and foreign markets, copyright owners should ensure that their copies intended for foreign distribution (1) bear a registered U.S. trademark; and (2) are physically and materially different from copies authorized for domestic sale.

A. Material Differences and Copyrighted Works

A finding of material differences can be based on differences in quality control, marketing methods, packaging, or customer support, or differences in the goods themselves. One court defined a material difference as "one that consumers consider relevant to a decision about whether to purchase a product," but noted that "the threshold of materiality must be kept low," and that any alteration "resulting in physical differences" should be considered material.[58]

Although the material differences standard applies to both imported and non-imported goods,[59] courts have established a particularly low threshold of materiality for gray market goods. Under this approach, even "subtle differences" can be material.[60] One court held that "any difference between the registrant's product and the allegedly infring-

---

[56] *K Mart*, supra note 1, 486 U.S. at 287–88; see also A. Bourjois & Co. v. Katzel, 275 F. 539 (2d Cir. 1921), *rev'd*, 260 U.S. 689 (1923).

[57] The trademark owner would lose control over the trademark in the foreign territory, which could undermine the value of its mark in the U.S. and other territories. Such an assignment could also involve considerable transaction costs, and could trigger unfavorable tax consequences, see 26 U.S.C. §§ 1231, 1253 (2012).

[58] *Davidoff*, supra note 32, 263 F.3d at 1301–2.

[59] A product is materially different if the item or its packaging has been altered since leaving the trademark owner's control, or if the post-manufacturing handling or quality control did not meet the trademark owner's requirements. See e.g. Prestonettes, Inc. v. Coty, 264 U.S. 359 (1924); *Davidoff*, supra note 32, 263 F.3d at 1301–3.

[60] *Société des Produits Nestle*, supra note 30, 982 F.2d at 641; *accord*, Zino Davidoff SA v. CVS Corp., 571 F.3d 238, 243–46 (2d Cir. 2009) ("In the context of gray-market goods . . . we apply a

ing gray good that consumers would likely consider to be relevant when purchasing a product creates a presumption of consumer confusion."[61] Examples include: different warranties;[62] Cabbage Patch dolls with birth certificates and adoption papers in Spanish rather than English;[63] different soap ingredients;[64] TIC TACS with a different size and calorie count;[65] chocolates with different shapes;[66] quality control differences;[67] packaging or labeling differences;[68] or different advertising participation or marketing methods.[69] It is not unusual for courts to find that a single gray market product embodies a multitude of material differences.[70] According to several courts, the use of packaging that identifies the country of origin does not reduce the likelihood of confusion arising from such material differences.[71] However, courts do not always agree on whether particular differences are material.[72]

The low threshold of materiality which applies to imported goods offers copyright owners an opportunity to block parallel imports by ensuring that any foreign-made copies they authorize are materially different from the domestically made copies that are sold under the same trademark. In the case of textbooks, for example, a simple

---

low threshold of materiality, requiring no more than a slight difference which consumers would likely deem relevant when considering a purchase of the product.").

[61] *Société des Produits Nestle, supra* note 30, 982 F.2d at 641.

[62] *Ibid.* at 639 n.7; Swatch S.A. v. New City, Inc., 454 F. Supp. 2d 1245, 1251 (S.D. Fla. 2006); Fender Musical Instr. Corp. v. Unlimited Music Ctr., Inc., No. 3:93CV2449 (AVC), 1995 U.S. Dist. LEXIS 15746 (D.Conn. February 16, 1995).

[63] *Original Appalachian Artworks, supra* note 30, 816 F.2d at 73.

[64] *Lever Bros. Co. v. United States*, 877 F.2d 101, 103, 108 (D.C. Cir. 1989); Dial Corp. v. Encina Corp., 643 F. Supp. 951, 955 (S.D. Fla. 1986).

[65] *Ferrero, supra* note 1, 753 F. Supp. at 1243, 1247.

[66] *Société des Produits Nestle, supra* note 30, 982 F.2d at 643.

[67] *Davidoff, supra* note 32, 263 F.3d at 1302 n.5 (nonimported goods); *Iberia Foods, supra* note 33, 150 F.3d at 302 (gray market goods); Warner-Lambert Co. v. Northside Dev. Corp., 86 F.3d 3, 5 (2d Cir. 1996) (nonimported goods); Polymer Tech. Corp. v. Mimran, 37 F.3d 74, 78–79 (2d Cir. 1994) (nonimported goods); Shell Oil Co. v. Commercial Petroleum, Inc., 928 F.2d 104, 106 (4th Cir. 1991) (nonimported goods); Phillip Morris, Inc. v. Allen Distributors, Inc., 48 F. Supp. 2d 844, 852–53 (S.D. Ind. 1999) (gray market goods); Adolph Coors Co. v. A. Genderson & Sons, Inc., 486 F. Supp. 131, 133 (D. Colo. 1980) (nonimported goods).

[68] *Zino Davidoff, supra* note 60, 571 F.3d at 243, 246 (removal of UPC codes from product packaging of gray market goods); *Davidoff & Cie, supra* note 32, 263 F.3d at 1299; *Shell Oil, supra* note 67, 928 F.2d at 106; *Lever Bros., supra* note 64, 877 F.2d at 103 (packaging and labeling differences were material); John Paul Mitchell Sys. v. Pete-N-Larry's, Inc., 862 F. Supp. 1020, 1027 (W.D.N.Y. 1994); PepsiCo, Inc. v. Nostalgia Prods. Corp., No. 90-C-7024, 1990 U.S. Dist. LEXIS 18990, at *4 (N.D. Ill. December 20, 1990); *Adolph Coors, supra* note 67, 486 F. Supp. at 133.

[69] *Nostalgia Prods., supra* note 68, 1990 LEXIS 18990, at *4; PepsiCo, Inc. v. Giraud, No. 87-01887 (JP), 1988 U.S. Dist. LEXIS 12864, at *7–8 (D.P.R. March 14, 1988).

[70] See e.g. PepsiCo, Inc. v. Reyes, 70 F. Supp. 2d 1057, 1058–59 (C.D. Cal. 1999); *Giraud, supra* note 69, 1988 LEXIS 12864, at *3–7.

[71] *Société des Produits Nestle, supra* note 30, 982 F.2d at 639; Ferrero U.S.A., Inc. v. Ozak Trading, Inc., 753 F. Supp. 1240, 1243 (D.N.J. 1991), *aff'd*, 935 F.2d 1281 (3d Cir. 1991).

[72] See Graham Webb Int'l Ltd. v. Emporium Drug Mart, Inc., 916 F. Supp. 909, 910 (E.D. Ark. 1995) (holding that removal of batch codes from hair care products was not a material difference where it did not significantly affect overall appearance of product, and thus would not materially affect consumer decision to purchase); John Paul Mitchell Systems v. Randall's Food Mkts. Inc., 17 S.W.3d 721, 721 (Tex. App. 2000) (similar).

difference in pagination would be a material difference. A student who uses a text that is paginated differently from the text that the professor has used in preparing the syllabus will encounter difficulty in completing the correct reading assignments; had the student known of the difference in pagination, this would almost certainly have influenced the purchasing decision. Other material differences might include changes in chapter headings or chapter sequence, re-numbering of problem sets, and the use of footnotes versus endnotes. Changing the color, fabric, or artwork used on the cover of the textbook, while a less substantial difference, might still qualify as material; even though these differences do not affect the content of the textbook, students who encounter both versions of the book could be confused as to whether they are purchasing the correct text.

With respect to books other than textbooks, including both fiction and nonfiction works, pagination differences might still be considered material under the low standard that courts have established for gray market goods. In addition, differences in covers, book jackets, and artwork might be more material for this class of works than for textbooks. Because these books are likely to be purchased at the consumer's own initiative, their visual appearance could influence the purchasing decision.[73] Other material differences could include chapter headings, design and placement of illustrations, and front matter and other supplementary content.

In the case of videogames or software,[74] differences in the warranty, documentation, language, or packaging are likely to qualify as material. For CDs and home video, material differences could arise from differences in "bonus" content, cover and interior art, packaging, and liner notes. For textiles, art reproductions, and other artistic or decorative works, differences in dimensions, design, manufacturing materials, or packaging could be material.

B. John Wiley & Sons Invokes Trademark Law against Parallel Imports

Textbook manufacturers have already turned to trademark law to combat parallel imports of copyrighted works. In November 2013, John Wiley & Sons (the unsuccessful plaintiff in *Kirtsaeng*) applied to CBP for *Lever* rule protection against unauthorized importation of eleven textbook titles bearing the registered trademarks WILEY and JW & DESIGN,[75] declaring that the imported books were materially different from the books authorized for domestic sale. On January 30, 2014, CBP granted the requested protection, reporting that

---

[73] In *Martin's Herend Imports*, *supra* note 31, the Fifth Circuit held that imported figurines infringed Martin's trademark where some were "completely different pieces" from those that Martin's had authorized for sale, and others "had painted patterns and colors different from those offered by Martin's." 112 F.3d at 1302. Even though, at the point of purchase, their outward appearance made them obviously different from the trademark owner's authorized goods, the court held that "[a]s a matter of law, such differences are material, since consumer choices for such artistic pieces are necessarily subjective or even fanciful, depending on each consumer's personal artistic tastes." *Ibid.*

[74] If a court finds that the software or videogame has been licensed rather than sold, then the first sale rule of copyright law will not apply in the first place. See e.g. Vernor v. Autodesk, 621 F.3d 1102 (9th Cir. 2010).

[75] JW & DESIGN, Registration No. 1,639,555 (Customs Recordation Number: TMK 06-01378); WILEY, Registration No. 1,003,988 (Customs Recordation No. TMK 06-01435).

the textbooks were physically and materially different from their counterparts authorized for sale in the U.S.; these differences included "product construction, design, quality, appearance, market pricing, and labeling."[76]

It is not clear whether CBP exercised any independent judgment in reaching this conclusion, or whether it simply parroted the publisher's assertions. Even considering the low threshold of materiality that courts apply to gray market goods, the CBP's assertion that "market pricing" constitutes a "physical and material difference" strains credibility. Nonetheless, rather than incur the costs of a legal battle, an unauthorized importer is likely to accept such a ruling and simply apply a *Lever* disclaimer in order to release the books for domestic distribution.

As noted earlier, the *Lever* label will not preclude John Wiley & Sons from pursuing remedies under the Lanham Act. In a Lanham Act claim, a court will have to evaluate whether, under all the facts and circumstances, the *Lever* label sufficiently negates the likelihood of confusion. In the meantime, students encountering the *Lever* disclaimer will have to decide whether the price differential offsets the risk of purchasing a text that might not fully conform to their course requirements. Some students might ignore the disclaimer completely. Indeed, the specific textbooks at issue in *Kirtsaeng* did bear a disclaimer, and apparently this did not dissuade the defendant or his customers from purchasing the books; unlike a *Lever* label, however, that disclaimer did not state that there were material differences between the domestic and foreign books.[77] Faced with a true *Lever* disclaimer, the more risk-averse student might decide to purchase the authorized text instead, thus handing a victory to the copyright/trademark owner.

VI. QUASI-PREEMPTION UNDER *DASTAR*?

The trademark strategy described above could be challenged as an impermissible end-run around the limitations of copyright law. Although copyright law generally does not preempt federal trademark law, the Supreme Court and some lower federal courts have disallowed certain applications of trademark law to copyrighted works when they frustrate the congressional intent underlying the copyright laws.

In *Dastar Corp. v. Twentieth Century Fox Film Corp.*,[78] the Supreme Court refused to apply section 43(a) to a claim of false designation of origin pertaining to an expressive work. When a television series produced by the plaintiff lost its copyright and entered the public domain, the defendant re-edited the series and released it on videocassette, using packaging that named the defendant as the producer and omitted any reference to the plaintiff.

In a typical section 43(a) claim, the defendant places the plaintiff's mark on the

---

[76] *General Notices*, 48 CUST. B. AND DEC., No. 7 (February 19, 2014).
[77] For example, one of the textbooks in *Kirtsaeng* contained the following warning: "This book is authorized for sale in Europe, Asia, Africa, and the Middle East only and may be not exported out of these territories. Exportation from or importation of this book to another region without the Publisher's authorization is illegal and is a violation of the Publisher's rights. The Publisher may take legal action to enforce its rights . . . Printed in Asia."
[78] Dastar Corp. v. Twentieth Century Fox Film Corp., 539 U.S. 23 (2003).

defendant's product. *Dastar*, however, involved a claim of "reverse passing off," because the defendant placed its own mark on the *plaintiff*'s product. The plaintiff claimed that the defendant had "bodily appropriat[ed]" the plaintiff's creative work; by replacing the plaintiff's trademark with its own, the defendant gave consumers the false impression that the defendant had created the series.[79]

The Supreme Court rejected this claim, holding that the term "origin" in section 43(a) refers to "the producer of the tangible goods that are offered for sale, and not to the author of any idea, concept, or communication embodied in those goods."[80] Acknowledging that, in general, section 43(a) encompasses claims of reverse passing off, the Court held that such a claim is limited to false designations of the producer of the *physical* goods, and cannot arise from failure to identify the origin of ideas or expression embodied in those goods.[81] Although *Dastar* concerned a work in which copyright had expired, courts have consistently held that *Dastar*'s reasoning applies equally to works still subject to copyright.[82]

Dastar, however, involved a claim of *reverse* passing off. As applied to expressive works, reverse passing off closely resembles a claim of copyright infringement. In contrast, the use of trademark law to prevent the importation or sale of materially different goods involves traditional passing off. So far, no court has held that *Dastar* precludes traditional passing off claims involving creative merchandise.[83] Thus, it appears that sections 32(1) and 43(a) will continue to permit a copyright owner to bring a trademark claim against a defendant that uses the copyright owner's trademark to sell copies that are materially different from the copies authorized for domestic sale.

VII. CONFLICT WITH COPYRIGHT POLICY

As in other situations where copyright and trademark law overlap, the possibility of using one regime to avoid the limitations of the other raises significant policy concerns. If copyright law prevents copyright owners from maintaining separate territorial markets for their works, should they be permitted to achieve a similar result through trademark law?

With respect to many non-copyrighted goods, trademark law's restrictions on gray market goods have strong policy justifications. Goods manufactured or packaged specifi-

---

[79] *Ibid.* at 28.
[80] *Ibid.* at 37.
[81] *Ibid.* at 31–32.
[82] See e.g. Zyla v. Wadsworth, 360 F.3d 243, 251–52 (1st Cir. 2004); Richard Feiner & Co. v. N.Y. Times Co., 07 Civ. 11218 (RMB) (RLE), 2008 U.S. Dist. LEXIS 58454, at *9–11 (S.D.N.Y. August 1, 2008); Thomas Publ'g Co., LLC v. Tech. Evaluation Ctrs., Inc., 06 Civ. 14212 (RMB), 2007 U.S. Dist. LEXIS 55086, at *6–7 (S.D.N.Y. July 27, 2007); Antidote Int'l Films, Inc. v. Bloomsbury Publ'g, PLC, 467 F. Supp. 2d 394, 389 (S.D.N.Y. 2007); Beckwith Builders, Inc. v. Depietri, No. 04-cv-282-SM, 2006 U.S. Dist. LEXIS 67060, at *12–14 (D.N.H. September 15, 2006); Auscape Int'l v. Nat'l Geographic Soc'y, 409 F. Supp. 2d 235, 250 (S.D.N.Y. 2004); Smith v. New Line Cinema, 03 Civ. 5274, 2004 U.S. Dist. LEXIS 18382, at *10–11 (S.D.N.Y. September 8, 2004); Williams v. UMG Recordings, 281 F. Supp. 2d 1177, 1185 (C.D. Cal. 2003).
[83] See e.g. King v. Innovation Books, 976 F.2d 824 (2d Cir. 1992); *Gilliam, supra* note 46; Lutz v. De Laurentis, 260 Cal. Rptr. 106 (Cal. Ct. App. 1989).

cally for foreign markets might have different ingredients, might be labeled or packaged differently, might be accompanied by different documentation (perhaps in a language other than English), might have been subjected to different levels of quality control during manufacturing, packaging, handling, or shipping, and might be covered by different warranties. Domestic consumers who purchase these unauthorized imports without knowing of these differences may be disappointed. Allowing trademark owners to segregate their domestic and foreign markets protects such consumers while enabling trademark owners to adjust their prices for each territory to reflect the costs of doing business and the specific risks and competitive conditions in those markets. Thus far, courts have treated trademark owners favorably by accepting even minor differences as material; in addition, they have not demanded a justification for the differences.

In the case of copyrighted works, some material differences between foreign and domestic versions may be unavoidable. Films released on home video, for example, may be dubbed or subtitled in different languages for different countries, or their content may be edited to satisfy local laws or preferences. Books may be translated into different languages. However, copyright owners can also introduce material differences that are unnecessary for meeting the demands of different markets. Because current law does not require a justification for material differences, arbitrary or artificial differences are just as effective in creating trademark liability as differences that are essential for meeting consumer demands.

The *Lever* disclaimer does not eliminate these concerns. While the use of the disclaimer can allow some materially different copies to be imported, it cannot insulate domestic resellers from liability for trademark infringement under the likelihood of confusion test. Thus, even if imports are permitted, retailers might be unwilling to stock the labeled goods based on liability concerns. A *Lever* label can also make goods more difficult to sell. Students alerted to material differences in a text could be concerned about their ability to complete assignments and prepare for examinations correctly. A warning of material differences could be particularly disconcerting to consumers contemplating the purchase of a book, DVD, CD, videogame or software package as opposed to the purchase of non-copyrighted goods such as candy or shampoo. The generally higher price of copyrighted works, together with the fact that many of them are non-returnable once opened, might make a *Lever* disclaimer more of a deterrent. Even if the product is returnable, consumers will have difficulty judging how the two versions are different unless they can compare them side by side, a comparison which, in the case of copyrighted works, most consumers will have neither the time nor the opportunity to undertake.[84]

Furthermore, a *Lever* disclaimer can impart useful information to consumers only as long as it remains attached to the merchandise. If the *Lever* label becomes separated from a product before its useful life is over, the product may be sold on the secondhand market to a purchaser who is unaware of the material differences. Copies of copyrighted works have longer useful lives than many other types of gray market goods (such as food or personal care products), and are also more likely to be sold secondhand. Because

---

[84] Cf. *Gilliam*, supra note 46, 538 F.2d at 24 (unauthorized editing of television programs harms the authors because "the public will have only the final product by which to evaluate the work" even if the network publicly takes responsibility for the editing).

the regulations governing *Lever* labels are not specific as to the manner of attachment, separation is possible, especially in the case of products with relatively long useful lives, such as copyrighted works. Consumers who purchase secondhand books, CDs, DVDs, videogames, or software packages might inadvertently purchase something materially different from the product they were seeking, and might not have the option of returning the item. Thus, the *Lever* label will not protect these downstream purchasers from being misled or confused.

In their ability to impede cross-border trade, material differences in copyrighted works are analogous to DVD region codes, which make commercially distributed DVDs that are coded for one territory unplayable in devices coded for other territories.[85] Region codes enable copyright owners to maintain separate markets by making unauthorized imports unappealing to consumers; in trademark terms, they easily qualify as material differences, and they are sometimes justified by goals other than price discrimination.[86] A consumer that is forewarned of the coding difference is likely to avoid the product, while the unaware consumer might purchase it and then experience the confusion and disappointment that are relevant to trademark infringement. Like other material differences, region codes effectuate a territorial restriction; however, region codes create a technological barrier, while most other material differences create only a legal one.[87] Although region codes can be circumvented by technological means,[88] only a policy-based legal challenge can overcome the effectiveness of other material differences.

The strategy of deliberately introducing differences between domestic and foreign editions solely to take advantage of trademark laws is an anticompetitive measure. It enables domestic copyright owners to maintain higher domestic prices by restricting competition from cheaper imports. However, because this strategy does not appear to violate any existing legal principles, it is unlikely to attract judicial scrutiny. Courts will be loath to dictate content to producers and publishers of copyrightable works, nor are they likely to find any legal basis for doing so. A court cannot compel a textbook publisher to use the same pagination in both Thailand and the U.S. Courts could, in theory, impose a higher threshold for assessing material differences in the context of copyrighted works. However, they would have to justify treating copyrightable works differently from other categories of gray market goods, possibly by noting the risk of an end-run around the first sale rule of copyright law. Because there are sometimes legitimate reasons for publishing different

---

[85] See Yu, *supra* note 16, at 194–95.

[86] Motion picture studios use DVD region codes to control the timing of movie releases in different countries to facilitate price discrimination, to satisfy local distributors' needs for customized content, packaging, and advertising, and to meet censorship requirements. Yu, *supra* note 16, at 200–216.

[87] Because they are a technological barrier, rather than a legal one, region codes have not been subjected to legal challenge in the U.S. At one time, however, their role in facilitating price discrimination prompted legal scrutiny under the competition laws of Australia and the European Union. Paul Sweeting, *Probes into Regional DVD Imperils Studio Strategy*, VARIETY (June 3, 2001), available at http://variety.com/2001/voices/columns/probes-into-regional-dvd-imperils-studio-strategy-1117800545/.

[88] Ryan Iwahashi, *How to Circumvent Technological Protection Measures Without Violating the DMCA: An Examination of Technological Protection Measures Under Current Legal Standards*, 26 BERKELEY TECH. L.J. 491, 506 (2011).

versions of a work in different countries, a heightened materiality standard would have to take account of the reasons for the material differences.

VIII. CONCLUSION

Although *Quality King* and *Kirtsaeng* have all but eliminated the copyright owner's right to control the importation of lawfully made copies under copyright law, publishers can now reclaim at least some of these rights under trademark law. This use of trademark law raises policy concerns because it has little or no connection to consumer protection. Although there are exceptions, many of the legitimate explanations for territory-based material differences in consumer goods have little application to copyrighted works. Furthermore, the CPB's recent application of the *Lever* rule to exclude copyrighted goods suggests that the agency applies little or no scrutiny to material differences claims.

Although Congress could address this problem through legislation, no industry groups are likely to lobby for such a change. Perhaps litigation will lead courts to reconsider the extremely low threshold of materiality they have applied to gray market goods. When copyright owners create material differences solely for the purpose of circumventing copyright law, courts should recognize that this practice is anticompetitive and inconsistent with federal copyright policy.

21. New developments in trademark exhaustion in Korea
*Byungil Kim**

I. INTRODUCTION

The "exhaustion of rights" doctrine[1] is one of the most fundamental limitations to intellectual property rights.[2] Under the theory of the exhaustion of rights, when an intellectual property right owner sells an article embodying those rights, they are exhausted with respect to that article. Thus, a purchaser can resell the article without being liable for infringement. Likewise, the owner of the intellectual property right cannot control the resale of a legally purchased good. Unless otherwise specified by law, subsequent acts of resale, rental, lending, or other forms of commercial use by third parties can no longer be controlled or opposed by the owner of the intellectual property or its licensee(s). There is a fairly broad consensus that this exhaustion principle applies at least within the context of the domestic market in most jurisdictions.

The exhaustion of rights doctrine takes on its greatest significance when goods embodying intellectual property rights are traded internationally. When rights are held for the same intellectual property right in multiple countries, the question that arises is whether, when, and which of, these rights are exhausted by sale of the products in a given national market with respect to other national markets.[3] In other words, one of the key issues associated with intellectual property protection is whether an intellectual property right owner can use intellectual property rights against the (re)importation of the protected products from another country, when these products have been first put onto the market in that country by the intellectual property owner herself or her licensees. At the present time,

---

* Professor of Law, School of Law, Hanyang University, Korea.

[1] It is also sometimes referred to as the "first sale doctrine." The domestic exhaustion principle holds that intellectual property rights (IPRs) are exhausted only by first sales within the territory of the granting state. This model is inconsistent with the rationale behind the move toward harmonization, namely, the abolition of national division for allocating IPRs. At the opposite end of the spectrum is international exhaustion. This option, although most beneficial to consumers, would be opposed by IPR owners. A third option is international exhaustion limited to certain types of product classes. This model would allow only IPRs attached to certain product classes to be internationally exhausted while protecting other products from such exhaustion. See Darren E. Donnelly, *Parallel Trade and International Harmonization of the Exhaustion of Rights Doctrine*, 13 COMPUTER & HIGH TECH. L.J. 487–510 (1997); Irene Calboli, *Trademark Exhaustion in the European Union: Community-Wide or International? The Saga Continues*, 6 MARQ. INTELL. PROP. L. REV. 47 (2002).

[2] Donnelly, *supra* note 1, at 448.

[3] Inherent in patent, trademark, and copyright protection is the right to prevent infringing imports. Typically, right owners use this protection against "pirated" copies, but the protection may also be effective to prevent the import of genuine goods. *Ibid.*

there is not a consensus as to whether this importation is lawful—in other words whether countries should adopt "international exhaustion" instead of national exhaustion regarding intellectual property rights.

The question of the acceptance of international exhaustion thus directly relates to the acceptance of the practice of parallel imports.[4] Parallel imports refer to the importation of goods from outside the distribution channels contractually negotiated by the manufacturer/intellectual property right owner. The manufacturer/intellectual property rights owner has no contractual connection with a parallel importer. Thus, based upon the right of preventing unauthorized importation that intellectual property rights may confer to the intellectual property owner, the latter may try to oppose such importation in order to control international product distribution and separate the national markets in which the products are distributed. If, however, national law provides that the distribution of the protected products in another country by the intellectual property rights owner, or with consent, leads to the exhaustion also of the domestic intellectual property rights, then the right to prevent the importation of these products is also exhausted and in turn can no longer be invoked against such parallel importation.

Manufacturers, publishers, and distributors who oppose parallel imports tend to raise a number of arguments against this practice. For example, they express concerns that parallel imports may include substandard products or even counterfeits, and may be difficult to support or service in a foreign country when these products are not distributed by authorized distributors. Critics of this practice also express concern that the inability to charge higher prices in some markets may undermine their ability to service products in those markets.[5] On the other hand, a variety of representatives of consumer interests' groups that support parallel imports say that measures to deal with substandard products or counterfeits can be addressed with or without parallel imports; that consumers' benefit from cross-border trade can be substantial, outweighing the risks of parallel imports; and that parallel imports permit smaller or less competitive markets to benefit from competition in more competitive markets.[6]

In general, the issue of parallel imports represented one of the most heated issues of debate in international intellectual property agreements and, to date, no global consensus has been reached on the issue.[7] Given the lack of global consensus, exhaustion policies

---

[4] Christopher Heath, *Legal Concept of Exhaustion and Parallel Imports*, in PARALLEL IMPORTS IN ASIA 18 (Christopher Heath ed., 2004).

[5] LAZAROS GRIGORIADIS, TRADE MARKS AND FREE TRADE: A GLOBAL ANALYSIS 20 (2014).

[6] Ansgar Ohly, *Trade Marks and Parallel Importation: Recent Developments in European Law*, 30 INT'L REV. INTELL. PROP. & COMPETITION L. 512 (1999).

[7] Under the World Trade Organization and the Agreement on Trade-Related Aspects of Intellectual Property Rights (TRIPS) rules, countries are permitted to decide for themselves how to handle parallel imports. The key section of TRIPS is art. 6, Exhaustion, which reads: "For the purposes of dispute settlement under this Agreement, subject to the provisions of Articles 35 and 46 nothing in this Agreement shall be used to address the issue of the exhaustion of intellectual property rights." Agreement on Trade-Related Aspects of Intellectual Property Rights, art. 6, April 15, 1994; Marrakesh Agreement Establishing the World Trade Organization, Annex 1C, Legal Instruments—Result of the Uruguay Rounds Vol. 31, 33 I.L.M. 83 (1994) [hereinafter TRIPS]. See also, Ohly, *supra* note 6.

vary widely across countries.[8] Different types of intellectual property may also be treated differently within a given country. Currently, it is up to individual countries to decide whether to allow or prohibit parallel imports. For example, several countries permit parallel imports while others restrict parallel imports except for certain types of goods.[9] Some countries regard efforts to discourage parallel imports as violations of anti-monopoly laws. Electronic commerce and the Internet are also contributing to increase the parallel imports between different jurisdictions.

The choice of one type of policy on intellectual property exhaustion versus another—i.e., national, regional, or international exhaustion—can have different implications for the country of importation. Under national exhaustion, rights end upon the first sale within a nation, but the intellectual property rights owner may prevent parallel trade with other countries. Where a country applies the concept of international exhaustion, rights are exhausted upon first sale anywhere and parallel imports are permitted. The concept of regional exhaustion permits parallel trade among a group of countries, but not from outside the region.

This chapter deals with the issues surrounding exhaustion of trademark rights in Korea, which so far permits the parallel importation of genuine goods—in other words, follows a principle of international exhaustion in trademark law.

II. EXHAUSTION OF TRADEMARK RIGHTS AND PARALLEL IMPORTS UNDER KOREAN LAW

There is no statutory law addressing the exhaustion of intellectual property rights in Korea. However, the Korean courts have held that intellectual property rights, including patent rights, design rights, and trademark rights, are exhausted if the product in question is made and/or sold by the rights owner.[10] Although a relatively new phenomenon

---

[8] See CARLOS M. CORREA, INTELLECTUAL PROPERTY RIGHTS, THE WTO AND DEVELOPING COUNTRIES: THE TRIPS AGREEMENT AND POLICY OPTIONS 83 (2003).

[9] Christopher Heath, *Patent Rights and the "Specific Mechanism" to Prevent Parallel Imports*, 45 INT'L REV. INTELL. PROP. & COMPETITION L. 399 (2014).

[10] Korean courts traditionally apply only national exhaustion with respect to patent rights. Interestingly, however, 20 years ago, there was one decision that held that the parallel import of patented products is not considered an infringement. The case, Ildong Pharmacie v. Farmatalia Carlo Erba S.p.a (Seoul District Court [Seoul Dist. Ct.], 81Ka967, March 14, 1981) ("*FCE*"), held that the first sale of a patented item outside of Korea also exhausts the patent rights in Korea. The case involved the parallel import of patented "Adriamycin" covered by Korean and Italian patents. Plaintiff FCE both manufactured its own "Adriamycin" and sold the patented article in Italy. A Swiss company (Rodian) imported them into Switzerland. The defendants purchased "Adriamycin" in Switzerland and imported them into Korea where FCE brought suit under its Korean patents. The Seoul-East District Court held that the first sale of a patented item outside of Korea also exhausts the patent rights in Korea. The court, thus, extended the doctrine of exhaustion of rights from those sales taking place in the destination country to all authorized sales. However, the court did not specify why a situation involving parallel imports of goods manufactured under a foreign patent did not infringe a corresponding Korean patent. Additionally, there was no explanation in the opinion concerning international exhaustion. In my opinion, it is questionable whether the Korean court attempted to support parallel import of patented goods under

in Korea, the relevance of parallel imports is growing in Korea and this issue has become more relevant, as the decisions analyzed below demonstrate.

Generally, the discussion on the exhaustion of intellectual property rights in Korea takes place within the framework of intellectual property law.[11] Hence, other provisions are also relevant in this area.[12]

A. The Legal Background: Trademark Law in Korea

Korea enacted the Trademark Act (TMA) in 1949, which was drafted under the military administration of the United States (U.S.). The 1949 TMA was replaced by the 1958 TMA, which was in effect until the latest version of the TMA became effective in 2009. Since then, the TMA has been revised thirty-seven times, including a complete overhaul in 1990. In particular, the TMA has been significantly amended in the last twenty years in order to comply with the Agreement on Trade-Related Aspects of Intellectual Property Rights (TRIPS),[13] the Protocol Relating to the Madrid Agreement Concerning the International Registration of Marks,[14] the Trademark Law Treaty,[15] and the South Korea-United States Free Trade Agreement.[16] Furthermore, enhanced protection of famous or well-known marks is provided under the Unfair Competition Prevention and Trade Secret Protection Act (UCPA).[17]

---

the theory of international exhaustion. Presently, Korea permits parallel imports of copyrighted products, but there is no decision on the parallel import of copyrighted goods.

[11] Patent Act [Teugheobeob], Act No. 950, December 31, 1961, *wholly amended by* Act No. 4207 on January 13, 1990 (S. Kor.); Utility Model Act [Silyongsinanbeob], Act No. 952, December 31, 1961, *wholly amended by* Act No. 7872 on March 3, 2006 (S. Kor.); Design Act [Designbohobeob], Act No. 951, December 31, 1961, *wholly amended by* Act No. 11848, on May 28, 2013 (S. Kor.); Trademark Act [Sangpyobeob], Act. No. 71, November 28, 1949 (S. Kor.), *wholly amended by* Act. No. 4210, January 13, 1990 (S. Kor.), *amended by* Act. No. 12751, June 11, 2014 (S. Kor.) (current version) [hereinafter TMA]; Copyright Act [Cheojakkweonbeob], Act. No. 432, January 28, 1957, *wholly amended by* Act No. 8101, on December 28, 2006 (S. Kor.). An English translation of all major intellectual property laws is available at Korea Legislation Research Institute, *Legislative Center* (2013), http://elaw.klri.re.kr/eng_service/main.do.

[12] Monopoly Regulation and Fair Trade Act [Dogjeom gyuje mich gongjeong georaee gwanhan beobryul], Act. No. 3320, December 31, 1980 (S. Kor.) [hereinafter MRFTA], *amended by* Act. No. 4198, January 13, 1990 (S. Kor.), *amended by* Act. No. 12708, May 28, 2014 (S. Kor.) (current version); Custom Act [Kwansebeob], Act. No. 67, November 23, 1949 (S. Kor.), *amended by* Act. No. 6305, December 29, 2000 (S. Kor.), *amended by* Act. No. 12847, December 23, 2014 (current version).

[13] See TRIPS, *supra* note 7.

[14] Protocol Relating to the Madrid Agreement Concerning the International Registration of Marks, June 27, 1989, [2001] A.T.S. 7.

[15] Trademark Law Treaty, October 27, 1994, 2037 U.N.T.S. 35.

[16] Free Trade Agreement Between the United States of America and the Republic of Korea, U.S.-S. Kor., June 30, 2007, Office of the U.S. Trade Representative, available at www.ustr.gov/trade-agreements/free-trade-agreements/korus-fta/final-text.

[17] Unfair Competition Prevention Act [Bujeong Gyeongjaeng Bangjibeob], Act. No. 911, December 30, 1961 (S. Kor.), *amended by* Act. No. 3897, December 31, 1986. The title of the Act was changed from "Unfair Competition Prevention Act" to "Unfair Competition Prevention and Trade Secret Protection Act" in Act. No. 5621, December 31, 1998 (S. Kor.), *amended by* Act. No. 11963, July 30, 2013 (S. Kor.).

Once a trademark right has been established by registration, the owner enjoys the right of exclusive use of the registered trademark on the designated goods, and can exclude others from using a mark identical with or similar to the registered trademark with respect to goods or services that are identical with or similar to the designated goods of the registered trademark.[18] The extent of protection is determined on the basis of the goods listed in the documents accompanying the application for registration of a trademark.[19]

The use of a trademark as an indication of source is the basic requirement for trademark infringement. "Use" comprises the acts of applying trademarks to goods or packages, sale, export, import, display, advertising, or distribution.[20]

In a civil action for trademark infringement, a plaintiff must prove that: (i) the plaintiff is an owner of the trademark registration; (ii) the defendant used the mark as a trademark which indicates source of specific goods or services; (iii) the usage of defendant falls within the category of acts specified in section 2(1)(vii); and (iv) the mark used by the defendant is identical with, or similar to, the registered trademark and the mark was used on goods which are identical with, or similar to, the designated goods of plaintiff.[21] The following acts are also deemed to constitute infringement of a trademark right according to section 66 of the TMA: (a) the act of delivering, selling, forging, imitating, or possessing a trademark identical with or similar to a registered trademark with the intent to use or to let others use the trademark; and (b) the act of manufacturing, delivering, selling, or possessing instruments with the intent to forge or imitate, or to let others forge or imitate a registered trademark of a third party.[22]

The first available defense to a claim of trademark infringement is that, due to dissimilarity of the trademarks or goods, confusion as to the origin or quality of the goods is not likely to occur. The next potential defense to an action for trademark infringement is set out in section 51 of the TMA (customary use, etc.).[23] The use of a trademark as an indication of source is the basic requirement for trademark infringement.[24] Thus, trademark infringers may attempt to defend their use claiming that the trademark is used as a shape of a product or as a decorative design.[25]

The TMA stipulates that an act of importing such goods or their packaging on which

---

[18] TMA, § 50.
[19] Ibid. § 52.
[20] Under § 2(1)(vii) of the TMA, the term "use of a trademark" means an act falling under any of the following items: (a) representing a trademark on goods or packages of goods; (b) transferring or delivering goods or packages of goods on which a trademark is represented, or displaying, exporting, or importing them for such purpose; (c) representing a trademark on advertisements on goods, price lists, transaction documents, signboards, or tags and displaying or distributing it. Ibid. § 2(1)(vii).
[21] Ibid. §§ 65, 66, 2(1)(vi). However, the test for trademark infringement in Korea is whether the marks in question are "confusingly similar" in the perception of consumers when used on similar goods, Supreme Court [S. Ct.], 85Hu65, February 11, 1986 (S. Kor.).
[22] Ibid. § 66. This type of infringement is generally referred to as "indirect infringement," which is different from the concept of contributory infringement under U.S. trademark law. There are no statutory causes of action for contributory infringement under Korean trademark law as such, and case law is rather unclear about the doctrine of contributory and vicarious liability.
[23] Ibid. § 51.
[24] Ibid. § 66.
[25] Ibid. § 7; see also ibid. § 51.

trademarks have been applied or displaying for the purposes of selling or delivering constitutes a "use of a trademark."[26] An act of importing goods bearing a registered or similar mark used on the designated or similar goods is considered infringement.[27] Thus, it will be unlawful to import into Korea if any merchandise of foreign manufacture, or the label, sign, print, package, wrapper, or receptacle bears counterfeit trademark. However, parallel import of genuine goods itself does not constitute trademark infringement or the licensee's exclusive right to use the trademark in Korea,[28] although importing goods that bear marks confusingly similar to registered marks is still not permissible.

In 1995, Korea began to actively discuss allowing parallel imports when the Korean Customs Services prohibited the importation of "Levi's Jeans" by the Price Club company. To settle this matter, the Korean government amended the public notice of the Fair Trade Commission and the regulations in the Customs Act to permit the parallel import of goods effective November 1, 1995.

B. Judicial Decisions on Parallel Imports of Trademarked Products

(1) *Polo* case

The *Polo* case,[29] decided in 1997, was the first Korean Supreme Court decision regarding the parallel importation into Korea of genuine goods protected by a trademark in Korea (the products at issue were not genuine even though defendant claimed that he mistakenly believed that the products were genuine). In particular, the Court held that the parallel importation of genuine goods manufactured by an authorized subcontractor unrelated to the trademark owner constituted an infringement of the registered exclusive licensee's rights in Korea.[30]

In the *Polo* case, Il-Kyung Company, Limited (hereinafter "Licensee") was registered as an exclusive licensee with the Korean Industrial Property Office (KIPO) to manufacture "POLO" trademark clothes. The Licensee was a Korean company, which was not related to the trademark owner. The Licensee invested a substantial amount of money to develop and market high quality POLO products designed especially for the Korean market. The defendant, Myung-Hee Kim, imported 2,050 pieces of counterfeit T-shirts bearing the POLO mark from the United States (U.S.) without consent of the trademark owner or Licensee. As a result, the Prosecutor's Office initiated a criminal action against the defendant for trademark infringement of the registered POLO mark.

Even though the defendant claimed that he mistakenly believed that the goods were genuine, the Court ultimately found that defendant committed trademark infringement. The Court also noted that if a third party would obtain less expensive, genuine POLO products, manufactured in a foreign country with inferior techniques and then began selling these products in Korea, this would also amount to infringement. In general, the

---

[26] *Ibid.* § 2(1)(vii).
[27] *Ibid.* §§ 50, 66.
[28] Seoul District Court [Seoul Dist. Ct.], 97Ghab32678, May 10, 1998 (S. Kor.).
[29] Supreme Court [S. Ct.], 96Do2191, October 10, 1997 (S. Kor.) ("*Polo*"). Byung–Il Kim, *Exhaustion and Parallel Imports in Korea*, in PARALLEL IMPORTS IN ASIA 73–83 (Christopher Heath ed., 2004).
[30] *Polo, supra* note 29.

Court stated that the quality of the products distributed by POLO's Licensee and the POLO products manufactured and first sold in a foreign country was not the same, and further that the source of the products manufactured by the exclusive Licensee was not the same.[31] The Court also stated that since there was no relationship between the Korean Licensee and the owner of the POLO trademark in the relevant foreign country, there was no likelihood that the trademark owner in the foreign country and the Licensee could jointly dominate the market.[32]

The Court defined the scope of permissible parallel imports as follows:

- The domestic exclusive licensee recorded with the KIPO had advertized the trademark ("POLO") with considerable cost of manufacture and sale of the trademarked goods in Korea.
- The goods marked with the same trademark sold in foreign countries were not only the ones that were manufactured in the country of the foreign trademark holder (in this case, U.S.), but also included many products manufactured in other countries on an original equipment manufacturer basis at low labour costs.
- There was no special relationship between the domestic exclusive licensee and the foreign trademark owner other than the exclusive licensing agreement. There were some differences in quality between the goods manufactured and sold in Korea by the domestic exclusive licensee, and the goods manufactured and sold in foreign countries. Further, it could not be said that the source of manufacture and sale of the goods of a domestic exclusive licensee and a foreign trademark owner were the same.
- Therefore, it was less likely that the trademark owner would abuse his trademark right in an unfair manner by using his power of management or control over the exclusive licensee.
- In conclusion, under these circumstances, even if the parallel imports of genuine goods did not constitute trademark infringement, such a case should not be permitted, and should be prevented from being an infringement of the domestic exclusive licensee's rights to use the trademark.[33]

As noted above, as a separate matter, the Supreme Court ruled that even if the parallel importer believed that the parallel import was permitted and that such importing did not infringe on the exclusive licensee's rights, such mistaken belief did not absolve the parallel importer from criminal liability for trademark infringement under the TMA.[34]

(2) *Burberry* case

The 2002 *Burberry* case[35] is the landmark case for parallel importing in Korea. The plaintiff, Burberry Limited, based in the United Kingdom (U.K.), registered and used the trademark of BURBERRY and the marks indicated in the schedules attached to the

---

[31] Ibid.
[32] Ibid.
[33] Ibid.
[34] Ibid.
[35] Supreme Court [S. Ct.], 99Da42322, September 24, 2002 (S. Kor.) ("*Burberry*").

original decision (collectively referred to as the Marks) in the U.K. and abroad. Euro Trade, Inc., executed an agency agreement with Burberry that stated that Euro Trade would have the exclusive right to import and sell the products manufactured by Burberry (the Products). In addition, Euro Trade actively conducted promotion and advertisement activities regarding the Products in Korea, and, thanks to such efforts, customers came to recognize the Products as a premium-brand product. The defendant imported (parallel import) the Products (so-called the Genuine Products) and provided them to domestic customers. For purposes of sales promotion, the defendant used BURBERRY signs outside its shops, used the marks on packaging, shopping bags and name cards, and published advertisements using the BURBERRY mark in fashion magazines. Burberry and Euro Trade jointly sued for trademark infringement.[36]

The Court in the *Burberry* case had to determine whether an act was deemed to infringe on a trademark right based on the basic function that a trademark performs. The two basic functions of trademarks are to indicate the source of the products bearing the trademark and to help customers trust the quality of the products. According to section 1 of the TMA, the purpose of the TMA is to contribute to industry development and to protect consumer interests by maintaining, through the protection of trademarks, the business credit of those persons using the trademarks.[37] The Court stated:

> [E]ven though the parallel importer's use of such trademark extends beyond the above scope of passive use, if he conducts promotion and advertisement activities by actively using the trademark, and if such activity use does not threaten to affect the above functions and does not cause domestic customers to mistake the source or the quality of the products bearing the trademark, such active use may not be deemed to constitute an infringement upon the TMA. In this regard, it is reasonable to conclude that the holder of trademark rights is not entitled to require the parallel importer to stop infringing upon the trademark right or destroy the products allegedly infringing upon the trademark right.[38]

The Court took the position that the act of parallel importing itself was a fair and legal act that did not constitute an infringement of any trademark right, and that a parallel importer's sales of products bearing the mark of the trademark owner should be permitted as long as such functions of the trademarks were not impaired.

The Korean Supreme Court decision in the *Burberry* case also addressed the extent to which a person can advertize a parallel imported product in Korea. The Supreme Court ruled that while the defendant's use of the BURBERRY trademark in connection with the sale of genuine Burberry products did not violate trademark law, such use may nevertheless violate unfair competition law if it is likely to cause consumer confusion with respect to the source of the product.[39]

Notably, the Court stated:

> Even though the parallel importer's active use of the trademark for the purpose of promotion and advertisement is deemed to be legal and fair and thus does not constitute an infringement

---

[36] *Ibid.*
[37] TMA, § 1.
[38] *Burberry, supra* note 35.
[39] *Ibid.*

upon the holder's trademark right, if the trademark used by the parallel importer serves as the operation mark in light of the circumstances of the usage, it may cause customers to mistake the parallel importer as an authorized sales agent of the foreign company. In such a case, the parallel importer's use falls within a category of acts causing public confusion concerning the owner of the trademark as set forth in Section 2(1)(b) of the UCPA and thus shall not be permitted.

(3) *Fujifilm* case

Korea also does not have any statutory regulations addressing the question of package modification with respect to imported products, even when the products are genuine. However, the issue was discussed in the *Fujifilm* case in 2003.[40] This case was the first court case where the products, or their packaging, had been modified by the importers.

Notably, the defendant in the business of selling disposable cameras collected empty disposable camera casings bearing the famous Japanese photo-film-maker's trademark "FUJIFILM," reloaded them with new film, and put them in new packaging. The defendant also put its trademark, "MIRACLE," in small font on the casing, but did not entirely remove the "FUJIFILM" mark from the casing. FUJIFILM Corporation brought a claim for trademark infringement, and the lower court ruled that the defendant had infringed FUJIFILM's trademark rights because the defendant had replaced the films and repackaged the disposable cameras. In particular, the court noted that reselling the altered disposable cameras was a new act of production, which fell outside the scope of the first sale doctrine.[41]

In this criminal case, the Supreme Court held that the defendant's conduct had substantially changed the quality and shape of the original product, and therefore the defendant infringed FUJIFILM's trademark rights, because: (i) the original trademark still remained in several places of the restored cameras; and (ii) there was an explicit notice in the original packaging that the camera body would not be returned after film development.[42] The ruling was based on the conclusion that the FUJIFILM mark functioned as a source identifier because the defendant's disposable cameras had the mark engraved into their casings. According to the decision, the defendant had collected empty casings of disposable cameras produced by FUJIFILM, reloaded them with new film and covered them with wrapping bearing the MIRACLE mark, thereby altering the packaging of the product.[43]

Generally, trademark rights in Korea are considered to be extinguished once the trademark owner transfers or sells the marked goods. In the *Fujifilm* case, however, the Supreme Court held that any processing or repair that results in altering the original shape of the goods is equivalent to new manufacturing, and, thus, could result in a finding of trademark infringement.[44]

The decision represents a possible recourse for trademark owners to protect their trademark rights even after marked products have been sold to third parties, and an exception to traditional trademark exhaustion theory.

---

[40] Supreme Court [S. Ct.], 2002Do3445, April 11, 2003 (S. Kor.) ("*Fujifilm*").
[41] Changwon District Court [Dist. Ct.], 2001 No. 2235, June 12, 2002 (S. Kor.).
[42] Ibid.
[43] Ibid.
[44] *Fujifilm, supra* note 40.

C. Analysis of the Current Statutory and Case Law

In light of the above decisions, parallel imports of original unaltered goods thus seem to be permissible in Korea. Unlike in Japan,[45] in Korea the answer (on the lawfulness of parallel imports) depends on the location where the goods were manufactured. In particular, the Supreme Court[46] stated that:

> [i]f a trademark owner manufactures and sells his branded goods within the territory of South Korea, the trademark owner can block parallel imports from another country . . . If a trademark owner does not manufacture his branded goods within the territory of South Korea, the trademark owner cannot block parallel imports.[47]

According to the Korean Supreme Court's rule, parallel imports are generally permitted in Korea when (i) the rightful trademark owner in a foreign country uses the mark on the imported products; (ii) there is a close legal or economic relationship between the foreign trademark owner and the Korean trademark owner; and (iii) there is no substantial difference in quality between the imported products and those of the Korean trademark right owner.[48]

The first basic requirement that allows for parallel imports under the Korean TMA is that the parallel imported goods should be genuine goods, which are legally labeled with the trademark at issue by the overseas trademark owners or a person who is lawfully licensed to do so.[49]

The most essential requirement for the permission of parallel imported products is that the trademark owner in Korea and the trademark owner overseas are the same or have a legally and/or economically close relationship so that the requirement that the sources of

---

[45] In Japan, trademark owners are generally precluded from using their rights against parallel imports of genuine goods, although under Japanese law it is not clear what "genuine" goods are. Osaka Chiho Saibansho [Osaka Dist. Ct.], February 27, 1970, 2 INT'L REV. INTELL. PROP. & COMPETITION L. 325 (1971) (Japan); Tōkyō Chihō Saibansho [Tōkyō Dist. Ct.], December 7, 1984, 543 Hanrei Times 323 (1985) (Japan); Nagoya Chihō Saibansho [Nagoya Dist. Ct.], March 25, 1988, 678 Hanrei Times 183 (1988) (Japan). See Christopher Heath, *From Parker to BBS: The Treatment of Parallel Imports in Japan*, 24 INT'L REV. INTELL. PROP. & COMPETITION L. 179 (1993).

[46] *Polo*, supra note 29.

[47] DUK-KYU CHOI, REPUBLIC OF KOREA, INTERNATIONAL EXHAUSTION OF INUSTRIAL PROPERTY RIGHTS 1–2, available at www.aippi.org/download/commitees/156/GR156rep_of_korea.pdf; www.aippi.org/download/commitees/156/GR156rep_of_korea.pdf. The permission to make parallel imports of genuine goods extends to those goods which were legitimately trademarked and distributed by a person who is the trademark right owner in Korea or who has a special relationship with the trademark right owner in Korea so that both persons can be regarded as one person. But if the source or quality indicated or guaranteed by the trademark attached to the goods thus distributed differs from the source or quality indicated or guaranteed by the trademark under petition, and the trademark as used by the parallel importer is considered to be separately used under circumstances similar to those of the petitioner's trademark, then in such cases those genuine goods should be excluded from Korea.

[48] Supreme Court [S. Ct.], 2012Da6059, August 20, 2014 (S. Kor.); Supreme Court [S. Ct.], 2006Da40423, October 13, 2006 (S. Kor.); Supreme Court [S. Ct.], 2002Da61965, June 9, 2005 (S. Kor.).

[49] Supreme Court [S. Ct.], 2012Da6059, August 20, 2014 (S. Kor); Supreme Court [S. Ct.], 2006Da40423, October 13, 2006 (S. Kor.).

the goods are perceived to be the same is satisfied.[50] A typical case where parallel import is permitted is when the trademark owners in Korea and overseas are the same or where they are closely related legally/economically, i.e., the trademark owner in Korea is the overseas trademark owner's general agent, exclusive distributor, or an affiliate, so that Korean consumers can recognize that the trademark attached to the parallel imported goods and that attached to the authentic imported goods indicate the same source. Even if parallel import is in violation of an agreement on distributable regions between the parties involved, this fact alone does not change the source of the parallel import, and, thus, does not result in the prohibition of parallel import of the product.

Furthermore, for the parallel imports to be permitted into Korea, there should be no practical difference in the quality of the parallel imported goods compared to the authorized goods imported into Korea by the trademark owner or its official distributors. In this respect, difference in quality signifies a difference in the functionality, durability, and the likeness of the product, not a difference in accompanying services, i.e., whether or not there is customer support, free-of-charge repairs, parts replacement, and the like. In the presence of any of these differences, the parallel imported goods would not be considered as genuine goods.

Moreover, parallel importing is not permitted in Korea under the UCPA if the trademark used by the parallel importer causes customer confusion with respect to the source/sponsorship/sales agent of the product.[51]

In Korea, it is not clear if contractual restrictions imposed by a trademark right owner can be used to limit the effect of international exhaustion.[52] In particular, if contractual restrictions are used to limit import of the genuine goods, it is preferable they are express in order to avoid any legal disputes.[53]

Furthermore, the "consent" giving rise to exhaustion is limited to specific arrangements, (for example, "a relationship with a subsidiary or affiliated company, or an agreement with a licensee"),[54] which is, in Korea, a question of fact. "However, if this 'consent' occurs in a parallel importation of [trademarked] products, the international exhaustion doctrine may apply to specific arrangements such as a relationship with a subsidiary or affiliated company, or an agreement with a licensee."[55]

---

[50] Supreme Court [S. Ct.], 2012Da6059, August 20, 2014 (S. Kor.); Supreme Court [S. Ct.], 2006Da40423, October 13, 2006 (S. Kor.); Supreme Court [S. Ct.], 2002Da61965, June 9, 2005 (S. Kor.).

[51] *Burberry*, *supra* note 35; Supreme Court [S. Ct.], 2008Da7462, January 30, 2009 (S. Kor.).

[52] The Japanese Supreme Court clearly stated that the extent of patent exhaustion is an issue of domestic patent law, having no relevance to the principles of territoriality and patent independence under the Paris Convention. Interestingly, the Supreme Court held that the patentee and the buyer have the right to contract to preclude international exhaution. See Jinzo Fujino, *Parallel Imports of Patented Goods: The Supreme Court Talks About Its Legality*, 22 A.I.P.P.I. J. 163 (1997) (translating and discussing the Japanese Supreme Court's decision in Jap-Auto Products v. BBS Kraftfahrzeug Technique A.G., Case No. Heisei 7(wo) 1988, delivered on July 1, 1997).

[53] DUK-KYU CHOI, *supra* note 47. In the case of trademarks, if contractual limitations are express, particular marking requirements should be compulsory, because the consumer should be protected from confusion as to sources of goods. If any marking to indicate some marketing restriction is removed or lost, a penalty or criminal remedy will be applied. TMA, § 95.

[54] DUK-KYU CHOI, *supra* note 47, at 2.

[55] *Ibid.* at 2. However, the "consent" for international exhaustion of trademarked goods is limited to a relationship with a subsidiary or affiliated company, or an agreement with a licensee.

III. PARALLEL IMPORTS AND COMPETITION LAW

A policy of national exhaustion is a government provided international restriction on vertical distribution. Each country that adopts this approach gives rights owners full rights to distribute goods themselves or through authorized dealers, including the right to exclude imports. Countries allowing parallel imports leave it to the market to determine commercial distribution channels. In Korea, however, commercial arrangements that result in vertical restrictions may be subject to competition laws to ensure that they do not result in anticompetitive outcomes.[56] In fact, strong competition laws may be a prerequisite to ensure that competitive market outcomes from parallel trade are realized. As in other jurisdictions, one's rights in a given trademark are limited by the Monopoly Regulation and Fair Trade Act (MRFTA) on anticompetitive practices. The MRFTA protects parallel imports to a certain extent, because they generally have the effect of enhancing competition in the Korean market. The basic presumption is that unfair obstruction of such parallel imports will constitute a violation of the MRFTA as an unfair business practice.[57] Further, a guideline of the Korean Fair Trade Commission (KFTC) provides for conditions under which parallel imports are permitted.

The KFTC announced guidelines on parallel imports in 1995,[58] and changed the Guidelines on Types of Unfair Trade Conducts Regarding Parallel Import in 1997,[59] 1998,[60] and 2009[61] to raise legal transparency regarding parallel imports by specifically illustrating major examples of unfair parallel imports.

The following are considered types of unfair conduct that interfere with parallel imports and are prohibited *inter alia*:

- interrupting the purchase of authentic goods from the foreign channels of distribution;
- restrictions against the distributors' handling of parallel imports;
- discriminatory treatment against sellers who deal with the parallel imports;
- suspension and refusal of product supply to sellers who deal with parallel imports; and
- restrictions on selling of the exclusively imported goods to a retailer who deals with the parallel imports.[62]

According to regulations of the Korean Fair Trade Committee (KFTC), the trademark owner cannot block the parallel imports under a relationship with a subsidiary or affiliated company, or an agreement with an exclusive licensee, KFTC Notification No. 23/2009, § 5.

[56] Since a third party other than a person who has an exclusive importing right imports authentic commercial goods through other distribution channels, parallel import generally has the effect of promoting competition, and thus unfairly impeding such will constitute a violation of the Korean competition law, KFTC Notification No. 23/2009, § 4(1).

[57] KFTC Notification No. 23/2009, § 4.
[58] KFTC Notification No. 10/1995.
[59] KFTC Notification No. 27/1997.
[60] KFTC Notification No. 19/1998.
[61] KFTC Notification No. 23/2009.
[62] KFTC Notification No. 23/2009, §§ 5–9.

The types of practices that could constitute an unfair trade practice are defined very broadly. Therefore, in principle, parallel imports are allowed in Korea under these Guidelines, and any action to unreasonably prevent parallel imports may be considered a violation of the MRFTA.

The Supreme Court held that in order to constitute this type of unfair trade practice, there must exist a reasonable causation between the act of a person with an exclusive importing right, having discovered the channel of purchase from the product number of parallel imports, etc., and the result preventing a person with the foreign trademark right from supplying products to his foreign customer who deals with the same products.[63]

The Court also pointed out that the existence of injustice must be determined after collectively examining various circumstances that may have surfaced in an individual case, such as the intention and purpose of the concerned exercise of rights; the impeding effect on price competitiveness; the characteristics of the concerned product and the situation of the market; the status of the person conducting the act in the market; the effect on the parallel importer, etc., in order to determine whether there is a danger of impeding fair trade. The burden of proof for this lies with the defendant.

IV. PARALLEL IMPORTS AND CUSTOMS LAW

Last, the Customs Tax Act (CTA), which provides for the protection of trademarks at the border, is also relevant to the practice of parallel imports. The Regulations[64] of the Korea Customs Office (KCS) were introduced because the enforcement measures enacted under the Customs Act to prevent the import of infringing goods were being used by exclusive licensors, licensees, and the KCS to prevent the parallel importation of genuine goods into Korea. The Regulations provide that the foreign trademark is affixed to the goods under the foreign trademark owner's authorization and either: (i) "the foreign and local trademark owners are the same or are in a relationship making them essentially the same entity," such as common ownership or control or an agency relationship; or (ii) the domestic trademark owner grants a "local exclusive license," the licensee being in a business relationship as described above, but excluding situations where the licensee is only involved in domestic manufacturing and sales of the trademarked goods.[65]

Here again, the crucial issue is the relationship between the foreign and domestic trademark owners. According to the Regulations of the KCS:

> if a trademark owner manufactures and sells his branded goods within the territory of Korea, the trademark owner may block parallel imports from another country, even if the imported goods have been put on the market in that country by the trademark owner or with his consent. However, if a trademark owner does not manufacture his branded goods within the territory of Korea, the trademark owner cannot block parallel imports.[66]

---

[63] Supreme Court [S. Ct.], 2000Du3184, May 2, 2002 (S. Kor.).
[64] Notifications for Import and Export Customs Clearance Procedures for Intellectual Property Rights (Korea Customs Office Notification), last revised in Notification No. 2014-57, effective 20 May 2014 [hereinafter KCS Notification].
[65] KCS Notification No. 57/2014, § 5.
[66] DUK-KYU CHOI, *supra* note 47, at 1–2.

Accordingly, an unrelated foreign trademark owner may be prohibited from importing its foreign trademarked goods. These Regulations are based on the economic and political aspects rather than legal aspects.

If a trademark owner learns about suspicious shipments of parallel importing or imitated products, the trademark right owner can seek protection through the KCS once the registered trademark has been recorded with the KCS by submitting an application for "Report of Trademark Right" and other required documents.[67] Then, custom clearance of the suspicious shipment is withheld for temporary detainment and the trademark owner can seek remedies through civil action, injunction against infringement, or criminal sanction.[68]

V. CONCLUSION

Parallel imports of trademarked products have recently become a subject of heated debate in Korea. Under Korean practice, without any specific provision on the issue, parallel imports are believed to promote competition, since these imports permit multiple parties to import the same product through different distribution channels. Accordingly, parallel imports are considered a legitimate business activity under the Trademark Act, the MRFTA, and the UCPA.

In contrast, trademark owners may file a claim to prohibit the sale of parallel imported products when a product is counterfeit, or if a product is of different quality and/or specification. Trademark owners may also oppose the sale of imported products where the parallel importer forges/falsifies the trademark or the actual origin of the product to mislead consumers into believing that such product is identical to the authorized products distributed in Korea.

However, it has been argued that the current legal system provides insufficient protection to well-known trademark owners. Korea is transitioning from a brand-importing country to a brand-exporting country. Current legal rules governing parallel import may need to be revised to achieve a careful balance between consumer interest and the trademark owners' proprietary interests, taking into account the globalization of international transactions involving multiple countries.[69]

---

[67] KCS Notification No. 57/2014, §§ 13–19.
[68] TMA, §§ 65–70, 93.
[69] Emma (Kyoung-Joo) Park, *Suggestions for Improving Korea's Parallel Importation System*, 13 ASIA-MENA COUNSEL (2015), available at www.inhousecommunity.com/controlPanel/download.php?id=1000306&download=1.

22. Trademark exhaustion and the Internet of resold things
Yvette Joy Liebesman* and Benjamin Wilson**

I. INTRODUCTION

Over the past ten years, casual resellers have migrated from garage sales, swap meets, and classified ads to eBay and Craigslist, turning side hobbies into lucrative businesses. Today, 30 million new ads are posted on Craigslist every month, and six million new listings are posted daily on eBay.[1] The explosive online market has affected the sales of new goods, troubling manufacturers[2] who seek to curtail the growth of this secondary market through several avenues—some legitimate, and others not so much. For example, to combat diversion to resellers outside of its official distribution chain, Tiffany, Inc., the well-known jeweler, attempted to institute a policy of limiting retail sales of identical items to lots of five or fewer, though this proved to be unsuccessful due to its sporadic enforcement.[3]

Manufacturers have also tried to stifle the resale market by suing resellers and auction sites for trademark and copyright infringement,[4] attempting wholesale removal of their goods on auction websites and other unauthorized distribution channels, and using auction site take-down notice procedures that are supposed to be reserved for removing counterfeit and infringing goods.[5] These actions go beyond trademark bullying and are more than merely stopping a merchant from using the owner's mark—the goal is to remove the reseller's goods from the market altogether. Courts have aided manufacturers

---

* Professor of Law, Saint Louis University School of Law.
** Associate at HeplerBroom LLC. This chapter is excerpted from an article originally published in the George Mason Law Review, *The Mark of a Resold Good*, 20 GEO. MASON L. REV. 157 (2012).

[1] reComparison Contributor, *eBay vs. Craigslist*, reComparison (2015), http://recomparison.com/comparisons/100646/ebay-vs-craigslist/; Tiffany (NJ) Inc. v. eBay, Inc., 576 F. Supp. 2d 463, 475 (S.D.N.Y. 2008), *aff'd in part*, 600 F.3d 93 (2d Cir. 2010).

[2] Ellie Mercado, Note, *As Long as "It" is Not Counterfeit: Holding eBay Liable for Secondary Trademark Infringement in the Wake of* LVMH *and* Tiffany Inc., 28 CARDOZO ARTS & ENT. L.J. 115, 116 (2010).

[3] See *Tiffany, supra* note 1, 576 F. Supp. 2d at 473 (stating that "rights holders . . . have obvious economic incentives to curtail the sale of . . . authentic goods on the Internet—after all, every sale . . . on eBay potentially represents a lost sales opportunity via [the manufacturer's] own authorized distribution channels").

[4] See Tiffany (NJ) Inc. v. eBay Inc., 600 F.3d 93, 96, 98 (2d Cir.), *cert. denied*, 131 S. Ct. 647 (2010) (noting that "[r]educing or eliminating the sale of all second-hand Tiffany goods, including genuine Tiffany pieces, through eBay's website would benefit Tiffany in at least one sense: [i]t would diminish the competition in the market for genuine Tiffany merchandise").

[5] See generally, Mary Kay, Inc. v. Weber, 601 F. Supp. 2d 632, 846 (N.D. Tex. 2009); *Tiffany, supra* note 1, 576 F. Supp. 2d at 481.

by ignoring the lack of confusion as to a good's source, and finding that online initial interest confusion as to sponsorship or affiliation of the distribution channel (even when the goods are the genuine goods of the mark owner) constitutes infringement. Under a claim of initial interest confusion, a mark owner is arguing that there is trademark infringement because, even though the consumers' confusion is "dispelled before an actual sale occurs," the end result is that the defendant "impermissibly capitalizes on the [good will] associated with a mark."[6] These courts' reasoning is contradicted by strong evidence showing that many consumers visit sites like eBay and Craigslist to find genuine goods at lower costs than they would find buying directly from the mark owner or authorized retailer, and are therefore not confused as to affiliation regarding distribution channel.[7]

Policies that advance the mark owner's ability to control all distribution channels harm consumers and disincentivize competition; manufacturers would have less motivation to innovate and improve their product when they control all distribution of goods beyond their first sale. Consumers would lose out on the competition that resellers provide.[8] We argue for an end to spurious claims of confusion where genuine goods are sold outside the manufacturer's distribution channel, as long as the reseller clearly disclaims any affiliation with the manufacturer or authorized distributor. Our suggestions would protect the lawful sale of goods in the secondary market while allowing manufacturers to prevent counterfeit products from being sold online.

II. THAT'S GONNA LEAVE A MARK

When one buys a Waterford crystal vase, the Waterford mark remains associated with the vase. No matter how many times that vase changes ownership, it remains identified as a Waterford vase. This serves a trademark's dual function of identifying the source of the vase and protecting the Waterford brand equity. "[T]rademark law protects the producer from pirates and counterfeiters" and others who would attempt to exploit the goodwill established by Waterford.[9] However, merely because the Waterford mark remains inextricably linked to its vases as a source indicator does not permit Waterford to control downstream sales of its goods outside its own distribution chains.[10] And while the Trademark

---

[6] Playboy Enters. v. Netscape Commc'ns Corp., 354 F.3d 1020, 1025 (9th Cir. 2004).

[7] See Eric Goldman, *Deregulating Relevancy in Internet Trademark Law*, 54 EMORY L.J. 507, 577 (2005). Prof. Goldman also discusses how customer surveys and other data show a variety of reasons for the use of trademark search terms, including finding distribution sources other than those authorized by the mark owner, and that there no evidence of confusion based on use of search terms. See *ibid.* at 522, 565.

[8] See generally, Mark A. Lemley & Mark P. McKenna, *Owning Mark(et)s*, 109 MICH. L. REV. 137, 187 (2010).

[9] See S. Rep. No. 100-515, at 4 (1988), *reprinted in* 1988 U.S.C.C.A.N. 5577, 5580 (stating trademark dual purpose of protecting "the public by making consumers confident that they can identify brands they prefer and can purchase those brands without being confused or misled" and protecting the brand equity of mark owners, who spend "conside[r]able time and money bringing a product to the marketplace.").

[10] Sebastian Int'l, Inc. v. Longs Drug Stores Corp., 53 F.3d 1073, 1074 (9th Cir. 1995) (per curiam).

Act of 1946 (Lanham Act) is intended to promote quality goods and services by protecting producers' goodwill, it is irrelevant whether the customer even knows the identity of the source. Consumers do not need to know that Kimberly-Clark makes "Huggies" disposable diapers, so long as the consumer recognizes that the "Huggies" mark identifies a single source of the good. As long as the customer is not confused as to the source of these genuine goods, then it should be irrelevant whether it was sold through the mark owner's own distribution channel or a reseller.[11]

A. Genuine Goods

The legislative history of the Lanham Act and related case law recognizes the need to protect consumers from passing off or otherwise confusing customers into purchasing goods that are not the genuine goods of the mark owner.[12] Trademarks serve to (1) foster competition in the marketplace;[13] (2) encourage manufacturers to maintain the quality of goods;[14] (3) "discourage those who hope to sell inferior products by capitalizing on a consumer's inability quickly to evaluate the quality of an item offered for sale;"[15] (4) help consumers locate products and services more efficiently;[16] and (5) serve as a "species of advertising."[17] And while trademark protection may have some anticompetitive consequences, "such protection may nevertheless remain justified so long as the mark improves the flow of otherwise indiscernible information concerning . . . the product to consumers, and . . . consumer desires to producers."[18]

B. Harsh Realities

Although it would appear that, based on nominative fair use and first sale/exhaustion principles, online secondary-sale merchants have a strong and valid affirmative defense against any claims of trademark infringement and should, thus, be free from interference by the mark owners, the reality of fighting these charges may be enough to shut down a secondary market business. The Internet Service Providers (ISPs) and auction sites also may face accusations of contributory infringement should they refuse to remove listings

---

[11] Mastercrafters Clock & Radio Co. v. Vacheron & Constantin-Le Coultre Watches, Inc., 221 F.2d 464, 466 (2d Cir. 1955); J. THOMAS MCCARTHY, MCCARTHY ON TRADEMARKS AND UNFAIR COMPETITION § 3:7 (4th ed. 2012).

[12] Park 'N Fly, Inc. v. Dollar Park and Fly, Inc., 469 U.S. 189, 198 (1985); S. Rep. No. 79-1333, at 3 (1946).

[13] S. Rep. No. 79-1333, at 4 ("To protect trade-marks, therefore, is to protect the public from deceit, to foster fair competition, and to secure to the business community the advantages of reputation and good will by preventing their diversion from those who have created them to those who have not.").

[14] *Park 'N Fly*, supra note 12, 469 U.S. at 198.

[15] ROGER E. SCHECHTER & JOHN R. THOMAS, INTELLECTUAL PROPERTY: THE LAW OF COPYRIGHTS, PATENTS AND TRADEMARKS § 25.3, at 547 (2003) (quoting Qualitex Co. v. Jacobson Products Co., 514 U.S. 159, 164 (1995)).

[16] See e.g. *Qualitex Co.*, supra note 15, 514 U.S. at 163–64.

[17] Northam Warren Corp. v. Universal Cosmetic Co., 18 F.2d 774, 774 (7th Cir. 1927).

[18] Glynn S. Lunney, Jr., *Trademark Monopolies*, 48 Emory L.J. 367, 431 (1999).

for the allegedly offending goods. Oftentimes, the small reseller cannot afford an attorney to defend itself.[19] Reseller-defendants may face the same fate as Veoh Networks, which, even though it was cleared of copyright infringement liability, was fatally wounded defending itself. "Veoh is legal, but Veoh is dead—killed by rightsowner lawfare that bled it dry."[20] Likewise, resellers may be dead right, but dead nonetheless if they attempt to fight big plaintiffs who are more concerned with shutting down competition than proving infringement.

III. WAGING LAWFARE

In addition to using threatening cease-and-desist letters, mark owners have not been shy about pursuing their claims in court.[21] The most common suits brought against online resellers are claims of either infringement or false designation of origin or description regarding the reseller's affiliation with the mark owner as an "authorized" distributor, often based on initial interest confusion.[22] Other claims sometimes alleged include trademark dilution, tortious interference with business relations, copyright infringement, and false advertising.[23]

A. Claiming All Sorts of Confusion

In her *prima facie* case, a plaintiff mark owner suing for trademark infringement must demonstrate that (1) she is the owner of a registered mark; (2) the defendant has used a mark in commerce in connection with goods or services as an indicator of source or sponsorship; and (3) this use is likely to cause customer confusion.[24] Of these elements, the last is the key in any infringement suit.[25] Supposedly, "likelihood" is not the mere possibility of confusion; customer confusion must be "probable," and the likelihood of confusion must affect an "appreciable or substantial number of consumers."[26] The eight factors adopted by the Second Circuit in *Polaroid Corp. v. Polarad Electronics Corp.* are typical of those

---

[19] Leah Chan Grinvald, *Shaming Trademark Bullies*, Wisc. L. Rev. 625, 647–48, 653 (2011); Ina Steiner, *David Versus Goliath: eBay Sellers Take on Corporate America*, ECommercebytes (August 5, 2003), available at www.ecommercebytes.com/cab/abn/y03/m08/i05/s02; Melvin Simensky & Eric C. Osterberg, *The Insurance and Management of Intellectual Property Risks*, 17 CARDOZO ARTS & ENT. L.J. 321, 337 (1999).
[20] See Eric Goldman, *UMG v. Shelter Capital: A Cautionary Tale of Rightsowner Overzealousness*, Tech. & Mktg. Law Blog (December 27, 2011), available at http://blog.ericgoldman.org/archives/2011/12/umg_v_shelter_c.htm.
[21] See William McGeveran, *Rethinking Trademark Fair Use*, 94 Iowa L. Rev. 49, 63–64 (2008).
[22] 15 U.S.C. § 1114(1) (2006); § 1125(a)(1); see also generally, Volkswagenwerk Aktiengesellschaft v. Church, 411 F.2d 350, 352 (9th Cir. 1969).
[23] 15 U.S.C. § 1125(c)(1); see e.g. Coastal Abstract Serv., Inc. v. First Am. Title Ins. Co., 173 F.3d 725, 733 (9th Cir. 1999) (tortious interference); see Sally Beauty Co. v. Beautyco, Inc., 304 F.3d 964, 970 (10th Cir. 2002) (false advertising).
[24] See e.g. Dep't of Parks & Recreation v. Bazaar del Mundo, Inc., 448 F.3d 1118, 1124 (9th Cir. 2006).
[25] Bird v. Parsons, 289 F.3d 865, 877 (6th Cir. 2002).
[26] Rodeo Collection, Ltd. v. West Seventh, 812 F.2d 1215, 1217 (9th Cir. 1987); Mushroom

used by other circuits. Courts consider: (1) the strength of the plaintiff's mark; (2) the degree of similarity between the plaintiff's and the defendant's marks; (3) the proximity of the products or services covered by the marks; (4) the likelihood that the plaintiff will bridge the gap; (5) evidence of actual confusion of consumers; (6) the defendant's good faith in adopting the mark; (7) the quality of the defendant's product or service; and (8) consumer sophistication.[27]

Resellers are usually accused of confusion as to affiliation or sponsorship; that is, the consumer is likely to think that the reseller is an authorized distributor or affiliated with the mark owner, even if, upon visiting the reseller's website, the consumer immediately realizes this is not the case.[28] In their assertions, mark owners often compare this initial interest confusion to a "bait and switch": the plaintiff claims that the defendant has used the plaintiff's mark in a way that gains the consumers' initial attention.[29] Initial interest confusion relies on the notion that, due to being initially drawn to the competitor:

> [e]ven though the consumer eventually may realize that the product is not the one originally sought, he or she may stay with the competitor. In that way, the competitor has captured the trademark holder's potential visitors or customers . . . Even if the consumer eventually becomes aware of the source's actual identity, or where no actual sale results, there is nonetheless damage to the trademark.[30]

Initial interest confusion is a controversial claim and has not been accepted by all circuits. On the one hand, the Ninth Circuit recognizes "that the use of another's trademark in a manner calculated 'to capture initial consumer attention, even though no actual sale is finally completed as a result of the confusion, may be still an infringement.'"[31] The Fourth Circuit, however, describes it as "relatively new and sporadically applied" and has refused to consider the doctrine as a legitimate claim under the Lanham Act.[32] The First Circuit also rejects initial interest confusion.[33]

The initial interest confusion doctrine "is at odds with the purpose, intent, and literal meaning of the Lanham Act"[34] and we should question the outright validity of the doctrine. As Professor Jennifer Rothman argues:

> [a]pplication of the initial interest confusion doctrine prevents comparative advertisements, limits information available to consumers, and shuts down speech critical of trademark holders

---

Makers, Inc. v. R.G. Barry Corp., 580 F.2d 44, 47 (2d Cir. 1978) (per curiam); Schechter and Thomas, *supra* note 15, § 29.1, at 638–40.

[27] Polaroid Corp. v. Polarad Electronics Corp., 287 F.2d 492, 495 (2d Cir. 1961); Schechter and Thomas, *supra* note 15, § 29.1, at 640.

[28] See 15 U.S.C. § 1125(a)(1); Designer Skin, LLC. v. S & L Vitamins, Inc., 560 F. Supp. 2d 811, 818 (D. Ariz. 2008).

[29] See Vail Assocs., Inc. v. Vend-Tel-Co., 516 F.3d 853, 872 (10th Cir. 2008). For a synopsis of the case history of initial interest confusion, see Jennifer E. Rothman, *Initial Interest Confusion: Standing at the Crossroads of Trademark Law*, 27 Cardozo L. Rev. 105, 114–21 (2005).

[30] Austl. Gold, Inc. v. Hatfield, 436 F.3d 1228, 1238–39 (10th Cir. 2006) (citations omitted).

[31] Brookfield Commc'ns, Inc. v. W. Coast Entm't Corp. 174 F.3d 1036, 1062 (9th Cir. 1999).

[32] Lamparello v. Falwell, 420 F.3d 309, 315–16 (4th Cir. 2005).

[33] See N. Light Tech., Inc. v. N. Lights Club, 97 F. Supp. 2d 96, 113 (D. Mass. 2000).

[34] Lisa M. Sharrock, *Realigning the Initial Interest Confusion Doctrine with the Lanham Act*, 25 Whittier L. Rev. 53, 54 (2003).

and their products and services . . . [It] undermines the free market system under a misguided notion that competition in and of itself is unfair.[35]

B. Acts of Aggression

Encouraged by the expansion of trademark protection in the courts, mark owners have become increasingly aggressive in policing their marks. Since:

> the middle part of the twentieth century, courts [have] expanded the range of actionable confusion beyond confusion over the actual source of a product—trademark law's traditional concern—to include claims against uses that might confuse consumers about whether the trademark owner sponsors or is affiliated with the defendant.[36]

Courts are finding liability even when consumers "couldn't possibly have been confused about the actual source of the defendants' products":[37]

> The actionable confusion, according to these courts, was not confusion that would have led consumers to buy the wrong product, or even to wrongly think they were buying from the trademark owner. Rather, the theory in [the examples described by Professors Lemley and McKenna] was that consumers would think there was some relationship between the trademark owner and the defendant based on the defendant's use of the trademark. The problem with this formulation is that it fails to specify the types of relationships about which confusion is relevant or the harm that supposedly flows from confusion about those relationships.[38]

Resellers are often at the mercy of spurious trademark and copyright infringement claims, and some courts have ignored affirmative defenses in finding infringement.[39] Some courts have accepted that confusion with regard to distribution of genuine goods is a valid form of trademark infringement, ignoring that there is no confusion as to the source of the goods—thus eviscerating the first sale affirmative defense. These forms of confusion, however, were not envisioned to apply to a competitor's use of the mark to sell the mark owner's own goods.[40] Rather, it "results when a consumer seeks a particular trademark holder's product and instead is lured to the product of a competitor by the competitor's use of the same or a similar mark."[41]

Thus, in spite of the genuineness of the article sold through resellers, these online resale businesses face the prospect of infringement suits due to courts' broadening interpretation of what constitutes actionable confusion. Indeed, since 1958, "the law's traditional willingness to permit a considerable degree of confusion in order to leave room for competitive imitation vanished, and courts began to seize on the slightest evidence of

---

[35] Rothman, *supra* note 29, at 108, 111 (arguing that "the doctrine is wrong as a matter of policy and . . . it represents an assault on the fundamental principles of trademark law").
[36] Mark A. Lemley & Mark McKenna, *Irrelevant Confusion*, 62 STAN. L. REV. 413, 414 (2010).
[37] *Ibid.* at 416–21.
[38] *Ibid.* at 421–22.
[39] Grinvald, *supra* note 19, at 660–61.
[40] Mary Kay, Inc. v. Weber, No. 3:08-CV-0776-G, 2009 WL 2569070, at *3 (N.D. Tex. August 14, 2009).
[41] Austl. Gold, Inc. v. Hatfield, 436 F.3d 1228, 1238 (10th Cir. 2006).

confusion as proof of infringement."[42] By rejecting a first sale defense based on initial interest confusion—which lowers the bar for a finding of a likelihood of confusion and, thus, infringement liability—"courts have made it very difficult to resell goods online."[43] In essence, the ability to successfully claim initial interest confusion based on the distribution channel eviscerates the first sale/exhaustion defense for Internet resellers, even when any confusion ends before the sale is consummated.[44] Such decisions seem contradictory to both congressional intent and Supreme Court precedent.

C. Mixing It Up

Mark owners have also sought to indirectly stifle resellers by accusing the resellers' web hosts of infringement through claims of contributory infringement.[45] ISPs and online auction sites would find it very useful if the Lanham Act had an Internet safe harbor provision similar to section 512 of the Copyright Act. Under this section, if a rights holder notifies a service provider such as eBay that infringing copyrighted material is stored in its system, in order to be immune from a suit for monetary damages, the service provider must promptly remove the allegedly infringing work. The limitations of copyright rights, however, should, in theory, thwart attempts to remove listings of genuine items for resale. However, this copyright misuse leaves the mark owners vulnerable to lawsuits under section 512(f) of the Digital Millennium Copyright Act (DMCA), which states that:

> [a]ny person who knowingly materially misrepresents under [section 512] . . . shall be liable for any damages, including costs and attorneys' fees, incurred by the alleged infringer . . . who is injured by such misrepresentation.

The Copyright Act of 1976 provides copyright owners the exclusive right to reproduce, make adaptations, distribute, publicly display, and publicly perform their works. Since photographing a three-dimensional copyrighted work results in a reproduction and adaptation of that work, photographing a Waterford vase, even for the purpose of using the photograph in an advertisement selling the vase, would theoretically infringe on the copyright owner's reproduction and adaptation right, and avail the copyright owner of the section 512 take-down provisions.[46] There are, however, several limitations on these exclusive rights, including 17 U.S.C. § 113(c), which declares that it is not copyright infringement for others to make and distribute pictures or photos of a useful article, such as our hypothetical Waterford vase, in connection with ads or commentaries related to the distribution or display of such articles, so long as the vase has been offered for sale or distributed to the public.

---

[42] Lunney, *supra* note 18, at 371, 385.
[43] Rothman, *supra* note 29, at 140–45.
[44] See Deborah F. Buckman, *Initial Interest Confusion Doctrine Under Lanham Trademark Act*, 183 A.L.R. Fed. 553, 607–8 (2003).
[45] Cf. John T. Cross, *Contributory Infringement and Related Theories of Secondary Liability for Trademark Infringement*, 80 Iowa L. Rev. 101, 101–2 (1994); Elizabeth K. Levin, *A Safe Harbor for Trademark: Reevaluating Secondary Trademark Liability After* Tiffany v. eBay, 24 Berkeley Tech. L.J. 491, 506 (2009).
[46] 17 U.S.C. §§ 106(1)–(2).

Even so, mark owners persist in bullying resellers to remove photographs of their items from websites based on a trademark likelihood of confusion claim, eviscerating the exception delineated in section 113.[47] For example, Standard Process separately sued two resellers of dietary supplements for trademark infringement, based in part on their use of photographs of Standard Process's products that were being resold online by the defendants. Standard Process sent cease-and-desist letters, stating that use of those photographs violated trademark law.[48] Yet there was no reason the defendants should have removed the photographs: in addition to section 113, the trademark first sale doctrine includes the ability to "stock, *display*, and resell"—posting photographs of products online amounts to displaying the products.[49] Their removal, according to Professor Rebecca Tushnet, is "caving to bullying" and unwarranted.[50]

Product photographs can actually help mark owners identify counterfeit products. So, ironically, by creating an environment in which product photographs cause liability, mark owners make it even more difficult—for themselves and consumers—to identify counterfeit products.[51] Of course, a major motive for removing photographs from the reseller's auction listings is that this will hurt sales. eBay even lists as one of its most effective strategies the use of "photos from a variety of angles."[52] If mark owners were able to claim that a reseller's use of photographs constitutes trademark infringement, this would be an end run around section 113 of the Copyright Act and eviscerate any protection it affords. Misusing copyright and trademark law points to a single objective: to decrease the competition of secondary markets. Small dealers are faced with either defending themselves or ceasing operations.[53]

D. Further Pursuits

In addition to attacking resellers, in their aggressive pursuit to shut down the Internet resale market, mark owners have also taken their fight to ISPs and online auction sites, alleging contributory infringement based on resellers' use of these sites to advertise the mark owners' goods. In their suits, mark owners allege that auction sites are not doing enough to stop counterfeiters; however, the mark owners also have the objective of

---

[47] See Rebecca Tushnet, *Supplemental Complaint: Internet Resale Case Survives Summary Judgment*, Rebecca Tushnet's 43(B)log (June 12, 2008), available at http://tushnet.blogspot.com/2008/06/supplemental-complaint-internet-resale.html.

[48] Standard Process, Inc. v. Total Health, Disc., Inc., 559 F. Supp. 2d 932, 936 (E.D. Wis. 2008); Standard Process, Inc. v. Banks, 554 F. Supp. 2d 866, 868 (E.D. Wisc. 2008).

[49] See Sebastian Int'l, Inc. v. Longs Drug Stores Corp., 53 F.3d 1073, 1076 (9th Cir. 1995) (per curiam) (emphasis added).

[50] Tushnet, *supra* note 47.

[51] Michelle C. Leu, Comment, *Authenticate This: Revamping Secondary Trademark Liability Standards to Address a Worldwide Web of Counterfeits*, 26 BERKELEY TECH. L.J. 591, 616–17 (2011); *How to Identify Counterfeit MAC Products: eBay Guides* (eBay October 26, 2011), available at www.ebay.com/gds/How-to-identify-fake-MAC-Cosmetics-Lipsticks-Viva-Glam-/10000000104967214/g.html.

[52] *Take Product Photos that Sell* (eBay 2015), http://pages.ebay.com/sellerinformation/tips-for-selling-online/effective-ebay-listings/product-photos.html.

[53] See Grinvald, *supra* note 19, at 647, 650–51.

removing genuine goods from this alternative distribution channel.[54] For example, in 2002, Tiffany & Co., the well-known jewelry company, began pressuring eBay to summarily remove Tiffany goods that met some general criteria (such as merchants selling more than five items) alleging that bulk sales outside Tiffany's normal distribution chain had to be counterfeit. When eBay refused to do so, Tiffany sued, contending that eBay was "facilitating and advertising the sale of 'Tiffany' goods that turned out to be counterfeit."[55]

eBay was successful in defending both direct and indirect infringement claims based on the defenses of nominative fair use and lack of control over the merchants who use the site. The Second Circuit declined to find eBay contributorily liable, stating "that eBay's practice was promptly to remove the challenged listing from its website, warn sellers and buyers, cancel fees it earned from that listing, and direct buyers not to consummate the sale of the disputed item."[56] While the court found that eBay did possess general knowledge that counterfeit items were listed on its website, it held that under the Supreme Court test outlined in *Inwood Laboratories, Inc. v. Ives Laboratories, Inc.*,[57] generalized knowledge was not sufficient "to impose upon eBay an affirmative duty to remedy the problem."[58] Other websites have also successfully defended themselves against similar suits.[59]

In spite of winning in court, these websites want to avoid suits for contributory infringement, and will take an unnecessarily strong conservative approach regarding accused listings. The hosts want to ensure that they are viewed merely as "conduits" between the buyer and seller with no direct control over the listed goods,[60] and will usually remove listings based on any accusation by the mark owner. If it is later proved (by the entity listing the good for sale) that it is indeed a genuine good and there is no confusion as to "distribution channel" affiliation, the item is relisted. This cycle of removing/disputing/relisting, however, costs the resellers of genuine goods time, money, and frustration and creates added burdens to both the reseller and the auction site, stifling the sale of goods for both parties.[61] Under the eBay model, every time an item is listed, the auction site earns a

---

[54] See e.g. Tiffany (NJ) Inc. v. eBay, Inc., 600 F.3d 93, 98, 101 (2d Cir.), *cert. denied*, 131 S. Ct. 647 (2010).

[55] *Ibid.* at 101. Tiffany claimed "direct and contributory trademark infringement, trademark dilution, and false advertising." *Ibid.* The allegation that bulk sales were counterfeit was rejected by both the district court and on appeal. *Ibid.* at 109 n.13.

[56] *Ibid.* at 103 (agreeing "with the district court that eBay's use of Tiffany's mark on its website and in sponsored links was lawful. eBay used the mark to describe accurately the genuine Tiffany goods offered for sale on its website. And none of eBay's uses of the mark suggested that Tiffany affiliated itself with eBay or endorsed the sale of its products through eBay's website."); *ibid.* at 106, 109 (holding that eBay was not contributorily liable because it had not continued "to supply its [service] to one whom it knows or has reason to know is engaging in trademark infringement" (quoting Inwood Labs., Inc. v. Ives Labs., Inc., 456 U.S. 844, 854 (1982)).

[57] 456 U.S. 844, 853–54 (1982).

[58] *Tiffany*, *supra* note 4, 600 F.3d at 107 (quoting Tiffany (NJ) Inc. v. eBay, Inc., 576 F. Supp. 2d 463, 508 (S.D.N.Y. 2008), *aff'd in part*, 600 F.3d 93 (2d Cir. 2010)).

[59] See e.g. GMA Accessories, Inc. v. BOP, LLC, 765 F. Supp. 2d 457, 465 (S.D.N.Y. 2011).

[60] See e.g. *Tiffany*, *supra* note 4, 600 F.3d at 98–99; Sellify, Inc. v. Amazon.com, Inc., 09 Civ. 10268 (JSR), 2010 WL 4455830, *4 (S.D.N.Y. November 4, 2010).

[61] Cf. *Tiffany*, *supra* note 1, 576 F. Supp. 2d at 474, 517 (noting that "Tiffany has occasionally been wrong [in alleging that an item listed on eBay was counterfeit] and later requested that listings

fee, and another fee is earned when the item is sold. Yet when a "take down" occurs, the listing fee is returned to the seller, depriving the host of the fee for a legitimate good.[62] If the reseller eventually gives up due to the burden of constantly having to defend legitimate auction listings to the host, then both the reseller and the host lose the income that is generated from the listing and sale of the good.[63]

A clearly defined and strong trademark first sale doctrine would give auction hosting sites less concern over potential lawsuits by mark owners who don't like their items being sold outside their authorized distribution channels.[64]

IV. GETTING DEFENSIVE

It has been repeatedly acknowledged that the producer of a good cannot prevent others from using the good's mark to truthfully describe the good. This basic belief is the foundation for both nominative fair use and first sale defenses, and "reflects the simple insight that anybody should be free to refer to goods and services by their brand names."[65]

A. Repackaged, Repaired, Resold

There are several ways to use another's mark in commerce that do not constitute infringement. These include, among others, when the vendor is (1) selling repackaged goods; (2) selling used or repaired goods; (3) reselling a genuine good. The repackager does not receive absolute protection under the first sale doctrine—the repackaging "can present a non-trivial harm to the producer's good will, and can deceive consumers who, in addition to identifying the trademark, have come to expect or rely upon a particular

---

be reinstated"). The Second Circuit noted that, since a substantial number of authentic Tiffany goods are sold on eBay, "[r]educing or eliminating the sale of all second-hand Tiffany goods, including genuine Tiffany pieces, through eBay's website would benefit Tiffany in at least one sense: It would diminish the competition in the market for genuine Tiffany merchandise." *Tiffany, supra* note 4, 600 F.3d at 98; *Tiffany, supra* note 1, 576 F. Supp. 2d. at 517 n. 39.

[62] *Standard Selling Fees* (eBay 2015), http://pages.ebay.com/help/sell/fees.html; *Why Did eBay Remove My Listing?* (eBay 2015), http://pages.ebay.com/help/sell/questions/listing-ended.html ("If we removed your listing because of a policy violation, we may or may not refund your fees for that listing, depending on the policy you violated and whether you've violated our policies in the past. If we refund your fees, all fees related to the removed listing will be automatically credited to your account within one billing cycle . . . If we agree that your item was removed in error, you can relist it. Unfortunately, you'll have to recreate the listing from scratch.").

[63] Cf. *Tiffany, supra* note 1, 576 F. Supp. 2d at 516 ("In addition to removing the [allegedly offending] listing, eBay also warned sellers and buyers, cancelled all fees associated with the listing, and directed buyers not to consummate the sale of the listed item.").

[64] "[T]rademark law needs a theory of trademark injury that distinguishes harm to legitimate interests the law should protect from a mere desire to capture a benefit enjoyed by another." Lemley and McKenna, *supra* note 8, at 137.

[65] See e.g. New Kids on the Block v. News Am. Publ'g, Inc., 971 F.2d 302, 307–8 (9th Cir. 1992); Michael Grynberg, *Things Are Worse Than We Think: Trademark Defenses in a "Formalist" Age*, 24 BERKELEY TECH. L.J. 897, 956 (2009).

type of packaging in their purchasing decisions."[66] When a "reseller's repackaging interferes with the trademark owner's ability to control the quality of its products . . . two harms can arise: harm to the consuming public in the form of deception and harm to the trademark owner in the form of loss of [goodwill]."[67] Thus, in order to avoid Lanham Act liability, when sellers purchase genuine goods and then repackage the goods for resale, these resellers generally must (1) disclose that they have repackaged the goods; (2) include their own name; (3) provide notice on the package that they are not affiliated with the manufacturer; and (4) must not give "undue prominence" to the good's mark. These rules for repackaged goods illustrate the underlying philosophy governing all sellers and resellers: an obligation to tell the truth regarding the source of the goods.[68]

A reseller who is selling a repaired good "has the right to resell the original product with the original trademark attached, as long as the reseller tells the truth about the origin of the repaired goods and about his responsibility for any repairs."[69] Just as a reseller must state that repackaged goods have been repackaged, a reseller of repaired goods must state that they have been repaired. At some point, however, repairs may be so extensive that the product "cannot properly be considered the same any longer" and the mark no longer truthfully describes the goods attached to it.[70]

B. Trademark Nominative Fair Use

Supposedly, "[u]se of the mark alone is not sufficiently probative of" an intent to deceive the public into believing that the mark owner endorsed or somehow supported the defendant's products or services,[71] and a defendant has a right to use a plaintiff's mark to truthfully describe the plaintiff's goods using the plaintiff's mark.[72] Yet in spite of its twenty-year history, the nominative fair use defense has mostly been confined to the Third, Fifth, and Ninth Circuits, and is not well understood in any of them.[73] Indeed, in the Ninth Circuit, it is not an affirmative defense; rather, it *replaces* likelihood of confusion in the plaintiff's *prima facie* case.[74] The First, Second, and Sixth Circuits have either rejected or declined to adopt nominative fair use,[75] and other courts have yet to

---

[66] Justin D. Swindells, *Repackaging Original Trademarked Goods: Trademark Exhaustion or Consumer Confusion?*, 7 FED. CIR. B.J. 391, 391–93 (1997).

[67] Ibid. at 402.

[68] SCHECHTER AND THOMAS, *supra* note 15, § 31.1.2, at 731. In the foundational nominative fair use case of Prestonettes, Inc. v. Coty, the Supreme Court recognized that when a "mark is used in a way that does not deceive the public," there is "no such sanctity in the word as to prevent its being used to tell the truth." Prestonettes, Inc. v. Coty, 264 U.S. 359, 368 (1924).

[69] David W. Barnes, *Free-Riders and Trademark Law's First Sale Rule*, 27 SANTA CLARA COMPUTER & HIGH TECH. L.J. 457, 486 (2011).

[70] SCHECHTER AND THOMAS, *supra* note 15, § 31.1.2, at 732; see also Champion Spark Plug Co. v. Sanders, 331 U.S. 125, 129 (1947).

[71] Century 21 Real Estate Corp. v. Lendingtree, Inc., 425 F.3d 211, 227 (3d Cir. 2005).

[72] New Kids on the Block v. News Am. Publ'g, Inc., 971 F.2d 302, 306 (9th Cir. 1992).

[73] See *Century 21 Real Estate*, *supra* note 71, 425 F.3d at 218.

[74] See e.g. Toyota Motor Sales, U.S.A., Inc. v. Tabari, 610 F.3d 1171, 1175 (9th Cir. 2010).

[75] Tiffany (NJ) Inc. v. eBay Inc., 600 F.3d 93, 102–3 (2d Cir.), *cert. denied*, 131 S. Ct. 647 (2010); Universal Commc'n Sys., Inc. v. Lycos, Inc., 478 F.3d 413, 424 (1st Cir. 2007); PACCAR

decide on its adoption or rejection.[76] In spite of this limited acceptance, nominative fair use is mentioned, albeit without a definition, in the Trademark Dilution Revision Act of 2006.[77]

The nominative fair use defense has been criticized for its analytical defects. As noted by Professor McGeveran, "[n]ominative fair use as it now exists has become ungainly and often unhelpful";[78] he succinctly summarizes the confused and inadequate state of the nominative fair use defense:

> [C]ourts have gradually larded up the simple idea of nominative fair use presented in *New Kids* to the point where it is excessively complex and minimally useful. By moving the doctrine away from any role as an early screening mechanism and closer in timing and substance to the likelihood of confusion determination, subsequent cases have destroyed nominative fair use.[79]

This muddled application of nominative fair use has adversely affected online resellers and unfairly strengthens mark owners' control over distribution channels for their goods beyond the initial sale to the public.[80]

C. That First Sale of a Genuine Good

The nominative fair use defense usually concerns comparative advertising or other instances where the defendant is selling its own goods and in some way refers to the mark owner's goods.[81] Under first sale/exhaustion, which could be considered a variation of nominative fair use, the defendant does not use the plaintiff's mark in an effort to sell the defendant's own goods, but rather uses the plaintiff's mark to refer to the plaintiff's goods, albeit with the intention of selling the plaintiff's goods. The first sale doctrine is

---

Inc. v. Telescan Techs., L.L.C., 319 F.3d 243, 256 (6th Cir. 2003), *overruled on other grounds by* KP Permanent Make-Up, Inc. v. Lasting Impression I, Inc., 543 U.S. 111, 121–23 (2004).

[76] The Fourth, Seventh, Eighth, Tenth, and Eleventh Circuits have to varying degrees declined to affirmatively state their position on nominative fair use. See Suntree Techs., Inc. v. EcoSense Int'l, Inc., 802 F. Supp. 2d 1273, 1282 (M.D. Fla. 2011); Teter v. Glass Onion, Inc., 723 F. Supp. 2d 1138, 1156 (W.D. Mo. 2010); Gennie Shifter, L.L.C. v. Lokar, Inc., No. 07-cv-01121, 2010 WL 126181, at *14 (D. Colo. January 12, 2010); Lorillard Tobacco Co. v. S & M Brands, Inc., 616 F. Supp. 2d 581, 589 (E.D. Va. 2009); DeVry Inc. v. Univ. of Med. & Health Sci.-St. Kitts, No. 08 CV 3280, 2009 WL 260950, at *5 (N.D. Ill. February 3, 2009).

[77] 15 U.S.C. § 1125(c)(3)(A) (2006). ("The following shall not be actionable as dilution by blurring or dilution by tarnishment under this subsection: . . . [a]ny fair use, including nominative . . . fair use, or facilitation of such fair use, of a famous mark by another person other than as a designation of source for the person's own goods or services.")

[78] McGeveran, *supra* note 21, at 89.

[79] *Ibid.* at 97.

[80] Cf. Mary Kay, Inc. v. Weber, 601 F. Supp. 2d 632, 857 (N.D. Tex. 2009) (applying the Ninth Circuit test to Ms. Weber's sale of Mary Kay products).

[81] See 15 U.S.C. § 1115(b)(4) (2006) ("[T]he right to use . . . [a] mark shall be subject to proof of infringement . . . and shall be subject to the following defenses or defects: . . . [t]hat the use . . . is descriptive of and used fairly and in good faith only to describe the goods or services of such party[.]"; Lindy Pen Co. v. Bic Pen Corp., 725 F.2d 1240, 1248 (9th Cir. 1984) ("[L]iability for infringement may not be imposed for using a registered trademark in connection with truthful comparative advertising.")).

based on the principle that trademark owners should not be able to control downstream sales of their goods.[82]

While first sale was legislatively created in the Copyright Act,[83] trademark and patent first sale (or exhaustion) affirmative defenses are long-recognized judicial constructs.[84] All three, however, serve a similar purpose: to "narrow the rights of the creator of intellectual property by creating competition between the creator and the reseller of the work."[85] As noted *supra*, the Supreme Court has recognized as early as 1924 that, even though it results in the secondary market merchant getting some advantage from the mark, a mark may be used by a refurbisher or reseller of a good in a way that does not deceive the public. Under the exhaustion doctrine:

> [t]he resale of genuine trademarked goods generally does not constitute infringement. This is for the simple reason that consumers are not confused as to the origin of the goods: the origin has not changed as a result of the resale . . . [T]he trademark protections of the Lanham Act are exhausted after the trademark owner's first authorized sale of that product. Therefore, even though a subsequent sale is without a trademark owner's consent, the resale of a genuine good does not violate the Act.[86]

It reflects a general public policy against restraints on alienation.[87] "[A]s a general matter, trademark law does not reach the sale of genuine goods bearing a true mark even though the sale is not authorized by the mark owner."[88] Thus, a reseller has the right to dispose of genuine goods that were originally produced under the authority of the mark owner, provided that the goods are not materially altered and the reseller does not give the impression it is affiliated with the manufacturer.[89] Because reselling the manufacturer's product can lead to some confusion as to the connection between the mark owner and the reseller, the first sale defense should not be:

---

[82] See *Sebastian Int'l, Inc. v. Longs Drug Stores Corp.*, 53 F.3d 1073, 1074 (9th Cir. 1995) (per curiam). For an in-depth discussion on the first sale rule and its rationale, see Barnes, *supra* note 70, at 461–69.

[83] 17 U.S.C. § 109(a) (2006). Patent law has a robust, but judicially created exhaustion principle. See *Quanta Computer, Inc. v. LG Elecs., Inc.*, 553 U.S. 617, 625 (2008).

[84] See e.g. *Champion Spark Plug Co. v. Sanders*, 331 U.S. 125, 129 (1947); *Prestonettes, Inc. v. Coty*, 264 U.S. 359, 360 (1924).

[85] Barnes, *supra* note 69, at 461.

[86] *Davidoff & Cie, S.A. v. PLD Int'l Corp.*, 263 F.3d 1297, 1301–2 (2001) (citations omitted); *Champion Spark Plug*, *supra* note 84, 331 U.S. at 129; see *Prestonettes*, *supra* note 84, 264 U.S. at 360.

[87] Barnes, *supra* note 69, at 458, 462 ("The first sale rule reflects property law's distaste for restraints on alienation and allows the holder of intellectual property rights to obtain the price for its creations only once.").

[88] *Bel Canto Design, Ltd. v. MSS HiFi, Inc.*, 837 F. Supp. 2d 208, 222 (S.D.N.Y. 2011) (quoting *Zip Int'l Grp., L.L.C. v. Trilini Imps., Inc.*, No. 09-CV-2437(JG)(VVP), 2011 WL 2132980, at *3 (E.D.N.Y. May 24, 2011)). MSS HiFi, however, had altered the goods' serial number, and the court found that these constituted "altered goods" which, as noted *supra*, are not genuine articles and "may generate consumer confusion about the source and quality of the trademarked product." *Ibid.* at 223 (citing *Beltronics USA*, 562 F.3d 1067, 1072 (April 9, 2009)).

[89] See *Champion Spark Plug Co.*, *supra* note 84, 331 U.S. at 129 ("[W]e would not suppose that one could be enjoined from selling a car whose valves had been reground and whose piston rings had been replaced unless he removed the name Ford or Chevrolet.").

rendered inapplicable merely because consumers erroneously believe the reseller is affiliated with or authorized by the producer. It is the essence of the "first sale" doctrine that a purchaser who does no more than stock, display, and resell a producer's product under the producer's trademark violates no right conferred upon the producer by the Lanham Act. When a purchaser resells a trademarked article under the producer's trademark, and nothing more, there is no actionable misrepresentation under the statute.[90]

Courts should tolerate more confusion than they typically do when the defendant is using a mark similar to the plaintiff's to sell the defendant's own goods.[91] As noted by David Barnes, courts tend to treat first sale "as an affirmative defense to what would otherwise be an infringement of the creator's rights ... [and] the trademark defendant has the burden of proving that it was reselling genuine and lawfully acquired goods."[92] However, it is the plaintiff's burden under the Lanham Act to establish likelihood of confusion as part of the *prima facie* case. Therefore, if the reason for the alleged likelihood of confusion claim is that the goods are not genuine, the plaintiff must prove that.[93] Exhaustion should apply equally to online sales as it does to brick-and-mortar stores. Courts, however, do not always do so, and (as discussed *infra*) by supporting plaintiffs' claims of trademark infringement, they extend control over the distribution channels of goods beyond the initial sale.[94]

V. CHALLENGING THE MARK OWNER'S DESIRE FOR TOTAL CONTROL

There is a need for comprehensive and definitive trademark nominative fair use and first sale doctrines with regard to online resale of genuine goods, along with more leeway regarding initial interest confusion related to distribution affiliation. Our solutions are supported by recent trademark scholarship advocating the need for a showing of actual injury, rather than "merely a benefit to someone else."[95]

---

[90] Sebastian Int'l, Inc. v. Longs Drug Stores Corp., 53 F.3d 1073, 1076 (9th Cir. 1995) (per curiam).
[91] *Ibid.* (applying the first sale doctrine despite consumer confusion).
[92] Barnes, *supra* note 69, at 465.
[93] KP Permanent Make-Up, Inc. v. Lasting Impression I, Inc., 543 U.S. 111, 121 (2004); Barnes, *supra* note 69, at 466–67.
[94] See e.g. Austl. Gold, Inc. v. Hatfield, 436 F.3d 1228, 1240–41 (10th Cir. 2006) (regarding a website); *Sebastian Int'l, Inc.*, *supra* note 90, 53 F.3d at 1076 (regarding a pharmacy); Lemley and McKenna, *supra* note 8, at 152–53.
[95] See Goldman, *supra* note 7, at 587; Lemley and McKenna, *supra* note 37, at 448–49; *supra* I.C; Lemley and McKenna, *supra* note 8, at 188. Professors Lemley and McKenna provide a two part test: "[T]rademark plaintiffs should have to demonstrate (1) that their injury flows from confusion about the actual source of the defendant's goods or about who is responsible for the quality of those goods; or (2) that the defendant's use causes confusion about some other relationship that is material to consumer purchasing decisions." *Ibid.*

A. Strengthening Available Defenses

There is a need for a rebalancing of the scales to prevent continued control by mark owners of the distribution of their products beyond the first sale. However, "[a]bsent congressional action, courts have only a limited ability to correct the imbalance between trademark liability and defenses."[96] For a legislative solution that would protect resellers of genuine goods without affecting a mark owner's ability to remove counterfeit goods from the marketplace, Congress could amend the Lanham Act by (1) codifying trademark first sale and nominative fair use as defenses under section 33(b); (2) eliminating the controversial claim of initial interest confusion regarding the sale of genuine goods; and (3) specifying a requirement of deceptive intent regarding distribution affiliation confusion for it to be an actionable claim.[97] This would generate uniformity among the circuits regarding nominative fair use, initial interest confusion, and the robustness of the first sale doctrine with regard to trademarks. Professor Michael Grynberg notes that when Congress passed the Trademark Anti-Dilution Act, it "enact[ed] specific safe harbors for activities that are unlikely to cause confusion or those that may cause confusion, but whose social utility is high enough that the benefits of immunizing the acts outweigh any costs."[98]

Since the trademark exhaustion doctrine has its roots in copyright law, an amendment to the Lanham Act could mimic section 109(a) of the Copyright Act:

> Notwithstanding the provisions of section 106(3) [the owner's exclusive right of distribution], the owner of a particular copy or phonorecord lawfully made under this title . . . is entitled, without the authority of the copyright owner, to sell or otherwise dispose of the possession of that copy or phonorecord.

Similar language would provide uniformity across these two oftentimes related intellectual property claims. If Lanham Act language clearly stated that the same first sale exception that applies for copyrights also applies for the use of the mark attached to the goods, this would give resellers more certainty in their use of the mark owner's brand when identifying the mark owner's goods during resale.

This solution should lead to less litigation; however, it may not stop the reality of cease-and-desist letters and threatened litigation. Penalties for threats of frivolous litigation are common, and are part of antitrust law, First Amendment protection, and copyright law.[99]

---

[96] Thompson v. N. Am. Stainless, L.P., 520 F.3d 644, 650 (6th Cir.) (Griffin, J., dissenting) (stating that courts tend to "legislate from the bench" only to implement what they believe is the intent of Congress), vacated, No. 07-5040, 2008 WL 6191996 (6th Cir. July 28, 2008); Grynberg, *supra* note 65, at 970.

[97] Cf. Lemley & McKenna, supra note 37, at 450 ("[T]he law should require that trademark owners claiming infringement based on confusion regarding anything other than source or responsibility for quality must demonstrate the materiality of that confusion to consumer purchasing decisions."); see also S&L Vitamins, Inc. v. Austl. Gold, Inc., 521 F. Supp. 2d 188, 202 (E.D.N.Y. 2007) ("Although the first sale doctrine traditionally applies as a defense to copyright infringement claims, courts have recognized it as a restraint on trademark infringement claims as well.").

[98] Grynberg, *supra* note 65, at 962.

[99] See 15 U.S.C. §§ 15(a)(1), 15a(1), 15c(a)(2)(A) (2006); Cal. Civ. Proc. Code §§ 425.16(a), (b)(1), (c)(1) (West 2012); 17 U.S.C. § 512(f) (2006).

Similarly worded language in the Lanham Act may prevent some of this bullying with regard to frivolous litigation.[100]

B. Expect Some Confusion

As noted *supra*, courts should move back towards their "traditional willingness to permit a considerable degree of confusion in order to leave room" for competition. Professor Glynn Lunney argues that, "we must limit actionable confusion to cases where, if the use is allowed to continue, a substantial number of purchasers or prospective purchasers will actually become confused concerning information that will materially influence their buying decisions."[101] Unless the mark owner can show actual deception on the part of the reseller, as a general rule plaintiffs should not be allowed to claim initial interest confusion with regard to alternative distribution channels of genuine goods. First, as long as there is no deception on the part of the reseller, any confusion as to "distribution channel" affiliation ends prior to the sale of the good.[102] Second, as noted earlier, many consumers visit sites like eBay and Craigslist for the purpose of finding genuine goods at lower costs than they would expect to find when buying directly from the mark owner or an authorized retailer.[103] Indeed, when a product is subject to first sale doctrine and the nominative fair use that accompanies it, some confusion should be expected. The Supreme Court declared in *KP Permanent Make-Up, Inc. v. Lasting Impressions I, Inc.* that:

> [s]ince the burden of proving likelihood of confusion rests with the plaintiff, and the fair use defendant has no free-standing need to show confusion unlikely, it follows . . . that some possibility of consumer confusion must be compatible with fair use, and so it is.[104]

Any initial confusion to the resale of a genuine good is related to the distribution source, not to the good itself; a claim of initial interest confusion should be a spurious allegation. An assertion of confusion as to the distributor's affiliation should be discounted—after all, there is no confusion as to the source of the good; the mark owner is truthfully the source of the good. And to hold a defendant liable for infringement where there may only be initial confusion as to whether the distribution channel is associated with the mark owner results in the mark owner controlling subsequent sales of his or her product.[105]

---

[100] Though it would do little to prevent the sending of threatening cease-and-desist letters, this matter is a problem faced by copyright and patent defendants as well and not an issue that will be discussed in this chapter. See Marketa Trimble, *Setting Foot on Enemy Ground: Cease-and-Desist Letters, DMCA Notifications and Personal Jurisdiction in Declaratory Judgment Actions*, 50 IDEA 777, 786–87 (2010).

[101] Lunney, *supra* note 18, at 478.

[102] Strange Music, Inc. v. Strange Music, Inc., 326 F. Supp. 2d 481, 492 (S.D.N.Y. 2004); Lemley and McKenna, *supra* note 37, at 448 (proposing that sponsorship or affiliation confusions should only be actionable if "they (1) are false or misleading and (2) materially affect consumer decisions").

[103] See Goldman, *supra* note 7, at 522–24 (discussing how search users can have a variety of reasons for the use of trademark search terms, including finding distribution sources other than those authorized by the mark owner).

[104] KP Permanent Make-Up, Inc. v. Lasting Impression I, Inc., 543 U.S. 111, 121–22 (2004).

[105] See Grynberg, *supra* note 65, at 907–8.

Although courts have declared that "[a]ffiliation confusion exists where use of a 'unique and recognizable identifier' could lead consumers to 'infer a relationship' between the trademark owner and the new product[,]"[106] this should not apply to the distribution of the goods after the initial sale, but rather only to the good itself. Otherwise, a finding of initial interest affiliation confusion because the seller is not affiliated with the mark owner would eviscerate any protection afforded through trademark law's first sale/exhaustion principle.[107]

We also should question whether initial interest affiliation confusion matters at all with regard to the secondary sale of goods. Courts have found such a claim spurious. In her concurrence in *Playboy Enterprises, Inc. v. Netscape Communications Corp.*, Judge Marsha Berzon contended that it was not "reasonable to find initial interest confusion when a consumer is never confused as to source or affiliation, but instead knows, or should know, from the outset that a product or web link is not related to that of the trademark holder because the list produced by the search engine so informs him."[108] Yet this form of confusion has been successfully asserted in Internet resale cases. Juries and judges have supported a finding of infringement based on initial interest affiliation confusion as to the distribution channel of the good, and have often discounted any first sale or nominative fair use defense.[109] Judges and juries seem to hold Internet sales to a different standard than consignment and resale shops in the brick-and-mortar world, where a plaintiff would face a much higher hurdle to show customer confusion with regard to distribution affiliation.[110]

There should be a presumption of non-infringement when a product's brand is used in the advertising for the reselling of an item, including in the description of it or use of a photograph of the item in an online sale. The plaintiff would have to overcome this presumption as part of his or her *prima facie* case.[111] Without a proven deception by the reseller, confusion as to affiliation with regard to distribution channels should be negated by the fact that the goods in question are genuine goods, and there is no confusion as to the actual source of the goods. "The words of the Lanham Act should not be stretched to cover matters that are typically of no consequence to purchasers."[112] As long as the goods are genuine, we must even question whether the purchaser is initially confused regarding the reseller's lack of affiliation with the mark owner.[113] The "point is not that consumers can never be harmed by confusion regarding non-quality-related relationships. Rather, the point is that the sort of attenuated confusion at issue in sponsorship and affiliation

---

[106] De Beers LV Trademark Ltd. v. DeBeers Diamond Syndicate, Inc. 440 F. Supp. 2d 249, 274 (S.D.N.Y. 2006) (quoting Star Indus., Inc. v. Bacardi & Co. Ltd., 412 F.3d 373, 384 (2d Cir. 2005)).
[107] Rothman, *supra* note 29, at 140.
[108] Playboy Enters., Inc. v. Netscape Commc'ns Corp., 354 F.3d 1020, 1034–35 (9th Cir. 2004) (Berzon, J., concurring).
[109] See Brookfield Commc'ns, Inc. v. W. Coast Entm't Corp., 174 F.3d 1036, 1062, 1065 (9th Cir. 1999) (ignoring the distribution channel); Mary Kay, Inc. v. Weber, 601 F. Supp. 2d 839, 858–59 (N.D. Tex. 2009) (ignoring first sale and fair use).
[110] See Rothman, *supra* note 29, at 169–70.
[111] McCann v. Newman Irrevocable Trust, 458 F.3d 281, 287 (3d Cir. 2006).
[112] Dastar Corp. v. Twentieth Century Fox Film Corp., 539 U.S. 23, 32–33 (2003).
[113] See Sharrock, *supra* note 34, at 65–66.

cases does not necessarily or even often harm consumers or the market for quality products[,]" and the costs of protecting consumers from this form of confusion is unreasonably high.[114] "In delineating the boundary between fair and unfair competition, we must keep firmly in mind that if competition is to remain an effective force for promoting social welfare, we must leave room for would-be competitors to operate."[115]

VI. CONCLUSION

Protecting the resale market increases consumer choice and spurs mark owners to innovate and bring new and improved products to the market. Legislatively-created first sale and nominative fair use doctrines, along with the elimination of initial interest confusion as a cause of action under the Lanham Act, would provide resellers and auction websites guidance in navigating the minefield of rights and duties with regard to Internet secondary-market sales, so that they more closely resemble the brick-and-mortar setting. This would support the economic policy goals underlying intellectual property[116] and spur competition and innovation in the marketplace.[117] These solutions would also benefit consumers looking for bargains and align trademark exhaustion in cyberspace with its application in brick-and-mortar settings.[118]

"The rights of a patentee or copyright holder are part of a 'carefully crafted bargain,' under which, once the patent or copyright monopoly has expired, the public may use the invention or work at will and without attribution." And both courts and Congress are loath to extend through trademark that which has been lost through the expiration of a patent or copyright.[119] For the first sale/exhaustion doctrine to be meaningful in copyright and patent law contexts, it must be equally robust as a trademark infringement defense. Nominative fair use must actually be accepted by the courts. In brick-and-mortar settings, there is no confusion as to affiliation with the mark owner with regard to distribution channels—it would be difficult to believe that a consumer would think that a consignment shop or antique store was affiliated with the mark owners of all the goods sold at such venues. The same should hold equally true in cyberspace.

---

[114] Lemley and McKenna, *supra* note 37, at 437–38 (emphasis omitted); *ibid.* at 438–42.
[115] Lunney, *supra* note 18, at 486.
[116] Fox Film Corp. v. Doyal, 286 U.S. 123, 127–28 (1932): "The sole interest of the United States and the primary object in conferring the monopoly lie in the general benefits derived by the public from the labors of authors. A copyright, like a patent, is 'at once the equivalent given by the public for benefits bestowed by the genius and meditations and skill of individuals, and the incentive to further efforts for the same important objects.'" (quoting Kendall v. Winsor, 62 U.S. 322, 328 (1858)). *Ibid.*
[117] See Lemley and McKenna, *supra* note 8, at 185.
[118] See generally, Sebastian Int'l, Inc. v. Longs Drug Stores Corp., 53 F.3d 1073, 1076 (9th Cir. 1995) (per curiam).
[119] Dastar Corp. v. Twentieth Century Fox Film Corp., 539 U.S. 23, 33–34 (2003) (citation omitted); see *Sebastian Int'l, Inc.*, *supra* note 118, 53 F.3d at 1075.

PART VI

SELECTED ISSUES (AND CHALLENGES) ON COPYRIGHT EXHAUSTION

23. How could the Taiwan Copyright Act follow the patent and trademark regime and adopt international copyright exhaustion?
Kung-Chung Liu*

I. INTRODUCTION

Since the 1980s, parallel imports of genuine goods protected by intellectual property rights, ranging from soft drinks, such as Coca-Cola, to automobiles, cosmetics, and consumer electronics and appliances, have become popular in Taiwan. This phenomenon has been driven by international price differentiation and, in turn, by parallel importers engaging in international arbitrage and importing lower priced products into Taiwan.[1] However, even though the Agreement on Trade-Related Aspects of Intellectual Property Rights (TRIPS) adopted under the framework of the World Trade Organization (WTO) expressly eschews the issue of exhaustion and leaves WTO members free to make their own decision pursuant to Article 6 of TRIPS,[2] Taiwan's intellectual property laws on parallel imports are not consistently in favor of these imports. To the contrary, Taiwan's intellectual property laws have been increasingly more concerned with safeguarding the interests of intellectual property rights holders, which has led to reducing the admissibility of parallel imports into Taiwan.

This chapter focuses on copyright exhaustion in the larger context of the disparity of treatment of parallel imports between copyright law and others areas of intellectual property in Taiwan. The chapter proceeds as follows. First, section II examines the application of the principle of exhaustion and the treatment of parallel imports under the Taiwan Integrated Circuit Layouts Act, the Trademark Act, the Patent Act, and the Plant Varieties Act. This section elaborates that these laws treat parallel imports differently, varying from accepting a system of international exhaustion to instead following national exhaustion. Second, section III reviews the Taiwan Copyright Act and highlights the strict approach against parallel imports that is currently adopted in the Act. The gist of this chapter culminates in section IV, which advocates for the adoption of the principle of international exhaustion also in copyright law, and in general across all areas of

---

* Research Fellow, Institutum Iurisprudentiae, Academia Sinica; External Director, Applied Research Center for Intellectual Assets and the Law in Asia (ARCIALA), Singapore Management University School of Law; Co-appointed professor, Institute of Law for Science and Technology, National Tsing Hua University.

[1] According to the observation of Professor Mao-Rong Huang, one of the founding commissioners of the Fair Trade Commission (FTC) between 1992 and 1995, serious international price discrimination exists in Taiwan. See Mao-Rong Huang, *Parallel Import, Intellectual Property and the Fair Trade Act*, 2 FAIR TRADE J. 1, 14 (1994).

[2] DANIEL GERVAIS, THE TRIPS AGREEMENT 222 (4th ed. 2012).

intellectual property law in Taiwan. In particular, this section explores how the Taiwan Copyright Act could follow the position adopted under the Taiwan Trademark Act and Patent Act, which currently follow the principle of international exhaustion.

II. THE PRINCIPLE OF EXHAUSTION UNDER INTELLECTUAL PROPERTY LAWS IN TAIWAN

Taiwan's intellectual property system is comprised of the Copyright Act, Patent Act, Trademark Act, Trade Secret Act, Integrated Circuit Layouts Protection Act, and the Plant Variety and Plant Seed Act. This system has gone through tremendous reforms in the last three decades, among other things due to pressure from Taiwan's major trading partners, mainly from the United States (U.S.) and the European Union (EU). This section summarizes the current law applicable in the areas of the protection of integrated circuit layouts, patents, trademarks, and plant varieties.

A. International Exhaustion Under the Taiwan Integrated Circuit Layouts Protection Act

After several years of deliberation, the Taiwan Integrated Circuit Layouts Protection Act was enacted in Taiwan in 1995.[3] The Integrated Circuit Layouts Protection Act was enacted primarily in order to boost the electronics and information industry in Taiwan, as integrated circuits are the "rice" (meaning "the staple") of the electronics and information industry. The Integrated Circuit Layouts Protection Act was also enacted in order to comply with TRIPS, as part of the requirements necessary for Taiwan to become a WTO member.

From the very beginning, the Integrated Circuit Layouts Protection Act took an unequivocal stance in favor of allowing parallel imports of legally made or acquired integrated circuits that were first marketed outside Taiwan. In particular, article 17(2) provides right holders with the exclusive right to prohibit the importation and distribution of layouts or integrated circuits incorporating layouts for commercial purposes.[4] Yet, the Integrated Circuit Layouts Protection Act explicitly provides for the exhaustion of this right after the first marketing of the products nationally or internationally.[5] Notably, Article 18 provides that the rights applicable to integrated circuits shall not apply to any of the following acts:

> (3) to import or distribute legally possessed circuit layouts or integrated circuits by an owner of legally reproduced circuit layouts or integrated circuits; (4) to import or distribute illegally produced integrated circuits by an owner who obtained without knowledge that the integrated circuits have infringed another's circuit layout rights.[6]

---

[3] Integrated Circuit Layouts Protection Act, August 11, 1995 (Taiwan).
[4] *Ibid.* art. 17(2).
[5] *Ibid.*
[6] Integrated Circuit Layout Protection Act, art. 18. However, according to art. 31 of the Act, if an owner as referred to under item 4 of art. 18 continues to import or distribute for commercial

The legislative reasoning behind the provision in the Integrated Circuit Layouts Protection Act is based on the consideration that the right of an integrated circuit owner would constitute a "serious impediment to the flow of ICs."[7] In this respect, it should be noted that such legislative reasoning also considered the provision in Article 6(5) of the World Intellectual Property Office (WIPO) Treaty on Intellectual Property in Respect to Integrated Circuits,[8] as well as legislation from the U.S. and Japan, and the respective notions of "first sale doctrine" and "exhaustion doctrine" that are used in these countries.

Still, despite the fact that the provisions in the Integrated Circuit Layouts Protection Act clearly favor a system of parallel imports and international exhaustion, the practical application of the Act has been very limited to date. In particular, no court decision on either the Integrated Circuit Layout Protection Act in general, nor on Article 18, has been adopted so far. In turn, the non-application of the Act in practice has diminished the impact that the adoption of the principle of international exhaustion in the Act could have had on other areas of intellectual property.

B. Moving Toward International Exhaustion Under the Taiwan Trademark Act and Taiwan Patent Act

The Taiwan Trademark Act also moved toward a system of international exhaustion in 2011. The Taiwan Patent Act followed a similar system in 2013.

(1) Taiwan Trademark Act

Throughout its history, the Taiwan Trademark Act[9] has never mentioned a specific right of importation for trademark owners, and in turn that Taiwan's trademark law would follow the principle of national trademark exhaustion.[10] Yet, problems soon arose concerning whether or not trademark holders could lawfully preclude third parties from parallel importing goods that bear their marks and had been lawfully sold or first distributed in a foreign market. This uncertainty was resolved when the Supreme Court issued an opinion ruling in favor of trademark exhaustion for parallel imported products. The decision of the Supreme Court was remarkable both because of the result (the judicial acceptance of the principle of international trademark exhaustion in Taiwan) and because it is unusual for Taiwan's Supreme Court, and for the judiciary in Taiwan in general, to develop and apply so firmly a legal theory without an existing statutory basis, and ahead of hearing support for such position from the academic community in Taiwan.

---

purposes after having received from the owner of the integrated circuit layout rights a written notice stating the facts of infringement and accompanied by an infringement assessment report of integrated circuits originally procured without notice of infringements, the owner of the integrated circuit layout rights may claim damages based on the usual royalties charged to use the infringed circuit layout. *Ibid.* art. 31.

[7] Legislative Yuan, Proceeding, 84 LEGISLATIVE YUAN GAZETTE 46, 22 (July 13, 1995).
[8] Washington Treaty on Intellectual Property in Respect to Integrated Circuits, art. 6(5), May 26, 1989, WIPO Lex. No. TRT/WASHINGTON/001.
[9] Trademark Act, January 1, 1931 (Taiwan).
[10] See e.g. the current art. 35(1) of the Trademark Act: "The proprietor of a registered trademark has the exclusive right in the trademark in relation to the designated goods or services." *Ibid.* art. 35(1).

In particular, in a landmark decision that was issued on October 22, 1992, the *Tai-Shan-Zi* case, the Fourth Civil Senate of the Supreme Court reasoned as follows:

> The parallel import of genuine goods harms neither the good will of the authorized user of the trade mark in this country nor the interest of consumers, prevents the authorized user of trade mark from monopolizing domestic market, controlling the price of goods, stimulates price competition and provides consumers with choices among the same goods; provided that the quality of which is equivalent to that of goods marketed by the authorized user in this country, and no danger of confusion or passing off among consumers is resulted in. The parallel import does not contravene the purpose of the Trademark Act and insofar does not constitute trade mark infringement.[11]

Subsequent decisions confirmed this position and, with it, the general favor of the Senates of the Supreme Court for the principle of international trademark exhaustion versus national exhaustion,[12] provided that the goods bearing the trademarks are resold in their original package[13] and the source of the goods is properly indicated so as to avoid consumer confusion.

One year later, in 1993, the judicial position in favor of international trademark exhaustion was formally codified in the Taiwan Trademark Act. Notably, paragraph 3 was added to the then article 23, which was renumbered as article 30(2) in 2003.[14] Today, article 30(2) of the Taiwan Trademark Act states that:

> Where goods bearing a registered trademark are traded or circulated in the marketplace by the trademark right holder or by an authorized person . . . the right holder shall not claim trademark rights on said goods. However, the aforementioned shall not apply in case of preventing deterioration or damage of goods or any other fair reasons.[15]

In addition, the current language of article 36(2) of the Taiwan Trademark Act, which was enacted in 2011, repeats the same wording almost verbatim, with minor revisions. In particular, article 36(2) reads:

> Where goods have been put on *the domestic or foreign market* under a registered trademark by the proprietor or with his consent, the proprietor is not entitled to claim trademark rights on

---

[11] Tai-Shan-Zi, 1992 Minshi Huibian (4th Civil Senate of the Supreme Court, October 22, 1992).

[12] The Supreme Court came to the same conclusion in 1993 in Tai-Shan-Zi No. 5380, 1993 Minshi Huibian (Supreme Court, October 8, 1993) and 1993 Tai-Shan-Zi No. 5607, 1993 Minshi Huibian (Supreme Court, October 21, 1993).

[13] It is, however, true that the repackage of imported genuine goods does not typically affect the original condition of the goods, but enhances their values and the importers have given due public notice of the fact that the product has been repacked. It is, thus, questionable to forbid parallel import solely for the sake of repackage. In Japan, for example, the package of goods is highly valued and sometimes even more important than the goods themselves. In other words, repackage of goods would have a value-added function. In contrast, the Court of Justice of the European Union (CJEU) is more tolerant towards parallel import of genuine goods that have been repackaged. See Jau-Hwa Chen, *Protection of Trade Mark and Free Trade Principle in European Union*, 17/18 SOCIOECONOMIC LAW & INST. REV. 223, 247–48 (1996).

[14] Trademark Act, art. 30(2).

[15] *Ibid.*

such goods, unless such claim is to prevent the condition of the goods from being changed or impaired *after they have been put on the market* or there exist other legitimate reasons.[16]

Besides the fact that article 36(2) expressly refers to "foreign market" in the text of the provision, the legislative reasoning behind the adoption of the provision clarifies that "the term 'market' includes the unspecified 'foreign market.'"[17] Furthermore, the wording "the domestic or foreign market" was inserted in the language of the provision to once again clarify that the position adopted in the Taiwan Trademark Act subscribes to the principle of international trademark exhaustion in Taiwan.[18]

Following the enactment of article 36(2) of the Taiwan Trademark Act, the courts have interpreted the provision in several decisions.[19] In particular, Taiwan's High Court-Taichung Branch addressed the issue of exhaustion in a case related to trademark infringement in 2012. In this case, the court stated that:

> However, once the trademark at issue has been licensed, the quality of clothes [note: designated goods] could not lead to an issue of trademark infringement as how the quality control over the legally produced products should be conducted is indeed an issue of agreement between the trademark owner and the licensee and beyond the knowledge and quality control of the owner of those clothing products acquired through market transaction.[20]

One year later, in 2013, the Intellectual Property Court of Taiwan rendered an additional interpretation of the provision. This interpretation, which the court rendered both in its capacity as a court of first[21] and second instance,[22] seems, however, less than convincing than the previous judicial opinions in this area. Notably, the court stated that:

> [What constitutes exception to exhaustion recognized by the] provision is that the products have been modified to the degree that it would objectively affect the willingness of relevant consumers to buy products or the price relevant consumers are ready to pay; the modified part of the products would lead relevant consumers into likelihood of confusion, and since there is substantial difference between the modified products and the original products the exhaustion doctrine does not apply.[23]

---

[16] *Ibid.* art. 36(2) (emphasis added).
[17] *Ibid.*
[18] *Ibid.*
[19] See e.g. Min-Shan-Shan-Yi-Zi No. 1 (Taiwan Intell. Prop. Ct. August 16, 2012).
[20] Zhi-Shan-Zi No. 2 (Taiwan High Ct. Taichung Branch, July 23, 2013).
[21] Min-Shan-Su-Zi No. 49 (Taiwan Intellectual Property Court, October 8, 2014).
[22] Min-Shan-Shan-Zi No. 17 (Taiwan Intell. Prop. Ct., April 30, 2015).
[23] *Ibid.*; see generally Min-Shan-Su-Zi No. 49, *supra* note 21. The legitimacy of the proviso in art. 36(2) leaves room for doubt. If it is for the preservation of quality of goods, then it is an issue that should be and is better dealt with by the consumers protection Act, (Taiwan) Consumer Protection Law, January 13, 1994. Even if it is for the preservation of the goodwill of trademark right holders, it is not justifiable to grant trademark right holders a superior position over the property rights of owners of the goods. If it is meant to protect trademark right holders against an intentional damage of the goods by their owners in order to diminish reputation of the former, then it can be sufficiently covered by art. 24 ("No enterprise shall, for the purpose of competition, make or disseminate any falsehood that is able to damage the business reputation of another.") or art. 25 ("In addition to what is provided for in this Law, no enterprise shall otherwise have any deceptive or obviously unfair conduct that is likely to affect trading order.") of the Fair Trade Act.

In particular, based on this decision, the Intellectual Property Court seemed to tie the notion of "likelihood of confusion" (the traditional standard for trademark infringement) with the notion of "substantial difference" between the modified products and the original products. The court, thus, (wrongfully in the opinion of this author) used the fact that the products were modified to deny that the trademark rights in the products had been exhausted. In turn, the court found that the unauthorized import of the products into Taiwan was not permitted under the Taiwan Trademark Act.

Despite this decision, the principle of international exhaustion continues to be the applicable system under the rule of the Taiwan Trademark Act to date. International exhaustion is certainly the default rule in all the instances in which the product quality is the same and has not been modified by the parallel importers. However, following the recent judicial decision above, parallel imports of products whose quality has been modified may no longer be considered lawful imports into Taiwan.

(2) Taiwan Patent Act

In 2003, the Taiwan Patent Act[24] recognized a patentee's right to import the products covered by her patent. The recognition of this right was one of the conditions that Taiwan had to satisfy in order to be admitted as a WTO member. The final text of the provision that introduced such right into Taiwan's patent law was modelled after Article 28 of TRIPS and considered the example of similar provisions adopted in the patent laws of the U.S., France, and Germany which were also followed. The newly introduced provision entered into force on January 1, 2002, the day when Taiwan became a member of the WTO.[25]

However, the introduction of the new importation right into the Taiwan Patent Act was coupled with the introduction of a clause on patent exhaustion.[26] In particular, the provision in article 57(1)(6)(f) of the Taiwan Patent Act prescribes:

> The validity of an invention patent does not cover the following: 6. After the sale of the patented goods *produced* by or with the consent of the patentee, the *use* or *resale* of the said goods. The aforementioned *production* and *sale* is not limited to this country.[27]

The legislative reasoning behind the introduction of this provision was "to codify the exhaustion doctrine in order to avoid controversies."[28] Yet, the interpretation of the

---

See Fair Trade Act, February 4, 1991, art. 24 (Taiwan); *ibid.* art. 25. Furthermore, it is dubious how trademark right holders can enforce their rights over the goods owned by others—to prohibit the continued sale or use of the trademarked goods or to assert trademark infringement for the continued sale or use of the goods?

[24] Patent Act, May 29, 1994 (Taiwan).
[25] World Trade Organization, *WTO Successfully Concludes Negotiations on Entry of the Separate Customs Territory of Taiwan, Penghu, Kinmen and Matsu*, Press/244 (September 18, 2001).
[26] The critique by MING-CHEN TSAI, THE STUDY ON INVENTION PATENTS 300 (1997) that the 1994 Patent Act did not recognize the distinction between the doctrine of exhaustion (of goods domestically made) and parallel import (of goods made in foreign countries) failed to understand that the object of exhaustion is the right to import and, therefore, has principally nothing to do with goods domestically made. See generally, *ibid.*
[27] According to arts. 103 and 117 of the Patent Act, utility models and design patents also enjoyed the right to import. Patent Act, arts. 103, 107 (emphasis added).
[28] Legislative Yuan, Proceedings, 82 LEGISLATIVE YUAN GAZETTE 71, 130 (December 9, 1993).

provision ultimately proved controversial, especially due to the fact that a related clause was introduced in article 57(2) of the Taiwan Patent Act, according to which "[t]he area in which the sale is allowed according to No. 6 of the preceding Paragraph is to be determined by courts in accordance with facts."[29] Notably, this latter clause essentially subjected, and subjects, the general principle of international patent exhaustion under article 57(1)(6) to the contractual agreement of the parties. In turn, in the instances of the absence of any agreement between the parties, the application of this principle is left to the discretion of the courts based upon the courts' interpretation of the facts of the case at issue.[30]

Not surprisingly, the provision in article 57(2) of the Taiwan Patent Act has been widely criticized based on the consideration that the regulation of patent exhaustion is an issue concerning public policy. In particular, it has been noted that the principle of patent exhaustion aims at striking a balance between the exclusive right of patentees and the exclusive rights of patent owners, and as such the extent of patent exhaustion should not be subject to private contracts. Moreover, it has been underlined that contractual agreements over the scope of patent exhaustion do not constitute legitimate public notice to third parties, and that these agreements may result in jeopardizing the certainty of patent transactions, more specifically transactions involving products or processes embodying the patent.[31]

Ultimately, as a result of these criticisms, the controversial provision in article 57(2) of the Taiwan Patent Act ("[t]he area in which the sale is allowed . . . is to be determined by courts in accordance with facts"[32]) was deleted as part of a series of patent reforms in 2011 (that included renumbering article 57 as article 59[33]), which took effect in 2013. The legislative reasoning behind the cancellation of the provision was that:

> [w]hile Article 57(1) No. 6 adopts the international exhaustion doctrine, Article 57(2) provides that courts are to determine the area of sale. Given that the decision on international exhaustion or domestic exhaustion is an issue of legislative policy and not for courts to determine according

---

Therefore, it is clearly wrong for Ming-Chen Tsai to have asserted in his book (MING-CHEN TSAI, *supra* note 26) that the 1994 Patent Act did not seem to have taken a clear international exhaustion stance and tended toward an implied license, because the sales of patented goods by the patentee to buyers implies a license for buyers to use such goods lawfully.

[29] Patent Act, art. 57(2). The legislators made no explanation as to the reason why the last sentences of arts. 57(2) and 118(2) were added. Some speculated that the fear of trade retaliation by the U.S. government was the unacknowledged ground for the mysterious U-turn when the legislators were about to introduce the international exhaustion doctrine, Sheng-Rong Zhuang, *Analyzing Parallel Import of Patented Products*, 46 LAW MONTHLY 4, 14 (1995).

[30] This understanding is confirmed by art. 35 of the Implementation Rules of the Patent Act: "The area in which sale is allowed according to the last sentence of Articles 57(2) and 118(2), is to be determined by contractual provisions; in cases where contracts are silent or unclear, the area is to be determined by [courts] according to the genuine intention of the parties, trading customs or other objective facts of trade." Enforcement Rules of the Patent Act, January 1, 1949 (Taiwan).

[31] For criticism of art. 57(2) of the Patents Act, see KUNG-CHUNG LIU, IPR ENFORCEMENT AND THE COMPETITION ACT 42 (2008).

[32] Patent Act, art. 59.

[33] According to arts. 120 and 142 of the Patent Act, art. 59 of the Patent Act can be applied *mutatis mutandis* to utility model patents and design patents. *Ibid.* arts. 120, 142.

to facts, this Paragraph expressly adopts the international exhaustion doctrine by deleting the last sentence of Article 57(2) to prevent controversy.[34]

Besides being relevant with respect to patent exhaustion, it should be noted that the (newly renumbered) article 59(1)(6) can also be relevant with respect to the exhaustion of utility patents. Notably, in a decision decided on April 2, 2009 in the case of *Tai-Shan-Zi*, the Supreme Court of Taiwan cautioned the lower courts to consider the application of this principle to utility patents and to determine the following points before excluding the application of (the newly renumbered) article 59(1)(6) by analogy to utility patents: (1) whether under the contract between the sales agent and the exclusive licensee to manufacture and sell the patented products where the exclusive licensee only manufactures the patented product upon notification of order from its sales agent this amounts to "sale"; (2) whether the patented products have been introduced into the market; and (3) whether the exclusive licensee has been rewarded.[35]

Finally, in a recent 2014 case, the Intellectual Property Court of Taiwan utilized the clause providing for no-retroactive application of later acquired patents against the "patented" products that had already been acquired by others under the exhaustion doctrine.[36] In this case, the court acted in its capacity as a court of first instance. Once again, the decision in this case proved the favor of the judiciary in Taiwan toward the principle of international exhaustion in patent law.

C. National Exhaustion Under the Taiwan Plant Variety and Plant Seed Act

At first, Taiwan's Plant Variety and Plant Seed Act (previously named the Plant Variety Act from its enactment in 1988 to 2004) introduced into Taiwan a broad "new variety right" (with a protection term of fifteen years) that consists of the exclusive right to disseminate, sell, and use the new variety "in order to protect the right of breeder and discoverer of new plant variety."[37] The original 1998 version of the Act was amended in 2004. As part of the amendments, the Act expanded the protection scope of this "new variety right" and included, among other rights, the introduction of an ad hoc right to import the plant variety at issue. In particular, the following language was introduced:

> The holder of a plant variety right shall have the exclusive right to preclude others from engaging, without the consent of the holder, in the following acts with respect to plant seeds to which the holder has the plant variety right: 1. Production or propagation, 2. Conditioning for the purpose of propagation, 3. Offering for sale, 4. Selling or otherwise marketing, 5. Importing or exporting, or 6. Holding for any of the purposes in the preceding five Subparagraphs.[38]

Moreover, in an effort to balance the rights of the general public in being able to use new plant varieties and to ensure food safety against the rights of the intellectual property

---

[34] Legislative Yuan, Proceedings,100 LEGISLATIVE YUAN GAZETTE 81, 160–61 (November 29, 2011).
[35] Tai-Shang-Zi No. 113, 2009 Minshi Huibian (Supreme Court, April 2, 2009).
[36] Min-Zhuan-Su-Zi 131 (Taiwan Intell. Prop. Ct., July 30, 2014).
[37] Plant Variety and Plant Seed Act, December 5, 1988, art. 8(1) (Taiwan); Legislative Yuan, Proceedings, 76 LEGISLATIVE YUAN GAZETTE 85, 17 (October 20, 1988).
[38] Plant Variety and Plant Seed Act, art. 24.

right holder,[39] a provision on the exhaustion of plant variety rights was introduced in article 26(1). Yet, the scope of the principle of exhaustion in this context is national exhaustion. Notably, the provision states that:

> The protection of a plant variety right shall not extend to: 6. Acts of *domestically* selling or otherwise circulating any material of a variety protected by a plant variety right, or its dependent variety, as undertaken voluntarily by or with the consent of the holder of the plant variety right, but not including acts of further propagation of such protected variety.[40]

The limitation of the principle of exhaustion to the national market is evident from the use of the word "domestically" contained in article 26(1). In addition, article 26(4)[41] does not exempt the act of exporting to a country that does not protect the plant genus or species to which the plant variety belongs because "[otherwise] the impact on the interests of holder of new plant variety would be greater."[42] This also indicates that the principle of exhaustion only applies within the national boundaries.

However, no court decision pertaining to this issue has been handed down to date, which to some extent reflects the practical irrelevance of this Act with respect to the issue of exhaustion in practice.

III. THE TAIWAN COPYRIGHT ACT: THE LAST STRONGHOLD OF NATIONAL EXHAUSTION

A. The Copyright Protection Agreement Between Taiwan and the U.S.

The ubiquitous nature of works protected by copyright law carries tremendous commercial interest in Taiwan, especially in the easy-to-reproduce era since the late 1970s. It is no wonder then that the scope of copyright protection was a priority for the U.S. trade negotiators during the trade talks between the U.S. and Taiwan. One of the major issues at stake in the trade talks context was the issue of parallel imports of copyrighted works into Taiwan. In particular, Article 14(1) of the Draft Agreement for the Protection of Copyright Between the Coordination Council for North American Affairs and the American Institute in Taiwan of 1989 (U.S.-Taiwan Copyright Protection Agreement, which took effect on 16 July 1993[43]) provides that:

> (1) Infringing copies of a work protected in accordance with this Agreement shall be liable to seizure in either territory where such work enjoys legal protection. An infringing copy shall mean

---

[39] Legislative Yuan, Proceedings, 93 LEGISLATIVE YUAN GAZETTE 17, 249 (March 23, 2004).
[40] Plant Variety and Plant Seed Act, art. 36(1) (emphasis added).
[41] Article 26(4) of the Act provides: "Acts under Subparagraph 6 . . . of Paragraph 1 shall not include acts of exporting propagating material of such protected variety to a country that does not protect the plant genus or species to which the plant variety belongs, provided that this provision shall not apply where the purpose is for final consumption." *Ibid.* art. 26(4).
[42] Legislative Yuan, Proceedings, 93 LEGISLATIVE YUAN GAZETTE 17, 302 (March 23, 2004).
[43] Agreement for the Protection of Copyright Between the Coordination Council for North American Affairs and the American Institute in Taiwan, July 16, 1993, Zhongwai Tiaoyue Jibian [hereinafter U.S.-Taiwan Copyright Protection Agreement].

a copy of such work that infringes any of the exclusive rights provided in domestic law and in this Agreement *including a copy which is imported into the territory represented by either Party where, if made in such territory by the importer, would constitute an infringement of the copyright.*[44]

The wording of Article 14 of the Agreement was somehow difficult to understand as no mention of "parallel imports" was made in the provision. Accordingly, it was not clear whether a "parallel imported copy" is automatically an infringing copy under the language of the provision. However, the very essence of the provision that was proposed by the U.S. could only lie in the banning of parallel imports of copyrighted products by U.S. copyright owners into Taiwan, as few companies and authors from Taiwan exported copyrighted products to the U.S. at that time.

B. Indirect Granting of the Right of Importation and Extremely Limited "Exceptions"

In 1992, Taiwan enacted a revolutionary Copyright Act, which, among other considerations, incorporated the U.S.-Taiwan Copyright Protection Agreement and its international obligations prior to the Agreement's ratification.[45] True to the verbatim translation of the draft of Article 14 of the U.S.-Taiwan Copyright Protection Agreement, article 87(3) of the Taiwan Copyright Act provided that the import into the jurisdiction of the Republic of China (Taiwan) of copies, the reproduction of which would violate copyright or plate right,[46] with an intention to distribute them in said jurisdiction, is deemed to be an "infringement of copyright or plate right."[47] The legislative reasoning behind the provision was, at best, succinct. In particular, it was stated that:

> In order to enhance the protection of copyright and plate right, certain circumstances are deemed to have infringed copyright or plate right, although as such they did not . . . Subparagraph 3 is a provision for the import of copies, the reproduction of which in this country violates copyright or plate right, into this country with an intention to distribute them domestically.[48]

However, no words about prohibiting "parallel imports" were written, spoken, or heard in the legislative reasoning and in the debates in the Taiwanese Congress leading to the adoption of the provision. Nevertheless, it is a logical consequence that, once the importation of copyrighted copies, whether genuine or counterfeit, was subjected to the approval of the right holders, copyright owners were already being indirectly granted the right of

---

[44] *Ibid.* art. 14(1) (emphasis added).
[45] In other words, the 1992 Copyright Act prematurely incorporated the draft U.S.-Taiwan Copyright Protection Agreement into the amendment, which is of course questionable.
[46] Copyright Act, May 14, 1928, (Taiwan). Article 79(1) and (2) of the Copyright Act stipulates: "(1) For a literary or artistic work that has no economic rights or for which the economic rights have been extinguished, a plate maker who arranges and prints the said literary work, or in the case of an artistic work, a plate maker who photocopies, prints, or uses a similar method of reproduction and first publishes such reproduction based on such original artistic work, and duly records it in accordance with this Act, shall have the exclusive right to photocopy, print, or use similar methods of reproduction based on the plate. (2)The rights of the plate maker shall subsist for ten years from the time the plate is completed." *Ibid.* arts. 79(1)–(2).
[47] *Ibid.* art. 87.
[48] Legislative Yuan, Proceedings, 81 Legislative Yuan Gazette 36, 123 (May 1, 1992).

importation over their copyrighted works.[49] As a result, parallel imports were de facto prohibited under the language (or lack thereof) of the Taiwan Copyright Act.

Not surprisingly, controversies erupted between the U.S. and Taiwan when the draft of the U.S.-Taiwan Copyright Protection Agreement underwent the parliamentary ratification review process in Taiwan. Accordingly, the Legislative Yuan attempted to resolve these disputes by deciding, on January 18, 1993, that "the Agreement be ratified under eight reservations, one of which was the dispute about whether Article 14 granted copyright owners 'right to import.'"[50] The Taiwanese government, eager to clarify the issue with the U.S. and to maintain Taiwan's reservation with respect to the importation right, sent representatives from Taiwan to the U.S. during the period of March 8–12, 1993 and again during April 7–8, 1993.[51] However, the response from the U.S. representatives was that the U.S. was deeply dismayed by the resolution adopted by the Legislative Yuan. Instead of agreeing with the resolution, the U.S. demanded the resolution be dropped and Article 87 be amended by the end of April 1993 to expressly introduce the wording related to the indirect right of importation as originally dictated in the U.S.-Taiwan Copyright Protection Agreement.[52] To the contrary, should Taiwan not implement the right of importation trade sanctions would be imposed by the U.S. on Taiwan.[53] As a result, the government of Taiwan adopted an amendment Bill to that effect on April 20, 1993. It took the Legislative Yuan only two days to pass the amendment on April 22, 1993,[54] but not without fierce protest from the opposition parties.

Still, the provision was adopted as agreed upon in the U.S.-Taiwan Copyright Protection Agreement. In particular, Article 87(3) implemented two clauses, both of which aim at "deterring the inflow of pirated copies and to indirectly granting the right to import to copyright owners to enhance their protection."[55] Specifically the provision states that:

(3) To import any copies produced without the authorization of the economic right holder or the plate right holder; (4): To import the original or any copies of a work legally reproduced abroad without the authorization of the economic right holder.[56]

---

[49] The Fifth Senate of the Supreme Court has incorrectly concluded in Tai-Fe-Zi No. 349, 1997 Minshi Huibian (5th Civil Senate of the Supreme Court, November 13, 1997) that the Copyright Act did not prohibit parallel import of genuine copyrighted works until the 1993 revision, which provided the new subparagraph 4 in art. 87.

[50] Soojin Kim, *In Pursuit of Profit Maximization by Restricting Parallel Imports: The U.S. Copyright Owner and Taiwan Copyright Law*, 5 PAC. RIM L. & POL'Y J. 205, 214 (1995).

[51] See generally *ibid.* at 215.

[52] According to the Chairman of the Copyright Committee (predecessor of the Taiwan Intellectual Property Office), Quan-Lu Wang, "The wording of Article 87 is the bottom line of the U.S.; and according to its intention, we are not allowed to amend it." See Legislative Yuan, Proceedings, 82 LEGISLATIVE YUAN GAZETTE 26, 579 (April 21, 1993).

[53] Kim, *supra* note 50, at 214.

[54] Legislative Yuan, Proceedings, 82 LEGISLATIVE YUAN GAZETTE 23, 3 (April 20, 1993); Legislative Yuan, Proceedings, 82 LEGISLATIVE YUAN GAZETTE 26, 565–67 (April 21, 1993); Legislative Yuan, Proceedings, 82 LEGISLATIVE YUAN GAZETTE 24, 70 (April 22, 1993).

[55] Legislative Yuan, Proceedings, 82 LEGISLATIVE YUAN GAZETTE 24, 55 (April 22, 1993).

[56] See U.S.-Taiwan Copyright Protection Agreement, *supra* note 43. The 4th Senate of the Supreme Court indicated in its decision in Tai-Fe- Zi No. 87, 1995 Minshi Huibian (4th Civil Senate of the Supreme Court 1995) that art. 87(3) of the 1992 Copyright Act is not exactly identical

Moreover, article 87*bis* was simultaneously added to the Taiwan Copyright Act "[t]o balance societal public interest" in the importation of genuine goods. The provision provides extremely and narrowly defined exceptions to the general right to importation, and states that:[57]

> The provisions of Subparagraph 4 of the preceding Article do not apply to any of the following circumstances:
> 1. Where the original or copies of a work are imported for the use of central or local government agencies; provided, this does not apply to import for use in schools or other educational institutions, or to the import of any audiovisual work for purposes other than archival use.
> 2. Where the original or a specified number of copies of any audiovisual works are imported in order to supply such works to nonprofit scholarly, educational or religious organizations for archival purposes, or where an original or specified number of copies of works other than audiovisual works are imported for library lending or archival purposes, provided that such copies are used in compliance with the provisions of Article 48.
> 3. Where the original or a specified number of copies of a work are imported for the private use of the importer, not for distribution, or where such import occurs because the original or copies form a part of the personal baggage of a person arriving from outside the territory.
> 4. Where the original or copies of a work incorporated into any legally imported goods, machinery, or equipment are imported in conjunction with the import of such items. Such original or copies of the work shall not be reproduced during the use or operation of the goods, machinery or equipment.
> 5. Where a user's manual or operational manual accompanying any legally imported goods, machinery, or equipment is imported; provided, this does not apply where the user's manual or operational manual are the principal objects of the importation.
> The "specified number" set forth in subparagraphs 2 and 3 of the preceding paragraph shall be prescribed by the competent authority.[58]

To further clarify the limited extent of these exceptions, the former Copyright Committee of Taiwan issued an ad hoc decree in 1993. The adoption of this decree followed and was prompted by the oral promise that a Taiwan representative had made to the U.S. representative. The decree provided that, for the purpose of the application of Article 87a(1)(2), the following number of works would qualify for the exception to the general principle of national exhaustion: one copy of an audiovisual work and five copies for other types of works. Likewise, the decree established that, for the purpose of the application of Article 87a(1)(3), one copy of any work at any one time was, and still is, allowed to be imported into Taiwan.[59]

Equally controversial, the violation of the new right of importation could lead to both civil and criminal remedies, namely, punishment of up to two years' imprisonment and/or a fine in the maximum amount of NT$100,000. This provision remained in effect until

---

to art. 87(4) of the 1993 Copyright Act, and the appellate court should apply the latter as it is the newer law.

[57] Article 87*bis*(1)(1)–(3) of the Taiwan Copyright Act clearly resembles § 602(a) of the U.S. Copyright Act. Copyright Act, art. 87*bis*(1); 17 U.S.C. § 602(a) (2015).

[58] Copyright Act, art. 87*bis*.

[59] Former Copyright Committees (predecessor of TIPO), Ministry of the Interior, Tai(82)-Nei-Zhu-Zi No. 8284870, April 24, 1993.

2003, when it was struck down through an amendment initiated by and during a "fractious negotiation meeting" in Taiwan.[60] Although this amendment was certainly welcome, the reasons behind the decriminalization of the violation of the right of importation remains unclear to date.[61]

C. Introduction of General Distribution Right and National Exhaustion

In addition to the right to importation, the 2003 amendment to the Taiwan Copyright Act formally introduces the general right to distribute and the principle of national exhaustion with respect to this right. Notably, article 28*bis* provides:

> (1) Except as otherwise provided in this Act, authors of works have the exclusive right to distribute their works through transfer of ownership. (2) Performers have the exclusive right to distribute their performances reproduced in sound recordings through transfer of ownership.[62]

The principle of national exhaustion is confirmed in article 59*bis* of the Taiwan Copyright Act, which additionally stipulates that "[a] person who has obtained ownership of the original of a work or a lawful copy thereof within the territory under the jurisdiction of the Republic of China may distribute it by means of transfer of ownership."[63]

D. The Fate of Legally Imported Genuine Copies: Resale No, Rental Yes

With respect to the application of article 87a(1)(3), it should also be noted that legally imported copies are not always bought and then resold by importers. Instead, these copies often journey further and are acquired by or enter into the possession of third parties via the resale or rental of the copies. However, the Supreme Court of Taiwan has ruled that the resale of these copyrighted copies is also not allowed. In particular, in its decision on January 14, 1999 in the case of *Tai-Fe-Zi No. 17*, a case involving a video shop reselling a legally imported laser disc imported by a third party, the Fifth Criminal Senate of the Supreme Court reasoned that:

> [t]he laser disc has been confirmed by the complainant to be genuine; circumstances for the application of Article 87a to exclude Article 87 Subparagraph 4 cannot be found, it is evident that the disc is an infringing copy. The defendant, knowing that it was an infringing copy, displayed it in his video shop with an intention to sell, violated Article 87 Subparagraph 2.[64]

---

[60] According to art. 68 of the Exercise of Functions of the Legislative Yuan Act, the Speaker of the Legislative Yuan can *ex officio* or upon application from factions of political parties convene factions negotiation meetings to solve disputes. Legislative Yuan, Proceedings, 96 LEGISLATIVE YUAN GAZETTE 83, 46–52 (November 30, 2007).
[61] According to art. 71 of the Exercise of Functions of the Legislative Yuan Act, factions negotiation meetings decide on the basis of consensus; the decision made by factions negotiation should be published, but not the reasoning. *Ibid.* art. 71.
[62] Copyright Act, art. 28*bis*.
[63] *Ibid.* art. 59*bis*.
[64] Tai-Fe-Zi No. 17, 1999 Xingshi Huibian (5th Criminal Senate of the Supreme Court, January 14, 1999).

Yet, adopting a position partially contradicting this decision, the Sixth Criminal Senate of the Supreme Court had previously upheld the lawfulness of rental of the legally imported copy in its December 10, 1998 decision in *Tai-Fe-Zi No. 397*.[65] The same year, the Seventh Criminal Senate of the Supreme Court issued a decision in a similar case concerning the rental of laser discs, which were legally imported by third parties and later were sold to the renter. In this case, the court confirmed that the copies could be lawfully rented and stated:

> [T]he final decision has specified that the owner of legal copies of works may rent such copies to others, as stipulated by Article 60. The fact that the 10 confiscated laser discs are legal copies of works has been confirmed by the defendant and the complainant as well. The defendant has acquired the ownership of those legal copies, and is legally allowed to display and rent the discs.[66]

Some commentators have criticized that the Supreme Court has not been consistent in its decisions in this area.[67] However, the seeming "inconsistency" of the Supreme Court can be easily explained by looking at the language of article 60 of the Taiwan Copyright Act, which clearly grants to the owners of originals of works and lawful copies of works the rental right of the works, except with respect to sound recording and computer programs. Notably, the provision clearly makes the rental of legal copies of works, whether imported or not, lawful.[68]

Still, it should be noted that the Supreme Court erred in banning the resale of legally imported genuine goods pursuant to article 87a(1)(3). Given that the allowed exception to the right of importation is extremely limited in the first place, the actual amount of legally imported genuine goods under the provision would be extremely limited. In turn, the resale of those goods could not pose any worth-mentioning harm to the interests of copyright holders.[69]

IV. HOW CAN THE TAIWAN COPYRIGHT ACT FOLLOW THE TAIWAN TRADEMARK AND PATENT ACT?

A. Building a General Theory of International Intellectual Property Exhaustion

Given the fact that Taiwanese citizens do not own many intellectual property rights in foreign countries and that Taiwan is primarily an import country of goods and services protected by intellectual property rights, the introduction of the exclusive right of importation that enables intellectual property holders to stop parallel import of intel-

---

[65] Tai-Fe-Zi No. 397, 1998 Xingshi Huibian (6th Criminal Senate of the Supreme Court, December 10, 1998).
[66] In a similar case, Tai-Fe-Zi No.158, 1998 Xingshi Huibian (7th Criminal Senate of the Supreme Court, June 4, 1998), the 7th Senate of the Supreme Court came to the same conclusion.
[67] Ming-Yang Shieh, *Does the Rental or Sale of Parallel Imported Laser Discs Violate Copyright?*, 7 TAIWAN LAW J. 62, 62 (February 2000).
[68] Copyright Act, art. 60.
[69] For a similar critique see Chung-Lun Shen, *The Manufacturing Lace and the Exhaustion Doctrine: The Reviews of Taiwanese Copyright Exhaustion Based on the U.S. Lessons*, 86 TAIPEI UNIV. LAW REV. 30 (June 2013).

lectual property protected products into Taiwan is at odds with Taiwan's interests as a whole. More specifically, the possibility to lawfully import intellectual property protected products into Taiwan under the principle of international exhaustion directly impacts the competitiveness of Taiwanese industries and the free flow of goods into Taiwan, both of which are vital to Taiwan's economic well-being. As Taiwan's Supreme Court adequately put it in its 1993 decision in *Tai Shan Zi 5380* (discussing trademark exhaustion):

> Parallel import of genuine goods . . . may prevent the market from being monopolized, facilitate intra-brand price competition, allow consumers to enjoy the benefit of reasonable prices, and so far as it does not contradict with the purpose of the Trademark Act shall be deemed to have been consented to by trademark right holders.[70]

Without doubt, articles 87(4) and 87*bis* of the Taiwan Copyright Act, and the administrative decree upheld by the Taiwan Intellectual Property Office (TIPO) taken together, favor the interests of U.S. copyright holders to a higher degree that they favor the interests of Taiwan's economy. In other words, labeling the current status quo as the result of blatant "U.S. economic imperialism" would not be an exaggeration. In effect, these provisions, along with the decision of the Supreme Court of Taiwan that disallows the resale of legally imported genuine goods, lead to the conclusion that the importation right in copyright law essentially is not subject to the principle of exhaustion.

Moreover, by and large, a large number of national systems of several countries are gravitating towards allowing parallel imports and adopting the international exhaustion doctrine. The recent landmark decision by the U.S. Supreme Court in *Kirtsaeng v. John Wiley & Sons, Inc.*, is another forceful example that confirms that the exhaustion doctrine applies to copies of copyrighted works lawfully made abroad[71] and international exhaustion prevails even in the U.S. itself despite the pressure by the U.S. to impose national exhaustion on other countries.

In Taiwan, the pro-parallel imports mindset is today the dominant trend. In addition to the favor of the academic community for parallel imports,[72] the Fair Trade Commission (FTC) has also taken a fairly parallel import-friendly attitude since its creation, despite the fact that the Fair Trade Act does not in itself contain any specific rule on parallel imports or intellectual property exhaustion. However, Interpretation No. 3 of the FTC clarifies that:[73]

---

[70] All decisions of courts are available at JUDICIAL YUAN, www.judicial.gov.tw.
[71] Kirtsaeng v. John Wiley & Sons, Inc., 133 S. Ct. 1358 (2013).
[72] Ming-Yang Shieh, *Importation Right of Patents and Parallel Import*, 2 TAIWAN LAW REV. 80, 84, 86 (June 1995); Chung-Lun Shen, *The Manufacturing Place and the Exhaustion Doctrine: The Reviews of Taiwanese Copyright Exhaustion Based on the U.S. Lessons*, 86 TAIPEI UNIV. LAW REV. 25 (June 2013); Chung-Lun Shen, *Licensing and Reasonable Transmission of Digitized Works: Epochal Application of the Exhaustion Doctrine*, 12 TAIWAN INTELL. PROP. REV. 33 (June 2014); Kuang-Cheng Chen, *Parallel Importation and Trademark Infringement*, 8 SHIH HSIN LAW J. 305–6 (June 2015).
[73] Fair Trade Commission, *Genuine Parallel Imports is a Violation of the Fair Trading Act*, available at www.ftc.gov.tw/internet/main/doc/docDetail.aspx?uid=223&docid=410.

While importing goods, which have been authorized by the original producer to be imported by his agent or manufactured by other producers, if the importing company has by active means misled consumers concerning the product's contents, source, name and address so as to give the impression that the goods come from the agent, this is the so-called free ride, then the "deception" or "obviously unfair" clause of Article 25 is invoked, because the domestic agent has invested huge marketing costs or expenditures to make the goods widely known to consumers.[74]

In other words, parallel import is permissible in Taiwan under the Fair Trade Act so long as the importer does not by active means mislead consumers into believing that the goods come from the agent instead of the importer.

In this respect, it should additionally be noted that the negative impact of banning parallel import of copies of copyrighted works has long been confirmed by the annual Survey on Monopoly over Imported Copyrighted Works conducted by the FTC. This survey began in 1994 under the mandate by the Legislative Yuan during the highly contentious introduction of the indirect right to import in the Taiwan Copyright Act.[75] The first survey compared the prices of imported computer software, LDs, CDs, books, magazines, and video games in three major cities in Taiwan (Taipei, Taichung, and Kaohsiung) and Los Angeles, New York, London, Paris, Hong Kong, Singapore, and Tokyo.[76] The survey demonstrated that prices of PC software, LDs, and magazines in Taiwan were indeed higher than those abroad, and the disappearance of the gray market after the ban of parallel imports is one of the reasons contributing to it.[77]

In summary, there is no obvious reason in Taiwan, and in the Taiwan Copyright Act, for not adhering to the principle of international exhaustion also in copyright law. The sooner Taiwan can shift its position towards international copyright exhaustion, the better.

Furthermore, it would be desirable to establish a coherent general theory of international exhaustion, not just in Taiwan, but also for the international community at large. In other words, it would be desirable to adopt international exhaustion as the overarching principle for all countries.[78] Equally important, it should be explicitly prohibited that the application of the international exhaustion doctrine be subject to contractual agreement, as national policies on exhaustion are clearly public-policy related and should not be contracted out by individual parties.[79] The Taiwan High Court has expressed a similar position in one of its decisions. In particular, the court stated that:

> According to the "exhaustion doctrine" of the intellectual property laws, a right holder has received remuneration for his creation and for products he made or made with his consent when they entered market for the first time, therefore should have lost the right to sell and use those products; any third party who has acquired the products lawfully is free to assign those products

---

[74] Ibid.
[75] Legislative Yuan, Proceedings, 82 LEGISLATIVE YUAN GAZETTE 24, 75 (April 22, 1993).
[76] FAIR TRADE COMMISSION, REPORT TO THE ECONOMIC AFFAIRS COMMITTEE OF THE LEGISLATIVE YUAN (No. 8361470, March 30, 1994). The surveys continued until 2001.
[77] Ibid.
[78] For a similar opinion see Kuang-Cheng Chen, *Parallel Importation and Trademark Infringement*, 8 SHIH HSIN LAW J. 305–6 (June 2015).
[79] This chapter rejects the stance taken by the U.S. Ninth Circuit Court in Vernor v. Autodesk, Inc., 671 F.3d 1102 (9th Cir. 2010), which allows contractual agreement to override the public policy represented by the exhaustion doctrine.

or make all kinds of use of those products, right holders may not interfere or assert rights; *this doctrine has become the axiom in the general theory of IP laws.*[80]

Last but not least, more attention should be paid to terminology in this area, as the use of appropriate terminology is certainly relevant as part of the general theory on the topic at issue. In particular, the use of the term "international exhaustion doctrine" should be preferred, rather than use of the (not so interchangeable) term "first sale doctrine." Using a clearer terminology would prove crucial, particularly with respect to the application of the principle of exhaustion in the digital context. As it turns out, in the digitalized and interconnected era of the Internet, "perpetual licenses" are more widely used just for the sole purpose of avoiding constituting the first "sale" and the resultant "exhaustion," illustrated by the decision in *UsedSoft GmbH v. Oracle International Corp.*[81] by the Court of Justice of the European Union (CJEU) in 2012.

B. Terminating the U.S.-Taiwan Copyright Protection Agreement

As with any international agreement, the U.S.-Taiwan Copyright Protection Agreement included a termination clause in Article 21, which states:

[t]his Agreement becomes effective on the date of the final signature thereafter and shall be valid until terminated by one Party upon notification to the other Party in writing at least six (6) months before the termination is to take effect.[82]

In light of this provision, Taiwan's government is encouraged to terminate the U.S.-Taiwan Copyright Protection Agreement as part of the process of negotiating a free trade agreement (FTA) with the U.S., and by adopting a provision similar to Chapter 10, Article 9 of the New Zealand-Taiwan FTA.[83] In particular, the U.S.-Taiwan Copyright

---

[80] Shan-I-Zi No. 20 (Taiwan High Court, December 23, 2014) (emphasis added).
[81] Case C-128/11, UsedSoft GmbH v. Oracle Int'l Corp., [2011] O.J. C194. The CJEU held that: "(1) Article 4(2) of Directive 2009/24/EC of the European Parliament and of the Council of 23 April 2009 on the legal protection of computer programs [[2009] O.J. L111/16, 18 (EN)] must be interpreted as meaning that the right of distribution of a copy of a computer program is exhausted if the copyright holder who has authorised, even free of charge, the downloading of that copy from the internet onto a data carrier has also conferred, in return for payment of a fee intended to enable him to obtain a remuneration corresponding to the economic value of the copy of the work of which he is the proprietor, a right to use that copy for an unlimited period. (2) Articles 4(2) and 5(1) of Directive 2009/24 must be interpreted as meaning that, in the event of the resale of a user license entailing the resale of a copy of a computer program downloaded from the copyright holder's website, that license having originally been granted by that right holder to the first acquirer for an unlimited period in return for payment of a fee intended to enable the right holder to obtain a remuneration corresponding to the economic value of that copy of his work, the second acquirer of the license, as well as any subsequent acquirer of it, will be able to rely on the exhaustion of the distribution right under Article 4(2) of that directive, and hence be regarded as lawful acquirers of a copy of a computer program within the meaning of Article 5(1) of that directive and benefit from the right of reproduction provided for in that provision." Directive 2009/24/EC, arts. 4(2), 5(1).
[82] U.S.-Taiwan Copyright Protection Agreement, art. 21.
[83] Chapter 10, Article 9 of the New Zealand-Taiwan FTA stipulates: "The Parties acknowledge the advice received from the Taipei Economic and Cultural Office and New Zealand Commerce

Protection Agreement should follow the example of Chapter 10, Article 3(4)(a) of the New Zealand-Taiwan FTA, which states that "[s]ubject to the international obligations that are applicable to each Party, the Parties affirm that each Party may: . . . provide for the international exhaustion of intellectual property rights."[84]

It should also be pointed out that no other FTA between the U.S. and other major trading partners in Asia (e.g., U.S.-South Korea and U.S.-Singapore) touch upon exhaustion issues. Singapore, for example, has been able to maintain its international exhaustion regime in copyright law even though Singapore entered into an FTA with the U.S.[85]

Finally, the U.S. could not legitimately oppose the termination of the U.S.-Taiwan Copyright Protection Agreement based on the fact that Taiwan would move from a system of national to international exhaustion. After all, the U.S. Supreme Court has recently clarified in its decision in *Kirtsaeng v. John Wiley & Sons, Inc.* that the U.S. also follows the principle of international copyright exhaustion. Accordingly, the U.S. would not lose "face" if Taiwan would terminate the U.S.-Taiwan Copyright Protection Agreement, for example, by joining, instead, the Trans-Pacific Partnership Agreement (TPP).[86]

V. CONCLUSION

Taiwan joined the WTO in 2002, and the country is long overdue for a comprehensive re-examination of its general policy on intellectual property exhaustion. At long last, the third draft of the amendment to the Taiwan Copyright Act, which was proposed by the TIPO in October 2015, abandons the national exhaustion doctrine in copyright law,[87] and follows the more free-trade friendly approach currently adopted in trademark and patent law. It is high time for Taiwan to break away from the out-of-date national exhaustion doctrine and the U.S.-Taiwan Copyright Protection Agreement and embrace the principle of international exhaustion as the general principle applicable to intellectual property law in Taiwan!

---

and Industry Office of their intention to terminate the following arrangements upon entry into force of this Agreement: a. Arrangement between the Taipei Economic and Cultural Office and the New Zealand Commerce and Industry Office, New Zealand, on the Reciprocal Protection and Enforcement of Copyright, done at Auckland on 15 June 1998; and b. Arrangement for the Protection of Industrial Property Rights between the Taipei Economic and Cultural Office in New Zealand and the New Zealand Commerce and Industry Office, done at Taipei on 20 October 1998." Agreement Between New Zealand and the Separate Customs Territory of Taiwan, Penghu, Kinmen, and Matsu on Economic Cooperation, ch. 10, art. 9 (July 2013), available at www.moea.gov.tw/TNE/main/home/Home.aspx.

[84] Ibid.
[85] See e.g. Copyright Act, §§ 32, 33 (providing that import of an article is legal so long as the making of the article was carried out with the consent of the owner of the copyright).
[86] Taiwan is not one of the 12 initiators of the Trans-Pacific Partnership (TPP). However, Taiwan is interested in joining the TPP and it is unlikely that Taiwan would be prevented from joining. The TPP does not touch the issue of exhaustion and leaves its members free to choose their preferred systems.
[87] The draft is available at TAIWAN INTELLECTUAL PROPERTY OFFICE, DRAFT AMENDMENT OF THE COPYRIGHT LAW, available at www.tipo.gov.tw/lp.asp?CtNode=7644&CtUnit=3743&BaseDSD=7&mp=1.

24. The Marrakesh Treaty and the targeted uses of copyright exhaustion
*Marketa Trimble**

I. INTRODUCTION

The Treaty to Facilitate Access to Published Works for Persons Who are Blind, Visually Impaired, or Otherwise Print Disabled, concluded by the WIPO Diplomatic Conference in Marrakesh in 2013 (the "Treaty"), states in Article 5(5) that "[n]othing in this Treaty shall be used to address the issue of exhaustion of rights."[1] This chapter analyzes whether, notwithstanding Article 5(5), the exhaustion principle could play a role in the implementation of the Treaty or whether, even if not directly playing a role in the implementation, the principle could assist in creating a regime that would be consistent with the Treaty's goals. The chapter does not claim that the exhaustion principle is necessarily the most suitable tool for implementing the Treaty;[2] the purpose of the chapter is to offer an analysis to those policy-makers and legislators who are considering the application of the exhaustion principle in the context of the Treaty.

The relevance of the exhaustion principle for the implementation of the Marrakesh Treaty is not readily apparent from the text of the Treaty, which treats the exhaustion principle in the same manner as the Agreement on Trade-Related Aspects of Intellectual Property Rights (TRIPS Agreement).[3] However, according to the recollections of the Treaty negotiators, the reasons for treating the principle in the Treaty in the same manner as in the TRIPS Agreement were not identical. The reason for the limited "agree to disagree"

---

* Samuel S. Lionel Professor of Intellectual Property Law, William S. Boyd School of Law, University of Nevada, Las Vegas. The author thanks Professors Irene Calboli and Mary LaFrance for suggesting the chapter topic; JUDr. Adela Faladova, Professor Justin Hughes, and the participants of the 2015 International Intellectual Property Scholars Roundtable at Duke Law School for their helpful comments and suggestions; Andrew Martineau at the Wiener-Rogers Law Library of the William S. Boyd School of Law for his excellent research support; and Gary A. Trimble for his valuable editing suggestions.

[1] Marrakesh Treaty to Facilitate Access to Published Works for Persons Who are Blind, Visually Impaired, or Otherwise Print Disabled, June 27, 2013, art. 5(5), available at www.wipo.int/treaties/en/text.jsp?file_id=301016 [hereinafter Marrakesh Treaty].

[2] For a discussion of the implementation of the cross-border exchange provisions of the Treaty see Marketa Trimble, *The Marrakesh Puzzle*, 45(7) INT'L REV. INTELL. PROP. & COMPETITION L. 768 (2014).

[3] Agreement on Trade-Related Aspects of Intellectual Property Rights, art. 13, April 15, 1994; Marrakesh Agreement Establishing the World Trade Organization, Annex 1C, Legal Texts: The Results of the Uruguay Round of Multilateral Trade Negotiations 320 (1999), 1869 U.N.T.S. 299, 33 I.L.M. 1197 (1994) [hereinafter TRIPS Agreement]; see *infra* note 19 and the accompanying text for a discussion of the differences between the Marrakesh Treaty and the TRIPS Agreement with respect to the exhaustion principle.

treatment of the exhaustion principle in the TRIPS Agreement was that the negotiators could not agree on which type of exhaustion principle should govern—the principle of national exhaustion or of international exhaustion—and for which rights.[4] Even at the time the Marrakesh Treaty was negotiated, countries were no closer to an agreement on a particular type of exhaustion principle, and it therefore made sense to leave the principle out of the Treaty. While the Marrakesh Treaty negotiators realized that opening the exhaustion principle debate would be fruitless, the Treaty negotiators, or at least some of them, also doubted that the exhaustion principle had any place in the Treaty because the principle did not seem to relate to the Treaty's content and subsequent implementation.[5]

This chapter suggests that the exhaustion principle might be relevant to the implementation of the Treaty. The analysis of the potential role for the exhaustion principle in the Treaty's implementation provides an opportunity to explore three matters that are not specific to the implementation of the Treaty. The first matter is a seldom-mentioned (and apparently never in depth investigated) relationship between the exhaustion principle and other limitations and exceptions to copyright. The second matter is the application of the three-step test[6] to limitations and exceptions that concern the distribution right in circumstances when distribution is expected to occur outside the country that is implementing the limitations or exceptions. Finally, the third matter is the "targeted uses" of the exhaustion principle; instances in which the exhaustion principle, also known as the "first sale doctrine" in the United States (U.S.), does not apply generally, as we would typically expect, but applies selectively because it is tailored to achieve particular goals.

II. THE MARRAKESH TREATY

The Marrakesh Treaty is the first international intellectual property treaty to focus on limitations and exceptions to copyright without simultaneously clarifying existing rights and/or adding new rights to international copyright law. The Treaty purports not to require that countries adopt limitations and exceptions extending beyond the three-step test framework established by earlier international treaties;[7] in several places, the Treaty reiterates the requirement that the limitations and exceptions under the Treaty must

---

[4] DANIEL GERVAIS, THE TRIPS AGREEMENT: DRAFTING HISTORY AND ANALYSIS 222, 226 (4th ed. 2012). See *infra* note 29 and the accompanying text for the difference between national and international exhaustion.

[5] See also Judith Sullivan, *Study on Copyright Limitations and Exceptions for the Visually Impaired*, WIPO, STANDING COMMITTEE ON COPYRIGHT AND RELATED RIGHTS, SCCR/15/7, February 20, 2007, 63 ("[P]rovision on exhaustion of rights is unlikely to be relevant to the legality of imports and exports of copies made under exceptions to copyright.").

[6] See *infra* note 77.

[7] On the history and versions of the three-step test see e.g. Justin Hughes, Fair Use and Its Politics: At Home and Abroad (draft, on file with the author); Christophe Geiger, Daniel Gervais, & Martin Senftleben, *The Three-Step Test Revisited: How to Use the Test's Flexibility in National Copyright Law*, 29(3) AM. U. INT'L L. REV. 581 (2014); Simonetta Vezzoso, *The Marrakesh Spirit: A Ghost in Three Steps?*, 45 INT'L REV. INTELL. PROP. & COMPETITION L. 796, 804–6 (2014); Andrew F. Christie & Robin Wright, *A Comparative Analysis of the Three-Step Tests in International Treaties*, 45(4) INT'L REV. INTELL. PROP. & COMPETITION L. 409 (2014).

comply with the pre-existing three-step test.[8] In being drafted to fit within the pre-existing three-step test framework, the Treaty appears to be more conservative than the TRIPS Agreement, which incorporated the three-step test from the Berne Convention but *de facto* extended the application of the test to allow for limitations and exceptions to rights that were not included in the Berne Convention.[9]

Notwithstanding the arguably conservative approach pursued by the Treaty, critics observed the adoption of the Treaty with significant concerns: the Marrakesh Treaty is the first treaty to dictate one specific purpose for which countries must utilize the limitations and exceptions that the three-step test framework permits. No longer may a country decide whether or not it will adopt limitations or exceptions for the benefit of the visually impaired; the Treaty mandates that countries implement limitations or exceptions for this specific purpose. Critics fear that the Treaty will be used as a template for future treaties that will mandate additional specific limitations and exceptions to copyright.[10]

The Treaty pursues two primary goals. First, it aims to facilitate easier and more rapid access to materials protected by copyright[11] for persons with visual impairments or other print disabilities. Second, it aims to protect the rights of copyright holders and authors.[12] To achieve these goals, the Treaty addresses two sets of problems: first, it provides for limitations and exceptions to facilitate access to materials domestically—within each country;[13] and second, it envisages a mechanism for cross-border exchange of materials so as to maximize access to materials internationally.[14] The cross-border exchange should assist in making materials more widely available because the possibility to export and import materials should eliminate the duplication of transaction and production costs that occurs when materials are produced in each country only for that country's own market.

The Treaty leaves it to the signatory countries to decide how they will implement their obligations under the Treaty. Countries are free to adopt any "measures necessary to ensure the application of [the] Treaty"[15] as long as the measures comply with the three-step test.[16] Countries may, but are not required to, use the template included in Article 4(2) for the implementation of the provisions concerning domestic access; the template implementation creates an exception to copyright that, presumably, is consistent with the

---

[8] Marrakesh Treaty, Preamble, fns. 4–6, art. 11.
[9] TRIPS Agreement, art. 13. Report of the Panel, *United States—Section 110(5) of the U.S. Copyright Act*, WT/DS160/R, para. 6.80 (June 15, 2000).
[10] See e.g. William New, *Negotiators, Stakeholders Tell Tale of WIPO Marrakesh Treaty Negotiation, Look to Implementation*, INTELL. PROP. WATCH (September 20, 2013), available at www.ip-watch.org/2013/09/20/negotiators-stakeholders-tell-tale-of-wipo-marrakesh-treaty-negotiation-look-to-implementation/; Kimberly Kindy, *Filmmakers' Group Tries to Reshape Treaty that Would Benefit the Blind*, WASHINGTON POST (June 22, 2013), available at www.washingtonpost.com/politics/filmmakers-group-tries-to-reshape-treaty-that-would-benefit-the-blind/2013/06/22/f98e6130-d761-11e2-9df4-895344c13c30_story.html.
[11] The materials are limited to particular "forms of works" and to particular formats of copies. Marrakesh Treaty, arts. 2(a) and (b). For the definition of "beneficiary persons" see *ibid.* art. 3.
[12] *Ibid.* Preamble.
[13] *Ibid.* art. 4.
[14] *Ibid.* arts. 5, 6, and 9.
[15] *Ibid.* art. 10(1).
[16] *Ibid.* art. 11.

three-step test. Additionally, countries may subject any limitation or exception that implements the Treaty to remuneration for copyright owners;[17] for example, countries may introduce a statutory licensing scheme to remunerate copyright owners.[18] Countries may also restrict limitations and exceptions so that the limitations and exceptions apply only when the materials at issue "cannot be obtained commercially under reasonable terms."[19] The Treaty offers an additional implementation template in Article 5(2), which concerns cross-border exchange of materials; countries may follow the template or implement cross-border exchange through other limitations or exceptions, but such other limitations and exceptions must comply with the three-step test.

Nowhere does the Treaty suggest that the principle of exhaustion of copyright should play a role in implementing the Treaty. Article 5(5) actually reads as though the negotiators intended to dissuade legislators from considering the exhaustion principle as a vehicle for the Treaty's implementation. Article 5(5) repeats a portion of Article 6 of the TRIPS Agreement, but the Treaty omits another part of the Article: Article 6 of the TRIPS Agreement prevents provisions of the TRIPS Agreement from being used "to address the issue of the exhaustion" "[f]or the purposes of dispute settlement under [the] Agreement." Article 6 has clear addressees: WTO dispute settlement bodies and countries that use the WTO dispute settlement mechanism to complain of TRIPS Agreement violations by other countries.[20] Article 5(5) of the Marrakesh Treaty has no "purposes" clause and therefore the Article lacks both specific addressees to which it is directed and identifiable purposes for which it is designed. Consequently, it is unclear who should refrain or for what purpose one should refrain from using the provisions of the Treaty to address the exhaustion principle.

It appears that the Treaty drafters intended to duplicate the result achieved by the TRIPS Agreement: repeat the countries' stipulation of disagreement regarding the exhaustion principle and declare the countries' agreement not to interpret the Treaty as dictating any particular type of exhaustion for any particular rights.[21] Article 5(5) of the Treaty is probably not designed to foreclose the possibility that a national legislature might utilize the exhaustion principle in implementing the Treaty; the language in the

---

[17] *Ibid.* art. 4(5). For countries that as of 2014 subjected exceptions and/or limitations for the benefit of the visually impaired to remuneration to copyright owners see Jingyi Li, *Copyright Exemptions to Facilitate Access to Published Works for the Print Disabled: The Gap Between National Laws and the Standards Required by the Marrakesh Treaty*, 45 INT'L REV. INTELL. PROP. & COMPETITION L. 740, 749–50 (2014).

[18] For criticism of the Treaty's approach in leaving to countries the decision whether or not to introduce remuneration see Jingyi Li & Niloufer Selvadurai, *Reconciling the Enforcement of Copyright with the Upholding of Human Rights: A Consideration of the Marrakesh Treaty to Facilitate Access to Published Works for the Blind, Visually Impaired and Print Disabled*, 36(10) E.I.P.R. 653, 661 (2014).

[19] Marrakesh Treaty, art. 4(4). On the debate regarding a potential requirement to check for commercial availability see Vezzoso, *supra* note 7, at 815–17.

[20] GERVAIS, *supra* note 4, at 222.

[21] Mihály J. Ficsor, *Commentary on the Marrakesh Treaty on Accessible Format Copies for the Visually Impaired*, October 11, 2013, 35, available at www.copyrightseesaw.net/archive/?sw_10_item=50. On the meaning of "the purposes of dispute settlement" in the TRIPS Agreement see JUSTIN MALBON, CHARLES LAWSON, & MARK DAVISON, THE WTO AGREEMENT ON TRADE-RELATED ASPECTS OF INTELLECTUAL PROPERTY RIGHTS: A COMMENTARY 175–77 (2014).

Treaty that emphasizes the freedom of countries to choose appropriate methods of implementation of the Treaty appears to support this interpretation.[22]

III. THE EXHAUSTION PRINCIPLE AND THE IMPLEMENTATION OF THE MARRAKESH TREATY

There are three reasons for which the exhaustion principle appears to be potentially relevant to the implementation of the Marrakesh Treaty. First, the exhaustion principle is a limitation on copyright: it limits the distribution right so that the right encompasses only the first sale or another act of first distribution by the copyright owner or with the copyright owner's authorization ("the first distribution").[23] The exhaustion principle therefore falls within the category of "limitations or exceptions," which the Treaty identifies as the tools that countries may use for the implementation of the Treaty. Second, the exhaustion principle concerns copies of works, and the Treaty also concerns copies—copies of certain types of works that are expressed in particular formats. Third, the exhaustion principle affects "subsequent distribution"—any and all distributions that follow the first distribution. As the next section of this chapter explains, the Treaty also affects such subsequent distribution.[24]

In addition to the reasons supporting any use of the exhaustion principle in implementing the Treaty, there are also several objections that could be raised against its use. The first and perhaps the strongest objection is that the exhaustion principle presupposes an act of first distribution that involves the copyright owner's (1) distribution of a copy of his work; and (2) collection of his reward, recovery of his investment,[25] or decision to forfeit his remuneration.[26] However, the first distribution based on a limitation or exception that is envisioned in the Treaty is not based on the copyright owner's decision; the first distribution does not even involve an act of distribution by the copyright owner. A later section in this chapter addresses this objection.

Another problem with using the exhaustion principle in implementing the Treaty is that the principle concerns only the right to distribute; the distribution right is separate from the right of reproduction, the right of making available to the public, and the right of public performance, all three of which should be covered by the limitations and exceptions

---

[22] Marrakesh Treaty, arts. 4(3), 5(3), 10(2), 11.
[23] For the definition of "first distribution" in the European Union see e.g. Benedetta Ubertazzi, *The Principle of Free Movement of Goods: Community Exhaustion and Parallel Imports*, in EU Copyright Law: A Commentary 41, 38–51 (Irini Stamatoudi & Paul Torremans eds., 2014); Laddie, Prescott & Vitoria, The Modern Law of Copyright and Designs paras. 33.21, 1512–15 (4th ed. 2011); Guido Westkamp, *Emerging Escape Clauses? Online Exhaustion, Consent and European Copyright Law*, in Intellectual Property at the Crossroads of Trade 59–61, 38–66 (Jan Rosén ed., 2012). For the definition of "first sale" under U.S. law see Goldstein on Copyright (2008) § 7.6.1.
[24] See *infra* for a further discussion of subsequent distribution under the Marrakesh Treaty.
[25] For the "reward theory of exhaustion" see Malbon, Lawson, & Davison, *supra* note 21, at 179.
[26] See Sullivan, *supra* note 5.

under the Treaty, in addition to the right of distribution.[27] Also, the exhaustion principle affects only subsequent distribution, while the Treaty covers all distributions—and arguably focuses on first distribution. Still another problem is that, although the Treaty covers electronic copies, in some countries the distribution right to electronic copies of all or some works does not exhaust.[28] It should be noted, however, that the exhaustion principle would not be (and could not be expected to be) the sole vehicle for the implementation of the Treaty; the implementation would have to be based on additional limitations or exceptions. But the exhaustion principle could be one of the implementing limitations or exceptions.

The exhaustion principle might further seem ill-suited for implementing the Treaty because the principle typically exists in two types: countries apply either the principle of national exhaustion or the principle of international exhaustion. Depending on which type of principle a country has adopted, first distribution either must occur within that country (for national exhaustion) or may occur anywhere in the world (for international exhaustion) for the distribution right to exhaust in that country. But the Treaty implementation would require a "Treaty country-wide" exhaustion, meaning that first distribution in any country that is party to the Treaty would result in exhaustion of the distribution right in all Treaty countries and permit further distribution without permission or license from the copyright owner within and among all Treaty countries. Although this design of the exhaustion principle does not fit the typical national and international exhaustion models, an international but territorially-limited exhaustion is not without precedent. In the European Union, copyright exhausts regionally; first distribution within the European Union exhausts copyright in all EU Member States.[29]

Another potential difficulty with the use of the exhaustion principle in implementing the Treaty is that the limitations and exceptions implementing the Treaty might have to be tailored to serve the particular purpose that the Treaty defines. The use of the exhaustion principle might therefore have to be targeted to serve particular authorized entities, beneficiary persons, and a particular purpose.[30] The exhaustion principle seems to be inconsistent with such targeting because the principle typically applies generally; arguably, an advantage of the principle is the generality of its application and the resulting ease with which even a layperson can understand this limitation on copyright. However, as one of the following sections points out, some targeted uses of the exhaustion principle already exist, and these uses limit the general applicability of the principle. In fact, targeted uses of the exhaustion principle are more common than might be realized.

---

[27] Marrakesh Treaty, art. 4(1).
[28] See also *infra* notes 65 and 66 and the accompanying text.
[29] On the exhaustion principle in the European Union see e.g. PAUL GOLDSTEIN & P. BERNT HUGENHOLTZ, INTERNATIONAL COPYRIGHT: PRINCIPLES, LAW AND PRACTICE 311–12 (3rd ed. 2013); LADDIE, PRESCOTT, AND VITORIA, *supra* note 23, paras. 33.13–33.16 and 33.21 at 1507–10 and 1512–15; Case C-479/04, Laserdisken ApS v. Kulturministeriet, [2006] E.C.R. I-8089, I-8120.
[30] Marrakesh Treaty, arts. 2(c), 3, 4(1), 5(1), 6.

IV. SUBSEQUENT DISTRIBUTION AND THE MARRAKESH TREATY

The exhaustion principle can be useful in the implementation of the Marrakesh Treaty only if the Treaty actually provides for subsequent distribution. If the Treaty concerns only first distribution the exhaustion principle will be of no assistance to the Treaty implementation although the principle could still serve to create a legal framework to fulfill the goals pursued by the Treaty—as long as such utilization of the principle complies with international copyright law obligations.

The Treaty does not state whether it concerns only first distribution or whether it also covers subsequent distribution. It seems logical that the Treaty should cover subsequent distribution; the Preamble to the Treaty mentions the need "to improve the circulation of [published] works," which seems to suggest that the Treaty covers not only first distribution but also subsequent distribution.[31] Article 4(1)(a) speaks of "facilitat[ing] the availability of works in accessible format copies for beneficiary persons" without specifying whether the facilitation should concern only first distribution or also subsequent distribution. Similarly, cross-border exchange under Article 5 does not appear to be limited to first distribution.

If we look at U.S. law as an example of corresponding national provisions, we see that the law seems to provide for both first distribution and subsequent distribution in its provision on limitations to copyright for the benefit of the visually impaired: section 121 of the U.S. Copyright Act provides for reproduction and distribution of copies and phonorecords by an authorized entity "for use by blind and other persons with disabilities," and the provision does not limit the distribution to first distribution. An authorized entity that makes a reproduction of copies or phonorecords in a specialized format may distribute the copies or phonorecords repeatedly (e.g., through lending),[32] and it may also subsequently distribute copies and phonorecords that were reproduced and first distributed by other authorized entities.

V. THE EXHAUSTION PRINCIPLE AND COPIES FIRST DISTRIBUTED UNDER EXCEPTIONS AND LIMITATIONS TO COPYRIGHT

Let us now return to the objection that the exhaustion principle cannot be used for copies distributed under the Treaty because the principle presupposes a voluntary act, or first distribution, by the copyright owner, an act that is missing when the first distribution is based on a limitation or exception to copyright.[33] Surprisingly, the relationship between the exhaustion principle and other limitations and exceptions to copyright has rarely been discussed in the literature.

---

[31] *Ibid.* Preamble.
[32] See 17 U.S.C. § 121(b)(2) (1997) for exceptions concerning computer programs and other works.
[33] See also *supra* note 5 and the accompanying text.

In general, for the exhaustion principle to apply, a copyright owner need not have possession or control of a particular copy of his work before or at the time the copy is first distributed, and the first distribution need not be based on the copyright owner's consent. The term "first sale doctrine," which is the term used in the U.S. for the doctrine that establishes the exhaustion principle, suggests that exhaustion may occur only with a first distribution by the copyright owner. However, the U.S. Copyright Act states that the principle applies to a "copy or phonorecord lawfully made under this title"[34]—a category that is broader than just copies first sold by copyright owners.[35] Similarly, the copyright laws of other countries do not limit the act of first distribution that is required for exhaustion to the first sale by the copyright owner.[36]

If the exhaustion principle were to apply only to copies first distributed by the copyright owner, the principle could never apply to copies that were reproduced and first distributed based on a limitation or exception to copyright. But the exhaustion principle *does* apply in some instances when the first distribution is based on a limitation or exception;[37] these are instances in which the copyright statute replaces the copyright owner's consent, dictates the scope of the consent, and mandates the remuneration, if any, to be paid to the copyright owner.

Consider the following example of the functioning of the exhaustion principle in cases of copies first distributed under one of the remunerated limitations included in the U.S. Copyright Act.[38] Remunerated limitations replace a copyright owner's consent to the first distribution of the copy and provide for remuneration in the form of a statutory royalty. One such limitation provides for a mechanical license for nondramatic musical works: When a performer obtains a mechanical license for a nondramatic musical work, the performer may record the work (record a cover, meaning reproduce the musical work) and distribute the phonorecord with the recording of the musical work.[39] The musical work remains an underlying work to the recording, and the first distribution of the phonorecord under the mechanical license exhausts the distribution right to the musical work; whoever purchases that particular phonorecord may resell the phonorecord without the permission of or a license from the owner of the copyright to the musical work[40] and the owner of the copyright to the musical work may not prevent the subsequent distribution of the particular phonorecord.

The exhaustion principle will not always apply to subsequent distribution of a copy when the first distribution of the copy is based on an exception or limitation, particularly if the exception does not provide for remuneration to the copyright owner. For example, an exception to copyright might allow a library to make a copy of an article and distribute

---

[34] 17 U.S.C. §109(a).
[35] For U.S. law see also *infra* note 57.
[36] Urheberrechtsgesetz, [Copyright Act], September 9, 1965, Bundesgesetzblatt [BGBl.] I, § 17(2) (Ger.); Copyright, Designs and Patents Act, 1988, ch. 48, § 18(3) (Eng.).
[37] 2-8 NIMMER ON COPYRIGHT § 8.12 ("The first sale doctrine may be claimed by any 'owner of a particular copy or phonorecord lawfully made,' and not just by those who acquired such ownership via a prior transfer from the copyright owner.").
[38] On the difference between an exception and a limitation see Ficsor, *supra* note 21, at 21.
[39] 17 U.S.C. § 115.
[40] See also 4 PATRY ON COPYRIGHT § 13:22 (2015). But see *infra* note 62.

the copy to a library patron;[41] however, the exception is typically not designed to permit subsequent distribution of the copy by the patron or a person who might obtain the copy from the patron.[42]

The determination of whether the exhaustion principle should apply to copies first distributed under a limitation or exception should depend on an assessment of the particular limitation or exception under the three-step test. In the above example of mechanical licenses, the statutory royalty may remunerate the copyright owner sufficiently for the limitation to comply with the three-step test. An exception to copyright that allows a library to make a copy of an article and distribute the copy to a library patron[43] might not meet the three-step test if it permits any subsequent distribution of the copy by the patron. However, the three-step test might be satisfied if a country were to adopt a statutory license to remunerate a copyright owner for the copies reproduced and distributed by libraries. Of course, remuneration alone will not always tilt the scales in favor of satisfying the three-step test.

When limitations and exceptions concern the distribution right, the possibility of the exhaustion of the right and the nature of subsequent distribution should be factored into the three-step-test analysis. A limitation or exception to copyright that concerns other rights will not require that subsequent distribution be factored into the three-step-test analysis. For example, when an exception permits a user to make a reproduction of a work for "private purposes,"[44] the law assumes no distribution of the copy made by the user, and there is no need to factor subsequent distribution in when the exception is evaluated under the three-step test.[45] When a limitation permits a user to reproduce and distribute a musical work,[46] unless subsequent distribution is limited in some manner, the law probably assumes that the distribution right exhausts with the first distribution under the limitation, and, therefore, the evaluation of the limitation under the three-step test must include a consideration of any subsequent distribution.

Typically when designing a limitation or exception that concerns the distribution right, a country will consider only subsequent *domestic* distribution and will then design the limitation or exception to comply with the three-step test when copies are subsequently distributed within the country. For example, a country designing an exception to copyright for the visually impaired might decide to opt for an unremunerated exception to reproduce and distribute specialized format copies but limit subsequent distribution by who may distribute (e.g., authorized entities) and to whom (e.g., to authorized entities or to the visually impaired). The country will typically not consider what the conditions might be for subsequent distribution if the copies will be exported to and distributed in other countries. This domestically-focused approach to designing the exception is

---

[41] 17 U.S.C. § 108(d).
[42] 17 U.S.C. § 108(d)(1), (e)(1), and (g)(2). Although isolated instances of subsequent distribution by patrons might be fair use or fall within the scope of another exception or limitation to copyright, repeated distributions of various copies by the same patron would be problematic.
[43] 17 U.S.C. § 108(d).
[44] Copyright Act, R.S.C. 1985, c. C-42, arts. 29, 29.22 (Can.).
[45] See *ibid.* art. 29.22(4) for a provision concerning subsequent distribution of the original from which the user made the reproduction.
[46] 17 U.S.C. § 115.

understandable and consistent with national legislating in other matters and other areas of law.[47] But while the approach is defensible when instances of subsequent distribution in foreign countries can be expected to present a few isolated outliers, the approach might be less defensible when the exception is explicitly supposed to serve not only domestic subsequent distribution but also foreign subsequent distribution. This point is important for further discussion later in this chapter.

VI. LIMITATIONS ON SUBSEQUENT DISTRIBUTION

If we conclude that the Treaty does cover subsequent distribution, and that the exhaustion principle may, in some circumstances, apply to copies whose first distribution was based on a limitation or exception to copyright, we may proceed to the question whether the Treaty will allow for unrestricted subsequent distribution of materials reproduced and first distributed under Treaty implementing provisions, or whether the Treaty limits subsequent distribution to distribution from authorized entities to authorized entities and/or beneficiaries and for the particular purpose defined in the Treaty.

Unless countries utilize the template provision in Article 4(2), the Treaty places no particular constraints on subsequent distribution with respect to domestic distribution. Compliance with the three-step test is the only constraint on both first domestic distribution and subsequent domestic distribution. National limitations and exceptions implementing Article 4(1) need not be restricted to distribution by authorized entities, or distribution by authorized entities to other authorized entities and beneficiaries. All the provision requires are limitations or exceptions "to facilitate the availability of works in accessible format copies for beneficiary persons."[48] Additionally, Article 12(1) permits countries to "implement . . . other copyright limitations and exceptions for the benefit of beneficiary persons";[49] such other limitations and exceptions need not limit distribution so that it will occur only from an authorized entity to another authorized entity or a beneficiary. Constraints do exist in the implementing provision template offered in Article 4(2), and the constraints will apply if a country decides to follow the template.

Whether subsequent domestic distribution of copies should be constrained by the same restrictions as first distribution, or whether subsequent domestic distribution should be unencumbered by the restrictions that apply to first distribution, will depend on an evaluation of the particular implementing limitation or exception according to the three-step test.[50] Unencumbered subsequent domestic distribution might be acceptable in countries that implement the Treaty through a limitation associated with remuneration to the copyright owner. However, permitting unencumbered subsequent domestic distribution might be problematic in countries that implement the Treaty through an unremunerated exception to copyright; even if such an unremunerated exception meets the three-step test

---

[47] See Marketa Trimble, *Advancing National Intellectual Property Policies in a Transnational Context*, 74 MD. L. REV. 203, 208–11 (2015).
[48] Marrakesh Treaty, art. 4(1).
[49] *Ibid.* art. 12(1).
[50] For the application of the three-step test to possible exceptions and limitations under the Treaty see Vezzoso, *supra* note 7, at 810–19.

for first distribution, the exception might fail the test when unencumbered subsequent distribution is factored in. The assessment is even more complicated because, as suggested earlier, the assessment should take into account *any* possible subsequent distribution, including subsequent distribution that may occur abroad following exportation of the copies.

For purposes of the three-step test, it would be helpful if countries could rely on certain parameters of subsequent distribution that would follow the exportation of copies to other countries. For this reason, it would have made sense for the Treaty to mandate such parameters, and the cross-border exchange provisions of the Treaty indeed appear to aim to provide certainty about the parameters of subsequent distribution of imported copies.

The cross-border exchange provision of Article 5(1) applies only to "accessible format cop[ies] made under a limitation or exception or pursuant to operation of law," and the provisions concern only distribution "by an authorized entity to a beneficiary person or an authorized entity in another Contracting Party."[51] Therefore, in cases of cross-border distribution, Article 5(1) restricts distribution across national borders (whether the distribution be the first distribution or a subsequent distribution) to distribution from authorized entities to authorized entities and/or beneficiaries and for the particular purpose defined in the Treaty.

Article 5(1), combined with other provisions of the Treaty, also dictates the conditions of a subsequent distribution of an imported copy. Authorized entities, in order to maintain their status as authorized entities, must "limit to beneficiary persons and/or authorized entities [their] distribution . . . of accessible format copies."[52] Therefore, if authorized entity A distributes a copy for the first time or a subsequent time across a border to authorized entity B, authorized entity B may, in turn, subsequently distribute the imported copy only to another authorized entity or a beneficiary. Through this mandated distribution chain, Article 5(1) affects domestic distribution when the distribution is a domestic distribution of copies that were imported in accordance with Article 5(1) and Article 6.

The obligation to maintain the chain in subsequent domestic distribution of imported copies under Article 5(1) applies only to authorized entities; beneficiaries are not constrained in their subsequent distribution of imported copies. Therefore, beneficiaries could theoretically break the chain and subsequently distribute to persons and entities other than beneficiaries and authorized entities. Of course, given the obligations of authorized entities to limit distribution to particular persons and entities, it is likely that authorized entities will include a contractual term in their transactions restricting subsequent distribution to beneficiaries or authorized entities. To what extent such a term will be enforceable in practice might be questionable.

An important caveat concerning subsequent distribution of imported copies is that Articles 10 and 12 of the Treaty could be interpreted as permitting subsequent distribution of imported copies even outside the mandated distribution chain, as long as the limitation or exception providing for such unrestricted subsequent distribution (1) complies with the three-step test, and (2) can be interpreted as both fulfilling countries' "rights

---

[51] Marrakesh Treaty, art. 5(1).
[52] *Ibid.* art. 2(c)(ii).

and obligations under [the] Treaty"[53] and being implemented "for the benefit of beneficiary persons."[54] The possibility for a country to avoid the mandated distribution chain should be welcomed particularly by countries that adhere to the principle of international exhaustion of copyright if those countries deem copies distributed under the Treaty to be first distributed for the purposes of the exhaustion principle. If such countries were to introduce the mandated distribution chain envisioned by Article 5(1), they would have to limit the application of the exhaustion principle for copies imported and subsequently distributed under the Treaty, with the incongruous result that while all other imported copies could be freely distributed, the subsequent distribution of copies imported under the Treaty would be limited.

The problem with the possibility of avoiding the implementation of the mandatory distribution chain for subsequent distribution of imported copies is that the possibility leaves a significant unknown in the three-step-test analysis: A country that legislates limitations or exceptions under which the copies are first distributed does not know what the parameters of subsequent distribution will be once the copies are exported to other countries. If that legislating country could rely on other countries to implement the mandated distribution chain for copies imported from the legislating country, the legislating country might, for example, introduce an unremunerated exception if, combined with a restricted subsequent distribution in all Treaty countries, the exception complied with the three-step test. If the parameters of subsequent distribution abroad are uncertain, the legislating country might opt to introduce a remunerated limitation that will more likely comply with the three-step test even if the copies happen to be exported and subsequently distributed in a country that places no restrictions on subsequent distribution of the imported copies.

VII. SUBSEQUENT DISTRIBUTION UNDER U.S. COPYRIGHT LAW

U.S. copyright law provides no instructive example with regard to constraints on subsequent distribution of copies first distributed under the exception for the visually impaired. The Copyright Act and its legislative history are silent about the relationship between the first sale doctrine (the exhaustion principle) under section 109(a) of the Copyright Act and the exception for the visually impaired under section 121. Section 121 refers to the distribution right in section 106 as limited by the first sale doctrine of section 109(a).[55] What the wordings of sections 121 and 109(a) mean is that a regular copy (meaning a copy that was not reproduced and distributed under section 121) that has been first distributed may be subsequently distributed to a visually impaired person without permission or a license; once the distribution right is exhausted, the distribution right no longer attaches to the particular copy, and section 121 need not apply for the copy to be available to the visually impaired. But does the first sale doctrine of section 109(a) apply to a subsequent

---

[53] *Ibid.* art. 10(3).
[54] *Ibid.* art. 12(1). Footnote 10 to art. 6 of the Marrakesh Treaty provides additional support for this interpretation.
[55] See also Kirtsaeng v. John Wiley & Sons, Inc., 133 S. Ct. 1351, 1367 (2013).

distribution of a copy that was reproduced and first distributed according to section 121? If the first sale doctrine does apply, the subsequent distribution is unencumbered by the restrictions of section 121; if the first sale doctrine does not apply, subsequent distribution may occur only under the restrictions of section 121.

Arguments in favor of the application of the first sale doctrine to specialized copies under section 121 can be inferred from the language and structure of the Copyright Act and from policy considerations. Section 121 does not state what its relationship to section 109(a) is, and it might therefore seem that the first sale doctrine in section 109(a) does not apply to copies that are reproduced and first distributed under the exception in section 121. But such a conclusion seems inconsistent with the fact that the first sale doctrine does apply to other exceptions and limitations in the same chapter of the Copyright Act, for example, to phonorecords recorded and first distributed under the section 115 mechanical license.[56] Also, at least some copies and phonorecords that are covered by the fair use doctrine under section 107 will be subject to the first sale doctrine.[57] From a policy perspective, the application of the first sale doctrine would facilitate the desired increased access to works by the visually impaired; because the Copyright Act would permit unrestricted subsequent distribution, the Act would allow for a secondary market to develop for copies and phonorecords in specialized formats that could enhance access to the copies by the visually impaired.

Other considerations weigh against the application of the first sale doctrine to specialized copies under section 121. The fact that the section 121 exception is not associated with remuneration to the copyright owner weighs against the application of the first sale doctrine to any copies reproduced and first distributed under the exception. Rather, the lack of remuneration suggests that subsequent distribution should be allowable only within the restrictions specified in section 121. A labeling provision in section 121 suggests that legislators intended for the restrictions in section 121 to constrain subsequent distribution; the section requires that copies and phonorecords in specialized formats bear not only a regular copyright notice but also a special notice distinguishing them from other, non-specialized format copies.[58] Such a special notice would seem to be useful if the restrictions of section 121 were intended to survive first distribution of the copies and continued to apply to subsequent distribution, although the notice also serves an informational purpose for first distribution.

The relationship between sections 121 and 109(a) of the U.S. Copyright Act has apparently not been the subject of litigation or other publicized disputes. One reason for the absence of disputes might be that effective physical measures have been in place to channel copies and phonorecords to subsequent distribution that complies with the restrictions of section 121. The specialized formatting of the copies and phonorecords creates a

---

[56] 17 U.S.C. §115.
[57] See also H. R. REP. NO. 94-1476 (1976) (For the first sale doctrine to apply, "a copy or phonorecord must have been 'lawfully made under this title,' though not necessarily with the copyright owner's authorization."). See also Kirtsaeng v. John Wiley & Sons, Inc., 133 S. Ct. 1351, 1361 (2013); GOLDSTEIN ON COPYRIGHT § 7.6.1 (2008) ("For example, copies made under section 107's fair use privilege or section 115's compulsory licensing provisions, although not authorized, are lawful and so come within the [first sale doctrine] exemption.").
[58] 17 U.S.C. § 121(b)(1)(B).

sufficient physical barrier to prevent uses of the copies and phonorecords by persons other than the visually impaired and has prevented the development of any market for the copies and phonorecords among users who are not visually impaired.[59] Without the development of a secondary market for users who are not visually impaired, no need has arisen to clarify the potential applicability of the first sale doctrine to copies distributed under the section 121 limitation.

Since the 2013 U.S. Supreme Court decision in *Kirtsaeng*[60] the United States has applied the principle of international exhaustion to copyright. Therefore, copies currently reproduced and distributed in countries outside the United States under existing limitations or exceptions that are designed in those countries for the benefit of the visually impaired may be imported to and further distributed in the United States without the permission of or a license from the copyright owner, and as long as U.S. courts consider such copies first distributed in the foreign countries, such subsequent distribution should be unencumbered by any limitations.

VIII. SUBSEQUENT DISTRIBUTION UNDER THE TARGETED EXHAUSTION PRINCIPLE

One objection to the use of the exhaustion principle to implement the Treaty is that in some circumstances countries will be required, or will want, to constrain subsequent distribution in some manner. Some constraints will have to be implemented in countries that utilize the template provisions of the Treaty; some constraints might also have to be included for other implementing limitations or exceptions to meet the three-step test. The need or desire for some constraints on subsequent distribution will be particularly strong if technological measures will no longer sufficiently protect access to copies to guarantee that copies will be used only by the visually impaired.

If the Treaty implementation requires constraints on subsequent distribution, the exhaustion principle would not seem to provide an adequately flexible tool of implementation if the principle were to apply generally, without limitation, to all copies and all first distributions. However, the general applicability imperative of the exhaustion principle is merely an illusion in modern copyright law.

Legislators and courts have created exceptions to the exhaustion principle and tailored the exceptions to either include or exclude particular types of works and particular uses. The resale right that some countries grant to authors is one such exception; based on the right, authors receive an additional royalty each time their works are resold for a price exceeding a certain amount. The right might be limited to resales made through certain types of persons or entities; for example, in the European Union only resales that involve "art market professionals, such as salesrooms, art galleries, and, in general, any dealers in

---

[59] See e.g. NLS Press Release, Library of Congress Braille and Talking-Book Program Releases Book Download App through Apple (September 24, 2013) available at www.loc.gov/nls/newsreleases/archive/2013-09-24.html; Daisy Consortium, *DAISY Standard*, www.daisy.org/daisy-standard. See also 142 Cong. Rec. S9061 (July 29, 1996) (remarks of Senator John Hubbard Chafee).

[60] Kirtsaeng v. John Wiley & Sons, Inc., 133 S. Ct. 1351 (2013).

works of art"[61] are subject to the payment of the resale royalty. The right does not limit exhaustion in the sense that it prevents subsequent resales altogether, but it does limit subsequent distribution *de facto* by imposing a tax on the resale price. The purpose of the resale right is to provide additional remuneration to authors who could not, at the time of the first sale, fully realize the full value of their work that had subsequently appreciated.

One set of exceptions to the exhaustion principle involves rights that affect the lending and rentals of copies, which are types of distribution of copies. Lending and rental rights survive first distribution and continue to be attached to a particular copy after first distribution. Countries may create the rights for specific types of works; international treaties require that countries provide for rental rights for computer programs, cinematographic works, and phonograms (with possible exceptions under certain circumstances).[62] The rights should assist in securing remuneration for copyright owners in an environment in which digital technologies enable the inexpensive creation of high quality copies. The existence of the rights evidences a recognition that copyright owners are likely losing remuneration when users borrow or rent copies, and subsequently reproduce the copies, instead of purchasing copies.

Computer programs are the object of another limitation to the exhaustion principle, a limitation that is also associated with a concern that digital technologies make it more difficult for copyright owners to fully benefit from their copyrights. In the United States, courts have accepted the position that copyright owners may use licenses to limit the first sale doctrine. In the U.S. Ninth Circuit, courts consider three factors in distinguishing a license from a sale: (1) specific language designating the license as such; (2) significant restrictions on the user's ability to transfer the software; and (3) notable use restrictions imposed by the copyright owner.[63] The courts thus provide guidelines for software licensors to follow if the licensors want only to license, and not to sell, their software; through licensing, the licensors exempt copies of the software from the exhaustion principle and exert continuing control over subsequent distribution of copies of the software.

The Court of Justice of the European Union has provided similar guidelines in its *UsedSoft* decision, in which the Court held that a software license will be considered a sale if the license provides for (1) a "payment of a fee intended to enable [the copyright owner] to obtain a remuneration corresponding to the economic value of the copy of the work," and (2) "a right [granted to the user] to use that copy for an unlimited period."[64] Although the court decisions in the U.S. on license or sale are not *per se* limited to software, the

---

[61] Directive 2001/84/EC of the European Parliament and of the Council of September 27, 2001 on the resale right for the benefit of the author of an original work of art, art. 1(2), [2001] O.J. L272 (EC).

[62] TRIPS Agreement, arts. 11 and 14(4); WIPO Copyright Treaty, December 20, 1996, art. 7; WIPO Performances and Phonograms Treaty, December 20, 1996, arts. 9, 13; 17 U.S.C. § 109(b). EU law provides for both lending and rental rights in Council Directive 2006/115 of the European Parliament and of the Council of December 12, 2006 on rental right and lending right and on certain rights related to copyright in the field of intellectual property, [2006] O.J. L376 (EC). See 17 U.S.C. § 109(b) and H.R. Res. 5586, 113th Cong. (2014) (a Bill to limit the limitation on the exhaustion principle in this case).

[63] Vernor v. Autodesk, Inc., 621 F.3d 1102 (9th Cir. 2010).

[64] Case C-128/11, UsedSoft GmbH v. Oracle Int'l Corp., 2012 EUR-Lex CELEX LEXIS 407, para. 1 (July 3, 2012).

courts seem to envision the application of their three-factor test primarily to software.[65] In the European Union, it has been disputed whether e-books should be treated in the same manner as software for purposes of the exhaustion principle.[66]

As the examples above demonstrate, it is possible to tailor the application of the exhaustion principle to serve various goals. To meet specific goals, legislators and courts have created constraints on the principle based on the type of beneficiary (e.g., an artist whose works are sold by "art market professionals" in the case of the resale right); the type of work for which copies are subject to distribution (e.g., computer programs); the type of distribution that is at issue (e.g., distribution through rental); and even the price that is paid for subsequent distribution (the minimal resale price in the case of the resale right). *De facto* exemptions to the exhaustion principle might be facilitated through courts' interpretations of what constitutes a sale for purposes of the application of the principle. With sufficient guidance from the courts, such as in the software examples mentioned above, copyright owners can exempt copies of their works from the exhaustion principle.

The examples above suggest that the general applicability of the exhaustion principle has been eroded to the point where limiting the application of the principle in cases of materials distributed under the limitations and exceptions implementing the Treaty does not seem like a particularly radical idea. The question is whether such a limited exhaustion principle is more suitable as an implementation tool than another limitation or exception to copyright that would cover subsequent distribution and impose the same constraints that the limited exhaustion principle would impose on subsequent distribution.

In cross-border exchange, the difference between the limited exhaustion and other limitations or exceptions might be based on the need to remunerate copyright owners for copies in the country of importation: when the distribution right is exhausted, subsequent distribution triggers no remuneration to the copyright owner. Therefore, the limited exhaustion principle would be a sensible implementation tool when the country of importation assumes that the author's remuneration was adequately satisfied in the country where the copies were first distributed. If the country of importation considers the author's remuneration not to be adequately satisfied by remuneration provided in the country where the copies were first distributed, the country of importation might want to subject the importation to remuneration to the copyright owner, and for that purpose, a limitation other than copyright exhaustion might be the more logical tool for Treaty implementation.[67] The problem for the country of importation will be that it will face a patchwork of solutions adopted by countries from which imported copies will originate, as different countries may adopt different limitations and exceptions for the first distribution. Unless technological measures make it straightforward for a country of importation

---

[65] UMG Recordings, Inc. v. Augusto, 628 F.3d 1175, 1180 (9th Cir. 2011) (recognizing that courts have addressed the issue "[p]articularly with regard to computer software").

[66] Oberlandesgericht Hamm [OLG Hamm], May 15, 2014, 22 U 60/13, 2014 (Ger.), available at http://dejure.org/dienste/vernetzung/rechtsprechung?Text=22%20U%2060/13; District Court of Amsterdam, July 21, 2014, KG 2014, 14-795 SP/MV (Nederlands Uitgeversverbond and Groep Algemene Uitgevers/Tom Kabinet) (Neth.).

[67] For a discussion of conflict-of-laws issues in the implementation of the Marrakesh Treaty see Trimble, *supra* note 2.

to differentiate between imported copies according to their country of origin, the country of importation might opt to adopt a more restrictive approach for all imported copies.

IX. CONCLUSION

Nothing in this chapter is intended as a criticism of the work of the negotiators of the Marrakesh Treaty. The negotiators worked under significant pressure and numerous constraints to achieve a highly socially desirable outcome—the improvement of access to copyrighted materials to persons who are visually impaired or otherwise print disabled.[68] A swift ratification of the Treaty should be a priority for all signatory countries; the act of ratification will serve not only as recognition of the significance of the Treaty's goals to the societies of the countries but also as confirmation that the countries are capable of agreeing on changes to copyright law that are prompted by the legitimate needs that their societies share. Potential implementation difficulties should not stand in the way of Treaty ratification.

However, the highly socially desirable mission of the Treaty should not overshadow the fact that the implementation of the Treaty presents some remarkable challenges. In fact, as this chapter attempts to demonstrate, analyzing the challenges may help uncover conceptual questions that are worth considering, not only in the context of the Treaty, but also generally: the relationship between the exhaustion principle and other limitations and exceptions to copyright, the functioning of the three-step test in a globalized world, and the current state of the exhaustion doctrine.

The practical effects of what might be perceived as the difficulties of Treaty implementation could prove to be minimal in practice. Technical means, existing or developed in the future, might provide sufficient protection to ensure that copies will be used only by those whom the Treaty intends as beneficiaries. Although the cross-border exchange provisions might initially serve to facilitate the exportation of mostly physical copies from countries where users now principally use electronic copies, future distribution might involve mainly electronic copies, for which (for better or for worse) the exhaustion principle might not apply at all or only in some circumstances. Finally, it will be a significant success of the Treaty if it sensitizes copyright owners and society at large to the needs of the visually impaired and prompts copyright owners to adjust their licensing practices to accommodate those needs.

---

[68] See *ibid*, at 769–72 for a discussion of the constraints.

25. From importation to digital exhaustion: a Canadian copyright perspective
*Pierre-Emmanuel Moyse**

I. INTRODUCTION

The issue of parallel importation questions the reach of intellectual property rights in a free trade context and is consubstantial to the broader theme of distribution.[1] Parallel importation refers to the importation for sale by a non-authorized distributor of genuine products outside the channels of distribution contractually organized by the owner of one or several intellectual property rights existing in said products.[2] A truism, most manufactured products are complex and contain one or more subject matters of intellectual property (shape, software, logo, etc.). The article or physical object becomes the *confluence* of various competing rights:[3] the rights pertaining to the ownership in the physical good and granted to its purchasers (customers, retailers, wholesalers, etc.) and the intellectual property rights. The rights over the article can affect the ways in which the embedded works are commercialized. This exposure to distinct, yet convergent, proprietary regimes translates into conflicts between different laws, the laws of common or civil law property and intellectual property laws. Hence, parallel importation cases are essentially conflict of law cases and not infringement cases *stricto sensu*. The object of contention is not the production of a counterfeited good by imitation or reproduction; it is, more precisely, a dispute over the authentic product, its circulation, and its market. Regional price discrimination and international demand and control over brand reputation are the principal drivers of strategic restrictions over parallel importation.[4] The advantages of leveraging

---

* Associate Professor, Faculty of Law, McGill University, Director of the Centre of Intellectual Property Policy (CIPP). An earlier version of this chapter was presented on April 14, 2015 at a workshop organized in Jerusalem by Professor Michal Shur-Ofry of Hebrew University. I am thankful to all participants of the workshop for their constructive comments and suggestions.

[1] WARWICK A. ROTHNIE, PARALLEL IMPORTS (1993). Amongst recent publications, see ROSE ANN MACGILLIVRAY, PARALLEL IMPORTATION (2010).

[2] Also referred to as "gray marketing" in the literature. See W. Lee Webster, *Restraining the Gray Marketer Policy and Practice*, 4 C.I.P.R. 211 (1987).

[3] The dichotomy between the two types of ownership is particularly well exposed under s. 202 of the U.S. Copyright Act (USCA): "[o]wnership of a copyright, or of any of the exclusive rights under a copyright, is distinct from ownership of any material object in which the work is embodied. Transfer of ownership of any material object, including the copy or phonorecord in which the work is first fixed, does not of itself convey any rights in the copyrighted work embodied in the object; nor, in the absence of an agreement, does transfer of ownership of a copyright or of any exclusive rights under a copyright convey property rights in any material object." *Ibid.*

[4] The seminal U.S. case of *Bobbs-Merrill* is a perfect example of the effect of price competition on distribution and the attempt to use intellectual property to regain control over the resale of books. Bobbs-Merrill Co. v. Isidor Straus & Nathan Straus, 210 U.S. 339 (1908). The question

control over the distribution of a product by relying on intellectual property are obvious. First, as intellectual property rights are territorially based, they allow for international and territorial divisions of ownership. Such divisions support the distribution network as organized contractually by the manufacturer. Second, as intellectual property rights apply *erga omnes*, they can restrain non-authorized dealers notwithstanding the absence of contractual ties. Not surprisingly, the inherent mapping power of intellectual property rights and their national or even protectionist overtones have posed a veritable threat towards the creation of a single European market. In response, the Court of Justice of the European Union (CJEU) developed a sophisticated jurisprudence to curb the exercise of intellectual property rights to fit the greater objective of the free circulation of goods within the European market. This is particularly true in copyright law. The CJEU relentlessly guards the principle of free circulation against the exercise of exclusive prerogatives granted by national copyright laws. When and where a national law prescribes a distribution right, the latter is limited to the putting into circulation (i.e., to the "first sale") of the copy.[5] Domestic restrictions affecting the circulation of goods are legitimate only:

> if they are . . . inseparably linked to the very existence of the exclusive rights. No such justification would exist if the restrictions on trade imposed or accepted by the national legislation were of such a nature as to constitute a means of arbitrary discrimination or a disguised measure to restrict trade.[6]

In effect, the construction of the single European market subjugated all intellectual property rights affecting the distribution to new paramount legal principles aimed at the collective enterprise. Servant to this very purpose, the exhaustion doctrine, first developed in Germany and the United States (U.S.),[7] became the strong arm of European integration policy. Once a commercial article is put into circulation by the right holder, or with his consent, within the European market, the use of intellectual property rights to limit the subsequent distribution of said article is neutralized.[8] The first sale doctrine is effectively

---

put to the Supreme Court was whether: "[the right to vend] intended to create a right which would permit the holder of the copyright to fasten by notice in a book or upon one of the articles mentioned within the statute, a restriction upon the subsequent alienation of the subject-matter of copyright after the owner had parted with the title to one who had acquired full dominion over it and had given a satisfactory price for it?" *Ibid.* at 349–50.

[5] The exhaustion principle has made its way into several Directives. See e.g. Directive 2001/29 on the harmonization of certain aspects of copyright and related rights in the information society, art. 4(1), [2001] O.J. L167/10 (EC). "Member States shall provide for authors, in respect of the original of their works or of copies thereof, the exclusive right to authorise or prohibit any form of distribution to the public by sale or otherwise." See also Directive 2009/24 on the legal protection of computer programs, art. 4(2), [2009] O.J. L111/16 (EC).

[6] Case 341/87, EMI Electrola GmbH v. Patricia Im, [1989] E.C.R. 00079, para. 12.

[7] Once the copyright owner "places a copyrighted item in the stream of commerce by selling it, he has exhausted his exclusive statutory right to control its distribution." Quality King Distribs., Inc. v. L'anza Research Int'l Inc., 523 U.S. 135, 152 (1998); more recently, see Kirtsaeng v. John Wiley & Sons, Inc., 133 S. Ct. 1351 (2013).

[8] Case 78/70, Deutsche Grammophon Gesellschaft mbH v. Metro-SB-Großmärkte GmbH & Co. KG., [1971] E.C.R. 59, 499–500, para. 12: "If a right related to copyright is relied upon to prevent the marketing in a Member State of products distributed by the holder of the right or with his consent on the territory of another Member State on the sole ground that such distribution did

the same.[9] The core idea behind exhaustion and the first sale doctrine is derived from liberal philosophy. Property was invented to support commerce and it must be unencumbered to circulate. All restrictions are, henceforth, suspicious and to be resisted.[10]

Compared to European legal engineering, Canadian law does not show the same level of engagement or sophistication. Canada is a signatory of many multilateral agreements aimed at regional integration—the latest being the Canada and European Union Comprehensive Economic and Trade Agreement (CETA) and the Trans-Pacific Partnership Agreement (TPP),[11] but none of these instruments address the thorny question of exhaustion. In fact, the leniency of Article 6 of the Agreement on Trade-Related Aspects of Intellectual Property Rights (TRIPS), labeled "Exhaustion," and part of the general provisions, parallels Canada's lack of interest in this matter. Article 6, reproduced almost verbatim in the freshly negotiated CETA (Article 20.4) and TPP (Article 18.12), reads as follows: "[F]or the purposes of dispute settlement under this Agreement [. . .] nothing in this Agreement shall be used to address the issue of the exhaustion of intellectual property rights."[12] And indeed, the Canadian Parliament has until now largely failed to assess the impact of intellectual property on importation and its repercussions on the Canadian market and consumers. Instead, the reflection on the contours of intellectual property rights and their impact on the distribution of cultural or complex products stems mainly from the courts.

The first part of this chapter will present the current statutory provisions dealing directly with the distribution of goods in which copyright resides. A particular attention will be given to the recent inclusion under section 3 of the Copyright Act[13] ("the Act") of a "first sale" right. The second part will examine the state of copyright law with respect to the importation provision in the aftermath of the 2007 Supreme Court decision in *Kraft Canada v. Euro-Excellence*. Finally, the difficult question of the distribution of

---

not take place on the national territory, such a prohibition, which would legitimize the isolation of national markets, would be repugnant to the essential purpose of the Treaty, which is to unite national markets into a single market." *Ibid.*

[9] PAUL GOLDSTEIN & P. BERNT HUGENHOLTZ, INTERNATIONAL COPYRIGHT: PRINCIPLES, LAW AND PRACTICE 305 (2d ed. 2010).

[10] According to the United States Patent and Trademark Office: "Indeed, the first sale doctrine implements the common law's abhorrence of restraints on alienation of property by providing that the distribution right does not generally prevent owners of lawfully made copies from alienating them in a manner of their own choosing." UNITED STATES PATENT AND TRADEMARK OFFICE (USPTO), INFORMATION INFRASTRUCTURE TASK FORCE, INTELLECTUAL PROPERTY AND THE NATIONAL INFORMATION INFRASTRUCTURE: A PRELIMINARY DRAFT OF THE REPORT OF THE WORKING GROUP ON INTELLECTUAL PROPERTY RIGHTS 69 (July 1994) [hereinafter PRELIMINARY DRAFT].

[11] Both the Canada and European Union Comprehensive Economic and Trade Agreement (CETA), concluded in August 2014, and the Trans-Pacific Partnership Agreement (TPP), signed on February 2016, are in the process of being reviewed for ratification. The consolidated text of CETA and the text of the TPP are available at http://www.international.gc.ca/trade-agreements-accords-commerciaux/agr-acc/fta-ale.aspx?lang=eng

[12] Agreement on Trade-Related Aspects of Intellectual Property Rights, April 15, 1994; Marrakesh Agreement Establishing the World Trade Organization, Annex 1C, Legal Instruments—Result of the Uruguay Rounds, vol. 31, 33 I.L.M. 83 (1994) [hereinafter TRIPS]. See Rajnish Kumar Rai & Srinath Jagannathan, *Parallel Imports und Unparallel Laws: Does the WTO Need to Harmonize the Parallel Import Law*, 3 J. WORLD TRADE 657–94 (2012).

[13] Copyright Act, R.S.C. 1985, c. C-42 (Can.).

works by electronic transmission will be addressed, including the possibility of a digital exhaustion.

II. THE STATUTORY RIGHTS

Void of any general distribution right, the Act nonetheless contains specific provisions dealing with the distribution of works or articles subject to copyright protection. Section 3(1)(h) and (i), for instance, establish a rental right for some categories of works such as computer programs, musical works, and sound recordings.[14] However, the importation remedies constitute the most important piece of the distribution regime. First, section 27.1 creates a special regime dealing specifically with the parallel importation of books. Secondly, section 27(2)(e), which is broader in its scope of application, reserves the right for the author to prevent the importation of any "copy" of work into Canada under certain conditions. Additionally, the legislature has recently adopted the right of "first sale."

A. The Parallel Importation of Books: Section 27.1

Section 27.1 lays down the foundations against parallel importation, an importation regime enjoyed by authors as well as distributors of books.[15] Introduced in 1997,[16] its origins are found in the colonial history of copyright law and the geopolitical situation of Canada with respect to the access of books and literary materials for Canadian readers (both French and English).[17] Section 27.1 creates a protected trade zone to benefit Canadian authors and their exclusive distributors against parallel imports. It concerns physical copies of literary works, i.e., books. Where there is an exclusive distributor of the book in Canada:[18]

---

[14] *Ibid.* s. 3(1)(h); *ibid.* s. 3(1)(i). We must also mention the existence of a public lending right program administered by the Canada Council of Arts and designed to compensate authors for the free public access to books in Canadian public libraries, see *Public Lending Right Program*, CANADA COUNCIL FOR THE ARTS (2015), available at http://canadacouncil.ca/writing-and-publishing/public-lending-right-office.

[15] Very little has been written on s. 27.1 of the Copyright Act. Interestingly, following its promulgation, public law scholars questioned its constitutionality. The provision voted by the Federal Parliament affects the commerce of goods (property) and therefore could fall under the Provincial jurisdiction as well. Jean Leclair, *La constitutionnalité des dispositions de la Loi sur les droits d'auteur relatives aux droits des distributeurs exclusifs de livres*, 10 CAHIERS DE PROPRIÉTÉ INTELLECTUELLE 141–55 (1997).

[16] An Act to Amend the Copyright Act, S.C. 1997, c. 24 (Can.). The Act to Amend the Copyright Act became effective on September 1, 1999.

[17] Pierre-Emmanuel Moyse, *Canadian Colonial Copyright: The Colony Strikes Back*, in AN EMERGING INTELLECTUAL PROPERTY PARADIGM, PERSPECTIVES FROM CANADA 107 (Ysolde Gendreau ed., 2008). See also, SARA BANNERMAN, THE STRUGGLE FOR CANADIAN COPYRIGHT: IMPERIALISM TO INTERNATIONALISM 1842–971 (2013).

[18] As a prerequisite, exclusive distributors and copyright holders must give "notice of exclusive distributor" as prescribed in the Regulations. Copyright Act, s. 4(1).

[i]t is an infringement of copyright in a book for any person to import the book where:
(a) copies of the book were made with the consent of the owner of the copyright in the book in the country where the copies were made, but were imported without the consent of the owner of the copyright in the book in Canada; and
(b) the person knows or should have known that the book would infringe copyright if it was made in Canada by the importer.[19]

In effect, the Act builds contractual distribution interests—the exclusive rights to import and distribute in Canada—into the copyright scheme in order to protect and stimulate the distribution market in Canada to the benefit of Canadian right holders. The interference with such agreement is characterized as an infringement. The definition of infringement has been modified accordingly, "infringing" act refers to "a copy that is imported in the circumstances set out in paragraph 27(2)(e) and section 27.1 but does not otherwise include a copy made with the consent of the owner of the copyright in the country where the copy was made."[20] Although expressly mentioned in the title, the Act contains no definition, nor explains what constitutes "parallel importation."

The function and pertinence of section 27.1 can seriously be questioned. It has never been a matter of litigation and there is no evidence that its scheme benefits Canadians.[21] The consensus within the Canadian book industry is also that it does not apply to digital books, for the reason that a book, under the current definition of the Act, "means a volume or a part or division of a volume, in printed form."[22]

B. The Importation Remedy Provision: Section 27(2)(e)

Section 27(2)(e) of the Act is the general provision regarding importation. It contemplates traditional trade where goods are shipped and distributed via regular distribution channels and networks. Contrary to the provision on the importation of books previously examined, the case law and literature under this title are far more robust. As we will see, its application has been found particularly problematic. Section 27(2)(e), which applies to all categories of works embodied in a physical medium reads as follows:

27(2) It is an infringement of copyright for any person to: . . .
(e) import into Canada for the purpose of doing anything referred to in paragraphs (a) to (c),
a copy of a work, sound recording or fixation of a performer's performance or of a communication signal that the person knows or should have known infringes copyright or would infringe copyright if it had been made in Canada by the person who made it.

---

[19] *Ibid.* s. 27.1(1)(a)–(b).
[20] *Ibid.* s. 2.
[21] The Canada Heritage Report also notes that "there is a widely held view within the book industry that the Regulations are not enforceable" in part due to the fact that the Government of Canada has no active role to play in enforcing the Regulations. Another reason is the cost and difficulty of tracking and assessing compliance. See GOVERNMENT OF CANADA, CANADIAN HERITAGE, REPORT ON PLANS AND PRIORITIES, TRADITIONAL BOOK RETAIL (July 11, 2013), available at www.pch.gc.ca/eng/1290026005966/1290026005968.
[22] Copyright Act, s. 2.

Paragraphs (a) to (c) referred to under 27(2)(e) contemplate the following situations:

(a) sell or rent out,
(b) distribute to such an extent as to affect prejudicially the owner of the copyright,
(c) by way of trade distribute, expose or offer for sale or rental, or exhibit in public[.]

Section 27(2)(e) of the Act, which establishes a remedy for unauthorized importation of a copy of work under certain conditions, contains an exhaustion rule only where the owner of a copyright in Canada, place of importation of the copy of the work, and in the country of its production are the same person. The provision provides for a limited or partial international exhaustion mechanism within the copyright statutory framework. A review of case law shows that its application has proved particularly problematic when the product itself only incidentally embodies a copyrighted element.[23] Section 27(2)(e) of the Act can ground a strategy to divert commercial power from the copyright law to control parallel importation of mass market products, an application that challenges the very objective of the legislation. The point was rightly made by Justice Fish in the landmark decision of the Supreme Court *Kraft Canada*,[24] a case where copyright was claimed by the manufacturer of chocolate in the logos affixed on the chocolate wrappers to prevent parallel importation.[25] Writing a concurring opinion, Justice Fish expresses "grave doubt whether the law governing the protection of intellectual property rights in Canada can be transformed in this way into an instrument of trade-control not contemplated by the Copyright Act."[26] In contrast, Justice Rothstein, in the majority opinion, refuses to limit the provision of section 27(2)(e) to a particular function, work, or destination:

> [T]he apparent purpose of s[ection] 27(2) (e) is to give Canadian copyright holders an added layer of protection where the Canadian copyright holder does not hold copyright in that work in foreign jurisdictions. Section 27(2) (e) protects Canadian copyright holders against "parallel importation" by deeming an infringement of copyright even where the imported works did

---

[23] See Volkswagen Canada Inc. v. Access Int'l Automotive Ltd., [2001] 3 F.C.R. 311, 2001 F.C.A. 79 (CanLII).

[24] Euro-Excellence Inc. v. Kraft Canada Inc., [2007] 3 S.C.R. 20, 2007 S.C.C. 37. In Australia, the issue was addressed by legislative intervention following a report underscoring the negative impact of relying on copyright law to thwart parallel importation of ordinary goods. COPYRIGHT LAW REVIEW COMMITTEE, *The Importation Provisions of the Copyright Act 1968* (1988), available at /www.worldlii.org/au/other/clrc/8/. Copyright Amendment Act (No. 1) 1998, Sch. 2 (Austl.). The Copyright Amendment Act has been effective since 2000.

[25] The fact pattern is summarized in the opinion of the Federal Court of Canada rendered by Justice Harrington in 2004, Kraft Canada Inc. v. Euro Excellence Inc., [2004] 4 F.C.R. 410, 2004 F.C. 652 (CanLII). The case concerned the parallel importation of Côte d'Or and Toblerone chocolate products produced in Europe by Kraft, imported and then distributed in Canada by its Canadian subsidiary. The defendant, Euro-Excellence, Inc., had been an authorized dealer for Canada for some time before its non-exclusive agreement was terminated in 2000. It, however, continued to buy and supply the Canadian market with genuine Côte d'Or and Toblerone products bought from unnamed, but authorized sources in Europe. In an effort to bar parallel imports and reclaim control over the Canadian market, the mother company, registered owner in Canada of the works "Elephant" and "Bear in the Mountain," granted an exclusive license to produce and reproduce the said logos to its subsidiary. Although the main arguments made by the defendant revolved around the notion of abuse of right, the case was ultimately decided on contractual grounds.

[26] *Ibid.* para. 56.

not infringe copyright laws in the country in which they were made. Without s[ection] 27(2) (e), the foreign copyright holder who could manufacture the work more cheaply abroad could flood the Canadian market with the work, thereby rendering the Canadian copyright worthless. Section 27(2) (e) thus represents Parliament's intention to ensure that Canadian copyright holders receive their just rewards even where they do not hold copyright abroad.[27]

The *Kraft Canada* decision questions the scope of section 27(2)(e) and has sparked animated debates[28] over the nature of copyright law, its objectives, and its impact on the distribution of branded products. It has also paved the way for emerging theories, such as abuse of intellectual property rights.[29] Despite these positive outcomes, section 27(2)(e) remains a convoluted provision and difficulties remain.

The first difficulty concerns the hypothetical maker test provided *in fine* under section 27(2)(e) of the Act. The provision refers specifically to the copy of a work (i.e., the imported copy) that would be infringing if made in Canada. The making is hypothetical and functions only as a condition to the remedy. Initially, the Act provides little guidance as to the identity of the person liable for the making of said copy, meaning that the scope of the importation remedy would vary depending on the status of the maker. Had the hypothetical maker been the importer, the law would have technically barred all parallel imports since the latter is rarely bestowed with the right to make the products he imports. Parliament removed the ambiguity by adding necessary clarifications. An infringement occurs if, and only if, the copy of the work imported into Canada would have been a counterfeited copy had it been made in Canada by the person who has made it in the country of origin. The hypothetical maker is not the importer, but the person who legally made the copy in the country of exportation. Hence, when the owners of copyrighted works that are embodied in a physical object, abroad and in Canada, are the same legal persons, the effect of the provision is neutralized. The asymmetry or territorial division of ownerships triggers the infringement remedy. Section 27(2)(e) of the Act aims at incentivizing the assignment of copyright to Canadian entities. It rewards both the Canadian owner and its foreign assignor by providing the legal means of controlling the domestic market of products legally made abroad, provided there is a Canadian owner.

Would a license to produce or to reproduce confer enough rights to a Canadian licensee in order for it to benefit from the importation remedy enjoyed by the Canadian owner? This issue was also discussed in *Kraft Canada*. The majority supported the view that "because a copyright owner cannot be liable to its exclusive licensee for infringement,

---

[27] *Ibid.* para. 21.
[28] See Pierre-Emmanuel Moyse, *Kraft Canada c. Euro-Excellence: l'insoutenable légèreté du droit*, 53 MCGILL L.J. 741 (2008). Many commentaries have been written on the case, including: Teresa Scassa, *Using Copyright Law to Prevent Parallel Importation: A Comment on Kraft Canada, Inc. v Euro Excellence, Inc.*, 85 CAN. B. REV. 409 (2007); Cameron J. Hutchinson, *Which Kraft of Statutory Interpretation? A Supreme Court of Canada Trilogy on Intellectual Property Law*, 46 ALTA L. REV. (2008); Carol Hitchman & Christopher Tan, *Case Commentary Euro-Excellence Inc. v. Kraft Canada Inc.*, 7 CAN. INT'L L. 118 (2007).
[29] See Pierre-Emmanuel Moyse, *L'abus de droit: L'anténorme Partie II*, 58 MCGILL L.J. 1 (2012).

there is no hypothetical infringement and thus no violation of Section 27(2) (e)."[30] Had the copyright been assigned, and not licensed, to the Canadian entity, the hypothetical maker test would have been met and, therefore, the infringement action granted. Interestingly, the definition of "exclusive license" provided in section 2.7 of the Act states that "[f]or the purposes of this Act, an exclusive licence is an authorization to do any act that is subject to copyright to the exclusion of all others *including the copyright owner* [. . .]".[31] The definition seems to defeat the majority opinion since the owner itself is bound to respect the contract exclusivity. The majority emphasized that such reading is incompatible with the inherent nature of copyright, which, if divisible, rests with the owner. In other words, the licensee enjoys a limited proprietary interest which, if not respected by the licensor-owner, could be remedied by a breach of contract action, but not infringement. This point has not resurfaced before Canadian courts, nor been seriously examined by Canadian doctrine. It remains, however, highly debatable. The interest conveyed to an exclusive-licensee could certainly be treated as what a civil law jurist would call a "dismemberment," an autonomous right opposable to all including to the owner.

Finally, the provision regarding importation seems rather obsolete in an era where cultural goods are directly ordered online by the consumers and shipped directly to their residence by postal mail, messenger, or electronic transmission. These business-to-consumer operations may amount to acts of importation not contemplated under section 27(2)(e). As previously mentioned, its scope is limited to importation for specific activities listed under section 27(2)(a) to (c). Moreover, section 44.01(2) of the Act, which refers to customs regulation, exempts private importation by individuals.[32]

C. A New Old First Sale Right: Section 3(1)(j)

The Copyright Modernization Act, effective since 2012, amended the Act's section 3(1) by adding a new paragraph 3(1)(j), which creates a "first sale" right in a context where no distribution rights exist. The new provision introduces a right to "sell or otherwise transfer ownership of tangible objects, as long as that ownership has never previously been transferred in or outside Canada with the authorization of the copyright owner." The makers of sound recordings enjoyed a similar prerogative under section 18(1). The new paragraph was introduced without official commentaries, nor clear rationale. It lays, amorphous, in the text as a reminder of Canadian tranquil obedience to international order. The provision partially borrows the language of the distribution provisions used in the 1996 World Intellectual Property Organization (WIPO) instruments, notably Article 6 of the WIPO Copyright Treaty (WCT) and Article 8 of the WIPO Performances and Phonograms Treaty (WPPT), which create a distribution right for authors and performers

---

[30] *Euro-Excellence, supra* note 24, para. 15.
[31] Copyright Act, s. 2(7) (emphasis added).
[32] *Ibid*, s. 44.01(2). Section 44.01 exempts from seizure: "(a) copies that are imported or exported by an individual in their possession or baggage if the circumstances, including the number of copies, indicate that the copies are intended only for their personal use; or (b) copies that, while being shipped from one place outside Canada to another, are in customs transit control or customs transhipment control in Canada."

limited to the transfer of ownership of copies.[33] However, since the distribution right is not expressly part of the bundle of rights listed under section 3(1), one should be careful not to hastily interpret this new addition as a transplant of foreign exhaustion theories. Canada will have to produce its own doctrine and study the economic impact of international exhaustion on its domestic market and its cultural policy. So far, scholars have left the field fallow. Again, the explicit reference to a place of first sale located "outside Canada" may call for an international exhaustion rule, but only in circumstances where its principle matches the specific exemption to the importation remedy pursuant to section 27(2)(e), i.e., when owners in the country of exportation and in Canada are the same person. Its constituting elements, the transfer of ownership in the copy of the work and the consent of the initial owner to said transfer—both notions extensively discussed in European law and under the concept of "lawful copy" in U.S. law—have received little attention in Canada. They can barely be sketched out of section 3(1)(j) of the Act. Again, the Canadian case law regarding these fundamental concepts is nonexistent. The Supreme Court of Canada came very close to establishing its own judicial doctrine on exhaustion in the 2002 case of *Théberge v. Galerie d'Art du Petit Champlain, Inc.*[34] In this case, Théberge sought compensation for the use of his work on posters put into circulation in Québec with his consent. The use at issue consisted in physically removing the poster's ink in order to transfer the image onto a canvas. No additional copy was produced since each poster became blank once the ink-removal operation completed. The Court, considering the right of the purchaser of the poster and that of the artist, made broad pronouncements in favor of the former:

> [t]he proper balance among these and other public policy objectives lies not only in recognizing the creator's rights but in giving due weight to their limited nature. In crassly economic terms it would be as inefficient to overcompensate artists and authors for the right of reproduction as it would be self-defeating to undercompensate them. Once an authorized copy of a work is sold to a member of the public, it is generally for the purchaser, not the author, to determine what happens to it. Excessive control by holders of copyrights and other forms of intellectual property may unduly limit the ability of the public domain to incorporate and embellish creative innovation in the long-term interests of society as a whole, or create practical obstacles to proper utilization.[35]

Finally, it is noteworthy to add that the *Théberge* decision stands in stark contrast with the recent CJEU decision in *Art & Allposters International BV v. Stichting Pictoright*.[36] The CJEU reached a different conclusion and decided that the replacement of the medium constitutes an "alteration of the copy of the protected work" and "a new reproduction of

---

[33] World Intellectual Property Organization, Copyright Treaty, art. 6, December 20, 1996, WIPO Doc. CRNR/DC/94 (1996) [hereinafter WIPO Copyright Treaty]. "(1) Authors of literary and artistic works shall enjoy the exclusive right of authorizing the making available to the public of the original and copies of their works through sale or other transfer of ownership." See also World Intellectual Property Organization, Performances and Phonograms Treaty, art. 8, April 12, 1997, S. Treaty Doc. No. 105-17 (1997) [hereinafter WPPT].
[34] Théberge v. Galerie d'Art du Petit Champlain Inc., [2002] 2 S.C.R. 336.
[35] *Ibid.* paras. 31, 32.
[36] Case C-419/13, Art & Allposters Int'l B.V. v. Stichting Pictoright, 2015 EUR-Lex 62013 (January 22, 2015), available at http://curia.europa.eu/juris/liste.jsf?num=C-419/13.

that work."[37] The notion of reproduction in relation to the distribution of works, as we will see in the next section, is at the juncture of a new exhaustion theory.

The *Théberge* decision was a marker of first importance towards the recognition of the right of the purchaser, paving the way to the new "first sale" provision.[38] However, it remains to be seen how the "first sale" rule will coexist with the general importation provision when "ownership of tangible objects has been transferred outside Canada with the authorization of the copyright owner."[39] Risk of contradictions exist between section 3(1)(j) and 27(2)(e) since the latter, as we have seen, allows for some control over international distribution.

III. THE CASE FOR DIGITAL EXHAUSTION

Jurists have been struggling for quite some time with the disappearance of copies and the dilution of notions imagined to deal with new uses and new distribution technologies (reproduction, broadcasting, cable distribution, etc.). Surprisingly, the old legal categories have resisted technological changes with few accommodations. This conceptual resilience has gravely complicated the transition towards simplifying the legal system. It is not that the law fails to find innovative ways to address the digital distribution of works, the problem instead is that right holders persist in relying on old concepts to preserve every inch of interest they have acquired in the analogical world. This section challenges some assumptions on which these claims or "rents" are built. First, the classic distinction entertained by jurists between the work and the copy of the work, as separate legal objects, may not hold true in the digital world. Indeed, digital goods do not lack physicality, which allows for the reconsideration of digital exhaustion. Secondly, the exhaustion theory and the limitations it imposes on the distribution right fit particularly well in the users' right movement recently initiated by the Supreme Court and which inspired a vibrant Canadian doctrine. Finally, digital *exhaustion*, at least as an intellectual exercise, should be given serious consideration.

A. Digital Goods: Simply Another Reality?

Exhaustion, when supported by Canadian statutory law, is limited to the specific situations examined above and concerns, as is the case in other jurisdictions, physical objects. Section 27(2)(e) of the Act employs the expression "copy of the work" where paragraphs

---

[37] The minority opinion in *Théberge* echoes the solution of the CJEU. "By transferring authorized reproductions of the respondent's works onto canvas, the appellants 'produce[d] or reproduce[d] [those] work[s] or any substantial part thereof in any material form whatever,' contrary to s[ection] 3(1) *C.A.*" *Théberge, supra* note 34, paras. 178–79. See also Copyright Act, s. 3.1.

[38] Approving the majority decision and for a discussion on national exhaustion in Canada, see Wendy A. Adams, *Secondary Markets for Copyrighted Works and the "Ownership Divide": Reconciling Competing Intellectual and Personal Property Rights*, 37 CAN. BUS. L.J. 321, 331, 335 (2002). *Contra*, Orit Fischman Afori, *Copyright Infringement Without Copying: Reflections on the Théberge Case*, 39 OTTAWA L. REV. 23 (2007).

[39] Copyright Act, s. 3(1)(j).

3(1)(j) and 18(1.1)(b) use "tangible object of copyright." Similarly, the rental rights prescribed pursuant to 3(h) and (i) apply to the embodiment of the work, either as a computer program or sound recording. Canadian law follows suit with international law as set in the WIPO Digital Treaties of 1996.[40] The agreed statement referring to the distribution right and the rental right section of the WCT reads as follows:

> [a]s used in these Articles, the expressions "copies" and "original and copies," being subject to the right of distribution and the right of rental under the said Articles, refer exclusively to fixed copies that can be put into circulation as tangible objects.[41]

As a result, exhaustion does not usually govern situations where the work is directly communicated to the public or otherwise transmitted in an intangible way or simply made available for streaming and viewing.[42] This proposition certainly stands true in Canadian law, but has never been explicitly formulated. It can only be inferred from the wording of the new section 3(1)(j), which specifically deals with tangible objects. This insistence on associating distribution with tangibility is far from being satisfactory and its justifications are weak.[43] The twentieth-century terminology based upon a certain idea of what is tangible seems rather out of place with the current reality of electronic transactions. Music, movies, and books, consumers believe, are, to all appearances, distributed or *sold* online whether they are subsequently shipped, imported, or downloaded and whether they are enjoyed in an e-format rather than in solid medium. The fact that online distribution services generate a new copy upon the user's demand, thus a reproduction, should not distract us from the applicability of the distribution right.[44] On the contrary, the idea of reproduction right is the intellectual legal heritage that has burdened the advancement of the legal system. It has prevented the useful allocation of liabilities amongst stakeholders in the diffusion of cultural goods online. Had the focus been on distribution, it would have been easier to engage intermediaries and telecommunication companies (currently

---

[40] WIPO Copyright Treaty, *supra* 33; WPPT, *supra* note 33.

[41] Similarly, see WIPO, WPPT, *Agreed Statements concerning WIPO Performances and Phonograms Treaty*, at arts. 2(e), 8, 9, 12, and 13.

[42] In European law, this principle has been established in the seminal cases Case 62/79, *S.A. Compagnie générale pour la diffusion de la télévision, Coditel & ors.* v. *Ciné/Vog Films & ors.*, [1980] E.C.R. 00881, 903–4., paras. 15–17. Case 262/81, Coditel S.A., Compagnie générale pour la diffusion de la télévision & ors. v. Ciné-Vog Films S.A. & ors, [1982] E.C.R. 03381, 3381–403.

[43] This is the conclusion we must reach upon the review of the early debate on the proper characterization of online transmission activities. The right of distribution for electronic transmission was a serious candidate before being abandoned, without much analysis, mostly as a result of pressures exercised at the international level from members of the European Union resistant to the idea of distribution originating from the U.S. The U.S. White Paper released in 1995 contained the following recommendation: "[t]he right to distribute copies of a work by transmission should be included both in the Berne Protocol and the New Instrument, perhaps as a separate right, as an aspect of a distribution right, as part of a right of communication to the public, or an aspect of the reproduction right." USPTO, INFORMATION INFRASTRUCTURE TASK FORCE, INTELLECTUAL PROPERTY AND THE NATIONAL INFORMATION INFRASTRUCTURE: REPORT OF THE WORKING GROUP ON INTELLECTUAL PROPERTY RIGHTS 150 (September 1995), available at www.uspto.gov/web/offices/com/doc/ipnii/ipnii.pdf [hereinafter U.S. White Paper].

[44] In fact, the right of distribution should be central and federate all rights. We defended this idea in our thesis, PIERRE-EMMANUEL MOYSE, LE DROIT DE DISTRIBUTION EN DROIT D'AUTEUR (2007).

excluded from all copyright liability[45]) in the construction and financing of a more balanced digital culture. It makes it onerous to innovative business models like UsedSoft or ReDigi.[46]

Digital goods have also become more *real* as their importance in our life grows stronger. The sense of ownership in objects made of alphanumerical data, including music files, remains unaffected by the informational nature of such objects. Property in a file is no less *real* by the new generation of users than a physical object for those born in the twentieth century. And, in fact, electrical impulses are real. The Civil Code of Québec itself took stock of this idea in 1994. Section 906 deems corporeal movables "waves or energy harnessed and put to use by man, whether their source is movable or immovable." In the world of electrical impulses, waves, and transistors, possession is simply experienced differently. The legal *doxa*, however, seems to deny the mere idea of *virtual possession*, which, all things considered, seems paradoxical. Drafters of end-user licensing agreements for online products have largely benefited from this conceptual ossification. They found in online distribution licensing practices a way to circumvent the exhaustion exemption.[47] Intangible objects, they advocate, are lent to us only for a limited time for limited uses and not sold despite all appearances.

We should resist this legal concatenation. The issue of digital exhaustion shows that time provoked the perversion of legal rules when their specific functions and the context in which they emerged are overlooked. Before jurists developed pathological overconceptualization tendencies, law was simply translating into words the ways we routinely interact with things, sometimes redressing negative and prejudicial habits. But, ultimately, law derived from experience, not from intellectual projections. When in compliance with the palpable reality, the language of law remains comprehensible and legible, safe from curiosities we poetically call "fictions of law." However, with the emergence of computer and information technology, the way we relate to "things," virtual or not, has been profoundly altered. And, to a certain extent, law fails to adequately describe new phenomena because our daily activities are increasingly performed in a virtual world. Our actions are not limited by the inherent properties of things that surround us. Digital objects are ubiquitous and polymorphous. But law and lawyers insist on organizing the legal science alongside fixed categories directly imbued with a rigid conception of what "reality" is when in fact we are moving seemingly to a world of endless possibilities. Hence, distinctions and rights based on the physicality of things or distinct technologies are encumbrances in the digital world. Neither technology nor law is neutral.[48] The best illustration of these

---

[45] Copyright Act, s. 31.1(1): "A person who, in providing services related to the operation of the Internet or another digital network, provides any means for the telecommunication or the reproduction of a work or other subject-matter through the Internet or that other network does not, solely by reason of providing those means, infringe copyright in that work or other subject-matter." *Ibid.*

[46] UsedSoft (2015), www.usedsoft.com/de; ReDigi (2015), www.redigi.com//site/index-invite.html.

[47] In fact, in 1994, the U.S. Green Paper expressly stated that: "[l]imitations on the exclusive rights, such as the first sale doctrine, fair use or library exemptions, may be overridden by contract." PRELIMINARY DRAFT, *supra* note 10.

[48] A theme dear to the Science and Technologies Studies. See S. JASANOFF, *Making Order: Law and Science in Action*, in HANDBOOK OF SCIENCE AND TECHNOLOGY STUDIES 761–86 (E. Hacket et al. eds., 3rd ed. 2007).

distortions is the challenge electronic distribution of works has posed to the legal community. Its characterization turned a simple and well-accepted reality into legal cubism: on the Internet, works are not imported, nor sold, or distributed, perhaps lent or transmitted, but are most certainly displayed, reproduced, and communicated or rendered available to the public. The difficulty is naturally that the above-captioned characterizations trigger different rights, creating as many layers of competing interests and, consequently, empowering as many right holders and, in its wake, a constellation of collective societies.[49] The convergence of the means of multiplying copies of a work, coupled with the endless capacity of transmission has confounded jurists and provoked the fragmentation of rights and interests. The exercise of characterization has become the work of an alchemist.

Recent court decisions have challenged the reflective nature of law and its resistance to changes. Law, at least in its statutory rendition, takes time to make, as evidenced by the sometime slow maturation process of legal concepts, allowing for reflection and innovation. The opportunity to review the exhaustion principle was first seized by the CJEU. The decision in the recent case of *Adobe* v. *UsedSoft*[50] marks a new development in copyright law as it relaxes the rigidity of the "tangibility" condition for exhaustion and weakened the concept of reproduction. The CJEU stirred away from the legal orthodoxy and deployed its own rationale to reinvent the exhaustion principle in the context of digital transmission of software. It reads "sell" where the right holder granted an unlimited and non-exclusive, non-transferable "license to use."[51] It followed that the downloading of a software by the licensed user exhausts the distribution right of the author and therefore lifts the ban to subsequently resell the right to use and update the software—when in fact, only the digital key to access to the Adobe platform was transferred to the third party. Applied for the first time in a case where no copies where distributed, but simply made available and downloaded by the end-user, the decision stands for the affirmation that the exhaustion mechanism neutralizes any and all rights that could have subsisted alongside the right to distribute the work. Indeed, and it is no little change in the Court's jurisprudence, even if the right to make available would have perhaps provided the right holder with an alternative ground of action to control the distribution of the software by a non-authorized dealer (like UsedSoft), the Court embraced the exhaustion mechanism. Adopting the point of view of the acquirer, the Court stressed that the online operation of downloading a copy of a software is equivalent to the acquisition of a lawful copy of a software on the secondary market:

> It makes no difference . . . whether the copy of the computer program was made available to the customer by the rightholder concerned by means of a download from the rightholder's website or by means of a material medium such as a CD-ROM or DVD. Even if, in the latter case too, the rightholder formally separates the customer's right to use the copy of the program supplied from

---

[49] ESTELLE DERCLAYE & MATTHIAS LEISTNER, INTELLECTUAL PROPERTY OVERLAPS: A EUROPEAN PERSPECTIVE (2010). See also Ariel Katz, *Commentary: Is Collective Administration of Copyrights Justified by the Economic Literature?*, in COMPETITION POLICY AND INTELLECTUAL PROPERTY 449 (Marcel Boyer, Michael Trebilcock, & David Vaver eds., 2009).

[50] Case C128/11, UsedSoft GmbH v. Oracle Int'l Corp., [2012] E.C.R. I-0000.

[51] The Court provides its own definition of sale: "[a]ccording to a commonly accepted definition, a 'sale' is an agreement by which a person, in return for payment, transfers to another person his rights of ownership in an item of tangible or intangible property belonging to him." *Ibid.* para. 42.

the operation of transferring the copy of the program to the customer on a material medium, the operation of downloading from that medium a copy of the computer program and that of concluding a licence agreement remain inseparable from the point of view of the acquirer, for the reasons set out in paragraph 44 above. Since an acquirer who downloads a copy of the program concerned by means of a material medium such as a CD-ROM or DVD and concludes a licence agreement for that copy receives the right to use the copy for an unlimited period in return for payment of a fee, it must be considered that those two operations likewise involve, in the case of the making available of a copy of the computer program concerned by means of a material medium such as a CD-ROM or DVD, the transfer of the right of ownership of that copy. Consequently, in a situation such as that at issue in the main proceedings, the transfer by the copyright holder to a customer of a copy of a computer program, accompanied by the conclusion between the same parties of a user licence agreement, constitutes a 'first sale . . . of a copy of a program' within the meaning of Article 4(2) of Directive 2009/24.[52]

In reconstructing the license as a sale, the Court challenged the assumption that copyright law ought to create various regimes depending on the medium—tangible or intangible— used to communicate the work. The dissection of a single operation, that of transmission, in a mosaic of legal variations (reproduction, communication, distribution, making available, exhibition, etc.) weakens the law's aspirations to efficiently regulate the commerce and exploitation of works. The micro-technical analysis, which has led to the overlapping of rights, is replaced by a subjective and macro-economical one. Henceforth, the Court instructs us that priority must be given to the acquirer's perception. It is no more sufficient for the author, to avoid the effect of exhaustion, to unilaterally assert that the work is licensed or that the right to reproduce the work remains with the author or further, that the work is communicated or made available to the public. The Court held that "the exhaustion of the distribution right under Article 4(2) of Directive 2009/24 concerns both tangible and intangible copies of a computer program" and, stretching its reasoning to the limits, subjected the right of making available to the exhaustion principle:

Moreover . . . in a situation such as that at issue in the main proceedings, the copyright holder transfers the right of ownership of the copy of the computer program to his customer. As the Advocate General observes in point 73 of his Opinion, it follows from Article 6(1) of the Copyright Treaty, in the light of which Articles 3 and 4 of Directive 2001/29 must, so far as possible, be interpreted . . . that the existence of a transfer of ownership changes an "act of communication to the public" provided for in Article 3 of that directive into an act of distribution referred to in Article 4 of the directive which, if the conditions in Article 4(2) of the directive are satisfied, can, like a "first sale . . . of a copy of a program" referred to in Article 4(2) of Directive 2009/24, give rise to exhaustion of the distribution right.[53]

B. Exhaustion as Users' Right: The Canadian School

If Australia has championed the issue of exhaustion in the common law context,[54] Canadian copyright law can boast having developed the users' right doctrine. The latest instalment of this emerging movement is heralded by the new section 29.21 of the 2012

---

[52] *UsedSoft*, *supra* note 50, paras. 47, 48.
[53] *Ibid.* para. 52.
[54] Copyright Amendment (Parallel Importation) Bill 2001 (Cth) (Austl.). A number of studies on parallel importing have been released by the Australian Competition and Consumer Commission

Copyright Act, the famous, or infamous, user-generated content provision that legitimizes the use and reproduction of copyrighted works for the creation of a new original work and "to authorize an intermediary to disseminate it" prescribing that the use is done solely for non-commercial purposes.[55] This provision is not an isolated or unrelated incident. It participates in a progressive movement of copyright reform initiated by the Supreme Court. In the landmark case *CCH Canada v. Law Society of Upper Canada*,[56] Chief Justice McLachlin ascertained that the fair dealing exception is a user's right. She concluded that:

> the fair dealing exception is perhaps more properly understood as an integral part of the Copyright Act than simply a defence. Any act falling within the fair dealing exception will not be an infringement of copyright. The fair dealing exception, like other exceptions in the Copyright Act, is a user's right. In order to maintain the proper balance between the rights of a copyright owner and users' interests, it must not be interpreted restrictively. As Professor Vaver . . . has explained, at p[age] 171: "User rights are not just loopholes. Both owner rights and user rights should therefore be given the fair and balanced reading that befits remedial legislation."[57]

The signal was hence given to an army of exegetes to expand and articulate more fully the notion of users' right. The Supreme Court reaffirmed the *CCH* findings in 2012, in *Society of Composers, Authors and Music Publishers of Canada v. Bell Canada*.[58] In the interval, and this is no coincidence, the concept of abuse of right made its way to Canadian jurisprudence: it was timidly dealt with in *Kraft Canada*, but its name was pronounced for the very first time and is now part of Canadian law.[59]

---

as well. For more information, see Australian Competition & Consumer Commission, Parallel Importing (June 21, 1999), available at www.accc.gov.au/speech/parallel-importing.

[55] Copyright Act, s. 29.21: "(1) It is not an infringement of copyright for an individual to use an existing work or other subject-matter or copy of one, which has been published or otherwise made available to the public, in the creation of a new work or other subject-matter in which copyright subsists and for the individual—or, with the individual's authorization, a member of their household—to use the new work or other subject-matter or to authorize an intermediary to disseminate it, if (a) the use of, or the authorization to disseminate, the new work or other subject-matter is done solely for non-commercial purposes; (b) the source—and, if given in the source, the name of the author, performer, maker or broadcaster—of the existing work or other subject-matter or copy of it are mentioned, if it is reasonable in the circumstances to do so; (c) the individual had reasonable grounds to believe that the existing work or other subject-matter or copy of it, as the case may be, was not infringing copyright; and (d) the use of, or the authorization to disseminate, the new work or other subject-matter does not have a substantial adverse effect, financial or otherwise, on the exploitation or potential exploitation of the existing work or other subject-matter—or copy of it—or on an existing or potential market for it, including that the new work or other subject-matter is not a substitute for the existing one." Ibid.

[56] CCH Canadian Ltd. v. Law Society of Upper Canada, [2004] 1 S.C.R. 339, 2004 S.C.C. 13 (Can.), available at www.canlii.org/en/ca/scc/doc/2004/2004scc13/2004scc13.html; see also Daniel Gervais, *The Purpose of Canadian Law in Canada*, 2 Univ. Ottawa Law & Tech. J. 315 (2005). "The Court tells us that users, who are also very often 'owners of a copy' of a protected work, have 'rights.'" Ibid. at 320.

[57] *CCH Canadian*, supra note 56, para. 58.

[58] Society of Composers, Authors and Music Publishers of Canada v. Bell Canada, 2012 S.C.C. 36, [2012] 2 S.C.R. 326, para. 11 (Can.).

[59] Justice Bastarache's opinion reserves further developments of the theory of abuse of right in intellectual property cases for the future: "As with the concept of *abus de droit*, my analysis renders

The articulation of fair dealing as a user's right has had a tremendous impact in the efforts to strive for a balanced policy of copyright. It has strengthened fair dealing, but has also given a new theoretical vehicle to shape and promote users' interests. It also raised the public attention to the political and social dimensions of copyright law: its scheme becomes inclusive and not just exclusive. The interests of the users, a now sizable and determinate public interest, must now be taken seriously when determining the limits to the importation remedies, as well as the scope of the new first sale provision. It supports the recognition of an international exhaustion rule and revives its applicability in the context of online distribution of files as the question of digital exhaustion, presented as a manifestation of users' rights, is becoming central.

C. Towards Digital Exhaustion?

In 2012, the Supreme Court of Canada, in what is now described as "the Pentalogy," rendered five important decisions in copyright law.[60] In *Rogers Communications Inc. v. Société canadienne des auteurs, compositeurs et éditeurs de musique* (2012),[61] the Court considered whether offering and streaming music online constituted acts subjected to the right of public communication by telecommunication pursuant to section 3(1)(f) of the Act. At stake was the imposition of a tariff to online music services to the benefit of members (authors and composers) of the collective society (Society of Composers, Authors and Music Publishers of Canada) in charge of the management of the right of communication to the public by telecommunication. The Court concluded that a *stream* of a musical work is an act contemplated under the right to communicate to the public, whether the public receives the communication in the same or in different places, at the same or at different times, or at their own or the sender's initiative. In a second decision, *Entertainment Software Association v. Society of Composers, Authors and Music Publishers of Canada* ("*ESA*"), rendered the same day, the Court dealt with the operation of downloading.[62] The Court deployed an unparalleled system of reasoning based upon the distinction between streaming and downloading. The Court concluded that the delivery of a videogame through downloading that contained musical works did not amount to an act of communication by telecommunication pursuant to the Act. It specifies that "[a]lthough a download and a stream are both 'transmissions' in technical terms (they both use 'data packet technology'), they are not both 'communications' for purposes of the Copyright Act."[63] The Court relied again on the balance of interests idea. The Court

---

an appeal to this developing doctrine unnecessary to deal with parallel importation of consumer goods. However, this is not to comment on the possible application of this doctrine in Canada; a determination on that issue is best left for another day." *Euro-Excellence*, *supra* note 24, para. 98.

[60] THE COPYRIGHT PENTALOGY: HOW THE SUPREME COURT OF CANADA SHOOK THE FOUNDATIONS OF CANADIAN COPYRIGHT LAW (Michael Geist ed., 2013).

[61] Rogers Communications Inc. v. Society of Composers, Authors and Music Publishers of Canada, 2012 C.S.C. 35, [2012] 2 R.C.S. 283 (Can.).

[62] Entm't Software Assoc. v. Society of Composers, Authors and Music Publishers of Canada, 2012 S.C.C. 34, [2012] 2 S.C.R. 231 ("*ESA*").

[63] *Ibid.* para. 28. The solution echoes that of the CJEU in *UsedSoft*: "the transfer by the copyright holder to a customer of a copy of a computer program, accompanied by the conclusion between the same parties of a user licence agreement, constitutes a 'first sale . . . of a copy of a

reiterated that "[t]he traditional balance between authors and users should be preserved in the digital environment"[64] to conclude that downloading a videogame is not an act of public communication of the musical work transferred with the videogame data. Instead, the operation amounts to the transmission of a copy of the work to the end-user in the same manner and with the same finality as if the said copy had been bought at a store:

> In our view, there is no practical difference between buying a durable copy of the work in a store, receiving a copy in the mail, or downloading an identical copy using the Internet. The Internet is simply a technological taxi that delivers a durable copy of the same work to the end user.[65]

The consequence of this finding is far-reaching. It remains to be seen how the decision will stand the test of time, especially since the passing of the new law, which was not effective at the time of the proceedings. The reform carries with it important amendments and, amongst other things, modernizes the public communication right to cover the making available of works. The Court will have to determine whether its views on file downloading, as an equivalent to the physical distribution of copy ("the same copy"), should prevail and override the application of all other competing rights, including notably that of making available, a position adopted by the CJEU in *UsedSoft*.[66] If it does uphold its position, Canada could become the first place where digital exhaustion occurs. Drawing on the conclusions reached by the Supreme Court in *Théberge*, reproduction under Canadian law requires an augmentation of the number of copies.[67] Technical solutions already exist that can mimic the distribution of tangible copies and avoid duplication (forward-and-delete technology).[68] Should the offering for resale of a music or movie file

---

program' within the meaning of Article 4(2) of Directive 2009/24." *Ibid.* para. 48. Further, "that the existence of a transfer of ownership changes an 'act of communication to the public' provided for in Article 3 of that directive into an act of distribution." *Entm't Software Assoc.*, supra note 62, para. 52.

[64] *Entm't Software Assoc.*, supra note 62, para. 8; Carys Craig, *Locking Out Lawful Users: Fair Dealing and Anti-Circumvention in Bill C-32*, in FROM "RADICAL EXTREMISM" TO "BALANCED COPYRIGHT": CANADIAN COPYRIGHT AND THE DIGITAL AGENDA 192 (Michael Geist ed., 2010).

[65] *Entm't Software Assoc.*, supra note 62, para. 5.

[66] The solution was expressly rejected in the U.S. case of *ReDigi*. The Court of the Southern District of New York categorically rejected the defense of digital exhaustion and confirmed the violation of both reproduction and distribution rights. With respect to the former, the Court stressed that: "[b]ecause the reproduction right is necessarily implicated when a copyrighted work is embodied in a new material object, and because digital music files must be embodied in a new material object following their transfer over the Internet, the Court determines that the embodiment of a digital music file on a new hard disk is a reproduction within the meaning of the Copyright Act." Capitol Records, L.L.C., v. ReDigi Inc., 934 F. Supp. 2d 640 (2013). See B. Makoa Kawabata, *Unresolved Textual Tension: Capitol Records v. ReDigi and a Digital First Sale Doctrine*, 21 UCLA ENT. L.R. 33, 55–71 (2014).

[67] *Théberge*, supra note 34, para. 42 (noting that "[a]s one would expect from the very word '*copy*right . . . reproduction' is usually defined as the act of producing *additional* or *new* copies of the work *in any material form*. Multiplication of the copies would be a necessary consequence of this physical concept of 'reproduction.'").

[68] A solution already envisaged and rejected in the U.S. White Paper: "[s]ome argue that the first sale doctrine should also apply to transmissions, as long as the transmitter destroys or deletes from his or her computer the original copy from which the reproduction in the receiving computer was made . . . In this case, without any doubt, a reproduction of the work takes place in the receiv-

lawfully acquired trigger the erasing of the original downloaded file, exhaustion could, under Canadian law, free the user of all contractual restrictions as well as from the application of the right of reproduction.[69]

We note, in passing, how prejudicial the antiquarian and omnipresent idea of reproduction is when applied in the realm of online transmission. Furthermore, notwithstanding the right of reproduction, which could be dealt with by relying on various defences (exhaustion, fair use or fair dealing, and all expressions of a user's right), the recasting of downloading as a mere distribution of copies should, in our opinion, dispose of all objections and restrictions that could limit the private enjoyment of files lawfully acquired. In other words, even if a new copy is generated (which is arguable as the Court in *ESA* considered that the same copy was distributed) at the moment of its transmission, it should not preclude exhaustion.[70] In short, the notion of distribution should neutralize and mute all other rights, including the new right of making available. Already, in many scholarly corners, hesitations have surfaced regarding the pertinence of the *making available* right with respect to the act of online distribution. Recently, Peter Menell concluded his historical review of the right of distribution under U.S. law by advocating that "to prove violation of copyright's distribution right, a copyright owner need merely show that a copyrighted work has been placed in a share folder that is accessible to the public."[71] Distribution, hence, includes the making available. This conclusion renders the question of exhaustion and the nature of the users' rights, both contractual and statutory, even more relevant.[72] Furthermore, the *ESA* decision invites us to reframe our comprehension of the technological processes behind the exploitation of works. The Court opted for a single characterization, which concords with the user's expectations and actual use. What seems to have influenced the Court is the fact that no music is enjoyed, played, or otherwise used during the downloading. The majority condemned the attempt by copyright owners to assert multiple rights for the same operation, characterized as "'double-dipping' by copyright owners in adjusting the two fees in such a way that 'divides the pie' between the collective societies administering reproduction rights, on the one hand, and

---

ing computer. To apply the first sale doctrine in such a case would vitiate the reproduction right." U.S. White Paper, *supra* note 43, at 93.

[69] As explained in the court's opinion, Media Manager, the software designed by ReDigi "continually runs on the user's computer and attached devices to ensure that the user has not retained music that has been sold or uploaded for sale." *ReDigi, supra* note 66, at 10.

[70] A position that seems incompatible with the solution recently adopted by the CJEU in the *Allposters* case, where it was decided that exhaustion applies only to the original and tangible copy of a work put on the market with the consent of the author, and not to the copy generated by the transfer of ink, suggesting that exhaustion does not affect the work itself, but only its embodiment produced under consent: "Consequently, the consent of the copyright holder does not cover the distribution of an object incorporating his work if that object has been altered after its initial marketing in such a way that it constitutes a new reproduction of that work. In such an event, the distribution right of such an object is exhausted only upon the first sale or transfer of ownership of that new object with the consent of the right holder." *Art & Allposters, supra* note 36, paras. 44–46.

[71] Peter S. Menell, *In Search of Copyright's Lost Ark: Interpreting the Right to Distribute in the Internet Age*, 59 J. COPYRIGHT SOC'Y U.S.A 201, 267 (2012).

[72] In *ReDigi*, the District Court refused to reassess the viability of the exhaustion doctrine in the context of the digital era. See *ReDigi, supra* note 66, at 655–56.

communication rights, on the other."[73] "This seems to us," writes the Court, "to undermine Parliament's purpose in creating the collective societies in the first place, namely to efficiently manage and administer different copyrights under the Act. This inefficiency harms both end users and copyright owners."[74]

The technical aspects of online operations may not be perfectly understood by the Court but its decision is sound at law. And here lies the most important contribution of the recent cases discussed above: what shapes the law and gears its application is the process by which the public comes to understand what is experienced by a user when downloading a digital content. This *general sentiment*, when unequivocal, generates institutions and establishes a legal normality. This is why we believe that the debate over the resurgence of digital exhaustion is far from being settled. Indeed, the jurisprudential momentum clearly empowers the users and not simply because we are in a consumerist world. The user engagement and rights with respect to most consumable electronic products must not be reduced to the licensed rights. Licensing agreements cannot take away rights created by courts or statutes. In some cases, the nature of the digital good and the context of the transaction dictate that copyright law supplements and overrides contractually constrained uses. This seems so obvious that no one has even raised the issue of works being transmitted by email or through mass media platforms.

IV. CONCLUSION

Two sets of conclusions can be drawn from this exploration into Canadian distribution law. First, the provisions on importation, patrons of the distribution rights, are no longer needed. Deficient and outdated, sections 27(2)(e) and 27.1 of the Act should be repealed or at least reformed. We must come to terms with the hypothetical maker test. Such reform could be modelled after the 2007 Israeli law, which opted for international exhaustion. The definition of "infringing copy" exempts a copy "which has been made outside of Israel, with the consent of the copyright owner in the country in which it was made."[75] The Canadian definition of infringement could easily be reworked to achieve a similar goal. The new first sale right prescribed under section 3(1)(j) of the Act, which applies to tangible objects "previously . . . transferred in or outside Canada with the authorization of the copyright owner," is certainly self-sufficient. Second, the users' right movement revives the idea of digital exhaustion as a possible articulation of said rights for the use of cultural products made available in an electronic file format and transmitted online, with the exclusion of streaming—a modern expression of "fair use." Exhaustion, in a digital

---

[73] *Entm't Software Assoc., supra* note 62, para. 11.

[74] *Ibid.* para. 11. The Court endorses the views expressed by A. Katz and quotes, "[t]he fragmentation of licences required for single activities among several monopolist-collectives generates inefficiencies, from which copyright owners as a whole also suffer." A similar conclusion was reached by the CJEU in the *Usedsoft* case, "[this] would allow the copyright holder to control the resale of copies downloaded from the internet and to demand further remuneration on the occasion of each new sale, even though the first sale of the copy had already enabled the rightholder to obtain an appropriate remuneration." *Usedsoft, supra* note 50, para. 63.

[75] Copyright Act, s. 1 (*as amended* July 28, 2011) (IL033) (IL).

context and under certain conditions, suppresses the licensing power used in *excess* and signals the contours of copyright: the point where the contract meets the public order. It does not mean that digital exhaustion must mirror exhaustion for tangible goods. It is not a blind authorization to deal with works acquired and downloaded in digital forms. It is an opportunity to revisit the idea of distribution by electronic transmission, once proposed, then abandoned,[76] to clarify the nature and scope of the exclusive rights for online exploitation of works in order to adequately reward authors and preserve users' rights. The idea of distribution becomes central as it allows, at last, to consider the responsibility—legal, financial, and moral—of the intermediaries such as telecommunication companies and service providers in the promotion of culture. They are distributing the works and have been the winners of the digital revolution to the detriment of authors.

---

[76] MIHÁLY FICSOR, THE LAW OF COPYRIGHT AND THE INTERNET 146 (2002): "[O]ne of the thorniest issues addressed during the preparatory work of the WCT and WPPT was the question of what right or rights should apply for interactive, on-demand transmission in digital networks. The main candidates were the right of distribution and the right of communication to the public." *Ibid.*

26. Exhaustion and the Internet as a distribution channel: the relationship between intellectual property and European law in search of clarification
Guido Westkamp*

I. INTRODUCTION

The expression "exhaustion," in intellectual property (IP), conveys a radical image, with broad connotations capping proprietary rights without a need to fall back on sector-specific exceptions. The term, with all its metaphorical imagery, is well-matched to European Union (EU) law as a system requiring flexible, yet normatively solid, principles that may still curtail national rights, very much in the sense of a collision clause. Broadly speaking, exhaustion occurs where a product is placed on the market by or with consent of the owner. Evidently, such rule is attractive as a generally restricting tool, especially as regards the creation of digital markets unfettered by exclusionary practises of IP owners. Indeed, the exhaustion *theory*,[1] as developed by German scholar Josef Kohler in the nineteenth century,[2] was arguably a rather broad concept.[3] It relied on the fundamental insight that any IP right was consumed by the first act of exploitation,[4] and relied much on an understanding of IP as a commercial, rather than a personality right. But the doctrine of exhaustion, which developed out of the implied consent doctrine,[5] was also known in

---

* Professor of Intellectual Property and Comparative Law and Co-Director, Queen Mary Intellectual Property Research Institute, Centre for Commercial Law Studies, Queen Mary University of London.

[1] See Guido Westkamp, *Emerging Escape Clauses? Online Exhaustion, Consent and European Copyright Law*, in INTELLECTUAL PROPERTY AT THE CROSSROADS OF TRADE (Jan Rosen ed., 2011).

[2] See JOSEF KOHLER, DAS AUTORRECHT: EINE ZIVILISTISCHE ABHANDLUNG 131 (1880).

[3] On the fundamental distinction between these two concepts, which gave rise to the exhaustion doctrine in Germany in the late nineteenth century, see Diethelm Klippel, *Historische Wurzeln und Funktionen von Immaterial- und Persönlichkeitsrechten im 19. Jahrhundert*, 4 ZEITSCHRIFT FÜR NEUERE RECHTSGESCHICHTE 132 (1982). Notably, Kohler never addressed the relationship between exhaustion and *product* market restrictions in licensing contracts. On this issue, see Helmut Haberstumpf, *Josef Kohler und die Erschöpfungslehre*, 6 ZEITSCHRIFT FÜR GEISTIGES EIGENTUM 470, 480 (2013).

[4] JOSEF KOHLER, LEHRBUCH DES PATENTRECHTS 132 (1908); see also Bundesgerichtshof (BGH, Federal Court of Justice), September 24, 1979, 1980 GRUR 38 (Ger.) "Fullplastverfahren" (acknowledging that exhaustion constitutes a general principle applicable to patent law even though the German Patent Act does not codify the rule).

[5] JOSEF KOHLER, DEUTSCHES PATENTRECHT 157–61 (1878). Kohler first developed the "implied consent" doctrine, according to which exhaustion would bar contractual claims against licensees only, and later expanded that concept towards a general exhaustion principle that could be relied upon by parties not bound by a contract with the patent owner.

other jurisdictions such as the United Kingdom (U.K).[6] It led to the formulation of a sole-standing exclusive right of distribution in German copyright law.[7]

In the EU, the completion of a digital single market is now a highly important target,[8] and exhaustion plays a vital part in securing an unobstructed development. Following the coming into force of the Treaty of Lisbon Amending the Treaty on European Union and the Treaty Establishing the European Community in 2007,[9] the (digital) single market aim is enshrined in the (partially new) EU provisions concerning the creation of an internal market.[10] Consequently, the EU has capacity to enact secondary legislation aiming at the harmonization of national laws under Article 114 of the Treaty on the Functioning of the European Union[11] (TFEU) and the specific new clause of Article 118 of the TFEU—though the question of "digital" exhaustion and the exclusion of Internet sales channels as such, have not yet been addressed by EU law-makers.

The exhaustion principle has been recently extended and applied to "intangible goods" by the Court of Justice of the European Union (CJEU) in *UsedSoft v. Oracle*,[12] regularly labeled as a revolutionary decision. Therein, the CJEU manifestly broadened the previously established concept of exhaustion as a regulatory tool to enforce concerns of the free movement of digital goods and the internal market's aim towards contemporary concerns of maintaining breathing space with regard to establishing a single digital market. Very similarly, the CJEU appears to reserve to itself much breathing space for future concerns regarding the establishment of a digital single market—preventing right owners excluding, broadly speaking, online channels unless such exclusion can be justified. This raises questions both of the level of interpreting harmonized IP law and, more critically, of the relationship between harmonized rights and primary EU law. It also questions the relationship between EU obligations under international copyright Convention law,

---

[6] Christopher Stothers, *Patent Exhaustion: A Comparative Analysis and Parallel Imports*, paper presented at 16th Conference on IP Law and Policy, Fordham University, New York (2008).

[7] Copyright Act 1911, 1 & 2 Geo. c. 46, s. 11 (Eng.); see Josef Kohler, *Neuerliche Auswüchse der Urheberrechtslehre*, 11 GEWERBLICHER RECHTSSCHUTZ UND URHEBERRECHT 269–72 (1906); see also Entscheidungen des Reichsgerichts in Zivilsachen (RGZ, German Empire Court) 63 Königs-Kursbuch 394; BGH, 1952 Parkstraße, GRUR 530 (531).

[8] See Communication from the Commission to the European Parliament, the Council, the Economic and Social Committee, and the Committee of the Regions, *Towards a Single Market Act for a Highly Competitive Social Market Economy, 50 Proposals for Improving our Work, Business and Exchanges with One Another*, COM(2010)608 final (October 27, 2010); Commission Communication to the European Parliament, the Council, the Economic and Social Committeeand the Committee of the Regions, *A Coherent Framework for Building Trust in the Digital Single Market for E-Commerce and Online Services*, COM(2012)942 final (January 11, 2012).

[9] Treaty of Lisbon Amending the Treaty on European Union and the Treaty Establishing the European Community, December 13, 2007, [2007] O.J. C306/1, 271 [hereinafter Treaty of Lisbon].

[10] See Consolidated Version of the Treaty on the Functioning of the European Union, art. 4(2)(a), May 9, 2008, [2008] O.J. C115/26–27 [hereinafter TFEU]. See also European Parliament Resolution of December 11, 2012 on Completing the Digital Single Market, Eur. Parl. Doc. (October 26, 2012), available at www.europarl.europa.eu/sides/getDoc.do?pubRef=-//EP//TEXT+TA+P7-TA-2012-0468+0+DOC+XML+V0//EN.

[11] TFEU, arts. 47–390.

[12] Case C-128/11, UsedSoft GmbH v. Oracle Int'l Corp., [2011] O.J. C194.

500 *Research handbook on intellectual property exhaustion and parallel imports*

in particular the World Intellectual Property Organization (WIPO) Copyright Treaty of 1996 (WCT).[13]

The digital single market objective is not mentioned as such in the Lisbon Treaty;[14] but the CJEU has adopted an approach that is highly motivated by the objective to create a wide flexibility for future decision-making. In this sense, the notion of a digital single market falls in line with the previous case law on exhaustion that was mostly concerned with territorial restrictions. Evidently, such continuance of a jurisprudence that seeks (rather subtly) to allow some freedom of judicial movement, causes concerns over the "legitimate" scope of IP rights if pitted against broad principles of (digital) market integration.

This chapter attempts to cast some light on the interplay between these concepts and its possible extension to what might be called "online exhaustion," though that terminology, as will be seen, is misleading.[15] To this end, I will try to clarify the different underlying rationales of exhaustion as a "dual" concept between EU market policy aims and IP regulation and to compare the approaches to online market freedoms under copyright law. In this area, the jurisprudence on exhaustion raises some uncomfortable questions for national law and the freedom to maintain judicial flexibility in sticking to traditional, yet possibly anachronistic, national IP rationales. As a result, some basic parameters may be distilled.

II. EXHAUSTION LANDSCAPE: CONTRACT, COMPETITION, CONSENT

The EU exhaustion landscape is wide and multifaceted. Exhaustion is a concept relevant to copious diverse circumstances. Whilst its individual elements seem, at first glance, rather articulate (requiring consent for the putting into circulation of goods protected by IP rights), the doctrine has had a long history, ranging from the application of competition law against attempts to segregate the common market geographically to questions of whether software manufacturers may control secondary markets in used software products. Following the concerns of establishing a single digital market, the doctrine can be seen as a general metaphor, which may be applied to restrict the exercise of rights where this is found to be incoherent with such aspiration, and which may therefore (at least on the basis of bringing into being a functional equivalent) apply to online "sales" above and beyond software copyright law.

Exhaustion is, and has always been, very much a concept of EU law that is probably more metaphorical than purely doctrinal in nature.[16] The jurisprudence of the CJEU

---

[13] WIPO Copyright Treaty, December 20, 1996, available at www.wipo.int/treaties/en/text.jsp?file_id=295166 [hereinafter WCT].
[14] On the changes to the economic principles, see PAUL CRAIG, THE LISBON TREATY 315 ff. (2d ed. 2013).
[15] See *infra* IV.
[16] The term "exhaustion" was first used in Case 102/77, Hoffmann-La Roche & Co. A.G. v. Centrafarm Vertriebsgesellschaft Pharmazeutischer Erzeugnisse mbH, [1978] E.C.R. 1139. The Court of Justice of the European Union (CJEU) did not, however, introduce the exhaustion

should principally be understood as having been concerned, predominantly, with policy concerns underlying the various legal principles that were applied to attempts to segregate product or territorial markets.[17] In that sense, it is apparent that the jurisprudence is not simply concerned with defining the scope of IP rights.

The emergence of exhaustion as a general tool for enforcing internal market aims prior to IP harmonization has been covered abundantly elsewhere;[18] a brief introduction into the structure of the matrix should suffice. At its heart, exhaustion is a broad concept that ultimately aims to exceed the mere prevention of parallel imports or, as the case may be, the exclusion of certain distribution channels, notably those based on online platform sales. Thus, whilst the exhaustion rule may be interpreted broadly, the scope may be limited significantly by contractual arrangements effectively eschewing the occurrence of exhaustion and allowing right holders to continue to exert control over dissemination channels.

Overall, the notion of exhaustion depends on a vexatious and partially indistinct interplay of (secondary) IP rules, contract, and competition law and the fundamental freedoms and policy aims as expressed under primary Treaty law. Indeed, the first wave of cases on parallel imports were decided either as matters of anticompetitive agreements[19] or as an abusive conduct.[20] It was only when the CJEU (then the European Court of Justice, or ECJ) took the more drastic step of limiting national IP rights by creating a collision clause under the (then) Article 36 of the Treaty Establishing the European Economic Community[21] that exhaustion became a broad normative principle against which the protection of "industrial and commercial property," as enshrined under Article 36, had to

---

principle as a novel, conceptual approach; rather, it stated that the principle had already existed in case law related to the Treaty Establishing the European Community, art. 30, August 31, 1992, [1992] O.J. C224 [hereinafter EC Treaty]; *ibid.* Subsequent case law then consistently and expressly reaffirmed the exhaustion rule. See Case C-200/96, Metronome Musik GmbH v. Music Point Hohkamp GmbH, [1998] E.C.R. I-1953; Case C-352/95, Phytheron Int'l S.A. v. Bourdon S.A., [1997] E.C.R. I-1729; Joined Cases C-267 & C-268/95, Merck & Co. v. Primecrown Ltd., [1996] E.C.R. I-6285; Joined Cases C-427, C-429, & C-436/93, Bristol-Myers Squibb v. Paranova A/S, [1996] E.C.R. I-3457; Case 9/93, IHT Internationale Heiztechnik GmbH v. Ideal-Standard GmbH, [1994] E.C.R. I-2789; Case 395/87, Ministère Pub. v. Tournier, [1989] E.C.R. 2521; Case 341/87, EMI Electrola GmbH v. Patricia Im, [1989] E.C.R. 79; Case 35/87, Thetford Corp. v. Fiamma, [1988] E.C.R. 3585; Case 19/84, Pharmon B.V. v. Hoechst A.G., [1985] E.C.R. 2281.

[17] Guido Westkamp, *Intellectual Property, Competition Rules and the Emerging External Market: Some Thoughts on the European Exhaustion Doctrine*, 11 MARQ. INTELL. PROP. LAW REV. 292, 316 (2007).

[18] See DAVID KEELING, INTELLECTUAL PROPERTY RIGHTS IN EU LAW, VOL. I, FREE MOVEMENT AND COMPETITION LAW 75 (2004); ULRICH JOOS, DIE ERSCHÖPFUNGSLEHRE IM URHEBERRECHT: EINE UNTERSUCHUNG ZU RECHTSINHALT UND AUFSPALTBARKEIT DES URHEBERRECHTS MIT VERGLEICHENDEN HINWEISEN AUF WARENZEICHENRECHT, PATENTRECHT UND SORTENSCHUTZ (1991); Gerhard Schricker, *Bemerkungen zur Erschöpfung im Urheberrecht*, *in* URHEBERRECHT, GESTERN, HEUTE MORGEN: FESTSCHRIFT FÜR ADOLF DIETZ ZUM 65. GEBURTSTAG 447–57 (Peter Ganea & Adolf Dietz eds., 2001); Jarrod Tudor, *Intellectual Property, the Free Movement of Goods and Trade Restraint in the European Union*, 6 J. BUS. ENTREPRENEURSHIP & L. ISS. 1 (2012).

[19] TFEU, art. 101.
[20] TFEU, art. 102.
[21] Today the clause is found in TFEU, arts. 34–36.

be justified.[22] In this regard, exhaustion was arguably considered as a rule that would ordinarily take precedence,[23] and it was only where the specific subject matter was adversely affected that the interests of IP owners would be recognized,[24] mainly in trademark law.[25] Importantly, the CJEU, then ECJ, made it clear that the constraints imposed upon national IP owners were, additionally, justified by the aim to create a common (later called "internal") market[26] and that both the provisions on competition law and the principle of free movement of goods[27] were, thus, to be considered as subsets of that overarching policy target.[28] In this context, the notion of consent became crucial.[29]

This interplay is complicated by the fact that the doctrine may be considered as either a general principle of EU law[30] with the aim of furthering market integration, or as a

---

[22] But see Clifford G. Miller, *Magill: Time to Abandon the "Specific Subject Matter" Concept*, 16 EUR. INTELL. PROP. REV. 415 (1994).

[23] Folkmar Koenigs, *Rechtsfolgen der Einheitlichen Europaeischen Akte fuer den Gewerblichen Rechtsschutz*, *in* LOHN DER LEISTUNG UND RECHTSSICHERHEIT 267, 270 (Bohlig ed., 1988).

[24] See Case 119/75, Société Terrapin v. Société Terranova C.A. Kapferer, [1976] E.C.R. 1039.

[25] See Directive 2008/95/EC of the European Parliament and of the Council of October 22, 2008 to approximate the laws of the Member States relating to trade marks, art. 7(2), [2008] O.J. L299/25 (EC) (replacing First Council Directive 89/104 of December 21, 1988 to approximate the laws of the Member States relating to trade marks, [1988] O.J. L40/1–7 (EC)), which allows the trademark owner to oppose further commercialization, which seemingly is a direct continuation of the specific subject matter test as formulated under previous case law. In 2015, a new Trade Mark Directive was adopted. See Directive (EU) 2015/2436 of the European Parliament and of the Council of December 16, 2015 to approximate the laws of the Member States relating to trade marks [2015] O.J. L336/1 (EU). According to Article 56, Article 15 will enter into force on January 15, 2019 and repeal Article 7 of Directive 2008/95/EC (the current provision on trademark exhaustion).

[26] This is because a violation of EC Treaty, art. 81 would, according to the jurisprudence of the CJEU, simultaneously violate TFEU, art. 34. Joined Cases 56/64 & 58/64, Établissements Consten, S.A.R.L. v. Commission, [1966] E.C.R. 299. The CJEU held that EC Treaty, art. 30 cannot restrict the application of EC Treaty, art. 81. *Ibid.* Subsequently, the CJEU emphasized that EC Treaty, art. 30 was applicable by way of analogy, but it referred to the occurrence of exhaustion. See also Case 24/67, Parke, Davis & Co. v. Probel, [1968] E.C.R. 55, 61.

[27] On the interplay between (now) arts. 101(1) and 36 TFEU see Case 119/75, Société Terrapin v. Société Terranova C.A. Kapferer, [1976] E.C.R. 1039.

[28] Case 78/70, Deutsche Grammophon v. Metro, [1971] E.C.R. 487; Case 24/67, Parke, Davis & Co. v. Probel, [1968] E.C.R. 55; Joined Cases 56/64 & 58/64, Établissements Consten, S.A.R.L. v. Commission, [1966] E.C.R. 299; but see Martin Schödermeier, *Die Ernte der "Maissaaat": Einige Anmerkungen zum Verhältnis von Art. 30 und 85 EWG-Vertrag*, GRUR INT. 85, 87 (1987).

[29] *Compare* with Joined Cases C-267/95 & C-268/95, Merck v. Primecrown, [1996] E.C.R. I-6285; Case 102/77, Hoffmann-La Roche v. Centrafarm, [1978] E.C.R. 1139. Subsequent case law then consistently and expressly reaffirmed the exhaustion rule. See Case C-200/96, Metronome Musik GmbH v. Music Point Hohkamp GmbH, [1998] E.C.R. I-1953; Case C-352/95, Phytheron Int'l S.A. v. Bourdon S.A., [1997] E.C.R. I-1729; Joined Cases C-267/95 & C-268/95, Merck & Co. v. Primecrown Ltd., [1996] E.C.R. I-6285; Joined Cases C-427/93, C-429/93, & C-436/93, Bristol-Myers Squibb v. Paranova A/S, [1996] E.C.R. I-3457; Case 9/93, IHT Internationale Heiztechnik GmbH v. Ideal-Standard GmbH, [1994] E.C.R. I-2789; Case 395/87, Ministère Pub. v. Tournier, [1989] E.C.R. 2521; Case 341/87, EMI Electrola GmbH v. Patricia Im, [1989] E.C.R. 79; Case 35/87, Thetford Corp. v. Fiamma, [1988] E.C.R. 3585; Case 19/84, Pharmon B.V. v. Hoechst A.G., [1985] E.C.R. 2281.

[30] Joined Cases 56/64 & 58/64, Établissements Consten, S.A.R.L. v. Commission, [1966] E.C.R. 299. See also Case 40/70, Sirena v. Eda, [1971] E.C.R. 69. A variety of cases have also applied the provisions of (now) arts. 34 and 36 of the TFEU (formerly arts. 28–30 of the EC Treaty, before

principle applicable as a matter of regulating discrete IP rights, to be assessed on the basis of interpreting secondary legislation and predominantly informed by national fixations. Further, secondary (harmonizing) IP legislation treats exhaustion in different ways. In trademark law, for example, exhaustion is the general rule. Further commercialization can be opposed where there are very specific circumstances, such as repackaging, which affects the origin function of the mark.[31] This is a specific exception, which links exhaustion with a justification based on the rationale of the respective IP right. But this specific exception is not, as such, present in copyright law, the specific topic of this chapter.

As I will elaborate in this chapter, as far as copyright law is harmonized, the relevant Directives do not offer, at first glance, much flexibility to apply the exhaustion rule (as opposed to an exhaustion *principle*) above and beyond the sale of works embodied in a physical form. From this perspective, exhaustion is understood as a rule more or less identical to the U.S. "first sale" doctrine[32] and is much rooted in underlying concepts of "things." In addition, the EU Copyright Directive (EUCD)[33] treats copyright protection as the norm. Thus, as a general rule, a high level of protection should be granted and exceptions and limitations where applied to digital uses in general should be treated with caution by national legislators. Exhaustion appears to be an exception to the general rule that a high level of protection should be provided, and therefore should be restricted to a physical copy embodying a work, rather than to intangible representations of works or to acts of communication in general.

If the exhaustion rule would be applied literally (e.g., by using the broad formulation of every time a copy of a work or product is put into circulation by or with consent of the owner), the control right would necessarily be curtailed drastically, especially so where exhaustion would be considered as a mandatory concept that cannot be easily eschewed by contract. However, this is decidedly not so. Arguments against such broad reading are plenty, and the key question concerns the relationship between contractual consent and permissible market segregations, now applied to online markets. But it remains undecided how precisely such conflicting positions interact with and inform the exhaustion rule.

Evidently, a brash and drastic imposition of constraints over online sales by third parties would naturally alleviate the problem by allowing the emergence of any market following an act of putting into circulation, as it were. But whilst geographical restraints such as bans on parallel imports could, at the time, been given a more cursory explanation by

---

that arts. 30–36 of the Treaty Establishing the European Economic Community, 1957 EUR-Lex CELEX LEXIS 1957E/TXT). See Case 9/93, IHT Internationale Heiztechnik GmbH v. Ideal-Standard GmbH, [1994] E.C.R. I-2789; Case 19/84, Pharmon B.V. v. Hoechst A.G., [1985] E.C.R. 2281; Case 144/81, Keurkoop B.V. v. Nancy Kean Gifts B.V., [1982] E.C.R. 2853; Case 187/80, Merck & Co. v. Stephar B.V., [1981] E.C.R. 2063; Joined Cases 55/80 & 57/80, Musik-Vertrieb Membran GmbH v. GEMA, [1981] E.C.R. 147; Case 15/74, Centrafarm B.V. v. Sterling Drug Inc., [1974] E.C.R. 1147.

[31] See Case-427/93, Bristol-Myers Squibb v. Paranova A/S, [1996] E.C.R. I-03457.
[32] See Capitol Records, L.L.C. v. ReDigi Inc., 934 F. Supp. 2d 640 (S.D.N.Y. 2013) (holding that there is no "online exhaustion" under §§ 106, 109 of the U.S. Copyright Act since offers for downloads do not constitute sales).
[33] Directive 2001/29/EC of the European Parliament and of the Council of May 22, 2001 on the harmonization of certain aspects of copyright and related rights in the information society, [2001] O.J. L167/10–19 (EC) [hereinafter EUCD].

relying on fundamental principles of market integration (derived from a resultant combination of competition law and the principle of the free movement of goods[34]) the issue of product market control is less easy to resolve because (as will be discussed in detail later[35]) the provisions under the EUCD[36] seem to expressly exclude exhaustion in relation to the exclusive rights of reproduction and communication to the public. Thus, the attempt to exclude "online" markets has become a test case for the aptitude of the exhaustion rule as a wider-restraining principle.

III. EXHAUSTION "ONLINE": COLLISION BETWEEN COPYRIGHT AND EU LAW?

Exhaustion may also apply for "used" digital goods that are protected under copyright law. The finer points are, however, far from being resolved. As it will be seen, some tendency to permit the application of the exhaustion doctrine was established by the CJEU in its guidance on exhaustion of computer programs downloaded for payment without particular restrictions as to the "period of use" rights. For other works, there is a major barrier to a finding of exhaustion, given that Article 4(2) of the EUCD,[37] in conjunction with recitals 28 and 29 to the EUCD,[38] appears to categorically rule out exhaustion for all avenues of exploitation except the distribution of physical goods. There is, therefore, uncertainty, particularly regarding whether the recent jurisprudence may be applied to works other than computer programs. Moreover, there is scope for a broader notion of exhaustion, especially when considering that the notion of exhaustion applied to downloads mirrors a commendable continuation of previous case law under primary EU law, with a high motivation to set the scene for a further use of the exhaustion rule as reflecting principles aiming at the digital market.

A. The Expansion of the Exhaustion Rule Towards Intangible Goods

In *UsedSoft*,[39] the CJEU held that, in general, the exhaustion rule, as enshrined in the Computer Software Directive, might apply where a copy of a program was acquired

---

[34] *Compare* with Joined Cases 56/64 & 58/64, Établissements Consten, S.A.R.L. v. Commission, [1966] E.C.R. 299. The CJEU later applied EC Treaty, art. 36, by way of analogy, to cases concerning art. 85 of the EC Treaty (now art. 81 of the TFEU). See Case 24/67, Parke, Davis & Co. v. Probel, [1968] E.C.R. 55. Then, it directly applied arts. 30–36 of the EC Treaty (now arts. 28–30 of the TFEU) to any exercise of intellectual property rights. See Case 16/74, Centrafarm B.V. v. Winthrop B.V., [1974] E.C.R. 1183; Case 192/73, Van Zuylen Frères v. Hag A.G., [1974] E.C.R. 731; Case 78/70, Deutsche Grammophon v. METRO-SB-GROSSMÄRKTE GmbH & Co. K.G., [1971] E.C.R. 487; Case 40/70, Sirena v. Eda, [1971] E.C.R. 69.
[35] See *infra* IV.
[36] Council Directive 2001/29 of the European Parliament and of the Council of May 22, 2001 on the harmonization of certain aspects of copyright and related rights in the information society, [2001] O.J. L167/10–19 (EC).
[37] EUCD, art. 4(2).
[38] *Ibid.* recitals 28, 29.
[39] Case C-128/11, UsedSoft GmbH v. Oracle Int'l Corp., [2011] O.J. C194.

by way of downloading from a platform operated by the right holder. It was therefore possible for acquirers to resell (usually older) program versions and thus to establish a secondary market.

The decision hinged upon two central considerations. First, the fact that the right holder had not imposed any specific conditions concerning a limit on the period of use meant that the agreement in question could be considered as a transfer within the meaning of Article 4 of the EU Computer Software Directive.[40] Second, it would follow that any necessary reproductions made by end-users were also covered by the lawful user provision therein. Thereby, the CJEU arrived at a conclusion that permits an expansion of the exhaustion rule above and beyond the sale of a physical carrier.

Unsurprisingly, the decision in *UsedSoft* is difficult to align with traditional copyright thinking. It could be discussed whether the decision lacks a proper investigation into the nature of computer programs versus a physical carrier embodying such program, or whether it indeed establishes a more general principle that can be applied, at least by way of analogy, to any digital work acquired by way of download. Further, the CJEU did not refer to the relationship between primary and secondary legislation and made no reference to an underlying rationale derived from any overriding principle of primary EU law. Nevertheless, it is suggested that (whilst the construction of the provisions under the Computer Software Directive as a matter of construing harmonized copyright law is debatable, at least) the decision does not entirely deviate from previous case law and that it offers enough flexibility for balancing copyright law with concerns of fundamental aims and principles. Indeed, such balancing test may, as will be discussed, also apply with respect to other forms of online uses.[41]

B. Construing Secondary Legislation: Exhaustion and Copyright Doctrine

The question of whether exhaustion may be applied to intangible goods, above and beyond software, remains open. Fundamentally, the conclusion can follow from both an intrinsic reading of copyright norms or a broader recognition of primary law, including aspects of the free movement of digital goods as a concern that is ultimately rooted in the internal market aim under Article 4(2)(a) of the TFEU. Notably, the CJEU did not expressly refer to an underlying principle but derived its conclusion from the text of the Computer Software Directive only, leaving aside a potential extension to other works.

There are many different lines of reasoning for and against such an extension. In short, the arguments against such extension predominantly rely on written copyright law and claim that exhaustion can only arise as a re-exception to the distribution right, which in turn would require a transfer of ownership by way of sale or otherwise. On that basis, it

---

[40] Directive 2009/24 of the European Parliament and of the Council of April 23, 2009 on the legal protection of computer programs (codified version), [2009] O.J. L111/16–22 (EC) [hereinafter Software Directive].

[41] See generally Chris Reed, *Online and Offline Equivalence: Aspiration and Achievement*, 18 INT'L J. INFO. L. & TECH. 248 (2006). On the notion of equal treatment, see Case C-128/11, UsedSoft GmbH v. Oracle Int'l Corp., [2011] O.J. C194/6; see generally TAKIS TRIDIMAS, THE GENERAL PRINCIPLES OF EU LAW 46 (1999); TREVOR HARTLEY, THE FOUNDATIONS OF EUROPEAN UNION LAW 145 (8th ed., 2014).

may also be concluded that international Convention excludes exhaustion by the same token. Further support for this conclusion can be found in Article 4(2) of and recital 29 to the EUCD, which exclude exhaustion in the case of services offering works for download.[42] This could lead to the result that the transfer of intangible data would exclusively be governed as an annex to the making available right.

In particular, those favoring an extension of exhaustion can argue, as a matter of statutory copyright law, in three ways. First, the distribution right may be applicable where the notion of ownership can be applied to data. Second, the exhaustion rule may be applied by way of analogy to digital transactions because it is equivalent to transferring goods embodied in physical carriers, as was the main contention in *UsedSoft*. Third, it can convincingly be argued that EU primary law requires a correction of secondary copyright legislation so as to more extensively avoid the portioning of the market and enforce concerns of a single digital market. In the following paragraphs, I will first address the fundamental copyright aspect of whether there is a coercive argument to apply the "making available" right. Building on this analysis, I will address the possible complexities that arise where the *UsedSoft* decision is found to be *contra legem* as regards the construction of secondary copyright law.

(1) *UsedSoft* as interpretation *contra legem*: lines of attack

General criticism of the *UsedSoft* decision holds that the decision is flawed. The first aspect of criticism concerns the allegedly misguided extension of the exhaustion rule to non-physical "goods" and the ensuing conclusion that the download in question cannot constitute a transfer as expressly required.

The notion of a *transfer*, as approached by the CJEU, is certainly debatable. In most jurisdictions, a transfer means a transfer of property in a physical embodiment of a work, meaning in a physical carrier. Consequentially, it is arguable whether the non-physical download of works can constitute an agreement concerning the transfer of physical property. Many commentators have taken the view that a software license, given the nature of software as an immaterial good, cannot be considered as containing an obligation to transfer such property status,[43] because the object consists of mere data. In other words, software cannot be "sold" because its very nature would exclude any notion of a contract for sale.[44] Others have taken the opposite view, arguing that software may constitute an

---

[42] EUCD, art. 4(4) and recital 29.
[43] In that sense, see the approach by the CJEU in Case C-456/06, Peek & Cloppenburg K.G. v. Cassina SpA, [2008] E.C.R. I-02731. Importantly, the Court reiterated that the notion of a sale as a transfer of property under art. 4(1) of the EUCD had to be construed in the light of art. 6 of the WCT since there was an obligation to interpret distribution right under EU law in accordance with international obligations, which is further supported by recital 15 of the EUCD. See also EUCD, art. 4(1); WCT, art. 6; EUCD, recital 15.
[44] Which under German law links the exhaustion rule, as a matter of the distribution right, directly with the definition of a contract for sale as expressly defined under art. 43 of the Civil Code in the version promulgated on January 2, 2002, Federal Law Gazette (Bundesgesetzblatt) 42, 2909, 2003, last amended by art. 4(5) of the Act of October 1, 2013, Federal Law Gazette I 3719, that is, as an obligation to transfer ownership in a physical thing. See Malte Stieper, *EuGH, Urt. v. 3.7.2012, Rs. C-128/11 – UsedSoft*, Zeitschrift für Urheber- und Medienrecht (ZUM) 668 (2012); Haberstumpf, *supra* note 3, at 482. Emma Linklater, *UsedSoft and the Big Bang Theory:*

object of a contract for the purchase of physical things.[45] Necessarily, these issues are intertwined with national preoccupations of contractual typology as applied to copyright law,[46] and such divergence is increasingly at odds with a notion of a single digital market. In the U.K., the acquisition of user rights in software has generally always been considered as a license,[47] rather than a purchase, whereas the debate in German law has, for a long time, been undecided.[48] The decision results, therefore, in uncertainty as to whether the exhaustion rule would apply to the program as a thing or whether it would apply to the licensed right of use.[49] Fundamentally, it is certainly correct that software is not a thing, and this consideration results in a broader applicability of the exhaustion rule that removes the strict reliance on a transfer by way of sale.[50]

(2) "Proper" solution under secondary software copyright law

Accordingly, the (allegedly) correct line of reasoning might look as follows: the dissemination of software by offering downloads constitutes an act of "making available," whilst the uses made by the acquirer constitute potentially various acts of reproduction. These rights are expressly not subject to exhaustion. For exhaustion to occur, the distribution right must be affected. Exhaustion, it follows, can only occur with respect to the physical embodiment. This physical embodiment is absent in the case of downloaded software since nothing in a physical form is conveyed and therefore, the free circulation of goods is not affected. In addition, some commentators pointed out that since the Computer Software Directive does not expressly provide for a "making available" in favor of software copyright owners, Article 3(1) of the EUCD[51] should have been applied in order to clarify twofold: (1) that download services are subject to the communication to the public right; and (2) that the service in question should exclusively be characterized as an act of making available. Thus, Article 1(2) of the EUCD,[52] which leaves the computer program

---

Is the Exhaustion Meteor About to Strike? (2013), available at http://papers.ssrn.com/sol3/papers.cfm?abstract_id=2271129; Ole Andreas Rognstad, *Legally Flawed But Politically Sound? Digital Exhaustion of Copyright in Europe After UsedSoft*, 1 OSLO LAW REV. (2014), available at www.journals.uio.no/index.php/oslawreview/article/view/977.

[45] See Paul Katzenberger, *Elektronische Printmedien und Urheberrecht*, ARCHIV FÜR PRESSERECHT (AFP) 434, 437 (1997).

[46] Especially so in Germany. See BGH, February 11, 2010, 9 GRUR 822 (Ger.); Kammergericht (Higher Regional Court Berlin) (2014) ZEITSCHRIFT FUER URHEBER- UND MEDIENRECHT – RECHTSPRECHUNGSDIENST (ZUM-RD) 504.

[47] See Ken Moon, *Resale of Digital Content: UsedSoft v. ReDigi*, 6 ENT. L. REV. 193 (2013).

[48] See Thomas Hoeren, *Überlegungen zur urheberrechtlichen Qualifizierung des elektronischen Abrufs, in* COMPUTER UND RECHT 517 (1996). See also BGH, 1988 GEWERBLICHER RECHTSSCHUTZ UND URHEBERRECHT 206, 211, in which exhaustion, broadly as a matter of principle was applied to the broadcasting right.

[49] It may also tentatively be argued that data can constitute a type of property which is capable of ownership. See THOMAS HOEREN & JONAS VOELKEL, BIG DATA UND RECHT 15 (Hoeren ed., 2014); Thomas Hoeren & Matthias Foersterling, *Onlinevertrieb gebrauchter Software – Hintergruende und Konsequenzen der EuGH-Entscheidung UsedSoft*, MULTIMEDIA UND RECHT (MMR) 642 (2012).

[50] See further Reto M. Hilty, Kaya Koklü, & Fabian Hafenbrädl, *Software Agreements: Stocktaking and Outlook: Lessons from the UsedSoft v. Oracle Case from a Comparative Law Perspective*, 44 INT'L REV. INTELL. PROP. & COMPETITION L. 263 (2013).

[51] EUCD, art. 3(1).

[52] *Ibid.* art. 1(2).

regulations intact as *lex specialis*,[53] does not apply with regard to the characterization of the claimant's service as "making available," which in turn relies on the protection granted to software copyright owners under Articles 6 and 8 of the WCT.[54] Software copyright is covered under both exclusive rights.

Therefore, it may be argued that Article 6 of the WCT[55] should not have been applied because, again, there is no physical transfer.[56] Thus, despite the fact that exhaustion remains a matter for national laws under Article 6(2) of the WCT,[57] the violation is deemed to be an improper characterization of the download "service" as a form of distribution. Exhaustion therefore, as matter of national implementation of these rules, cannot occur. In other words, there would not have been any scope left for assessing the impact of the distribution right and its "proper" interpretation under Article 6 of the WCT[58] because Articles 6 and 8 of the WCT are considered mutually exclusive.[59] Consequentially, because the Computer Software Directive does not afford a right of "making available," as applies to other works under Article 3(1) of the EUCD,[60] the CJEU should have clarified instead that the transaction in question was subject to the "making available" right so as to allow software copyright owners to enjoy this right fully. These objections deserve a closer inspection.

(3) Redundancy of contractual typologies

It is obvious that the notion of a transfer, and thereby sale, is open to criticism. Specifically under German copyright law, the exhaustion rule would only apply with respect to the concrete copy put into circulation. It is a different matter, however, how far that criticism is sound as a matter of developing the exhaustion rule.

The fact that the claimant herself labeled the transaction as a license was irrelevant.[61] However, the Court did not expressly interpret the notion of a transfer of property. It explained that the transaction in question should be regarded as a sale. The notion of a sale itself therefore becomes, apparently, an autonomous principle that does not necessarily require a transfer of property but may be understood in a broader way. Moreover,

---

[53] See MATTHIAS LEISTNER, DIE METHODIK DES EUGH UND DIE GARANTENFUNKTION DER NATIONALEN GERICHTE BEI DER FORTENTWICKLUNG DES EUROPÄISCHEN URHEBERRECHTS (2015), available at www.jura.uni-bonn.de/fileadmin/Fachbereich_Rechtswissenschaft/Einrichtungen/Lehrstuehle/Zivilrecht4/Manuskripte_Leistner/Die_Methodik_des_EuGH_und_die_Garantenfunktion_der_nationalen_Gerichte_bei_der_Fortentwicklung_des_europaeischen_Urheberrechts.pdf.

[54] WCT, arts. 6, 8.

[55] *Ibid.* art. 6.

[56] See Oberlandesgericht (OLG, Hamm Regional Higher Court) 2014 GRUR 853 (Ger.) (rejecting exhaustion in relation to audiobooks solely on the basis of the absence of a physical embodiment and asserting that art. 8 of the WCT prevents an application of the exhaustion by way of analogy).

[57] WCT, art. 6(2).

[58] *Ibid.* art. 6.

[59] In that sense, inaccurately, BRIGGITE LINDNER & TED SHAPIRO, COPYRIGHT IN THE INFORMATION SOCIETY: A GUIDE TO NATIONAL IMPLEMENTATION OF THE EUROPEAN DIRECTIVE 21 (2011) (noting that where the making available right is implicated, there cannot be a concurrent scope for the distribution right).

[60] EUCD, art. 3(1).

[61] See also BGH, July 11, 2013, KOMMUNIKATION & RECHT (K&R) 252 (Ger.).

at least in some Member States, including Germany, the question as to whether software may be an object of a contract for sale (within the meaning of the relevant sections of the German Civil Code) had been debated. That debate has little to say on exhaustion in a European context since it is first and foremost concerned with questions of liability under contract law. Third, deliberations on whether software may constitute "a thing" do not exhaustively resolve the issue. The ontological qualification of computer programs in law cannot determine, with absolute precision, its treatment across all legal branches and questions of copyright protection must rest on the underlying rationale of copyright in the first place.

Finally, the terminologies used are not identical. The fact that certain transactions are classified as a "sale" under national laws with a specific connotation cannot derogate from the insight that, nevertheless, exhaustion can occur in a broader sense, that is, as a principle limiting the control right over specific subsequent uses.

Therefore, the criticism claiming an improper construction of the notion of a transfer is unpersuasive. Again, exhaustion (as mentioned) may well have a different, more metaphorical meaning under EU law than it has under national law. Therefore, the question as to whether exhaustion applies to a specific type of transfer (which must, under national law, correspond with the connotation of a sale) is largely irrelevant from the perspective of EU law. As was shown in relation to trademark exhaustion, national law (or a manifest legal tradition of construction under national law) may be subject to correction in case there is a conflict with primary law. After all, the construction of EU law can exceed an interpretation limited by the connotation of a provision's wording—though under that premise further complexities lie in wait.

IV. EXHAUSTION AND DIGITAL MARKETS

This finding is also true with regard to an initially more compelling disapproving position. This argument proceeds on the basis that the CJEU misinterpreted the scope of the various exclusive rights and, in doing so, also confused the categories of goods (to which exhaustion, as a European principle, applies) and rights in the communication of works, which would fall under the umbrella of services (to which exhaustion cannot apply). Following this reasoning, it may then be asserted that, regarding services, exhaustion cannot occur whenever works are made available since such making available constitutes "a service," thus, the decision could be considered noncompliant with basic values under primary EU law. This argument can, in turn, rely on the allegedly express exclusion of exhaustion in relation to services under recital 29 of the EUCD.[62]

However, these two questions should not be confused and each will be addressed in turn. First, does it follow, as a matter of interpreting secondary copyright law, that a download service must inevitably be governed by the "making available" right? Secondly, if "yes," can it be argued that because of the distinction under primary EU law regarding the freedom of services and the free movement of goods, exhaustion, in an absolute sense, does not apply in the context of a service? In other words, a clear distinction should be

---

[62] EUCD, recital 29.

drawn between the intrinsic construction of copyright law and the concerns of primary law.

That line of reasoning ultimately accuses the CJEU of acting *contra legem* in interpreting secondary Union law, and concurrently disregarding an obligation under public international law (Article 8 of the WCT and Article 10 of the WIPO Performances and Phonograms Treaty (WPPT)) which are binding.[63]

A. Exclusion of Exhaustion for Services Under EU Law

First, from the perspective of EU law, the distinction between goods and services and the consequential denial of exhaustion as a principle that must exclusively be confined to the free movement of goods regime appears unfounded. Both regimes may easily converge[64] and there is no indication that exhaustion (as a tool for allowing the CJEU to evaluate conflicts between national law and fundamental freedoms) may not occur in a context similar to territorial constraints. Therefore, the fact that, as a matter of terminology, the genesis of a European exhaustion doctrine was intrinsically linked to the principle of the free movement of goods is, as such, not a persuasive counter-argument for excluding exhaustion where it concerns services. Indeed, reliance on exhaustion probably requires a more refined approach in decision-making because the structure of the "freedom of service" regime does not include a possible justification for the protection of "industrial and commercial property."[65] Another justification is Article 36 of the TFEU,[66] which formed, ultimately, the basis permitting the CJEU to develop the exhaustion doctrine both as a re-exception and as a general proportionality test.[67] But that does not mean that exhaustion is strictly confined to the free movement of goods regime. Regarding Article 36 of the TFEU,[68] the Court was not concerned with the construction of the scope of national exclusive rights under copyright law[69] but with the interpretation of primary EU law.[70]

In this regard, a related proposition seeking to exclude exhaustion in cases of services is based on the decision in *Coditel*,[71] in which the CJEU stated that the "cable right" is not

---

[63] See *ibid.* recital 15.
[64] See Case C-35/95 & C-36/95, Konsumentombudsmannen (KO) v. De Agostini (Svenska) Förlag A.B., [1997] E.C.R. I-3843.
[65] Albert Bleckmann, *Zur Problematik der Cassis de Dijon-Rechtsprechung des Europäischen Gerichtshofs*, GRUR INT. 172, 174 (1986); PAUL DEMARET, PATENTS, TERRITORIAL RESTRICTIONS AND EEC LAW 14 (1978).
[66] TFEU, art. 36.
[67] Ulrich Loewenheim, *Schallplattenimporte und freier Warenverkehr im Gemeinsamen Markt*, 95 ARCHIV FÜR URHEBER-, FILM-, FUNK- UND THEATERRECHT 41, 44 (1983).
[68] TFEU, art. 36.
[69] Herman Cohen Jehoram, *Articles 30–36 EEC and Intellectual Property*, SOCIAAL-ECONOMISCH WETGEVING (TIJDSCHRIFT VOOR EUROPEES EN ECONOMISCH RECHT) (SEW) 374 (1982).
[70] Westkamp, *supra* note 17, at 291.
[71] See Case C-62/79, S.A. Compagnie générale pour la diffusion de la télévision, Coditel & ors. v. Ciné Vog Films & ors., [1980] E.C.R. 881; Case C-262/81, Coditel S.A., Compagnie générale pour la diffusion de la télévision & ors. v. Ciné-Vog Films S.A. & ors., [1982] E.C.R. 3381 (*"Coditel II"*); Case C-158/86, Warner Bros. v. Christensen, [1988] E.C.R. 2605; Case C-395/87, Ministère Public v. Tournier, [1989] E.C.R. 2521; Case C-61/97, Videogramdistributorer v. Laserdisken, [1998]

exhausted because the showing of movies can be infinitely repeated. However, the Court also clarified that it was the very specific characteristics of the commercial exploitation of films in cinemas and television that were decisive in allowing copyright protection to surpass the freedom to provide services, since the public is always present in such cases. In other words, the *Coditel* decision should not be generalized as a basis for excluding exhaustion, or a functionally equivalent rule constraining national copyright, in unconditional terms. In sum, nothing under European law would prevent the imposition of the exhaustion rule where a specific conduct based on exercising national IP rights is found to be in conflict with aims such as the internal market. At least, such cases are open to balancing and proportionality assessments.

In sum, the characterization as "goods" or "services" under primary EU law does not immediately impact the reasoning that excludes exhaustion as regards the "making available" right. The primary law therefore is indifferent to the qualification of exclusive rights under copyright law.

B. Online Exhaustion and the Supremacy of Primary Union Law

The second hurdle is more daunting to overcome and should be analyzed here, in particular, as regarding the notion of "making available" as a service under copyright law. The main problem with a broader contention that exhaustion can apply to downloads lies, consequentially, in international copyright Convention law; Article 3(1) of the EUCD[72] literally transposes Article 8 of the WCT[73] as an obligation of the EU.[74] In this case, the question of exhaustion must be clearly distinguished between a matter of Convention law applicable to traditional copyright thinking, on the one hand, and the imposition of exhaustion on works for the benefit of European principles and aims, on the other.

If it was correct to allocate any act of "making available," including any subsequent transmission of "works by download" in totality to the "making available right" as enshrined in Article 8 of the WCT,[75] the *UsedSoft* decision (and, naturally, any attempt to extend it to other categories of work) would thus be noncompliant with international obligations. As regards computer programs, as mentioned, a "making available right" does not apply. Nevertheless, Article 8 of the WCT[76] affords that right to any "work." Accordingly, some commentators have argued that Article 1(2)(a) of the EUCD is inapplicable,[77] and that, instead, that lacuna should be filled on the basis of Article 4(2) of the EUCD.[78] The question of a violation of the norms under the WCT thus hinges, first,

---

E.C.R. I-5171. This position was broadly followed, prior to the coming into force of the EUCD, in *Green Paper on Copyright and Related Rights in the Information Society* 57, COM(1995)382 final (July 27, 1995).

[72] EUCD, art. 3(1).
[73] WCT, art. 8.
[74] See EUCD, recital 15.
[75] WCT, art. 8.
[76] *Ibid.*
[77] Linklater, *supra* note 44; Rognstad, *supra* note 44.
[78] EUCD, art. 4(2).

on the "proper" construction of the scope of the "making available right" as opposed to the distribution right.

There are two main arguments that might, consequentially, support the view that the notion of "online exhaustion" conflicts with international obligations. Both may be based on the wording of Article 8 of the WCT[79] and Article 3(1) of the EUCD.[80] The "making available right," in that sense, is to be considered as one "limb" of a general right of communication to the public and that right encompasses any transmission of works by wire or wireless means, with the exception of public performances. Therefore, it would follow that Article 6 of the WCT,[81] which obliges the contracting parties to guarantee a right of distribution,[82] but leaves the question of exhaustion under that provision to national laws,[83] must be solely concerned with physical copies. It would then follow that offering works for download falls within the public communication right, and thus, that exhaustion cannot occur because the subsequent transmission (upon the request of the individual user) of an "intangible copy" is part of that right. The second argument relates to that verdict: because Article 4(2) of the EUCD[84] expressly excludes exhaustion under European law and thus outlines the scope of the distribution right, exhaustion is likewise confined to physical copies as a matter of secondary EU law. In essence, these two arguments claim that the extension of exhaustion to intangible goods is incompatible with both international law and secondary European legislation, by construing the right of distribution excessively. This raises interesting and cumbersome questions, both as regards the relationship between primary EU and international law, as well as between primary and secondary law, to which I will return later.

(1) Compliance with international Convention law

However, and before questions of normative hierarchies should be addressed, the conclusion reached here can very arguably be supported as a matter of copyright law. First, nothing under Article 6 of the WCT[85] compels a reading of "download services" as falling under Article 8 of the WCT,[86] and therefore the distribution right, upon which the *UsedSoft* decision relied, can initially be extended to intangible goods. Second, that finding can be combined with a construction of Article 3(1) of the EUCD[87] and Article 8 of the WCT[88] which focuses on the subsequent transmission of the work. That transmission can be evaluated as an act independent of any "making available" to the public. In the case of downloads, that act may, additionally, be qualified as a monetary transaction.

---

[79] WCT, art. 8.
[80] EUCD, art. 3(1).
[81] WCT, art. 6.
[82] See also *Records of the Diplomatic Conference on Certain Copyright and Neighboring Rights Questions*, WIPO PUBLICATION NO. 348 (E) 195–97 (1996).
[83] See generally MIHALY FICSOR, CURRENT ISSUES OF EXHAUSTION OF RIGHTS (KIRTSAENG & QUALITY KING, REDIGI V. USEDSOFT) (2014), available at www.copyrightseesaw.net/archive/?sw_10_item=55.
[84] EUCD, art. 4(2).
[85] WTC, art. 6.
[86] *Ibid.* art. 8.
[87] EUCD, art. 3(1).
[88] WCT, art. 8.

Thus, even where that subsequent transmission was classified as a "transmission by wire or wireless means," the "making available" right cannot apply to it since the act of downloading is not an interactive act; it also does not constitute an act of *public* communication since it is instigated by an individual user, and therefore cannot constitute any act "to the public."

Hence, the subsequent transmission is consumed by the exercise of the "making available" right, but hardly bars a finding of exhaustion. And even if the download constituted an act that forms part of the "communication to the right" (which concerns an issue that transcends the scope of this chapter[89]) the immediate finding is not one of mutual exclusivity between the distribution right and the communication to the public right, but a conclusion that there may be a conflict where the download simply substitutes for a physical transaction. Therefore, the central issue concerns the characterization of the transaction rather than the technological process involved. Further, nothing under secondary copyright legislation prevents a finding that seeks to balance the interests between copyright owners and (as a matter of intrinsic copyright construction) the rights of individual users.[90] Certainly, copyright law is to be interpreted purposively and that approach is to be based upon a balancing of interests.[91] In sum, the imposition of exhaustion upon intangible goods neither means that the right to communicate works to the public is exhausted nor that an appropriate purposive construction of the relevant copyright legislation exceeds established patterns of interpretation. The conclusion that exhaustion may occur thus may follow from an intrinsic interpretation of copyright law, and evidently the CJEU saw no need to engage with a more principled approach above and beyond giving guidance on the text of the EUCD. It is therefore ultimately irrelevant whether the exclusive rights of distribution or communication are mutually exclusive as a matter of international copyright law, or whether they may be considered as converging. The decision is also clearly commensurate with the jurisprudence on exhaustion prior to the enactment of secondary harmonizing legislation and offers, in that sense, freedom of movement for the CJEU to react to technological development. The CJEU therefore sought to accommodate interests that are expressly enshrined in the EUCD, namely, the aim of providing a high degree of protection and the need to strike a balance between copyright protection and other conflicting interests. In this case, arguably, the conflicting interests are the concerns of a digital single market. The approach in *UsedSoft* is, ultimately, commendable for delineating the notion of transactions and the scope of exclusive right in general.

---

[89] See JORG REINBOTHE & SILKE VON LEWINSKI, THE WIPO TREATIES 1996, § 21, art. 8 (2002). It should be noted that Council Directive 96/6/EC of the European Parliament and of the Council of March 11, 1996 on the legal protection of databases, [1996] O.J. L77/20–28 (EC) [hereinafter Database Directive] left the characterization of online uses largely open. Member States were thus at liberty to attach such uses to the distribution right. See Database Directive, recitals 25–27; see MICHEL WALTER & SILKE VON LEWINSKI, EUROPEAN COPYRIGHT LAW: A COMMENTARY paras. 9.5.22, 11.3.36 (2010).
[90] See Case C-456/06, Peek & Cloppenburg K.G. v. Cassina SpA, [2008] E.C.R. I-0273 (clearly demonstrating that right holders cannot infinitely rely on the "high level of protection" that is to be granted under the EUCD).
[91] Case C-275/06, Productores de Música de España (Promusicae) v. Telefónica de España S.A.U., [2008] E.C.R. I-00271, para. 70.

(2) Flexibilities of interpretation: the continued relevance of primary law

Yet even if the opposite view was taken—that the extension of the exhaustion principle to tangible goods must be considered as incompatible with the wording and/or *telos* of both the relevant Directives and international obligations—that view would eschew arguments based on the relationship between primary law, on the one hand, and secondary European and international law, on the other. As far as the methodology employed is concerned, the Court generally takes a more purposive or teleological, rather than literal, approach.[92] However, that methodology has limits. It may, as many commentators have implicitly claimed, be argued that the notion of "intangible goods" exceeds the outer limits of the wording used in secondary legislation or that the pairing of the two terms should even be considered paradoxical, and thus beyond acceptable purposive patterns of construction. In addition, such an argument may be made on the basis that harmonizing measures ultimately concretize primary law, and that, therefore, the scope of full harmonization is conclusive in the sense of delineating the boundaries between primary law under the Treaty and secondary law under the Directives. Thus, the *UsedSoft* decision would go beyond the accepted canon of interpretation of secondary law. It is indeed a recognized principle that the CJEU must neither interpret a norm under secondary union law *contra legem* nor may the Court interfere, in doing so, with political concerns,[93] such as nebulous implications of a digital single market.[94] The traditional construction of the exhaustion rule as applicable only to physical goods finds much support in national legal traditions, especially, as seen, in Germany; it may also be argued that such traditions ultimately shaped the distinction between "making available" and "distribution" under Convention law. Arguably, the same applies in cases where the EU legislator accepted, to some degree, that secondary legislation might conflict with primary law in the future.[95]

There is an immediate fallacy in that argument. A concretized *rule* is necessarily narrow in scope and, therefore, is more static than generalized principles. Indeed, the interpretation of EU law in conformity with primary law is an accepted method of teleological and systematic interpretation.[96] In essence, then, arguments based on the wording or static *telos* of a particular norm of secondary legislation remove the ability to react to specifi-

---

[92] LEISTNER, *supra* note 53.

[93] See generally, Stefan Leible & Ronny Domroese, *Die primaerrechtskonforme Auslegung*, in KARL RIESENHUBER, EUROPAEISCHE METHODENLEHRE (2010).

[94] In fact, the issue underlying that argument is complex: where the wording of a particular norm leaves space for interpretation such as under art. 4(c) of the Software Directive, clearly the CJEU has capacity to concretize such norms; conversely, it has been argued that the Court should exercise caution in cases where it is uncertain whether the Union legislator reserved the right to regulate a specific question. At the time when the decision was rendered it was rather clear that the Commission had commenced to initialize a program for copyright reform, and likewise there was much activity regarding the program for establishing a digital single market. See generally, Christian Calliess, *Rechtsfortbildung und Richterrecht in der EU*, GOETTINGER ONLINE-BEITRAEGE ZUM EUROPARECHT 28 (2005).

[95] Case 314/85, Foto-Frost v. Hauptzollamt Luebeck-Ost, [1987] E.C.R. 4199, 4230–32. See also Martin Höpner, *Von der Lückenfüllung zur Vertragsumdeutung – Ein Vorschlag zur Unterscheidung von Stufen der Rechtsfortbildung durch den Europäischen Gerichtshof*, 1 DER MODERNE STAAT – ZEITSCHRIFT FÜR PUBLIC POLICY, RECHT UND MANAGEMENT (DMS) 165, 171 (2010).

[96] See Case C-315/92, Verband Sozialer Wettbewerb eV v. Clinique Laboratoires S.N.C. & Estée Lauder Cosmetics GmbH, [1994] E.C.R. I-317, para. 1.

cally technological development and thereby hinder a meaningful evolution of the law.[97] In addition, such reading appears anachronistic and inconclusive; it largely ignores important aspects under European law. Although (deplorably) the decision in *UsedSoft* does not expressly refer to underlying principles of primary EU law, and does also not expose a clear deduction from specific primary aims, it does not immediately follow that secondary legislation must take precedence even where secondary legislation is considered as fully harmonizing, and thus as concretizing, principles under primary Union law.[98] If so, the same principles must also apply where there is a collision between international law binding the EU and implemented by way of secondary legislation, on the one hand, and an alleged misinterpretation of such rules for the benefit of enforcing primary aims, on the other. In general, obligations under public international law rank lower than primary law, and have, therefore, the same status as secondary legislation. This debate, which ultimately concerns the normative hierarchy under EU law and the related division of powers, cannot be fully addressed here.[99] However, there is certainly very little secondary copyright legislation that would support such a view, especially since the decision, in expressly noting the extension based on an economic equivalence argument, appears as a convincing continuation of the previous jurisprudence on the free movement of goods, which can now rely upon the digital single market as part of the "general internal market aim" of Article 4(2)(a) of the TFEU.[100]

C. Capacities and Parameters: Exhaustion in a Multi-Layered System

Therefore, the CJEU has the capacity to develop secondary legislation via general balancing approaches as it had done prior to harmonizing IP legislation coming into force, and as the CJEU does regularly.[101] Regarding a future approach, the decision in *UsedSoft* might offer some initial guidance on the allocation of interests within such a balancing exercise. Consent appears to remain the decisive criterion. The underlying motivation, here, clearly was to address a form of contradictory conduct by traders, who, on the one hand, benefited from the opening of markets but who, on the other hand, sought advantage by exercising national IP rights so as to repartition the common market.[102]

It is obvious that such a fundamental proposition can effortlessly be applied to the notion of a digital single market. It follows that any consent generally, and as a matter of principle, leads to exhaustion, as it does under trademark law. Regarding copyright, the central arguments supporting that view are as follows: first, as mentioned, the transaction in question is equivalent to a physical transfer and therefore should not be evaluated differently. Second, the copyright owner has no legitimate interest in controlling

---

[97] See, as regards the need for a dynamic interpretation of Union law, Case 283/31, CILFIT v. Ministry of Health, [1982] E.C.R. 3415, para. 20.
[98] See e.g. Case 315/92, Verband Sozialer Wettbewerb eV v. Clinique Laboratoires S.N.C. & Estée Lauder Cosmetics GmbH, [1994] E.C.R. I-317, para. 13 ff.
[99] See Martin Nettesheim, *Normenhierarchien im EU-Recht*, 6 EUROPARECHT (EuR) 737 (2007).
[100] TFEU, art. 4(2)(a).
[101] See LEISTNER, *supra* note 53.
[102] See also the reliance on "implied consent" in BGH GEWERBLICHER RECHTSSCHUTZ UND URHEBERRECHT 628 (2010). See also Westkamp, *supra* note 1.

secondary markets where such equivalence is present and where there is, in accordance with the *UsedSoft* decision, only one user, so that the first acquirer still must erase their copy. Third, the notion of consent is obviously and generally intertwined with notions of legal certainty. The jurisprudence of the CJEU regarding the notion of the public, in relation to the public communication right under Article 3 of the EUCD,[103] appears to support that view: here, the Court emphasizes whether a new public is reached.[104] Such new public is present only where the defendant interferes with the communication process and where, consequentially, such use deviates from the previous expression of consent. Notably, as mentioned, the CJEU emphasized in this respect that such finding could be derived from balancing.[105] The fact that, according to *UsedSoft*, a simple contractual condition in a licensing agreement which limits the right to use in time might allow right holders to avoid exhaustion[106] does not appear to pose a serious obstacle to favoring exhaustion,[107] again as a normative *principle* embedded in EU primary (competition) law.[108]

V. CONCLUSION

This chapter has shown that the extension of the exhaustion principle to intangible goods can follow immediately from concerns of primary EU law over secondary law, and therefore the decision can effortlessly be legitimized by internal market considerations—though undergoing that doctrinaire effort seems unwarranted. The same inference can be reached under an integral construction of normative copyright law. However, the CJEU has not expressly clarified how far concerns about the establishment of a digital single market actually underscore that extension, if at all; neither is a proper analysis of the construction of the exclusive rights that are present. Still, exhaustion remains an important tool in opening up avenues of dynamic decision-making and must be considered a principled medium allowing internal market targets to be recognized. Accordingly, the

---

[103] EUCD, art. 3.
[104] By way of example on the notion of both a "new" public and a commercial implication as preconditions for construing the "public," see e.g. Case C-607/11, ITV Broadcasting Ltd., ITV 2 Ltd. et al. v. TV Catchup Ltd., [2013] 3 C.M.L.R. 1; Case C-135/10, Società Consortile Fonografici (SCF) v. Marco Del Corso, [2012] O.J. C133/3; see also, Poorna Mysoor, *Unpacking the Right of Communication to the Public: A Closer Look at International and EU Copyright Law*, 166 INTELL. PROP. Q. 166 (2013).
[105] Case C-275/06, Productores de Música de España (Promusicae) v. Telefónica de España S.A.U., [2008] E.C.R. I-00271, para. 70.
[106] See Christopher Stothers, *When is Copyright Law Exhausted by a Software License? UsedSoft v Oracle*, 11 EUR. INTELL. PROP. REV. 11 (2012).
[107] See also BGH, November 3, 2005, 493 GRUR 435 (Ger.) *Microsoft OEM* (limiting the effect of a software license restricting licensees to sell software only as part of new PCs, rather than on individual carriers, under art. 31(1) of the Copyright Act of September 9, 1965, 1 FEDERAL LAW GAZETTE 1273 [hereinafter the German Authors Right Act 1965]).
[108] The decision in *UsedSoft*, therefore, does not conclusively remove any control right but allows the determination of exceptions. These should predominantly address competition law. See also Arne Nordmeyer, *Lizenzantiquitaetenhandel – Der Handel Mit "Gebrauchter" Software aus Kartellrechtlicher Perspektive*, GRUR INT. 489 (2012).

decision displays the same metaphorical understanding as in previous case law. In that sense, "online" exhaustion falls in the accepted categories of primary law, which in turn allows the CJEU to promote a meaningful and dynamic progression of EU law.

However, there are also frustrations, as, necessarily, the open standard of construction diminishes legal certainty, at least concerning those cases where the normative content in secondary law builds upon national legal traditions or is derived from international convention law. Whilst it is true that the CJEU, especially as regards trademarks, places much emphasis on the underlying rationales of the IP right in question, which, as mentioned, give potentially more freedom to traders where the origin function must be preserved, such reliance on a particular function of copyright can hardly be ascertained in its jurisprudence. This is not surprising in a system that combines numerous divergent preoccupations with copyright and/or *droit d'auteur* principles in national laws that have adopted, in general, highly heterogeneous normative rules and principles. These normative rules and principles are necessarily also informed by more fundamental doctrines from contract, tort, or property law.

In addition, the typical brevity and apodictic statements in the context of preliminary rulings eschew an unequivocal categorization of the principles voiced by the CJEU. This is problematic precisely because the logic inherent in this system of decision-making cannot precisely delineate the scope of interpretation, and thus cannot address sufficiently possible exceptions, or assert more precisely which parameters should be employed in a balancing test. Generally, such tests, where profoundly predisposed by specific European aims under primary law, will inevitably lead to conflicts with international harmonization in copyright law, the norms of which, as explained, are subordinate in rank. In addition, there is, in contrast to trademark law, no clear understanding of the role of competition law within copyright exhaustion; trademark law thus shows that, ultimately, the exercise of IP rights by and large is subject to judicial control based on primary principles. Those principles include a reasoning very strictly focused on the function and rationale of the right in questions. Here, the fact that no common understanding of copyright's fundamental rationale has been developed hinders a similar approach.

Nevertheless, there is a clear signal that the CJEU, in general, will continue to intervene and advance, resting assured in its very own self-conception as the "motor of integration," now with a clearer perception of the need to remove barriers resulting from the exercise of IP rights in digital markets. At this moment, all that can be ascertained is a modest tendency; there is certainly nothing wrong in trouncing increasingly anachronistic national concepts. However, things are different for national courts, especially where the legislative text under secondary legislation is predominantly identical to, and informed by, legislative language from national law. National courts can hardly relinquish traditional concepts by broad references to European integration aims. The result is a piecemeal development that may, via preliminary rulings, incrementally inform national law, but such approach can hardly establish solid doctrinal frameworks. It might seem, then, advisable to adopt specific "exhaustion" legislation regulating, in detail, the conditions and exception relating to a dedicated European exhaustion rule across all branches of IP, which may well be combined with considerations drawn from competition law with which this notion of exhaustion must rather urgently be fused.

27. Digital copyright exhaustion and personal property
Aaron Perzanowski* and Jason Schultz**

I. INTRODUCTION

Typically, copyright law is understood as a set of rules that governs intangible expression. But for consumers, copyright law governs the otherwise autonomous and intimate realm of our personal possessions. As invasive as it might seem, copyright law can tell us where we can play our records, to whom we can display our paintings, and whether we can resell our books. And as more and more of our possessions are digital, it can also tell us what devices we can use them on, where we can access them, and with whom we can share them. In this way copyright law serves as both a bridge and a barrier between intellectual and personal property, attempting to balance the competing interests of both regimes.[1] For more than a century, copyright law mediated the tension between these two interests through the principle of exhaustion: the rights holder's power to prevent distributing, using, or sometimes even reproducing a work yields to the personal property interests of consumers once they lawfully acquired a copy of a work. As a result, exhaustion enables libraries to lend their books, museums to display their paintings, and consumers to fill up their bookshelves, borrow DVDs, and back up their software.

Rather than an idiosyncratic carve out, exhaustion is an inherent part of copyright law's balance between the rights of creators and the rights of the public. It is a fundamental component of almost every intellectual property system, one that recognizes that the rights of consumers are not at odds with the goals of the copyright system, but at its core. Meaningful consumer rights to use and transfer personal property are essential to the ultimate goals of the copyright system, public access to, and enjoyment of, new creative works.[2] Exhaustion also helps preserve copyright's legitimacy and lawful markets for copyrighted works by encouraging consumers to pay supra-competitive prices in exchange for the right to use, alienate, and under certain conditions, modify their copy.[3]

---

* Professor of Law, Case Western Reserve University School of Law.
** Professor of Clinical Law, New York University School of Law. This chapter borrows from our article, *Reconciling Intellectual & Personal Property*, 90 NOTRE DAME L. REV. 1213 (2015).

[1] See Wendy J. Gordon, *An Inquiry into the Merits of Copyright: The Challenges of Consistency, Consent, and Encouragement Theory*, 41 STAN. L REV. 1343, 1422 (1989) (noting that "intellectual property rights often operate to restrain the owners of tangible things from their ordinarily privileged uses of those things").

[2] See Aaron Perzanowski & Jason Schultz, *Digital Exhaustion*, 58 UCLA L. REV. 889, 893–901 (2011) (discussing the benefits of exhaustion).

[3] See Masakazu Ishihara & Andrew Ching, *Dynamic Demand for New and Used Durable Goods Without Physical Depreciation: The Case of Japanese Video Games*, ROTMAN SCH. OF MGMT., WORKING PAPER NO. 2189871, 10 (2012), available at http://ssrn.com/abstract=2189871 (finding

Nonetheless, exhaustion has become controversial as of late, with many commentators and copyright owners arguing that it is nothing more than a legacy loophole or market inefficiency that allows consumers to make unauthorized uses of intellectual property rightly controlled by the copyright owner. And in recent years, rights holders have taken aggressive steps to undermine exhaustion and weaken consumer property interests in an effort to shift the property balance in their favor. They have argued that exhaustion does not apply to goods imported into the United States[4] or to copies manufactured abroad;[5] they have developed technologies to block the resale and use of pre-owned media;[6] they have used spurious complaints to remove legitimate used items from secondary markets like eBay.[7] These efforts have met with mixed success.

But two legal and technological trends have proven much more effective in curtailing exhaustion and threatening consumer interests. The first is a set of copyright holder efforts that seek to redefine the notion of ownership by characterizing certain consumer transactions as licenses even when they "buy" the work. Second, technology has shifted consumer purchases in copyright markets away from tangible copies. Rather than picking up books and records from store shelves, we stream, download, and store content in the Cloud. These shifts have created something of a crisis for the exhaustion doctrine. In an economy premised on tangible goods, exhaustion is a concept so deeply engrained that it often goes unnoticed. But in the digital marketplace we increasingly occupy, exhaustion risks being dismissed as an anachronism, a concept that simply can not be ported into the economy of bits. According to copyright holders, you do not own the digital media you purchase online.[8] According to the Ninth Circuit, you do not own the plastic disc on which your software programs are encoded.[9] And according to General Motors and John Deere, you do not own the software embedded in your car or your tractor.[10] In short, the very notion of personal property is under attack.

This chapter, building on our earlier work, attempts to find a way forward for the exhaustion doctrine.[11] We suggest that the equilibrium between personal and intellectual property enabled by exhaustion depends on assumptions about the copyright

---

future resale opportunities increase consumers' willingness-to-pay for new copies of videogames and elimination of used markets would reduce publisher profits on average by 10 percent per game); Hsunchi Chu & Shuling Liao, *Buying While Expecting to Sell: The Economic Psychology of Online Resale*, 63 J. BUS. RES. 1073, 1073–78 (2010), available at http://dx.doi.org/10.1016/j.jbusres.2009.03.023 (finding significant estimated resale return to be a positive influence over consumer purchasing decisions).

[4] Quality King Distribs., Inc. v. L'anza Research Int'l, Inc., 523 U.S. 135, 145–54 (1998).
[5] Kirtsaeng v. John Wiley & Sons, Inc., 133 S. Ct. 1351, 1355–56 (2013).
[6] See U.S. Patent Application No. 13/611,243, at A-1 (filed September 12, 2012, published January 3, 2013) (describing Sony's "Electronic Content Processing System").
[7] See UMG Recordings Inc. v. Augusto, 628 F.3d 1175, 1178–83 (9th Cir. 2011).
[8] See *infra* notes 143–56 and accompanying text.
[9] See Vernor v. Autodesk, Inc., 621 F.3d 1102, 1111 (9th Cir. 2010).
[10] See Kyle Wiens, *We Can't Let John Deere Destroy the Very Idea of Ownership*, WIRED (April 21, 2015), www.wired.com/2015/04/dmca-ownership-john-deere.
[11] See Perzanowski and Schultz, *supra* note 2, at 892, 926–45; Aaron Perzanowski & Jason Schultz, *Copyright Exhaustion and the Personal Use Dilemma*, 96 MINN. L. REV. 2067, 2076–77, 2112–33 (2012); Aaron Perzanowski & Jason Schultz, *Legislating Digital Exhaustion*, 29 BERKELEY TECH. L.J. 1535, 1536–58 (2015); Perzanowski & Schultz, *supra* note 2.

marketplace that are quickly becoming outdated. And we argue that consumer rights must be preserved, but in a manner that recognizes the differences between digital and analog distribution.

II. THE EROSION OF OWNERSHIP

The exhaustion doctrine had a long history before the U.S. Supreme Court first applied it to copyrighted works in *Bobbs-Merrill*. From the Court's perspective in 1908, the questions of personal property and copy ownership were simple ones. The Court understood that a publisher's attempt to restrain subsequent alienation of books through a printed notice did not undermine the personal property interests of book owners.[12] Despite the publisher's attempt to limit resale, those who bought books owned them.[13] A century later, the question of whether unilateral restrictions announced by copyright holders are sufficient to subvert copy ownership has become plagued by confusion and uncertainty. In large part, that uncertainty emerged from disputes over computer software. This section describes the courts' treatment of copy ownership in the software cases and offers two explanations for their endorsement of efforts by copyright holders to characterize software transactions as licenses rather than sales.

A. The Software Ownership Cases

Disputes over copy ownership arise in two related contexts in software copyright law. Sections 109 and 117 of the Copyright Act both offer copy owners defenses for otherwise infringing acts. Again, the first sale doctrine allows for resale or other distribution of a copy by its owner.[14] Section 117 offers targeted protection to owners of copies of computer programs, permitting them to make copies or adaptations essential to the use or backup of the program.[15] Under both of these exhaustion rules, the core question is the same: whether the defendant is the owner of a copy of the software program.

Courts have struggled to answer this seemingly straightforward question, adopting a range of inconsistent approaches without clearly embracing any underlying principle.[16] The least nuanced cases allow copyright holders to avoid exhaustion by unilaterally declaring that they are licensing, rather than selling, their products.[17] As long as they utter the "magic words," copyright holders can control copies even after an apparent sale.[18] Other courts probe the specifics of license terms more meaningfully, holding

---

[12] Bobbs-Merrill Co. v. Straus, 210 U.S. 339, 350 (1908).
[13] *Ibid.*
[14] 17 U.S.C. § 109(a).
[15] *Ibid.* § 117(a).
[16] See Brian W. Carver, *Why License Agreements Do Not Control Copy Ownership: First Sales and Essential Copies*, 25 BERKELEY TECH. L.J. 1887, 1892–930 (2010).
[17] See e.g. MAI v. Peak, 991 F.2d 511 (9th Cir. 1993); Microsoft Corp. v. Harmony Computers & Elecs., 846 F. Supp. 208, 213 (E.D.N.Y. 1994); Wall Data Inc. v. L.A. Cnty. Sheriff's Dep't, 447 F.3d 769, 785 (9th Cir. 2006).
[18] See Carver, *supra* note 16, at 1899.

that where an agreement specifies a fixed duration, requires ongoing payments, or the return or destruction of the copies, they are licensed not sold.[19] Still other courts have turned to the Uniform Commercial Code to decide whether defendants hold title to their copy.[20]

Finally, some courts have been willing to look beyond licensing terms and formal title transfer to interrogate the nature of the transaction between the rights holder and consumer. Transactions characterized by single payments and perpetual rights of possession and use have been deemed sales regardless of the rights holder's contentions to the contrary.[21] According to the Second Circuit, it would be "anomalous for a user whose degree of ownership of a copy is so complete that he may lawfully use it and keep it forever, or if so disposed, throw it in the trash" to be treated as a non-owner.[22] The question is "whether the party exercises sufficient incidents of ownership over a copy of the program to be sensibly considered the owner of the copy."[23]

Without a consistent rule, or at least clear competing theories, the copy ownership cases are difficult to reconcile. Their seemingly ad hoc outcomes offer consumers little certainty or predictability about their rights in the copies they acquire. For most of the twentieth century, courts would have rejected out of hand the contention that a printed notice attached to a chattel could prevent a transfer of ownership. But today courts entertain and often accept that very characterization, particularly in cases involving software.

B. Software Exceptionalism

One reason courts may be more tolerant of limitations on consumer ownership in this context is the sense, however vague, that software is somehow different; that the rules that govern ownership of other copies (and chattels generally) do not apply to the thoroughly modern stuff that is computer software.

The Ninth Circuit offers the clearest illustration of this sort of software exceptionalism. On June 7, 2010, Judges Canby, Callahan, and Ikuta heard oral arguments in two cases, both of which turned on the question of copy ownership.[24] Both involved the allegedly unlawful resale of copies of protected works in violation of the terms of license agreements. And in both cases, the copies were lawfully made and the licenses imposed similar restrictions. But the court reached very different conclusions relying on two seemingly inconsistent approaches. One case was about software; the other was not.

UMG v. Augusto involved the resale of promotional CDs given away to music reviewers

---

[19] See Novell, Inc. v. Unicom Sales, Inc., No. 03-2785, 2004 WL 1839117, at *9, 12 (N.D. Cal. August 17, 2004) (finding a license where the agreement required ongoing payments and return of the copies to the rights holder).
[20] See Synergistic Techs., Inc. v. IDB Mobile Commc'ns, Inc., 871 F. Supp. 24, 29 (D.D.C. 1994); Mahru v. Superior Court, 237 Cal. Rptr. 298, 300 (Cal. Ct. App. 1987); U.C.C. § 2-401 (2012) (providing that a seller's reservation of title to goods shipped or delivered to a buyer is, at best, considered a reservation of a security interest).
[21] Softman Prods. Co., v. Adobe Sys., Inc., 171 F. Supp. 2d 1075, 1085 (C.D. Cal. 2001).
[22] Krause v. Titleserv, Inc., 402 F.3d 119, 123 (2d Cir. 2005).
[23] *Ibid.* at 124.
[24] See UMG Recordings Inc. v. Augusto, 628 F.3d 1175 (9th Cir. 2011); Vernor v. Autodesk, Inc., 621 F.3d 1102 (9th Cir. 2010).

and other industry insiders.[25] The defendant purchased used CDs from local record stores and resold them on eBay. He argued that as the owner of the discs, his resale was protected by the first sale doctrine. But the record label insisted that Augusto was not the owner of those discs because of a notice printed on the discs declaring that they were the property of the label. Despite the label's insistence, the Ninth Circuit held that title to the discs transferred to their recipients upon delivery and, eventually, to Augusto, entitling him to invoke the first sale doctrine.[26]

Vernor v. Autodesk centered on the resale of software discs.[27] Autodesk argued that the notice accompanying its discs meant that customers who paid thousands of dollars for a copy of its software did not own those discs, but merely "licensed" them. Rather than apply the rule that governed *Augusto*, however, the court announced a three-part test that asks: first, "whether the copyright owner specifies that a user is granted a license"; second, "whether the copyright owner significantly restricts the user's ability to transfer the software"; and third, "whether the copyright owner imposes notable use restrictions."[28] Since the terms contained the necessary language, the court concluded that Autodesk owned the discs.

The court applied two very different frameworks in these cases. In *Augusto*, it focused on the practical reality of the transaction, regardless of the purported licensing terms. But in *Vernor*, it was concerned almost exclusively with the text of the license. What's more, if we apply the *Vernor* test to the facts of *Augusto*, each prong is satisfied: UMG characterized the transaction as a license; it prohibited recipients from transferring the discs to others; and it confined them to "personal" use of the discs.[29] This inconsistency suggests that the Ninth Circuit has created two parallel regimes for distinguishing licenses from sales. In software cases, it applies a test that turns on factors entirely within the control of the rights holder. In non-software cases, it adopts a more consumer-friendly approach that turns on the nature of the transaction.

If these divergent approaches are motivated by software exceptionalism, the court's basic intuition is easy to forgive. Software is different from other sorts of copyrighted works in important ways. First, software code is not written for its aesthetic beauty; it is written to do work. This deeply functional nature of software code is difficult to square with copyright law's exclusion of any "procedure, process, system, [or] method of operation."[30] Second, copies of software have little intrinsic value. Unlike a book or painting, you can stare at a CD-ROM or floppy disk all day and learn nothing about the work it contains. The value of a copy of a program is only realized within a computer's operating environment, where running the program requires the creation of additional copies.[31]

---

[25] *Augusto, supra* note 24, 628 F.3d at 1177.
[26] *Ibid.* at 1180.
[27] *Vernor, supra* note 24, 621 F.3d at 1103.
[28] *Ibid.* at 1110–11.
[29] *Augusto, supra* note 24, 628 F.3d at 1177–78. The Ninth Circuit attempted to distinguish *Augusto* and *Vernor* on the grounds that UMG, unlike Autodesk, had no mechanism in place to enforce its restrictions. *Ibid.* at 1183. But Autodesk likewise lacked any means of terminating consumers' possession of the discs. *Vernor, supra* note 24, 621 F.3d at 1107.
[30] *Ibid.* § 102(b).
[31] These copies may or may not implicate the reproduction right. See Aaron Perzanowski, *Fixing RAM Copies*, 104 Nw. U.L. Rev. 1067, 1104–5 (2010).

Third, licensing has been a component of software transactions since mass markets for programs emerged. By introducing licensing at the outset, the software industry helped shape the expectations of consumers and courts. A key feature of early software licenses was "the provision that the developer retains title to—that is, licenses and does not sell—the individual copy of the program itself."[32] Those provisions were, and are, a strategic effort to undermine exhaustion, control secondary markets, and limit competition.[33]

These characteristics might help to explain software exceptionalism, but they don't justify it. First, the imperfect fit of software within the copyright system suggests we should be particularly careful about strategies that would enable copyright holders to leverage their statutory rights in a way that harms consumers. Second, section 117 of the Copyright Act strongly suggests that consumer ownership and exhaustion are more important given the need to copy and adapt computer programs. Third, the fact that software licenses are commonplace tells us very little about the wisdom of allowing them to undermine ownership. But these three characteristics are not the whole story. As the next section explains, the tendency to embrace "licensing" particular copies has its roots in a deeper uncertainty about the nature of property rights.

C. Shifting Views on Property

In the century separating *Bobbs-Merrill* from the contemporary debate over copy ownership, our understanding of property has undergone a dramatic shift, from the certainty of Blackstonian absolutism to the more equivocal bundle of rights. Despite the merits of a more nuanced relational theory of property, that shift enabled a blurring of the distinction between property and contract, which in turn bolstered efforts to redefine copy ownership through licensing terms.

Early twentieth century thinking was dominated by a tradition rooted in natural rights and encapsulated in Blackstone's oft-quoted—if oft-misunderstood—description of property as "that sole and despotic dominion which one man claims and exercises over the external things of the world, in total exclusion of the right of any other individual in the universe."[34] Within that framework, property rights were rights in things, held by a single owner, with a nearly absolute right to exclude.[35]

Beginning with Hohfeld's taxonomy of jural relations, however, our picture of property became more complex. Hohfeld advanced the idea that property rights were not rights in things, but rights against people.[36] Under this view, rights *in personam*, like those arising under contract, apply to specified individuals. Rights *in rem*, like those arising under

---

[32] Michael J. Madison, *Reconstructing the Software License*, 35 Loy. U. Chi. L.J. 275, 314 (2003).

[33] *Ibid.* at 281 ("[T]he software license is designed to defeat copyright law's doctrine of first sale.").

[34] William Blackstone, 2 Commentaries on the Laws of England 1 (John L. Wendell ed., 1857).

[35] See Abraham Bell & Gideon Parchomovsky, *A Theory of Property*, 90 Cornell L. Rev. 531, 543–44 (2005) (describing the central elements of this conception of property).

[36] Wesley Newcomb Hohfeld, *Fundamental Legal Conceptions as Applied in Judicial Reasoning*, 26 Yale L.J. 710, 718 (1917).

a property regime, apply to a much larger, less specific class.[37] A property right, then, does not describe the relationship between an owner and a thing, but the aggregation of relationships between individuals. Decades later, Honoré's eleven incidents of ownership further disaggregated our notion of property into discrete component parts, no one of which is necessary for ownership.[38] Taken together, these insights form the core of the "bundle of rights" conception of property that largely defined property orthodoxy in recent decades.[39]

Critics charge that this view results in a notion of property that is infinitely malleable,[40] lacking any core or essence,[41] conceptually unmoored,[42] fragmented,[43] and ultimately meaningless.[44] If property rights are nothing more than a collection of relationships between individuals, infinitely divisible and alienable, and if we lack any articulable criteria for which discrete rights render one an owner, property lacks any distinctive character that sets it apart from other modes of allocating resources.

Capitalizing on this perceived breakdown, some economists offer a reassuringly simple take on the role of property. From this perspective, property rights do little more than establish default entitlements to be allocated through private bargaining.[45] If property rights are nothing more than *in personam* rights writ large, property law should embrace the same flexibility and granularity we see in the realm of privately negotiated agreements.[46] And if so, property rights become indistinguishable from contractual ones.[47] Once property is viewed from this angle, the use of standardized contractual terms to "license" a tangible copy looks less like an anomaly inconsistent with the hundreds of

---

[37] Ibid.

[38] A.M. Honoré, *Ownership*, in Oxford Essays in Jurisprudence 107, 112–28 (A.G. Guest ed., 1961).

[39] See Bell & Parchomovsky, *supra* note 35, at 546.

[40] Ibid. at 545–46.

[41] James E. Penner, *The "Bundle of Rights" Picture of Property*, 43 UCLA L. Rev. 711, 770 (1996) ("The bundle of rights view leads to a 'concept' of property . . . with no definable essence, and no guidelines for definition which might in any way govern its application in particular circumstances.").

[42] Ibid. at 731 ("[P]roperty is to float free from any anchorage to the concept of a 'right to a thing.'").

[43] Adam Mossoff, *What is Property? Putting the Pieces Back Together*, 45 Ariz. L. Rev. 371, 376 (2003) (rejecting "the fragmentation of property achieved by the bundle theory").

[44] Edward L. Rubin, *Due Process and the Administrative State*, 72 Calif. L. Rev. 1044, 1086 (1984) ("[I]t is now commonplace to acknowledge that property is simply a label for whatever 'bundle of sticks' the individual has been granted.").

[45] See Yoram Barzel, Economic Analysis of Property Rights 33 (2d ed. 1997) ("At the heart of the study of property rights lies the study of contracts."); Steven N.S. Cheung, *The Structure of a Contract and the Theory of a Non-Exclusive Resource*, 13 J.L. & Econ. 49, 67 (1970) (noting that the principal significance of property is to establish the right to contract); Thomas W. Merrill & Henry E. Smith, *What Happened to Property in Law and Economics?*, 111 Yale L.J. 357, 359–60 (2001) ("Coase implied that property has no function other than to serve as the baseline for contracting or for collectively imposing use rights in resources.").

[46] See Thomas W. Merrill & Henry E. Smith, *The Property/Contract Interface*, 101 Colum. L. Rev. 773, 800 (2001).

[47] Ibid. at 376 ("For modern economists, property rights are primarily regarded as a prerequisite for exchange.").

years of common law rejecting equitable servitudes on chattels, and more like an example of property formalism yielding to market efficiency.

Copyright law lends itself to the bundle of rights characterization, and perhaps by extension, to the substitution of property rights with contractual ones. The exclusive rights of a copyright holder are an explicitly enumerated bundle.[48] And those rights are infinitely divisible, as the Act makes clear.[49] Given the malleability of this bundle, copyright's notion of ownership of the work is correspondingly fuzzy. If copyright holders are free to disassemble and parcel their rights into any configuration they choose, granting some rights to use the work while withholding others, it is easier to understand how courts might buy into the myth of licensing particular copies of the work. Why should rights holders be denied the flexibility to distribute copies to the public while retaining ownership of them if the function of property rights is merely to set the stage for private bargaining?

D. The Shrinking Software Divide

Courts have endorsed attempts to characterize purchases as licenses in the software context, but have proven far less open to that characterization when it comes to movies, music, and books.[50] This fact might suggest that the effects of the software licensing paradigm will be contained. But there are two reasons to think this licensing model will have ripple effects across the copyright economy.

First, the copyright marketplace is rife with examples of rights holders and their intermediaries insisting that consumers do not actually own the copies they buy. According to Amazon's Terms of Use for the Kindle Store, consumers who hit the "Buy now with 1-click®" button do not own a copy of the book they download.[51] This is at odds with what consumers reasonably understand the word "buy" to mean. Apple's iTunes Store, the largest music retailer in the world, is somewhat more conflicted in how it characterizes transactions with consumers.[52] After describing those transactions as "purchases" and noting that "[a]ll sales . . . are final," Apple insists that consumers agree not to "rent, lease, loan, sell, [or] distribute" their purchases.[53] Amazon's competing MP3 store offers similar terms.[54]

---

[48] 17 U.S.C. § 106 (2012).
[49] *Ibid.* § 201(d). "Transfer of ownership" is defined as "an assignment, mortgage, exclusive license, or any other conveyance, alienation, or hypothecation of a copyright or of any of the exclusive rights comprised in a copyright, whether or not it is limited in time or place of effect, but not including a nonexclusive license." *Ibid.* § 101.
[50] UMG Recordings, Inc. v. Augusto, 628 F.3d 1175, 1183 (9th Cir. 2011) (concerning audio CDs); United States v. Wise, 550 F.2d 1180, 1192 (9th Cir. 1977) (concerning film prints); Classic Concepts, Inc. v. Linen Source, Inc., Nos. 04-8088 & 04-8457, 2006 WL 4756377, at *17 (C.D. Cal. April 27, 2006) (concerning copyrighted design on a rug); Middlebrooks v. Comm'r of Internal Revenue, 34 T.C.M. (CCH) 1187 (T.C. 1975) (concerning magazines); Old West Realty, Inc. v. Idaho State Tax Comm'n, 716 P.2d 1318, 1320–21 (Idaho 1986) (concerning books).
[51] *Kindle Store Terms of Use*, www.amazon.com/gp/help/customer/display.html?nodeId=201014950.
[52] See *iTunes Store Sets New Record with 25 Billion Songs Sold*, APPLE (February 6, 2013), www.apple.com/pr/library/2013/02/06iTunes-Store-Sets-New-Record-with-25-Billion-Songs-Sold.html.
[53] *Terms and Conditions*, APPLE, www.apple.com/legal/internet-services/itunes/us/terms.html.
[54] *Ibid.*

These efforts are not confined to digital downloads. Beachbody, the makers of the popular P90X home workout routine, insists that its customers do not own the DVDs they purchase from the company's website. According to the Beachbody Terms of Use, "[y]ou may not, without the express written permission of Beachbody or the respective copyright owner . . . sell [or] resell . . . services or products obtained through [its] Sites."[55] Beachbody has aggressively targeted individual consumers who resold legitimate copies of its DVDs on eBay, threatening litigation and demanding exorbitant compensation.[56] It is easy to understand why Beachbody would want to prevent customers from reselling their workout videos after their New Year's resolve runs out. As reasonable as three easy payments of U.S.$39.95 may be,[57] used DVDs on the secondary market would introduce unwanted downward price pressure. What is harder to see is how this restraint on alienation can be squared with the principle of exhaustion or consumer property interests more generally.

Second, the gap between software and other classes of copyrighted works is shrinking. In its early days, software was a thing unto itself in the copyright landscape. But as traditional forms of expression—books, music, visual art—become more interactive, they are becoming indistinguishable from software. The line between programs and data has always been a largely artificial one.[58] But today that distinction is increasingly blurred. Some videogames are best described as interactive films.[59] E-books offer levels of responsiveness to user input impossible with the printed page.[60] And artists like Jay Z,[61] Lady Gaga,[62] and Bjork[63] have all released new music embedded in smartphone applications. This blurring renders efforts to maintain the current bifurcated approach to licensing untenable. That problem is compounded by the shifting nature of the copy itself.

---

[55] *Terms of Use*, BEACHBODY, www.beachbody.com/product/about_us/terms_of_use.do.

[56] See e.g. *If I Purchase a Set of P90x Workout Dvds is It Legal for Me to Resell Them if I Want or Can They Restrict My Right to Resell*, AVVO, www.avvo.com/legal-answers/if-i-purchase-a-set-of-p90x-workout-dvds-is-it-leg-124160.html; *I Tried to Sell a P90x on eBay. I Got Removed for Copyright Infringement. Then I Got a Call and Email from an Attorney*, AVVO, www.avvo.com/legal-answers/i-tried-to-sell-a-p90x-on-ebay—i-got-removed-for—439679.html.

[57] See *P90X3® is Available Now*, BEACHBODY, www.beachbody.com/category/video.do?bclid=6614435001.

[58] See MARTIN DAVIS, THE UNIVERSAL COMPUTER 164–65 (2012) (describing the distinction between program and data as an illusion).

[59] Matt Miller, *Heavy Rain and the Birth of Interactive Film*, GAME INFORMER (February 10, 2010, 11:00 am), available at www.gameinformer.com/blogs/editors/b/gimiller_blog/archive/2010/02/10/heavy-rain-and-the-birth-of-interactive-film.aspx (describing the videogame *Heavy Rain* as "interactive storytelling" that is "more film than it is game").

[60] See Avi Itzkovitch, *Interactive eBook Apps: The Reinvention of Reading and Interactivity*, UX MAG. (April 12, 2012), available at http://uxmag.com/articles/interactive-ebook-apps-the-reinvention-of-reading-and-interactivity.

[61] Evan Minsker, *Jay-Z Announces New LP Magna Carta Holy Grail*, PITCHFORK (June 16, 2013, 9:39 pm), available at http://pitchfork.com/news/51187-jay-z-announces-new-lp-magna-carta-holy-grail.

[62] Alice Vincent, *Lady Gaga Announces ARTPOP, Her New Album App Release*, TELEGRAPH (July 12, 2013, 11:01 am), available at www.telegraph.co.uk/culture/music/music-news/10175597/Lady-Gaga-announces-ARTPOP-her-new-album-app-release.html.

[63] *Bjork, Damon Albarn, Snoop Dogg for Manchester International Festival*, NME (March 17, 2011), available at www.nme.com/news/bjork/55508.

III. THE EROSION OF THE COPY

The copy, needless to say, has been an essential concept in the law of copyright for centuries, and part of copyright law in the United States (U.S.) since its inception. Central to contemporary copyright thinking is the notion that copies and their statutory companions, phonorecords, are material objects distinct from the intangible works that the copyright grant is meant to encourage.

Much like the once clear, but increasingly opaque notion of ownership, the copy is now a concept plagued by uncertainty. Changes in storage and distribution technologies alongside shifting media consumption patterns have profoundly altered the way in which we interact with copyrighted works. The tangible copy, once the primary means of distribution, has been displaced by cloud storage, streaming, and software-as-a-service. Copies were once finite, stable, and valuable. But the unitary copy—the hardcover, the LP, the film reel—has been largely displaced. Today's marketplace is characterized by ubiquitous, temporary instantiations of works. Copyright law has struggled to assimilate these developments. This section first describes those changes and then turns to the efforts by courts to make sense of them and their implications for the distinction between the copy and the work.

Dramatic improvements in computational capacity and storage, along with increasingly fast and pervasive data connectivity, allow consumers to acquire, store, and access media in new ways. We can download our media collections to computers and mobile devices. We can choose between Cloud storage services from Amazon, Apple, Dropbox, Google, and Microsoft, among others, at nearly no cost. Amazon's MP3 Store enables consumers to buy, save, and play their purchases directly from its Cloud Player without ever downloading a permanent file to their laptop or mobile device, let alone handling a plastic disc.[64] Software-as-a-service offerings, like Adobe Creative Cloud, prove that the functionality that once local copies provided can be achieved by remotely accessing data.[65] These technological developments have been accompanied and partly driven by changing consumer preferences. The skyrocketing popularity of subscription streaming services like Netflix and Spotify demonstrate that many consumers would rather access a library of streaming titles than purchase tangible copies. These changes offer great promise to consumers. But they also threaten to destabilize our understanding of the copy and its place in the copyright system.

This risk is evident in a number of recent cases. In *Cartoon Network v. CSC Holdings, Inc.*, the court had to decide whether instantiations of a work were too temporary to count as copies.[66] Cablevision was sued for offering consumers a Remote Storage Digital Video Recorder system (RS-DVR) that functioned similarly to a set-top home DVR but stored programs centrally at a Cablevision data center. The RS-DVR system briefly loaded videostreams into its buffer memory, for as much as 1.2 seconds before relaying the data to hard drives that stored recorded programs. Cartoon Network alleged this

---

[64] See *Get Started at Amazon MP3*, AMAZON, www.amazon.com/b?node=2658409011.
[65] *Features: Tools and Services*, ADOBE, www.adobe.com/products/creativecloud/tools-and-services.html.
[66] Cartoon Network LP, LLLP v. CSC Holdings, Inc., 536 F.3d 121, 127 (2d Cir. 2008).

buffering infringed their copyrighted television programs. The case turned on whether the buffer data were fixed in a tangible medium and met the statutory definition of copies. Unlike earlier courts, the Second Circuit recognized that fixation entails two distinct requirements. First, the work must be sufficiently embodied to be perceived, reproduced, or communicated. And second, that embodiment must persist for more than a transitory duration. Because "[n]o bit of data remains in any buffer for more than a fleeting 1.2 seconds . . . [and] each bit of data here is rapidly and automatically overwritten as soon as it is processed," the court was satisfied that the "works in this case are embodied in the buffer for only a 'transitory' period" and thus not copies.[67]

Although we applaud the Second Circuit's careful statutory and factual analysis, it highlights an important conceptual difficulty for copyright law. If, as the court rightly concluded, buffer data are not copies, what exactly are they? They are not the intangible work, but seem to occupy some interstitial space within the copy/work dichotomy. The uncertain status of embodiments like these suggests a growing difficulty in identifying where copies end and where non-copies begin. And if copyright law cannot tell us what embodiments even count as copies, copy ownership faces a significant challenge.

In *Capitol v. ReDigi*, we saw yet another challenge to our understanding of the copy—or in this case, the phonorecord.[68] There, ReDigi created a platform for the resale of pre-owned digital music. If a consumer who bought a copy of "The Sign" by Swedish pop group Ace of Base from the iTunes Music Store in a fit of 1990s nostalgia later regretted that purchase, ReDigi would allow her to recapture some of her investment by transferring her interest in the song to another equally nostalgic buyer. According to ReDigi, its software verifies that the music was legitimately purchased before uploading the seller's file to its Cloud Locker, where the file is stored until purchased by another user. The technical design of ReDigi's upload process introduces an important wrinkle in the copyright analysis. ReDigi argues that the upload does not create a new copy, it merely migrates the file from one location to another. As each packet of information that comprises the file is uploaded to the Cloud, it is deleted from the user's local drive. And "at the end of the process, the digital music file is located in the Cloud Locker and not on the user's computer."[69] Finally, the software deletes any additional local copies, mimicking the consequences of an analog sale, a transfer of ownership that terminates the rights of one party and establishes the rights of another. Capitol Records sued ReDigi for reproducing its protected works. The question was whether the copy on ReDigi's server should be understood as distinct from the one on the seller's hard drive, or instead, as a single copy that was moved from one storage location to the next.

The court held that the migration process created a new material object and thus, a new phonorecord.[70] In doing so, the court drew a sharp distinction between the copyrighted sound recording—the work—and the "appropriate segment of the hard disk"—the phonorecord.[71] According to the court, this conclusion was not only demanded by the

---

[67] *Ibid.* at 129–30.
[68] Capitol Records, L.L.C. v. ReDigi Inc., 934 F. Supp. 2d 640 (S.D.N.Y. 2013).
[69] *Ibid.*; see also U.S. Patent No. 8,627,500 (filed December 31, 2010).
[70] *Capitol Records, supra* note 68, 934 F. Supp. 2d at 650–51.
[71] *Ibid.* at 649.

Copyright Act, but dictated by the limits of technology.[72] But far from confirming the alignment of the rules imposed by the law of physics, the *ReDigi* opinion underscores the mismatch between our current technological capability and copyright law's preoccupation with the unitary copy. Digital consumers are awash in a sea of copies. Copies flit into and out of existence. They are created, used, discarded, and created yet again. Cloud computing and streaming free us from the burden of the unitary copy. Consumers no longer need to lug their digital media collections with them everywhere they go; they simply need a data connection. The notion that we can identify the particular copy that a consumer purchased from iTunes is hard to square with the reality of networked distribution. Yet the *ReDigi* court felt a need to pin the tail on the proverbial donkey and identify particular phonorecords within the ReDigi system.

Finally, in *UsedSoft GmbH v. Oracle*, the European Court of Justice approached the question of the identity of the copy very differently.[73] There, Oracle sued UsedSoft for allowing users to purchase second-hand software licenses. Oracle claimed that when these consumers subsequently downloaded the software from its servers, along with patches and updates, they illegally reproduced the code. The Court rejected this theory, holding that the doctrine of exhaustion applied not only to the initial download, but to all subsequent updates and patches, even if downloaded by a subsequent user. The court reasoned that the sale was not tied to a particular download or copy, but rather extended to any "functional equivalent" so long as payment was initially made to Oracle.[74] In other words, the Court was less concerned with particular copies, that is, particular downloads to particular material objects, than it was with the rights of subsequent transferees to access the work. If exhaustion applied, it did so regardless of the identity of any particular copy.[75]

Together, these cases signal a growing uncertainty about the definition of the copy and the legal status of those instantiations of a work that occupy that middle ground between the tangible copy and the intangible work. Historically, copyright law has conceptualized consumer rights as situated in particular copies. As the role of the unitary copy is diminished, the exhaustion principle and the values it serves are at risk.

IV. THE FUNCTIONS OF COPY OWNERSHIP

Without a stable understanding of the copy or a meaningful notion of copy ownership, copyright law's exhaustion doctrine, as it has been historically understood and applied

---

[72] Ibid. at 649–50 ("This understanding is, of course, confirmed by the laws of physics. It is simply impossible that the same 'material object' can be transferred over the Internet.").
[73] Case C-128/11, UsedSoft GmbH v. Oracle Int'l Corp., [2012] E.C.R. 407, para. 52 (July 3, 2012), available at http://eur-lex.europa.eu/legalcontent/EN/TXT/PDF/?uri=CELEX:62011CJ0128&from=EN.
[74] Ibid. para. 61.
[75] A subsequent decision by a German court has clarified that *UsedSoft*'s interpretation is based entirely on art. 51 of the EU Computer Programs Directive and therefore would not apply to other types of digital copyrighted works, such as e-books. See Case No. 4 O 191/11, Landgericht Bielefeld (LG, German Regional Court) (Ger.), available at www.boersenverein.de/sixcms/media.php/976/LG_Bielefeld_vom_05.03.13_Klage_Verbraucherzentralen.pdf.

by courts, faces a crisis. Although some rights holders would celebrate the end of first sale and other exhaustion rules, our prognosis is not quite so dire. Rather than give up altogether on the consumer rights that flow from copy ownership, this section identifies the functions copy ownership has served in order to reformulate the exhaustion principle in a way that preserves its crucial role in the copyright system.

The copyright system has relied on copy ownership as one of many tools for delineating the scope of copyright holders' control over their works and balancing that power against the interests of the public in using and deriving value from those creations. Here we consider why. What is it about the relationship between the rights holder, the work, and the consumer that justifies extending rights to copy owners that would otherwise fall within the exclusivity of the copyright holder?

We argue that copy ownership serves as a proxy for a cluster of related considerations that together justify distinguishing copy owners from the public at large as a matter of copyright policy. These core functions of copy ownership explain why copyright law confers special status on some users of protected works. But they do not dictate how. With a clearer understanding of the reasons we privilege copy owners, we detail an approach to copyright exhaustion that legislators and courts can use to more transparently balance the competing interests of consumers and creators.

A. Author Incentives

The creation of economic incentives for creative production is an important constitutional and instrumental objective of U.S. copyright law. Because creative works are public goods, copyright theory worries that, absent some legal intervention to limit competition and create artificial scarcity, creators will under-invest in new works.[76] Through legal exclusivity, "copyright supplies the economic incentive to create and disseminate ideas."[77]

For most of history, the financial and popular success of copyrighted works has been a function of the sale of copies. As a general rule, authors who sell more copies make more money. As a result, copy ownership provides a strong indication that compensation paid to the author is sufficient. The exclusive right of initial distribution gives copyright holders the power to set sale prices. Once that price has been paid, we should assume that the copyright holder has reaped a fair reward, and continued exclusivity can no longer be justified.[78]

An exhaustion rule triggered by copy ownership strikes a balance between the rights of authors and the rights of the public, a balance calibrated to preserve creative incentives. Exhaustion applies only to lawfully made copies disposed of at an initial price set by the

---

[76] See WILLIAM M. LANDES & RICHARD A. POSNER, THE ECONOMIC STRUCTURE OF INTELLECTUAL PROPERTY LAW 40 (2003).
[77] Harper & Row, Publrs., Inc. v. Nation Enters., 471 U.S. 539, 558, 105 S. Ct. 2218 (1985).
[78] Brilliance Audio, Inc. v. Haights Cross Commc'ns, Inc., 474 F.3d 365, 373–74 (6th Cir. 2007); Platt & Munk Co., Inc., v. Republic Graphics, Inc., 315 F.2d 847, 854 (2d Cir. 1963) (quoting United States v. Masonite Corp., 316 U.S. 265, 278 (1942)) (internal quotation marks omitted)); Parfums Givenchy, Inc. v. C & C Beauty Sales, Inc., 832 F. Supp. 1378, 1389 (C.D. Cal. 1993); Burke & Van Heusen, Inc. v. Arrow Drug, Inc., 233 F. Supp. 881, 884 (E.D. Pa. 1964).

rights holder.[79] This ensures that the rights holder receives a measure of compensation sufficient to justify its investment. In this way, copy ownership functions as a limit on copyright holder authority, but one that respects the incentive structure of the copyright system.

B. Consumer Incentives

Creative incentives are not an end unto themselves.[80] As Jessica Litman put it:

> [t]he most important reason we encourage creators to make, and distributors to disseminate, works of authorship is so that people will read the books, listen to the music, look at the art, and watch the movies . . . That is the way that copyright law promotes the Progress of Science.[81]

Copyright law has developed a number of tools—limited duration, fair use, statutory licenses, and other exceptions and limitations—meant to serve these two seemingly inconsistent objectives. But it relies primarily on market mechanisms to both encourage creation and ensure consumption. Consumer participation in the copyright market is crucial.

Copy ownership benefits the copyright system as a whole. The practical and legal advantages that copy ownership extends to consumers provide strong reasons to participate in lawful markets for copyrighted content. In order for copyright incentives to do their job, consumers must be willing to pay supra-competitive prices for protected works despite their widespread availability at near-zero marginal cost. The struggle facing the copyright system is convincing consumers that a lawful copy is more desirable than an unlawful one. The most obvious way to do that is through the "stick" of infringement liability.

But the "carrot" is equally important. A clear exhaustion principle that entitles consumers to use and alienate copies makes the value proposition presented by copyright compliance more attractive. Copy ownership and exhaustion offer consumers real value. They can resell the copy and recoup some of its value.[82] They can also preserve, loan, and modify their copy to suit their needs.[83] When lawfully available copies lack the freedoms consumers expect, they are less desirable.[84] And unlawful copies are necessarily more attractive in comparison. But when consumers can rely on getting something of value for

---

[79] See Kirtsaeng v. John Wiley & Sons, Inc., 133 S. Ct. 1351, 1354–55 (2013) (describing the relation between the "first sale doctrine" and exhaustion).

[80] See Sony Corp. of Am. v. Universal City Studios, Inc., 464 U.S. 417, 429 (1984) (noting that copyright and patent rights are "intended to motivate the creative activity of authors and inventors by the provision of a special reward, and to allow the public access to the products of their genius after the limited period of exclusive control has expired.").

[81] Jessica Litman, *Real Copyright Reform*, 96 IOWA L. REV. 1, 13 (2010).

[82] Ishihara and Ching, *supra* note 3, at 1; Chu and Liao, *supra* note 3, at 1073.

[83] See generally Benedict G.C. Dellaert & Pratibha A. Dabholkar, *Increasing the Attractiveness of Mass Customization: The Role of Complementary On-Line Services and Range of Options*, 13 INT'L J. ELEC. COM. 43 (2009); Nickolaus Franke & Martin Schreier, *Why Customers Value Self-Designed Products: The Importance of Process Effort and Enjoyment*, 27 J. PRODS. MGMT. 1020 (2010).

[84] When Microsoft initially announced its Xbox One console, it was roundly criticized for plans to restrict the use of secondhand games. Because of this overwhelmingly negative feedback,

their money, they are more likely to opt into the copyright economy. In short, first sale and related rights steer consumers towards lawful markets, those that promise compensation to rights holders. In doing so, consumer property rights help copyright law serve its dual objectives of incentivizing creative production and encouraging access to the resulting creative output.

C. Copies and Information Costs

Exhaustion also helps consumers navigate the marketplace for protected works by limiting information costs. Unlike contract law, which imposes no limits on creative permutations of rights, exchanges of property rights are limited to an identifiable number of standard forms.[85] This commitment to a closed set of property forms, or the principle of *numerus clausus*, not only helps distinguish property regimes from private contractual ordering, it is one of property's principle advantages. By favoring sales and discouraging idiosyncratic transfers of rights in copies, exhaustion rules limit information costs.

One justification for standardizing property transactions is a concern over restraints on alienation.[86] Unpredictable bundles of rights increase transaction costs in a way that could discourage transfers of property and hinder more valuable uses. Even setting aside the impact of idiosyncratic configurations of rights on parties to a transaction, nonstandard bundles impose information cost externalities on third parties. Even if "clear-eyed" parties with equal bargaining power agree to a bespoke bundle of rights, that choice has costs for other market participants who must investigate the details of property transactions with much greater scrutiny. Once on notice that property bundles deviating from the standard forms are accepted, those acquiring property interests or hoping to avoid infringing them, bear the burden of uncovering their potentially unique characteristics.[87]

This concern is not new.[88] But it is a particularly pressing one today in markets for copyrighted works given the increasing complexity of license terms and the escalating information costs they impose.[89] The current iTunes terms are over 19,000 words, translating into fifty-six pages of fine print. If the Chief Justice of the Supreme Court cannot

---

Microsoft eventually relented. Don Mattrick, *Your Feedback Matters—Update on Xbox One*, XBOX WIRE (June 19, 2013, 2:00 pm), available at http://news.xbox.com/2013/06/update.

[85] Thomas W. Merrill & Henry E. Smith, *Optimal Standardization in the Law of Property: The Numerus Clausus Principle*, 110 YALE L.J. 1, 3 (2000).

[86] See Carol M. Rose, *What Government Can Do for Property (and Vice Versa)*, in THE FUNDAMENTAL INTERRELATIONSHIPS BETWEEN GOVERNMENT AND PROPERTY 209, 214–15 (Nicholas Mercuro & Warren J. Samuels eds., 1999); Michael A. Heller, *The Boundaries of Private Property*, 108 YALE L.J. 1163, 1199 (1999) (describing the century long concern of alienation in regard to property).

[87] Merrill & Smith, *supra* note 46, at 777.

[88] Keppell v. Bailey, (1834) 39 Eng. Rep. 1042, (Ch.D.) 1049 ("[G]reat detriment would arise and much confusion of rights if parties were allowed to invent new modes of holding and enjoying real property . . . [I]t would hardly be possible to know what rights the acquisition of any parcel conferred, or what obligation it imposed.").

[89] See Christina Mulligan, *A Numerus Clausus Principle for Intellectual Property*, 80 TENN. L. REV. 235, 249 (2013).

expend the effort to wade through those terms, we should not expect the average consumer to take on those costs either.[90]

The *numerus clausus* principle avoids these problems by refusing to recognize certain transactional forms.[91] Assured that non-standard "fancies" are not lurking in the marketplace, parties are relieved of the burden of investigating the particulars of each transaction. Instead, they need only gather enough information to identify a property interest as fitting within one of the few established forms. Traditionally, those accepted forms have been limited with respect to real property, and constrained even more so when it comes to personal property.[92]

But the *numerus clausus* principle is largely absent from intellectual property law.[93] Exhaustion, perhaps because it mediates the border between intellectual and personal property, is one notable exception. A functioning exhaustion rule—one that incorporates a robust notion of copy ownership—serves as copyright's expression to the *numerus clausus* principle.[94] Exhaustion is an effort to limit the permissible forms of transfers of copies and prevent the proliferation of idiosyncratic interests and the negative consequences that flow from them.

The statutory basis for this reading begins with the distribution right itself, which provides that copyright holders have the exclusive right "to distribute copies or phonorecords of the copyrighted work to the public *by sale or other transfer of ownership, or by rental, lease, or lending*."[95] This language suggests a bifurcated universe of copy transfer. First, we have transfers of ownership, which entail a perpetual right to possess and use the copy: sales or gifts. Second, we have transfers of limited duration: rental, lease, or lending. If we take exhaustion and *numerus clausus* seriously, transactions must fall within one of these two categories. Certainly, many licenses are easy enough to characterize as rentals, leases, or lendings. A consumer is not the owner of a book she borrows from the library. Nor does a Netflix subscriber own the physical or digital copies of movies she watches. Copyright holders, under our reading, retain considerable flexibility to devise subscription, streaming, and other business models not premised on the sale of copies. But distribution by license is not among the standard forms of transfers of copies recognized by copyright law.[96]

Taken together, these three functions of copy ownership—safeguarding authorial incentives, encouraging consumer participation in copyright markets, and reducing information costs—explain why copyright law privileges copy owners over consumers at large. Next, we consider how to preserve those basic functions within a marketplace that deemphasizes the copy and a legal system that has diluted the notion of consumer ownership.

---

[90] Mike Masnick, *Supreme Court Chief Justice Admits He Doesn't Read Online EULAs or Other "Fine Print,"* TECHDIRT (October 22, 2010, 9:48 am), available at www.techdirt.com/articles/20101021/02145811519/ supreme-court-chief-justice-admits-he-doesn-t-read-online-eulas-or-other-fine-print.shtml.
[91] See Merrill & Smith, *supra* note 85, at 13–14.
[92] *Ibid.* at 17.
[93] Mulligan, *supra* note 89.
[94] *Ibid.* at 252.
[95] 17 U.S.C. § 106(3) (2012) (emphasis added).
[96] Carver, *supra* note 16, at 1948 (arguing "there is simply no such thing as distribution of a copy by means of a *license*.").

V. FREEING EXHAUSTION FROM THE COPY

Although exhaustion has been tied to the copy historically, none of the functions detailed above are dependent on any particular medium of expression or method of distribution. These functions, like any property right, help define and structure the relationships between parties. All three are intended to construct a functioning marketplace in which creators and consumers are encouraged to participate. But the success of that market does not depend on the transfer of unitary copies. Instead, it depends on the exchange of rights between consumers and creators and an appropriate legal mechanism for ensuring the right balance between them.

The copy, because of the technological limitations that prevailed for most of copyright's history, was a helpful tool for calibrating those incentives. Ownership of a copy served as a sort of "talisman" that reassured courts that a defendant's behavior was not a threat to the system. The copy was a token representing a set of rights that entitle copy owners to make otherwise prohibited uses of a work, not because the copy itself has any special inherent virtue, but because it signifies that those uses satisfy a broader set of policy considerations. But the copy can no longer serve that role effectively. Courts need a new way to think through conflicts between the rights of consumers and the rights of creators. We can take away the copy, and we can even dispense with the preoccupation with ownership, so long as we have some other means of verifying that consumers stand in a privileged relation to the work.

The distinction between rights to the copy and rights in the work, and the related conceptual division between personal and intellectual property, have been useful constructs in copyright law. But both have served as proxies for a more complicated calculus weighing the respective rights of creators and consumers. These heuristics helped courts and policy-makers balance those competing interests without undertaking an individualized analysis of the impact on the incentives and costs associated with each contested use. But at the same time, those heuristics have obscured the policy considerations that underlie the contest between intellectual and personal property rights. And because of shifts in technology and the marketplace, those proxies are an increasingly unreliable measure of the interests they once incorporated. Although the Copyright Office continues to see it as a "defining element" of exhaustion, the copy looks increasingly like a "mere relic."[97]

Thinking about the copy as a proxy ultimately reveals how little separates personal and intellectual property rights. At bottom, the difference between personal and intellectual property is simply who prevails. When the interests of consumers are given more weight, we speak in terms of personal property. When the interests of copyright holders carry the day, we invoke intellectual property. But the rights themselves are not qualitatively different. The rights to distribute, reproduce, and display, for example, are equally at stake in both personal and intellectual property. Nor can one meaningfully distinguish between these two categories by insisting that personal property concerns copies while intellectual property protects the work. Tying the consumer's right to her particular copy has been a convenient and easily understood way of articulating the limits of the consumer's rights

---

[97] U.S. COPYRIGHT OFFICE, DMCA SECTION 104 REPORT 86 (2001).

to exploit the underlying work. But it doesn't change the fact that intellectual and personal property regulate the same sets of behaviors and relationships.

Characterizing the statutory interests that the Copyright Act establishes for creators and consumers as "property" ultimately states a conclusion about the degree to which the law will vindicate them.[98] But that label alone does not help us resolve conflicts between those rights. Proponents of broader and stronger intellectual property protection frequently leverage the rhetorical force of the property label.[99] By recognizing that both creators and consumers can lay equal claim to the property mantle, policy-makers might be better equipped to thoughtfully consider the merits of proposals which expand intellectual property.

Exhaustion rules allocate usage rights to a defined group of consumers to make particular uses of a work without the permission of the copyright holder. But that allocation is constrained in important respects. Gifts, lending, and resale are limited to the number of copies acquired.[100] Public displays are limited to the location where the copy is housed.[101] Archival copies cannot be retained after the transfer of the originally acquired copy.[102] In each case, these rights and their limitations are justified in reference to a set of underlying policy considerations rooted in costs and incentives.

Historically, copy ownership has served a dual role in this system. It has identified the class of consumers granted these usage rights. And it has helped to define and reinforce the limitations of those rights. For the reasons we have documented here, copy ownership can no longer effectively serve those functions. Copyright law needs a new way to identify this class of consumers. And it needs to formulate new limitations on consumer usage rights that are sensitive to the three policies we have described and their application to a marketplace defined by digital distribution.

Elsewhere, we have argued that courts and policy-makers should replace the current rigid statutory exhaustion rules with a more flexible approach. In deciding whether a transaction triggers exhaustion, we suggest courts consider three key factors: the duration of consumer possession or access; whether the payment structure is one-time or ongoing; and the characterization of the transaction communicated to the consumer, including whether it is referred to as a sale or purchase in marketing materials.[103] Once exhaustion is triggered, courts need to decide whether particular uses of a work are within its scope.

---

[98] See Arnold S. Weinrib, *Information and Property*, 38 U. TORONTO L.J. 117, 120 (1988) ("It also makes plain the conclusory nature of the term 'property': it is a legal characterization, a statement that the court has chosen to assign a particular form of protection to the interest in question." (footnote omitted)); JEREMY BENTHAM, THE THEORY OF LEGISLATION 113 (C. K. Ogden ed., 1950) ("Property and law are born together, and die together. Before laws were made there was no property; take away laws, and property ceases.").

[99] See Margaret Jane Radin, *Information Tangibility*, in ECONOMICS, LAW AND INTELLECTUAL PROPERTY 395, 400 (Ove Granstrand ed., 2003) (noting that "analogies to physical property, and invasion of physical property are showstoppers of persuasion"); David Fagundes, *Property Rhetoric and the Public Domain*, 94 MINN. L. REV. 652, 659 (2010) (examining the use of property as a "rhetorical trope").

[100] 17 U.S.C. § 109(a) (2012).
[101] *Ibid.* § 109(c).
[102] *Ibid.* § 117(a).
[103] Perzanowski & Schultz, *supra* note 2.

A workable digital exhaustion doctrine cannot be limited to the distribution right alone. The doctrine should also permit limited acts of reproduction, and even the creation of derivative works, to the extent necessary to enable transfers across competing technology platforms. But purchasers of digital content cannot be given free rein to exploit works simply because they bought a single copy. In assessing consumer behavior, courts should consider: whether the purchaser fully parted with possession of or access to the work; whether the use deprives rights holders of a fair return; and whether the purchaser has materially altered the underlying expression.[104]

VI. CONCLUSION

The approach we advocate is consistent with the policy concerns motivating exhaustion rules. In the future we envision, copyright exhaustion would not be tied to a particular copy but would grant an identifiable subset of consumers' limited rights to use, modify, and alienate their interests in a work, regardless of its embodiment in any particular tangible form. This model offers the consumer incentives and low information costs of the traditional property-based approach. And if properly limited, it would maintain creative incentives by ensuring fair rewards for the sale of well-defined transferable interests in works to the public.

The contours of the copyright law, and by extension the respective rights of creators and consumers, have been shaped by the interactions of both unchanging policy commitments and the contingencies of existing technology, markets, and practices. As that backdrop changes, copyright law should and must adapt. But it should do so with an eye to its underlying purposes and justifications. The transition to digital distribution of information demands a change to our approach to copyright exhaustion. But that transition should not be exploited as an opportunity to do away with a key component of copyright's balance between the creators and the public. The approach we outlined above helps ensure that the exhaustion principle and the policy commitments at its core outlive the paperback.

---

[104] *Ibid.* (noting that when the underlying expression is altered, fair use would generally be a more appropriate doctrinal tool).

Index

Abbott, Frederick M. 264, 268
active pharmaceutical ingredients (APIs) 148–49, 150
Acts of Accession 178
Adams v. Burke judgment (1873) 17–18
"affiliate exception" to gray market imports 99
aggression, acts of 427–28, 429
Agreement on Trade-Related Aspects of Intellectual Property Rights *see* TRIPS Agreement (Agreement on Trade-Related Aspects of Intellectual Property Rights)
American Banana Co. v. United Fruit Co. judgment (1909) 231
analogue copies 64–65
ancillary restraints 42
Andean Community of Nations (Andean Pact) xix, 211–13
Anti-Counterfeiting Trade Agreement (ACTA), pharmaceutical products 162, 163
antiretrovirals 146–47
antitrust law, and case against exhaustion 28–29, 32–34
Anti-Unfair Competition Law, China 316–17
arbitrage 32, 85, 112, 115, 282
 cross-border 33, 107
Aronson v. Quick Point judgment (1979) 8–11
Art & Allposters International BV v. Stiching Pictoright judgment (2015) 486–87
ASEAN (Association of Southeast Asian Nations) 195, 377
 Agreement on the Common Effective Preferential Tariff Scheme for the ASEAN Free Trade Area 378–79
 ASEAN Declaration (1967) 377
 "ASEAN Way" 378
 current members 378, 384
 Economic Community Blueprint 378, 385
 Framework Agreement (1995) 379
 trademark exhaustion and free movement of goods 367, 377–83
 see also European Economic Area (EEA); European Union (EU); NAFTA (North American Free Trade Agreement)
Australia, national exhaustion rule 104
author incentives, functions of copy ownership 530–31

Bangkok Declaration (1967) 377
Bauer v. O'Donnell (1913) 59
Berne Convention for the Protection of Literary and Artistic Works (Berne Convention) 91–92
 Appendix 95, 96
Betts v. Willmott judgment (1871) 290
bilateral agreements 249
biotechnology
 biological material, and general exhaustion rules 296–97
 Biotechnology Directive (Directive 98/44/EC of the European Parliament and Council on the Legal Protection of Biotechnological Inventions) 296, 302, 303, 305, 306
 EPSPS enzymes 292, 293, 304–5
 expansion of intellectual property protections xviii
Bloomer v. McQuewan judgment (1852) 17
Bobbs-Merrill v. Strauss judgment (1908) 11, 15, 18, 57, 58, 66
 digital exhaustion 520, 523
Bodenhausen, G. H. C. 92
Boesch v. Graff judgment (1890) 241, 242, 276–77
Bowman v. Monsanto judgment (2013)
 analysis
  general exhaustion and biological material 296–97
  "making" and self-replication 298–99
  plant variety protection and saving seeds 299–301
 case history 294
 decision 294–95
 incentives theory, and intellectual property exhaustion 4, 10, 11, 19, 21
 see also Monsanto Company (publicly traded American multinational agrochemical and agricultural biotechnology corporation)
brand differentiation strategies 360, 362, 366
Brazilian Industrial Property Law 206
Brazilian Intellectual Property Code 297
Bristol-Myers Squibb v. Paranova judgment (1997) 101, 171–72, 174, 191, 348, 349–50, 351–52, 357, 360, 503
Brulotte v. Thys judgment (1964) 8–9, 10

Brunei Darussalam 380
Burberry judgment (Supreme Court of South Korea, 2002) 413–14

calibration tool, parallel importation as 96, 105
Cambodian Law concerning Marks, Trade Names and Acts of Unfair Competition 380, 386
Canada
  case law of importance
    CCH Canada v. Law Society of Upper Canada (2004) 492
    Kraft Canada v. Euro-Excellence (2007) 30, 480, 483, 484, 492
    Rogers Communications Inc. v. Société canadienne des auteurs, compositeurs et éditeurs de musique (2012) 493
    Society of Composers, Authors and Music Publishers of Canada v. Bell Canada (2012) 492
    Théberge v. Galerie d'Art du Petit Champlain, Inc. (2002) 486, 487, 494
  copyright 478–97
    Act to Amend the Copyright Act (1997) 481
    Copyright Act 480, 481–87
    importation remedy provision (s. 27(2)(e) of Copyright Act) 482–85
    new old first sale right (s. 3(1)(j) of Copyright Act) 485–87
    parallel importation of books (s. 27.1 Copyright Act) 481–82
  digital exhaustion, case for 487–96
    digital goods 487–91
    exhaustion as users' right 491–93
  distribution law 496
  and EU Comprehensive Economic and Trade Agreement (2014) 480
  international exhaustion 375, 376
  statutory rights 481–87
  trademark infringement 377
  Trans-Pacific Partnership Agreement (2016) 480
Capitol Records, LLC v. ReDigi Inc. judgment (2013) 66, 68, 71, 74–75, 528
Cartagena Agreement (1973) 211
cartels 165
Cartoon Network v. CSC Holdings, Inc. judgment (2008) 527–28
CCH Canada v. Law Society of Upper Canada pharmaceutical products judgment (2004) 492
cDNA (artificially produced sequences) 140
Centrafarm B.V. v. American Home Products Corp. judgment (1978) 173, 360

Central American Integration System (SICA) 213, 214
Chafee, Zechariah 55–56
chattel servitudes 44, 54, 55, 56, 59, 60, 525
Chen, Yeh-ning 185
Chen, Yongmin 117
Chile 201
China 308–23
  Anti-Unfair Competition Law 316–17
  Customs Office 317
  Customs Regulation on IPRs 317–18
  as developing country 312
  economic effects, parallel imports 318–22
    impact on authorized importers or distributors 319
    impact on consumers 319–20
    impact on patentees 320
    parallel imported cars in the Shanghai Free-Trade Zone 320–22
    permitting parallel imports in China 319–20
  international exhaustion, adoption of 311
  IP position 136, 142
  legal framework 309–18
    Anti-Unfair Competition Law 316–17
    Customs Regulation on IPRs 317–18
    Third Amendment to Chinese Patent Law, changes before and after 309–16
  as member of WTO 309
  patent exhaustion, development 308–23
  Shanghai Free-Trade Zone (SFTZ), parallel imported cars in 320–22
  State Intellectual Property Office 312, 313
  Third Amendment to Chinese Patent Law, changes before and after 308, 309–16
    current Patent Law of 2008 and current regulation of parallel imports 311–12, 322
    legislation background 312–15
    legislation basis (without prejudice to international agreements) 315–16
    state of patent law prior to 309–11
  and TRIPS 310
  and United States 141–42
CJEU *see* Court of Justice of the European Union (CJEU)
CNL-SUCAL N.V. v. Hag G.F. A.G (Hag II) judgment (1990) 175
Coase Theorem and transaction costs 40–41
Colomer, Ruiz-Jarabo (Advocate General) 260, 261, 359
Columbia Broadcasting System, Inc. v. Scorpio Music Distributors, Inc. judgment (1984) 234, 235, 236

Commerce Department, U.S. 285, 287
Committee on International Trade Law, International Law Association 146
common law
  in Australia 491
  chattels 525
  first sale doctrine 23, 334, 335, 340
  implied licenses 295
  passing off 191
  patent exhaustion 16
  peaceful enjoyment of property 57
  restraint of trade 41, 42
  and restrictions on alienation of private property 334, 340, 343, 480
  servitudes 44, 47, 48, 52, 54–5, 60, 63
    and origins of intellectual property exhaustion 56–9
  trademark infringement 394, 396
  in United States 273, 274
Common Market of the South (MERCOSUR) *see* MERCOSUR (Common Market of the South)
common-enterprise argument, market-communitarian conflict 142
Compagnie générale pour la diffusion de la télévision & ors. v. Ciné-Vog Films S.A. & ors (*Coditel II* judgment) (1982) 488, 510–11
competition law
  European Union
    free movement of goods 344–45
    and parallel trade in pharmaceuticals 255–62
    principle of European exhaustion and EU competition law 253–55
    and trademark exhaustion 343–89
    wider integration of competition concerns in exhaustion doctrine 352–63
  "interbrand" price competition 250, 251
  Korea 419–20
  and parallel trade in pharmaceuticals 255–62
    Greek and Spanish *GlaxoSmithKline* judgments 256–58, 261, 262
    innovation vs. parallel trade in pharmaceuticals 260–61
    no benefits for consumers created by parallel trade 259–60
    regulation of pharmaceutical markets in the Member States 258–59
  see also European Union (EU); parallel trade; pharmaceutical products; trademark exhaustion
Comprehensive Economic and Trade Agreement (CETA), 2014 480

compulsory licensing
  and India 332, 337
  pharmaceutical products
    consent and reward 156–57
    lawful placement 158–59
    and TRIPS 94, 95
confusion, trademarks 423, 425–27
  challenging mark owner's desire for total control 437–39
  likelihood of 448
consent, Latin American parallel imports 201–2
consumers
  China, patent exhaustion in 319–20
  incentives for 531–32
  and parallel trade 259–60
contract law
  and efficient distribution 35
  and patents 8, 9
  redundancy of contractual typologies 508–9
  sales contracts, digital products 66
contributory infringement claims, trademark exhaustion 428
Copad v. Christian Dior judgment (2009) 356–57
copies
  analogue 64–65
  cases 527–28
  copyright exhaustion, U.S. 12–13
  functions of ownership 532–33
  imported, first sale rule in U.S. 390–407
  and information costs 532–33
  infringing 496
  legally imported genuine, in Taiwan 455–56
  under Marrakesh Treaty (2013) 467–70
  pirated 408
  see also copyright; copyright exhaustion; digital products/digital exhaustion
copy
  erosion of 527–29
  freeing exhaustion from 534–36
  functions of ownership 529–33
    author incentives 530–31
    consumer incentives 531–32
    freeing exhaustion from the copy 534–36
copyright
  in Canada *see* Canadian copyright
  conflict with trademark policy 404–7
  Copyright Directive (Directive 2001/29/EC), EUCD 503, 507, 509, 511, 512, 513
  first sale doctrine 23
  in Germany 499
  "interim" harmonized standard 143
  Kirtsaeng v. John Wiley decision, impact 391, 392, 393, 457, 460, 474

vs. paradigmatic possessory property rights in tangible objects 45
parallel imports 107, 391–93
pharmaceutical trade 153
and public domain works 7
servitudes 57–58
software as copyright-relevant activity 73, 77
and tangible objects 45
term extension 5, 6, 7
trademark law as a copyright alternative 393–94
WIPO Copyright Treaty (WCT) 70, 485–86, 500, 508, 512
see also first sale doctrine; *Kirtsaeng v. John Wiley & Sons* judgment (2013); patents; trademarks
copyright exhaustion
and copyright doctrine 505–9
digital *see* digital copyright exhaustion
patent exhaustion distinguished 17
pirated or counterfeited goods *see* counterfeit goods
United States 11–16
contemporary version 14
copies 12–13
Copyright Act 1976, s. 109 12–13, 234, 473–74
first sale doctrine 12, 14, 15, 17
industry practices 13–14
multi-territorial conduct, context of 234–38
sale based on economic and business realities of a transaction 13
see also United States
see also incentives theory, and intellectual property exhaustion
copyrighted works
Lanham Act remedies, applying to 400–403
and material differences 400–402
cost-benefit analysis 37–39
Coty Prestige Lancaster Group GmbH v. Simex Trading A.G. judgment (2010) 349
counterfeit goods 15, 16, 421, 422, 423, 429, 430, 436, 452
domestic sale 394–95
and non-counterfeit 264, 390, 394, 395
trademarked 382, 413
see also trademark exhaustion; trademarks
Court of Justice of the European Union (CJEU) 101, 479, 499
Canadian copyright perspective 486, 487, 490, 493, 494, 495, 496
and digital products/digital age 64, 69, 70, 72, 74, 76, 79, 80, 81

and internal market 170, 171, 172, 173, 175, 177, 178, 179, 180, 181, 184
Internet and exhaustion 500–501, 502, 504, 505, 506, 510, 513, 517
patent exhaustion
pharmaceutical products 253, 254, 255, 265, 266, 267
self-replicating technologies 269, 290, 301, 302, 304, 305, 306
and pharmaceutical products 157, 160, 165
patent exhaustion 253, 254, 255, 265, 266, 267
and Taiwan 446, 459
trademark exhaustion 344, 347, 364, 365
competition concerns 353, 354, 355, 356, 357, 358, 359, 360, 363
free movement of goods 368, 369, 372, 384
Trade Mark Directive and exhaustion 348, 349, 350, 352
see also European Court of Justice (ECJ)
covenants, real 47
Craigslist site 422, 423, 437
cross-border arbitrage 33, 107
Cuba 201, 207
Curb v. MCA Records, Inc. judgment (1995) 233
Curtiss Aeroplane & Motor Corp. v. United Aircraft Engineering Corp. judgment (1920) 277
Customs and Border Protection (CBP), U.S. 394, 396–97, 399, 402–3, 407
Customs Regulation on IPRs, China 317–18

Daimler Manufacturing Co. v. Conklin judgment (1909) 277
Danzon, Patricia M. 120, 121
Dastar Corp. v. Twentieth Century Fox Film Corp (2003), quasi-preemption under 403–4
data exclusivity, pharmaceutical trade 153–54
De Mattos v. Gibson (1858) 54, 57
dead-hand control, property law 44, 50–51
dealer investment, parallel trade 31–32
Deepsouth Packing Co. v. Laitram Corp. judgment (1972) 238, 239
Deutsche Grammophon v. Metro judgment (1971) 170
Dickerson v. Matheson judgment (1893) 277
Digital Millennium Copyright Act (DMCA) 428
Section 104 Report 75
digital products/digital exhaustion xix, 64–82, 487–91

Index 541

analogue copies, use of (first period) 64–65
benefits of shifting from hard copy distribution 393
case law of importance
   Bobbs-Merrill v. Strauss (1908) 66
   Capitol Records, LLC v. ReDigi Inc. (2013) 66, 68, 71, 74–75, 528
   UMG v. Augusto (2001) 521–22
   UsedSoft v. Oracle (2012) *see UsedSoft v. Oracle* judgment (2012)
copy, erosion of 527–29
digital future 21–22
digital markets and exhaustion 509–16
Digital Millennium Copyright Act 75, 428
downloading of works by user himself on own device (second period) 65, 66, 72
e-books 74, 75, 78–79, 80
evaluation of digital age 76–81
exhaustion
   in Canada 493–96
   in first period of digital age 66–72
first period of digital age 64–65, 66, 73
   exhaustion in 66–72
first sale doctrine 66, 68, 69, 70, 71
hybrid business models 66, 68
implied license theory 67, 76, 78
incentives theory, and intellectual property exhaustion 14
InfoSoc Directive (Directive 2001/29) 64, 69, 74
opinions and evaluation 68–72
outlook, digital age 81–82
ownership, erosion of 520–26
   property, shifting views on 523–25
   software divide, shrinking 525–26
   software exceptionalism 521–23
   software ownership cases 520–21
and personal property 518–36
   erosion of copy 527–29
   erosion of ownership 520–26
physical carriers, use of (in first period) 64–65, 71
pure enjoyment criterion 77
reality of 489
sales contracts 66
second period of digital age 65
   exhaustion in 66–72
   first sale doctrine 70
   vs. third period 68
software, opinions regarding works other than 74–76
Software Directive (Directive 2009/24) 64, 72, 74, 80, 81, 504, 507
streaming, downloading works by 65
technical developments in 64–66
technical protections measures, purposes 80–81
terminology 66–68
third period of digital age 65, 77
   vs. second period 68
   transfer of capacity to be a licensee in 72–81
transfer of capacity to be a licensee in the third period 72–81
undesired use activities, hindering 78
in United States 68–9
see also copies; Internet, and trademark exhaustion; Internet and exhaustion as a distribution channel; software
Dispute Settlement Understanding (DSU), Latin America 203–4
distribution
   Canadian law 496
   and exhaustion 34–36, 137–38
   integrity of selective distribution systems 358
   introduction of a general distribution right, in Taiwan 455
   Marrakesh Treaty (2013) *see* Marrakesh Treaty (2013)
   patents, initial authorized sale terminating patent owner's rights to control 99
   subsequent (under Marrakesh Treaty) 467
      limitations on 470–72
      under targeted exhaustion principle 474–77
      under U.S. copyright law 472–74
   vertical pricing and distributor-level parallel trade 116–18
   see also distributional problem; Internet and exhaustion as a distribution channel
distributional problem
   addressing 136–38
   exhaustion 129–33
   IPR harmonization 134–36, 140–43
DNA 140
   self-replicating technologies 292, 293, 301, 302, 306
Doha Ministerial Declaration on TRIPs and Public Health (2001) 128, 135, 137, 147, 159, 284, 331
Dominican Republic 201, 202
   Industrial Property Law 205–6
Doncaster Pharmaceuticals v. Bolton Pharmaceutical Co. (2006) 175–76
Dr. Miles Medical Co. v. John D. Park & Sons (1911) 55, 58
drug approval 149–50
   see also pharmaceutical products
drug regulatory authority (DRA) 149
Duffy, John 60

easements 47
eBay site 422, 423, 430–31, 437
e-books *see* electronic books (e-books)
ECJ *see* European Court of Justice (ECJ)
economic factors
   parallel importation 115–18
   parallel trade 251–53
   profit-increasing parallel imports 115–16
   rationale for exhaustion *see* economic rationale, exhaustion
economic integration schemes, parallel imports in (Latin America) 207–13
   Andean Community of Nations (Andean Pact) 211–13
   Central American Integration System (SICA) 213, 214
   Common Market of the South (MERCOSUR) 207–13
economic rationale, exhaustion 23–43
   antitrust scholarship, limited relevance to exhaustion 32–34
   case against exhaustion 28–34
      parallel trade 30–32
   case for exhaustion 25–28
   conflicting views, reconciling
      efficient distribution 34–36
      margin, focus on 36–37
      short-term and long-term costs and benefits 37–39
   distributional problem 129–30
   exhaustion as sticky default rule 40–42
   first sale doctrine, formulations 24
   limited relevance of antitrust scholarship to exhaustion question 32–34
efficiency
   distribution 34–36
   dynamic 26–27
   IPRs, efficiency-based 130, 131, 134, 139
   "purist" approach 141
   static 25–26
Eldred v. Ashcroft judgment (2003) 6–8
electronic books (e-books) 393, 476, 526, 529
   digital products/digital exhaustion 74, 75, 78–79, 80
EMI Records v. United Kingdom judgment (1976) 177
Enlarged Board of Appeal, European Patent Office 300
EPSPS enzymes 292, 293, 304–5
equitable servitudes 47
erosion
   of copy 527–29
   of general applicability of exhaustion principle 476
   of ownership

property, shifting views on 523–25
software divide, shrinking 525–26
software exceptionalism 521–23
software ownership cases 520–21
of traditional limitations on land servitudes 54
Etablissements Consten, S.A.R.L. & Grundig-Verkaufs GmbH v. Commission (1966) (*"Consten and Grundig"*) judgment 344, 346, 348, 354, 356, 365
European Commission 109
European Council, *New Approach to Technical Harmonization and Standards* 371
European Court of Justice (ECJ) 253, 344, 501, 529
   trademark exhaustion and free movement of goods 368, 369–70
   see also Court of Justice of the European Union (CJEU)
European Economic Area (EEA) xix
   Agreement on 169, 170, 371
   goods not put on the market in 177–78
   trademark exhaustion and free movement of goods 367, 368–73
European Medicines Agency (EMA) 148
European Patent Convention (EPC) 300
European Patent Office (EPO), Enlarged Board of Appeal 300
European Union (EU)
   Acts of Accession 178
   Biotechnology Directive (Directive 98/44/EC) 296, 302, 303, 305, 306
   case law of importance
      Art & Allposters International BV v. Stiching Pictoright (2015) 486–87
      Compagnie générale pour la diffusion de la télévision & ors. v. Ciné-Vog Films S.A. & ors (*Coditel II*) (1982) 488, 510–11
      Merck v. Stephar (1981) 255
      Syfait v. GlaxoSmithKline (2005) 256
      UsedSoft v. Oracle (2012) *see UsedSoft v. Oracle* judgment (2012)
   competition law and parallel trade in pharmaceuticals 255–62
   Greek and Spanish *GlaxoSmithKline* judgments 256–58, 261, 262
   innovation vs. parallel trade in pharmaceuticals 260–61
   no benefits for consumers created by parallel trade 259–60
   regulation of pharmaceutical markets in the Member States 258–59
Comprehensive Economic and Trade Agreement (2014) 480

Copyright Directive (Directive 2001/29/EC), EUCD 503, 507, 509, 511, 512, 513
data exclusivity, pharmaceutical industry 153
exclusion of exhaustion for services under EU law 510–11
exhaustion landscape 500–504
InfoSoc Directive *see* InfoSoc Directive (Directive 2001/29)
parallel trade
  competition law on restraints 253–62
  jurisdictional approaches to parallel importation 100–102
  negative and positive integration 254
  pharmaceutical products 255–62
  Regulations 100
pharmaceutical products 153
principle of European exhaustion and EU competition law 251, 253–55
regulation of pharmaceutical markets in the Member States 258–59
Software Directive *see* Software Directive (Directive 2009/24)
Trade Mark Directive *see under* trademarks
trademark exhaustion and free movement of goods 368–73
transit of pharmaceuticals, dealing with 264–69
  appropriate legal regime 267–69
  legal situation in EU 264–67
  whether collision between copyright and EU law 504–9
exchange rate variations, East Asia 110
exclusive dealing 29
exhaustion of rights doctrine, intellectual property
  application of doctrine 125
  benefit-cost optimization 129–30
  case against 28–34
  case for 25–28
  Coase Theorem and transaction costs 40–41
  common law origins 56–59
  copyright *see* copyright exhaustion
  definitions 125–26, 498
  developed nations' position 130–31, 132, 136
  digital exhaustion, case for (Canada) 487–96
  and digital markets 509–16
    capacities and parameters 515–16
    compliance with international Convention law 512–13
    exclusion of exhaustion for services under EU law 510–11
    interpretation flexibilities 514–15
    online exhaustion and supremacy of primary Union law 511–15
    primary law, continued relevance 514–15

distributional problem 129–33
in domestic law, and parallel importing 85
economic rationale for 23–43, 129–30
effects on static efficiency 25–26
erosion of 476
EU exhaustion landscape 500–504
European exhaustion and competition law 251, 253–55
general exhaustion and biological material 296–97
geographic scope (United States) 226–27
  and national treatment principle 227–28, 229–31
  and territoriality 231–44
and German copyright law 499
global policies 114
and implied consent doctrine 498
and incentives *see* incentives, and intellectual property
intangible property *see* intangible property
international diversity 409–10
international exhaustion *see* international exhaustion
international harmony, working towards 138–40
and Internet as a distribution channel 498–517
in Latin America *see* Latin America
and Marrakesh Treaty 465–66
in a multi-layered system 515–16
national *see* national exhaustion
one-size-fits-all 138–39
online exhaustion and supremacy of primary Union law 511–15
and parallel importation 106–24
patent *see* patent exhaustion
principles 11, 13, 169, 424, 503
"red wine" fallacy 34
regional *see* regional exhaustion
and resale right 67
and right to use 67
secondary markets 129–30
in Singapore *see* Singapore
as sticky default rule 40–42
in Taiwan *see* Taiwan
terminology 67, 68
and Trade Mark Directive 348–52, 363, 364
triggering events 125
and TRIPS 126–29
as users' right 491–93
whether collision between copyright and EU law 504–9
wider integration of competition concerns in doctrine 352–63

"Exhaustion Plus," internal market 171–84
  "*BMS* conditions" 172, 173
  examples of relevant goods
    changed condition 171–73
    not put on the market by the proprietor or with his consent 175–77
    not put on the market in the EEA 177–78
    put on the market under a different mark 173–75
    right holder not objecting quickly enough 178–81
  packaging 171–73
  services 181–84
  Specific Mechanism 179, 180
externalities, servitudes 52–53, 61

fair dealing, users' right 493
farmer's privilege, plant variety protection 299
FDA *see* Food and Drug Administration (FDA)
finished pharmaceutical products (FPPs) 148–9, 150
first marketing theory *see* implied license theory
first sale doctrine 23, 25, 27, 58, 67, 156, 408
  Canada 485–7
  common law 23, 334, 335, 340
  copyright exhaustion, U.S. 12, 14, 15, 17
  digital age 66, 68, 69, 70, 71, 503
  distinguished from exhaustion principle 88–89
  effects on dynamic efficiency 26–27
  first unconditional sale 24
  first-authorized sale 24
  formulations 24
  genuine goods 433–35
  international intellectual property rules and exhaustion 88–89
  and material differences 395–96
  see also copyright exhaustion; exhaustion; horizontal restraints; post-sale restraints; United States; vertical restraints
Food and Drug Administration (FDA) 148, 152, 283, 285, 286
Football Assoc. Premier League v. QC Leisure judgment (2011) 181
free movement of goods
  and competition law 344–45
  in GATT 86
  mutual recognition principle 370, 372
  and trademark exhaustion 352, 367–89
  see also trademark exhaustion
free riding 33, 129, 136, 362
  parallel trade/imports 31, 33, 109, 121, 361

free trade agreements (FTAs) 199, 200, 211, 249
French, Susan 49
Fuji Photo Film Co., v. Jazz Photo Corp (*Jazz Photo II*) judgment (2005) 186, 242, 277
Fujifilm judgment (Supreme Court of South Korea, 2003) 416
full appropriation of creative work/invention 5

Ganslandt, Mattias 110, 111, 117, 185, 280
General Agreement on Tariffs and Trade (GATT) 96, 155, 271
  Article V 266
  Article IX 90
  Article XX 90, 91
    exceptions 89, 91
  free movement of goods 86
  pre-TRIPS 89–91
  provisions 89
General Court of the European Union 359
genetic material, "function" 304–5
genuine goods 424, 431
  first sale doctrine 433–5
  in Singapore 188, 189
  see also goods
Germany 499
Gilead (drug company) 154, 155
GlaxoSmithKline judgments, Greek and Spanish 256–58, 262
globalization 108
Good Manufacturing Practices (GMP) 148
goods
  changed condition 171–73
  counterfeit *see* counterfeit goods 394–95
  digital xix, 487–91
  free movement of
    and competition law 344–45
    and trademark exhaustion 367–89
  genuine *see* genuine goods
  intangible, expansion of exhaustion rule towards 504–5
  labeling 163, 376, 377, 385, 401, 403, 473
  not put on the market by the proprietor or with his consent 175–77
  not put on the market in the EEA 177–78
  positional 32
  put on the market under a different mark 173–75
  relabeling 360, 372, 377
  repackaging *see* repackaging of goods
  resold, and Internet 422–39
  right holder not objecting quickly enough 178–81
  used or repaired, selling 431, 432
  see also services

Google France, Google Inc. v. Louis Vuitton Malletier; Google France v. Viaticum Luteciel; Google France v. CNRRH Pierre Alexis Thonet Bruno Raboi Tiger judgment (2010) 354
gray market 98, 99
  see also parallel trade
gray market goods *see* parallel imports (PI)/ parallel importation
Grossman, Gene M. 121, 281
Guatemala 201, 202
  Copyright Law 206

harmony, international
  context 125–29
  definitions 125–26
  distributional problem 129–38
  exhaustion 138–40
    under and after TRIPS, and transnational IPRs 126–29
  intellectual property rights 134–36, 140–43
  IPR harmonization 134–36, 140–43
  Kirtsaeng v. John Wiley & Sons (2013) 126–27, 133, 138
  realpolitik of parties' respective bargaining positions 134
  transnational IPRs 126–29
  working towards 125–44
Heald, Paul 7
Heller, Michael 51–52
Henry v. A. B. Dick Co. (1912) 58, 59
Hoffmann-La Roche v. Centrafarm judgment (1978) 171, 347, 350, 358
Holiday v. Mattheson judgment (1885) 241
Holmes, Oliver Wendell (Justice) 45
Honda Giken v. Maria Patmanidi judgment (2013) 364, 365
Hong Kong 186
horizontal restraints 28, 29
Hynes, Richard 60

IHT Internationale Heiztechnik v. Ideal-Standard judgment (1994) 175, 346
implied consent doctrine, and exhaustion 498
implied license theory
  common law 295
  digital products/digital exhaustion 67, 76, 78
  patent exhaustion 289, 290–91
  terminology 67
  see also licensing
import controls, pharmaceutical products 150
Incandescent Gaslight Co. v. Cantelo (1895) 59
incentives theory, and intellectual property exhaustion 3–22
  author incentives, functions of copy ownership 530–31
  case law of importance
    Adams v. Burke (1873) 17–18
    Aronson v. Quick Point (1979) 8–11
    Bloomer v. McQuewan (1852) 17
    Bobbs-Merrill v. Strauss (1908) 11, 15, 18
    Bowman v. Monsanto (2013) 4, 10, 11, 19
    Brulotte v. Thys (1964) 8–9, 10
    Eldred v. Ashcroft (2003) 6–8
    Kirtsaeng v. John Wiley & Sons judgment (2013) 14–15
    Quality King v. L'Anza (1997) 14, 15
    Quanta v. LG Electronics (2008) 18–19, 20, 242
    United States v. Univis Lens Co. (1942) 18
  consumer incentives 531–32
  contract law 8, 9, 10
  copyright exhaustion 11–16
  criticism of IP incentives 5
  digital future 21–22
  direct rewards 5
  gauging incentives 6–7
  incentives-based justification for intellectual property 3, 6, 7
  inventions, nonpatentable 9, 10
  limitations of incentives theory 3–4
  monetary rewards 4, 5, 9
  patent exhaustion 16–21
  pre-emption issue 8–11
  randomness and serendipity 5
  size of incentives 5
  U.S. approach to copyright and patent exhaustion 11–21
India, patent exhaustion in 324–40
  ambiguities in patient exhaustion doctrine 326–29
  compulsory licensing 332, 337
  and Copyright Act (1957) 334
  development of exhaustion doctrine 324–25
  fixing patent law on "international exhaustion" 333–35
  and international exhaustion 326, 333–35
  legal interpretation vs. legal construction 325–26
  legislative amendments and lack of judicial guidance 326–29
  and national exhaustion 335–39
  policy style reasoning of exhaustion law 330–33
  Rajagopal Ayyangar Report 326
  Statement of Objects and Reasons of 2002 Amendment to Patents Act 327
  strict legal construction 335–39
  teleological interpretation 330–33

and Trade Marks Act (1999) 334, 337, 338
and TRIPS 325, 330, 331, 332, 334
Waiver Decision (2003) 331
Indian Patents Act (1970) 326
   2002 Amendment 327
   2005 Amendment 328
   section 107A 327
   section 107A(b) 328, 329, 330, 332, 340
      reworking 333–35
      whether referring to national exhaustion 335–39
Indonesia 380
Industrial Revolution, land-use planning needs 47
information costs, servitudes 44, 47–50, 61
InfoSoc Directive (Directive 2001/29 of the European Parliament and of the Council of May 22, 2001 on the harmonization of certain aspects of copyright and related rights in the information society) 64, 74
   Recitals 28 and 29 69
innovation
   "Innovation Wetlands" 28
   vs. parallel trade in pharmaceuticals 260–61
   producer-centric view of 27
intangible property 56, 88, 490, 499
   expansion of exhaustion rule towards 504–5
intellectual property (IP)
   developed nations' position 136
   "different strokes for different intellectual property (IP) folks" approach 186, 195–96
   exhaustion *see* exhaustion of rights doctrine, intellectual property; incentives theory, and intellectual property exhaustion
   exhaustion in domestic IP context 129
   as an intangible property right 88
   internal politics and particular IP regimes 142–43
   international rules *see* international intellectual property rules
   and pharmaceutical products *see under* pharmaceutical products
   see also intangible property; intellectual property rights (IPRs)
intellectual property rights (IPRs)
   efficiency-based 130, 131, 134
   exclusive, deadweight loss resulting from grant of 25
   harmonization 134–36, 140–43
   intangible 88
   Latin America, provisions in legislation relating to imports of products protected by 215–25
   market-based 141–42
   as matter of trade policy, ignoring 107–8
   transnational 126–29
   TRIPS standards 142
   see also intellectual property (IP); TRIPS Agreement (Agreement on Trade-Related Aspects of Intellectual Property Rights)
"interbrand" price competition 250, 251
internal market 169–84
   case law of importance
      Bristol-Myers Squibb v. Paranova (1997) 171–72
      Centrafarm v. American Home Products (1978) 173
      CNL-SUCAL N.V. v. Hag G.F. A.G (*Hag II*) (1990) 175
      Deutsche Grammophon v. Metro (1971) 170
      Doncaster Pharmaceuticals v. Bolton Pharmaceutical Co. (2006) 175–76
      EMI Records v. United Kingdom (1976) 177
      Football Assoc. Premier League v. QC Leisure (2011) 181
      Hoffmann-La Roche v. Centrafarm (1978) 171, 347, 350, 358
      IHT Internationale Heiztechnik v. Ideal-Standard (1994) 175, 346
      Merck v. Sigma (2015) 179, 180
      Peak Holdings v. Axolin-Elinor (2004) 177
      Pharmacia & Upjohn v. Paranova (1999) 174, 360
      Silhouette Int'l v. Harlauer (1998) 177, 364
      Speciality European Pharma v. Doncaster Pharmaceuticals Ltd (2015) 175
      Van Zuylen Frerese v. Hag (*Hag I*) (1974) 175, 344, 346
   European framework 169–71
   "Exhaustion Plus" *see* "Exhaustion Plus," internal market
   TRIPs-plus 169
international exhaustion
   acceptance 409
   Canada 375, 376
   China 311
   defined 106
   India 326, 333–35
   and international non-exhaustion 128, 131, 132, 135, 143
   lawful placement 158
   and patents 151–52, 154
      argument for international patent exhaustion 273–75
      China 311, 314
      regulatory responses to 271–88

pharmaceutical products 263
Taiwan
  under Patent Act 448–50
  under Taiwan Integrated Circuits Layouts Protection Act 444–45
  under Taiwan Trademark Act 445–48
  theory building 456–59
  and TRIPS 250, 251
  United States xviii, 375–76
international intellectual property rules 85–105
  Berne Convention 91–92
    Appendix 95, 96
  case law of importance
    Japan—Customs Duties, Taxes and Labelling Practices on Imported Wines and Alcoholic Beverages (1983) 91
    United States—Imports of Certain Automotive Spring Assemblies (1983) 90
    United States—Section 337 of the Tariff Act of 1930 (1989) 90
  exhaustion and first sale doctrine 88–89
  General Agreement on Tariffs and Trade 96
  prior to TRIPS 89–91
  and parallel imports 85–105
  Paris Convention 91–92
  TRIPS Agreement 92–96
International Law Association, Committee on International Trade Law 146
International Trade Commission (ITC), U.S. 90, 285
  Summary Notice of Determination 86
International Trademark Association (INTA) 380
International Union for the Protection of Plant Varieties (UPOV) 297
  Convention 299, 300
Internet, resales and trademark exhaustion 422–39
  challenging mark owner's desire for total control 435–39
  confusion 437–39
  strengthening available defenses 436–37
  defenses
    available, strengthening 436–37
    first sale of a genuine good 433–35
    repackaged goods, selling 431, 432
    reselling a genuine good 431
    trademark nominative fair use 432–33
    used or repaired goods, selling 431, 432
  litigation 425–31
    aggression, acts of 427–28, 429
    confusion, claiming 423, 425–27
    contributory infringement claims 428

Copyright Act 1976 428
ISPs and online auction sites 429–31
Standard Process 429
Waterford mark example 423
Internet and exhaustion as a distribution channel 437, 498–517
  EU exhaustion landscape 500–504
  exhaustion and digital markets 509–16
    capacities and parameters 515–16
    compliance with international Convention law 512–13
    exclusion of exhaustion for services under EU law 510–11
    interpretation flexibilities 514–15
    online exhaustion and supremacy of primary Union law 511–15
    primary law, continued relevance 514–15
  "Internet of things" xviii
  whether collision between copyright and EU law 504–9
    exhaustion and copyright doctrine 505–9
    intangible goods, expansion of exhaustion rule towards 504–5
    "proper" solution under secondary software copyright law 507–8
    redundancy of contractual typologies 508–9
    secondary legislation, construing 505–9
    UsedSoft judgment as interpretation *contra legem* 506–7
  see also digital products/digital exhaustion; distribution; Internet, resales and trademark exhaustion
Internet Service Providers (ISPs) 424
  and online auction sites 429–31
inventions
  nonpatentable 9, 10
  restrictions on use of chattels embodying 59
  see also patent exhaustion; patents
Inwood Laboratories, Inc. v. Ives Laboratories judgment (1982) 430
IPRs *see* intellectual property rights (IPRs)
ISPs *see* Internet Service Providers (ISPs)
Israel, parallel importation, jurisdictional approaches 102–4
ITC *see* International Trade Commission (ITC), U.S.

Japan
  copyright law 127–28
  national exhaustion 106
  Japan—Customs Duties, Taxes and Labelling Practices on Imported Wines and Alcoholic Beverages (1983) 91

Jazz Photo Corp. v. International Trade Commission judgment (2001) 242, 243, 244, 277
Jefferson, Thomas 51
John D. Park & Sons v. Hartman (1907) 54, 58

K Mart Corp v. Cartier, Inc. judgment (1988) 98
Keppel v. Bailey (1834) 48
Kirtsaeng v. John Wiley & Sons judgment (2013) xvii–xviii, 30, 138
 and copyright law 391, 392, 393, 457, 460, 474
 details of case xvii, 234
 impact of, for international exhaustion 391, 392, 393
 incentives theory, and intellectual property exhaustion 14–15
 international harmony, working towards 126–27, 133
 patent exhaustion 276, 288
 territoriality and geographic scope of exhaustion 234, 236, 237, 238, 241, 242, 243, 245
 and trademark law 393
 transnational IPRs and exhaustion 126–27
Kohler, Josef 291, 292, 295, 296, 498
Koninklijke Philips Elecs. v. Lucheng Meijing Indus. Co. & Nokia Corp. v. Her Majesty's Commissioners of Revenue and Customs (*Philips and Nokia*) judgment (2011) 265, 267, 269
Korea *see* South Korea, trademark exhaustion in
Korea Customs Office (KCS) 420, 421
Korean Fair Trade Commission (KFTC) 419
KP Permanent Make-Up, Inc. v. Lasting Impressions I. Inc. judgment (2004) 437

labeling of goods 163, 376, 377, 385, 401, 403, 473
 see also goods; relabeling of goods
Lai, Edwin L.-C. 121, 281
laissez faire approach, trademark exhaustion 373–83
land servitudes 46, 47, 61, 62
Lanham Act (Trademark Act 1946), U.S.
 aims 423–4
 genuine goods 424
 parallel importation 99
 remedies, applying to copyrighted works 400–403
 trademark exhaustion and Internet 423–24, 428, 435, 439
 trademark infringement 394, 396
 see also United States

Lao PDR 380–81, 386
Latin America
 exhaustion of rights in 198–225
 free trade agreements 199, 200, 211
 parallel importation *see* Latin American parallel imports
 provisions in legislation relating to imports of products protected by IPRs (Table) 215–25
 and TRIPS 198, 199, 202
Latin American parallel imports
 Argentine Patent Law 202, 203
 Dispute Settlement Understanding 203–4
 in economic integration schemes 207–13
 Implementing Regulations 205
 Industrial Property Law 204, 205–6
 under national legislation 201–7
  consent not given 202–6
  consent-based approach 201–2
  exhaustion within national market 206–7
 see also MERCOSUR (Common Market of the South)
least developed countries (LDCs) 126, 128
 and India 330, 331
Leegin Creative Leather Prods, Inc. v. PSKS, Inc (2007) 358
Lemley, Mark 7
Lever Bros Co. v. United States (*Lever II*) judgment (1993) 99, 163
Lexmark International, Inc. v. Impression Products, Inc. judgment (2014) 243, 278
licensing
 compulsory 94, 95, 156–59, 332
 consent and reward 156–57
 escalator clauses, conditional on patent grant 5
 implied license theory 67, 289, 290–91
 lawful placement 158–59
 pharmaceutical products 154–59
 transfer of capacity to be a licensee in the third period of digital age 72–81
 voluntary, and differential pricing 154–56
Lisbon Treaty (2007) 353, 499
L'Oréal S.A. v. eBay International A.G. (2011) 349
Los Angeles News Service v. Reuters judgment (1998) 232–33

Madison, James 51
Madrid Agreement for the Repression of False or Deception Indications of Source 91
Mahoney, Julia 50
Malaysia Trademark Act (1976) 382–83
Malueg, David A. 114, 280

manufacturing, pharmaceutical products 148–49
margin, focus on 36–37
market-communitarian conflict, common-enterprise argument 142
Markus, Keith 185
Marrakesh Treaty (2013) 461–77
  copies first distributed under exceptions and limitations to copyright 467–70
  critics 463
  evaluation 477
  goals 463
  implementation of obligations under 463–64
  and exhaustion principle 465–66
  subsequent distribution under limitations on 470–72
  under targeted exhaustion principle 474–77
  and U.S. law 467, 472–74
  three-step test 469, 470, 471
  and TRIPS 461, 462, 464
Maskus, Keith E. 110, 111, 117, 280
material differences
  and copyrighted works 400–402
  and first sale doctrine 395–96
Merck v. Sigma judgment (2015) 179, 180
Merck v. Stephar judgment (1981) 255
MERCOSUR (Common Market of the South) xix, 207–13
  admissibility of parallel imports 210
  Andean Community of Nations (Andean Pact) 211–13
  Central American Integration System 213
  Protocol for the Harmonization of Intellectual Property Provisions on Trademarks, Indications of Source and Appellations of Origin (2000) 207–8
  Protocol on Basic Principles and General Rules on Intellectual Property (MERCOSUR Protocol 2008) 208, 209
  Protocol on Harmonization of Norms in the Field of Industrial Design (1998) 208
  Resolution 1/00 210
  Treaty of Asunción, established by (1991) 207
  see also Latin America; Latin American parallel imports
Merrill, Thomas W. 48, 53
Mexico 201, 205, 206, 384, 385
  Industrial Property Law 222, 376, 377
  and NAFTA 373, 376, 377
Microsoft v. AT&T judgment (2007) 240
Monopoly Regulation and Fair Trade Act (MRFTA), Korea 419, 420, 421
Monsanto Company (publicly traded American multinational agrochemical and agricultural biotechnology corporation)
  Canadian Supreme Court decision in *Monsanto v. Schmeisser* (2004) 293, 294, 299
  European Court of Justice decision in *Monsanto v. Cefetra et al* (2010) 290
  case history 301–2
  decision 302–3
  self-replicating technology as patented by 292–94
  U.S. Supreme Court decision in *Bowman v. Monsanto* (2013)
    analysis 296–301
    case history 294
    decision 294–95
    incentives theory, and intellectual property exhaustion 4, 10, 11, 19, 21
Monsanto v. Cefetra et al judgment (2010) 290
  analysis
    "function" of genetic material 304–5
    possible scope of protection outside Europe 305–6
    scope of protection and contribution to society 306–7
  case history 301–2
  decision 302–3
  see also Monsanto Company (publicly traded American multinational agrochemical and agricultural biotechnology corporation)
Monsanto v. Schmeisser judgment (2004) 293, 294, 299
Motion Picture Patents Co. v. Universal Film Manufacturing Co. (1917) 59
Mulligan, Christina M. 27
mutual recognition principle 370, 372, 387
Myanmar 380

NAFTA (North American Free Trade Agreement)
  members 384–85
  trademark exhaustion and free movement of goods 367, 368, 373–77
  and TRIPS 373, 374
  see also ASEAN (Association of Southeast Asian Nations); European Economic Area (EEA); European Union (EU)
Nash bargaining 114
National Economic Research Associates (NERA) 109
national exhaustion
  defined 106, 126
  India 335–39

Taiwan 450–51, 455
United States xviii
National Office of Industrial Property of Vietnam 381–82
national treatment principle
 and geographic scope of exhaustion 229–31
 and TRIPS 229
Nat'l Phonograph Co. of Australia v. Menck judgment (1911) 290–91
New Zealand, parallel importation, jurisdictional approaches 102–4
Nokia Corp v. Her Majesty's Commissioners of Revenue & Customs judgment (2009) 265
nominative fair use defense, trademarks 432–33
non-governmental organizations (NGOs) 158
North American Free Trade Agreement *see* NAFTA (North American Free Trade Agreement)
notice, servitudes 44, 47–50
numerus clausus principle 27, 533

online auction sites, and Internet Service Providers 429–31
ordre public 143
Organization for Economic Cooperation and Development (OECD) 107

packaging 171–73
Panama 202
Pan-West (Pte.) Ltd. v Grand Bigwin Pte. Ltd judgment (2003) 192, 195, 196
Paraguay 202
parallel imports (PI)/parallel importation
 "affiliate exception" to gray market imports 99
 in Australia 104
 as a calibration tool 96, 105
 in Canada (books, under s. 27.1 of Copyright Act) 481–82
 case law of importance
  K Mart Corp v. Cartier, Inc. (1988) 98
  Lever Bros Co. v. United States (Lever II) (1993) 99, 163
 in China
  economic effects of permitting 319–20
  regulation of parallel imports 311–12
 and competition law (Korea) 419–20
 copyright 107, 391–93
 and customs law (Korea) 420–21
 Dastar Corp. v. Twentieth Century Fox Film Corp (2003), quasi-preemption under 403–4
 definitions 390, 478
 economic perspectives 106–24

empirical evidence 110–12
 in European Union 100–102
 exchange rate variations, East Asia 110
 and exhaustion of rights in domestic law 85
 few international rules concerning 85
 free riding 31, 33, 109, 121, 361
 international intellectual property rules 85–105
  Berne Convention 91–92, 95, 96
  General Agreement on Tariffs and Trade 89–91, 96
  Paris Convention 91–92, 94
  prior to TRIPS Agreement 89–91
  TRIPS Agreement 92–96
 intra-EU 109
 in Israel 102–4
 John Wiley & Sons, invoking of trademark law against parallel imports 402–3
 jurisdictional approaches to 97–104
  in Australia 104
  in European Union 100–102
  in Israel 102–4
  in New Zealand 102–4
  in Singapore 102–4
  in United States 97–100
 in Korea 417, 418, 419–21
 lack of harmonization/coordination among developed countries 85–86
 lack of multilateral agreed rule, effect 87
 Lever rule 396–97, 402, 403, 405, 406, 407
  uncertain impact of *Lever* disclaimers on trademark infringement claims 397–99
 liberalized copyright rules on 391–93
 in New Zealand 102–4
 and North-South divide 97, 121
 profit-increasing parallel imports 115–16
 rationales for allowing 87–88
 rationales for preventing 87
 in Singapore 102–4, 190, 191
 stylized facts 109–10
 trademark exhaustion 360–61
 trademark remedies against
  Tariff Act remedies 399–400
  trademark infringement 394–99
 and TRIPS 88, 93
 in United States 97–100, 118
 see also European Union (EU); parallel trade; United States
parallel trade
 and competition 117
 distortion by regulation 145
 distributor-level 110–11
 and vertical pricing 116–18

economics of 251–53
European Union (EU)
   competition law on restraints 253–62
   jurisdictional approaches to parallel importation 100–102
   negative and positive integration 254
   pharmaceutical products 255–62
   Regulations 100
free riding 31, 33
impact on local dealer investment 31–32
as international community arbitrage 112
no benefits for consumers created by 259–60
in pharmaceutical products xx, 145–65
   dealing with internationally 262–64
   and EU competition law 255–62
   future for parallel trade in medicine 164–65
   Greek and Spanish *GlaxoSmithKline* judgments 256–58, 261, 262
   innovation vs. parallel trade in pharmaceuticals 260–61
   no benefits for consumers created by parallel trade 259–60
   regulation of pharmaceutical markets in EU Member States 258–9
post-sale restraints 32
and price controls 119–22
price discrimination 30–31
R&D models 118–19
restraints 32, 251, 252
   EU competition law 253–62
trademarks/trademark exhaustion 152–53, 358
see also parallel imports (PI)/parallel importation
Parfums Christian Dior SA v. Dior v. Evora judgment (1997) 351, 352, 355
Paris Convention for the Protection of Industrial Property (Paris Convention) 91–92, 94, 158
patent exhaustion
   China 308–23
      economic effects 318–22
      legal framework 309–18
   copyright exhaustion distinguished 17
   defined 16–17
   escalator clauses, licensing arrangements 5
   implied license theory 289, 290–91
   India
      ambiguities in patient exhaustion doctrine 326–29
      hermeneutics of 324–40
      and international exhaustion 333–35
      legal construction 335–39

      legislative amendments and lack of judicial guidance 326–29
      teleological interpretation 330–33
   international
      argument for 273–75
      and India 333–35
      regulatory responses to 271–88
   origins (U.S.) 17–19
   patent owner's exclusive right to sale and right to use 17
   and regional exhaustion 286, 308, 324
   remuneration by first marketing theory 291–92
   self-replicating technologies 289–307
      European Court of Justice decision in *Monsanto* v. *Cefetra et al* (2010) 301–7
      as patented by Monsanto 292–94
      U.S. Supreme Court decision in *Bowman v. Monsanto* 294–301
   theories 290–92
   United States 16–21, 100, 275–87
      access, role of regulation in (pharmaceutical industry) 283–87
      origins of patent exhaustion 17–19
      questioning benefits of geographic price discrimination 278–83
      recent Supreme Court developments 19–21
      Sherman Act 1990 18
patents
   and contract law 8, 9
   initial, authorized sale terminating patent owner's rights to control distribution 99
   and international exhaustion 151–52, 154
   parallel importation, jurisdictional approaches 102
   pharmaceutical trade 151–52
   territorial 99–100
   and TRIPS 93
   see also copyright; patent exhaustion; trademarks
Peak Holdings v. Axolin-Elinor judgment (2004) 177
per se rules, vertical restraints 29
personal property servitudes 54–56
Perzanowski, Aaron 25, 60
Pfizer (drug company) 152
pharmaceutical products
   access, role of regulation in 283–87
   active pharmaceutical ingredients (APIs) 148–49, 150
   Anti-Counterfeiting Trade Agreement 162, 163
   antiretrovirals 146–47

brand names 153
case law of importance
   GlaxoSmithKline judgments, Greek and Spanish 256–58, 262
   Koninklijke Philips Elecs. v. Lucheng Meijing Indus. Co. & Nokia Corp. v. Her Majesty's Commissioners of Revenue and Customs (*Philips and Nokia*) (2011) 265, 267, 269
   Lever Bros Co. v. United States (Lever II) (1993) 99, 163
   Nokia Corp v. Her Majesty's Commissioners of Revenue & Customs (2009) 265
   Sisvel v. Sosecal (2008) 265
   Sot. Lélos kai Sia (2008) 259, 260, 359–60
complexities of medicines trade 147–50
compulsory licensing *see* compulsory licensing
differential pricing and voluntary licensing 154–56
Doha Ministerial Declaration on TRIPS and Public Health (2001) 128
drug approval aspects 149–50
forms of intellectual property relevant to
   copyright 153
   data exclusivity 153–54
   patents 151–52
   trademarks 152–53
future for parallel trade in medicine 164–65
global regulation 145
historical perspective 146–47
import controls 150
licensing
   compulsory 156–59
   voluntary 154–56
manufacturing aspects 148–49
monetary value of patents 151
originator pharmaceutical companies 154–55
over-the-counter drugs 149
parallel trade in xx, 145–65
   dealing with internationally 262–64
   and EU competition law 255–62
   future for parallel trade in medicine 164–65
   Greek and Spanish *GlaxoSmithKline* judgments 256–58, 262
   imports 111
   innovation vs. parallel trade in pharmaceuticals 260–61
   no benefits for consumers created by parallel trade 259–60
   regulation of pharmaceutical markets in EU Member States 258–59

patent exceptions, Canadian 93
patent protection 249–70
price controls 150, 159–61
regulatory measures 161–62
research-based firms 118
selling price/resale price 151–52
Supplementary Protection Certificate (SPC) 179, 180, 268
transit of, dealing with 264–69
   appropriate legal regime 267–69
   Border Measures Regulation 264, 265, 266, 267
   legal situation in EU 264–67
Trans-Pacific Partnership Agreement 162, 163
and TRIPS 153, 159, 283, 284
unlawful subsidies 160
Pharmacia & Upjohn S.A. v. Paranonova A/S judgment (1999) 174, 360
Philippines, Intellectual Property Code (2013) 382
phonorecords, prohibition of rental market for 13
plant variety protection 299–301
Playboy Enterprises, Inc. v. Netscape Communications Corp. judgment (2004) 438
Png, Ivan 185
Polaroid Corp. v. Polarad Electronics Corp. judgment (1961) 425–26
Polo judgment (Supreme Court of South Korea, 1997) 413–14
positional goods 32
post-sale restraints 23, 32
   and case against exhaustion 28
   economic benefits/justifications 36–37, 38
   and price discrimination 31
   short-term 24
   see also horizontal restraints; vertical restraints
PP v. Teoh Ai Nee judgment (1993) 187–88, 195
pre-emption, incentives and intellectual property 8–11
price controls
   and parallel trade 119–22
   pharmaceutical products 150, 159–61
price differentiation 154–56, 258
price discrimination
   arbitrage 32, 33, 112
   effects on global well-being 113
   first-degree 112, 279
   general economic benefits 272
   international 112–15

parallel trade 30–31
and post-sale restraints 31
questioning benefits of geographic price
    discrimination 278–83
second-degree 112, 279
third-degree 112–14, 115, 279, 280
ubiquitous nature 112
unofficial 25
privacy, consumer 27
problem of the future 47, 50–52, 53, 54
see also servitudes, personal property
product lifecycle 37
profit-increasing parallel imports 115–16
property
    common law, and restrictions on alienation
        of private property 334, 340, 343,
        480
    dead-hand control, property law 44,
        50–51
    rights *in personam* 523, 524
    rights *in rem* 523–24
    shifting views on 523–25
public domain works 7

Quality King v. L'Anza judgment (1997) 14, 15,
    235, 236, 391–92, 407
Quanta v. LG Electronics judgment (2008)
    18–19, 20, 242

Raff, Horst 116
rebranding 360–62
ReDigi judgment *see Capitol Records, LLC v.
    ReDigi Inc.* judgment (2013)
reference-pricing 123
regional exhaustion xix, xx, 89, 126, 151, 226
    internal market 171, 177, 178
    parallel imports and exhaustion, economic
        perspectives 106, 110, 114, 123
    and patent exhaustion 286, 308, 324
    and trademark exhaustion 364, 365, 368,
        383, 384, 386–87, 410
    whether exceptions to rule for reasons
        related to competition 363–65
relabeling of goods 360, 372, 377
see also goods; labeling of goods
"remote-control" property interests, and
    servitudes 45–46, 49, 50, 62
remuneration by first marketing theory, patent
    exhaustion 291–92
repackaging of goods 102, 163, 173, 181, 191,
    431–32
    conditions for 171–72, 174
    trademark exhaustion 347, 349, 350, 351–52,
        360, 377
    unauthorized 372

see also Bristol-Myers Squibb v. Paranova
    judgment (1997); trademark exhaustion;
    trademarks
resale price maintenance (RPM) 29, 31
resales and Internet *see* Internet, resales and
    trademark exhaustion
research and development (R&D) models, and
    parallel trade 118–19
restraints
    ancillary 42
    competition law on 253–62
    historical treatment of agreements in
        restraint of trade 41–42
    horizontal 28, 29
    parallel trade 32, 251, 252
        EU competition law 253–62
    post-sale *see* post-sale restraints
    reasonable 41–42
    restraint of trade 41–42
    vertical 28–29, 31, 33
Richardson, Martin 114
Robinson, Glen 56, 60
*Rogers Communications Inc. v. Société
    canadienne des auteurs, compositeurs et
    éditeurs de musique* judgment (2012) 493
Rose, Carol 47, 50
Rothman, Jennifer 426–27
Roussel Uclaf S.A. v. Hockley Int'l Ltd
    judgment (1996) 291
rule of reason analysis, trademark exhaustion
    347, 357–58

Saggi, Kamal 281
Schmitt, Nicolas 116
Schultz, Jason 25, 60
Schwartz, Marius 114, 280
SCM Agreement (Agreement on Subsidies and
    Countervailing Measures), 1994 87
secondary markets, exhaustion 129–30
seed-saving, and plant variety protection
    299–301
self-replicating technologies
    case law of importance
        Betts v. Willmott (1871) 290
        Bowman v. Monsanto (2013) *see* below
        Monsanto v. Cefetra et al judgment (2010)
            see below
        Monsanto v. Schmeisser (2004) 293, 294,
            299
        *Nat'l Phonograph Co. of Australia v.
            Menck* (1911) 290–91
        Roussel Uclaf S.A. v. Hockley Int'l Ltd
            (1996) 291
        *United Wire Ltd. v. Screen Repair Services
            (Scotland)* (2000) 296

DNA 292, 293, 301, 302
European Court of Justice decision in
    Monsanto v. *Cefetra et al* (2010) 290
    analysis 304–7
    case history 301–2
    decision 302–3
    general exhaustion and biological material 296–97
    "making" and self-replication 298–99
    and patent exhaustion rules 289–307
    as patented by Monsanto 292–94
    plant variety protection and saving seeds 299–301
    theories of patent exhaustion 20
        implied license 290–91
        remuneration by first marketing 291–92
    U.S. Supreme Court decision in *Bowman v. Monsanto* (2013) 4, 294–301
        analysis 296–301
        case history 294
        decision 294–95
        incentives theory, and intellectual property exhaustion 4, 10, 11, 19, 21
    see also Monsanto Company (publicly traded American multinational agrochemical and agricultural biotechnology corporation); patent exhaustion
serfdom, feudal 51
services
    exclusion of exhaustion for, under EU law 510–11
    "Exhaustion Plus," internal market 181–84
    see also goods
servitudes, personal property 44–63
    case law of importance
        Bauer. v. O'Donnell (1913) 59
        Bobbs-Merrill v. Strauss (1908) 57, 58
        De Mattos v. Gibson (1858) 54, 57
        Dr. Miles Medical Co. v. John D. Park & Sons (1911) 55, 58
        Henry v. A. B. Dick Co. (1912) 58, 59
        Incandescent Gaslight Co. v. Cantelo (1895) 59
        John D. Park & Sons v. Hartman (1907) 54, 58
        Keppel v. Bailey (1834) 48
        Motion Picture Patents Co. v. Universal Film Manufacturing Co. (1917) 59
        Straus v. Victor Talking Machine Co. (1917) 59
        Taddy & Co v. Sterious & Co (1904) 54, 57
        Tulk v. Moxhay (1848) 48, 54, 55
        White-Smith Music Publishing v. Apollo (1908) 45

chattel servitudes 44, 54, 55, 56, 59, 60, 525
common law 44, 47, 48, 52, 54–55, 60, 63
    and origins of intellectual property exhaustion 56–59
contemporary critiques 59–62
copyright context 57–58
dead-hand control in property law 44, 50–51
definitions 46
easements 47
equitable 47
externalities 52–53, 61
free alienation policy 55
history 44, 45–56
land 46, 47, 61, 62
notice and information costs 44, 47–50, 61
personal property 54–56
problem of the future 47, 50–52, 53, 54
real covenants 47
and "remote-control" property interests 45–46, 49, 50, 62
Restatement (Third) of Property: Servitudes (2000) 49, 53
tangible property 62, 63
third parties 52–53
transaction-cost-insulated 51–52
use restriction "annexed to a chattel" 58
Shanghai Free-Trade Zone (SFTZ, China)
    Administrative Committee 321
    parallel imported cars in 320–22
    Shanghai Municipal Commission of Commerce, notice on parallel imported cars 320–21
    see also China
SICA (Central American Integration System) 213, 214
Silhouette Int'l v. Harlauer judgment (1998) 177, 364
Simes, Lewis 50–51
Singapore
    asymmetries 195–96
    case law of importance
        Pan-West (Pte.) Ltd. v. Grand Bigwin Pte. Ltd (2003) 192, 195, 196
        PP v. Teoh Ai Nee (1993) 187–88, 195
        Société des Produits Nestlé S.A. v. Petra Foods Ltd [2014] 189
    Copyright Act (1987) 187–90, 191, 195
    exhaustion doctrine in 187–95
    "genuine" products 188, 189
    and Hong Kong 186
    Imperial Copyright Act (1911) 187
    parallel importation
        jurisdictional approaches 102–4
        Trade Marks Act (1998) 190, 191
    Patents Act (1994) 186, 193–95

Select Committee on the Copyright Bill 187
Trade Marks Act (1998) 186, 190–92, 381
Trade Marks Ordinance (1938) 190
and United Kingdom Patents Ordinance (1937) 193
and WTO Decision of August 30, 2003 193, 194
see also ASEAN (Association of Southeast Asian Nations)
Single European Act (1986) 253, 254
Sisvel v. Sosecal judgment (2008) 265
Smith, Henry E. 48, 53
Société des Produits Nestlé S.A. v. Petra Foods Ltd judgment [2014] 189
Society of Composers, Authors and Music Publishers of Canada v. Bell Canada judgment (2012) 492
software
 as copyright-relevant activity 73
 digital age 72–74
  opinions regarding works other than software 74–76
 divide, shrinking 525–26
 exceptionalism 521–23
 ownership cases 520–21
 rental market, prohibition 13
 Software Directive (2009) 64
 use of as a copyright-relevant activity 67, 77
 see also digital products/digital exhaustion; Internet, and trademark exhaustion; Internet and exhaustion as a distribution channel
Software Directive (Directive 2009/24 of the European Parliament and of the Council of April 23, 2009 on the legal protection of computer programs) 72, 80, 81, 504, 507
 lex specialis character 64, 74
Sot. Lélos kai Sia judgment (2008) 259, 260, 359–60
 see also GlaxoSmithKline judgments, Greek and Spanish
South Africa
 public health policy 147
 South African Medicines Amendment Act (1997) 146
South Korea, trademark exhaustion in 408–21
 case law of importance
  Burberry (2002) 414–16
  Fujifilm (2003) 416
  Polo (Supreme Court, 1997) 413–14
 competition law and parallel imports 419–20
 customs law and parallel imports 420–21
 exhaustion of trademark rights and parallel imports under Korean law 410–18

current statutory and case law, analysis 417–18
 judicial decisions on parallel imports of trademarked products 413–16
 legal background 411–13
 parallel imports and competition law 419–20
and Korea Customs Office 420, 421
Monopoly Regulation and Fair Trade Act (MRFTA) 419, 420, 421
parallel imports 417, 418, 419–21
Trademark Act (TMA), 1949 411, 412–13
and TRIPS 411
Unfair Competition Prevention and Trade Secret Protection Act (UCPA) 411, 418, 421
Speciality European Pharma v. Doncaster Pharmaceuticals Ltd judgment (2015) 175
State Intellectual Property Office (SIPO), China 312, 313
statin drugs 152
Straus v. Victor Talking Machine Co. (1917) 59
streaming, downloading works by 65
Strix Ltd. v. Maharaja Appliances Ltd judgment (2009) 328–29
Subafilms, Ltd. v. MGM-Pathe Communications Co. judgment (1994) 231, 233
Supplementary Protection Certificate (SPC) 179, 180, 268
Syfait v. GlaxoSmithKline judgment (2005) 256, 257, 258

Taddy & Co v. Sterious & Co judgment (1904) 54, 57
Taiwan 443–60
 cases 450, 455, 456, 457
 Copyright Act 456–60
 Copyright Committee, former 454
 exhaustion principle under intellectual property laws 444–51
 indirect granting of right of importation and limited "exceptions" 452–55
 Intellectual Property Court 447, 448
 international exhaustion
  under Patent Act 448–50
  under Taiwan Integrated Circuits Layouts Protection Act 444–45
  under Taiwan Trademark Act 445–48
 theory building 456–59
 introduction of general distribution right and national exhaustion 455
 legally imported genuine copies 455–56

national exhaustion
   and introduction of a general distribution right 455
   under Taiwan Plant Variety and Plant Seed Act 450–51
Patent Act
   and Copyright Act 456–60
   international exhaustion under 448–50
   Survey on Monopoly over Imported Copyrighted Works 458
Trademark Act
   and Copyright Act 456–60
   international exhaustion under 445–48
   and TRIPS 443
   U.S.–Taiwan Copyright Protection Agreement (1993) 451–52, 453
   terminating 459–60
Taiwan Intellectual Property Office (TIPO) 457
tangible property 334, 490
   servitudes 62, 63
Tariff Act remedies, trademark infringement (U.S.) 399–400
TEC *see* Treaty Establishing the European Community (TEC)
term of copyright, extending 5, 6, 7
territoriality and geographic scope of exhaustion, United States
   Copyright Act 231–38
   impact of territoriality principle 228
   Patent Act 238–44
TFEU *see* Treaty on the Functioning of the European Union (TFEU)
Thai Central Intellectual Property and International Trade court 383
Thai Supreme Court 383
Théberge v. Galerie d'Art du Petit Champlain, Inc. judgment (2002) 486, 487, 494
Third Amendment to Chinese Patent Law, changes before and after 309–16
   current Patent Law of 2008 and current regulation of parallel imports 311–12, 322
   legislation background 312–15
   legislation basis (without prejudice to international agreements) 315–16
   state of patent law prior to 309–11
tiered pricing 108
Torrance, Andrew W. 28
TPP *see* Trans-Pacific Partnership Agreement (TPP), 2016
trademark exhaustion
   in ASEAN 377–83
   brand differentiation strategies 360, 362, 366
   case law of importance
      Bristol-Myers Squibb v. Paranova (1997) 101, 171–72, 174, 191, 348, 349–50, 351–52, 357, 360, 503
      Centrafarm B.V. v. American Home Products Corp. (1978) 173, 360
      Copad v. Christian Dior (2009) 356–57
      Coty Prestige Lancaster Group GmbH v. Simex Trading A.G. (2010) 349
      Etablissements Consten, S.A.R.L. & Grundig-Verkaufs GmbH v. Commission (1966) ("*Consten and Grundig*") 344, 346, 348, 354, 356, 365
      Google France, Google Inc. v. Louis Vuitton Malletier; Google France v. Viaticum Luteciel; Google France v. CNRRH Pierre Alexis Thonet Bruno Raboi Tiger (2010) 354
      Honda Giken v. Maria Patmanidi (2013) 364, 365
      Inwood Laboratories, Inc. v. Ives Laboratories (1982) 430
      KP Permanent Make-Up, Inc. v. Lasting Impressions I. Inc. (2004) 437
      Leegin Creative Leather Prods, Inc. v. PSKS, Inc. (2007) 358
      L'Oréal S.A. v. eBay International A.G. (2011) 349
      Parfums Christian Dior SA v. Dior v. Evora (1997) 351, 352, 355
      Pharmacia & Upjohn S.A. v. Paranonova A/S (1999) 174, 360
      Playboy Enterprises, Inc. v. Netscape Communications Corp. (2004) 438
      Polaroid Corp. v. Polarad Electronics Corp (1961) 425–26
      Viking Gas A/S v. Kosan Gas A/S (2011) 353–54
   comparison of EU/EEA, NAFTA and ASEAN 367, 368, 383–88
   Copyright Act (1976) 428
   in EU/EEA 368–73
   and free movement of goods 352, 367–89
   genuine goods 424
   interface with EU competition law 343–89
   and Internet
      challenging mark owner's desire for total control 435–39
      defenses 431–35
      ISPs and online auction sites 429–31
      litigation 425–31
   and Internet (of re-sold things) 422–39
   in Korea *see* Korea, trademark exhaustion in
   laissez faire approach 373–83
   Lanham Act (Trademark Act 1946), U.S. 423–24, 428

litigation 425–31
  aggression, acts of 427–28, 429
  confusion, claiming 423, 425–27
  contributory infringement claims 428
in NAFTA 373–77
parallel imports 360–61
rebranding 360–62
and regional exhaustion 364, 365, 368, 383, 384, 386–87, 410
rule of reason analysis 347, 357–58
Standard Process 429
teleology 355–56
trademark nominative fair use 432–33
see also repackaging of goods; trademarks
trademarks
  Andean Community of Nations (Andean Pact) 212
  conflict with copyright policy 404–7
  essential function and specific subject matter 345–48
  gray market goods 98
  impairment of a trademark function 352
  infringement 394–99
    contributory, claims of 428
    first sale rule and material differences 395–96
    importation and *Lever* rule 396–97, 402, 403, 405, 406, 407
    uncertain impact of *Lever* disclaimers on claims 397–99
  and integrity of selective distribution systems 358
  parallel trade/imports 100, 152–53
    remedies against parallel imports 394–400
  pharmaceutical trade 152–53
  primary purpose of protection 369–70
  remedies against parallel imports 394–400
    Tariff Act remedies 399–400
    trademark infringement 394–99
  Trade Mark Directive (Directive 2008/95/EC)
    exhaustion and the TMD system 348–52, 363
    and goods in transit 100
    internal market 170–71
  trademark law as a copyright alternative 393–94
  using trademark law to override copyright's first sale rule for imported copies (U.S.) 390–407
  Waterford mark example 423–24
  see also copyright; patents
transaction-cost-insulated servitudes 51–52

Trans-Pacific Partnership Agreement (TPP), 2016 xvii, 460, 480
  pharmaceutical products 162, 163
Treaty Establishing the European Community (TEC) 253–54, 256, 260, 501
  trademark exhaustion 345, 348, 350, 352–53
Treaty of Lisbon (2007) 353, 499
Treaty on the Functioning of the European Union (TFEU) 169
  Internet and exhaustion as a distribution channel 499, 510
  patent exhaustion 253, 254, 256, 260
  trademark exhaustion 343, 348, 350, 353
Treaty to Facilitate Access to Published Works for Persons Who are Blind, Visually Impaired or Otherwise Print Disabled (2013) *see* Marrakesh Treaty (2013)
TRIPS Agreement (Agreement on Trade-Related Aspects of Intellectual Property Rights)
  Article 6 provisions xviii, 106, 115, 128, 198
    and China 310, 312, 315
    and India 330, 331, 334
    international exhaustion 250, 251
    pharmaceutical products 262, 263, 270
  and China 310, 312, 315
  data exclusivity, pharmaceutical industry 153
  distributional issues 136, 137
  exhaustion under and after 126–29
  failure of negotiators to agree on IPR exhaustion 127–28, 143
  flexibilities 213
  GATT prior to 89–91
  grace-period extension 128, 134, 135
  and India 325, 330, 331, 332, 334
  international harmony, working towards 127, 128, 131
  international intellectual property rules 91, 92–96
  international patent exhaustion 274
  IPR standards 142
  and Korea 411
  and Latin America 198, 199, 202
  and Marrakesh Treaty 461, 462, 464
  minimum standards 199
  and NAFTA 373, 374
  and national treatment principle 229
  and parallel importing 88, 93
  pharmaceutical products 153, 159, 283, 284
  post-TRIPS WTO negotiations 135
  purpose 85–86
  and Taiwan 443
  "TRIPS-plus" provisions 136, 169, 184
  see also Doha Ministerial Declaration on TRIPs and Public Health (2001)

Tulk v. Moxhay (1848) 48, 54, 55
Tushnet, Rebecca 429
tying, practice of 29, 31, 55, 135, 355, 534

UMG v. Augusto judgment (2001) 521–22
Unfair Competition Prevention and Trade Secret Protection Act (UCPA), Korea 411, 418, 421
Uniform Commercial Code (UCC) 60, 521
United Kingdom Patents Ordinance (1937) 193
United States
   case law of importance
      American Banana Co. v. United Fruit Co. (1909) 231
      Boesch v. Graff (1890) 241, 242, 276–77
      Columbia Broadcasting System, Inc. v. Scorpio Music Distributors, Inc. (1984) 234, 235, 236
      Curb v. MCA Records, Inc. (1995) 233
      Curtiss Aeroplane & Motor Corp. v. United Aircraft Engineering Corp. (1920) 277
      Daimler Manufacturing Co. v. Conklin (1909) 277
      Deepsouth Packing Co. v. Laitram Corp. (1972) 238, 239
      Dickerson v. Matheson (1893) 277
      Environmental Defense Fund, Inc. v. Massey (1993) 237
      Fuji Photo Film Co. v. Jazz Photo Corp (Jazz Photo II) (2005) 186, 242, 277
      Holiday v. Mattheson (1885) 241
      Jazz Photo Corp. v. International Trade Commission (2001) 242, 243, 244, 277
      Kirtsaeng v. John Wiley & Sons (2013) see *Kirtsaeng v. John Wiley & Sons* judgment (2013)
      Lexmark International, Inc. v. Impression Products, Inc. (2014) 243, 278
      Los Angeles News Service v. Reuters (1998) 232–33
      Microsoft v. AT&T (2007) 240
      Quality King v. L'Anza (1997) 14, 15, 235, 236, 391–92, 407
      Subafilms, Ltd. v. MGM-Pathe Communications Co. (1994) 231, 233
   and China 141–42
   common law 273, 274
   Copyright Act xviii, 127, 231–38
      extra-territoriality and multi-territorial conduct under 232–34
   copyright exhaustion 11–16
      contemporary version 14
      copies 12–13
      Copyright Act 1976, s. 109 12–13, 234, 473–74
      industry practices 13–14
      multi-territorial conduct, context of 234–38
      sale based on economic and business realities of a transaction 13
   Customs and Border Protection 394, 396–97, 399, 402–3, 407
   data exclusivity, pharmaceutical industry 153
   digital goods 68–69
   exhaustion of intellectual property rights 228–31
      copyright exhaustion 11–16, 234–38
      national treatment rule and geographic scope of exhaustion 229–31
      patent exhaustion 16–21, 241–44
   extra-territoriality
      under Copyright Act 232–34
      and multi-territorial conduct 232–34, 238–41
      under Patent Act 238–41
   Food and Drug Administration (FDA) 148, 152
   geographic scope of exhaustion 226–27
      and national treatment rule 227, 229–31
      and territoriality 228, 231–44
   international exhaustion xviii, 375–76
   International Trade Commission 86
   Lanham Act remedies, applying to copyrighted works 400–403
   and Marrakesh Treaty 467, 472–74
   multi-territorial conduct
      under Copyright Act 232–34
      copyright exhaustion in context of 234–38
      and extra-territoriality 232–34, 238–41
      under Patent Act 238–41
      patent exhaustion in context of 241–44
   national exhaustion xviii
   parallel importation
      jurisdictional approaches to 97–100
      pharmaceutical products 118
   Patent Act xviii, 140, 238–44
      amendment (1996) 99
      extra-territoriality and multi-territorial conduct under 238–41
   patent exhaustion 16–21, 100
      access, role of regulation in (pharmaceutical industry) 283–87
      international exhaustion 275–87
      multi-territorial conduct, context of 241–44
      origins 17–19
      questioning benefits of geographic price discrimination 278–83

recent Supreme Court developments 19–21
Sherman Act 1990 18
pharmaceutical products 153
Restatement of Property (1944) 49
Restatement (Third) of Property: Servitudes (2000) 49, 53
Science, State, Justice, Commerce, and Related Agencies Appropriations Act 200
Tariff Act remedies, trademark infringement 399–400
territoriality and geographic scope of exhaustion 226–27, 228
  Copyright Act 231–38
  Patent Act 238–44
trademark infringement 377
trademark law, using to override copyright's first sale rule for imported copies 390–407
TRIPS Agreement and national treatment principle 229
U.S.–Taiwan Copyright Protection Agreement (1993) 451–52, 453
  terminating 459–60
  see also first sale doctrine; International Trade Commission (ITC), U.S.; Lanham Act (Trademark Act 1946), U.S.
United States Patent and Trademark Office (USPTO) 8
United States v. Univis Lens Co. judgment (1942) 18
United States—Imports of Certain Automotive Spring Assemblies (1983) 90
United States—Section 337 of the Tariff Act of 1930 (1989) 90
United Wire Ltd. v. Screen Repair Services (Scotland) judgment (2000) 296, 333
UPOV *see* International Union for the Protection of Plant Varieties (UPOV)
Uruguay 202

Uruguay Round Communication 339, 340
UsedSoft v. Oracle judgment (2012) 64, 68, 70, 72, 76, 79, 81, 184, 459, 475, 490, 494, 499, 504, 505, 514, 515, 516, 529
  as interpretation *contra legem* 506–7
USPTO (U.S. Patent and Trademark Office) 98, 230

Valletti, Tommaso M. 119
Van Zuylen Frerese v. Hag (Hag I) judgment (1974) 175, 344, 346
Veoh Networks 425
vertical integration 35, 366
  imperfect/incomplete 23, 36, 43
vertical price control (VPC) 117
vertical pricing and distributor-level parallel trade 116–18
vertical restraints 28–29, 31, 33
Vietnam Intellectual Property Law (2009) 381
Viking Gas A/S v. Kosan Gas A/S judgment (2011) 353–54
Von Hippel, Eric 28

Waiver Decision (2003) 158, 331
White-Smith Music Publishing v. Apollo judgment (1908) 45
World Intellectual Property Office (WIPO) 445
  WIPO Copyright Treaty (WCT) 70, 485–86, 500, 508, 512
  WIPO Performances and Phonograms Treaty (WPPT) 485–86, 488, 510
World Trade Organization (WTO)
  Decision of August 30, 2003 193, 194
  dispute settlement mechanism 92–93
  Doha Ministerial Conference 266
  Prequalification Program 148
  see also TRIPS Agreement (Agreement on Trade-Related Aspects of Intellectual Property Rights)

Yu, Peter K. 136, 137, 281